SHAKESPEARE SAID IT

WILLIAM DODGE LEWIS

SHAKESPEARE SAID IT

TOPICAL QUOTATIONS FROM THE WORKS OF
SHAKESPEARE SELECTED AND ANNOTATED BY

WILLIAM DODGE LEWIS

WITH AN INTRODUCTION BY
WILLIAM P. TOLLEY

SYRACUSE : *SYRACUSE UNIVERSITY* : MCMLXI

TO MY DAUGHTER
JESSIE LOUISE LEWIS

INTRODUCTION

THE DEEPEST AND most enduring pleasures are those of the mind. Music may move us deeply and art may thread thoughts together for us in unusual ways, but it is in the greatest literature that art and idea unite to achieve maximum power. William Dodge Lewis knew this from a lifetime of study. He knew too the capacity of such literature to stir the mind and imagination of the reader.

In Oxford's Bodleian Library is a copy of the first translation into English of Plutarch's *Lives*. It contains handwritten notes thought to be those of William Shakespeare. Whether they actually are his or not it is nevertheless clear that Shakespeare's whole group of plays set in classical civilization dates from a period immediately succeeding the appearance of that translation. It is entirely appropriate that this should be the last book by William Dodge Lewis, for as the imagination of Shakespeare was whetted by reading, so too the life of William Dodge Lewis was quickened and shaped by his love of books.

He was born in the "north country" of New York State in Saint Lawrence County, on January 17, 1870. By his lineage from early American settlers he inherited the open heartiness of the Dutch on his mother Ann Van Ornam's side, and from his father John Edward Lewis's side the poetry of Wales and steadfastness of England. As a college student at Syracuse University he served as Assistant Editor of *The Onondagan*, the year book, presaging his career. In 1892 he graduated with Phi Beta Kappa honors, and in September of that year married his college classmate Louise Graff of Utica, New York.

His early career was spent in the public schools of Syracuse where his gifts were soon recognized. He served as Principal of the Prescott School, Chairman of the Department of English at Central High School, and Principal of the new North High School. Meanwhile, in 1895, he had earned his Master of Arts degree at the University.

In 1910 he left Syracuse for a distinguished Principalship in Philadelphia at the William Penn High School for Girls, and he remained in that post until 1919, when he became Deputy Superintendent of Public Instruction in charge of Secondary Education for the Commonwealth of Pennsylvania. In that year he was also given high recognition by his professional colleagues who elected him President of the National Association of Secondary School Principals.

Out of this rich experience he published in 1914 his first book entitled, *Democracy's High School*. From his intimate knowledge of young people he saw the need for more effective cultivation of the skill and habits of good reading. He served as joint author of three more books and four particularly significant series of readers. The books were: *Practical English for High Schools, Knowing and Using Words*, and *English for Use*. The foundations for present developments in remedial reading were laid by the four series of readers, *Silent Reading Series, The New Silent Readers, The Reading Hour Series*, and *English for Elementary Schools*. They earned him wide recognition as a distinguished pedagogue. In 1917 Syracuse University conferred upon him the honorary degree of Doctor of Pedagogy, and in 1921 Susquehanna University added the laureate of Doctor of Literature. His alma mater awarded him, in 1952, the Arents Medal for excellence in the field of education.

In 1923 he left the Pennsylvania Department of Education to become the Editor-in-Chief of the John C. Winston Company, Philadelphia publisher. There he served as joint editor of the *Winston Simplified Dictionary* and its advanced edition as well as the *Dictionary for Schools*. His immense scholarly energy and his zeal for sharing the very best led him to edit numerous classic English texts and to contribute articles to the most widely read journals of his day such as the *Outlook Magazine, Ladies Home Journal*, and the *Saturday Evening Post*. Although he retired from his position as Editor-in-Chief at the John C. Winston Company in 1940, he continued for twenty more years to enjoy his exceptional clarity and vigor of mind.

Always a cordial host and one who gave his friendship with genuine warmth, he served many good causes. He was a Trustee of his Methodist Church and of the Lake Placid Club Educational Foundation. It was at Lake Placid, where he spent most of the last thirty summers of his life, that his final illness came upon him. He passed away on November 14, 1960, just two months before his ninety-first birthday at his home in Lansdowne, Pennsylvania.

To his son, Frederick Howard Lewis, his daughter, Jessie Louise Lewis, with whom he made his home, and all who were privileged to know him, he left a rich heritage of personal affection and the love of learning. Miss Lewis deserves special recognition for the care she has taken as his literary executor to see this book through to publication.

WILLIAM PEARSON TOLLEY
Chancellor, Syracuse University

PREFACE

IN PREPARING THE present volume of excerpts from the plays and poems of the immortal Bard, the compiler has had in mind the almost universal interest in Shakespeare's portrayal of human life. Recognition of the vitality of his work wins enthusiastic response from pupils in higher grammar school grades, youth in the secondary schools, and adults even of limited formal education.

The sample passages offered under hundreds of topic headings may provide the stimulus in encouraging first-hand perusal of the plays and poems. For example, the king in *Love's Labour's Lost* characterizes the voluble Don Adriano as,

> One whom the music of his own vain tongue
> Doth ravish like enchanting harmony.

Again, in the same play Biron compliments feminine charm in these words:

> A wither'd hermit, fivescore winters worn,
> Might shake off fifty, looking in her eye.

A single illustration of the poet's wise comments on human life must represent thousands of others:

The web of our life is of a mingled yarn, good and ill together: our virtues would be proud, if our faults whipped them not; and our crimes would despair, if they were not cherished by our virtues.

Topic headings are arranged in alphabetical order. With a few exceptions, entries appear in alphabetical order by source, and in chronological sequence when more than one entry is supplied from the same source. Sources are given by act, scene, and line or lines. A quotation appearing under one heading may include topics relating to other headings; cross references have been provided in these cases. Many of the same quotations reappear under alternate headings in abbreviated or more complete form.

One basic idea in the present volume is the explanation of archaic or unfamiliar words, phrases, and sentences. These notes are placed conveniently right after each entry. There are literally hundreds of such instances, ranging from the use of *his* for *its* or often *fond* for *foolish* to such words as *excrement* for *hair* or *beard*. There are also important words referring to customs of Elizabethan times. In agony of remorse for the murder of his brother, King Claudius cries:

> O limed soul, that struggling to be free
> Art more engaged!

The word *limed* refers to a rural method of catching birds. A sticky substance called *birdlime* was smeared on branches where birds habitually roosted. As the victims struggled, their wings were caught and they were "more engaged," only to await the club of the rustic seeking a dinner.

Among the many sources consulted in preparing this work, one of the most important was *Shakespeare, Red Letter Edition*, edited by Frederick D. Losey. The quotations are identified in accordance with *Works of William Shakespeare* (Globe Edition, 1891), edited by William George Clark and William Addis Wright. Of great assistance were *William Shakespeare, Dramas*, edited by William J. Rolfe; *Shakesperian Grammar*, by Edwin A. Abbott; *Complete Concordance of Shakespeare*, by John Bartlett; *Standard Book of Shakespeare Quotations*, edited by Burton Stevenson; *The Oxford Shakespeare Glossary*, by Charles T. Onions. The superb scholarship shown in the fourth edition of Alexander Schmidt's *Shakespeare-Lexicon* has seldom failed to give satisfactory information. The court of last resort has been the *Variorum Edition* of Horace Howard Furness.

The frequent inclusion of complete or sometimes condensed scenes is a unique feature of this volume. The compiler believes that these excerpts may furnish a lure to the reader, perhaps to the secondary school or grammar school student.

In justification of the claim that grammar school pupils can appreciate Shakespeare, I have personal evidence. When I was Principal of Prescott School in Syracuse, New York, more than fifty years ago, I often read Shakespeare to seventh and eighth-year classes. I then had little technical scholarship—only enthusiastic devotion to Shakespeare. Some ability to read orally was my chief resource. Unless I am greatly mistaken, the general reaction of pupils was favorable—with some, enthusiastic. I bought an edition of individual plays, and pupils were permitted to borrow them. Many were taken out and read. One boy read twenty-two plays in a single year.

Shortly after I became head of the English department of Central High School in Syracuse, Dr. Frederick D. Losey came to Syracuse University. His classes were an inspiration, and I discovered what scholarship in Shakespeare meant. My close lifelong friendship with this great teacher nurtured my devotion to the Bard.

It is the compiler's hope that this addition to the annual crop of Shakespeare books may help others to enjoy the heritage of the greatest literary genius of all time.

WILLIAM DODGE LEWIS

Lansdowne, Pennsylvania
May 25, 1960

SHAKESPEARE SAID IT

SHAKESPEARE SAID IT

ABSENCE

CLEOPATRA. Noblest of men, woo 't die?
Hast thou no care of me? shall I abide
In this dull world, which in thy absence is
No better than a sty?
Antony and Cleopatra, IV, 13:59

ORLANDO. For these two hours, Rosalind,
I will leave thee.
ROSALIND. Alas! dear love. I cannot lack
thee two hours.
As You Like It, IV, 1:181

PORTIA. I am glad this parcel of wooers
are so reasonable, for there is not one among
them but I dote on his very absence.
Merchant of Venice, I, 2:118

BIANCA. What! keep a week away? seven
days and nights?
Eight score eight hours? and lovers' absent
hours,
More tedious than the dial[1] eight score
times?
O weary reckoning!
Othello, III, 4:173

[1] dial: clock face.

Were I with her, the night would post too
soon;
But now are minutes added to the hours;
To spite me now, each minute seems a
moon;[1]
Passionate Pilgrim, 1:205

[1] moon: month.

O absence! what a torment would'st thou
prove,
Were it not thy sour leisure gave sweet leave
To entertain the time with thoughts of love,
Sonnet 39

Sometime, all full with feasting on your
sight,
And by and by clean starved for a look;
Sonnet 75

How like a winter hath my absence been
From thee, the pleasure of the fleeting year!

What freezings have I felt, what dark days
seen!
What old December's bareness every where!
Sonnet 97

O! never say that I was false of heart,
Though absence seem'd my flame to qual-
ify.[1]
As easy might I from myself depart
As from my soul, which in thy breast doth
lie:
That is my home of love: if I have rang'd,
Like him that travels, I return again,
Sonnet 109

[1] qualify: abate.

VALENTINE. O thou that dost inhabit in
my breast,
Leave not the mansion so long tenantless,
Lest, growing ruinous, the building fall
And leave no memory of what it was!
Repair me with thy presence, Silvia!
Two Gentlemen of Verona, V, 4:7

CAMILLO. They have seemed to be together, though absent, shook hands, as over
a vast,[1] and embraced, as it were, from the
ends of opposed winds.
Winter's Tale, I, 1:31

[1] vast: a boundless sea.

ABUSE

BERTRAM. Here comes my clog.
HELENA. I have, sir, as I was commanded
from you,
All's Well That Ends Well, II, 5:58

CLEOPATRA. Rogue! thou hast liv'd too
long.
Draws a knife.
Antony and Cleopatra, II, 5:73

FALSTAFF. A king's son! If I do not beat
thee out of thy kingdom with a dagger of
lath, and drive all thy subjects afore thee
like a flock of wild geese, I'll never wear
hair on my face more. You Prince of Wales!
. . . . .

PRINCE. These lies are like their father that begets them; gross as a mountain, open, palpable. Why, thou clay-brained guts, thou knotty-pated fool, thou whoreson, obscene, greasy tallow-ketch.[1]
I Henry IV, II, 4:150, 249
[This exchange is a sample of the good-natured raillery between FALSTAFF and PRINCE HAL.]
[1] tallow-ketch: fat rolled into a lump.

K. HENRY. Lay not thy hands on me; forbear, I say:
Their touch affrights me as a serpent's sting.
Thou baleful messenger, out of my sight!
Upon thy eye-balls murderous tyranny
Sits in grim majesty to fright the world.
II Henry VI, III, 2:46

OSWALD. What dost thou know me for?
KENT. A knave, a rascal, an eater of broken meats; a base, proud, shallow, beggarly, three-suited, hundred-pound, filthy, worsted-stocking knave; a lily-livered,[1] action-taking[2] knave; a whoreson, glass-gazing, super-serviceable,[3] finical rogue; one-trunk-inheriting slave; one that would'st be a bawd, in a way of good service, and art nothing but the composition of a knave,
King Lear, II, 2:13
[1] lily-livered: cowardly; the liver was believed to be the seat of courage. [2] action-taking: going to law rather than personal combat. [3] super-serviceable: over-officious.

BRABANTIO [to RODERIGO]. I have charg'd thee not to haunt about my doors:
In honest plainness thou hast heard me say
My daughter is not for thee; and now, in madness,
Being full of supper and distempering[1] draughts,
Upon malicious bravery dost thou come
To start[2] my quiet.
Othello, I, 1:96
[1] distempering: intoxicating. [2] start: disturb.

THERSITES. To be a dog, a mule, a cat, a fitchew,[1] a toad, a lizard, an owl, a puttock,[2] or a herring without a roe, I would not care; but to be Menelaus! I would conspire[3] against destiny.
Troilus and Cressida, V, 1:66
[1] fitchew: polecat. [2] puttock: a bird of prey. [3] conspire . . . destiny: fight to avoid being Menelaus.

ACCIDENT

OBERON. Think no more of this night's accidents

But as the fierce vexation of a dream.
Midsummer Night's Dream, IV, 1:71

ACCUSATION

CRANMER. I do beseech your lordships
That in this case of justice, my accusers,
Be what they will, may stand forth face to face,
And freely urge against me.
Henry VIII, V, 3:45

FRIAR. Then shall he mourn,
If ever love had interest in his liver,[1]
And wish he had not so accused her,
No, though he thought his accusation true.
Much Ado About Nothing, IV, 1:232
[1] Liver: sometimes believed seat of the emotions.

DUCHESS OF YORK.[1] Thou toad, thou toad, where is thy brother Clarence,
And little Ned Plantagenet, his son?
Q. ELIZABETH. Where is the gentle Rivers, Vaughan, Grey?
DUCHESS. Where is kind Hastings?
K. RICHARD. A flourish, trumpets! strike alarum, drums!
Let not the heavens hear these tell-tale women
Rail on the Lord's anointed. Strike, I say!
Flourish. Alarums.
Richard III, IV, 4:145
[1] Duchess of YORK: Mother of K. RICHARD, to the KING.

DUCHESS [to K. RICHARD]. No, by the holy rood,[1] thou know'st it well,
Thou cam'st on earth to make the earth my hell.
A grievous burden was thy birth to me;
Tetchy[2] and wayward was thy infancy;
Thy school-days frightful, desperate, wild and furious;
Thy prime of manhood daring, bold and venturous;
Thy age confirm'd,[3] proud, subtle, sly, and bloody,
More mild, but yet more harmful, kind[4] in hatred:
What comfortable hour canst thou name
That ever grac'd me with thy company?
Richard III, IV, 4:165
[1] rood: cross. [2] Tetchy: fretful. [3] age confirm'd: riper age. [4] kind of hatred: outwardly kind to those he hated.

ACHIEVEMENT

HELENA. Oft expectation fails, and most oft there

Where most it promises; and oft it hits
Where hope is coldest and despair most fits.
All's Well That Ends Well, II, 1:145

ANTONY. To business that we love we rise betime,[1]
And go to 't with delight.
Antony and Cleopatra, IV, 4:20
[1] betime: early.

MESSENGER. And many strokes, though with a little axe,
Hew down and fell the hardest-timber'd oak.
III Henry VI, II, 1:54

PORTIA. If to do were as easy as to know what were good to do, chapels had been churches, and poor men's cottages princes' palaces.
Merchant of Venice, I, 2:13

AARON. So must you resolve,
That what you cannot as you would achieve,
You must perforce accomplish as you may.
Titus Andronicus, II, 1:104

ULYSSES. To have done[1] is to hang
Quite out of fashion, like a rusty mail
In monumental mockery. Take the instant[2] way;
For honour travels in a strait so narrow
Where one but goes abreast:[3] keep then the path.
Troilus and Cressida, III, 3:151
[1] To have done . . . mockery: mere record of achievement is like rusty mail. [2] instant: the task offering itself right now. [3] Where . . . abreast: where one goes alone depending entirely upon himself.

ACT

HELENA. It is not so with him that all things knows,
As 't is with us that square[1] our guess by shows;
But most it is presumption in us when
The help of heaven we count the act of men.
All's Well That Ends Well, II, 1:152
[1] square . . . shows: decide by appearances.

PANDULPH. This act[1] so evilly borne shall cool the hearts
Of all his people and freeze up their zeal,
That none[2] so small advantage shall step forth
To check his reign, but they will cherish it.
King John, III, 4:149
[1] This act: probable murder of ARTHUR.

[2] none . . . cherish: no one will fail to prize an opportunity to attack JOHN's reign.

PEMBROKE. This act[1] is as an ancient tale new told,
And in the last repeating troubles me.
King John, IV, 2:18
[1] act: JOHN's second crowning.

BASTARD. Be great in act, as you have been in thought;
Let not the world see fear and sad distrust
Govern the motion of a kingly eye:
Be stirring as the time; be fire with fire;
Threaten the threatener, and outface the brow
Of bragging horror: so shall inferior eyes
That borrow their behaviours from the great,
Grow great by your example and put on
The dauntless spirit of resolution.
King John, V, 1:45

LADY MACBETH. Art thou afeard
To be the same in thine own act and valour
As thou art in desire?
Macbeth, I, 7:39

ISABELLA. His act did not o'ertake his bad intent,
And must be buried but as an intent
That perish'd by the way.
Measure for Measure, V, 1:456

ACTING—ACTOR

JAQUES. I must have liberty
Withal,[1] as large a charter as the wind,
To blow on whom I please; for so fools have:
And they that are most galled with my folly,
They most must laugh. And why, sir, must they so?
The 'why' is plain as way to parish church:
He that a fool doth very wisely hit,
Doth very foolishly, although he smart,
Not to seem senseless of the bob.[2]
As You Like It, II, 7:47
[1] Withal: with it. [2] bob: jibe.

HAMLET. He that plays the king shall be welcome; his majesty shall have tribute of me; the adventurous knight shall use his foil and target;[1] the lover shall not sigh gratis; the humorous man shall end his part in peace; the clown shall make those laugh[2] whose lungs are tickle o' the sere.[3]
Hamlet, II, 2:332
[1] target: shield. [2] laugh . . . sere: laugh easily; metaphor of shooting. [3] sere: the trigger of a gun.

HAMLET [to the players]. Speak the speech, I pray you, as I pronounced it to you, trippingly on the tongue; but if you mouth it, as many of your players do, I had as lief the town-crier spoke my lines. Nor do not saw the air too much with your hand, thus; but use all gently: for in the very torrent, tempest, and, as I may say, the whirlwind of passion, you must acquire and beget a temperance that may give it smoothness. O! it offends me to the soul to hear a robustious periwig-pated[1] fellow tear a passion to tatters, to very rags, to split the ears of the groundlings,[2] who for the most part are capable of nothing but inexplicable dumbshows and noise: I would have such a fellow whipped for o'erdoing Termagant;[3] it outherods Herod:[4] pray you, avoid it.

. . . . .

Be not too tame neither, but let your own discretion be your tutor: suit the action to the word, the word to the action; with this special observance, that you o'erstep not the modesty[5] of nature; for anything so overdone is from the purpose of playing, whose end, both at the first and now, was and is, to hold, as 't were, the mirror up to nature; to show virtue her own feature, scorn her own image, and the very age and body of the time his form and pressure. Now, this overdone, or come tardy off, though it make the unskilful laugh, cannot but make the judicious grieve; the censure of the which one must in your allowance o'erweigh a whole theatre of others.
Hamlet, III, 2:1, 18
[1] periwig-pated: wearing a wig. [2] groundlings: people in the pit, the cheapest part of Shakespeare's theater. [3] Termagant: an imaginary violent god of the Mohammedans. [4] Herod: a blustering tyrant in mystery plays. [5] modesty: moderation.

BOTTOM. An[1] I may hide my face, let me play Thisby too. I'll speak in a monstrous little voice, 'Thisne, Thisne.' 'Ah! Pyramus, my lover dear; thy Thisby dear, and lady dear!'

. . . . .

Let me play the lion too. I will roar, that I will do any man's heart good to hear me;

. . . . .

ALL. That would hang us, every mother's son.
BOTTOM. I grant you friends, if that you should fright the ladies out of their wits, they would have no more discretion but to hang us; but I will aggravate[2] my voice so that I will roar you as gently as any sucking dove; I will roar you an 't were any nightingale.
Midsummer Night's Dream, I, 2:54, 72, 79
[1] An: if. [2] aggravate: BOTTOM's blunder, possibly for abate.

BUCKINGHAM. Tut! I can counterfeit the deep tragedian,
Speak, and look back, and pry on every side.
Tremble and start at wagging of a straw,
Intending[1] deep suspicion: ghastly looks
Are at my service, like enforced smiles;
And both are ready in their offices,
At any time to grace my stratagems.
Richard III, III, 5:5
[1] Intending: pretending.

ULYSSES. A strutting player, whose conceit[1]
Lies in his hamstring, and doth think it rich
To hear the wooden dialogue and sound
'Twixt his stretch'd footing and the scaffoldage,—
Troilus and Cressida, I, 3:153
[1] conceit: thought.

ADAPTATION

Q. MARGARET. Why, courage then! what cannot be avoided
'T were childish weakness to lament or fear.
III Henry VI, V, 4:36

BIRON. At Christmas I no more desire a rose
Than wish a snow in May's new-fangled mirth;
But like of each thing that in season grows.
Love's Labour's Lost, I, 1:105

PORTIA. How many things by season[1] season'd are
To their right praise and true perfection!
Merchant of Venice, V, 1:106
[1] season, etc.: by fitness of occasion adapted for appreciation.

GAUNT. All places that the eye of heaven visits
Are to a wise man ports and happy havens.
Richard II, I, 3:275

ADDER

HERMIA. And hast thou kill'd him sleeping? O brave touch!
Could not a worm, an adder, do so much?
An adder did it; for with doubler tongue
Than thine, thou serpent, never adder stung.
Midsummer Night's Dream, III, 2:70

K. RICHARD. Yield stinging nettles to mine enemies;

And when they from thy bosom pluck a
    flower,
Guard it, I pray thee, with a lurking adder
Whose double tongue may with a mortal
    touch
Throw death upon thy sovereign's enemies.
Richard II, III, 2:18

CALIBAN. Sometime am I
All wound with adders, who with cloven
    tongues
Do hiss me into madness.
Tempest, II, 2:13

She starts, like one that spies an adder
Wreath'd up in fatal folds just in his way,
The fear whereof doth make him shake and
    shudder.
Venus and Adonis, 878

ADMIRATION

HAMLET. Saw who?
HORATIO. My lord, the king your father.
HAMLET. The king my father!
HORATIO. Season[1] your admiration[2] for a
    while
With an attent ear, till I may deliver,
Upon the witness of these gentlemen,
This marvel to you.
Hamlet, I, 2:190
[1] Season: hold back. [2] admiration: wonder,
amazement; no sense of approval.

With more than admiration[1] he admir'd
Her azure veins, her alabaster skin
Her coral lips, her snow-white dimpled
    chin.
Rape of Lucrece, 417
[1] admiration: the present meaning.

FERDINAND. Admir'd Miranda!
Indeed the top of admiration; worth
What's dearest to the world!
Tempest, III, 1:37

CAMILLO. I should leave[1] grazing, were I
    of your flock,
And only live by gazing.
PERDITA. Out, alas!
You'd be so lean, that blasts of January
Would blow you through and through.
Winter's Tale, IV, 4:109
[1] leave: stop.

FLORIZEL [to PERDITA]. What you do
Still betters what is done. When you speak,
    sweet,
I'd have you do it ever: when you sing,
I'd have you buy and sell so; so give alms;
Pray so; and, for the ordering your affairs,
To sing them too: when you do dance, I
    wish you

A wave o' the sea, that you might ever do
Nothing but that.
Winter's Tale, IV, 4:135

ADOLESCENCE

CLEOPATRA. My salad days,
When I was green in judgment.
Antony and Cleopatra, I, 5:73

HOTSPUR. The nimble-footed madcap
    Prince of Wales,
And his comrades, that daff'd[1] the world
    aside,
And bid it pass?
I Henry IV, IV, 1:96
[1] daff'd: put off, from doffed, literally, do-off.

PORTIA [to NERISSA]. I'll hold thee any
    wager,
When we are both accoutred like young
    men,
I'll prove the prettier fellow of the two,
And wear my dagger with the braver grace,
And speak between the change of man and
    boy
With a reed voice, and turn two mincing
    steps
Into a manly stride, and speak of frays
Like a fine bragging youth, and tell quaint
    lies,
How honourable ladies sought my love,
Which I denying, they fell sick and died;
I could not do withal;[1] then I'll repent,
And wish, for all that, that I had not kill'd
    them.

    . . . . .

I have within my mind
A thousand raw tricks of these bragging
    Jacks,
Merchant of Venice, III, 4:62, 76
[1] withal: with it.

ANTONIO. Scrambling,[1] outfacing,[2] fash-
    ion-mong'ring boys,
That lie and cog[3] and flout, deprave and
    slander,
Go anticly,[4] show outward hideousness,
And speak off half a dozen dangerous
    words,
How they might hurt their enemies, if they
    durst.
Much Ado About Nothing, V, 1:94
[1] Scambling: contentious. [2] outfacing: swag-
gering. [3] cog: cheat, deceive. [4] anticly: fan-
tastically.

OLIVIA. Of what personage and years is
    he?[1]
MALVOLIO. Not yet old enough for a man.

nor young enough for a boy; as a squash[2] is before 't is a peascod, or a codling[3] when 't is almost an apple: 't is with him in standing water, between boy and man. He is very well-favoured,[4] and he speaks very shrewishly:[5] one would think his mother's milk were scarce out of him.

Twelfth Night, I, 5:164

[1] he: VIOLA, disguised as a man. [2] squash: unripe peascod, husk of peas. [3] codling: unripe apple. [4] well-favoured: good-looking. [5] shrewishly: sharply, pertly.

ADULTERY

GHOST. Ay, that incestuous, that adulterate beast,[1]
With witchcraft of his wit, with traitorous gifts,
O wicked wit and gifts, that have the power
So to seduce! won to his shameful lust
The will of my most seeming-virtuous queen.

Hamlet, I, 5:42

[1] beast: CLAUDIUS, brother of HAMLET's father, and king after the murder.

QUEEN. What have I done that thou dar'st wag thy tongue
In noise so rude against me?
HAMLET. Such an act
That blurs the grace and blush of modesty,
Calls virtue hypocrite, takes off the rose[1]
From the fair forehead of an innocent love
And sets a blister[2] there, makes marriage vows
As false as dicers' oaths; O! such a deed
As from the body of contraction[3] plucks
The very soul, and sweet religion makes
A rhapsody of words; heaven's face doth glow,
Yea, this solidity[4] and compound mass,
With tristful[5] visage, as against the doom,
Is thought-sick at the act.

Hamlet, III, 4:38

[1] rose: symbol of innocent love. [2] blister: symbol of prostitute, sometimes so branded. [3] contraction: the marriage contract. [4] solidity, etc.: the earth. [5] tristful: sorrowful.

QUEEN. Ay me! what act,
That roars so loud and thunders in the index?
HAMLET. Look here, upon this picture, and on this;
The counterfeit presentment of two brothers.
See, what a grace was seated on this brow;
Hyperion's curls, the front of Jove himself,
An eye like Mars, to threaten and command,
A station like the herald Mercury
New-lighted on a heaven-kissing hill,

A combination and a form indeed,
Where every god did seem to set his seal,
To give the world assurance of a man.
This was your husband: look you now, what follows.
Here is your husband; like a mildew'd ear,
Blasting his wholesome brother. Have you eyes?
Could you on this fair mountain leave to feed,
And batten on this moor? Ha! have you eyes?
You cannot call it love, for at your age
The hey-day in the blood is tame, it 's humble,
And waits upon the judgment; and what judgment
Would step from this to this? Sense, sure, you have,
Else could you not have motion; but sure, that sense
Is apoplex'd; for madness would not err,
Nor sense[1] to ecstasy[2] was ne'er so thrall'd
But it reserv'd some quantity of choice,
To serve in such a difference. What devil was't
That thus hath cozen'd[3] you at hoodman-blind?
Eyes without feeling, feeling without sight,
Ears without hands or eyes, smelling sans[4] all,
Or but a sickly part of one true sense
Could not so mope.
O shame! where is thy blush? Rebellious hell,
If thou canst mutine in a matron's bones,
To flaming youth let virtue be as wax,
And melt in her own fire.

. . . . .

QUEEN. O Hamlet! speak no more;
Thou turn'st mine eyes into my very soul;
And there I see such black and grained spots
As will not leave their tinct.
HAMLET. Nay, but to live
In the rank sweat of an enseamed bed,
Stew'd in corruption, honeying and making love
Over the nasty sty,—
QUEEN. O! speak to me no more;
These words like daggers enter in mine ears;
No more, sweet Hamlet!
HAMLET. A murderer and a villain;
A slave that is not twentieth part the tithe
Of your precedent lord; a vice of kings;
A cut-purse of the empire and the rule,
That from a shelf the precious diadem stole,
And put it in his pocket!
QUEEN. No more!
HAMLET. A king of shreds and patches,—

Hamlet, III, 4:51

[1] sense: thought. [2] ecstasy: insanity. [3] cozen'd: deceived. [4] sans: without.

Enter GHOST.

Save me, and hover o'er me with your
    wings,
You heavenly guards! What would your
    gracious figure?
    QUEEN. Alas! he 's mad.
    HAMLET. Do you not come your tardy
son to chide,
That, laps'd in time and passion, lets go by
The important acting of your dread com-
    mand?
O! say.
    GHOST. Do not forget: this visitation
Is but to whet thy almost blunted purpose.
But, look! amazement on thy mother sits;
O! step between her and her fighting soul;
Conceit in weakest bodies strongest works:
Speak to her, Hamlet.
    HAMLET. How is it with you, lady?
    QUEEN. Alas! how is 't with you,
That you do bend your eye on vacancy
And with the incorporal air do hold dis-
    course?
Forth at your eyes your spirits wildly peep;
And, as the sleeping soldiers in the alarm,
Your bedded hair, like life in excrements,[1]
Starts up and stands an end. O gentle son!
Upon the heat and flame of thy distemper
Sprinkle cool patience. Whereon do you
    look?
    HAMLET. On him, on him! Look you,
how pale he glares!
His form and cause conjoin'd, preaching to
    stones,
Would make them capable. Do not look
    upon me;
Lest with this piteous action you convert
My stern effects: then what I have to do
Will want true colour; tears perchance for
    blood.
    QUEEN. To whom do you speak this?
    HAMLET. Do you see nothing there?
    QUEEN. Nothing at all; yet all that is I see.
    HAMLET. Nor did you nothing hear?
    QUEEN. No, nothing but ourselves.
    HAMLET. Why, look you there! look!
how it steals away;
My father, in his habit as he liv'd;
Look! where he goes, even now, out at the
    portal.
                        Exit GHOST.
                Hamlet, III, 4:104
[1] excrements: often used for beard or hair.

    QUEEN. This is the very coinage of your
brain:
This bodiless creation ecstasy[1]
Is very cunning in.
    HAMLET. Ecstasy!
My pulse, as yours, doth temperately keep
    time
And makes as healthful music. It is not mad-
    ness

That I have utter'd: bring me to the test,
And I the matter will re-word, which mad-
    ness
Would gambol from. Mother, for love of
    grace,
Lay not that flattering unction to your soul,
That not your trespass but my madness
    speaks;
It will but skin and film the ulcerous place,
Whiles rank corruption, mining all within,
Infects unseen. Confess yourself to heaven;
Repent what's past; avoid what is to come;
And do not spread the compost[2] on the
    weeds
To make them ranker. Forgive me this my
    virtue;
For in the fatness of these pursy times
Virtue itself of vice must pardon beg,
Yea, curb and woo for leave to do him good.
    QUEEN. O Hamlet! thou hast cleft my
        heart in twain.
    HAMLET. O! throw away the worser part
        of it,
And live the purer with the other half.
Good night: but go not to mine uncle's bed;
Assume a virtue, if you have it not.
That monster, custom, who all sense doth
    eat,
Of habits devil, is angel yet in this,
That to the use of actions fair and good
He likewise gives a frock or livery,
That aptly is put on. Refrain to-night;
And that shall lend a kind of easiness
To the next abstinence: the next more easy;
For use[3] almost can change the stamp of na-
    ture,
And either master the devil, or throw him
    out
With wondrous potency. Once more, good
    night:
And when you are desirous to be bless'd,
I'll blessing beg of you. For this same lord,
                Pointing to POLONIUS.
I do repent: but heaven hath pleas'd it so,
To punish me with this, and this with me,
That I must be their scourge and minister.
I will bestow him, and will answer well
The death I gave him. So, again, good night.
I must be cruel only to be kind:
Thus bad begins and worse remains behind.
One word more, good lady.
    QUEEN. What shall I do?
    HAMLET. Not this, by no means, that I
        bid you do:
Let the bloat king tempt you again to bed;
Pinch wanton on your cheek; call you his
    mouse;
And let him, for a pair of reechy kisses,
Or paddling in your neck with his damn'd
    fingers,
Make you to ravel all this matter out,
That I essentially am not in madness,

But mad in craft. 'T were good you let him
   know;
For who that's but a queen, fair, sober, wise,
Would from a paddock,[4] from a bat, a gib,[5]
Such dear concernings hide? who would do
   so?
No, in despite of sense and secrecy,
Unpeg the basket on the house's top,
Let the birds fly, and, like the famous ape,
To try conclusions, in the basket creep,
And break your own neck down.
   QUEEN. Be thou assur'd, if words be made
      of breath,
And breath of life, I have no life to breathe
What thou hast said to me.
                              Hamlet, III, 4:137

[1] ecstasy: madness.   [2] compost: fertilizer.
[3] use: habit.   [4] paddock: toad.   [5] gib: tom-cat.

   QUEEN. Ah! my good lord, what have I
      seen tonight.
   KING. What, Gertrude? How does Ham-
      let?
   QUEEN. Mad as the sea and wind, when
      both contend
Which is the mightier. In his lawless fit,
Behind the arras hearing something stir,
Whips out his rapier, cries, 'A rat! a rat!'
And, in this brainish apprehension, kills
The unseen good old man.[1]
                              Hamlet, IV, 1:5

[1] man: POLONIUS.

   K. LEAR. Ay, every inch a king:
When I do stare, see how the subject quakes.
I pardon that man's life. What was thy
   cause?
Adultery?
Thou shalt not die: die for adultery! No:
The wren goes to 't, and the small gilded fly
Does lecher in my sight.
Let copulation thrive; for Gloucester's bas-
   tard son
Was kinder to his father than my daughters
Got 'tween the lawful sheets.
                              King Lear, IV, 6:109

   EMILIA. Why, who would not make her
husband a cuckold[1] to make him a monarch?
I should venture purgatory for 't.
   DESDEMONA. Beshrew me, if I would do
      such a wrong
For the whole world.
                              Othello, IV, 3:76

[1] cuckold: husband of a faithless wife.

   LEONTES. She's an adulteress, . . .
A bed-swerver, even as bad as those
That vulgars give bold'st titles.
                              Winter's Tale, II, 1:88, 93

ADVERSITY

   DUKE. Sweet are the uses of adversity,
Which like the toad, ugly and venomous,

Wears yet a precious jewel in his head;
                              As You Like It, II, 1:12

   ADRIANA. A wretched soul, bruis'd with
      adversity,
We bid be quiet when we hear it cry;
But were we burden'd with like weight of
   pain,
As much or more we should ourselves com-
   plain.
                              Comedy of Errors, II, 1:34

   FIRST KEEPER. This is the quondam[1] king;
      let's seize upon him.
   K. HENRY. Let me embrace thee, sour ad-
      versity.
For wise men say it is the wisest course.
                              III Henry VI, III, 1:23

[1] quondam: one-time.

   FRIAR LAURENCE. Thou fond[1] mad man,
      hear me but speak a word.
   ROMEO. O! thou wilt speak again of ban-
      ishment.
   FRIAR LAURENCE. I'll give thee armour to
      keep off that word;
Adversity's sweet milk, philosophy,
To comfort thee, though thou art banished.
                              Romeo and Juliet, III, 3:52

[1] fond: foolish.

ADVICE

   COUNTESS. Love all, trust a few,
Do wrong to none: be able for thine enemy
Rather in power than use, and keep thy
   friend
Under thy own life's key: be check'd[1] for
   silence,
But never tax'd[2] for speech.
                              All's Well That Ends Well, I, 1:73

[1] check'd: rebuked.   [2] tax'd: censured.

   POLONIUS. Yet here, Laertes! aboard,
      aboard, for shame!
The wind sits in the shoulder of your sail,
And you are stay'd[1] for. There; my blessing
   with thee!
And these few precepts in thy memory
See thou character.[2] Give thy thoughts no
   tongue,
Nor any unproportion'd thought his[3] act.
Be thou familiar, but by no means vulgar;
The friends thou hast, and their adoption
   tried,
Grapple them to thy soul with hoops of
   steel;
But do not dull thy palm with entertain-
   ment
Of each new-hatch'd, unfledg'd comrade.
   Beware
Of entrance to a quarrel, but being in,

Bear't that the opposed may beware of thee.
Give every man thine ear, but few thy
  voice;
Take each man's censure[4] but reserve thy
  judgment.
Costly thy habit as thy purse can buy,
But not express'd in fancy; rich, not gaudy;
For the apparel oft proclaims the man,
And they in France of the best rank and sta-
  tion
Are most select and generous, chief in that.
Neither a borrower nor a lender be:
For loan oft loses both itself and friend,
And borrowing dulls the edge of hus-
  bandry.[5]
This above all: to thine own self be true,
And it must follow, as the night the day,
Thou canst not then be false to any man.
Farewell; my blessing season this in thee!
  Hamlet, I, 3:55
[1] stay'd: waited.   [2] character: write.   [3] his:
its.   [4] censure: opinion, not necessarily criti-
cism.   [5] husbandry: economy.

Fool.[1] Have more than thou showest,
Speak less than thou knowest,
Lend less than thou owest.[2]
  King Lear, I, 4:131
[1] Fool: jester.   [2] owest: ownest.

Fool. When a wise man gives thee better
counsel, give me mine again: I would have
none but knaves follow it, since a fool
gives it.
That sir which serves and seeks for gain,
And follows but for form,
Will pack when it begins to rain,
And leave thee in the storm.
But I will tarry; the fool will stay,
And let the wise man fly:
The knave turns fool that runs away;
The fool no knave, perdy.
  Kent. Where learned you this, fool?
  Fool. Not i' the stocks, fool.
  King Lear, II, 4:75

Gratiano. But fish not, with this melancholy bait,
For this fool-gudgeon,[1] this opinion.
  Merchant of Venice, I, 1:101
[1] gudgeon: a fish easily caught.

Portia. It is a good divine that follows his
own instructions: I can easier teach twenty
what were good to be done, than be one of
the twenty to follow mine own teaching.
  Merchant of Venice, I, 2:16

Whereas thine eye hath chose the dame,
And stall'd the deer that thou should'st
  strike,

· · · · ·

Take counsel of some wiser head,
Neither too young nor yet unwed.
  Sonnets to Sundry Notes
  of Music, IV: 89, 93

AFFECTION

Celia. Come, come, wrestle with thy affections.
Rosalind. O! they take the part of a better wrestler than myself.
  As You Like It, I, 3:21

Laertes. Keep you in the rear of your af-
  fection,
Out of the shot and danger of desire.
  Hamlet, I, 3:34

King. Love! his affections do not that
  way tend.
  Hamlet, III, 1:170

Shylock. Affection,
Mistress of passion, sways it to the mood
Of what it likes, or loathes.
  Merchant of Venice, IV, 1:50

Affection is my captain, and he leadeth;
And when his gaudy banner is display'd,
The coward fights and will not be dismay'd.
  Rape of Lucrece, 271

I have debated, even in my soul,
What wrong, what shame, what sorrow I
  shall breed;
But nothing can affection's course control,
Or stop the headlong fury of his speed.
I know repentant tears ensue the deed,
  Rape of Lucrece, 498

Duke. How will she love, when the rich
  golden shaft
Hath kill'd the flock of all affections else
That live in her; when liver, brain, and
  heart,
These sovereign thrones, are all supplied,
  and fill'd
Her sweet perfections with one self[1] king.
  Twelfth Night, I, 1:35
[1] self: absolute.

Affection is a coal that must be cool'd;
Else, suffer'd, it will set the heart on fire.
The sea hath bounds, but deep desire hath
  none;
  Venus and Adonis, 387

AFFLICTION

Gloucester. O you mighty gods!
This world I do renounce, and in your
  sights

Shake patiently my great affliction off.
King Lear, IV, 6:34

GLOUCESTER. Henceforth I'll bear
Affliction till it do cry out itself
'Enough, enough,' and die.
King Lear, IV, 6:75

COSTARD. Welcome the sour cup of prosperity! Affliction may one day smile again; and till then, sit thee down, sorrow!
Love's Labour's Lost, I, 1:315

LEONTES. This affliction has a taste as sweet
As any cordial[1] comfort.
Winter's Tale, V, 3:76
[1] cordial: a soothing drink or medicine.

AGE

CLEOPATRA. Though age from folly could not give me freedom,
It does from childishness.
Antony and Cleopatra, I, 3:57

ENOBARBUS. Age cannot wither her,[1] nor custom stale
Her infinite variety; other women cloy
The appetites they feed, but she makes hungry
Where most she satisfies;
Antony and Cleopatra, II, 2:240
[1] Her: CLEOPATRA.

Unregarded age in corners thrown.
As You Like It, II, 3:42

HAMLET. The age is grown so picked[1] that the toe of the peasant comes so near the heel of the courtier, he galls his kibe.
Hamlet, V, 1:150
[1] picked: fastidious.   [2] kibe: sore heel.

BASTARD. Sweet, sweet, sweet poison for the age's tooth:
King John, I, 1:213

GREMIO. Skipper,[1] stand back: 't is age that nourisheth.
TRANIO. But youth in ladies' eyes that flourisheth.
Taming of the Shrew, II, 1:341
[1] Skipper: flighty fellow.

AIR

HAMLET. The air bites shrewdly; it is very cold.
HORATIO. It is a nipping and an eager[1] air.
Hamlet, I, 4:1
[1] eager: keen; often used for sour.

GHOST. But soft! methinks I scent the morning air;
Brief[1] let me be.
Hamlet, I, 5:58
[1] Brief, etc.: refers to belief that ghosts could appear only at night.

TITANIA. I will purge thy mortal grossness so
That thou shalt like an airy spirit go.
Midsummer Night's Dream, III, 1:163

LUCENTIO. Tranio, I saw her coral lips to move,
And with her breath she did perfume the air;
Sacred and sweet was all I saw in her.
Taming of the Shrew, I, 1:179

ALONE

K. HENRY. I and my bosom must debate awhile,
And then I would no other company.
Henry V, IV, 1:31

CASSIUS. Ye gods, it doth amaze me
A man of such a feeble temper should
So get the start of the majestic world,
And bear the palm alone.
Julius Caesar, I, 2:128

JULIET. My dismal scene I needs must act alone.
Romeo and Juliet, IV, 3:19

Now counting best to be with you alone,
Then better'd that the world may see my pleasure:
Sometime, all full with feasting on your sight,
And by and by clean starved for a look;
Sonnet 75

OLIVIA. Give us the place alone: we will hear this divinity.
Twelfth Night, I, 5:235

ALTERNATIVE

OCTAVIUS CAESAR. But I had rather fast from all four days
Than drink so much in one.
Antony and Cleopatra, II, 7:108

ELINOR. Whether hadst thou rather be a Faulconbridge
And like thy brother,[1] to enjoy thy land,
Or the reputed son of Coeur-de-Lion,
Lord[2] of thy presence and no land beside?
King John, I, 1:134

[1] like . . . brother: in place of brother. [2] Lord . . . presence: confident in command of your personality.

CLAUDIO. Is there no remedy?
ISABELLA. None, but such remedy, as to save a head,
To cleave a heart in twain.
Measure for Measure, III, 1:61

ISABELLA. I had rather my brother die by the law than my son should be unlawfully born.
Measure for Measure, III, 1:195

ANNE PAGE. Alas! I had rather be set quick[1] i' the earth
And bowl'd to death with turnips.
Merry Wives of Windsor, III, 4:90
[1] quick: alive.

AMBITION

[Song] ALL. Who doth ambition shun,
And loves to live i' the sun,
Seeking the food he eats
And pleas'd with what he gets,
Come hither, come hither, come hither:
Here shall he see
No enemy
But winter and rough weather.
As You Like It, II, 5:40

ARVIRAGUS. What should we speak of
When we are old as you? when we shall hear
The rain and wind beat dark December, how
In this our pinching cave shall we discourse
The freezing hours away? We have seen nothing;
Cymbeline, III, 3:35

HAMLET. O God! I could be bounded in a nutshell, and count myself a king of infinite space, were it not that I have bad dreams.
GUILDENSTERN. Which dreams indeed are ambition, for the very substance of the ambitious is merely the shadow of a dream.
HAMLET. A dream itself is but a shadow.
ROSENCRANTZ. Truly, and I hold ambition of so airy and light a quality that it is but a shadow's shadow.
Hamlet, II, 2:260

PRINCE.[1] Ill-weav'd ambition, how much art thou shrunk!
When that this body did contain a spirit,
A kingdom for it was too small a bound;
But now two paces of the vilest earth
Is room enough: this earth, that bears thee dead,

Bears not alive so stout[2] a gentleman.
I Henry IV, V, 4:88
[1] About HOTSPUR, whom he has killed. [2] stout: bold, resolute.

PLANTAGENET. Here dies the dusky torch of Mortimer,
Chok'd with ambition of the meaner sort.
I Henry VI, II, 5:122

DUCHESS.[1] Put forth thy hand, reach at the glorious gold.[2]
What! is 't too short? I'll lengthen it with mine;
And, having both together heav'd it up,
We'll both together lift our heads to heaven,
And never more abase our sight so low.
As to vouchsafe one glance unto the ground.

. . . . .

Were I a man, a duke, and next of blood,
I would remove these tedious stumbling-blocks
And smooth my way upon their headless necks;
And, being a woman, I will not be slack
To play my part in Fortune's pageant.
II Henry VI, I, 2:11, 63
[1] To her husband, GLOUCESTER, not the future RICHARD III. [2] gold: crown.

GLOUCESTER[1] [soliloquy]. Why then, I do but dream on sovereignty;
Like one that stands upon a promontory,
And spies a far-off shore where he would tread,
Wishing his foot were equal with his eye;
And chides the sea that sunders him from thence,

. . . . .

Then, since this earth affords no joy to me
But to command, to check,[2] to o'erbear such
As are of better person than myself,
I'll make my heaven to dream upon the crown;
And, whiles I live, to account this world but hell,
Until my misshap'd trunk that bears this head
Be round impaled with a glorious crown.
III Henry VI, III, 2:134, 165
[1] Later KING RICHARD III. [2] check: reprove.

BUCKINGHAM. The devil speed him! no man's pie is freed
From his ambitious finger.
Henry VIII, I, 1:52

WOLSEY. Cromwell,[1] I charge thee, fling away ambition:
By that sin fell the angels: how can man then,
The image of his Maker, hope to win by 't?

Love thyself last: cherish those hearts that
   hate thee:
Corruption wins not more than honesty.
Still in thy right hand carry gentle peace,
To silence envious tongues: be just and fear
   not.
Let all the ends thou aim'st at be thy coun-
   try's,
Thy God's, and truth's: then if thou fall'st,
   O Cromwell!
Thou fall'st a blessed martyr. Serve the king;
And,—prithee, lead me in:
There take an inventory of all I have,
To the last penny: 't is the king's: my robe
And my integrity to heaven is all
I dare now call mine own. O Cromwell,
   Cromwell!
Had I but serv'd my God with half the zeal
I serv'd my king, he would not in mine age
Have left me naked to mine enemies.
                              Henry VIII, III, 2:441
[1] CROMWELL: servant to WOLSEY.

Ross. 'Gainst nature still!
Thriftless ambition, that wilt ravin up
Thine own life's means!
                              Macbeth, II, 4:28

GLOUCESTER.[1] If not to answer, you might
   haply[2] think
Tongue-tied ambition, not replying, yielded
To bear the golden yoke of sovereignty,
Which fondly[3] you would here impose on
   me.
                              Richard III, III, 7:144
[1] Later KING RICHARD III.   [2] haply: perchance.
[3] fondly: foolishly.

ANGEL

HAMLET. Angels and ministers of grace
   defend us!
                              Hamlet, I, 4:39

HORATIO. Now cracks a noble heart. Good
   night, sweet prince,
And flights of angels sing thee to thy rest!
                              Hamlet, V, 2:370

BUCKINGHAM [as he is led to execution].
Go with me, like good angels, to my end;
And, as the long divorce of steel falls on me,
Make of your prayers one sweet sacrifice;
And lift my soul to heaven.
                              Henry VIII, II, 1:75

MALCOLM. Angels are bright still, though
   the brightest fell;
Though all things foul would wear the
   brows of grace,
Yet grace must still look so.
                              Macbeth, IV, 3:22

BOYET. 'For,' quoth the king, 'an angel
   shalt thou see;
Yet fear not thou, but speak audaciously.'
The boy replied, 'An angel is not evil;
I should have fear'd her had she been a
   devil.'
                              Love's Labour's Lost, V, 2:103

GRATIANO. Poor Desdemona! I am glad
   thy father's dead.
Thy match was mortal to him, and pure
   grief
Shore his old thread in twain: did he live
   now,
This sight would make him do a desperate
   turn,
Yea, curse his better angel from his side,
And fall to reprobance.
                              Othello, V, 2:204

K. RICHARD. God for his Richard hath in
   heavenly pay
A glorious angel: then, if angels fight,
Weak men must fall, for heaven still[1] guards
   the right.
                              Richard II, III, 2:60
[1] still: always, as often in Shakespeare, usually
with a sense of continued action.

ROMEO. She speaks;
O! speak again, bright angel: for thou art
As glorious to this night, being o'er my
   head,
As is a winged messenger of heaven
Unto the white-upturned wond'ring eyes
Of mortals, that fall back to gaze on him
When he bestrides the lazy-pacing clouds,
And sails upon the bosom of the air.
                              Romeo and Juliet, II, 2:20

Two loves I have of comfort and despair,
Which like two spirits do suggest[1] me still:[2]
The better angel is a man, right fair,
The worser spirit a woman, colour'd ill.
To win me soon to hell, my female evil
Tempteth my better angel from my side,
And would corrupt my saint to be a devil,
Wooing his purity with her foul pride.
And whether that my angel be turn'd fiend
Suspect I may, yet not directly tell;
But being both from[3] me, both to each
   friend,
I guess one angel in another's hell:
Yet this shall I ne'er know, but live in doubt,
Till my bad angel[4] fire my good one out.
                              Sonnet 144
[1] suggest: tempt. [2] still: continuously. [3] from:
away from.   [4] bad angel: probably the dark
lady.

VALENTINE. Is she not a heavenly saint?
PROTEUS. No; but she is an earthly paragon.
                              Two Gentlemen of Verona, II, 4:145

ANGER

Mecaenas. Never anger
Made good guard for itself.
Antony and Cleopatra, IV, 1:9

Volumnia. Anger's my meat; I sup upon
myself.
And so shall starve with feeding.
Coriolanus, IV, 2:50

Norfolk. Anger is like
A full-hot horse, who being allow'd his way,
Self-mettle tires him.

. . . . .

Be advis'd;
Heat not a furnace for your foe so hot
That it do singe yourself.
Henry VIII, I, 1:132, 139

Brutus. When you are over-earnest with
your Brutus,
He'll think your mother chides, and leave
you so.
Julius Caesar, IV, 3:123

Iago. But men are men; the best sometimes
forget:
Though Cassio did some little wrong to him,
As men in rage strike those that wish them
best.
Othello, II, 3:241

Katharina. My tongue will tell the anger
of my heart,
Or else my heart, concealing it, will break.
Taming of the Shrew, IV, 3:77

Timon. Yond man is ever angry.
Go, let him have a table by himself,
For he does neither affect[1] company,
Nor is he fit for it, indeed.
Timon of Athens, I, 2:28
[1] affect: enjoy.

Paulina. If I prove honey-mouth'd, let
my tongue blister,
And never to my red-look'd anger be
The trumpet any more.
Winter's Tale, II, 2:34

ANSWER

Countess. Marry, that's a bountiful answer that fits all questions.
Clown. It is like a barber's chair that fits
all buttocks.
All's Well That Ends Well, II, 2:15

Countess. I will be a fool in question,
hoping to be the wiser by your answer.
All's Well That Ends Well, II, 2:41

Isabella. If that be sin, I'll make it my
morn prayer
To have it added to the faults of mine,
And nothing of your answer.
Measure for Measure, II, 4:71

Duke. If his own life answer the straitness[1] of his proceeding, it shall become him
well; wherein if he chance to fail, he hath
sentenced himself.
Measure for Measure, III, 2:269
[1] straitness: strictness.

Proteus. A silly answer and fitting well
a sheep.
Two Gentlemen of Verona, I, 1:81

APE

Imogen. What makes your admiration?
Iachimo. It cannot be i' the eye; for apes
and monkeys
'Twixt two such shes would chatter this
way and
Contemn with mows[1] the other.
Cymbeline, I, 6:38
[1] mows: grimaces.

Beatrice. He that is less than a man, I am
not for him: therefore I will even take
sixpence in earnest[1] of the bear-ward,[2] and
lead his apes[3] into hell.[4]
Much Ado About Nothing, II, 1:41
[1] earnest: payment ahead of time. [2] bear-
ward: in some editions, bear-herd. [3] apes:
apes rode on the bears. [4] hell: refers to the
saying that unmarried women were doomed
to lead apes in hell.

APPEARANCE

Aufidius. Say, what's thy name?
Thou hast a grim appearance, and thy face
Bears a command in 't; though thy tackle's
torn,
Thou show'st a noble vessel.[1]
Coriolanus, IV, 5:65
[1] vessel: ship; metaphor for personal appear-
ance.

Falstaff. Bardolph, am I not fallen away
vilely since this last action? do I not bate?[1]
do I not dwindle? Why, my skin hangs
about me like an old lady's loose gown; I am
withered like an old apple-john.[2]
I Henry IV, III, 3:1
[1] bate: shrink. [2] apple-john: an apple that
withers badly.

O! do but think
You stand upon the rivage[1] and behold

A city on the inconstant billows dancing;
For so appears this fleet majestical.
Henry V, Prologue to Act III: 13
[1] rivage: shore.

K. HENRY. All his senses have but human conditions: his ceremonies laid by, in his nakedness he appears but a man.
Henry V, IV, 1:108

'But woe is me! too early I attended[1]
A youthful suit, it was to gain my grace,
Of one by nature's outwards so commended,
That maidens' eyes stuck over all his face.
A Lover's Complaint, 78
[1] attended . . . suit: followed a youthful fancy.

BANQUO [to the WITCHES]. I' the name of truth,
Are ye fantastical,[1] or that indeed
Which outwardly ye show?
Macbeth, I, 3:52
[1] fantastical: imaginary.

DUKE. O! what may man within him hide,
Though angel on the outward side:
Measure for Measure, III, 2:285

GLOUCESTER.[1] Sweet prince, the untainted virtue of your years
Hath not yet div'd into the world's deceit:
Nor more can you distinguish of a man
Than of his outward show; which, God he knows,
Seldom or never jumpeth[2] with the heart.
Richard III, III, 1:7
[1] Gloucester, later KING RICHARD III. [2] jumpeth: agrees.

APPETITE

POMPEY. Let witchcraft join with beauty, lust with both!
Tie up the libertine[1] in a field of feasts,
Keep his brain fuming; Epicurean cooks
Sharpen with cloyless sauce his appetite,
That sleep and feeding may prorogue his honour
Even till a Lethe'd[2] dulness!
Antony and Cleopatra, II, 1:22
[1] libertine: ANTONY. [2] Lethe: a river in Hades; its water caused forgetfulness.

DROMIO EPHESUS. Methinks, your maw,[1] like mine, should be your clock
And strike you home without a messenger.
Comedy of Errors, I, 2:66
[1] maw: stomach.

HAMLET. She would hang on him,
As if increase of appetite had grown
By what it fed on.
Hamlet, I, 2:143

O appetite, from judgment stand aloof!
The one a palate hath that needs will taste,
Though reason weep, and cry, 'It is thy last.'
A Lover's Complaint, 166

MACBETH. Now, good digestion wait on appetite,
And health on both.
Macbeth, III, 4:38

SALARINO. O! ten times faster Venus' pigeons fly
To seal love's bonds new-made, than they are wont
To keep obliged faith unforfeited.
GRATIANO. That ever holds: who riseth from a feast
With that keen appetite that he sits down?
Merchant of Venice, II, 6:5

ULYSSES. And appetite an universal wolf,
So doubly seconded with will and power,
Must make perforce an universal prey,
And last eat up himself.
Troilus and Cressida, I, 3:12

APRIL

ANTONY. The April's in her eyes; it is love's spring,
And these the showers to bring it on.
Antony and Cleopatra, III, 2:43

SERVANT. A day in April never came so sweet,
To show how costly summer was at hand,
As this fore-spurrer comes before his lord.
Merchant of Venice, II, 9:93

When proud-pied[1] April, dress'd in all his trim,
Hath put a spirit of youth in every thing.
Sonnet 98
[1] proud-pied: in many colors.

PANDARUS. I'll be sworn 't is true: he will weep you, an 't[1] were a man born in April.
CRESSIDA. And I'll spring up in his tears, an 't were a nettle against May.
Troilus and Cressida, I, 2:188
[1] an 't: as if.

IRIS. Thy banks with pioned and twilled brims,
Which spongy April at thy hest betrims,
To make cold nymphs chaste crowns.
Tempest, IV, 1:64

ARGUMENT

SICINIUS. With rigorous hands: He[1] hath resisted law,

And therefore law shall scorn him further
  trial
Than the severity of the public power,
Which he so sets at nought.
                        Coriolanus, III, 1:267
[1] He: CORIOLANUS.

GUILDENSTERN. O! there has been much
throwing about of brains.
                        Hamlet, II, 2:375

FALSTAFF. Well, thou wilt be horribly
chid[1] tomorrow when thou comest to thy
father; if thou love me, practise an answer.
  PRINCE. Do thou stand for my father, and
examine me upon the particulars of my life.
  FALSTAFF. Shall I? content: this chair shall
be my state, this dagger my sceptre, and this
cushion my crown.

                . . . . .

[Pretending to speak for KING HENRY].
And yet there is a virtuous man whom I
have often noted in thy company, but I
know not his name.
  PRINCE. What manner of man, an[2] it like
your majesty?
  FALSTAFF. A goodly portly man, i' faith,
and a corpulent; of a cheerful look, a pleasing eye, and a most noble carriage; and, as
I think, his age some fifty, or, by 'r[3] lady,
inclining to threescore; and now I remember me, his name is Falstaff: if that man
should be lewdly given, he deceiveth me;
for, Harry, I see virtue in his looks. If then
the tree may be known by the fruit, as the
fruit by the tree, then peremptorily I speak
it, there is virtue in that Falstaff: him keep
with, the rest banish.
                        1 Henry IV, II, 4:410, 459
[1] chid: scolded. [2] an . . . like: if it please.
[3] by 'r lady: a mild oath, "by our lady," the
Virgin Mary.

PRINCE HAL [pretending to be the KING,
his father]. There is a devil haunts thee in
the likeness of an old fat man; a tun of man
is thy companion. Why dost thou converse
with that trunk of humours,[1] that bolting-
hutch[2] of beastliness, that swoln parcel of
dropsies, that huge bombard[3] of sack, that
stuffed cloak-bag of guts, that roasted Manningtree[4] ox with the pudding in his belly,
that reverend vice, that grey iniquity, that
father ruffian, that vanity in years? Wherein
is he good but to taste sack and drink it?
wherein neat and cleanly but to carve a capon and eat it? wherein cunning but in
craft? wherein crafty but in villany?
wherein villanous but in all things? wherein
worthy but in nothing?
                        1 Henry IV, II, 4:492

[1] humours: caprices. [2] bolting-hutch: flour-
bin. [3] bombard: leather container for liquor.
[4] Manningtree: a town where a whole ox was
roasted at a fair.

FALSTAFF [speaking as KING]. If to be old
and merry be a sin, then many an old host
that I know is damned: if to be fat be to be
hated, then Pharaoh's lean kine are to be
loved. No, my good lord; banish Peto, banish Bardolph, banish Poins; but for sweet[1]
Jack Falstaff, kind Jack Falstaff, true Jack
Falstaff, valiant Jack Falstaff, and therefore
more valiant, being, as he is, old Jack Falstaff, banish not him thy Harry's company:
banish plump Jack, and banish all the world.
                        1 Henry IV, II, 4:518
[1] sweet: this word was frequently used in a
way that would now be offensive.

HOLOFERNESS. He draweth out the thread
of his verbosity finer than the staple of his
argument.
                        Love's Labour's Lost, V, 1:18

[Arguments determine many important de-
cisions of Shakespeare's characters. LADY MAC-
BETH knows her husband well. After reading
his letter telling of the prophecy of the
witches, she says:]
Hie thee hither,
That I may pour my spirits in thine ear,
And chastise with the valour of my tongue
All that impedes thee from the golden
  round,[1]
Which fate and metaphysical[2] aid doth seem
To have thee crown'd withal.
                        Macbeth, I, 5:26
[1] golden round: the crown. [2] metaphysical:
supernatural.

[In this great soliloquy MACBETH argues with
himself about the murder of DUNCAN. A solilo-
quy expresses the speaker's true thought and
feeling.]
  MACBETH. If[1] it were done when 't is done,
    then 't were well
It were done quickly; if the assassination
Could trammel[2] up the consequence, and
    catch
With his surcease success; that but this blow
Might be the be-all and the end-all here,
But here, upon this bank and shoal of time,
We'd jump[3] the life to come. But in these
    cases
We still[4] have judgment here; that we but
    teach
Bloody instructions, which, being taught, re-
    turn
To plague the inventor; this even-handed
    justice
Commends the ingredients of our poison'd
    chalice

To our own lips. He 's here in double trust:
First, as I am his kinsman and his subject,
Strong both against the deed; then, as his
    host,
Who should against his murderer shut the
    door,
Not bear the knife myself. Besides, this Dun-
    can
Hath borne his faculties so meek, hath been
So clear in his great office, that his virtues
Will plead like angels trumpet-tongued
    against
The deep damnation of his taking-off;
And pity, like a naked new-born babe,
Striding the blast, or heaven's cherubin,
    hors'd
Upon the sightless⁵ couriers of the air,
Shall blow the horrid deed in every eye,
That tears shall drown the wind. I have no
    spur
To prick the sides of my intent, but only
Vaulting ambition, which o'erleaps itself
And falls on the other—
                                    Macbeth, I, 7:1
¹ If, etc.: if the murder meant the crown and
safety. ² trammel . . . success: catch as in a
net and with his (its) surcease (conclusion).
³ jump: risk. ⁴ still: always, as often in Shake-
speare. ⁵ sightless: invisible.

                                    Enter LADY M.
    MACBETH. We will proceed no further in
        this¹ business:
He hath honour'd me of late; and I have
    bought
Golden opinions from all sorts of people,
Which would be worn now in their newest
    gloss,
Not cast aside so soon.
    LADY M. Was the hope drunk
Wherein you dress'd yourself? hath it slept
    since,
And wakes it now, to look so green and
    pale
At what it did so freely? From this time
Such I account thy love. Art thou afeard
To be the same in thine own act and valour
As thou art in desire?
                        . . . . .
    MACBETH. Prithee, peace.
I dare do all that may become a man;
Who dares do more is none.
    LADY M. What beast was 't then
That made you break this enterprise to me?
When you durst do it then you were a man;
And, to be more than what you were, you
    would
Be so much more the man. Nor time nor
    place²
Did then adhere, and yet you would make
    both:
They have made themselves, and that their
    fitness now

Does unmake you. I have given suck, and
    know
How tender 't is to love the babe that milks
    me:
I would, while it was smiling in my face,
Have pluck'd my nipple from his boneless
    gums,
And dash'd the brains out, had I so sworn
    as you
Have done to this.
                        . . . . .
    MACBETH. If we should fail,—
    LADY M. We fail.
But screw your courage to the sticking-
    place,
And we 'll not fail. When Duncan is asleep,
Whereto the rather shall his day's hard jour-
    ney
Soundly invite him, his two chamberlains
Will I with wine and wassail so convince³
That memory, the warder of the brain,
Shall be a fume, and the receipt of reason
A limbeck⁴ only; when in swinish sleep
Their drenched natures lie as in a death,
What cannot you and I perform upon
The unguarded Duncan? what not put upon
His spongy officers, who shall bear the guilt
Of our great quell?⁵
    MACBETH. Bring forth men-children only;
For thy undaunted mettle should compose
Nothing but males. Will it not be receiv'd,
When we have mark'd with blood those
    sleepy two
Of his own chamber and us'd their very
    daggers,
That they have done 't?
    LADY M. Who dares receive it other,
As we shall make our griefs and clamour
    roar
Upon his death?
    MACBETH. I am settled, and bend up
Each corporal⁶ agent to this terrible feat.
Away, and mock the time with fairest show:
False face must hide what the false heart
    doth know.
                                    Macbeth, I, 7:31, 45
¹ this business: the murder of DUNCAN. ² nor
time nor place: a much debated passage; con-
sensus is, a time before the play opens. ³ con-
vince: overcome. ⁴ limbeck: a still. ⁵ quell:
murder. ⁶ corporal: bodily.

    BASSANIO. In my school-days, when I had
        lost one shaft,
I shot his fellow of the self-same flight
The self-same way with more advised
    watch,
To find the other forth; and by adventuring
    both,
I oft found both. I urge this childhood
    proof,
Because what follows is pure innocence.
                        Merchant of Venice, I, 1:140

LAUNCELOT GOBBO. I will try confusions[1]
with him.
Merchant of Venice, II, 2:38
[1] confusions: LAUNCELOT's mistake for conclusions.

GRATIANO. You must not deny me: I must
go with you to Belmont.
BASSANIO. Why, then you must. But hear
thee, Gratiano;
Thou art too wild, too rude and bold of
voice.

. . . . .

GRATIANO. Signior Bassanio, hear me:
If I do not put on a sober habit,[1]
Talk with respect, and swear but now and
then,
Wear prayer-books in my pocket, look demurely,
Nay more, while grace is saying, hood mine
eyes
Thus with my hat, and sigh, and say 'amen,'
Use all the observance of civility,
Like one well studied in a sad ostent[2]
To please his grandam, never trust me more.
Merchant of Venice, II, 2:188, 198
[1] habit: costume.   [2] ostent: appearance, show.

MOWBRAY. 'Tis not the trial of a woman's
war,
The bitter clamour of two eager tongues,
Can arbitrate this cause betwixt us twain.
Richard II, I, 1:48

GLOUCESTER.[1] With lies well steel'd with
weighty arguments.
Richard III, I, 1:148
[1] Later KING RICHARD III.

How can my Muse want[1] subject to invent,
While thou dost breathe, that pour'st into
my verse
Thine own sweet argument, too excellent
For every vulgar paper to rehearse?
Sonnet 38

[1] want: lack.

O! know, sweet love, I always write of you,
And you and love are still[1] my argument.
Sonnet 76
[1] still: always.

MALVOLIO.[1] Let thy tongue twang with
arguments of state.
Twelfth Night, III, 4:78
[1] Quoting from MARIA's letter.

ARISTOCRACY

KING. Strange is it that our bloods,
Of colour, weight, and heat, pour'd all together,

Would quite confound[1] distinction, yet
stand off
In differences so mighty

. . . . .

From lowest place when virtuous things
proceed,
The place is dignified by the doer's deed.
All's Well That Ends Well, II, 3:125, 132
[1] confound: overcome, make impossible.

CORIOLANUS. Thus we debase
The nature of our seats, and make the rabble
Call our cares fears; which will in time
break ope
The locks o' the senate, and bring in the
crows
To peck the eagles.

. . . . .

At once pluck out
The multitudinous tongue; let them not lick
The sweet which is their poison. Your dishonour
Mangles true judgment, and bereaves the
state
Of that integrity which should become it,
Not having the power to do the good it
would,
For[1] the ill which doth control 't.
Coriolanus, III, 1:135, 156
[1] For: because of.

ULYSSES. O! when degree[1] is shak'd,[2]
Which is the ladder to all high designs,
The enterprise is sick. How could communities,
Degrees in schools, and brotherhoods in cities,
Peaceful commerce from dividable shores,
The primogenitive[3] and due of birth,
Prerogative of age, crowns, sceptres, laurels,
But by degree, stand in authentic place?
Troilus and Cressida, I, 3:101
[1] degree: class or caste, military rank.   [2] shak'd: laid aside.   [3] primogenitive: right of oldest son.

ARREST

HAMLET. Had I but time, as this fell[1] sergeant, Death,
Is strict in his arrest, O! I could tell you,—
Hamlet, V, 2:347
[1] fell: cruel.

MISTRESS QUICKLY.[1] A hundred mark is a
long one for a poor lone woman to bear;
and I have borne, and borne, and borne; and
have been fubbed[2] off, and fubbed off, and
fubbed off, from this day to that day.

. . . . .

Please your grace, I am a poor widow of Eastcheap, and he[3] is arrested at my suit.

CHIEF JUSTICE. For what sum?

M. QUICKLY. It is more than for some, my lord; it is for all, all I have. He hath eaten me out of house and home; he hath put all my substance into that fat belly of his.

. . . . .

Thou[4] didst swear to me then, as I was washing thy wound, to marry me and make me my lady thy wife.

. . . . .

And didst thou not kiss me and bid me fetch thee thirty shillings?

. . . . .

By this heavenly ground I tread on, I must be fain to pawn both my plate and the tapestry of my dining-chambers.

. . . . .

FALSTAFF. Let it be ten pound if thou canst. Come, an 't were not for thy humours, there 's not a better wench in England. Go, wash thy face, and draw[5] thy action. Come, thou must not be in this humour with me.

. . . . .

M. QUICKLY. Prithee, Sir John, let it be but twenty nobles: i' faith, I am loath to pawn my plate, so God save me, la!

FALSTAFF. Let it alone; I'll make other shift: you'll be a fool still.

M. QUICKLY. Well, you shall have it, though I pawn my gown. I hope you'll come to supper. You'll pay me all together?

II Henry IV, II, 1:34, 76, 98, 109, 143, 151, 160, 165

[1] FALSTAFF's hostess. [2] fubbed off: put off.
[3] he: FALSTAFF. [4] To FALSTAFF. [5] draw . . . action: withdraw arrest for debt.

ELBOW. I do lean upon justice, sir, and do bring in here before your good honour two notorious benefactors.[1]

Measure for Measure, II, 1:48

[1] benefactors: ELBOW's error for malefactors.

DOGBERRY. One word, sir. Our watch, sir, have indeed comprehended two aspicious persons, and we would have them this morning examined before your worship.

Much Ado About Nothing, III, 5:49

ARROGANCE

MENENIUS. The tartness of his face sours ripe grapes: when he[1] walks, he moves like an engine, and the ground shrinks before his treading: he is able to pierce a corslet with

his eye; talks like a knell, and his hum is a battery. He sits in his state, as a thing made for Alexander. What he bids be done is finished with his bidding. He wants[2] nothing of a god but eternity and a heaven to throne in.

Coriolanus, V, 4:18

[1] he: CORIOLANUS. [2] wants: lacks.

SURREY. Can ye endure to hear this arrogance?

And from this fellow? If we live thus tamely,

To be thus jaded by a piece of scarlet,

Farewell nobility.

Henry VIII, III, 2:278

ULYSSES. Pride hath no other glass

To show itself but pride, for supple knees

Feed arrogance and are the proud man's fees.

Troilus and Cressida, III, 3:47

ASS

DROMIO EPHESUS. By the wrongs I suffer and the blows I bear,

I should kick, being kick'd; and being at that pass,

You would keep from my heels and beware of an ass.

Comedy of Errors, III, 1:16

FIRST CLOWN. Cudgel thy brains no more about it, for your dull ass will not mend his pace with beating.

Hamlet, V, 1:63

ANTONY. Then take we down his load, and turn him[1] off,

Like to the empty ass to shake his ears,

And graze in commons.

Julius Caesar, IV, 1:24

[1] him: LEPIDUS, one of the three men ruling Rome.

FALSTAFF. I do begin to perceive that I am made an ass.

Merry Wives of Windsor, V, 5:124

CONRADE. Away! you are an ass; you are an ass.

DOGBERRY. Dost thou not suspect[1] my place? Dost thou not suspect my years? O that he were here to write me down an ass! but masters, remember that I am an ass; though it be not written down, yet forget not that I am an ass. No, thou villain, thou art full of piety,[2] as shall be proved upon thee by good witness.

. . . . .

And, masters, do not forget to specify, when
time and place shall serve, that I am an ass.
Much Ado About Nothing, IV, 2:75
and V, 1:263

[1] suspect: respect. [2] piety: the crime DOG-
BERRY means is anyone's guess.

IAGO. Make the Moor thank me, love me,
and reward me,
For making him egregiously an ass.
Othello, II, 1:317

CALIBAN. What a thrice-double ass
Was I, to take this drunkard for a god,
And worship this dull fool!
Tempest, V, 1:295

AUTHORITY

CORIOLANUS. Behold! these are the trib-
unes of the people,
The tongues o' the common mouth: I do
despise them;
For they do prank them in authority
Against all noble sufferance.[1]
Coriolanus, III, 1:21

[1] sufferance: endurance.

CORIOLANUS. My soul aches
To know, when two authorities are up,
Neither supreme, how soon confusion
May enter 'twixt the gap of both and take
The one by the other.
Coriolanus, III, 1:108

FLAVIUS. Hence! home, you idle creatures,
get you home:
Is this a holiday?

. . . . .

MARULLUS. But what trade art thou? Answer me directly.
SECOND COMMONER. A trade, sir, that I
hope I may use with a safe conscience;
which is, indeed, sir a mender of bad soles.

. . . . .

I am, indeed, sir, a surgeon to old shoes;
when they are in great danger, I recover
them.
Julius Caesar, I, 1:1, 12, 27

KENT. You have that in your countenance
which I would fain call master . . . Authority.
King Lear, I, 4:29

CLAUDIO. Thus can the demi-god Authority
Make us pay down for our offence by
weight.
Measure for Measure, I, 2:124

ISABELLA. Man, proud man,
Drest in a little brief authority,
Most ignorant of what he 's most assur'd,[1]
His glassy essence,[2] like an angry ape,
Plays such fantastic tricks before high
heaven
As make the angels weep.
Measure for Measure, II, 2:118

[1] assur'd: certain. [2] glassy essence: nature like
a glass reflecting thoughts of others.

ISABELLA. Authority, though it err like
others,
Hath yet a kind of medicine in itself,
That skins the vice o' the top.
Measure for Measure, II, 2:134

Art made tongue-tied by authority.
And folly doctor-like controlling skill.
Sonnet 66

PETRUCHIO. I say it is the moon.
KATHARINA. I know it is the moon.
PETRUCHIO. Nay, then you lie; it is the
blessed sun.
KATHARINA. Then God be bless'd, it is the
blessed sun:
But sun it is not when you say it is not,
And the moon changes even as your mind.
What you will have it nam'd, even that it is;
And so it shall be so for Katharine.
Taming of the Shrew, IV, 5:16

CLOWN.[1] Though authority be a stubborn
bear, yet he is oft led by the nose with gold.
Winter's Tale, IV, 4:830

[1] CLOWN: a rustic.

BABE

HELENA. He that of greatest works is fin-
isher
Oft does them by the weakest minister:
So holy writ in babes hath judgment shown.
All's Well That Ends Well, II, 1:139

POLONIUS. Marry,[1] I'll teach you: think
yourself a baby,
That you have ta'en these tenders[2] for true
pay,
Which are not sterling.
Hamlet, I, 3:105

[1] Marry: indeed; originally an oath, "by
Mary." [2] tenders: offers.

HAMLET. That great baby[1] you see there
is not yet out of his swaddling-clouts.
ROSENCRANTZ. Happily he's the second
time come to them; for they say an old man
is twice a child.
Hamlet, II, 2:400

[1] baby: POLONIUS.

Q. ELIZABETH. Stay yet; look back with me unto the Tower.
Pity, you ancient stones, those tender babes
Whom envy hath immur'd within your walls,
Rough cradle for such little pretty ones!
Rude ragged nurse, old sullen playfellow
For tender princes, use my babies well.
So foolish sorrow bids your stones farewell.
Richard III, IV, 1:98

Q. ELIZABETH. Ah! my poor princes, ah! my tender babes,
My unblown flowers, new-appearing sweets,
If yet your gentle souls fly in the air
And be not fix'd in doom perpetual,
Hover about me with your airy wings,
And hear your mother's lamentation.
Richard III, IV, 4:9

ANTIGONUS. Come on, poor babe:
Some powerful spirit instruct the kites and ravens
To be thy nurses!
Winter's Tale, II, 3:185

BACHELOR

KING. Fair maid, send forth thine eye: this youthful parcel
Of noble bachelors stand at my bestowing.
All's Well That Ends Well, II, 3:58

IACHIMO. Can my sides hold, to think that man, who knows
By history, report, or his own proof,
What woman is, yea, what she cannot choose
But must be, will his free hours languish for
Assured bondage?
Cymbeline, I, 6:69

CINNA. Wisely I say, I am a bachelor.
CITIZEN. That's as much as to say, they are fools that marry.
Julius Caesar, III, 3:17

BENEDICK. That a woman conceived me, I thank her; that she brought me up, I likewise give her most humble thanks. . . . Because I will not do them the wrong to mistrust any, I will do myself the right to trust none, and the fine[1] is, for the which I may go the finer,[2] I will live a bachelor.
Much Ado About Nothing, I, 1:240
[1] fine: end.   [2] finer: better.

DON PEDRO. I shall see thee, ere I die, look pale with love.
BENEDICK. With anger, with sickness, or with hunger, my Lord; not with love: prove that ever I lose more blood with love than I will get again with drinking, pick out mine

eyes with a ballad-maker's pen, and hang me up at the door of a brothel-house for the sign of blind Cupid.
Much Ado About Nothing, I, 1:250

DON PEDRO. 'In time the savage bull doth bear the yoke.'
BENEDICK. The savage bull may; but if ever the sensible Benedick bear it, pluck off the bull's horns and set them in my forehead.
Much Ado About Nothing, I, 1:263

BENEDICK. When I said I would die a bachelor, I did not think I should live till I were married.
Much Ado About Nothing, II, 3:253

DON PEDRO. He hath twice or thrice cut Cupid's bowstring, and the little hangman dare not shoot at him. He hath a heart as sound as a bell, and his tongue is the clapper; for what his heart thinks his tongue speaks.
Much Ado About Nothing, III, 2:12

DON PEDRO. How dost thou, Benedick, the married man?
Much Ado About Nothing, V, 4:100

No, lady, no; my heart longs not to groan,
But soundly sleep, while now it sleeps alone.
Venus and Adonis, 785

BALLAD

JAQUES. And then the lover,
Sighing like furnace, with a woeful ballad
Made to his mistress' eyebrow.
As You Like It, II, 7:147

FALSTAFF.[1] Go hang thyself in thine own heir apparent garters![2] If I be ta'en I'll peach[3] for this. An[4] I have not ballads made on you all, and sung to filthy tunes, let a cup of sack be my poison.
I Henry IV, II, 2:45
[1] To PRINCE HAL, heir to the throne.   [2] garters: pun on Knight of the Garter.   [3] peach: turn king's evidence.   [4] An: if.

HOTSPUR. I had rather be a kitten, and cry mew
Than one of these same metre ballad-mongers;
I had rather hear a brazen canstick turn'd,
Or a dry wheel grate on the axle-tree;
And that would set my teeth nothing on edge.
I Henry IV, III, 1:128

SERVANT. O master! if you did but hear the pedlar at the door, you would never dance again after a tabor and pipe; no, the bagpipe could not move you. He sings several tunes faster than you'll tell[1] money: he utters them as he had eaten ballads and all men's ears grew to his tunes.

CLOWN.[2] He could never come better: he shall come in. I love a ballad but even too well, if it be doleful matter merrily set down, or a very pleasant thing indeed and sung lamentably.[3]

Winter's Tale, IV, 4:181

[1] tell: count.   [2] CLOWN: rustic.   [3] lamentably: sadly.

BANISHMENT

K. RICHARD. We banish you our territories:
You, cousin Hereford,[1] upon pain of life,
Till twice five summers have enrich'd our fields,
Shall not regreet our fair dominions,
But tread the stranger paths of banishment.

Richard II, I, 3:139

[1] HEREFORD: another name for BOLINGBROKE, later KING HENRY IV.

BOLINGBROKE. This must my comfort be,
The sun that warms you here shall shine on me;
And those his golden beams to you here lent
Shall point on me and gild my banishment.

Richard II, I, 3:144

K. RICHARD. Norfolk, for thee remains a heavier doom,
Which I with some unwillingness pronounce:
The sly slow hours shall not determinate
The dateless limit of thy dear exile;
The hopeless word of 'never to return'
Breathe I against thee, upon pain of life.

Richard II, I, 3:148

BOLINGBROKE.[1] By this time, had the king permitted us,
One of our souls had[2] wander'd in the air,
Banish'd this frail sepulchre of our flesh,
As now our flesh is banish'd from this land.

Richard II, I, 3:194

[1] To MOWBRAY.   [2] had: would have.

BOLINGBROKE. Where'er I wander, boast of this I can,
Though banish'd, yet a true-born Englishman.

Richard II, I, 3:308

BOLINGBROKE. And sigh'd my English breath in foreign clouds,
Eating the bitter bread of banishment.

Richard II, III, 1:20

JULIET. 'Tybalt is dead, and Romeo banished!'
That 'banished,' that one word 'banished,'
Hath slain ten thousand Tybalts. Tybalt's death
Was woe enough, if it had ended there.

Romeo and Juliet, III, 2:112

ROMEO. There is no world without Verona walls,
But purgatory, torture, hell itself.
Hence banished is banish'd from the world,
And the world's exile is death; then 'banished'
Is death mis-term'd. Calling death 'banished,'
Thou cutt'st my head off with a golden axe,
And smil'st upon the stroke that murders me.

. . . . .

'T is torture, and not mercy: heaven is here,
Where Juliet lives; and every cat and dog
And little mouse, every unworthy thing,
Live here in heaven and may look on her;
But Romeo may not: more validity,
More honourable state, more courtship lives
In carrion flies than Romeo: they may seize
On the white wonder of dear Juliet's hand,
And steal immortal blessing from her lips,
Who, even in pure and vestal modesty,
Still blush, as thinking their own kisses sin;
But Romeo may not; he is banished.

Romeo and Juliet, III, 3:17, 29

ROMEO. Hadst thou no poison mix'd, no sharp-ground knife,
No sudden mean of death, though ne'er so mean,
But 'banished' to kill me? 'Banished'!
O friar! the damned use that word in hell;
Howlings attend it: how hast thou the heart,
Being a divine, a ghostly confessor,
A sin-absolver, and my friend profess'd,
To mangle me with that word 'banished'?

FRIAR LAWRENCE. Thou fond[1] mad man, hear me.

Romeo and Juliet, III, 3:44

[1] fond: foolish.

BANQUET

[Before the guests arrive, LADY M. says to her husband:]
Gentle my lord, sleek o'er your rugged looks;
Be bright and jovial among your guests tonight.

Macbeth, III, 2:27

[As the guests are seated, MACBETH goes to the door to talk with BANQUO's murderer.]
MACBETH. There's blood upon thy face.

24

BANQUET

MURDERER. 'T is Banquo's then.
MACBETH. 'T is better thee without than
he within.
Is he dispatch'd?
MURDERER. My lord, his throat is cut; that
I did for him.

. . . . .

MURDERER. Most royal sir,
Fleance is 'scap'd.
MACBETH. Then comes my fit again: I had
else been perfect;
Whole as the marble, founded as the rock,
As broad and general as the casing air:
But now I am cabin'd, cribb'd, confin'd,
bound in
To saucy doubts and fears.

. . . . .

[BANQUO's ghost enters and takes MACBETH's
chair but is seen only by MACBETH.]
MACBETH. Which of you have done this?
LORDS. What, my good lord?
MACBETH. Thou canst not say I did it:
never shake
Thy gory locks at me.
ROSS. Gentlemen, rise; his highness is not
well.
Macbeth, III, 4:12, 20, 48

LADY M. [aside to MACBETH]. Are you a
man?
MACBETH. Ay, and a bold one, that dare
look on that
Which might appal the devil.
LADY M. O proper stuff!
This is the very painting of your fear;
This is the air-drawn dagger which, you
said,
Led you to Duncan. O! these flaws¹ and
starts,
Impostors² to true fear, would well become
A woman's story at a winter's fire,
Authoriz'd by her grandam. Shame itself!
Why do you make such faces? When all's
done
You look but on a stool.
MACBETH. Prithee, see there! behold!
look! lo! how say you?
Why, what care I? If thou canst nod, speak
too.
If charnel-houses and our graves must send
Those that we bury back, our monuments³
Shall be the maws of kites.
Ghost vanishes.
LADY M. What! quite unmann'd in folly?
MACBETH. If I stand here, I saw him.
Macbeth, III, 4:58

¹ flaws: storms of passion. ² impostors: compared with true fears. ³ monuments . . .
kites: burial places, the stomachs of birds of
prey.

MACBETH. The time has been,
That, when the brains were out, the man
would die,
And there an end; but now they rise again,
With twenty mortal murders on their
crowns,
And push us from our stools.
Macbeth, III, 4:79

Re-enter Ghost.
MACBETH. Avaunt! and quit my sight! Let
the earth hide thee!
Thy bones are marrowless, thy blood is
cold;
Thou hast no speculation in those eyes
Which thou dost glare with.
LADY M. Think of this, good peers,
But as a thing of custom: 't is no other;
Only it spoils the pleasure of the time.
MACBETH. What man dare, I dare:
Approach thou like the rugged Russian bear,
The arm'd rhinoceros, or the Hyrcan tiger;
Take any shape but that, and my firm nerves
Shall never tremble: or be alive again,
And dare me to the desert with thy sword;
If¹ trembling I inhabit then, protest me
The baby of a girl. Hence, horrible shadow!
Unreal mockery, hence!
Ghost vanishes.
Why, so; being gone,
I am a man again. Pray you, sit still.
LADY M. You have displac'd the mirth,
broke the good meeting,
With most admir'd² disorder

. . . . .

I pray you, speak not; he grows worse and
worse;
Question enrages him. At once, good night:
Stand not upon the order of your going,
But go at once.
LENOX. Good night; and better health
Attend his majesty!
LADY M. A kind good night to all!
Exeunt Lords and Attendants.
MACBETH. It will have blood, they say;
blood will have blood;
Stones³ have been known to move and trees
to speak;
Augurs⁴ and understood relations have
By magot-pies⁵ and choughs and rooks
brought forth
The secret'st man of blood.

. . . . .

For mine own good
All causes shall give way: I am in blood
Stepp'd in so far, that, should I wade no
more,
Returning were as tedious as go o'er.
Strange things I have in head that will to
hand,

Which must be acted ere they may be scann'd.

    Lady M. You lack the season of all natures, sleep.

               Macbeth, III, 4:93, 117, 135

[1] If . . . inhabit: a much disputed passage; possibly, if I tremble, or if I stay within doors. [2] admir'd: wonderful. [3] Stones . . . move: possibly referring to rocking stones indicating guilt. [4] Augurs . . . relations: another much discussed passage; possibly, the relations understood by soothsayers (Delius). [5] magot-pies, etc.: talking birds.

BARGAIN

    Posthumus. My ring I hold dear as my finger; 't is part of it.

    Iachimo. You are afraid, and therein the wiser. If you buy ladies' flesh at a million a dram, you cannot preserve it from tainting.

    . . . . .

    Iachimo. Your hand; a covenant. We will have these things set down by lawful counsel, and straight away for Britain lest the bargain should catch cold and starve.

               Cymbeline, I, 4:145, 179

    Hotspur. I'll give thrice so much land
To any well-deserving friend;
But in the way of bargain, mark ye me,
I'll cavil[1] on the ninth part of a hair.

               I Henry IV, III, 1:137

[1] cavil: argue persistently.

    Shylock. He hates our sacred nation, and he rails,
Even there where merchants most do congregate,
On me, my bargains, and my well-won thrift,
Which he calls interest. Cursed be my tribe,
If I forgive him!

            Merchant of Venice, I, 3:49

    Paris. Fair Diomed, you do as chapmen[1] do,
Dispraise the thing that you desire to buy;
But we in silence hold this virtue well,
We'll but commend what we intend to sell.

           Troilus and Cressida, IV, 1:75

[1] chapmen: buyers or sellers, merchants.

BASTARD

    Queen. Calmly, good Laertes.

    Laertes. That drop of blood that's calm proclaims me bastard,
Cries cuckold to my father, brands the harlot

Even here, between the chaste unsmirched brows
Of my true mother.

               Hamlet, IV, 5:115

    Suffolk. Blunt-witted lord, ignoble in demeanour!
If ever lady wrong'd her lord so much,
Thy mother took into her blameful bed
Some stern untutor'd churl, and noble stock
Was graft with crab-tree slip; whose fruit thou art,
And never of the Nevils' noble race.

             II Henry VI, III, 2:210

    Bastard. Brother, take you my land, I'll take my chance,
Your face hath got five hundred pound a year,
Yet sell your face for five pence and 't is dear.

    . . . . .

Brother by the mother's side, give me your hand:
My father[1] gave me honour, yours gave land.
Now blessed be the hour, by night or day,
When I was got, Sir Robert was away!

             King John, I, 1:151, 163

[1] father: Richard Coeur-de-Lion.

    Bastard. Sir Robert might have eat his part in me
Upon Good-Friday and ne'er broke his fast.

               King John, I, 1:234

    Edmund [soliloquy, showing Edmund's character]. Thou, Nature, art my goddess; to thy law
My services are bound. Wherefore should I
Stand in the plague of custom, and permit
The curiosity of nations to deprive me,
For that I am some twelve or fourteen moonshines
Lag[1] of a brother? Why bastard? wherefore base?
When my dimensions are as well compact,
My mind as generous, and my shape as true,
As honest madam's issue? Why brand they us
With base? with baseness? bastardy? base, base?
Who in the lusty stealth of nature take
More composition and fierce quality
Than doth, within a dull, stale, tired bed,
Go to the creating a whole tribe of fops,
Got 'tween asleep and wake? Well then,
Legitimate Edgar, I must have your land:
Our father's love is to the bastard Edmund
As to the legitimate. Fine word, 'legitimate'!
Well, my legitimate, if this letter speed,[2]
And my invention thrive, Edmund the base

Shall top the legitimate. I grow, I prosper;
Now, gods, stand up for bastards!
King Lear, I, 2:1
[1] Lag: later than. [2] speed: succeed.

THERSITES. I am a bastard too; I love bastards; I am a bastard begot, bastard instructed, bastard in mind, bastard in valour, in everything illegitimate. One bear will not bite another, and wherefore should one bastard?
Troilus and Cressida, V, 7:16

BATTLE

SCAURUS. The greater cantle[1] of the world is lost
With very ignorance; we have kiss'd away
Kingdoms and provinces

. . . . .

Yon ribaudred[2] nag of Egypt,
Whom leprosy o'ertake! i' the midst o' the fight,
When vantage like a pair of twins appear'd,
Both as the same, or rather ours the elder,
The breese upon her, like a cow in June,
Hoists sails and flies.

. . . . .

She once being loof'd.[3]
The noble ruin of her magic, Antony,
Claps on his sea-wing, and like a doting mallard,
Leaving the fight in height, flies after her.
I never saw an action of such shame;
Experience, manhood, honour, ne'er before
Did violate so itself.
Antony and Cleopatra, III, 8:16, 27
[1] cantle: part, comet.   [2] ribaudred: lewd.
[3] loof'd: usually luffed, brought close to the wind; CLEOPATRA took her ships out of the battle and ANTONY followed.

K. HENRY. Once more unto the breach, dear friends, once more;
Or close the wall up with our English dead.

. . . . .

Hold hard the breath, and bend up every spirit
To his[1] full height! On, on, you noble English.
Henry V, III, 1:1, 16
[1] his: its.

WILLIAMS. I am afeard there are few die well that die in a battle; for how can they charitably dispose of any thing when blood is their argument?
Henry V, IV, 1:148

REIGNIER. I think, by some odd gimmals[1] or device
Their arms are set like clocks, still[2] to strike on;
Else ne'er could they hold out so as they do.
1 Henry VI, I, 2:41
[1] gimmals: gimcracks.   [2] still: continued action.

K. HENRY. This battle fares like to the morning's war,
When dying clouds contend with growing light,
What time the shepherd, blowing of his nails,
Can neither call it perfect day nor night.
Now sways it this way, like a mighty sea
Forc'd by the tide to combat with the wind;
Now sways it that way, like the self-same sea
Forc'd to retire by fury of the wind:
Sometimes the flood prevails, and then the wind;
Now one the better, then another best;
Both tugging to be victors, breast to breast,
Yet neither conqueror nor conquered:
So is the equal poise of this fell[1] war.
III Henry VI, II, 5:1
[1] fell: cruel.

MACBETH. Make all our trumpets speak; give them all breath,
Those clamorous harbingers[1] of blood and death.
Macbeth, V, 6:9
[1] harbingers: forerunners.

BEAR

BRUTUS. He's a lamb indeed, that baes like a bear.
Coriolanus, II, 1:12

K. LEAR. Thou'dst shun a bear;
But if thy flight lay toward the roaring sea,
Thou'dst meet the bear i' the mouth.
King Lear, III, 4:9

THESEUS. In the night, imagining some fear,
How easy is a bush suppos'd a bear!
Midsummer Night's Dream, V, 1:21

OTHELLO. Hang her! I do but say what she is. So delicate with her needle! An admirable musician! O! she will sing the savageness out of a bear.
Othello, IV, 1:198

BEARD

TOUCHSTONE. Stand you both forth now: stroke your chins, and swear by your beards that I am a knave.

CELIA. By our beards, if we had them, thou art.
As You Like It, I, 2:77

KING. You must not think
That we are made of stuff so flat and dull
That we can let our beard be shook with danger
And think it pastime.
Hamlet, IV, 7:30

FALSTAFF. I will sooner have a beard grow in the palm of my hand than he shall get one on his cheek.
II Henry IV, I, 2:23

GOWER. What a beard of the general's cut and a horrid suit of the camp will do among foaming bottles and ale-washed wits, is wonderful to be thought on.
Henry V, III, 6:8

KATHARINA. A wife? A beard, fair health, and honesty;
With three-fold love I wish you all these three.
Love's Labour's Lost, V, 2:834

BEATRICE. Lord! I could not endure a husband with a beard on his face: I had rather lie in the woollen.[1]
LEONATO. You may light on a husband that hath no beard.
BEATRICE. What should I do with him? dress him in my apparel and make him my waiting-gentlewoman?
Much Ado About Nothing, II, 1:31
[1] lie . . . woollen: blankets without sheets.

CLAUDIO. The old ornament of his cheek hath already stuffed tennis-balls.
Much Ado About Nothing, III, 2:46

CLOWN. Now Jove, in his next commodity of hair, send thee a beard!
Twelfth Night, III, 1:50

NESTOR. I'll hide my silver beard in a gold beaver,[1]
And in my vantbrace[2] put this wither'd brawn.
Troilus and Cressida, I, 3:296
[1] beaver: face-guard of a helmet. [2] vantbrace: armour for the arm.

BEAST

HAMLET. O God! a beast, that wants[1] discourse of reason,
Would have mourn'd longer,—married with my uncle.
Hamlet, I, 2:150
[1] wants: lacks.

HAMLET. What is a man,
If his chief good and market of his time
Be but to sleep and feed? a beast, no more.
Hamlet, IV, 4:33

HAMLET.[1] 'T is a vice to know him. He hath much land, and fertile: let a beast be lord of beasts, and his crib shall stand at the king's mess: 't is a chough;[2] but, as I say, spacious in the possession of dirt.
Hamlet, V, 2:86
[1] About OSRIC, a foppish courtier. [2] chough: a chattering bird.

FALSTAFF. O powerful love! that, in some respects, makes a beast a man; in some other, a man a beast.
Merry Wives of Windsor, V, 5:5

DEMETRIUS. I'll run from thee and hide me in the brakes,
And leave thee to the mercy of wild beasts.
HELENA. The wildest hath not such a heart as you.
Midsummer Night's Dream, II, 1:227

TIMON. Timon will to the woods; where he shall find
The unkindest beast more kinder than mankind.
Timon of Athens, IV, 1:35

BEAUTY

ROSALIND. Beauty provoketh thieves sooner than gold.
As You Like It, I, 3:112

ROSALIND [to PHEBE]. What though you have no beauty,—
As by my faith, I see no more in you
Than without candle may go dark[1] to bed—
Must you be therefore proud and pitiless?
As You Like It, III, 5:37
[1] dark, etc.: no one anxious to see her.

ROSALIND. 'Tis not your inky brows, your black silk hair,
Your bugle[1] eyeballs, nor your cheek of cream,
That can entame my spirits to your worship,
You foolish shepherd, wherefore do you follow her,
Like foggy south puffing with wind and rain?
As You Like It, III, 5:46
[1] bugle: black glass bead.

FIRST LORD. Her beauty and her brain go not together; she's a good sign, but I have seen small reflection of her wit.
Cymbeline, I, 2:31

Posthumus. Let her beauty
Look through a casement to allure false
    hearts
And be false with them.
                                    Cymbeline, II, 4:33

Hamlet. If you be honest[1] and fair, your
honesty should admit no discourse to your
beauty.
    Ophelia. Could beauty, my lord, have
better commerce than with honesty?
    Hamlet. Ay, truly; for the power of
beauty will sooner transform honesty from
what it is to a bawd than the force of honesty can translate beauty into his[2] likeness:
this was sometime a paradox, but now the
time gives it proof. I did love you once.
                                    Hamlet, III, 1:106
[1] honest: chaste. [2] his: its.

Suffolk. O, stay! I have no power to let
    her pass;
My hand would free her, but my heart
    says no.
As plays the sun upon the glassy streams,
Twinkling another counterfeited beam,
So seems this gorgeous beauty to mine eyes.
Fain would I woo her, yet I dare not speak:
I'll call for pen and ink and write my mind.
                                    1 Henry VI, V, 3:60

K. Henry. By heaven, she[1] is a dainty one.
    Sweetheart,
I were unmannerly to take you out,
And not to kiss you. A health, gentlemen!
                                    Henry VIII, I, 4:94
[1] she: Anne Bullen.

Biron. A wither'd hermit, five-score win-
    ters worn,
Might shake off fifty, looking in her eye.
                                    Love's Labour's Lost, IV, 3:242

Claudio. Let every eye negotiate for itself
And trust no agent; for beauty is a witch
Against whose charms faith melteth into
    blood.
                                    Much Ado About Nothing, II, 1:185

Iago. He hath a daily beauty in his life
That makes me ugly;
                                    Othello, V, 1:19

Beauty is but a vain and doubtful good;
A shining gloss that vadeth suddenly:
A flower that dies when first it 'gins to bud;
A brittle glass that's broken presently:
A doubtful good, a gloss, a glass, a flower,
Lost, vaded, broken, dead within an hour.
And as goods lost are seld[1] or never found,
As vaded gloss no rubbing will refresh,
As flowers dead lie wither'd on the ground,
As broken glass no cement can redress,

So beauty blemish'd once 's for ever lost,
In spite of physic,[2] painting, pain, and cost.
                                    Passionate Pilgrim, 169
[1] seld: seldom. [2] physic: medicine.

Beauty itself doth of itself persuade
The eyes of men without an orator;
                                    Rape of Lucrece, 29

All orators are dumb when beauty pleadeth.
                                    Rape of Lucrece, 268

Romeo. Here lies Juliet, and her beauty
    makes
This vault a feasting presence full of light.
                                    Romeo and Juliet, V, 3:85

From fairest creatures we desire increase,
That thereby beauty's rose might never die.
                                    Sonnet 1

When I behold the violet past prime,
And sable curls all silver'd o'er with white;
When lofty trees I see barren of leaves,
Which erst[1] from heat did canopy the herd,
And summer's green all girded up in
    sheaves,
Borne on the bier with white and bristly
    beard,
Then of thy beauty do I question make,
That thou among the wastes of time
    must go,
                                    Sonnet 12
[1] erst: formerly.

O! how much more doth beauty beauteous
    seem
By that sweet ornament which truth doth
    give:
The rose looks fair, but fairer we it deem
For that sweet odour which doth in it live.
                                    Sonnet 54

Thy outward thus with outward praise is
    crown'd;
But those same tongues, that give thee so
    thine own,
In other accents do this praise confound
By seeing farther than the eye hath shown.
They look into the beauty of thy mind,
And that, in guess, they measure by thy
    deeds.
                                    Sonnet 69

When in the chronicle of wasted time
I see descriptions of the fairest wights,
And beauty making beautiful old rhyme
In praise of ladies dead and lovely knights
Then, in the blazon of sweet beauty's best
Of hand, of foot, of lip, of eye, of brow,
I see their antique pen would have express'd
Even such a beauty as you master now.

So all their praises are but prophecies
Of this our time, all you prefiguring;
Sonnet 106

TROILUS. Her hand,
In whose comparison all whites are ink,
Writing their own reproach; to whose soft seizure
The cygnet's[1] down is harsh.
Troilus and Cressida, I, 1:55

[1] cygnet: young swan.

ULYSSES. Fie, fie upon her!
There's language in her eye, her cheek, her lip.
Nay, her foot speaks; her wanton spirits look out
At every joint and motive of her body.
Troilus and Cressida, IV, 5:54

VIOLA. 'Tis beauty truly blent, whose red and white
Nature's own sweet and cunning hand laid on:
Lady, you are the cruell'st she alive,
If you will lead these graces to the grave
And leave the world no copy.
Twelfth Night, I, 5:257

POLIXENES. This is the prettiest low-born lass[1] that ever
Ran on the green-sward: nothing she does or seems
But smacks of something greater than herself;
Too noble for this place.
CAMILLO. He tells her something
That makes her blood look out. Good sooth, she is
The queen of curds and cream.
Winter's Tale, IV, 4:156

[1] lass: PERDITA.

BED

GHOST. Let not the royal bed of Denmark be
A couch for luxury[1] and damned incest.
Hamlet, I, 5:82

[1] luxury: lust.

CLIFFORD. If dreams prove true.
WARWICK. You were best to go to bed and dream again.
II Henry VI, V, 1:196

IAGO. There's millions now alive
That nightly lie in those unproper beds
Which they dare swear peculiar.
Othello, IV, 1:68

JULIET. Go, ask his name.—If he be married,

My grave is like to be my wedding bed.
NURSE. His name is Romeo, and a Montague;
The only son of your great enemy.
Romeo and Juliet, I, 5:136

Weary with toil, I haste me to my bed,
The dear repose for limbs with travel tir'd;
Sonnet 27

KATHARINA. Young budding virgin, fair and fresh and sweet,
Whither away, or where is thy abode?
Happy the parents of so fair a child;
Happier the man, whom favourable stars
Allot thee for his lovely bed-fellow!
Taming of the Shrew, IV, 5:37

SIR TOBY. Not to be a-bed after midnight is to be up betimes.[1] . . . To be up after midnight and to go to bed then, is early; so that to go to bed after midnight is to go to bed betimes.
Twelfth Night, II, 3:1

[1] betimes: early.

LUCIANA. 'Tis double wrong, to truant with your bed,
And let her read it in thy looks at board.
Comedy of Errors, III, 2:17

BEES

CANTERBURY. Therefore doth heaven divide
The state of man in divers functions,
Setting endeavour in continual motion;
To which is fixed, as an aim or butt,
Obedience: for so work the honey-bees,
Creatures that by a rule in nature teach
The act of order to a peopled kingdom.
They have a king and officers of sorts;
When some, like magistrates, correct at home,
Others, like merchants, venture trade abroad,
Others, like soldiers, armed in their stings,
Make boot upon the summer's velvet buds;
Which pillage they with merry march bring home
To the tent-royal of their emperor:
Who, busied in his majesty, surveys
The singing masons building roofs of gold,
The civil citizens kneading up the honey,
The poor mechanic porters crowding in
Their heavy burdens at his narrow gate,
The sad-ey'd justice, with his surly hum,
Delivering o'er to executors pale
The lazy yawning drone.
Henry V, I, 2:183

WARWICK. The commons, like an angry hive of bees

that want their leader, scatter up and down,
And care not who they sting in his revenge.
II Henry VI, III, 2:125

Воттом. Mounsieur Cobweb, good mounsieur, get you your weapons in your hand, and kill me a red-hipped humble-bee on the top of a thistle; and, good mounsieur, bring me the honey-bag.
Midsummer Night's Dream, IV, 1:10

THIRD FISHERMAN. We would purge the land of these drones, that rob the bee of her honey.
Pericles, II, 1:50

BEGGAR—BEGGING

FALSTAFF. What! a young knave, and beg! Is there not wars? is there not employment? doth not the king lack subjects? do not the rebels want soldiers? Though it be a shame to be on any side but one, it is worse shame to beg than to be on the worst side.
II Henry IV, I, 2:84

GLOUCESTER. Is it a beggar-man?
He has some reason, else he could not beg.
I' the last night's storm I such a fellow saw,
Which made me think a man a worm!
King Lear, IV, 1:31

BANQUO. Speak then to me, who neither beg nor fear
Your favours nor your hate.
Macbeth, I, 3:60

PORTIA. I see, sir, you are liberal in offers:
You taught me first to beg, and now me-thinks
You teach me how a beggar should be an-swer'd.
Merchant of Venice, IV, 1:438

BELIEF

CLOWN.[1] He that will believe all that they say, shall never be saved by half that they do.
Antony and Cleopatra, V, 2:257
[1] CLOWN: a rustic.

ORLANDO. Fair youth, I would I could make thee believe I love.
ROSALIND. Me believe it! you may as soon make her that you love believe it; which, I warrant, she is apter to do than to confess she does.
As You Like It, III, 2:404

ORLANDO. I sometimes do believe, and sometimes do not;
As those that fear they hope, and know they fear.
As You Like It, V, 4:3

BRUTUS. Believe me for mine honour, and have respect to mine honour, that you may believe.
Julius Caesar, III, 2:16

When my love swears that she is made of truth
I do believe her, though I know she lies.
Sonnet 138

MARIA. There is no Christian, that means to be saved by believing rightly, can ever believe such impossible passages of gross-ness.
Twelfth Night, III, 2:75

BELL

FRENCH GENERAL.[1] Hark! hark! the Dau-phin's drum, a warning bell,
Sings heavy music to thy timorous soul,
And mine shall ring thy dire departure out.
I Henry VI, IV, 2:39
[1] To English GENERAL TALBOT.

YORK. Ring, bells, aloud; burn bonfires, clear and bright,
To entertain great England's lawful king.
II Henry VI, V, 1:3

SURREY. I'll startle you
Worse than the sacring bell,[1] when the brown wench
Lay kissing in your arms, lord cardinal.
Henry VIII, III, 2:294
[1] sacring bell: hand bell used in the Mass.

BASTARD. Bell,[1] book, and candle shall not drive me back
When gold and silver becks me to come on.
King John, III, 3:12
[1] Bell, etc.: implements used in excommunica-tion.

K. JOHN. The midnight bell
Did, with his iron tongue and brazen mouth,
Sound one into the drowsy race of night.
King John, III, 3:37

BIRD

K. HENRY. Thou art a summer bird,
Which ever in the haunch[1] of winter sings
The lifting up of day.
II Henry IV, IV, 4:91
[1] haunch: later part.

K. Henry. The bird that hath been limed[1]
in a bush,
With trembling wings misdoubteth every
bush;
III Henry VI, 6:13
[1] limed: caught in sticky substance smeared on
bushes.

While Philomela[1] sits and sings, I sit and
mark,
And wish her lays were tuned like the lark;
For she doth welcome daylight with her
ditty,
And drives away dark dismal-dreaming
night:
Passionate Pilgrim, 197
[1] Philomela: the nightingale.

BIRTH

Laertes [to Ophelia]. Perhaps he loves
you now,
And now no soil nor cautel[1] doth besmirch
The virtue of his will; but you must fear,
His greatness weigh'd, his will is not his
own,
For he himself is subject to his birth;
He may not, as unvalu'd persons do,
Carve[2] for himself, for on his choice depends
The safety and the health of the whole state;
Hamlet, I, 3:14
[1] cautel: deceit. [2] Carve: decide selfishly.

K. Henry.[1] The owl shriek'd at thy birth,
an evil sign;
The night-crow cried, aboding luckless
time;
Dogs howl'd, and hideous tempest shook
down trees;
The raven rook'd her on the chimney's top,
And chattering pies[2] in dismal discords sung.
III Henry VI, V, 6:44
[1] To Gloucester, later Richard III. [2] pies:
magpies.

K. Lear. Thou must be patient; we came
crying hither:
Thou know'st the first time that we smell
the air
We waul and cry.

. . . . .

When we are born, we cry that we are come
To this great stage of fools.
King Lear, IV, 6:182

Beatrice. There was a star danced, and
under that I was born.
Much Ado About Nothing, II, 1:348

Othello. I fetch my life and being
From men of royal siege,[1] and my demerits
May speak unbonneted to as proud a for-
tune
As this that I have reach'd; for know, Iago,
But that I love the gentle Desdemona,
I would not my unhoused free condition
Put into circumscription and confine
For the sea's worth.
Othello, I, 2:21
[1] siege: rank.

BLESSING

Belarius. The benediction of these cover-
ing heavens
Fall on their heads like dew! for they are
worthy
To inlay heaven with stars.
Cymbeline, V, 5:350

Hamlet [to his mother]. And when you
are desirous to be blessed,
I'll blessing beg of you.
Hamlet, III, 4:171

Archbishop of Canterbury. God and his
angels guard your sacred throne,
And make you long become it!
Henry V, I, 2:7

One. Forsooth, a blind man at Saint Al-
ban's shrine,
Within this half hour hath receiv'd his sight;
A man that ne'er saw in his life before.
K. Henry. Now, God be prais'd, that to
believing souls
Gives light in darkness, comfort in despair!
II Henry VI, II, 1:63

Duchess of York.[1] God bless thee! and
put meekness in thy mind,
Love, charity, obedience, and true duty,
Gloucester. Amen; [Aside] and make
me die a good old man!
That is the butt-end of a mother's blessing;
I marvel that her grace did leave it out.
Richard III, II, 2:107
[1] Mother of Gloucester, later Richard III.

Gaunt. The world's ransom, blessed
Mary's son.
Richard II, II, 1:56

BLOOD

Menenius. 'True is it, my incorporate
friends,' quoth he,
'That I receive the general food at first,
Which you do live upon; and fit it is,
Because I am the store-house and the shop
Of the whole body: but, if you do remem-
ber,

I send it through the rivers of your blood,
Even to the court, the heart, to the seat o'
    the brain;
And, through the cranks[1] and offices of man,
The strongest nerves and small inferior
    veins
From me receive that natural competency
Whereby they live.'
                              Coriolanus, I, 1:134
[The speaker—the belly—describes the circu-
lation of the blood.]
[1] cranks, etc.: parts of the body.

COMINIUS. He was a thing of blood,
    whose every motion
Was tim'd with dying cries.
                              Coriolanus, II, 2:112

MENENIUS. The blood he[1] hath lost,
Which, I dare vouch, is more than that he
    hath,
By many an ounce, he dropp'd it for his
    country;
And what is left, to lose it by his country,
Were to us all, that do 't and suffer it,
A brand to th' end o' the world.
                              Coriolanus, III, 1:299
[1] he: CORIOLANUS.

KING. What if this cursed hand
Were thicker than itself with brother's
    blood,
Is there not rain enough in the sweet heav-
    ens
To wash it white as snow?
                              Hamlet, III, 3:43

K. JOHN. There is no sure foundation set
    on blood,
No certain life achiev'd by other's death.
                              King John, IV, 2:104

LUCIO. Lord Angelo; a man whose blood
Is very snow-broth; one who never feels
The wanton stings and motions of the sense,
But doth rebate and blunt his natural edge
With profits of the mind, study and fast.
                              Measure for Measure, I, 4:57

SHYLOCK. I say my daughter is my flesh
    and blood.
SALARINO. There is more difference be-
    tween thy flesh and hers than between
    jet and ivory; more between your
    bloods than there is between red wine
    and Rhenish.
                              Merchant of Venice, III, 1:40

BOLINGBROKE. He[1] did plot the Duke of
    Gloucester's death,

                    . . . . .

Sluic'd out his innocent soul through streams
    of blood:
Which blood, like sacrificing Abel's, cries,
Even from the tongueless caverns of the
    earth
To me for justice and rough chastisement.
                              Richard II, I, 1:100
[1] He: MOWBRAY.

HECTOR. Is your blood
So madly hot that no discourse of reason,
Nor fear of bad success in a bad cause,
Can qualify[1] the same?
                              Troilus and Cressida, II, 2:115
[1] qualify: moderate, temper.

BLUSH

K. HENRY. Put off your maiden blushes;
avouch the thoughts of your heart with the
looks of an empress; take me by the hand,
and say 'Harry of England, I am thine.'
                              Henry V, V, 2:252

SURREY. Now, if you can blush and cry
    'guilty,' cardinal,
You'll show a little honesty.
WOLSEY. Speak on, sir;
I dare your worst objections: if I blush,
It is to see a nobleman want[1] manners.
                              Henry VIII, III, 2:305
[1] want: lack.

CLAUDIO. O! what authority and show of
    truth
Can cunning sin cover itself withal.[1]
Comes not that blood as modest evidence
To witness simple virtue? Would you not
    swear,
All you that see her, that she were a maid,
By these exterior shows? But she is none:
She knows the heat of a luxurious[2] bed;
Her blush is guiltiness, not modesty.
                              Much Ado About Nothing, IV, 1:36
[1] withal: with. [2] luxurious: lustful.

BRABANTIO. A maiden never bold;
Of spirit so still and quiet, that her motion
Blush'd at herself.
                              Othello, I, 3:94

JULIET. Thou know'st the mask of night
    is on my face,
Else would a maiden blush bepaint my cheek
For that which thou hast heard me speak
    to-night.
                              Romeo and Juliet, II, 2:85

ROMEO. And steal immortal blessing from
    her lips,
Who, even in pure and vestal modesty,
Still blush, as thinking their own kisses sin;
                              Romeo and Juliet, III, 3:37

PETRUCHIO. Has thou beheld a fresher
  gentlewoman?
Such war of white and red within her
  cheeks!
  Taming of the Shrew, IV, 5:29

AARON. Fie, treacherous hue! that will be-
  tray with blushing
The close enacts and counsels of the heart.
  Titus Andronicus, IV, 2:117

PERDITA. I should blush
To see you so attired.
  Winter's Tale, IV, 4:12

BOASTER

PAROLLES. Who knows himself a braggart,
Let him fear this; for it will come to pass
That every braggart shall be found an ass.
  All's Well That Ends Well, IV, 3:370

POLONIUS. Hath there been such a time,
  I'd fain know that,
That I have positively said ' 'T is so,'
When it prov'd otherwise?
KING. Not that I know.
POLONIUS [pointing to his head and shoul-
  der]. Take this from this, if this be
  otherwise.
If circumstances lead me, I will find
Where truth is hid, though it were hid in-
  deed
Within the centre.
  Hamlet, II, 2:153

FALSTAFF. There live not three good men
unhanged in England, and one of them is fat
and grows old.
  I Henry IV, II, 4:144

GLENDOWER. At my nativity
The front of heaven was full of fiery shapes,
Of burning cressets;[1] and at my birth
The frame and huge foundation of the earth
Shak'd like a coward.
HOTSPUR. Why, so it would have done at
the same season, if your mother's cat had but
kittened, though yourself had never been
born.
  I Henry IV, III, 1:13
[1] cressets: fires in the sky.

GLENDOWER. I say the earth did shake
  when I was born.
HOTSPUR. And I say the earth was not of
  my mind,

  . . . . .

GLENDOWER. I can call spirits from the
  vasty deep.

HOTSPUR. Why, so can I, or so can any
  man;
But will they come when you do call for
  them?
  I Henry IV, III, 1:21, 53

GLENDOWER. And all the courses of my
  life do show
I am not in the roll of common men.
Where is he living, clipp'd[1] in with the sea
That chides the banks of England, Scotland,
  Wales,
Which calls me pupil, or hath read[2] to me?
  I Henry IV, III, 1:42
[1] clipp'd: enclosed. [2] read to me: lectured or
instructed me.

FALSTAFF. Here, travel-tainted as I am,
have, in my pure and immaculate valour,
taken Sir John Colevile of the dale, a most
furious knight and valorous enemy. But
what of that? he saw me, and yielded; that I
may justly say with the hook-nosed fellow[1]
of Rome, 'I came, saw, and overcame.'
  II Henry IV, IV, 3:40
[1] fellow: Julius Caesar.

FALSTAFF. If you do not all show like gilt
two-pences to[1] me, and I in the clear sky of
fame o'ershine you as much as the full moon
doth the cinders of the element, which show
like pins' head to her, believe not the word
of the noble.
  II Henry IV, IV, 3:55
[1] to: compared with.

ORLEANS. The Dauphin longs for morn-
ing.
RAMBURES. He longs to eat the English.
CONSTABLE. I think he will eat all he kills.
  Henry V, III, 7:98

BASTARD. Here's a stay[1]
That shakes the rotten carcass of old death
Out of his rags! Here's a large mouth, in-
  deed,
That spits forth death and mountains, rocks
  and seas,
Talks as familiarly of roaring lions
As maids of thirteen do of puppy-dogs.
What cannoneer begot this lusty blood?
He speaks plain cannon fire, and smoke, and
  bounce;[2]
He gives the bastinado[3] with his tongue;
Our ears are cudgell'd; not a word of his
But buffets better than a fist of France.
'Zounds! I was never so bethump'd with
  words
Since I first call'd my brother's father dad.
  King John, II, 1:455
[1] stay: this is a much discussed word; possibly
a storm of passion. [2] bounce: slap-bang. [3] bas-
tinado: a sound beating.

GRATIANO. As who should say, 'I am Sir
  Oracle,
And when I ope my lips let no dog bark!'
Merchant of Venice, I, 1:93

BODY

AUFIDIUS. Let me twine
Mine arms about that body, where against
My grained ash an hundred times hath
  broke,
And scarr'd the moon with splinters.
Coriolanus, IV, 5:112

RICHARD. Like rich hangings in a homely
  house,
So was his will in his old feeble body.
But, noble as he is, look where he comes.
II Henry VI, V, 3:12

GLOUCESTER. But when the fox hath once
  got in his nose,
He'll soon find means to make the body follow.
III Henry VI, IV, 7:25

WARWICK. I must yield my body to the
  earth,
And, by my fall, the conquest to my foe.
Thus yields the cedar to the axe's edge,
Whose arms gave shelter to the princely
  eagle,
Under whose shade the ramping lion slept,
Whose top branch overpeer'd Jove's spread-
ing tree
And kept low shrubs from winter's power-
ful wind.
III Henry VI, V, 2:9

PORTIA. By my troth, Nerissa, my little
body is aweary of this great world.
Merchant of Venice, I, 2:1

IAGO. Our bodies are our gardens, to the
which our wills are gardeners . . . either to
have it sterile with idleness or manured with
industry.
Othello, I, 3:323

My body or my soul, which was the dearer,
When the one pure, the other made divine?
Rape of Lucrece, 1163

BOND—TRIAL

SHYLOCK. Go with me to a notary, seal
me there
Your single bond; and, in a merry sport,
If you repay me not on such a day,
In such a place, such sum or sums as are
Express'd in the condition, let the forfeit

Be nominated for an equal pound
Of your fair flesh, to be cut off and taken
In what part of your body pleaseth me.
  ANTONIO. Content, i' faith: I'll seal to such
  a bond,
And say there is much kindness in the Jew.
Merchant of Venice, I, 3:145

  DUKE. How shalt thou hope for mercy,
  rendering none?
  SHYLOCK. What judgment shall I dread,
  doing no wrong?
You have among you many a purchas'd
  slave,
Which, like your asses and your dogs and
  mules,
You use in abject and in slavish parts,
Because you bought them: shall I say to you,
Let them be free, marry them to your heirs?
Why sweat they under burdens? let their
  beds
Be made as soft as yours, and let their pal-
ates
Be season'd with such viands? You will an-
swer:
'The slaves are ours': so do I answer you:
The pound of flesh, which I demand of him,
Is dearly bought; 'tis mine, and I will have it.
If you deny me, fie upon your law!
There is no force in the decrees of Venice.
I stand for judgment: answer; shall I
  have it?
Merchant of Venice, IV, 1:88

BELLARIO's *letter*.[1] I beseech you, let his
lack of years be no impediment to let him
lack a reverend estimation, for I never knew
so young a body with so old a head.
Merchant of Venice, IV, 1:161
[1] About PORTIA, who comes as judge in the
trial.

PORTIA. The quality of mercy is not
  strain'd,
It droppeth as the gentle rain from heaven
Upon the place beneath: it is twice bless'd;
It blesseth him that gives and him that takes:
'Tis mightiest in the mightiest; it becomes
The throned monarch better than his
  crown;
His sceptre shows the force of temporal
  power,
The attribute to awe and majesty,
Wherein doth sit the dread and fear of
  kings;
But mercy is above this sceptred sway,
It is enthroned in the hearts of kings,
It is an attribute to God himself.
And earthly power doth then show likest
  God's
When mercy seasons justice. Therefore,
  Jew,
Though justice be thy plea, consider this,

That in the course of justice, none of us
Should see salvation: we do pray for mercy.
And that same prayer doth teach us all to render
The deeds of mercy. I have spoke thus much
To mitigate the justice of thy plea,
Which if thou follow, this strict court of Venice
Must needs give sentence 'gainst the merchant there.
Merchant of Venice, IV, 1:184

SHYLOCK. My deeds upon my head! I crave the law,
The penalty and forfeit of my bond.
Merchant of Venice, IV, 1:206

PORTIA. Why, this bond is forfeit;
And lawfully by this the Jew may claim
A pound of flesh, to be by him cut off
Nearest the merchant's heart.
Merchant of Venice, IV, 1:230

SHYLOCK. I charge you by the law,
Whereof you are a well-deserving pillar,
Proceed to judgment: by my soul I swear
There is no power in the tongue of man
To alter me. I stay here on my bond.
ANTONIO. Most heartily I do beseech the court
To give the judgment.
PORTIA. Why then, thus it is:
You must prepare your bosom for his knife.
SHYLOCK. O noble judge! O excellent young man!
Merchant of Venice, IV, 1:238

PORTIA. Have by some surgeon, Shylock, on your charge,
To stop his wounds, lest he do bleed to death.
SHYLOCK. Is it so nominated in the bond?
PORTIA. It is not so express'd; but what of that?
'T were good you do so much for charity.
SHYLOCK. I cannot find it: 'tis not in the bond.
Merchant of Venice, IV, 1:257

PORTIA. You, merchant, have you any thing to say?
ANTONIO. But little: I am arm'd and well prepar'd.
Give me your hand, Bassanio: fare you well!
Grieve not that I am fallen to this for you;
For herein Fortune shows herself more kind
Than is her custom: it is still[1] her use
To let the wretched man outlive his wealth,
To view with hollow eye and wrinkled brow
An age of poverty; from which lingering penance
Of such a misery doth she cut me off.
. . . . .

Repent but[2] you that you shall lose your friend,
And he repents not that he pays your debt;
For if the Jew do cut but deep enough,
I'll pay it instantly with all my heart.
Merchant of Venice, IV, 1:263, 278
[1] still . . . use: always her custom. [2] but: only.

SHYLOCK. We trifle time; I pray thee, pursue sentence.
PORTIA. A pound of that same merchant's flesh is thine:
The court awards it, and the law doth give it.
SHYLOCK. Most rightful judge!
PORTIA. And you must cut this flesh from off his breast:
The law allows it, and the court awards it.
SHYLOCK. Most learned judge! A sentence! Come, prepare!
PORTIA. Tarry a little: there is something else.
This bond doth give thee here no jot of blood;
The words expressly are 'a pound of flesh':
Take then thy bond, take thou thy pound of flesh;
But, in the cutting it, if thou dost shed
One drop of Christian blood, thy lands and goods
Are, by the laws of Venice, confiscate
Unto the state of Venice.
GRATIANO. O upright judge! Mark, Jew: O learned judge!
SHYLOCK. Is that the law?
PORTIA. Thyself shalt see the act;
For, as thou urgest justice, be assur'd
Thou shalt have justice, more than thou desirest.
Merchant of Venice, IV, 1:298

PORTIA. Therefore prepare thee to cut off the flesh.
Shed thou no blood; nor cut thou less, nor more,
But just a pound of flesh: if thou tak'st more,
Or less, than a just pound, be it but so much
As makes it light, or heavy, in the substance,
Or the division of the twentieth part
Of one poor scruple, nay, if the scale do turn
But in the estimation of a hair,
Thou diest and all thy goods are confiscate.
GRATIANO. A second Daniel, a Daniel, Jew!
Now, infidel, I have thee on the hip.
PORTIA. Why doth the Jew pause? take thy forfeiture.
SHYLOCK. Give me my principal, and let me go.

BASSANIO. I have it ready for thee; here it is.

PORTIA. He hath refus'd it in the open court:

He shall have merely justice, and his bond.

. . . . .

If it prov'd against an alien
That by direct or indirect attempts
He seek the life of any citizen,
The party 'gainst the which he doth contrive
Shall seize one half his goods; the other half
Comes to the privy coffer of the state;
And the offender's life lies in the mercy
Of the duke only, 'gainst all other voice.

Merchant of Venice, IV, 1:324, 349

BOOK

DUKE SR. And this our life, exempt from public haunt,
Finds tongues in trees, books in the running brooks,
Sermons in stones, and good in every thing.

As You Like It, II, 1:15

BIRON. Small have continual plodders ever won,
Save base authority from others' books.

Love's Labour's Lost, I, 1:87

MESSENGER. I see, lady, the gentleman is not in your books.

BEATRICE. No; an[1] he were, I would burn my study.

Much Ado About Nothing, I, 1:78

[1] an: if.

K. RICHARD. I'll read enough
When I do see the very book indeed
Where all my sins are writ, and that's myself.

Richard II, IV, 1:273

PROSPERO. Me, poor man, my library was dukedom large enough.

. . . . .

Knowing I lov'd my books, he[1] furnish'd me
From my own library with volumes that
I prize above my dukedom.

Tempest, I, 2:109, 165

[1] he: GONZALO.

CALIBAN. Remember
First to possess his books; for without them
He's but a sot, as I am, nor hath not
One spirit to command.

Tempest, III, 2:100

PROSPERO. I'll break my staff,
Bury it certain fathoms in the earth,

And, deeper than did ever plummet sound,
I'll drown my book.

Tempest, V, 1:54

BORES

BASTARD. I'll take that burden from your back,
Or lay on that shall make your shoulders crack.

AUSTRIA. What cracker is this same[1] that deafs our ears
With this abundance of superfluous breath?

King John, II, 1:145

[1] this same: PHILIP THE BASTARD.

BEATRICE. O Lord! he will hang upon him like a disease: he is sooner caught than the pestilence, and the taker runs presently[1] mad.

Much Ado About Nothing, I, 1:86

[1] presently: immediately.

DON PEDRO. Thou wilt be like a lover presently,[1]
And tire the hearer with a book of words.

Much Ado About Nothing, I, 1:308

[1] presently: at once.

OLIVIA. If it be aught to the old tune, my lord,
It is as fat and fulsome to mine ear
As howling after music.

Twelfth Night, V, 1:111

BORROWING

POLONIUS. Neither a borrower nor a lender be;
For loan oft loses both itself and friend.

Hamlet, I, 3:75

DOGBERRY. [He] borrows money in God's name; the which he hath used so long and never paid, that now men grow hardhearted, and will lend nothing for God's sake.

Much Ado About Nothing, V, 1:321

TIMON. I will dispatch you severally:[1] you to Lord Lucius; to Lord Lucullus you; I hunted with his honour to-day; you, to Sempronius. Commend me to their loves; and, I am proud, say, that my occasions have found time to use 'em toward a supply of money: let the request be fifty talents.

Timon of Athens, II, 2:196

[1] severally: separately.

FLAVIUS. They answer, in a joint and corporate voice,

That now they are at fall,[1] want[2] treasure, cannot
Do what they would; are sorry; you are honourable;
But yet they could have wished—they know not—
. . . . .
Would all were well—'tis pity.
Timon of Athens, II, 2:213, 218
[1] fall: ebb.   [2] want: lack.

Lucius. Commend me bountifully to his good lordship; and I hope his honour will conceive the fairest of me, because I have no power to be kind: and tell him this from me, I count it one of my greatest afflictions, say, that I cannot pleasure such an honourable gentleman. Good Servilius, will you befriend me so far as to use mine own words to him?
Timon of Athens, III, 2:57

BOUNTY

Soldier. Enobarbus,[1] Antony
Hath after thee sent all thy treasure, with
His bounty overplus: the messenger
Came on my guard; and at thy tent is now
Unloading of his mules.
. . . . .
Enobarbus. I am alone the villain of the earth,
And feel I am so most. O Antony!
Thou mine of bounty, how would'st thou have paid
My better service, when my turpitude
Thou dost so crown with gold.
Antony and Cleopatra, IV, 5:20, 30
[1] Enobarbus has deserted to Caesar.

K. Henry to Wolsey. I presume
That as my hand has open'd bounty to you,
My heart dropp'd love.
Henry VIII, III, 2:183

Clown. Sir, let your bounty[1] take a nap,
I will awake it anon.
Twelfth Night, V, 1:50
[1] bounty: benevolence.

BOY

Rosalind. Boys and women are for the most part, cattle of this colour.
As You Like It, III, 2:435

Oliver. 'The boy is fair,
Of female favour,[1] and bestows himself
Like a ripe forester.'
As You Like It, IV, 3:86
[1] favour: countenance.

Gobbo. Marry, God forbid! the boy was the very staff of my age, my very prop.
Merchant of Venice, II, 2:69

Gobbo. Pray you, sir, stand up. I am sure you are not Launcelot, my boy.
Launcelot. Pray you, let's have no more fooling about it, but give me your blessing: I am Launcelot, your boy that was, your son that is, your child that shall be.
Merchant of Venice, II, 2:87

Scroop. Boys, with women's voices,
Strive to speak big, and clap their female joints
In stiff unwielding arms against thy crown.
Richard II, III, 2:113

Gloucester. O! 'tis a parlous[1] boy;
Bold, quick, ingenious, forward, capable:
He's all the mother's, from the top to toe.
Richard III, III, 1:154
[1] parlous: mischievous.

Clown. When that I was and a little tiny boy,
With hey, ho, the wind and the rain;
A foolish thing was but a toy,
For the rain it raineth every day.
But when I came to man's estate,
With hey, ho, the wind and the rain;
'Gainst knaves and thieves men shut their gates,
For the rain it raineth every day.
Twelfth Night, V, 1:398

Polixenes. We were, fair queen,
Two lads that thought there was no more behind
But such a day to-morrow as to-day,
And to be boy eternal.
Winter's Tale, I, 2:63

BRAIN

Caesar. It 's monstrous labour, when I wash my brain,
And it grows fouler.
Antony and Cleopatra, II, 7:105

Rosalind. Woman's gentle brain
Could not drop forth such giant-rude invention,
Such Ethiop words, blacker in their effect
Than in their countenance.
As You Like It, IV, 3:33

Polonius. I do think, or else this brain of mine
Hunts not the trail of policy so sure
As it hath us'd to do, that I have found
The very cause of Hamlet's lunacy.
Hamlet, II, 2:46

FOOL. If a man's brains were in 's heels,
were't not in danger of kibes?[1]
King Lear, I, 5:8

[1] kibes: sore heels.

FALSTAFF. Well, if I be served such another trick, I'll have my brains ta'en out and
buttered, and give them to a dog for a new
year's gift.
Merry Wives of Windsor, III, 5:7

FALSTAFF. Have I laid my brain in the
sun and dried it, that it wants[1] matter to
prevent so gross o'er-reaching as this? Am
I ridden with a Welsh goat too?
Merry Wives of Windsor, V, 5:143

[1] wants: lacks.

THESEUS. Lovers and madmen have such
seething brains,
Such shaping fantasies, that apprehend
More than cool reason ever comprehends.
Midsummer Night's Dream, V, 1:4

BENEDICK. Shall quips and sentences and
these paper bullets of the brain awe a man
from the career of his humour?
Much Ado About Nothing, II, 3:248

NESTOR. His brain as barren
As banks of Libya.
Troilus and Cressida, I, 3:327

THERSITES. Here's Agamemnon, an hon-
est fellow enough, and one that loves quails,[1]
but he has not so much brain as ear-wax.
Troilus and Cressida, V, 1:57

[1] quails: loose women.

BRAVERY

OCTAVIUS CAESAR. Antony,
Leave thy lascivious wassails. When thou
once
Wast beaten from Modena, where thou
slew'st
Hirtius and Pansa, consuls, at thy heel
Did famine follow, whom thou fought'st
against,
Though daintily brought up, with patience
more
Than savages could suffer.

· · · · ·

And all this,
It wounds thine honour that I speak it now,
Was borne so like a soldier, that thy cheek
So much as lank'd[1] not.
Antony and Cleopatra, I, 4:55, 68

[1] lank'd: shrank.

CELIA. O! that's a brave man. He writes
brave verses, speaks brave words, swears

brave oaths, and breaks them bravely, quite
traverse, athwart the heart of his lover.
As You Like It, III, 4:43

TITUS. No, Caius Marcius;
I'll lean upon one crutch and fight with
t'other,
Ere stay behind this business.
Coriolanus, I, 1:246

BELARIUS. I never saw
Such noble fury in so poor a thing;
Such precious deeds in one that promis'd
nought
But beggary and poor looks.
Cymbeline, V, 5:8

CHATILLON. In brief, a braver choice of
dauntless spirits
Than now the English bottoms have waft
o'er
Did never float upon the swelling tide.
King John, II, 1:72

SERGEANT. All's too weak;
For brave Macbeth—well he deserves that
name.
Macbeth, I, 2:15

ROSS. The Thane of Cawdor, began a dis-
mal conflict;
Till that Bellona's[1] bridegroom,[2] lapp'd in
proof,[3]
Confronted him with self-comparisons,
Point against point rebellious, arm 'gainst
arm.
Curbing his lavish spirit.
Macbeth, I, 2:53

[1] Bellona: Roman goddess of war. [2] bridegroom: MACBETH. [3] lapp'd in proof: clad in
proved armour.

BREAST

IAGO. Who has a breast so pure
But some uncleanly apprehensions
Keep leets[1] and law-days, and in session sit
With meditations lawful?
Othello, III, 3:138

[1] leets: sessions of court.

BREATH

IACHIMO. 'T is her breathing that
Perfumes the chamber thus; the flame o' the
taper
Bows toward her, and would under-peep
her lids,
To see the enclosed lights, now canopied
Under these windows, white and azure lac'd
With blue of heaven's own tinct.
Cymbeline, II, 2:18

K. Henry. O hard condition!
Twin-born with greatness, subject to the breath
Of every fool.
Henry V, IV, 1:250

Shylock. Shall I bend low, and in a bond-man's key,
With bated breath, and whispering humbleness.
Merchant of Venice, I, 3:124

Bottom. And, most dear actors, eat no onions nor garlic, for we are to utter sweet breath.
Midsummer Night's Dream, IV, 2:42

Benedick. If her breath were as terrible as her terminations,[1] there were no living near her; she would infect to the north star.
Much Ado About Nothing, II, 1:256
[1] terminations: words.

Othello. O balmy breath, that dost almost persuade
Justice to break her sword! One more, one more.
Othello, V, 2:16

York. Direct not him whose way himself will choose:
'Tis breath thou lack'st, and that breath wilt thou lose.
Richard II, II, 1:29

Speed. She is not to be kissed fasting, in respect of her breath.
Two Gentlemen of Verona, III, 1:326

BREVITY

Polonius. Since brevity is the soul of wit,
And tediousness the limbs and outward flourishes,
I will be brief.
Hamlet, II, 2:90

Ophelia. 'Tis brief, my lord.
Hamlet. As woman's love.
Hamlet, III, 2:163

Falstaff. But what says she to me? be brief, my good she-Mercury.[1]
Merry Wives of Windsor, II, 2:81
[1] Mercury: the messenger of the gods.

Brakenbury. What! so brief?
Second Murderer. 'Tis better, sir, than to be tedious.
Richard III, I, 4:88

Friar Laurence. I will be brief, for my short date of breath
Is not so long as is a tedious tale.
Romeo and Juliet, V, 3:229

BRIDEGROOM

Portia. Then music is . . .
As are those dulcet sounds at break of day
That break into the dreaming bridegroom's ear,
And summon him to marriage.
Merchant of Venice, III, 2:56

K. Lear. I will die bravely, like a smug bridegroom. What!
I will be jovial: come, come; I am a king,
My masters, know you that?
King Lear, IV, 6:202

Deiphobus. Let us make ready straight.
Aeneas. Yea, with a bridegroom's fresh alacrity.
Troilus and Cressida, IV, 4:147

BROTHER

Arviragus. Are we not brothers?
Imogen. So man and man should be,
But clay and clay differs in dignity,
Whose dust is both alike.
Cymbeline, IV, 2:4

Hamlet. Here is your husband; like a mildew'd ear,
Blasting his[1] wholesome brother.
Hamlet, III, 4:64
[1] His: its.

Boy. Nym and Bardolph are sworn brothers in filching, and in Calais they stole a fire-shovel; I knew by that piece of service the men would carry coals.[1] They would have me as familiar with men's pockets as their gloves or their handkerchers.
Henry V, III, 2:47
[1] carry coals: endure affronts.

Isabella. Better it were a brother died at once,
Than that a sister, by redeeming him,
Should die for ever.
Measure for Measure, II, 4:106

Beatrice. Who is his companion now? He hath every month a new sworn brother.
Much Ado About Nothing, I, 1:73

Timon. Twinn'd brothers of one womb,
Whose procreation, residence, and birth,

Scarce is dividant, touch them with several fortunes,
The greater scorns the lesser.
Timon of Athens, IV, 3:3

BROW

NORTHUMBERLAND. Yea, this man's brow, like to a title-leaf,
Foretells the nature of a tragic volume:
So looks the strand whereon the imperious flood
Hath left a witness'd usurpation.
II Henry IV, I, 1:60

CALUMNY

COUNTESS. Wilt thou ever be a foul-mouthed and calumnious knave?
All's Well That Ends Well, I, 3:61

LAERTES. Virtue itself 'scapes not calumnious strokes.
Hamlet, I, 3:38

HAMLET. Be thou as chaste as ice, as pure as snow, thou shalt not escape calumny.
Hamlet, III, 1:140

LEONTES. The shrug, the hum or ha, these petty brands
That calumny doth use—O, I am out!—
That mercy does, for calumny will sear
Virtue itself: these shrugs, these hums and ha's,
When you have said 'she's goodly,' come between
Ere you can say 'she's honest.'[1]
Winter's Tale, II, 1:71
[1] honest: chaste.

CANKER

GLOUCESTER. O Nell, sweet Nell, if thou dost love thy lord,
Banish the canker of ambitious thoughts.
II Henry VI, I, 2:17

PROSPERO. He's something stain'd
With grief that's beauty's canker.
Tempest, I, 2:415

PROTEUS. Yet writers say, as in the sweetest bud
The eating canker dwells, so eating love
Inhabits in the finest wits of all.
VALENTINE. And writers say, as the most forward bud
Is eaten by the canker ere it blow.
Two Gentlemen of Verona, I, 1:42

CANNON

K. JOHN. Be thou as lightning in the eyes of France;
For ere thou canst report I will be there,
The thunder of my cannon shall be heard.
So hence! Be thou the trumpet of our wrath.
King John, I, 1:24

K. JOHN. The cannons have their bowels full of wrath,
And ready mounted are they to spit forth
Their iron indignation 'gainst your walls:
King John, II, 1:210

BASTARD. By east and west let France and England mount
Their battering cannon charged to the mouths,
Till their soul-fearing clamours have brawl'd down
The flinty ribs of this contemptuous city:
King John, II, 1:381

IAGO. Can he be angry? I have seen the cannon,
When it hath blown his ranks into the air,
And, like the devil, from his very arm
Puff'd his own brother.
Othello, III, 4:134

CAPTAIN

ISABELLA. That in the captain's but a choleric word,
Which in the soldier is flat blasphemy.
Measure for Measure, II, 2:130

MERCUTIO. O! he is the courageous captain of compliments.
Romeo and Juliet, II, 4:20

CAPTIVE

ENOBARBUS. Our courteous Antony,
Whom ne'er the word of 'No' woman heard speak,
Being barber'd ten times o'er, goes to the feast,
And for his ordinary[1] pays his heart
For what his eyes eat only.
Antony and Cleopatra, II, 2:227
[1] ordinary: meal, repast.

PISTOL. What is thy name? discuss.
FRENCH SOLDIER. *O Seigneur Dieu!*
PISTOL. O, Signieur Dew should be a gentleman:
Perpend my words, O Signieur Dew, and mark:
O Signieur Dew, thou diest on point of fox,[1]

Except, O signieur, thou do give me
Egregious ransom.
                              Henry V, IV, 4:5
[1] fox: sword.

MOWBRAY. Never did captive with a
   freer heart
Cast off his chains of bondage and embrace
His golden uncontroll'd enfranchisement,
More than my dancing soul doth celebrate
This feast of battle with mine adversary.
                              Richard II, I, 3:88

CARE

JOAN [OF ARC]. Care is no cure, but rather
   corrosive,
For things that are not to be remedied.
                              1 Henry VI, III, 3:3

GLOUCESTER. Thus sometimes hath the
   brightest day a cloud;
And after summer evermore succeeds
Barren winter with his wrathful nipping
   cold:
So cares and joys abound, as seasons fleet.[1]
                              II Henry VI, II, 4:1
[1] fleet: pass quickly.

MACBETH. The innocent sleep,
Sleep that knits up the ravell'd sleave of
   care.
                              Macbeth, II, 2:37

GRATIANO. You look not well, Signior
   Antonio;
You have too much respect upon the world:
They lose it that do buy it with much care:
Believe me, you are marvellously chang'd.
   ANTONIO. I hold the world but as the
   world, Gratiano;
A stage where every man must play a part,
And mine a sad one.
                              Merchant of Venice, I, 1:73

CLAUDIO. What though care killed a cat,
thou hast mettle enough in thee to kill care.
   Much Ado About Nothing, V, 1:132

YORK. Things past redress are now with
   me past care.
                              Richard II, II, 3:170

FRIAR LAURENCE. Care keeps his watch in
   every old man's eye,
And where care lodges, sleep will never lie.
                              Romeo and Juliet, II, 3:35

CAT

HAMLET. Let Hercules himself do what
   he may,
The cat will mew and dog will have his day.
                              Hamlet, V, 1:314

FALSTAFF. Tut, never fear me: I am as vig-
ilant as a cat to steal cream.
   PRINCE. I think to steal cream indeed, for
thy theft hath already made thee butter.
                              1 Henry IV, IV, 2:64

FIRST WITCH. Thrice the brinded cat hath
   mew'd.
   SECOND WITCH. Thrice and once the
   hedge-pig whin'd.
                              Macbeth, IV, 1:1

GOWER. The cat, with eyne of burning
   coal,
Now couches fore the mouse's hole:
                Pericles, Introduction to Act III: 5

MERCUTIO. Tybalt, you rat-catcher, will
you walk?
   TYBALT. What would'st thou have with
me?
   MERCUTIO. Good king of cats, nothing
but one of your nine lives, that I mean to
make bold withal.[1]
                              Romeo and Juliet, III, 1:78
[1] withal: with it.

ANTONIO. They'll take suggestion as a cat
   laps milk;
They'll tell[1] the clock to any business that
We say befits the hour.
                              Tempest, II, 1:288
[1] tell: count.

CAUSE

HAMLET. A dull and muddy-mettled rascal, peak,[1]
Like John-a-dreams,[2] unpregnant[3] of my
   cause,
And can say nothing; no, not for a king,
Upon whose property and most dear life
A damn'd defeat was made.
                              Hamlet, II, 2:593
[1] peak: pine away. [2] John-a-dreams: a dreamy,
idle fellow. [3] unpregnant: dull to all action.

HAMLET. On him, on him![1] Look you,
   how pale he glares!
His form and cause conjoin'd, preaching to
   stones,
Would make them capable.
                              Hamlet, III, 4:125
[1] him: HAMLET's father's ghost.

FLUELLEN. There is occasions and causes
why and wherefore in all things.
                              Henry V, V, 1:3

K. HENRY. And poise the cause in justice'
   equal scales,
Whose beam stands sure, whose rightful
   cause prevails.
                              II Henry VI, II, 1:204

CAUTION

SECOND LORD. [I] therefore dare not
Say what I think of it, since I have found
Myself in my incertain grounds to fail
As often as I guess'd.
All's Well That Ends Well, III, 1:13

VENTIDIUS. Better to leave undone than
  by our deed
Acquire too high a fame when him we serve
  's away.
Who does i' the wars more than his captain
  can

. . . . .

Becomes his captain's captain; and ambition,
The soldier's virtue, rather makes choice of
  loss
Than gain which darkens him.
Antony and Cleopatra, III, 1:14, 21

PANDULPH. And he that stands upon a
  slippery place
Makes nice[1] of no vile hold to stay[2] him up:
King John, III, 4:137
[1] nice: fastidious distinctions. [2] stay: hold.

CEREMONY

K. HENRY [soliloquy]. O ceremony!
  show me but thy worth:
What is thy soul of adoration?
Art thou aught else but place, degree, and
  form,
Creating awe and fear in other men?
Wherein thou art less happy, being fear'd,
Than they in fearing.
What drink'st thou oft, instead of homage
  sweet,
But poison'd flattery? O! be sick, great
  greatness,
And bid thy ceremony give thee cure.
Think'st thou the fiery fever will go out
With titles blown from adulation?
Will it give place to flexure and low-bend-
  ing?
Canst thou, when thou command'st the beg-
  gar's knee,
Command the health of it? No, thou proud
  dream,
That play'st so subtly with a king's repose;
I am a king that find thee; and I know
'T is not the balm,[1] the sceptre and the ball,
The sword, the mace, the crown imperial,
The intertissued robe of gold and pearl,
The farced title running fore the king,
The throne he sits on, nor the tide of pomp
That beats upon the high shore of this
  world,
No, not all these, thrice-gorgeous cere-
  mony,

No, not all these, laid in bed majestical,
Can sleep so soundly as the wretched slave,
Who with a body fill'd and vacant mind
Gets him to rest, cramm'd with distressful
  bread;
Never sees horrid night, the child of hell,
But, like a lackey, from the rise to set
Sweats in the eye of Phoebus,[2] and all night
Sleeps in Elysium; next day after dawn,
Doth rise and help Hyperion[3] to his horse,
And follows so the ever-running year
With profitable labour to his grave:
And, but for ceremony, such a wretch,
Winding up days with toil and nights with
  sleep,
Had the fore-hand and vantage of a king.
The slave, a member of the country's peace,
Enjoys it; but in gross brain little wots[4]
What watch the king keeps to maintain the
  peace,
Whose hours the peasant best advantages.
Henry V, IV, 1:261
[1] balm and next lines: symbols of monarch.
[2] Phoebus: the sun god. [3] Hyperion: another
name for the sun god; the Greeks thought of
the sun god as riding in a horse-drawn chariot.
[4] wots: knows.

BRUTUS. When love begins to sicken and
  decay,
It useth an enforced ceremony.
Julius Caesar, IV, 2:20

LADY MACBETH. To feed were best at
  home;
From thence, the sauce to meat is ceremony.
Macbeth, III, 4:35

TIMON. Nay, my lords, ceremony was
  but devis'd at first
To set a gloss on faint deeds, hollow wel-
  comes,
Recanting goodness, sorry ere 't is shown;
But where there is true friendship, there
  needs none.
Timon of Athens, I, 2:15

CERTAINTY

KING. Upon thy certainty and confidence[1]
What dar'st thou venture?
HELENA. Tax[2] of impudence,
A strumpet's boldness, a divulged shame,
Traduc'd by odious ballads.
All's Well That Ends Well, II, 1:172
[1] confidence: that she can cure him. [2] Tax:
accusation.

DUKE. Not a semblance, but a certainty.
Measure for Measure, IV, 2:203

JESSICA. Who are you? Tell me for more
  certainty,

Albeit I'll swear that I do know your
   tongue.
LORENZO. Lorenzo, and thy love.
JESSICA. Lorenzo, certain; and my love in-
   deed,
Merchant of Venice, II, 6:26

CAMILLO. Swear his thought over
By each particular star in heaven and
By all their influences, you may as well
Forbid the sea for to obey the moon
As or[1] by oath remove or counsel shake
The fabric of his folly, whose foundation
Is pil'd[2] upon his faith, and will continue
The standing[3] of his body.
Winter's Tale, I, 2:424
[1] or . . . or: either . . . or.   [2] pil'd: built.
[3] standing: permanence.

CHALLENGE

PLANTAGENET [YORK]. Let him that is a
true-born gentleman
And stands upon the honour of his birth,
If he suppose that I have pleaded truth,
From off this brier pluck a white rose
   with me.
SOMERSET. Let him that is no coward nor
   no flatterer,
But dare maintain the party of the truth,
Pluck a red rose from off this thorn with
   me.
WARWICK. I love no colours, and without
   all colour
Of base insinuating flattery
I pluck this white rose with Plantagenet.
SUFFOLK. I pluck this red rose with young
   Somerset,
I Henry VI, II, 4:27

And here I prophesy: this brawl to-day,
Grown to this faction in the Temple gar-
   den,
Shall send between the red rose and the
   white
A thousand souls to death and deadly night.
I Henry VI, II, 4:124

LEONATO. Know, Claudio, to thy head,
Thou hast so wrong'd mine innocent child
   and me
That I am forc'd to lay my reverence[1] by,
And, with grey hairs and bruise of many
   days,
Do challenge thee to trial of a man.
Much Ado About Nothing, V, 1:62
[1] reverence: consideration of old age.

SIR ANDREW. 'T were as good a deed as
to drink when a man's a-hungry, to challenge him to the field, and then to break
promise with him and make a fool of him.
Twelfth Night, II, 3:135

SIR TOBY. Go, write it in a martial hand;
be curst[1] and brief; it is no matter how
witty, so it be eloquent and full of invention: taunt him with the license of ink: if
thou thou'st him some thrice, it shall not be
amiss; and as many lies as will lie in thy
sheet of paper.
Twelfth Night, III, 2:45
[1] curst: waspish.

SIR TOBY [reading the challenge]. Thou
comest to the Lady Olivia, and in my sight
she uses thee kindly: but thou liest in thy
throat; that is not the matter I challenge
thee for.
FABIAN. Very brief, and to exceeding
good sense-less.
SIR TOBY. I will waylay thee going home;
where, if it be thy chance to kill me,—
FABIAN. Good.
SIR TOBY. Thou killest me like a rogue
and a villain,
FABIAN. Still you keep o' the windy[1] side
of the law: good.
SIR TOBY. Fare thee well; and God have
mercy upon one of our souls! He may have
mercy upon mine, but my hope is better;
and so look to thyself. Thy friend, as thou
usest him, and thy sworn enemy, Andrew
Aguecheek.
Twelfth Night, III, 4:170
[1] windy: safe.

VIOLA. I have heard of some kind of men
that put quarrels purposely on others to
taste[1] their valour; belike this is a man of
that quirk.
Twelfth Night, III, 4:268
[1] taste: test.

CHANCE

OCTAVIUS CAESAR [to CLEOPATRA]. The
   record of what injuries you did us,
Though written in our flesh, we shall re-
   member
As things but done by chance.
Antony and Cleopatra, V, 2:118

CORIOLANUS. Tell these sad women[1]
'T is fond[2] to wail inevitable strokes
As 't is to laugh at 'em. My mother, you wot
   well
My hazards still[3] have been your solace.
Coriolanus, IV, 1:25
[1] women: his wife and his mother. [2] fond:
foolish. [3] still: always.

ARCHBISHOP. Against ill chances men are
   ever merry,
But heaviness[1] foreruns the good event.
WESTMORELAND. Therefore be merry,
   coz; since sudden sorrow

Serves to say thus, 'Some good thing comes to-morrow.'
II Henry IV, IV, 2:81
[1] heaviness: low spirits.

MACBETH [aside]. If chance will have me king, why, chance may crown me,
Without my stir.
Macbeth, I, 3:143

MOROCCO. If Hercules and Lichas[1] play at dice
Which is the better man, the greater throw
May turn by fortune from the weaker hand:
So is Alcides[2] beaten by his page.
Merchant of Venice, II, 1:32
[1] Lichas: his servant.   [2] Alcides: another name for Hercules.

K. RICHARD. Slave! I have set my life upon a cast,
And I will stand the hazard of the die.[1]
Richard III, V, 4:9
[1] die: cast of dice.

FLORIZEL. We profess
Ourselves to be the slaves of chance and flies
Of every wind that blows.
Winter's Tale, IV, 4:531

CHANGE

ANTONY. The hated, grown to strength,
Are newly grown to love.
Antony and Cleopatra, I, 3:48

GLOUCESTER. The seasons change their manners, as[1] the year
Had found some months asleep and leap'd them over.
II Henry IV, IV, 4:123
[1] as: as if.

CADE. Was ever feather so lightly blown to and fro as this multitude?
II Henry VI, IV, 8:57

LYSANDER. Swift as a shadow, short as any dream,
Brief as the lightning in the collied[1] night,
That, in a spleen, unfolds both heaven and earth,
And ere a man hath power to say 'Behold!'
The jaws of darkness do devour it up:
So quick bright things come to confusion.
Midsummer Night's Dream, I, 7:144
[1] collied: darkened.

TITANIA. The seasons alter: hoary-headed frosts
Fall in the fresh lap of the crimson rose,
And on old Hiems'[1] thin and icy crown
An odorous chaplet of sweet summer buds

Is, as in mockery, set. The spring, the summer,
The chiding autumn, angry winter, change
Their wonted liveries, and the mazed world,
By their increase, now knows not which is which.
And this same progeny of evils comes
From our debate, from our dissension.
Midsummer Night's Dream, II, 1:107
[1] Hiems: personification of winter.

MERCUTIO. O flesh, flesh, how art thou fishified!
Romeo and Juliet, II, 4:41

CAPULET. All things that we ordained festival,
Turn from their office to black funeral;
Our instruments to melancholy bells,
Our wedding cheer to a sad burial feast,
Our solemn hymns to sullen dirges change,
Our bridal flowers serve for a buried corse,
And all things change them to the contrary.
Romeo and Juliet, IV, 5:84

VALENTINE. Why, how know you that I am in love?
SPEED. Marry, by these special marks. First, you have learned, like Sir Proteus, to wreathe your arms, like a malecontent; to relish a love-song, like a robin-redbreast; to walk alone, like one that had the pestilence; to sigh, like a school-boy that had lost his A B C; to weep, like a young wench that had buried her grandam; to fast, like one that takes diet; to watch, like one that fears robbing; to speak puling, like a beggar at Hallowmas. You were wont, when you laughed, to crow like a cock; when you walked, to walk like one of the lions; when you fasted, it was presently after dinner; when you looked sadly, it was for want of money: and now you are metamorphosed with a mistress, that, when I look on you, I can hardly think you my master.
Two Gentlemen of Verona, II, 1:17

PROTEUS. Even as one heat another heat expels,
Or as one nail by strength drives out another,
So the remembrance of my former love
Is by a newer object quite forgotten.
At first I did adore a twinkling star,
But now I worship a celestial sun.
Two Gentlemen of Verona, II, 4:192

CHARACTER

ENOBARBUS. Antony will use his affection where it is; he married but his occasion here.
Antony and Cleopatra, II, 6:138

OLIVER. I hope I shall see an end of him;[1] for my soul, yet I know not why, hates nothing more than he. Yet he's gentle, never schooled and yet learned, full of noble device, of all sorts enchantingly beloved, and indeed so much in the heart of the world, and especially of my own people, who best know him, that I am altogether misprised.

As You Like It, I, 1:170

[1] him: ORLANDO.

FIRST CITIZEN. Though soft-conscienced men can be content to say it was for his country, he did it to please his mother, and to be partly proud; which he is, even to the altitude of his virtue.

Coriolanus, I, 1:37

FALSTAFF. I do remember him[1] at Clement's Inn like a man made after supper of a cheese-paring: when a' was naked he was for all the world like a forked radish, with a head fantastically carved upon it with a knife: a' was so forlorn that his dimensions to any thick sight were invincible: a' was the very genius of famine; yet lecherous as a monkey.

II Henry IV, III, 2:330

[1] him: JUSTICE SHALLOW.

K. HENRY. He[1] hath a tear for pity and a hand
Open as day for melting charity;
Yet notwithstanding, being incens'd, he 's flint,
As humorous[2] as winter, and as sudden
As flaws[3] congealed in the spring of day.
His temper therefore must be well observ'd:
Chide him for faults, and do it reverently,
When you perceive his blood inclin'd to mirth;
But, being moody, give him line and scope,
Till that his passions, like a whale on ground,
Confound themselves with working.

II Henry IV, IV, 4:31

[1] He: PRINCE HENRY, later HENRY V.   [2] humorous: changeable, uncertain.   [3] flaws . . . day: gusts carrying ice in spring.

GRIFFITH. His[1] overthrow heap'd happiness upon him;
For then, and not till then, he felt himself,
And found the blessedness of being little:
And, to add greater honours to his age
Than man could give him, he died fearing God.

Henry VIII, IV, 2:64

[1] His: WOLSEY'S.

CHATILLON. Rash, inconsiderate, fiery voluntaries,[1]
With ladies' faces and fierce dragons' spleens,
Have sold their fortunes at their native homes,
Bearing their birthrights proudly on their backs,
To make a hazard of new fortunes here.

King John, II, 1:67

[1] voluntaries: volunteers.

BRUTUS. I am not gamesome: I do lack some part
Of that quick spirit that is in Antony.

Julius Caesar, I, 2:28

CAESAR. Let me have men about me that are fat;
Sleek-headed men and such as sleep o' nights.
Yond Cassius has a lean and hungry look;
He thinks too much: such men are dangerous.

. . . . .

Would he were fatter! But I fear him not:
Yet if my name were liable to fear,
I do not know the man I should avoid
So soon as that spare Cassius. He reads much;
He is a great observer, and he looks
Quite through the deeds of men; he loves no plays,
As thou dost, Antony; he hears no music;
Seldom he smiles, and smiles in such a sort
As if he mock'd himself, and scorn'd his spirit
That could be mov'd to smile at any thing.
Such men as he be never at heart's ease
Whiles they behold a greater than themselves.

Julius Caesar, I, 2:192

CASCA. O! he[1] sits high in all the people's hearts:
And that which would appear offence in us,
His countenance, like richest alchemy,
Will change to virtue and to worthiness.

Julius Caesar, I, 3:157

[1] he: BRUTUS.

ANTONY. This[1] was the noblest Roman of them all:
All the conspirators save only he
Did that they did in envy of great Caesar;
He only, in a general honest thought
And common good to all, made one of them.
His life was gentle, and the elements
So mix'd in him that Nature might stand up
And say to all the world, 'This was a man!'

Julius Caesar, V, 5:69

[1] This: BRUTUS.

Enter LADY M. [reading a letter].
They met me in the day of success; and I
have learned by the perfectest report, they
have more in them than mortal knowledge.
When I burned in desire to question them
further, they made themselves air, into
which they vanished. Whiles I stood rapt
in the wonder of it, came missives from the
king, who all-hailed me 'Thane of Cawdor';
by which title, before, these weird sisters
saluted me, and referred me to the coming
on of time, with 'Hail, king that shalt be!'
Macbeth, I, V:1

LADY M. [soliloquy]. Glamis thou art,
and Cawdor; and shalt be,
What thou art promis'd. Yet do I fear thy
nature;
It is too full o' the milk of human kindness[1]
To catch the nearest way; thou would'st be
great,
Art not without ambition, but without
The illness should attend it; what thou
would'st highly,
That would'st thou holily; would'st not
play false,
And yet would'st wrongly win; thou 'dst
have, great Glamis,
That which cries 'Thus thou must do, if
thou have it';
And that which rather thou dost fear to do
Than wishest should be undone.
Macbeth, I, 5:16
[1] kindness: nature.

DUKE. Angelo,
There is a king of character in thy life,
That to the observer doth thy history
Fully unfold.
Measure for Measure, I, 1:27

PROVOST. A man that apprehends death
no more dreadfully but as a drunken sleep;
careless, reckless, and fearless of what's past,
present, or to come; insensible of mortality,[1]
and desperately mortal..
Measure for Measure, IV, 2:148
[1] mortality: death.   [2] mortal: subject to common fate of man.

DUKE.[1] O! your desert speaks loud; and I
should wrong it
To lock it in the wards of covert[2] bosom,
When it deserves, with characters of brass,
A forted residence 'gainst the tooth of time
And razure[3] of oblivion.
Measure for Measure, V, 1:9
[1] To ANGELO.   [2] covert: secret.   [3] razure: de-
struction.

BEATRICE. How tartly that gentleman
looks! I never can see him but I am heart-
burned an hour after.
Much Ado About Nothing, II, 1:3

OTHELLO. My parts, my title, and my per-
fect soul
Shall manifest me rightly.
Othello, I, 2:31

IAGO. The Moor is of a free and open na-
ture,
That thinks men honest that but seem to
be so,
And will as tenderly be led by the nose
As asses are.
Othello, I, 3:405

AGAMEMNON. When rank Thersites opes
his mastick[1] jaws,
We shall hear music, wit, and oracle.
Troilus and Cressida, I, 3:73
[1] mastick: mastiff.

ULYSSES [about TROILUS]. The youngest
son of Priam, a true knight;
Not yet mature, yet matchless; firm of
word,
Speaking of deeds and deedless in his
tongue;
Not soon provok'd nor being provok'd
soon calm'd:
His heart and hand both open and both free;
For what he has he gives, what thinks he
shows;
Yet gives he not till judgment guide his
bounty,
Nor dignifies an impure thought with
breath.
Troilus and Cressida, IV, 5:96

OLIVIA. I suppose him virtuous, know
him[1] noble,
Of great estate, of fresh and stainless youth;
In voices well divulg'd, free, learn'd, and
valiant;
And in dimension and the shape of nature
A gracious person.
Twelfth Night, I, 5:277
[1] him: DUKE ORSINO.

MARIA. An affectioned[1] ass, that cons
state[2] without book, and utters it by great
swarths: the best persuaded of himself; so
crammed, as he thinks, with excellencies,
that it is his ground of faith that all that
look on him love him.
Twelfth Night, II, 3:160
[1] affectioned: affected.   [2] state: dignity of de-
portment.

CHARITY

OPHELIA. To the noble mind
Rich gifts wax[1] poor when givers prove unkind.
Hamlet, III, 1:100
[1] wax: grow.

Biron. Charity itself fulfils the law;
And who can sever love from charity?
Love's Labour's Lost, IV, 3:364

Portia. 'T were good you do so much for charity.
Shylock. I cannot find it: 'tis not in the bond.
Merchant of Venice, IV, 1:261

Timon. 'Tis not enough to help the feeble up,
But to support him after.
Timon of Athens, I, 1:107

CHARM

Katharine. I saw him at the Duke Alencon's once;
And much too little of that good I saw
Is my report to his great worthiness.
Rosaline. Another of these students at that time
Was there with him, if I have heard a truth:
Biron they call him; but a merrier man,
Within the limit of becoming mirth,
I never spent an hour's talk withal.[1]
His eye begets occasion for his wit;
For every object that the one doth catch
The other turns to a mirth-moving jest,
Which his fair tongue, conceit's[2] expositor,
Delivers in such apt and gracious words,
That aged ears play truant at his tales,
And younger hearings are quite ravished;
So sweet and voluble is his discourse.
Love's Labour's Lost, II, 1:61
[1] withal: with.   [2] conceit's: thought's.

Second Witch. For a charm of powerful trouble
Like a hell-broth boil and bubble.
Macbeth, IV, 1:18

Claudio. In her[1] youth
There is a prone and speechless dialect,
Such as move men.
Measure for Measure, I, 2:187
[1] her: Isabella's.

Lorenzo. Beshrew me, but I love her[1] heartily;
For she is wise, if I can judge of her,
And fair she is, if that mine eyes be true,
And true she is, as she hath prov'd herself;
And therefore, like herself, wise, fair, and true,
Shall she be placed in my constant soul.
Merchant of Venice, II, 6:52
[1] her: Jessica.

Mistress Quickly. Surely, I think you have charms, la; yes, in truth.

Falstaff. Not I, I assure thee; setting the attraction of my good parts aside, I have no other charms.
Merry Wives of Windsor, II, 2:109

Florizel. My good Camillo,
She is as forward of her breeding as
She is i' the rear o' our birth.
Camillo. I cannot say 't is pity
She lacks instructions, for she seems a mistress
To most that teach.
Winter's Tale, IV, 4:589

CHASTITY

Mariana. The honour of a maid is her name, and no legacy is so rich as honesty.[1]
All's Well That Ends Well, III, 5:12
[1] honesty: chastity, as frequently in Shakespeare.

Diana. My chastity 's the jewel of our house,
Bequeathed down from many ancestors,
Which were the greatest obloquy i' the world
In me to lose.
All's Well That Ends Well, IV, 2:46

Coriolanus. Chaste as the icicle
That's curded[1] by the frost from purest snow,
And hangs on Dian's[2] temple.
Coriolanus, V, 3:65
[1] curded: congealed.   [2] Diana, the moon goddess.

Imogen. Away! I do condemn mine ears that have
So long attended thee. If thou wert honourable,
Thou would'st have told this tale for virtue, not
For such an end thou seek'st; as base as strange.
Cymbeline, I, 6:141

Posthumus. I thought her
As chaste as unsunn'd snow.
Cymbeline, II, 5:12

Iachimo. He spake of her as[1] Dian[2] had hot[3] dreams,
And she alone were cold.
Cymbeline, V, 5:180
[1] as: as if.   [2] Dian: Diana, Greek goddess.
[3] hot: lascivious.

Laertes. Then weigh what loss your honour may sustain,
If with too credent ear you list his songs,

Or lose your heart, or your chaste treasure
    open
To his unmaster'd importunity.
Fear it, Ophelia, fear it, my dear sister,
                                    Hamlet, I, 3:29

When he most burn'd in heart-wish'd lux-
    ury,[1]
He preach'd pure maid and prais'd cold
    chastity.
                            Lover's Complaint, 314
[1] luxury: lust.

ANGELO. What would you do?
ISABELLA. As much for my poor brother
    as myself:
That is, were I under the terms of death,
The impression of keen whips I'd wear as
    rubies,
And strip myself to death, as to a bed
That longing have been sick for, ere I'd
    yield
My body up to shame.
                        Measure for Measure, II, 4:98

MISTRESS PAGE. Well, I will find you
twenty lascivious turtles ere one chaste man.
        Merry Wives of Windsor, II, 1:82

FORD. She dwells so securely on the ex-
cellency of her honour, that the folly of my
soul dares not present itself.
        Merry Wives of Windsor, II, 2:251

LYSANDER. One turf shall serve as pillow
    for us both;
One heart, one bed, two bosoms, and one
    troth.
HERMIA. Nay, good Lysander; for my
    sake, my dear,
Lie further off yet, do not lie so near.

                . . . . .

But, gentle friend, for love and courtesy
Lie further off; in human modesty,
Such separation as may well be said
Becomes a virtuous bachelor and a maid,
So far be distant; and good night, sweet
    friend.
        Midsummer Night's Dream, II, 2:41, 56

TITANIA. The moon methinks looks with
    a watery eye;
And when she weeps, weeps every little
    flower,
Lamenting some enforced chastity.
        Midsummer Night's Dream, III, 1:202

HERO. If I know more of any man alive
Than that which maiden modesty doth war-
    rant,
Let all my sins lack mercy!
        Much Ado About Nothing, IV, 1:180

To win his heart, she touch'd him here and
    there:
Touches so soft still[1] conquer chastity.
                        Passionate Pilgrim, 49
[1] still: always.

LYSIMACHUS. Had I brought hither a cor-
    rupted mind,
Thy speech had[1] alter'd it.
                        Pericles, IV, 6:111
[1] had: would have.

BOULT. The nobleman would have dealt
with her like a nobleman, and she sent him
away as cold as a snowball; saying his prayers too.
                        Pericles, IV, 6:146

This hot desire converts to cold disdain:
Pure Chastity is rifled of her store,
And Lust, the thief, far poorer than before.
                        Rape of Lucrece, 691

ROMEO. She will not stay[1] the siege of
    loving terms,
Nor bide the encounter of assailing eyes,
Nor ope her lap to saint-seducing gold.
                    Romeo and Juliet, I, 1:218
[1] stay: abide.

The little Love-god lying once asleep
Laid by his side his heart-inflaming brand,
Whilst many nymphs that vow'd chaste life
    to keep
Came tripping by; but in her maiden hand
The fairest votary took up that fire
Which many legions of true hearts had
    warm'd;
And so the general[1] of hot desire
Was sleeping by a virgin hand disarm'd.
                                Sonnet 154
[1] general . . . desire: commander of passion.

ANTIGONUS. For every inch of woman in
    the world,
Ay, every dram of woman's flesh is false,
If she be.
                        Winter's Tale, II, 1:137

CHILD

K. LEAR. How sharper than a serpent's
    tooth it is
To have a thankless child!
                            King Lear, I, 4:310

LADY M. 'Tis the eye of childhood
That fears a painted devil.
                            Macbeth, II, 2:54

MISTRESS QUICKLY. You may know one
another's mind, and the boy never need to

understand anything: for 't is not good that children should know any wickedness; old folks, you know, have discretion, as they say, and know the world.
Merry Wives of Windsor, II, 2:131

THIRD CITIZEN. Woe to that land that's govern'd by a child.
Richard III, II, 3:11

JULIET. So tedious is this day
As is the night before some festival
To an impatient child that hath new robes
And may not wear them.
Romeo and Juliet, III, 2:28

Or who is he so fond[1] will be the tomb
Of his self-love, to stop posterity?
Thou art thy mother's glass, and she in thee
Calls back the lovely April of her prime;
So thou through windows of thine age shalt see,
Despite of wrinkles, this thy golden time.
Sonnet 3

[1] fond: foolish.

That's for thyself to breed another thee,
Or ten times happier, be it ten for one;
Ten times thyself were happier than thou art,
If ten of thine ten times refigur'd thee;
Then what could death do, if thou should'st depart,
Leaving thee living in posterity?
Sonnet 6

CHOICE

BERTRAM. At first I stuck my choice upon her, ere my heart
Durst make too bold a herald of my tongue.
All's Well That Ends Well, V, 3:44

TOUCHSTONE. A poor virgin, sir, an ill-favoured[1] thing, sir, but mine own.
As You Like It, V, 4:59

[1] ill-favoured: homely.

QUEEN. Come hither, my good Hamlet, sit by me.
HAMLET.[1] No, good mother, here's metal more attractive.
Hamlet, III, 2:113

[1] Going to OPHELIA.

K. HENRY. I shall be well content with any choice
Tends to God's glory and my country's weal.
I Henry VI, V, 1:26

FRANCE.[1] Fairest Cordelia, that art most rich, being poor;

Most choice, forsaken; and most lov'd, despis'd!
King Lear, I, 1:253

[1] FRANCE: KING OF FRANCE.

PORTIA. In terms of choice I am not solely led
By nice[1] direction of a maiden's eyes;
Besides, the lottery of my destiny
Bars me the right of voluntary choosing:
But if my father had not scanted[2] me
And hedg'd me by his wit, to yield myself
His wife who wins me by that means I told you,
Yourself, renowned prince, then stood as fair
As any comer I have look'd on yet.
Merchant of Venice, II, 1:13

[1] nice: fastidious. [2] scanted: limited.

PORTIA. Go, draw aside the curtains, and discover
The several caskets to this noble prince.
Now make your choice.
MOROCCO. The first, of gold, who this inscription bears:
Who chooseth me shall gain what many men desire.
The second, silver, which this promise carries:
Who chooseth me shall get as much as he deserves.
This third, dull lead, with warning all as blunt:
Who chooseth me must give and hazard all he hath.
How shall I know if I do choose the right?
PORTIA. The one of them contains my picture, prince:
If you choose that, then I am yours withal.

. . . . .

But here an angel in a golden bed
Lies all within. Deliver me the key:
Here do I choose, and thrive I as I may!
PORTIA. There, take it, prince; and if my form lie there,
Then I am yours.
He unlocks the golden casket.
MOROCCO. O hell! what have we here?
A carrion Death, within whose empty eye
There is a written scroll. I'll read the writing.
All that glisters is not gold;
Often have you heard that told:
Many a man his life hath sold
But my outside to behold:
Gilded tombs do worms infold.
Had you been as wise as bold,
Young in limbs, in judgment old,
Your answer had not been inscroll'd:
Fare you well; your suit is cold.
Cold, indeed; and labour lost:

Then, farewell, heat, and welcome, frost!
Portia, adieu. I have too griev'd a heart
To take a tedious leave: thus losers part.
Merchant of Venice, II, 7:1, 58

ARRAGON. Well, but to my choice:
*Who chooseth me shall get as much as he
    deserves.*
I will assume desert. Give me a key for this,
And instantly unlock my fortunes here.
                    He opens the silver casket.
    PORTIA. Too long a pause for that which
        you find there.
        ARRAGON. What's here? the portrait of a
            blinking idiot,
Presenting me a schedule! I will read it.
How much unlike art thou to Portia!
How much unlike my hopes and my de-
    servings!
*Who chooseth me shall have as much as he
    deserves.*
Did I deserve no more than a fool's head?
Is that my prize? are my deserts no better?
    PORTIA. To offend, and judge, are distinct
        offices,
And of opposed natures.
    ARRAGON. What is here?
*The fire seven times tried this:
Seven times tried that judgment is
That did never choose amiss.
Some there be that shadows kiss;
Such have but a shadow's bliss:
There be fools alive, I wis,
Silver'd o'er; and so was this.
Take what wife you will to bed,
I will ever be your head:
So be gone, sir: you are sped.*
Still more fool I shall appear
By the time I linger here:
With one fool's head I came to woo,
But I go away with two.
                    Merchant of Venice, II, 9:49

    PORTIA *to* BASSANIO. I pray you, tarry:
        pause a day or two
Before you hazard; for, in choosing wrong,
I lose your company: therefore forbear
    awhile.
There's something tells me, but it is not
    love,
I would not lose you; and you know your-
    self,
Hate counsels not in such a quality.
                    Merchant of Venice, III, 2:1

    BASSANIO. Let me to my fortune and the
        caskets.
    PORTIA. Away then! I am lock'd in one of
        them:
If you do love me, you will find me out.
Nerissa and the rest, stand all aloof.
Let music sound while he doth make his
    choice;
Then, if he lose, he makes a swan-like end,

Fading in music: that the comparison . . .
A Song, whilst BASSANIO *comments on the
                        caskets to himself.*
Tell me where is fancy[1] bred,
Or in the heart or in the head?
How begot, how nourished?
Reply, reply.
It is engender'd in the eyes,
With gazing fed; and fancy dies
In the cradle where it lies.
Let us all ring fancy's knell:
I'll begin it,—Ding, dong, bell.
    ALL. Ding, dong, bell.
    BASSANIO. So may the outward shows be
        least themselves:
The world is still deceiv'd with ornament.
In law, what plea so tainted and corrupt
But, being season'd with a gracious voice,
Obscures the show of evil?

                    . . . . .

    BASSANIO. What find I here?
                    Opening the leaden casket.
Fair Portia's counterfeit! What demi-god
Hath come so near creation? Move these
    eyes?
Or whether, riding on the balls of mine,
Seem they in motion? Here are sever'd lips,
Parted with sugar breath; so sweet a bar
Should sunder such sweet friends. Here in
    her hairs
The painter plays the spider, and hath
    woven
A golden mesh to entrap the hearts of men
Faster than gnats in cobwebs: but her
    eyes!—
How could he see to do them? having made
    one,
Methinks it should have power to steal both
    his
And leave itself unfurnish'd: yet look, how
    far
The substance of my praise doth wrong this
    shadow
In underprizing it, so far this shadow
Doth limp behind the substance. Here's
    the scroll,
The continent and summary of my fortune.
*You that choose not by the view,
Chance as fair and choose as true!
Since this fortune falls to you,
Be content and seek no new.
If you be well pleas'd with this
And hold your fortune for your bliss,
Turn you where your lady is
And claim her with a loving kiss.*
A gentle scroll. Fair lady, by your leave;
I come by note, to give and to receive.
                    Merchant of Venice, III, 2:39, 63, 115
[1] fancy: love.

    BASSANIO. So, thrice-fair lady, stand I,
        even so

As doubtful whether what I see be true,
Until confirm'd, sign'd, ratified by you.

   PORTIA. You see me, Lord Bassanio, where
     I stand,
Such as I am: though for myself alone
I would not be ambitious in my wish,
To wish myself much better; yet for you
I would be trebled twenty times myself;
A thousand times more fair, ten thousand
   times
More rich;
That only to stand high in your account,
I might in virtues, beauties, livings, friends,
Exceed account: but the full sum of me
Is sum of nothing; which, to term in gross,
Is an unlesson'd girl, unschool'd, unpractis'd;
Happy in this, she is not yet so old
But she may learn; happier than this,
She is not bred so dull but she can learn;
Happiest of all is that her gentle spirit
Commits itself to yours to be directed,
As from her lord, her governor, her king.
Myself and what is mine to you and yours
Is now converted: but now I was the lord
Of this fair mansion, master of my servants,
Queen o'er myself; and even now, but now,
This house, these servants, and this same my-
   self
Are yours, my lord. I give them with this
   ring;
Which when you part from, lose, or give
   away,
Let it presage the ruin of your love,
And be my vantage to exclaim on you.
       Merchant of Venice, III, 2:147

   GRATIANO. My Lord Bassanio and my gen-
    tle lady,
I wish you all the joy that you can wish;
For I am sure you can wish none from me:
And when your honours mean to solemnize
The bargain of your faith, I do beseech you,
Even at that time I may be married too.

   BASSANIO. With all my heart, so thou canst
    get a wife.

   GRATIANO. I thank your lordship, you
    have got me one.
My eyes, my lord, can look as swift as
   yours:
You saw the mistress, I beheld the maid;
You lov'd, I lov'd for intermission.
No more pertains to me, my lord, than you.
Your fortune stood upon the caskets there,
And so did mine too, as the matter falls;
For wooing here until I sweat again,
And swearing till my very roof was dry
With oaths of love, at last, if promise last,
I got a promise of this fair one here
To have her love, provided that your for-
   tune
Achiev'd her mistress.

   PORTIA. Is this true, Nerissa?

   NERISSA. Madam, it is, so you stand
    pleas'd withal.

   BASSANIO. And do you, Gratiano, mean
    good faith?

   GRATIANO. Yes, faith, my lord.

   BASSANIO. Our feast shall be much hon-
    our'd in your marriage.

   GRATIANO. We'll play with them the first
    boy for a thousand ducats.
       Merchant of Venice, III, 2:191

   HORTENSIO. There's small choice in rotten
apples.
       Taming of the Shrew, I, 1:139

CHRISTIAN

   K. HENRY. We are no tyrant but a Chris-
    tian King.
       Henry V, I, 2:241

   SHYLOCK. O father Abram! what these
    Christians are,
Whose own hard dealings teaches them sus-
   pect
The thoughts of others.
       Merchant of Venice, I, 3:161

   SHYLOCK. If a Jew wrong a Christian,
what is his humility? Revenge. If a Christian
wrong a Jew, what should his sufferance be
by Christian example? Why, revenge.
       Merchant of Venice, III, 1:71

   JESSICA. I shall be saved by my husband;
he hath made me a Christian.

   LAUNCELOT GOBBO. Truly, the more to
blame he: we were Christians enow[1] before;
e'en as many as could well live one by another. This making of Christians will raise
the price of hogs: if we grow all to be pork-
eaters, we shall not shortly have a rasher on
the coals for money.
       Merchant of Venice, III, 5:21

[1] enow: enough.

   RIVERS. A virtuous and a Christian-like
    conclusion,
To pray for them that have done scath to us.
       Richard III, I, 3:316

CHURCH

   JAQUES. The 'why' is plain as way to
    parish church.
       As You Like It, II, 7:52

   JAQUES. Get you to church, and have a
good priest that can tell what marriage is.
       As You Like It, III, 3:86

FALSTAFF. An[1] I have not forgotten what the inside of a church is made of, I am a pepper-corn, a brewer's horse: the inside of a church! Company, villanous company, hath been the spoil of me.
I Henry IV, III, 3:8
[1] An: if.

GLOUCESTER. And ne'er throughout the year to church thou go'st
Except it be to pray against thy foes.
I Henry VI, I, 7:42

CIRCUMSTANCE

HAMLET. And so, without more circum-stance at all,
I hold it fit that we shake hands and part.
Hamlet, I, 5:127

KING. And can you, by no drift of cir-cumstance,
Get from him why he puts on this con-fusion,
Grating so harshly all his days of quiet
With turbulent and dangerous lunacy?
Hamlet, III, 1:1

VIOLA. If nothing lets[1] to make us happy both
But this my masculine usurp'd attire,
Do not embrace me till each circumstance
Of place, time, fortune, do cohere and jump
That I am Viola.
Twelfth Night, V, 1:256
[1] lets: prevents.

CITIZENS

FIRST LORD.[1] Sweep on, you fat and greasy citizens;
'Tis just the fashion; wherefore do you look
Upon that poor and broken bankrupt there?
As You Like It, II, 1:55
[1] Quoting JAQUES.

CLASS HATRED

FIRST CITIZEN. We are accounted poor citizens, the patricians, good. What author-ity surfeits on would relieve us. If they would yield us but the superfluity, while it were wholesome, we might guess they re-lieved us humanely; but they think we are too dear: the leanness that afflicts us, the object of our misery, is an inventory to particularize their abundance; our suffer-ance[1] is a gain to them. Let us revenge this with our pikes, ere we become rakes:[2] for

the gods know I speak this in hunger for bread, not in thirst for revenge.

. . . . .

Care for us! True, indeed! They ne'er cared for us yet: suffer us to famish, and their storehouses crammed with grain; make edicts for usury, to support usurers; repeal daily any wholesome act established against the rich, and provide more piercing statutes daily to chain up and restrain the poor. If the wars eat us not up, they will; and there's all the love they bear us.
Coriolanus, I, 1:15, 82
[1] sufferance: meekness, patience.   [2] rakes: starvelings.

MARCIUS.[1] They said they were an-hun-gry; sigh'd forth proverbs:
That hunger broke stone walls; that dogs must eat;
That meat was made for mouths; that the gods sent not
Corn for the rich men only.
Coriolanus, I, 1:209
[1] Later CORIOLANUS.

CLOTHES

LAFEU. The soul of this man is his clothes.
All's Well That Ends Well, II, 5:48

ROSALIND. Good my complexion! dost thou think, though I am comparisoned[1] like a man, I have a doublet[2] and hose in my disposition?
As You Like It, III, 2:204
[1] comparisoned: dressed.   [2] doublet and hose: male costume.

FALSTAFF. Pray . . . that our armies join not in a hot day; for, by the Lord, I take but two shirts out with me, and I mean not to sweat extraordinarily.
II Henry IV, I, 2:233

SLY. Ne'er ask me what raiment I'll wear, for I have no more doublets than backs, no more stockings than legs, nor no more shoes than feet; nay, sometime more feet than shoes.
Taming of the Shrew, Induction, 2:9

PETRUCHIO. To me she's[1] married, not unto my clothes.
Could I repair what she will wear in me
As I can change these poor accoutrements,
'T were well for Kate and better for myself.
But what a fool am I to chat with you
When I should bid good-morrow to my bride,
And seal the title with a lovely kiss!
Taming of the Shrew, III, 2:119
[1] she: KATHARINA.

PETRUCHIO. Will we return unto thy fa-
    ther's house,
And revel it as bravely[1] as the best,
With silken coats and caps and golden rings,
With ruffs and cuffs and farthingales[2] and
    things;
With scarfs and fans and double change of
    bravery,
With amber bracelets, beads and all this
    knavery.
                Taming of the Shrew, IV, 3:53
[1] bravely: ostentatiously.   [2] farthingales:
hooped petticoats.

PETRUCHIO. Well, come, my Kate; we will
    unto your father's,
Even in these honest mean habiliments.
Our purses shall be proud, our garments
    poor:
For 'tis the mind that makes the body rich;
And as the sun breaks through the darkest
    clouds,
So honour peereth in the meanest habit.[1]
What is the jay more precious than the lark
Because his feathers are more beautiful?
Or is the adder better than the eel
Because his painted skin contents the eye?
O, no, good Kate; neither art thou the worse
For this poor furniture[2] and mean array.
                Taming of the Shrew, IV, 3:171
[1] habit: costume.   [2] furniture: equipment.

SERVANT. You would think a smock[1] were
a she-angel, he so chants to the sleeve-hand[2]
and the work about the square[3] on't.
                Winter's Tale, IV, 4:210
[1] smock: a woman's undergarment.   [2] sleeve-
hand: a cuff.   [3] square: embroidery.

CLOUD

ANTONY. Sometime we see a cloud that's
    dragonish;
A vapour sometime like a bear or lion,
A tower'd citadel, a pendent rock,
A forked mountain or blue promontory
With trees upon 't, that nod unto the world
And mock our eyes with air: thou hast seen
    these signs;
They are black vesper's[1] pageants.
                Antony and Cleopatra, IV, 14:2
[1] vesper's: evening's.

CHARMIAN. Dissolve, thick cloud, and
    rain; that I may say,
The gods themselves do weep.
                Antony and Cleopatra, V, 2:302

PRINCE. Yet herein will I imitate the sun,
Who doth permit the base contagious clouds
To smother up his beauty from the world,
                I Henry IV, I, 2:220

HECATE. Hark! I am call'd; my little spirit
    see,
Sits in a foggy cloud, and stays[1] for me.
                Macbeth, III, 5:34
[1] stays: awaits.

DEMETRIUS. These things seem small and
    undistinguishable,
Like far-off mountains turned into clouds.
                Midsummer Night's Dream, IV, 1:191

GLOUCESTER.[1] And all the clouds that
    lour'd upon our house
In the deep bosom of the ocean buried.
                Richard III, I, 1:3
[1] Later K. RICHARD III.

THIRD CITIZEN. When clouds are seen,
    wise men put on their cloaks;
                Richard III, III, 2:32

TRINCULO. Yond same black cloud, yond
huge one, looks like a foul bombard[1] that
would shed his[2] liquor. If it should thunder
as it did before, I know not where to hide
my head: yond same cloud cannot choose
but fall by pailfuls.
                Tempest, II, 2:20
[1] bombard: a leather jug for liquor.   [2] his: its.

Coal-black clouds that shadow heaven's
    light
Do summon us to part and bid good night.
                Venus and Adonis, 533

CLOWN

[The word *clown* in Shakespeare usually
means a simple rustic. Sometimes it means a
jester. The clown occasionally shows a sly
humor.]
SECOND LORD. My lord, the roynish[1]
    clown, at whom so oft
Your grace was wont to laugh, is also miss-
    ing.
                As You Like It, II, 2:8
[1] roynish: paltry, mean.

TOUCHSTONE. Holla, you clown!
ROSALIND. Peace, fool: he's not thy kinsman.
                As You Like It, II, 4:66

TOUCHSTONE. It is meat and drink to me
to see a clown.
                As You Like It, V, 1:11

COLD

BERTRAM. You are no maiden, but a monu-
    ment:

When you are dead you should be such a one
As you are now, for you are cold and stern;
All's Well That Ends Well, IV, 2:7

K. HENRY. My blood hath been too cold and temperate,
Unapt to stir at these indignities,
I Henry IV, I, 3:10

K. HENRY. Blunt not his love,
Nor lose the good advantage of his grace
By seeming cold or careless of his will.
II Henry IV, IV, 4:27

K. JOHN. Make his bleak winds kiss my parched lips
And comfort me with cold.
King John, V, 7:39

FOOL.[1] Nay, an[2] thou canst not smile as the wind sits, thou'lt catch cold shortly.
King Lear, I, 4:112
[1] Fool: jester.   [2] an: if.

FALSTAFF. My belly's as cold as if I had swallowed snowballs for pills.
Merry Wives of Windsor, III, 5:24

COMFORT

ADAM. He that doth the ravens feed,
Yea, providently caters for the sparrow,
Be comfort to my age!
As You Like It, II, 3:43

SUFFOLK. Comfort, my sovereign! gracious Henry, comfort!
K. HENRY. What! doth my Lord of Suffolk comfort me?
Came he right now to sing a raven's note,
Whose dismal tune bereft my vital powers,
And thinks he that the chirping of a wren,
By crying comfort from a hollow breast,
Can chase away the first-conceived sound?
Hide not thy poison with such sugar'd words.
II Henry VI, III, 2:38

CAPUCIUS. The king's request that I would visit you;
Who grieves much for your weakness, and by me
Sends you his princely commendations,
And heartily entreats you take good comfort.
Q. KATHARINE. O! my good lord, that comfort comes too late;
'T is like a pardon after execution:
That gentle physic,[1] given in time, had[2] cur'd me;

But now I am past all comforts here but prayers.
Henry VIII, IV, 2:116
[1] physic: medicine, remedy.   [2] had: would have.

MARIANA. Here comes a man of comfort, whose advice
Hath often still'd my brawling discontent.
Measure for Measure, IV, 1:8

CLEON. If heaven slumber while their creatures want,
They may awake their helps to comfort them.
Pericles, I, 4:16

YORK. Comfort's in heaven; and we are on the earth,
Where nothing lives but crosses, cares, and grief.
Richard II, II, 2:78

DUCHESS. Thou art a widow; yet thou art a mother,
And hast the comfort of thy children left thee:
Richard III, II, 2:55

As a decrepit father takes delight
To see his active child do deeds of youth,
So I, made lame by fortune's dearest spite,
Take all my comfort of thy worth and truth:
Sonnet 37

SEBASTIAN. He receives comfort like cold porridge.
Tempest, II, 1:10

PROSPERO. A solemn air and the best comforter
To an unsettled fancy, cure thy brains,
Now useless, boil'd within thy skull!
Tempest, V, 1:58

COMMAND

K. HENRY. Canst thou, when thou command'st the beggar's knee.
Command the health of it?
Henry V, IV, 1:273

CLAUDIO. Or whether that the body public be
A horse whereon the governor doth ride,
Who, newly in the seat, that it may know
He can command, lets it straight feel the spur;
Measure for Measure, I, 2:163

Duke. Command these fretting waters
from your eyes
With a light heart.
Measure for Measure, IV, 3:151

Arragon. O! that estates, degrees, and of-
fices
Were not deriv'd corruptly, and that clear
honour
Were purchas'd by the merit of the wearer.
How many then should cover that stand
bare;
How many be commanded that command;
Merchant of Venice, II, 9:41

COMMUNISM

Cade. Be brave then; for your captain is
brave, and vows reformation. There shall
be in England seven halfpenny loaves sold
for a penny; the three-hooped[1] pot shall
have ten hoops; and I will make it felony to
drink small beer. All the realm shall be in
common, and in Cheapside shall my palfrey
go to grass. And when I am king, as king I
will be,—
All. God save your majesty!
Cade. I thank you, good people: there
shall be no money; all shall eat and drink
on my score; and I will apparel them all in
one livery, that they may agree like brothers, and worship me their lord.
II Henry VI, IV, 2:69
[1] three-hooped pot: the drinking measure.

Dick. I have a suit unto your lordship.
Cade. Be it a lordship, thou shalt have
it for that word.
Dick. Only that the laws of England
may come out of your mouth.

. . . . .

Cade. I have thought upon it; it shall be
so. Away! burn all the records of the realm:
my mouth shall be the parliament of England.

. . . . .

And henceforward all things shall be in
common.
II Henry VI, IV, 7:4, 15, 20

Gonzalo. I' the commonwealth I would
by contraries
Execute all things; for no kind of traffic[1]
Would I admit; no name of magistrate;
Letters should not be known; riches, pov-
erty,
And use of service, none; contract, succes-
sion,
Bourn, bound of land, tilth, vineyard, none;
No use of metal, corn, or wine, or oil;

No occupation, all men idle, all;
And women too, but innocent and pure;
No sovereignty;—
Sebastian. Yet he would be king on 't.
Antonio. The latter end of his common-
wealth forgets the beginning.
Gonzalo. All things in common nature
should produce
Without sweat or endeavour: treason, fel-
ony,
Sword, pike, knife, gun, or need of any
engine,
Would I not have; but nature should bring
forth,
Of it own kind, all foison,[2] all abundance,
To feed my innocent people.
Tempest, II, 1:147
[1] traffic: trade, commerce. [2] foison: plenty.

COMPANION

Celia. If she[1] be a traitor,
Why so am I; we still[2] have slept together,
Rose at an instant, learn'd, play'd, eat to-
gether;
And wheresoe'er we went, like Juno's swans,
Still we went coupled and inseparable.
As You Like It, I, 3:74
[1] she: Rosalind. [2] still: always; continued ac-
tion, as often in Shakespeare.

Antipholus, Syracuse. A trusty villain,[1]
sir, that very oft,
When I am dull with care and melancholy,
Lightens my humour with his merry jests.
Comedy of Errors, I, 2:19
[1] villain: here a term of endearment.

Chief Justice. Well, God send the prince
a better companion!
Falstaff. God send the companion a better prince! I cannot rid my hands of him.
II Henry IV, I, 2:223

Warwick. My gracious lord, you look[1]
beyond him[2] quite:
The prince but studies his companions
Like a strange tongue, wherein, to gain the
language.
II Henry IV, IV, 4:67
[1] look beyond: misunderstand. [2] him: Prince
Henry.

K. Lear. Upon such sacrifices, my Cor-
delia,
The gods themselves throw incense. Have I
caught thee?
He that parts us shall bring a brand from
heaven,
And fire us hence like foxes.
King Lear, V, 3:20

Portia. In companions
That do converse and waste the time to-
gether,
Whose souls do bear an equal yoke of love,
There must be needs a like proportion
Of lineaments, of manners, and of spirit;
Which makes me think that this Antonio,
Being the bosom lover of my lord,
Must needs be like my lord.
Merchant of Venice, III, 4:11

Mercutio. Why, is not this better now
than groaning for love? now art thou sociable, now art thou Romeo; now art thou
what thou art, by art as well as by nature.
Romeo and Juliet, II, 4:92

COMPANY

Duke Senior. Why, how now, monsieur!
what a life is this,
That your poor friends must woo your
company?
As You Like It, II, 7:9

Jaques. I thank you for your company;
but, good faith, I had as lief have been myself alone.
Orlando. And so had I; but yet, for fashion sake, I thank you too for your society.
Jaques. God be wi' you: let's meet as little as we can.
Orlando. I do desire we may be better
strangers.
As You Like It, III, 2:268

Falstaff. It is certain that either wise
bearing or ignorant carriage is caught, as
men take diseases, one of another: therefore
let men take heed of their company.
II Henry IV, V, 1:85

Duchess.[1] What comfortable hour canst
thou name
That ever grac'd me with thy company?
Richard III, IV, 4:173
[1] To her son, King Richard III.

Ceres. Her[1] and her blind boy's[2] scandal'd
company I have forsworn.
Tempest, IV, 1:90
[1] Her: Venus.   [2] boy: Cupid.

COMPARISON

Imogen. He[1] never can meet more mischance than come
To be but nam'd of[2] thee. His meanest garment,
That ever hath but clipp'd his body, is
dearer

In my respect than all the hairs above thee,
Were they all made such men.
Cymbeline, II, 3:137
[1] He: Posthumus.   [2] of: by.

K. Lear. But where the greater malady is
fix'd,
The lesser is scarce felt. Thou'dst shun a
bear;
But if thy flight lay toward the roaring sea,
Thou'dst meet the bear i' the mouth.
King Lear, III, 4:8

Constance. As like
As rain to water, or devil to his dam.
King John, II, 1:127

Boyet. Be now as prodigal of all dear
grace
As Nature was in making graces dear
When she did starve the general world be-
side,
And prodigally gave them all to you.
Love's Labour's Lost, II, 1:9

Dogberry. Comparisons are odorous.
Much Ado About Nothing, III, 5:18

Benvolio. Compare her face with some
that I shall show,
And I will make thee think thy swan a crow.
Romeo and Juliet, I, 2:91

Tranio. He is my father, sir; and, sooth
to say,
In countenance somewhat doth resemble
you.
Biondello [Aside]. As much as an apple
doth an oyster, and all one.
Taming of the Shrew, IV, 2:99

Agamemnon. Light boats sail swift,
though greater hulks draw deep.
Troilus and Cressida, II, 3:277

CONCEIT

Falstaff. His wit 's as thick as Tewksbury mustard: there's no more conceit[1] in
him than is in a mallet.
II Henry IV, II, 4:262
[1] conceit: mental faculty.

Edgar. And yet I know not how conceit[1]
may rob
The treasury of life when life itself
Yields to the theft; had he been where he
thought
By this had thought been past.
King Lear, IV, 6:42
[1] how conceit: whether imagination, etc.;
Edgar's father thinks he has fallen from a
great height.

LORENZO. You have a noble and a true conceit[1]
Of god-like amity; which appears most strongly
In bearing thus the absence of your lord.
Merchant of Venice, III, 4:2
[1] conceit: idea.

IAGO. Dangerous conceits[1] are in their natures poisons,
Which at the first are scarce found to distaste,
But with a little act upon the blood,
Burn like the mines of sulphur.
Othello, III, 3:326
[1] conceits: ideas.

DUKE. Proteus, the good conceit[1] I hold of thee,
For thou hast shown some sign of good desert,
Makes me the better to confer with thee.
Two Gentlemen of Verona, III, 2:17
[1] conceit: opinion.

CONDOLENCE

ANTONY. Fulvia[1] is dead.

．　．　．　．　．

ENOBARBUS. Indeed the tears[2] live in an onion that should water this sorrow.
Antony and Cleopatra, I, 2:162, 176
[1] Fulvia: ANTONY'S wife. [2] tears . . . onion: onion can cause artificial tears.

LEONATO. Patch grief with proverbs.
Much Ado About Nothing, V, 1:17

LEONATO. Men
Can counsel and speak comfort to that grief
Which they themselves not feel;

．　．　．　．　．

Charm ache with air and agony with words.
Much Ado About Nothing, V, 1:20, 26

LEONATO. No, no; 'tis all men's office to speak patience
To those that wring under the load of sorrow,
But no man's virtue nor sufficiency
To be so moral when he shall endure
The like himself.
Much Ado About Nothing, V, 1:27

PAULINA. What's gone and what's past help
Should be past grief.
Winter's Tale, III, 2:223

CONFESSION

HAMLET. Confess yourself to heaven;
Repent what's past; avoid what is to come.
Hamlet, III, 4:149

ANGELO. O my dread lord!
I should be guiltier than my guiltiness,
To think I can be undiscernible,
When I perceive your grace, like power divine,
Hath look'd upon my passes.[1] Then, good prince,
No longer session[2] hold upon my shame,
But let my trial be mine own confession:
Immediate sentence then and sequent[3] death
Is all the grace I beg.
Measure for Measure, V, 1:371
[1] passes: acts. [2] session: court. [3] sequent death: death that follows.

BASSANIO. Promise me life, and I'll confess the truth,
PORTIA. Well then, confess and live.
BASSANIO. 'Confess' and 'love'
Had been the very sum of my confession.
Merchant of Venice, III, 2:34

BENEDICK. I may chance have some old quirks and remnants of wit broken on me, because I have railed so long against marriage; but doth not the appetite alter? A man loves the meat in his youth that he cannot endure in his age. Shall quips and sentences and these paper bullets of the brain awe a man from the career of his humour?[1] No; the world must be peopled. When I said I would die a bachelor, I did not think I should live till I were married. Here comes Beatrice. By this day! she's a fair lady: I do spy some marks of love in her.
Much Ado About Nothing, II, 3:245
[1] humour: cast of mind, temper.

CONFUSION

DROMIO EPHESUS. The capon burns, the pig falls from the spit,
The clock hath strucken twelve upon the bell;
My mistress made it one upon my cheek:
She is so hot because the meat is cold;
The meat is cold because you come not home;
You come not home because you have no stomach;
You have no stomach having broke your fast;
But we that know what 't is to fast and pray
Are penitent for your default to-day.
Comedy of Errors, I, 2:44

BASTARD. I am amaz'd,[1] methinks, and lose
  my way
Among the thorns and dangers of this
  world.
                                        King John, IV, 3:140
[1] amaz'd: confused, puzzled.

MALCOLM. Nay, had I power, I should
Pour the sweet milk of concord into hell,
Uproar the universal peace, confound
All unity on earth.
                                        Macbeth, IV, 3:97

THESEUS. Where I have come, great
  clerks[1] have purposed
To greet me with premeditated welcomes;
Where I have seen them shiver and look
  pale,
Make periods in the midst of sentences,
Throttle their practis'd accent in their fears,
And, in conclusion, dumbly have broke off,
Not paying me a welcome. Trust me, sweet,
Out of this silence yet I pick'd a welcome.
                        Midsummer Night's Dream, V, 1:93
[1] clerks: scholars.

OTHELLO. Why, how now, ho! from
  whence ariseth this?
Are we turn'd Turks, and to ourselves do
  that
Which heaven hath forbid the Ottomites?[1]
For Christian shame put by this barbarous
  brawl;
He that stirs next to carve[2] for his own rage
Holds his soul light; he dies upon his motion.
Silence that dreadful bell! it frights the isle
From her propriety. What is the matter,
  masters?
                                        Othello, II, 3:169
[1] Ottomites: Turks.   [2] carve: indulge in personal rage.

SERVANT. Madam, the guests are come,
supper served up, you called, my young
lady asked for, the nurse cursed in the pantry, and every thing in extremity.
                                Romeo and Juliet, I, 3:100

THERSITES. Why, he[1] stalks up and down
like a peacock, a stride and a stand; rumi-
nates like an hostess that hath no arithmetic
but her brain to set down her reckoning;
bites his lip with a politic regard, as who
should say 'There were wit in this head, an[2]
't would out'; and so there is, but it lies as
coldly in him as fire in a flint, which will
not show without knocking.
                        Troilus and Cressida, III, 3:251
[1] he: AJAX.   [2] an: if.

VIOLA [in male disguise]. I am all the
  daughters of my father's house,
And all the brothers too.
                                Twelfth Night, II, 4:123

CONSCIENCE

CORNELIUS. But I beseech your grace,
  without offence,
My conscience bids me ask, wherefore you
  have
Commanded of me these most poisonous
  compounds,
Which are the movers of a languishing
  death,
But though slow, deadly?
                                        Cymbeline, I, 5:7

POLONIUS. 'T is too much prov'd, that
  with devotion's visage[1]
And pious action we do sugar o'er
The devil himself.
  KING [Aside]. O! 'Tis too true;
How smart a lash that speech doth give my
  conscience!
The harlot's cheek, beautied with plaster-
  ing art,
Is not more ugly to[2] the thing that helps it
Than is my deed to my most painted word:
O heavy burden!
                                        Hamlet, III, 1:47
[1] devotion's visage: appearance of worship.
[2] to: compared with.

HAMLET. Thus conscience does make
  cowards of us all.
                                        Hamlet, III, 1:83

PRINCE. Now, my masters, for a true face
and good conscience.
FALSTAFF. Both which I have had; but
their date is out, and therefore I'll hide me.
                                        I Henry IV, II, 4:550

PRINCE HENRY. By heaven, Poins, I feel
  me much to blame,
So idly to profane the precious time,
When tempest of commotion, like the south,
Borne with black vapour, doth begin to melt
And drop upon our bare unarmed heads.
Give me my sword and cloak. Falstaff, good
  night.
                                        II Henry IV, II, 4:390

LORD CHAMBERLAIN. It seems the marriage
  with his brother's wife
Has crept too near his conscience.
  SUFFOLK. No; his conscience
Has crept too near another lady.
                                        Henry VIII, II, 2:17

WOLSEY. I know myself now; and I feel
  within me
A peace above all earthly dignities,
A still and quiet conscience. The king has
  cur'd me,
I humbly thank his grace; and from these
  shoulders,

These ruin'd pillars, out of pity, taken
A load would sink a navy, too much hon-
    our:
O! 'tis a burden, Cromwell, 'tis a burden
Too heavy for a man that hopes for heaven.
                            Henry VIII, III, 2:378

ISABELLA. Go to your bosom;
Knock there, and ask your heart what it
    doth know
That's like my brother's fault: if it confess
A natural guiltiness such as is his,
Let it not sound a thought upon your tongue
Against my brother's life.
                    Measure for Measure, II, 2:136

LAUNCELOT GOBBO. Certainly my conscience will serve me to run from this Jew
my master. The fiend is at mine elbow, and
tempts me, saying to me, 'Gobbo, Launcelot
Gobbo, good Launcelot,' or 'good Gobbo,'
or 'good Launcelot Gobbo, use your legs,
take the start, run away.' My conscience
says, 'No; take heed, honest Launcelot.

                    . . . . .

Certainly . . . my conscience is but a kind
of hard conscience, to offer to counsel me
to stay with the Jew. The fiend gives the
more friendly counsel: I will run, fiend; my
heels are at your commandment; I will run.
                    Merchant of Venice, II, 2:1, 27

BASSANIO. Let me choose,
For as I am, I live upon the rack.
    PORTIA. Upon the rack, Bassanio! then
    confess
What treason there is mingled with your
    love.
    BASSANIO. None but that ugly treason of
    mistrust,
Which makes me fear the enjoying of my
    love:
There may as well be amity and life
'Tween snow and fire, as treason and my
    love.
    PORTIA. Ay, but I fear you speak upon the
    rack,
Where men enforced do speak any thing.
    BASSANIO. Promise me life, and I'll confess
    the truth.
    PORTIA. Well then, confess and live.
    BASSANIO. 'Confess' and 'love'
Had been the very sum of my confession.
                    Merchant of Venice, III, 2:24

IAGO. Though in the trade of war I have
    slain men,
Yet do I hold it very stuff o' the conscience
To do no contriv'd[1] murder: I lack iniquity
Sometimes to do me service.
                            Othello, I, 2:1
[1] contriv'd: plotted.

SECOND MURDERER. I'll not meddle with
it;[1] it makes a man a coward; a man cannot
steal, but it accuseth him; a man cannot
swear, but it checks[2] him; a man cannot lie
with his neighbour's wife, but it detects him:
't is a blushing shame-fast spirit, that mutinies in a man's bosom; it fills a man full of
obstacles . . . and every man that means to
live well endeavors to trust to himself and
live without it.
                            Richard III, I, 4:141
[1] it: his conscience.   [2] checks: reproves.

K. RICHARD. My conscience hath a thou-
    sand several[1] tongues,
And every tongue brings in a several tale,
And every tale condemns me for a villain.
                            Richard III, V, 3:193
[1] several: separate.

K. RICHARD. By the apostle Paul, shadows
    to-night
Have struck more terror to the soul of
    Richard
Than can the substance of ten thousand sol-
    diers
Armed in proof,[1] and led by shallow Rich-
    mond.
                            Richard III, V, 3:216
[1] proof: tested armour.

K. RICHARD. Conscience is but a word
    that cowards use,
Devis'd at first to keep the strong in awe:
Our strong arms be our conscience, swords
    our law.
                            Richard III, V, 3:309

ALONSO. O! it is monstrous; monstrous!
Methought the billows spoke and told me
    of it;
The winds did sing it to me; and the thun-
    der,
That deep and dreadful organ-pipe,[1] pro-
    nounc'd
The name of Prosper.
                            Tempest, III, 3:95
[1] organ-pipe: voice.

TROILUS. I'll haunt thee like a wicked
    conscience still,[1]
That mouldeth goblins swift as frenzy's[2]
    thoughts.
                    Troilus and Cressida, V, 10:28
[1] still: always.   [2] frenzy's: insanity's.

CONSPIRACY

BRUTUS. O conspiracy!
Sham'st thou to show thy dangerous brow
    by night,

When evils are most free? O! then by day
Where wilt thou find a cavern dark enough
To mask thy monstrous visage? Seek none,
  conspiracy;
Hide it in smiles and affability:
For if thou path[1] thy native semblance on,
Not Erebus itself were dim enough
To hide thee from prevention.
                                    Julius Caesar, II, 1:77
[1] path: put.

ANTONIO. For all the rest,
They'll take suggestion as a cat laps milk;
They'll tell[1] the clock to any business that
We say befits the hour.
SEBASTIAN. Thy case, dear friend,
Shall be my precedent: as thou gott'st
  Milan,
I'll come by Naples. Draw thy sword: one
  stroke
Shall free thee from the tribute which thou
  pay'st;
And I the king shall love thee.

                        · · · · ·

ARIEL.[2] While you here do snoring lie,
Open-eyed Conspiracy
His time doth take.
If of life you keep a care,
Shake off slumber and beware:
Awake! awake!
                        Tempest, II, 1:287, 300
[1] tell: count.   [2] Singing in GONZALO's ear.

CONSTANCY

PORTIA. O constancy! be strong upon my
  side;
Set a huge mountain 'tween my heart and
  tongue;
                        Julius Caesar, II, 4:6

CONTEMPLATION

FABIAN. Contemplation makes a rare tur-
key-cock of him: how he jets under his
advanced plumes.
                        Twelfth Night, II, 5:35

CONTEMPT

ANTONY. What our contempts do often
  hurl from us
We wish it ours again.
                Antony and Cleopatra, I, 2:127

MARCIUS.[1] The common file,—a plague!
  tribunes[2] for them!

The mouse ne'er shunn'd the cat as they did
  budge
From rascals worse than they.
                        Coriolanus, I, 6:43
[1] Later, CORIOLANUS.   [2] tribunes: officers to
protect the rights of the common people or
plebes, here called the common file.

CORIOLANUS. Most sweet voices!
Better it is to die, better to starve,
Than crave the hire which first we do de-
  serve.
Why in this woolvish toge[1] should I stand
  here,
To beg of Hob and Dick, that do appear,
Their needless vouches?[2]
                        · · · · ·
SECOND CITIZEN. Amen, sir. To my poor
  unworthy notice,
He mock'd us when he begg'd our voices.
THIRD CITIZEN. Certainly.
He flouted us downright.
                        Coriolanus, II, 3:119, 167
[1] toge: toga, a costume.   [2] vouches: votes.

CORIOLANUS. For the mutable, rank-
  scented many, let them
Regard me as I do not flatter, and
Therein behold themselves.
                        Coriolanus, III, 1:66

BRUTUS. You speak o' the people
As if you were a god to punish, not
A man of their infirmity.
                        Coriolanus, III, 1:80

FALSTAFF. No more, Pistol: I would not
have you go off here. Discharge yourself of
our company, Pistol.
                        II Henry IV, II, 4:146

BASTARD. Madam, an if my brother had
  my shape,
And I had his, Sir Robert his, like him;
And if my legs were two such riding rods,
My arms such eel-skins stuff'd, my face so
  thin
That in mine ear I durst not stick a rose
Lest men should say 'Look, where three-
  farthings[1] goes!'
And, to[2] his shape, were heir to all this land,
Would I might never stir from off this place,
I'd give it every foot to have this face:
I would not be Sir Nob[3] in any case.
                        King John, I, 1:138
[1] three-farthings: a coin bearing a rose.   [2] to:
in addition.   [3] Sir Nob: his mother's husband,
not BASTARD's father.

GONERIL. I must change arms at home,
  and give the distaff
Into my husband's hands.
                        King Lear, IV, 2:17

JULIA [to PROTEUS]. Thou subtle, per-
   jur'd, false, disloyal man!
Think'st thou I am so shallow, so conceit-
   less,[1]
To be seduced by thy flattery,
That hast deceiv'd so many with thy vows?
Return, return, and make thy love amends.
For me, by this pale queen of night I swear,
I am so far from granting thy request
That I despise thee for thy wrongful suit,
And by and by intend to chide myself
Even for this time I spend in talking to thee.
   Two Gentlemen of Verona, IV, 2:95
[1] conceitless: unable to think.

CONTENTMENT

DUKE SENIOR. Now, my co-mates and
   brothers in exile,
Hath not old custom made this life more
   sweet
Than that of painted pomp? Are not these
   woods
More free from peril than the envious
   court?
Here feel we but the penalty of Adam,
The seasons' difference; as the icy fang
And churlish chiding of the winter's wind,
Which, when it bites and blows upon my
   body,
Even till I shrink with cold, I smile and say
'This is no flattery: these are counsellors
That feelingly persuade me what I am.'
Sweet are the uses of adversity,
Which like the toad, ugly and venomous,
Wears yet a precious jewel[1] in his head;
And this our life, exempt from public haunt,
Finds tongues in trees, books in the running
   brooks,
Sermons in stones, and good in every thing.
   As You Like It, II, 1:1
[1] jewel, etc.: referring to a common supersti-
tion.

ANTIPHOLUS, SYRACUSE. He that com-
   mends me to mine own content
Commends me to the thing I cannot get.
   Comedy of Errors, I, 2:33

GLENDOWER. She bids you on the wanton
   rushes lay you down
And rest your gentle head upon her lap,
And she will sing the song that pleaseth you,
And on your eyelids crown the god of
   sleep,
Charming your blood with pleasing heavi-
   ness,
Making such difference 'twixt wake and
   sleep
As is the difference betwixt day and night

The hour before the heavenly-harness'd
   team
Begins his golden progress in the east.
   I Henry IV, III, 1:214

IDEN. Lord! who would live turmoiled in
   the court,
And may enjoy such quiet walks as these?
This small inheritance my father left me
Contenteth me, and worth a monarchy.
I seek not to wax[1] great by others' waning,
Or gather wealth I care not with what envy:
Sufficeth that I have maintains my state,
And sends the poor well pleased from my
   gate.
   II Henry VI, IV, 10:18
[1] wax . . . waning: profit by others' loss.

ANNE. I swear, 't is better to be lowly
   born,
And range with humble livers in content,
Than to be perk'd up in a glistering[1] grief
And wear a golden[2] sorrow.
   Henry VIII, II, 3:19
[1] glistering: shining. [2] golden sorrow: the
crown. ANNE is thinking of QUEEN KATHARINE.

MACBETH [soliloquy]. Nought's had, all's
   spent,
Where our desire is got without content:
'T is safer to be that which we destroy
Than by destruction dwell in doubtful joy.
   Macbeth, III, 2:5

CONTRAST

JAQUES. O knowledge ill-inhabited,[1] worse
   than Jove in a thatched house!
   As You Like It, III, 3:10
[1] inhabited: housed.

IACHIMO. Had I this cheek
To bathe my lips upon; this hand, whose
   touch,
Whose every touch, would force the feeler's
   soul
To the oath of loyalty; this object, which
Takes prisoner the wild motion of mine eye,
Fixing it only here; should I, damn'd then,
Slaver with lips as common as the stairs
That mount the Capitol.
   Cymbeline, I, 6:99

BISHOP OF ELY. The strawberry grows
   underneath the nettle,
And wholesome berries thrive and ripen
   best
Neighbour'd by fruit of baser quality.
   Henry V, I, 1:60

GENTLEMAN. The to-and-fro conflicting
   wind and rain.
   King Lear, III, 1:11

OSWALD. What most he should dislike
  seems pleasant to him;
What like, offensive.
                          King Lear, IV, 2:10

GRATIANO. How like a younker[1] or a
  prodigal
The scarfed[2] bark puts from her native bay,
Hugg'd and embraced by the strumpet
  wind!
How like the prodigal doth she return,
With over-weather'd ribs and ragged sails,
Lean, rent, and beggar'd by the strumpet
  wind!
                  Merchant of Venice, II, 6:14
[1] younker: stripling.   [2] scarfed: flag-adorned.

THESEUS. A tedious brief scene of young
  Pyramus
And his love Thisbe; very tragical mirth.
Merry and tragical! tedious and brief!
That is, hot ice and wondrous strange snow.
How shall we find the concord of this dis-
  cord?
                Midsummer Night's Dream, V, 1:56

ROMEO. Here's much to do with hate, but
  more with love:
Why then, O brawling love! O loving hate!
O any thing! of nothing first created.
O heavy lightness! serious vanity!
Misshapen chaos of well-seeming forms!
Feather of lead, bright smoke, cold fire, sick
  health!
Still-waking sleep, that is not what it is!
This love feel I, that feel no love in this.
                    Romeo and Juliet, I, 1:181

ALEXANDER. He[1] is as valiant as the lion,
churlish as the bear, slow as the elephant; a
man into whom nature hath so crowded
humours[2] that his valour is crushed into
folly, his folly sauced with discretion: there
is no man hath a virtue that he hath not a
glimpse[3] of, nor any man an attaint[4] but he
carries some stain of it. He is melancholy
without cause, and merry against the hair.[5]
                  Troilus and Cressida, I, 2:20
[1] He: AJAX.   [2] humours: caprices.   [3] glimpse
of: trace of.   [4] attaint: evil.   [5] hair: grain.

COQUETTE

BERTRAM. She knew her distance and did
  angle for me,
Madding my eagerness with her restraint,
As all impediments in fancy's course
Are motives of more fancy;[1] and, in fine,[2]
Her infinite cunning, with her modern
  grace.
Subdued me to her rate: she got the ring.
                All's Well That Ends Well, V, 3:212
[1] fancy: love.   [2] fine: the end.

CLEOPATRA. Where is he?[1]
CHARMIAN. I did not see him since.
CLEOPATRA. See where he is, who's with
  him, what he does;
I did not send you: if you find him sad,
Say I am dancing; if in mirth, report
That I am sudden sick: quick, and return.

          . . . . .

CHARMIAN. In each thing give him way;
cross him in nothing.
CLEOPATRA. Thou teachest like a fool; the
way to lose him.
                Antony and Cleopatra, I, 3:1, 9
[1] he: ANTONY.

CLEOPATRA. I will betray
Tawny-finn'd fishes; my bended hook shall
  pierce
Their slimy jaws; and, as I draw them up,
I'll think them every one an Antony,
And say 'Ah, ha! you're caught.'
                Antony and Cleopatra, II, 5:11

CLEOPATRA. That time—O times!—
I laugh'd him out of patience; and that night
I laugh'd him into patience: and next morn,
Ere the ninth hour, I drunk him to his bed;
Then put my tires[1] and mantles on him,
  whilst
I wore his sword Philippan.
                Antony and Cleopatra, II, 5:18
[1] tires: headdresses.

HAMLET. I have heard of your paintings
too, well enough; God hath given you one
face, and you make yourselves another; you
jig, you amble, and you lisp, and nickname
God's creatures, and make[1] your wantonness
your ignorance. Go to, I'll no more on 't; it
hath made me mad.
                          Hamlet, III, 1:148
[1] make . . . ignorance: pretend ignorance as
mask for wantonness.

ROSALINE. How I would make him fawn,
  and beg, and seek,
And wait the season, and observe the times,
And spend his prodigal wits in bootless
  rhymes,
And shape his service wholly to my hests,
And make him proud to make me proud
  that jests!
So potent-like would I o'ersway his state
That he should be my fool, and I his fate.
                  Love's Labour's Lost, V, 2:62

FALSTAFF. I spy entertainment in her; she
discourses, she carves, she gives the leer of
invitation.
                Merry Wives of Windsor, I, 3:48

CRESSIDA. Women are angels, wooing;
Things won are done; joy's soul lies in the
doing:
That she belov'd knows nought that knows
not this:
Men prize the thing ungain'd more than it is.
Troilus and Cressida, I, 2:312

Bid me discourse, I will enchant thine ear,
Or like a fairy trip upon the green,
Or like a nymph, with long dishevell'd hair,
Dance on the sands, and yet no footing seen:
Venus and Adonis, 145

CORRUPTION

HELENA. How do you mean?
May be the amorous count solicits her
In the unlawful purpose.
WIDOW. He does indeed;
And brokes[1] with all that can in such a suit
Corrupt the tender honour of a maid:
But she is arm'd for him and keeps her
guard
In honestest defence.
All's Well That Ends Well, III, 5:71
[1] brokes: bargains.

MARCELLUS. Something is rotten in the
state of Denmark.
Hamlet, I, 4:90

KING. In the corrupted currents of this
world
Offence's gilded hand may shove by justice,
And oft 't is seen the wicked prize itself
Buys out the law; but 't is not so above.
Hamlet, III, 3:57

HAMLET. Rank corruption, mining all
within
Infects unseen.
Hamlet, III, 4:148

Q. MARGARET. Thy sale of offices and
towns in France,
If they were known, as the suspect is great,
Would make thee quickly hop without thy
head.
II Henry VI, I, 3:138

DUKE. My business in this state
Made me a looker-on here in Vienna,
Where I have seen corruption boil and bub-
ble
Till it o'er-run the stew:[1] laws for all faults,
But faults so countenanc'd,[2] that the strong
statutes
Stand like the forfeits[3] in a barber's shop,
As much in mock as mark.
Measure for Measure, V, 1:318
[1] stew: cauldron. [2] countenanc'd: overlooked,
not punished.   [3] forfeits . . . mark: penalties
as much a mockery as a statement of law.

SCRIVENER. Who is so gross[1]
That cannot see this palpable[2] device?
Yet who so bold but says he sees it not?
Richard III, III, 6:10
[1] gross: dull. [2] palpable: easily seen.

COUNSEL—COUNSELLOR

DUKE SENIOR. These are counsellors
That feelingly persuade me what I am.
As You Like It, II, 1:10

K. HENRY. Friendly counsel cuts off
many foes.
I Henry VI, III, 1:185

CADE. Can he that speaks with the tongue
of an enemy be a good counsellor?
II Henry VI, IV, 2:181

BUCKINGHAM. This holy fox,[1]
Or wolf, or both, for he is equal ravenous
As he is subtle, and as prone to mischief
As able to perform 't, his mind and place
Infecting one another, yea, reciprocally,
Only to show his pomp as well in France
As here at home, suggests the king our mas-
ter
To this last costly treaty.
Henry VIII, I, 1:158
[1] fox: WOLSEY.

POMPEY. Good counsellors lack no
clients.
Measure for Measure, I, 2:111

POMPEY. I thank your worship for your
good counsel.
Measure for Measure, II, 1:266

LEONATO. I pray thee, cease thy counsel,
Which falls into mine ears as profitless
As water in a sieve.
Much Ado About Nothing, V, 1:3

PERICLES. Fit counsellor and servant for a
prince,
Who by thy wisdom mak'st a prince thy
servant.
Pericles, I, 2:63

AARON. Two may keep counsel when the
third's away.
Titus Andronicus, IV, 2:144

COURAGE

ENOBARBUS. Now he[1] 'll outstare the
lightning. To be furious
Is to be frighted[2] out of fear, and in that
mood

The dove will peck the estridge;[3] and I see still,
A diminution in our captain's brain
Restores his heart. When valour preys on reason
It eats the sword it fights with.
Antony and Cleopatra, III, 11:195
[1] he: Antony. [2] frighted . . . fear: frightened until one no longer is afraid. [3] estridge: ostrich.

Rosalind. I must comfort the weaker vessel, as doublet and hose ought to show itself courageous to petticoat: therefore, courage.
As You Like It, II, 4:6

Posthumus. Our countrymen
Are men more[1] order'd than when Julius Caesar
Smil'd at their lack of skill, but found their courage
Worthy his frowning at; their discipline,
Now mingled with their courages, will make known
To their approvers[2] they are people such
That mend[3] upon the world.
Cymbeline, II, 4:20
[1] more order'd: better disciplined. [2] approvers: those who test them. [3] mend . . . world: improve.

Hotspur. Doomsday is near; die all, die merrily.
I Henry IV, IV, 1:134

Bourbon. Normans, but bastard Normans, Norman bastards!
Mort de mai vie![1] if they march along
Unfought withal, but I will sell my dukedom,
To buy a slobbery[2] and a dirty farm
In that nook-shotten[3] isle of Albion.
Henry V, III, 5:10
[1] *Mort . . . vie:* an oath, death of my life. [2] slobbery: wet and foul. [3] nook-shotten: abounding in capes and bays of England.

K. Henry. Gloucester, 't is true that we are in great danger;
The greater therefore should our courage be.
Henry V, IV, 1:1

K. Henry. Ah! cousin York, would thy best friends did know
How it doth grieve me that thy head is here.
Q. Margaret. My lord, cheer up your spirits: our foes are nigh.
And this soft courage[1] makes your followers faint.
III Henry VI, II, 2:54
[1] soft courage: lack of courage.

K. Lewis. Yield not thy neck
To fortune's yoke, but let thy dauntless mind
Still[1] ride in triumph over all mischance.
III Henry VI, III, 3:16
[1] still: continued action, as often in Shakespeare.

Q. Margaret. Great Lords, wise men ne'er sit and wail their loss,
But cheerly seek how to redress their harms.
What though the mast be now blown overboard,
The cable broke, the holding-anchor lost,
And half our sailors swallow'd in the flood;
Yet lives our pilot still: is 't meet that he
Should leave the helm and like a fearful lad
With tearful eyes add water to the sea,
And give more strength to that which hath too much;
Whiles in his moan the ship splits on the rock,
Which industry and courage might have sav'd?
III Henry VI, V, 4:1

Bastard. Shall a beardless boy,[1]
A cocker'd[2] silken wanton,[3] brave our fields,
And flesh his spirit in a war-like soil,
Mocking the air with colours idly spread,
And find no check? . . . to arms.
King John, V, 1:69
[1] boy: Lewis, the Dauphin. [2] cocker'd: pampered. [3] wanton: effeminate.

Lewis [the Dauphin]. The day shall not be up so soon as I,
To try the fair adventure of to-morrow.
King John, V, 5:21

First Senator. He 's truly valiant that can wisely suffer
The worst that man can breathe, and make his wrongs
His outsides, to wear them like his raiment, carelessly,
And ne'er prefer[1] his injuries to his heart,
To bring it into danger.
Timon of Athens, III, 5:31
[1] prefer: present, lay before.

COURT

Touchstone. Wast ever in court, shepherd?
Corin. No, truly,
Touchstone. Then thou art damned.
Corin. Nay, I hope.
Touchstone. Truly, thou art damned like an ill-roasted egg, all on one side.
Corin. For not being at court? Your reason?

TOUCHSTONE. Why, if thou never wast at court, thou never sawest good manners; if thou never sawest good manners, then thy manners must be wicked; and wickedness is sin, and sin is damnation. Thou art in a parlous state, shepherd.

CORIN. Not a whit, Touchstone: those that are good manners at the court are as ridiculous in the country as the behaviour of the country is most mockable at the court.

As You Like It, III, 2:34

BELARIUS. The art o' the court,
As hard to leave as keep, whose top to climb
Is certain falling, or so slippery that
The fear 's as bad as falling;

Cymbeline, III, 3:46

K. HENRY. Down, royal state! all you
sage counsellors, hence!
And to the English court assemble now,
From every region, apes of idleness!

II Henry IV, IV, 5:121

AARON. The emperor's court is like the
house of Fame,
The palace full of tongues, of eyes, of ears.

Titus Andronicus, II, 1:126

COURTESY

IMOGEN. Dissembling courtesy! How fine
this tyrant[1]
Can tickle where she wounds!

Cymbeline, I, 1:84

[1] tyrant: the QUEEN.

FRENCHMAN. Sir, we have known together
in Orleans.
POSTHUMUS. Since when I have been
debtor to you for courtesies, which I will
be ever[1] to pay and yet pay still.

Cymbeline, I, 4:35

[1] ever . . . pay still: always paying but never
pay fully.

HOTSPUR. Why, what a candy deal of
courtesy
This fawning greyhound then did proffer
me!
And 'gentle Harry Percy,' and 'kind cousin';
O! the devil take such cozeners.[1]

I Henry IV, I, 3:251

[1] cozeners: deceivers.

SECOND GENTLEMAN. The mirror of all
courtesy.[1]

Henry VIII, II, 1:53

[1] mirror . . . courtesy: BUCKINGHAM.

DUKE. Give me your hand,
And let the subject see, to make them know
That outward courtesies would fain pro-
claim
Favours that keep within.

Measure for Measure, V, 1:13

BOLINGBROKE [kneeling]. My gracious
lord,—
K. RICHARD. Fair cousin, you debase your
princely knee
To make the base earth proud with kissing
it:
Me rather had my heart might feel your love
Than my unpleas'd eye see your courtesy.
Up, cousin, up; your heart is up, I know,
Thus high at least, although your knee be
low.

Richard II, III, 3:189

ULYSSES. The elephant hath joints, but
none for courtesy: his legs are legs for
necessity, not for flexure.

Troilus and Cressida, II, 3:113

COURTIER

JAQUES. He hath been a courtier, he
swears.
TOUCHSTONE. If any man doubt that, let
him put me to my purgation.[1] I have trod a
measure;[2] I have flattered a lady; I have been
politic with my friend, smooth with mine
enemy; I have undone three tailors; I have
had four quarrels, and like to have fought
one.

As You Like It, V, 4:42

[1] purgation: proof. [2] measure: dance.

FIRST GENTLEMAN. Not a courtier,
Although they wear their faces to the bent
Of the king's looks, hath a heart that is not
Glad at the thing they scowl at.

Cymbeline, I, 1:12

AENEAS. Courtiers as free, as debonair,[1]
unarm'd,
As bending angels; that 's their fame in
peace:
But when they would seem soldiers, they
have galls,[2]
Good arms, strong joints, true swords.

Troilus and Cressida, I, 3:235

[1] debonair: gentle, affable. [2] galls: bitterness
of mind for fighting.

AUTOLYCUS. Whether it like[1] me or no, I
am a courtier. Seest thou not the air of the
court in these enfoldings? hath not my gait
in it the measure of the court? receives not
thy nose court-odour from me? reflect I not
on thy baseness court-contempt? Thinkest
thou, for that I insinuate, or touse[2] from thee
thy business, I am therefore no courtier? I

am courtier cap-a-pe;[3] and one that will either push on or pluck back thy business
there: whereupon I command thee to open
thy affair.

Winter's Tale, IV, 4:753

[1] like . . . no: please me or not.   [2] touse:
wrench.   [3] cap-a-pe: head to foot.

COURTSHIP

OTHELLO. I will a round unvarnish'd tale
    deliver
Of my whole course of love; what drugs,
    what charms,
What conjuration, and what mighty magic,
For such proceeding I am charg'd withal,
I won his daughter

. . . . .

[I] found good means
To draw from her a prayer of earnest heart
That I would all my pilgrimage dilate,
Whereof by parcels she had something
    heard,
But not intentively: I did consent;
And often did beguile her of her tears,
When I did speak of some distressful stroke
That my youth suffer'd. My story being
    done,
She gave me for my pains a world of sighs:
She swore, in faith, 't was strange, 't was
    passing[1] strange;
'T was pitiful, 't was wondrous pitiful:
She wish'd she had not heard it, yet she
    wish'd
That heaven had made her such a man; she
    thank'd me.
And bade me, if I had a friend that lov'd
    her,
I should but teach him how to tell my story,
And that would woo her. Upon this hint I
    spake:
She lov'd me for the dangers I had pass'd,
And I lov'd her that she did pity them.
This only is the witchcraft I have us'd:
Here comes the lady; let her witness it.

Othello, I, 3:90, 151

[1] passing: surpassingly.

ROMEO [to JULIET]. If I profane with my
    unworthiest hand
This holy shrine, the gentle fine[1] is this;
My lips, two blushing pilgrims, ready stand
To smooth that rough touch with a tender
    kiss.
JULIET. Good pilgrim, you do wrong
    your hand too much,
Which mannerly devotion shows in this;
For saints have hands that pilgrims' hands
    do touch,
And palm to palm is holy palmers' kiss.

ROMEO. Have not saints lips, and holy
    palmers too?
JULIET. Ay, pilgrim, lips that they must
    use in prayer.
ROMEO. O! then, dear saint, let lips do
    what hands do;
They pray, grant thou, lest faith turn to de-
    spair.
JULIET. Saints do not move, though grant
    for prayers' sake.
ROMEO. Then move not, while my
    prayer's effect I take.
Thus from my lips, by thine, my sin is
    purg'd.

Kissing her.

JULIET. Then have my lips the sin that
    they have took.
ROMEO. Sin from my lips? O trespass
    sweetly urg'd!
Give me my sin again.
JULIET. You kiss by the book.

Romeo and Juliet, I, 5:95

[1] fine: punishment, or payment for a fault.

ROMEO. He jests at scars that never felt a
    wound.

JULIET appears above at a window.

But, soft! what light through yonder win-
    dow breaks?
It is the east, and Juliet is the sun!
Arise, fair sun, and kill the envious moon,

. . . . .

She speaks, yet she says nothing: what of
    that?
Her eye discourses; I will answer it.
I am too bold, 't is not to me she speaks:
Two of the fairest stars in all the heaven,
Having some business, do entreat her eyes
To twinkle in their spheres till they return.

. . . . .

See! how she leans her cheek upon her hand:
O! that I were a glove upon that hand
That I might touch that cheek.

Romeo and Juliet, II, 2, 1:11, 23

JULIET. O Romeo, Romeo! wherefore art
    thou Romeo?
Deny thy father, and refuse thy name;
Or, if thou wilt not, be but sworn my love,
And I 'll no longer be a Capulet.
ROMEO [aside]. Shall I hear more, or shall
    I speak at this?
JULIET. 'T is but thy name that is my
    enemy;
Thou art thyself, though not a Montague.
What's Montague? it is nor hand, nor foot,
Nor arm, nor face, nor any other part,
Belonging to a man. O! be some other name:
What's in a name? that which we call a rose
By any other name would smell as sweet;

So Romeo would, were he not Romeo
    call'd,
Retain that dear perfection which he owes[1]
Without that title. Romeo, doff[2] thy name;
And for thy name, which is no part of thee,
Take all myself.
Romeo and Juliet, II, 2:33

[1] owes: owns. [2] doff: put off.

Romeo. With love's light wings did I o'er
    perch these walls;
For stony limits cannot hold love out,
And what love can do that dares love at-
    tempt;
Therefore thy kinsmen are no stop to me.
Romeo and Juliet, II, 2:66

Juliet. O gentle Romeo!
If thou dost love, pronounce it faithfully:
Or if thou think'st I am too quickly won,
I'll frown and be perverse and say thee nay,
So thou wilt woo; but else, not for the
    world.
In truth, fair Montague, I am too fond,
And therefore thou may'st think my hav-
    iour light:
But trust me, gentleman, I'll prove more
    true
Than those that have more cunning to be
    strange.[1]
Romeo and Juliet, II, 2:93

[1] strange: coyly aloof.

Romeo. Lady, by yonder blessed moon I
    swear
That tips with silver all these fruit-tree
    tops—
    Juliet. O! swear not by the moon, the
    inconstant moon,
That monthly changes in her circled orb,
Lest that thy love prove likewise variable.
Romeo and Juliet, II, 2:107

Juliet. Although I joy in thee,
I have no joy of this contract to-night:
It is too rash, too unadvis'd, too sudden;
Too like the lightning, which doth cease
    to be
Ere one can say it lightens. Sweet, good
    night!
This bud of love, by summer's ripening
    breath,
May prove a beauteous flower when next
    we meet.
Good night! good night! as sweet repose
    and rest
Come to thy heart as that within my breast!
Romeo and Juliet, II, 2:116

Juliet. My bounty is as boundless as the
    sea,
My love as deep; the more I give to thee,
The more I have, for both are infinite.
Romeo and Juliet, II, 2:133

Romeo. O blessed, blessed night! I am
    afeard,
Being in night, all this is but a dream,
Too flattering-sweet to be substantial.
Romeo and Juliet, II, 2:139

Re-enter Juliet, *above.*
Juliet. Three words, dear Romeo, and
    good night indeed.
If that thy bent of love be honourable,
Thy purpose marriage, send me word to-
    morrow,
By one that I 'll procure to come to thee,
Where, and what time, thou wilt perform
    the rite;
And all my fortunes at thy foot I'll lay,
And follow thee my lord throughout the
    world.
Romeo and Juliet, II, 2:143

Juliet. Hist! Romeo, hist! O! for a fal-
    coner's voice,
To lure this tassel[1]-gentle back again.
Bondage is hoarse, and may not speak aloud,
Else would I tear the cave where Echo lies,
And make her airy tongue more hoarse than
    mine,
With repetition of my Romeo's name.
Romeo and Juliet, II, 2:159

[1] tassel-gentle: Juliet means *tercel*, a bird that
can be called by the falconer.

Juliet. 'T is almost morning; I would
    have thee gone;
And yet no further than a wanton's bird,
Who lets it hop a little from her hand,
Like a poor prisoner in his twisted gyves,
And with a silk thread plucks it back again,
So loving-jealous of his liberty.
    Romeo. I would I were thy bird.
    Juliet. Sweet, so would I:
Yet I should kill thee with much cherishing.
Good night, good night! parting is such
    sweet sorrow
That I shall say good night till it be morrow.
Romeo and Juliet, II, 2:177

Ferdinand [to Miranda]. My prime re-
    quest,
Which I do last pronounce, is, O you won-
    der!
If[1] you be maid or no?
Tempest, I, 2:425

[1] If: whether.

Prospero. This swift business
I must uneasy make, lest too light winning
Make the prize light.
Tempest, I, 2:450

Miranda.[1] There's nothing ill can dwell in
    such a temple:

If the ill spirit have so fair a house
Good things will strive to dwell with 't.
Tempest, I, 2:457
[1] About FERDINAND.

FERDINAND [entering with a log]. There
   be some sports are painful, and their
   labour
Delight in them sets off: some kinds of base-
   ness
Are nobly undergone, and most poor mat-
   ters
Point to rich ends. This my mean task
Would be as heavy to me as odious, but
The mistress which I serve quickens what 's
   dead
And makes my labours pleasures.
Tempest, III, 1:1

MIRANDA. If you 'll sit down,
I 'll bear your logs the while. Pray, give me
   that:
I 'll carry it to the pile.
FERDINAND. No, precious creature;
I had rather crack my sinews, break my
   back,
Than you should such dishonour undergo,
While I sit lazy by.

. . . . .

MIRANDA. You look wearily,
FERDINAND. No, noble mistress; 't is fresh
   morning with me
When you are by at night. I do beseech
   you—
Chiefly that I might set it in my prayers—
What is your name?
Tempest, III, 1:23, 32

MIRANDA. Hence, bashful cunning!
And prompt me, plain and holy innocence!
I am your wife, if you will marry me;

. . . . .

FERDINAND. Ay, with a heart as willing
As bondage e'er of freedom: here's my
   hand.
Tempest, III, 1:81, 89

PROSPERO. Look thou be true. Do not give
   dalliance
Too much the rein: the strongest oaths
   are straw
To the fire i' the blood. Be more abstemious,
Or else good night your vow.
FERDINAND. I warrant you, sir;
The white cold virgin snow upon my heart
Abates the ardour of my liver.[1]
Tempest, IV, 1:51
[1] liver: believed to be the seat of sexual desire.

COWARD

PAROLLES. He excels his brother for a
coward, yet his brother is reputed one of
the best that is. In a retreat he outruns any
lackey; marry, in coming on he has the
cramp.
All's Well That Ends Well, IV, 3:321

IMOGEN. Plenty and peace breeds cow-
   ards, hardness ever
Of hardiness is mother.
Cymbeline, III, 6:21

BELARIUS. Cowards father cowards, and
   base things sire base:
Cymbeline, IV, 2:26

HAMLET [soliloquy]. Am I a coward?
Who calls me villain? breaks my pate
   across?
Plucks off my beard and blows it in my
   face?
Tweaks me by the nose? gives me the lie i'
   the throat
As deep as to the lungs? Who does me this?
   Ha!
'Swounds! I should take it, for it cannot be
But I am pigeon-liver'd, and lack gall
To make oppression bitter, or ere this
I should have fatted all the region kites
With this slave's offal. Bloody, bawdy vil-
   lain!
Remorseless, treacherous, lecherous, kind-
   less[1] villain!
Hamlet, II, 2:598
[1] kindless: unnatural.

ROSENCRANTZ. Many wearing rapiers are
afraid of goose quills.
Hamlet, II, 2:359

FALSTAFF. He will not swagger with a
Barbary hen if her feathers turn back in any
show of resistance.
II Henry IV, II, 4:107

BARDOLPH. On, on, on, on, on! to the
breach, to the breach!
NYM. Pray thee, corporal, stay: the
knocks are too hot; and for mine own part,
I have not a case of lives: the humour of it
is too hot, that is the very plain-song[1] of it.
Henry V, III, 2:1
[1] plain-song: a simple melody.

WARWICK. Welcome, Somerset: I hold it
   cowardice
To rest mistrustful where a noble heart
Hath pawn'd an open hand in sign of love;
III Henry VI, IV, 2:7

NYM. I dare not fight; but I will wink
and hold out mine iron. It is a simple one;

but what though? it will toast cheese, and it will endure cold as another man's sword will: and there's an end.

. . . . .

Men may sleep, and they may have their throats about them at that time; and some say knives have edges.
Henry V, II, 1:7, 23

CLIFFORD. So cowards fight when they can fly no further;
So doves do peck the falcon's piercing talons;
So desperate thieves, all hopeless of their lives,
Breathe out invectives 'gainst the officers.
III Henry VI, I, 4:40

BASTARD. You[1] are the hare of whom the proverb goes,
Whose valour plucks dead lions by the beard.
King John, II, 1:137
[1] You: DUKE OF AUSTRIA.

CONSTANCE. O Austria![1] thou dost shame
That bloody spoil: thou slave, thou wretch, thou coward!
Thou little valiant, great in villany!
Thou ever strong upon the stronger side!
Thou Fortune's champion, that dost never fight
But when her humorous[2] ladyship is by
To teach thee safety!

. . . . .

Thou wear a lion's hide! doff[3] it for shame,
And hang a calf's-skin on those recreant limbs.
King John, III, 1:114, 128
[1] Austria: DUKE OF AUSTRIA.   [2] humorous: capricious.   [3] doff: do off, put off.

CAESAR. Cowards die many times before their deaths;
The valiant never taste of death but once.
Julius Caesar, II, 2:32

BASSANIO. How many cowards, whose hearts are all as false
As stairs of sand, wear yet upon their chins
The beards of Hercules and frowning Mars,
Who, inward search'd, have livers white as milk;
Merchant of Venice, III, 2:85

DUCHESS. That which in mean men we entitle patience
Is pale cold cowardice in noble breasts.
Richard II, I, 2:33

CLOWN.[1] Not a more cowardly rogue in all Bohemia: if you had but looked big and spit at him, he 'd have run.
Winter's Tale, IV, 3:112
[1] CLOWN: a simple rustic; about AUTOLYCUS.

CRIME

K. HENRY. If little faults, proceeding on distemper,[1]
Shall not be wink'd at, how shall we stretch our eye
When capital crimes, chew'd, swallow'd, and digested
Appear before us?
Henry V, II, 2:54
[1] distemper: drunkenness.

GONERIL. By day and night he[1] wrongs me; every hour
He flashes into one gross crime or other,
That sets us all at odds: I'll not endure it.
King Lear, I, 3:3
[1] he: KING LEAR, her father.

K. LEAR. Tremble, thou wretch,
Thou hast within thee undivulged crimes,
Unwhipp'd of justice; hide thee, thou bloody hand,
Thou perjur'd, and thou simular[1] of virtue.
King Lear, III, 2:51
[1] simular: counterfeit.

DUKE.[1] I come to visit the afflicted spirits
Here in the prison: do me the common right
To let me see them and to make me know
The nature of their crimes, that I may minister
To them accordingly.
Measure for Measure, II, 3:4
[1] Disguised as a friar.

CRISPIAN DAY

K. HENRY. This day is called the feast of Crispian:
He that outlives this day, and comes safe home,
Will stand a tip-toe when this day is nam'd,
And rouse him at the name of Crispian.
He that shall live this day, and see old age,
Will yearly on the vigil feast his neighbours,
And say 'To-morrow is Saint Crispian':
Then will he strip his sleeve and show his scars,
And say 'These wounds I had on Crispin's day.'
Old men forget; yet all shall be forgot,
But he'll remember with advantages
What feats he did that day. Then shall our names

Familiar in his mouth as household words,
Harry the king, Bedford and Exeter,
Warwick and Talbot, Salisbury and
    Gloucester,
Be in their flowing cups freshly remember'd.
This story shall the good man teach his son;
And Crispin Crispian shall ne'er go by,
From this day to the ending of the world,
But we in it shall be remembered;
We few, we happy few, we band of broth-
    ers;
For he to-day that sheds his blood with me
Shall be my brother; be he ne'er so vile
This day shall gentle his condition:
And gentlemen in England now a-bed
Shall think themselves accurs'd they were
    not here,
And hold their manhoods cheap whiles any
    speaks
That fought with us upon Saint Crispin's
    day.
                                        Henry V, IV, 3:40

CRITICISM

JAQUES. Will you sit down with me? and
we two will rail against our mistress the
world, and all our misery.
ORLANDO. I will chide no breather in the
world but myself, against whom I know
most faults.
                                As You Like It, III, 2:293

FLUELLEN. If I find a hole in his coat, I
will tell him my mind.
                                        Henry V, III, 6:88

WOLSEY. If I am
Traduc'd[1] by ignorant tongues, which nei-
    ther know
My faculties nor person, yet will be
The chronicles of my doing, let me say
'T is but the fate of place, and the rough
    brake
That virtue must go through. We must not
    stint
Our necessary actions, in the fear
To cope[2] malicious censurers; which ever,
As ravenous fishes, do a vessel follow.
                                        Henry VIII, I, 2:71
[1] Traduc'd: abused.   [2] cope: encounter.

BENEDICK. Happy are they that hear their
detractions[1] and can put them to mending.
            Much Ado About Nothing, II, 3:238
[1] detractions: defamations.

HERO. Disdain and scorn ride sparkling in
    her eyes,
Misprising what they look on.
            Much Ado About Nothing, III, 1:51

CROWN

K. HENRY. Uneasy lies the head that
    wears a crown.
                                II Henry IV, III, 1:31

PRINCE. Why doth the crown lie there
    upon his[1] pillow,
Being so troublesome a bedfellow?
O polish'd perturbation! golden care!
That keep'st the ports of slumber open wide
To many a watchful night! sleep with it
    now!
Yet not so sound and half so deeply sweet
As he whose brow with homely biggin[2]
    bound
Snores out the watch of night.
                                II Henry IV, IV, 5:21
[1] his: its.   [2] biggin: nightcap.

K. HENRY. God knows, my son,
By what by-paths and indirect crook'd ways
I met this crown; and I myself know well
How troublesome it sat upon my head.

            . . . . .

Therefore, my Harry,
Be it thy course to busy giddy minds
With foreign quarrels; that action, hence
    borne out,
May waste the memory of the former days.
                            II Henry IV, IV, 5:184, 213

RICHARD.[1] How sweet a thing it is to wear
    a crown,
Within whose circuit is Elysium,[2]
And all that poets feign of bliss and joy.
                                III Henry VI, I, 2:29
[1] RICHARD: son of YORK, brother of KING
EDWARD IV, later DUKE OF GLOUCESTER and
KING RICHARD III.   [2] Elysium: paradise.

K. HENRY. My crown is in my heart, not
    on my head;
Not deck'd with diamonds and Indian
    stones,
Nor to be seen: my crown is call'd content;
A crown it is that seldom kings enjoy.
                                III Henry VI, III, 1:62

GLOUCESTER [soliloquy]. I'll make my
    heaven to dream upon the crown;
And, whiles I live, to account this world but
    hell,
Until my misshap'd trunk that bears this
    head
Be round impaled with a glorious crown.
And yet I know not how to get the crown,
For many lives stand between me and home:
And I, like one lost in a thorny wood,
That rends the thorns and is rent with the
    thorns,
Seeking a way and straying from the way;

Not knowing how to find the open air,
But toiling desperately to find it out,
Torment myself to catch the English
    crown;
And from that torment I will free myself,
Or hew my way out with a bloody axe.
Why, I can smile, and murder whiles I smile,
And cry 'Content' to that which grieves my
    heart,
And wet my cheeks with artificial tears,
And frame my face to all occasions.
I'll drown more sailors than the mermaid
    shall;
I'll slay more gazers than the basilisk;
I'll play the orator as well as Nestor,
Deceive more slily than Ulysses could,
And, like a Sinon, take another Troy.
I can add colours to the chameleon,
Change shapes with Proteus for advantages,
And set the murd'rous Machiavel to school.
Can I do this, and cannot get a crown?
Tut! were it further off, I'll pluck it down.
    III Henry VI, III, 2:168
[1] Later RICHARD III.

MACBETH [soliloquy]. Upon my head
    they[1] plac'd a fruitless crown,
And put a barren sceptre in my gripe,
Thence to be wrench'd with[2] an unlineal
    hand,
No son of mine succeeding.
    Macbeth, III, 1:61
[1] they: the witches.   [2] with: by.

COUNT.[1] A thousand flatterers sit within
    thy crown,
Whose compass is no bigger than thy head;
And yet, incaged in so small a verge,[2]
The waste is no whit lesser than thy land.
    Richard II, II, 1:100
[1] To KING RICHARD.   [2] verge: the extent of the
KING's court, twelve miles.

CUCKOLD

CLOWN. He that comforts my wife is the
cherisher of my flesh and blood; he that
cherishes my flesh and blood loves my flesh
and blood; he that loves my flesh and blood
is my friend: *ergo*, he that kisses my wife is
my friend.
    All's Well That Ends Well, I, 3:51

FORESTERS. What shall he have that kill'd
    the deer?
His leather skin and horns to wear.
Then sing him home . . .
Take thou no scorn to sear the horn;[1]
It was a crest ere thou wast born:
Thy father's father wore it,
And thy father bore it:
The horn, the horn, the lusty horn

Is not a thing to laugh to scorn.
    As You Like It, IV, 2:11
[1] horn: symbol of a cuckold, the husband of a
faithless wife.

LUCIO. Your highness said even now, I
made you a duke: good my lord, do not
recompense me in making me a cuckold.
    Measure for Measure, V, 1:522

FALSTAFF. Of what quality was your love
then?
FORD.[1] Like a fair house built upon another man's ground.
    Merry Wives of Windsor, II, 2:223
[1] In disguise.

FALSTAFF. Hang him, mechanical salt-butter[1] rogue! I will stare him out of his wits;
I will awe him with my cudgel: it shall hang
like a meteor o'er the cuckold's horns.
    Merry Wives of Windsor, II, 2:290
[1] Salt-butter rogue: a huckster.

FALSTAFF. Fate, ordaining he should be a
cuckold, held his hand.
    Merry Wives of Windsor, III, 5:107

LEONTES. There have been,
Or I am much deceiv'd, cuckolds ere now;
And many a man there is, even at this pres-
    ent,
Now, while I speak this, holds his wife by
    the arm,
That little thinks she has been sluic'd in 's
    absence.
And his pond fish'd by his next neighbour,
    by
Sir Smile, his neighbour.
    Winter's Tale, I, 2:190

LEONTES. Should all despair
That have revolted wives, the tenth of man-
    kind
Would hang themselves. Physic[1] for 't there
    is none.
    Winter's Tale, I, 2:198
[1] Physic: medicine, cure.

CUCKOO

WORCESTER. And being fed by us you us'd
    us so
As that ungentle gull, the cuckoo's bird,[1]
Useth the sparrow: did oppress our nest,
Grew by our feeding to so great a bulk
That even our love durst not come near
    your sight.
    I Henry IV, V, 1:59
[1] cuckoo's bird: the young cuckoo; referring
to this bird's habit of laying its eggs in the
nests of other birds and having its young fed
with their nestlings.

FOOL. For you know, nuncle,[1]
The hedge-sparrow fed the cuckoo so long
That it had it[2] head bit off by it[2] young.
                                        King Lear, I, 4:234
[1] nuncle: the customary address of a jester to
his superior.   [2] it: an old possessive for its,
which is seldom used by Shakespeare.

I

When daisies pied and violets blue
And lady-smocks all silver-white
And cuckoo-buds of yellow hue
Do paint the meadows with delight,
The cuckoo then, on every tree,
Mocks married men; for thus sings he,
Cuckoo;
Cuckoo, cuckoo: O word of fear,
Unpleasing to a married ear!

II

When shepherds pipe on oaten straws,
And merry larks are ploughmen's clocks,
When turtles tread, and rooks, and daws,
And maidens bleach their summer smocks,
The cuckoo then, on every tree,
Mocks married men; for thus sings he,
Cuckoo;
Cuckoo, cuckoo: O word of fear,
Unpleasing to a married ear!
                                Love's Labour's Lost, V, 2:904

CUPID

ROSALIND. No; that same wicked bastard
of Venus that was begot of thought, conceived of spleen, and born of madness, that
blind rascally boy that abuses every one's
eyes because his own are out, let him be
judge how deep I am in love.
                                        As You Like It, IV, 1:216

K. LEAR. Dost thou squiny at me? No, do
thy worst, blind Cupid; I'll not love.
                                        King Lear, IV, 6:140

BIRON. And I—
Forsooth in love! I, that have been love's
whip;
A very beadle to a humorous sigh;
A critic, nay, a night-watch constable,
A domineering pedant o'er the boy.[1]
                                Love's Labour's Lost, III, 1:174
[1] boy: Cupid.

BIRON. This wimpled, whining, purblind,
wayward boy,
This senior-junior, giant-dwarf, Dan Cupid;
Regent of love-rhymes, lord of folded arms,
The anointed sovereign of sighs and groans,
Liege of all loiterers and malecontents,
Dread prince of plackets,[1] king of cod-
pieces,[2]

Sole imperator and great general
Of trotting paritors:[3] O my little heart!
And I to be a corporal of his field,
And wear his colours like a tumbler's hoop!
                                Love's Labour's Lost, III, 1:181
[1] plackets: slits in skirts or petticoats.   [2] cod-
pieces: items of men's costume.   [3] paritors:
officers of bishop's court.

OBERON. But I might see young Cupid's
fiery shaft
Quench'd in the chaste beams of the wat'ry
moon,
And the imperial votaress[1] passed on,
In maiden meditation, fancy-free[2]
Yet mark'd I where the bolt of Cupid fell:
It fell upon a little western flower,
Before milk-white, now purple with love's
wound,
And maidens call it Love-in-idleness.
                                Midsummer Night's Dream, II, 1:161
[1] imperial votaress: Q. ELIZABETH.   [2] fancy-
free: not in love.

PUCK. Here she[1] comes, curst[2] and sad:
Cupid is a knavish lad,
Thus to make poor females mad.
                                Midsummer Night's Dream, III, 2:439
[1] she: HERMIA.   [2] curst: shrewish.

HERO. My talk to thee must be how Bene-
dick
Is sick in love with Beatrice: of this matter
Is little Cupid's crafty arrow made.
                                Much Ado About Nothing, III, 1:20

ROMEO. Well, in that hit you miss: she[1] 'll
not be hit
With Cupid's arrow; she hath Dian's wit;
And, in strong proof of chastity well arm'd,
From love's weak childish bow she lives un-
harm'd.
                                        Romeo and Juliet, I, 1:213
[1] she: the one ROMEO loved before meeting
JULIET.

MERCUTIO. Speak to my gossip Venus
one fair word,
One nickname for her purblind[1] son and
heir,
Young Adam Cupid, he that shot so trim
When King Cophetua lov'd the beggar-
maid.
                                        Romeo and Juliet, II, 1:11
[1] purblind: blind or partly blind.

MERCUTIO. Alas! poor Romeo, he is already dead; stabbed with a white wench's
black eye; shot through the ear with a love-
song; the very pin[1] of his heart cleft with
the blind bow-boy's butt-shaft.
                                        Romeo and Juliet, II, 4:13
[1] pin: center of a target.

Iris. Her[1] waspish-headed son[2] has broke his arrows,
Swears he will shoot no more, but play with sparrows,
And be a boy right out.
Tempest, IV, 1:99
[1] Her: Venus. [2] son: Cupid.

CURE

Imogen. If you'll be patient, I'll no more be mad;
That cures us both.
Cymbeline, II, 3:108

Macbeth. The labour we delight in physics[1] pain.
Macbeth, II, 3:55
[1] physics: acts as a remedy.

Macbeth. If thou could'st, doctor, cast[1]
The water of my land, find her disease,
And purge it to a sound and pristine health,
I would applaud thee to the very echo,
That should applaud again.
Macbeth, V, 3:50
[1] cast: find disorder by inspecting water.

Benvolio. Tut! man, one fire burns out another's burning,
One pain is lessen'd by another's anguish;
Turn giddy, and be holp[1] by backward turning;
One desperate grief cures with another's languish:
Take thou some new infection to thy eye,
And the rank poison of the old will die.
Romeo and Juliet, I, 2:46
[1] holp: helped.

Past cure I am, now reason is past care,
And frantic-mad with evermore unrest;
My thoughts and my discourse as madmen's are,
At random from the truth, vainly express'd;
For I have sworn thee fair and thought thee bright,
Who art as black as hell, as dark as night.
Sonnet 147

Polixenes. He makes a July's day short as December,
And with his varying childness cures in me
Thoughts that would thick my blood.
Winter's Tale, I, 2:169

CURSE

Marcius. All the contagion of the south light on you,
You shames of Rome! you herd of—Boils and plagues

Plaster you o'er, that you may be abhorr'd
Further than seen, and one infect another
Against the wind a mile! You souls of geese,
That bear the shapes of men, how have you run
From slaves that apes would beat!
Coriolanus, I, 4:30

Suffolk. Poison be their drink!
Gall, worse than gall, the daintiest that they taste!
Their[1] sweetest shade a grove of cypress trees![2]
Their chiefest prospect murdering basilisks!
Their softest touch as smart as lizards' stings!
Their music frightful as the serpent's hiss,
And boding screech-owls make the concert full!
All the foul terrors in dark-seated hell.
II Henry VI, III, 2:321
[1] Their: the lords that have defeated him.
[2] cypress trees: emblems of mourning. [3] basilisks: serpents that killed by their look.

Lear [about Cordelia]. Unfriended, new-adopted to our hate,
Dower'd with our curse, and stranger'd with our oath.
King Lear, I, 1:206

K. Lear. Hear, Nature, hear! dear goddess, hear!
Suspend thy purpose, if thou didst intend
To make this creature[1] fruitful!
Into her womb convey sterility!
Dry up in her the organs of increase,
And from her derogate body never spring
A babe to honour her! If she must teem,[2]
Create her child of spleen, that it may live
And be a thwart disnatur'd torment to her!
Let it stamp wrinkles in her brow of youth,
With cadent tears fret channels in her cheeks,
Turn all her mother's pains and benefits
To laughter and contempt, that she may feel
How sharper than a serpent's tooth it is
To have a thankless child!
King Lear, I, 4:297
[1] creature: Goneril. [2] teem: bear a child.

K. Lear. You nimble lightnings, dart your blinding flames
Into her[1] scornful eyes! Infect her beauty,
You fen-suck'd fogs, drawn by the powerful sun,
To fall and blast her pride!
King Lear, II, 4:167
[1] her: Regan.

Q. Margaret.[1] A little joy enjoys the queen thereof;

For I am she, and altogether joyless.
I can no longer hold me patient.
Hear me, you wrangling pirates, that fall
out
In sharing that which you have pill'd[2] from
me!
Which of you trembles not that looks
on me?
If not, that, I being queen, you bow like sub-
jects,
Yet that, by you depos'd, you quake like
rebels?
Ah! gentle villain,[3] do not turn away.

. . . . .

GLOUCESTER. Have done thy charm, thou
hateful wither'd hag!
Q. MARGARET. And leave out thee? stay,
dog, for thou shalt hear me.
If heaven have any grievous plague in store
Exceeding those that I can wish upon thee,
O! let them keep it till thy sins be ripe,
And then hurl down their indignation
On thee, the troubler of the poor world's
peace.
Richard III, I, 3:155, 215
[1] Widow of Henry VI.   [2] pill'd: plundered.
[3] villain: GLOUCESTER, later KING RICHARD III.

MISTRESS PAGE. Curses all Eve's daughters,
of what complexion soever.
Merry Wives of Windsor, IV, 2:24

Q. MARGARET. The worm of conscience
still begnaw thy soul!
Thy friends suspect for traitors while thou
livest,
And take deep traitors for thy dearest
friends!
No sleep close up that deadly eye of thine,
Unless it be while some tormenting dream
Affrights thee with a hell of ugly devils!
Thou elvish-mark'd, abortive, rooting hog!
Thou that wast seal'd in thy nativity
The slave of nature and the son of hell!
Richard III, I, 3:222

BUCKINGHAM. Curses never pass
The lips of those that breathe them in the
air.
Q. MARGARET. I will not think but they
ascend the sky,
And there awake God's gentle-sleeping
peace.
Richard III, I, 3:285

Q. MARGARET. Earth gapes, hell burns,
fiends roar, saints pray,
To have him suddenly convey'd from
hence.
Cancel his bond of life, dear God: I pray,
That I may live and say, The dog[1] is dead.
. . . . .

DUCHESS [OF YORK].[2] Either thou wilt die
by God's just ordinance,
Ere from this war thou turn a conqueror,
Or I with grief and extreme age shall perish
And never more behold thy face again.
Therefore take with thee my most grievous
curse;
Which, in the day of battle, tire thee more
Than all the complete armour that thou
wear'st!
My prayers on the adverse party fight;
And there the little souls of Edward's chil-
dren
Whisper[3] the spirits of thine enemies
And promise them success and victory.
Bloody thou art, bloody will be thy end.
Richard III, IV, 4:75, 183
[1] dog: KING RICHARD.   [2] Mother of EDWARD IV,
CLARENCE, and RICHARD III; to RICHARD III.
[3] Whisper: whisper to.

SEBASTIAN. A pox[1] o' your throat, you
bawling, blasphemous, incharitable dog!
BOATSWAIN. Work you, then.
Tempest, I, 1:44
[1] pox: a venereal disease; term often used as
curse.

CALIBAN. As wicked dew as e'er my
mother[1] brush'd
With raven's feather from unwholesome fen
Drop on you both! a south-west blow on ye
And blister you all o'er!
PROSPERO. For this, be sure, to-night thou
shalt have cramps,
Side-stitches that shall pen thy breath up;
urchins[2]
Shall forth at vast of night that they may
work
All exercise[3] on thee; thou shalt be pinch'd
As thick as honeycomb, each pinch more
stinging
Than bees that made them.
Tempest, I, 2:321
[1] mother: the witch Sycorax.   [2] urchins:
hedge-hogs.   [3] exercise: characteristic mischief.

CALIBAN. You taught me language, and
my profit on 't
Is, I know how to curse.
Tempest, I, 2:263

TIMON. Plagues, incident to men,
Your potent and infectious fevers heap
On Athens, ripe for stroke! Thou cold sci-
atica,
Cripple our senators, that their limbs may
halt
As lamely as their manners! Lust and liberty
Creep in the minds and marrows of our
youth,

That 'gainst the stream of virtue they may
strive,
And drown themselves in riot!
Timon of Athens, IV, 1:21

CALIBAN. All the infections that the sun
sucks up
From bogs, fens, flats, on Prosper fall and
make him
By inch-meal[1] a disease!
Tempest, II, 2:1

[1] inch-meal: every inch.

TIMON [soliloquy]. Let me look back
upon thee. O thou wall,
That girdlest in those wolves, dive in the
earth,
And fence not Athens! Matrons, turn in-
continent!
Obedience fail in children! Slaves and fools,
Pluck the grave wrinkled senate from the
bench,
And minister in their steads!
Timon of Athens, IV, 1:1

TIMON. Would thou wert clean enough to
spit upon!
APEMANTUS. A plague on thee! thou art
too bad to curse.
Timon of Athens, IV, 3:364

CUSTOM

CORIOLANUS. What custom wills, in all
things should[1] we do 't.
The dust on antique time would lie un-
swept,
And mountainous error be too highly
heap'd
For truth to o'erpeer.
Coriolanus, II, 3:125

[1] should: if we should.

HAMLET. That monster, custom, who all
sense doth eat,
Of habits devil, is angel yet in this,
That to the use of actions fair and good
He likewise gives a frock or livery,
That aptly is put on. Refrain to-night;
And that shall lend a kind of easiness
To the next abstinence: the next more easy;
For use[1] almost can change the stamp of
nature.
Hamlet, III, 4:161

[1] use: custom, habit.

K. HENRY. O Kate! nice[1] customs court'sy
to great kings. Dear Kate, you and I cannot
be confined within the weak list of a country's fashion: we are the makers of manners,
Kate.
Henry V, V, 2:293

[1] nice: prudish, exacting.

SANDS. New customs,
Though they be never so ridiculous,
Nay, let 'em be unmanly, yet are follow'd.
Henry VIII, I, 3:2

OTHELLO. The tyrant custom, most grave
senators,
Hath made the flinty and steel couch of war
My thrice-driven bed of down.
Othello, I, 3:230

SLENDER. All his successors gone before
him hath done 't; and all his ancestors that
come after him may.
Merry Wives of Windsor, I, 1:14

DAGGER

GUIDERIUS. Thy words, I grant, are big-
ger, for I wear not
My dagger in my mouth.
Cymbeline, IV, 2:78

FALSTAFF. And now is this Vice's dagger[1]
become a squire, and talks as familiarly of
John a Gaunt as if he had been sworn
brother to him; and I'll be sworn a'[2] ne'er
saw him but once in the Tilt-yard.
II Henry IV, III, 2:342

[1] Vice's dagger: Vice, a character in morality
plays, carried a dagger of lath. [2] a': he, JOHN
A GAUNT.

K. HENRY. Thou hid'st a thousand daggers in thy thoughts,
Which thou hast whetted on thy stony
heart.
II Henry IV, IV, 5:107

DAMNED

HAMLET. When he is drunk asleep, or in
his rage,
Or in the incestuous pleasure of his bed,
At gaming, swearing, or about some act
That has no relish of salvation in 't;
Then trip him, that his heels may kick at
heaven,
And that his soul may be as damn'd and
black
As hell, whereto it goes.
Hamlet, III, 4:89

PISTOL. I'll see her damned first; to Pluto's[1]
damned lake, to the infernal deep, with Erebus[2] and tortures vile also.
II Henry IV, II, 4:171

[1] Pluto: the god of the lower world. [2] Erebus:
hell, a place of darkness.

BASTARD. Thou'rt damn'd as black; nay,
nothing is so black;

Thou art more deep damn'd than Prince
  Lucifer:
There is not yet so ugly a fiend of hell
As thou shalt be, if thou didst kill this child.[1]
  HUBERT. Upon my soul—
  BASTARD. If thou didst but consent
To this most cruel act, do but despair;
And if thou want'st a cord, the smallest
  thread
That ever spider twisted from her womb
Will serve to strangle thee; a rush will be a
  beam
To hang thee on; or would'st thou drown
  thyself,
Put but a little water in a spoon,
And it shall be as all the ocean,
Enough to stifle such a villain up.
                              King John, IV, 3:121
[1] child: PRINCE ARTHUR.

DANCING

DUKE SENIOR. Play, music! and you brides
  and bridegrooms all,
With measure heap'd in joy, to the measures[1] fall.
                              As You Like It, V, 4:184
[1] measures: dancing.

THESEUS. Come now; what masques,
  what dances shall we have,
To wear away this long age of three hours
Between our after-supper and bed-time?
Where is our usual manager of mirth?
What revels are in hand? Is there no play,
To ease the anguish of a torturing hour?
                      Midsummer Night's Dream, V, 1:32

MARGARET. God match me with a good
dancer!
BALTHAZAR. Amen.
MARGARET. And God keep him out of my
sight when the dance is done!
              Much Ado About Nothing, II, 1:111

QUEEN. My legs can keep no measure in
  delight
When my poor heart no measure keeps in
  grief:
Therefore, no dancing, girl.
                              Richard II, III, 4:7

GLOUCESTER.[1] He capers nimbly in a
  lady's chamber
To the lascivious pleasing of a lute.
                              Richard III, I, 1:12
[1] Later KING RICHARD III.

ROMEO. Not I, believe me: you have
  dancing shoes
With nimble soles; I have a soul of lead
So stakes me to the ground I cannot move.
                      Romeo and Juliet, I, 4:13

CAPULET. For you and I are past our
  dancing days.
                      Romeo and Juliet, I, 5:33

FLORIZEL. When you do dance, I wish you
A wave o' the sea, that you might ever do
Nothing but that; move still, still so,
And own no other function.
                      Winter's Tale, IV, 4:140

DANGER

ADAM. Why would you[1] be so fond[2] to
  overcome
The bonny priser[3] of the humorous[4] duke?
                              As You Like It, II, 3:7
[1] you: ORLANDO.   [2] fond: foolish.   [3] priser:
prize fighter.   [4] humorous: capricious.

HAMLET. Thou wretched, rash, intruding
  fool, farewell!
I took thee for thy better:[1] take thy fortune;
Thou find'st to be too busy is some danger.
                              Hamlet, III, 4:31
[1] better: the KING.

WORCESTER. And to your quick-conceiv-
  ing discontents
I'll read you matter deep and dangerous
As full of peril and adventurous spirit
As to o'er-walk a current, roaring loud,
On the unsteadfast footing of a spear.
                              1 Henry IV, I, 3:189

HOTSPUR. Send danger from the east unto
  the west,
So honour cross it from the north to south
And let them grapple: O! the blood more
  stirs
To rouse a lion than to start a hare.
                              1 Henry IV, I, 3:195

K. JOHN. A fearful eye thou hast: where
  is that blood
That I have seen inhabit in those cheeks?
So foul a sky clears not without a storm.
                              King John, IV, 2:106

CAESAR. Danger knows full well
That Caesar is more dangerous than he:
We are two lions litter'd in one day,
And I the elder and more terrible.
                              Julius Caesar, II, 2:44

Q. MARGARET.[1] They that stand high have
  many blasts to shake them,
And if they fall, they dash themselves to
  pieces.
                              Richard III, I, 3:259
[1] Widow of KING HENRY VI.

Titus. For now I stand as one upon a rock
Environ'd with a wilderness of sea,
Who marks the waxing[1] tide grow wave by
  wave,
Expecting ever when some envious surge
Will in his[2] brinish bowels swallow him.
Titus Andronicus, III, 1:93
[1] waxing: rising. [2] his: its.

The path is smooth that leadeth on to dan-
  ger;
I hate not love, but your device in love.
Venus and Adonis, 788

Polixenes. I conjure thee . . .
. . . that thou declare
What incidency thou dost guess of harm
Is creeping toward me; how far off, how
  near;
Which way to be prevented if to be;
If not, how best to bear it.
Winter's Tale, I, 2:400

DAUGHTER

Imogen. Would I were
A neat-herd's daughter, and my Leonatus
Our neighbour shepherd's son!
Cymbeline, I, 1:148
[1] neat-herd: cowherd.

Polonius.[1] What might you think? No, I
  went round [2] to work,
And my young mistress thus I did bespeak;
'Lord Hamlet is a prince, out of thy star;
This must not be': and then I precepts gave
  her.
Hamlet, II, 2:139
[1] To the King and Queen. [2] round: promptly.

Polonius. What a treasure had he, my
  lord?
Hamlet. Why,
One fair daughter, and no more,
The which he loved passing[1] well.
Polonius [aside]. Still on my daughter.
Hamlet, II, 2:426
[1] passing: exceedingly.

K. Lear. Tell me, my daughters,
Since now we will divest us both of rule,
Interest of territory, cares of state,
Which of you shall we say doth love us
  most?
That we our largest bounty may extend
Where nature doth with merit challenge.

. . . . .

Goneril. Sir, I love you more than words
  can wield the matter;
Dearer than eye-sight, space, and liberty;
Beyond what can be valued, rich or rare.

. . . . .

Regan. I am made of that self metal as
  my sister,
And prize me at her worth.

. . . . .

Cordelia. Unhappy that I am, I cannot
  heave
My heart into my mouth: I love your maj-
  esty
According to my bond; no more nor less.
K. Lear. How, how, Cordelia! mend your
  speech a little
Lest you may mar your fortunes.

. . . . .

Cordelia. Why have my sisters husbands,
  if they say
They love you all? Haply, when I shall
  wed,
That lord whose hand must take my plight
  shall carry
Half my love with him, half my care and
  duty.
Sure I shall never marry like my sisters,
To love my father all.
King Lear, I, 1:49, 56, 71, 93, 101

K. Lear. Darkness and devils!
Saddle my horses; call my train together.
Degenerate bastard! I'll not trouble thee:
Yet have I left a daughter.
King Lear, I, 4:273

Regan. I pray you, father, being weak,
  seem so.
If, till the expiration of your month,
You will return and sojourn with my sister,
Dismissing half your train, come then to me;
I am now from home, and out of that provi-
  sion
Which shall be needful for your entertain-
  ment.
K. Lear. Return to her? and fifty men
  dismiss'd?
No, rather I abjure all roofs, and choose
To wage against the enmity o' the air;
To be a comrade with the wolf and owl,
Necessity's sharp pinch!
King Lear, II, 4:203

Brabantio. How got she out? O! treason
  of the blood:
Fathers, from hence trust not your daugh-
  ters' minds
By what you see them act.
Othello, I, 1:170
Baptista. What, will my daughter prove a
  good musician?
Hortensio. I think she'll sooner prove a
  soldier:
Iron may hold with her, but never lutes.
Taming of the Shrew, II, 1:145

SHEPHERD. Fie, daughter! when my old
  wife liv'd, upon
This day she was both pantler,[1] butler, cook;
Both dame and servant; welcom'd all, serv'd
  all.
                              Winter's Tale, IV, 4:55
[1] pantler: servant in charge of pantry.

DAY

IRAS. The bright day is done,
And we are for the dark.
                    Antony and Cleopatra, V, 2:193

PISANIO. Hath Britain all the sun that
  shines? Day, night,
Are they not but in Britain?
                              Cymbeline, III, 4:139

BEDFORD. The day begins to break, and
  night is fled,
Whose pitchy mantle over-veil'd the earth.
                              I Henry VI, II, 2:1

CAPTAIN. The gaudy, blabbing, and re-
  morseful day
Is crept into the bosom of the sea,
And now loud-howling wolves arouse the
  jades
That drag the tragic melancholy night;
Who with their drowsy, slow, and flagging
  wings
Clip dead men's graves, and from their
  misty jaws
Breathe foul contagious darkness in the air.
                              II Henry VI, IV, 1:1

MACBETH. So foul and fair a day I have
  not seen.
                              Macbeth, I, 3:38

SALISBURY. One day too late, I fear me,
  noble lord,
Hath clouded all thy happy days on earth.
O! call back yesterday, bid time return.
                              Richard II, III, 2:67

ROMEO. Night's candles are burnt out,
  and jocund day
Stands tiptoe on the misty mountain tops:
                              Romeo and Juliet, III, 5:9

DEATH

ENOBARBUS. Cleopatra, catching but the
least noise of this, dies instantly; I have seen
her die twenty times upon far poorer moment. I do think there is mettle in death
which commits some loving act upon her,
she hath such a celerity in dying.
                    Antony and Cleopatra, I, 2:143

ANTONY. I will be
A bridegroom in my death, and run into 't
As to a lover's bed.
                    Antony and Cleopatra, IV, 14:99

ANTONY. I am dying, Egypt, dying; only
I here importune death awhile, until
Of many thousand kisses the poor last
I lay upon thy lips.
                    Antony and Cleopatra, IV, 15:18

CLEOPATRA. Where art thou, death?
Come hither, come! come, come, and take a
  queen
Worth many babes and beggars!

                    . . . . .

Shall they hoist me up
And show me to the shouting variety
Of censuring Rome? Rather a ditch in
  Egypt
Be gentle grave unto me! rather on Nilus'
  mud
Lay me stark naked, and let the water-flies
Blow me into abhorring! rather make
My country's high pyramides my gibbet,
And hang me up in chains!
                    Antony and Cleopatra, V, 2:46, 58

CLEOPATRA. If thou and nature can so gen-
  tly part,
The stroke of death is as a lover's pinch,
Which hurts, and is desir'd.

                    . . . . .

Come, thou mortal wretch,
To the asp, which she applies to her breast.
With thy sharp teeth this knot intrinsicate
Of life at once untie; poor venomous fool,
Be angry, and dispatch.
                    Antony and Cleopatra, V, 2:297, 307

MENENIUS.[1] And, being angry, does forget that ever
He heard the name of death.
                              Coriolanus, III, 1:259
[1] About CORIOLANUS.

POSTHUMUS. Cur'd
By the sure physician, death, who is the key
To unbar these locks.
                              Cymbeline, V, 4:6

POSTHUMUS. I am merrier to die than
  thou art to live.
FIRST GAOLER. Indeed, sir, he that sleeps
  feels not the toothache.
                              Cymbeline, V, 4:175

HAMLET [soliloquy]. To die, to sleep;
To sleep: perchance to dream: ay, there's
  the rub;

For in that sleep of death what dreams may
   come,
When we have shuffled off this mortal coil,

    . . . . .

Must give us pause.
The undiscover'd country from whose
   bourn
No traveller returns.
                  Hamlet, III, 1:64, 79

HAMLET [soliloquy]. To my shame, I see
The imminent death of twenty thousand
   men,
That, for a fantasy and trick of fame,
Go to their graves like beds, fight for a plot
Whereon the numbers cannot try the cause.
                   Hamlet, IV, 4:59

HAMLET. Imperious Caesar, dead and
   turn'd to clay,
Might stop a hole to keep the wind away:
O! that that earth, which kept the world in
   awe,
Should patch a wall to expel the winter's
   flaw.[1]
                   Hamlet, V, 1:237

[1] flaw: wind.

QUEEN. Sweets to the sweet: farewell!
                  Scattering flowers.
I hop'd thou should'st have been my Ham-
   let's wife;
I thought thy bride-bed to have deck'd,
   sweet maid,
And not have strew'd thy grave.
                   Hamlet, V, 1:266

PRINCE. Why, thou owest God a death.
FALSTAFF. 'Tis not due yet: I would be
loath to pay him before his day. What need
I be so forward with him that calls not
on me?
                 I Henry IV, V, 1:127

PISTOL. Then death rock me asleep,
   abridge my doleful days!
Why then, let grievous, ghastly, gaping
   wounds
Untwine the Sisters Three![1] Come, Atropos.[2]
                II Henry IV, II, 4:211
[1] Sisters Three: the three goddesses of man's
destiny. [2] Atropos: the one who cuts the
thread of life.

SHALLOW. Death is certain. Is old Double
of your town living yet?
SILENCE. Dead, sir.
SHALLOW. Jesu! Jesu! dead! a'[1] drew a
good bow; and dead! a' shot a fine shoot:

John a Gaunt loved him well, and betted
much money on his head. Dead!
                II Henry IV, III, 2:45
[1] a': he.

HOSTESS. As ever you came of women,
come in quickly to Sir John. Ah! poor heart,
he is so shaked of a burning quotidian tertian,[1] that it is most lamentable to behold.
Sweet men, come to him.
NYM. The king hath run bad humours on
the knight; that's the even of it.
PISTOL. Nym, thou hast spoke the right;
His heart is fracted[2] and corroborate.[3]
                 Henry V, II, 1:122
[1] quotidian tertian: fever paroxysms every 3rd
day; HOSTESS is confused. [2] fracted: broken.
[3] corroborate: critics are uncertain what PISTOL
means; he may use a word he does not understand.

BARDOLPH. Would I were with him,[1]
   wheresom'er he is, either in heaven or in
   hell!
HOSTESS. Nay, sure, he 's not in hell: he 's
in Arthur's[2] bosom, if ever man went to Arthur's bosom. A'[3] made a finer end and went
away an[4] it had been any christom[5] child; a'
parted even just between twelve and one,
even at the turning o' the tide: for after I
saw him fumble with the sheets and play
with flowers and smile upon his fingers'
ends, I knew there was but one way; for his
nose was as sharp as a pen, and a' babbled of
green fields. 'How now, Sir John?' quoth I:
'what, man! be o' good cheer.' So a' cried
out 'God, God, God!' three or four times:
now I, to comfort him, bid him a' should
not think of God, I hoped there was no need
to trouble himself with any such thoughts
yet.
                 Henry V, II, 3:7
[1] him: FALSTAFF. [2] Arthur: HOSTESS' error for
Abraham. [3] A': he. [4] an: if. [5] christom
child: the chrisom was a white cloth put on a
child after baptism; HOSTESS refers to use of
term for one dying within the month of
christening.

MORTIMER. But now the arbitrator of de-
   spairs,
Just death, kind umpire of men's miseries,
With sweet enlargement[1] doth dismiss me
   hence.
                I Henry VI, II, 5:28
[1] enlargement: a setting free.

TALBOT. Thou antic[1] Death, which
   laugh'st us here to scorn.
                I Henry VI, IV, 7:18
[1] antic: a buffoon.

K. HENRY. Ah! what a sign it is of evil
    life
Where death's approach is seen so terrible.
                            II King Henry VI, III, 3:5

GRIFFITH. Full of repentance,
Continual meditations, tears, and sorrows,
He[1] gave his honours to the world again,
His blessed part to heaven, and slept in
    peace.
                            Henry VIII, IV, 2:27
[1] He: WOLSEY.

CONSTANCE. Death, death: O amiable
    lovely death!
Thou odoriferous stench! sound rottenness!
Arise forth from the couch of lasting night,
Thou hate and terror to prosperity,
And I will kiss thy detestable bones,
And put my eyeballs in thy vaulty brows,
And ring these fingers with thy household
    worms,
And stop this gap of breath with fulsome
    dust,
And be a carrion monster like thyself:
Come, grin on me; and I will think thou
    smil'st
And buss thee as thy wife! Misery's love,
O! come to me.
                            King John, III, 4:25

PRINCE HENRY. Death, having prey'd
    upon the outward parts,
Leaves them, invisible; and his siege is now
Against the mind, the which he pricks and
    wounds
With many legions of strange fantasies,
Which, in their throng and press to that last
    hold,
Confound themselves.
                            King John, V, 7:15

BRUTUS. That we shall die, we know; 't is
    but the time
And drawing days out, that men stand upon.
    CASSIUS. Why, he that cuts off twenty
    years of life
Cuts off so many years of fearing death.
                            Julius Caesar, III, 1:99

EDGAR. O! our lives' sweetness,
That we the pain of death would hourly die
Rather than die at once!
                            King Lear, V, 3:184

K. LEAR. Howl, howl, howl, howl! O! you
    are men of stones:
Had I your tongues and eyes, I'd use
    them so
That heaven's vault should crack. She 's
    gone for ever.
I know when one is dead, and when one
    lives;

She 's dead as earth. Lend me a looking-
    glass;
If that her breath will mist or stain the
    stone,
Why, then she lives.
                            King Lear, V, 3:257

KENT. Vex not his ghost: O! let him pass;
    he hates him
That would upon the rack of this tough
    world
Stretch him out longer.
                            King Lear, V, 3:313

MALCOLM. Nothing in his[1] life
Became him like the leaving it; he died
As one that had been studied in his death
To throw away the dearest thing he ow'd[2]
As 't were a careless trifle.
                            Macbeth, I, 4:7
[1] his: CAWDOR'S.   [2] ow'd: owned.

SEYTON. The queen, my lord, is dead.
    MACBETH. She should[1] have died hereafter;
There would have been a time for such a
    word.
To-morrow, and to-morrow, and to-mor-
    row,
Creeps in this petty pace from day to day,
To the last syllable of recorded time;
And all our yesterdays have lighted fools
The way to dusty death. Out, out, brief
    candle!
Life 's but a walking shadow, a poor player
That struts and frets his hour upon the
    stage,
And then is heard no more; it is a tale
Told by an idiot, full of sound and fury,
Signifying nothing.
                            Macbeth, V, 5:16
[1] should: would; sometimes used interchange-
ably by Shakespeare.

MACBETH. I will not be afraid of death and
    bane
Till Birnam forest come to Dunsinane.

                                . . . . .

                            Enter a Messenger.
Thou com'st to use thy tongue; thy story
    quickly.
    MESSENGER. Gracious my lord,
I should report that which I say I saw,
But know not how to do it.
    MACBETH. Well, say, sir.
    MESSENGER. As I did stand my watch
    upon the hill,
I look'd toward Birnam, and anon, me-
    thought,
The wood began to move.
    MACBETH. Liar and slave!
    MESSENGER. Let me endure your wrath if
    't be not so:

Within this three mile may you see it com-
ing;
I say, a moving grove.
  MACBETH. If thou speak'st false,
Upon the next tree shalt thou hang alive,
Till famine cling[1] thee; if thy speech be
  sooth,
I care not if thou dost for me as much.
I pull in[2] resolution, and begin
To doubt the equivocation of the fiend
That lies like truth; 'Fear not till Birnam
  wood
Do come to Dunsinane'; and now a wood
Comes toward Dunsinane. Arm, arm, and
  out!
If this which he avouches does appear,
There is nor flying hence nor tarrying here.
I 'gin to be aweary of the sun,
And wish the estate o' the world were now
  undone.
Ring the alarum-bell! Blow, wind! come
  wrack!
At least we 'll die with harness on our back.
          Macbeth, V, 3:59 and V, 5:29
[1] cling: wither. [2] pull in: like stopping a horse.

  MACBETH. They have tied me to a stake; I
  cannot fly,
But bear-like[1] I must fight the course.
  What 's he
That was not born of woman? Such a one
Am I to fear, or none.
                Macbeth, V, 7:1
[1] bear-like . . . course: for bear-baiting, the
bear was tied to a stake and a certain number
of dogs attacked at once; each attack was a
course.

             Enter MACDUFF.
  MACDUFF. Turn, hell-hound, turn!
  MACBETH. Of all men else I have avoided
  thee:
But get thee back, my soul is too much
  charg'd
With blood of thine already.
  MACDUFF. I have no words;
My voice is in my sword, thou bloodier vil-
  lain
Than terms can give thee out!
                They fight.
  MACBETH. Thou losest labour:
As easy may'st thou the intrenchant[1] air
With thy keen sword impress as make me
  bleed:
Let fall thy blade on vulnerable crests;
I bear a charmed life, which must not yield
To one of woman born.
  MACDUFF. Despair thy charm;
And let the angel whom thou still[2] hast
  serv'd
Tell thee, Macduff was from his mother's
  womb
Untimely ripp'd.

  MACBETH. Accursed be that tongue that
  tells me so,
For it hath cow'd[3] my better part of man:
And be these juggling fiends no more be-
  liev'd,
That palter with us in a double sense;
That keep the word of promise to our ear,
And break it to our hope. I'll not fight with
  thee.
  MACDUFF. Then yield thee, coward,
And live to be the show and gaze o' the
  time:
We 'll have thee, as our rarer monsters are,
Painted[4] upon a pole, and underwrit,
'Here may you see the tyrant,'
  MACBETH. I will not yield,
To kiss the ground before young Malcolm's
  feet,
And to be baited with the rabble's curse.
Though Birnam wood be come to Dunsi-
  nane,
And thou oppos'd, being of no woman born,
Yet I will try the last: before my body
I throw my war-like shield. Lay on, Mac-
  duff,
And damn'd be him that first cries 'Hold,
  enough!'
              Exeunt, fighting.
                Macbeth, V, 7:33
[1] intrenchant: not to be cut. [2] still: progres-
sive action, always. [3] cow'd: depressed with
fear. [4] Painted . . . pole: on cloth hung from
pole.

  ISABELLA [to CLAUDIO]. Lord Angelo,
  having affairs to heaven,
Intends you for his swift ambassador,

        · · · · ·

Therefore your best appointment make
  with speed;
To-morrow you set on.
        Measure for Measure, III, 1:56, 60

  ISABELLA. The sense of death is most in
  apprehension,[1]
And the poor beetle, that we tread upon,
In corporal sufferance finds a pang as great
As when a giant dies.

        · · · · ·

  CLAUDIO. If I must die,
I will encounter darkness as a bride,
And hug it in mine arms.
        Measure for Measure, III, 1:78, 83
[1] apprehension: forethought, imagination.

  CLAUDIO. Ay, but to die, and go we know
  not where;
To lie in cold obstruction and to rot;
This sensible warm motion to become
A kneaded clod; and the delighted spirit
To bathe in fiery floods, or to reside

In thrilling region of thick-ribbed ice;
To be imprison'd in the viewless winds,
And blown with restless violence round
    about
The pendent[1] world; or to be worse than
    worst
Of those that lawless and incertain thoughts
Imagine howling: 't is too horrible!
The weariest and most loathed worldly life
That age, ache, penury and imprisonment
Can lay on nature is a paradise
To what we fear of death.
                  Measure for Measure, III, 1:118
[1] pendent: hanging in the universe.

OTHELLO [soliloquy beside the bed where
    DESDEMONA is asleep].
It is the cause, it is the cause, my soul;
Let me not name it to you, you chaste stars!
It is the cause. Yet I'll not shed her blood,
Nor scar that whiter skin of hers than snow,
And smooth as monumental alabaster.
Yet she must die, else she 'll betray more
    men.
Put out the light, and then put out the light:
If I quench thee, thou flaming minister,
I can again thy former light restore,
Should I repent me; but once put out thy
    light,
Thou cunning'st pattern of excelling nature,
I know not where is that Promethean heat
That can thy light relume. When I have
    pluck'd the rose,
I cannot give it vital growth again,
It needs must wither: I'll smell it on the
    tree.
                                        Kisses her.
O balmy breath, that dost almost persuade
Justice to break her sword! One more, one
    more.
Be thus when thou art dead, and I will kill
    thee,
And love thee after. One more, and this the
    last:
So sweet was ne'er so fatal. I must weep,
But they are cruel tears; this sorrow 's heav-
    enly,
It strikes where it doth love.
                                        She wakes.
                              Othello, V, 2:1

DESDEMONA. Will you come to bed, my
    lord?
OTHELLO. Have you pray'd to-night, Des-
    demona?
DESDEMONA. Ay, my lord.
OTHELLO. If you bethink yourself of any
    crime
Unreconcil'd as yet to heaven and grace,
Solicit for it straight.
DESDEMONA. Alas! my lord, what may
    you mean by that?

OTHELLO. Well, do it, and be brief; I will
    walk by:
I would not kill thy unprepared spirit;
No; heaven forfend! I would not kill thy
    soul.
DESDEMONA. Talk you of killing?
OTHELLO. Ay, I do.
DESDEMONA. Then heaven
Have mercy on me!
OTHELLO. Amen! with all my heart.
                              Othello, V, 2:25

[After he has smothered her, OTHELLO learns
that DESDEMONA was innocent.]
OTHELLO. Where should Othello go?
Now how dost thou look now? O ill-starr'd
    wench!
Pale as thy smock! when we shall meet at
    compt,[1]
This look of thine will hurl my soul from
    heaven,
And fiends will snatch at it. Cold, cold, my
    girl!
Even like thy chastity.
O! cursed, cursed slave. Whip me, ye devils,
From the possession of this heavenly sight!
Blow me about in winds! roast me in sul-
    phur!
Wash me in steep-down gulfs of liquid fire!
O Desdemona! Desdemona! dead!
O! oh! oh!
                              Othello, V, 2:271
[1] compt: final accounting.

LODOVICO. O thou Othello! that wert once
    so good,
Fall'n in the practice of a damned slave,
What shall be said to thee?
OTHELLO. Why, any thing:
An honourable murderer, if you will;
For nought did I in hate, but all in honour.

                    . . . . .

Speak of me as I am; nothing extenuate,
Nor set down aught in malice: then must
    you speak
Of one that lov'd not wisely but too well;
Of one not easily jealous, but, being
    wrought,
Perplex'd in the extreme; of one whose
    hand,
Like the base Indian, threw a pearl away
Richer than all his tribe.

                    . . . . .

And say besides, that in Aleppo once,
Where a malignant and a turban'd Turk
Beat a Venetian and traduc'd the state,
I took by the throat the circumcised dog,
And smote him, thus.
                                Stabs himself.

OTHELLO. I kiss'd thee ere I kill'd thee; no
way but this,
Falling upon DESDEMONA.
Killing myself to die upon a kiss.
Dies.
Othello, V, 2:291, 342, 352

GAUNT.[1] My oil-dried lamp and time-be-
wasted light
Shall be extinct with age and endless night;
My inch of taper will be burnt and done,
And blindfold death not let me see my son.
Richard II, I, 3:221
[1] GAUNT: father of BOLINGBROKE who has been
banished for six years.

NORTHUMBERLAND.[1] His tongue is now a
stringless instrument;

. . . . .

K. RICHARD. The ripest fruit first falls, and
so doth he.
Richard II, II, 1:149, 153
[1] About JOHN OF GAUNT.

[ROMEO has heard that JULIET is dead. With a
deadly poison for himself he reaches her tomb
just before she revives from the sleeping po-
tion.]
CHORUS. From forth the fatal loins of
these two foes
A pair of star-cross'd lovers take their life;
Romeo and Juliet, Prologue, 5

ROMEO. Here lies Juliet, and her beauty
makes
This vault a feasting presence full of light.
. . . . .

Death, that hath suck'd the honey of thy
breath,
Hath had no power yet upon thy beauty:
Thou art not conquer'd; beauty's ensign yet
Is crimson in thy lips and in thy cheeks,
And death's pale flag is not advanced there.
Romeo and Juliet, V, 3:85, 92

ROMEO. Eyes, look your last!
Arms, take your last embrace! and lips, O
you,
The doors of breath, seal with a righteous
kiss
A dateless bargain to engrossing death!
Come, bitter conduct, come, unsavoury
guide!
Thou desperate pilot, now at once run on
The dashing rocks thy sea-sick weary bark!
Here's to my love!
Drinks.
O true apothecary!
Thy drugs are quick. Thus with a kiss I die.
Dies.
. . . . .

JULIET. Yea, noise? then I'll be brief. O
happy dagger!
Seizes ROMEO's *dagger and stabs herself.*
This is thy sheath;
There rest, and let me die.
Dies.
Romeo and Juliet, V, 3:112, 169

CAPULET. Death lies on her like an un-
timely frost
Upon the sweetest flower of all the field.
Romeo and Juliet, IV, 5:28

LORD. Grim death, how foul and loathsome is thine image!
Taming of the Shrew, Induction, 1:35

TITUS. Sleep in peace, slain in your country's wars!

. . . . .

In peace and honour rest you here, my sons;
Rome's readiest champions, repose you here
in rest,
Secure from worldly chances and mishaps!
Titus Andronicus, I, 1:91, 150

CLOWN. Come away, come away, death,
And in sad cypress let me be laid;
Fly away; fly away, breath;
I am slain by a fair cruel maid.
My shroud of white, stuck all with yew,
O! prepare it:
My part of death, no one so true
Did share it.
Not a flower, not a flower sweet,
On my black coffin let there be strown;
Not a friend, not a friend greet
My poor corpse, where my bones shall be
thrown.
A thousand thousand sighs to save,
Lay me, O! where
Sad true lover never find my grave,
To weep there.
Twelfth Night, II, 4:52

'Hard-favour'd[1] tyrant, ugly, meagre, lean,
Hateful divorce of love,' thus chides she
Death,
Grim-grinning ghost, earth's worm, what
dost thou mean
To stifle beauty and to steal his[2] breath,
Who when he liv'd, his breath and beauty
set
Gloss on the rose, smell to the violet?
Venus and Adonis, 931
[1] Hard-favour'd: ugly looking.   [2] his: its.

DECEPTION

CHARMIAN. 'T was merry when
You wager'd on your angling; when your
diver

Did hand a salt-fish on his hook, which he
With fervency drew up.
Antony and Cleopatra, II, 5:15

ADRIANA. My heart prays for him, though
my tongue do curse.
Comedy of Errors, IV, 2:28

KATHARINE. *O bon Dieu! les langues des
hommes sont pleines de tromperies.*
K. HENRY. What says she, fair one? that
the tongues of men are full of deceits?
Henry V, V, 2:118

Q. MARGARET. Fair lords, cold snow melts
with the sun's hot beams.
Henry my lord is cold in great affairs,
Too full of foolish pity; and Gloucester's
show
Beguiles him as the mournful crocodile[1]
With sorrow snares relenting passengers;
Or as the snake, roll'd in a flowering bank,
With shining checker'd slough, doth sting a
child
That for the beauty thinks it excellent.
II Henry VI, III, 1:223
[1] crocodile . . . passengers: refers to "croco-
dile tears."

K. HENRY. And when the lion fawns upon
the lamb,
The lamb will never cease to follow him.
III Henry VI, IV, 8:49

CICERO. Men may construe things after
their fashion,
Clean from the purpose of the things themselves.
Julius Caesar, I, 3:34

KATHARINE. For he hath wit to make an
ill shape good,
And shape to win grace though he had no
wit.
Love's Labour's Lost, II, 1:59

LUCIO. Thou concludest like the sanctimonious pirate, that went to sea with the
Ten Commandments, but scraped one out
of the table.[1]
Measure for Measure, I, 2:7
[1] table: list.

BASSANIO. So may the outward shows be
least themselves:
The world is still[1] deceiv'd with ornament.
In law, what plea so tainted and corrupt
But, being season'd with a gracious voice,
Obscures the show of evil? In religion,
What damned error, but some sober brow
Will bless it and approve it with a text,
Hiding the grossness with fair ornament?

There is no vice so simple but assumes
Some mark of virtue on his[2] outward parts.
How many cowards, whose hearts are all as
false
As stairs of sand, wear yet upon their chins
The beards of Hercules and frowning Mars,
Who, inward search'd, have livers white as
milk;
And these assume but valour's excrement[3]
To render them redoubted! Look on
beauty,
And you shall see 'tis purchas'd by the
weight;
Which therein works a miracle in nature,
Making them lightest that wear most of it:
So are those crisped snaky golden locks
Which make such wanton gambols with the
wind,
Upon supposed fairness, often known
To be the dowry of a second head,
The skull that bred them in the sepulchre.
Thus ornament is but the guiled shore
To a most dangerous sea; the beauteous
scarf
Veiling an Indian beauty; in a word,
The seeming truth which cunning times
put on
To entrap the wisest.
Merchant of Venice, III, 2:92
[1] still: always.   [2] his: its.   [3] excrement: beard or
hair.

FALSTAFF. I would all the world might be
cozened,[1] for I have been cozened and
beaten too. If it should come to the ear of
the court how I have been transformed, and
how my transformation hath been washed
and cudgelled, they would melt me out of
my fat drop by drop, and liquor fishermen's
boots with me.
Merry Wives of Windsor, IV, 5:95
[1] cozened: deceived.

BALTHAZAR [singing]. Sigh no more, la-
dies, sigh no more,
Men were deceivers ever,
One foot in sea, and one on shore,
To one thing constant never.
Then sigh not so,
But let them go,
And be you blithe and bonny,
Converting all your sounds of woe
Into Hey nonny, nonny.
Sing no more ditties, sing no mo,
Of dumps so dull and heavy;
The fraud of men was ever so,
Since summer first was leavy.
Then sigh not so,
But let them go,
And be you blithe and bonny,
Converting all your sounds of woe
Into Hey nonny, nonny.
Much Ado About Nothing, II, 3:64

CLAUDIO. O! what authority and show of truth
Can cunning sin cover itself withal.[1]
> *Much Ado About Nothing*, IV, 1:36

[1] withal: with.

IAGO. She did deceive her father, marrying you;
And when she seem'd to shake and fear your looks
She lov'd them most.
OTHELLO. And so she did.
IAGO. Why, go to, then;
She that so young could give out such a seeming.
To seel her father's eyes up close as oak.
> *Othello*, III, 3:206

And my true eyes have never practis'd how
To cloak offences with a cunning brow.
> *Rape of Lucrece*, 748

DUCHESS.[1] Ah! that deceit should steal such gentle shape,
And with a virtuous vizard[2] hide deep vice.
> *Richard III*, II, 2:27

[1] Mother of RICHARD III, about him. [2] vizard: mask.

JULIET. O serpent heart, hid with a flowering face!
Did ever dragon keep so fair a cave?
Beautiful tyrant! fiend angelical!
Dove-feather'd raven! wolvish-ravening lamb!
Despised substance of divinest show!
Just opposite to what thou justly seem'st;
A damned saint, an honourable villain!
O nature! what hadst thou to do in hell
When thou didst bower the spirit of a fiend
In mortal paradise of such sweet flesh?
Was ever book containing such vile matter
So fairly bound? O! that deceit should dwell
In such a gorgeous palace.
> *Romeo and Juliet*, III, 2:73

Thou blind fool, Love, what dost thou to mine eyes,
That they behold, and see not what they see?
That know what beauty is, see where it lies,
Yet what the best is take the worst to be.
If eyes, corrupt by over-partial looks,
Be anchor'd in the bay where all men ride,
Why of eyes' falsehood hast thou forged hooks,
Whereto the judgment of my heart is tied?
> *Sonnet* 137

When my love swears that she is made of truth,
I do believe her, though I know she lies.
> *Sonnet* 138

As testy sick men, when their deaths be near,
No news but health from their physicians know.
> *Sonnet* 140

GRUMIO. Here 's no knavery! See, to beguile[1] the old folks, how the young folks lay their heads together!
> *Taming of the Shrew*, I, 2:138

[1] beguile: deceive.

DEED

HAMLET. Foul deeds will rise,
Though all the earth o'erwhelm them, to men's eyes.
> *Hamlet*, I, 2:257

QUEEN. O! what a rash and bloody deed is this.
HAMLET. A bloody deed! almost as bad, good mother,
As kill a king, and marry with his brother.
> *Hamlet*, III, 4:27

LANCASTER.[1] As a false favourite doth his prince's name,
In deeds dishonourable? You have ta'en up,
Under the counterfeited zeal of God,
The subjects of his substitute, my father;
And both against the peace of heaven and him
Have here upswarm'd them.
> *II Henry IV*, IV, 2:25

[1] To the ARCHBISHOP OF YORK.

MACBETH. I have done the deed. Didst thou not hear a noise?
LADY M. I heard the owl scream and the crickets cry.
> *Macbeth*, II, 2:15

LADY M. These deeds must not be thought
After these ways; so, it will make us mad.
> *Macbeth*, II, 2:33

MACBETH. Ere the bat hath flown
His cloister'd flight, ere to black Hecate's summons
The shard-borne beetle with his drowsy hums
Hath rung night's yawning peal, there shall be done
A deed of dreadful note.
LADY M. What 's to be done?
MACBETH. Be innocent of the knowledge, dearest chuck,
Till thou applaud the deed. Come, seeling night,
Scarf up the tender eye of pitiful day,
And with thy bloody and invisible hand
Cancel and tear to pieces that great bond

Which keeps me pale! Light thickens, and
  the crow
Makes wing to the rooky wood;
Good things of day begin to droop and
  drowse,
Whiles night's black agents to their preys
  do rouse.
Thou marvell'st at my words: but hold thee
  still;
Things bad begun make strong themselves
  by ill.
                Macbeth, III, 2:40

MACBETH. How now, you secret, black,
  and midnight hags!
WITCHES. A deed without a name.
                Macbeth, IV, 1:48

MACBETH [aside]. Time, thou anticipat'st
  my dread exploits;
The flighty purpose never is o'ertook
Unless the deed go with it; from this mo-
  ment
The very firstlings of my heart shall be
The firstlings of my hand. And even now,
To crown my thoughts with acts, be it
  thought and done:
The castle of Macduff I will surprise;
Seize upon Fife; give to the edge o' the
  sword
His wife, his babes, and all unfortunate souls
That trace him in his line. No boasting like
  a fool;
This deed I'll do before this purpose cool.
              Macbeth, IV, 1:144

TYRREL. The tyrannous and bloody act[1]
  is done;
The most arch deed of piteous massacre
That ever yet this land was guilty of.
Dighton and Forrest, whom I did suborn
To do this piece of ruthless butchery, . . .
Melted with tenderness and mild compas-
  sion,
Wept like to children in their deaths' sad
  story.
              Richard III, IV, 3:1

[1] Murder of princes.

DEFECT

HAMLET. So oft it chances in particular
  men
That, for some vicious mole of nature in
  them,
      . . . . .
Carrying, I say, the stamp of one defect,
Being nature's livery or fortune's star,
Their virtues, else, be they as pure as grace,
As infinite as man may undergo,
Shall in the general censure[1] take corruption
From that particular fault.
            Hamlet, I, 4:23, 31

[1] censure: opinion.

K. HENRY [to PRINCE HAL]. Defect of
  manners, want of government,
Pride, haughtiness, opinion, and disdain:
The least of which haunting a nobleman
Loseth men's hearts and leaves behind a
  stain
Upon the beauty of all parts besides,
           1 Henry IV, III, 1:183

FERDINAND. For several virtues
Have I lik'd several women; never any
With so full soul but some defect in her
Did quarrel with the noblest grace she
  ow'd[1]
And put[2] it to the foil.
              Tempest, III, 1:42

[1] ow'd: owned. [2] put . . . foil: tested for a
fault.

DEFENCE

DAUPHIN. In cases of defence 't is best to
  weigh
The enemy more mighty than he seems.
              Henry V, II, 4:43

PRINCE. My royal father, cheer these no-
  ble lords,
And hearten those that fight in your de-
  fence.
Unsheathe your sword, good father: cry,
  'Saint George!'
             III Henry VI, II, 2:78

MISTRESS PAGE. Be not amazed; call all
your senses to you: defend your reputation,
or bid farewell to your good life for ever.
      Merry Wives of Windsor, III, 3:125

DEFIANCE

ANTONY. Fortune knows
We scorn her most when most she offers
  blows.
       Antony and Cleopatra, III, 11:74

CYMBELINE. Our subjects, sir,
Will not endure his[1] yoke; and for ourself
To show less sovereignty than they, must
  needs
Appear unkinglike.
             Cymbeline, III, 5:4

[1] his: Caesar's.

LAERTES. How came he dead? I'll not be
  juggled with.
To hell, allegiance! vows, to the blackest
  devil!
Conscience and grace, to the profoundest
  pit!

I dare damnation. To this point I stand,
That both the worlds I give to negligence,
Let come what comes; only I 'll be reveng'd
Most throughly[1] for my father.
Hamlet, IV, 5:130
[1] throughly: thoroughly, as often in Shakespeare.

K. HENRY.[1] My people are with sickness
much enfeebled,
My numbers lessen'd, and those few I have
Almost no better than so many French;
Who when they were in health, I tell thee,
herald,
I thought upon one pair of English legs
Did march three Frenchmen.

. . . . .

Yet, God before, tell him we will come on,
Though France himself and such another
neighbour
Stand in our way. There's for thy labour,
Montjoy.
Go bid thy master well advise himself:
If we may pass, we will; if we be hinder'd,
We shall your tawny ground with your red
blood
Discolour: and so, Montjoy, fare you well.
Henry V, III, 6:154, 165
[1] To the French herald demanding surrender.

WARWICK. I had rather chop this hand off
at a blow,
And with the other fling it at thy face,
Than bear so low a sail to strike to thee.
III Henry VI, V, 1:50

BIANCA. I am no breeching scholar[1] in the
schools;
I 'll not be tied to hours nor 'pointed times,
But learn my lessons as I please myself.
Taming of the Shrew, III, 1:18
[1] breeching scholar: schoolboy liable to be
flogged.

AENEAS [to Greek DIOMEDES]. Health to
you, valiant sir,
During all question of the gentle truce;
But when I meet you arm'd, as black defiance
As heart can think or courage execute.
Troilus and Cressida, IV, 1:10

PAULINA.[1] What studied torments, tyrant,
hast for me?
What wheels? racks? fires? what flaying?
boiling
In leads or oils? what old or newer torture
Must I receive, whose every word deserves
To taste of thy most worst? Thy tyranny,
Together working with thy jealousies,
Fancies too weak for boys, too green and
idle

For girls of nine, O! think, what they have
done,
And then run mad indeed, stark mad!

. . . . .

A thousand knees
Ten thousand years together, naked, fasting,
Upon a barren mountain, and still winter
In storm perpetual, could not move the
gods
To look that way thou wert.
Winter's Tale, III, 2:176, 211
[1] To LEONTES.

DELAY

MESSENGER. But yet, madam,—
CLEOPATRA. I do not like 'but yet,' it does
allay[1]
The good precedence; fie upon 'but yet'!
'But yet' is as a gaoler to bring forth
Some monstrous malefactor. Prithee, friend,
Pour out the pack of matter to mine ear,
The good and bad together.
Antony and Cleopatra, II, 5:49
[1] allay . . . precedence: spoil the favorable report made before.

ROSALIND. One inch of delay more is a
South-sea[1] of discovery; I prithee, tell me
who is it, quickly, and speak apace. I would
thou could'st stammer, that thou might'st
pour this concealed man out of thy mouth,
as wine comes out of a narrow-mouthed
bottle; either too much at once, or none at
all. I prithee, take the cork out of thy
mouth, that I may drink thy tidings.
As You Like It, III, 2:207
[1] South-sea . . . discovery: referring to fabulous tales current in Shakespeare's time.

HAMLET. The law's delay,
The insolence of office, and the spurns
That patient merit of the unworthy takes.
Hamlet, III, 1:72

ALENCON. Delays have dangerous ends.
I Henry VI, III, 2:33

PORTIA. I speak too long; but 't is to peise[1]
the time,
To eke it and draw it out in length.
Merchant of Venice, III, 2:22
[1] peise: best defined by second line.

K. RICHARD. Come; I have learn'd that
fearful[1] commenting
Is leaden servitor to dull delay;
Delay leads impotent and snail-pac'd beggary:
Then fiery expedition be my wing.
Richard III, IV, 3:51
[1] fearful . . . delay: comments full of fear lead
to delay.

MERCUTIO. In delay
We waste our lights in vain, like lamps by
    day.
                           Romeo and Juliet, I, 4:45

DESPAIR

ENOBARBUS. I fight against thee! No: I
    will go seek
Some ditch wherein to die; the foul'st best
    fits
My latter part of life.
                    Antony and Cleopatra, IV, 6:37

O sun! thy uprise shall I see no more;
Fortune and Antony part here; even here
Do we shake hands. All come to this? The
    hearts
That spaniel'd me at heels, to whom I gave
Their wishes, do discandy,[1] melt their
    sweets
On blossoming Caesar; and this pine is
    bark'd,
That overtopp'd them all. Betray'd I am.
O this false soul of Egypt! this grave charm,
Whose eye beck'd forth my wars, and call'd
    them home,
Whose bosom was my crownet, my chief
    end,
Like a right gipsy, hath, at fast and loose,
Beguil'd me to the very heart of loss.
                   Antony and Cleopatra, IV, 12:18
[1] discandy: dissolve.

CLEOPATRA. The crown o' the earth doth
    melt. My lord!
O! wither'd is the garland of the war,
The soldier's pole is fall'n: young boys and
    girls
Are level now with men; the odds is gone,
And there is nothing left remarkable
Beneath the visiting moon.
                   Antony and Cleopatra, IV, 15:63

CLEOPATRA. His legs bestrid the ocean; his
    rear'd arm
Crested the world; his voice was propertied
As all the tuned spheres, and that to friends;
But when he meant to quail and shake the
    orb,
He was as rattling thunder. For his bounty,
There was no winter in 't, an autumn 't was
That grew the more by reaping; his delights
Were dolphin-like, they show'd his back
    above
The element they liv'd in; in his livery
Walk'd crowns and crownets, realms and is-
    lands were
As plates dropp'd from his pocket.
                    Antony and Cleopatra, V, 2:81

HAMLET [soliloquy]. O! that this too too
    solid flesh would melt,

Thaw and resolve itself into a dew;
Or that the Everlasting had not fix'd
His canon 'gainst self-slaughter! O God!
    God!
How weary, stale, flat, and unprofitable
Seem to me all the uses of this world.
Fie on 't! ah fie! 't is an unweeded garden,
That grows to seed; things rank and gross
    in nature
Possess it merely.[1] That it should come to
    this!
But two months dead: nay, not so much,
    not two:
So excellent a king; that was, to this,
Hyperion[2] to[3] a satyr;[4] so loving to my
    mother
That he might not beteem the winds of
    heaven
Visit her face too roughly. Heaven and
    earth!
Must I remember? why, she would hang on
    him,
As if increase of appetite had grown
By what it fed on; and yet, within a month,
Let me not think on 't: Frailty, thy name is
    woman!
A little month; or ere those shoes were old
With which she follow'd my poor father's
    body,
Like Niobe, all tears: why she, even she—
O God! a beast, that wants[5] discourse of
    reason,
Would have mourn'd longer,—married with
    my uncle,
My father's brother, but no more like my
    father
Than I to Hercules: within a month,
Ere yet the salt of most unrighteous tears
Had left the flushing in her galled eyes,
She married. O! most wicked speed, to post
With such dexterity to incestuous sheets.
It is not nor it cannot come to good;
But break, my heart, for I must hold my
    tongue!
                                Hamlet, I, 2:129
[1] merely: absolutely.   [2] Hyperion: god of the
Sun.   [3] to: compared with.   [4] satyr: part man
and part goat.   [5] wants: lacks.

K. HENRY. O! beat away the busy med-
    dling fiend
That lays strong siege unto this wretch's
    soul
And from his bosom purge this black de-
    spair.
                            II Henry VI, III, 3:21

K. PHILIP.[1] Look! who comes here; a
    grave unto a soul;
Holding the eternal spirit, against her will,
In the vile prison of afflicted breath.
                             King John, III, 4:17
[1] As CONSTANCE enters.

PRINCE HENRY. How fares your majesty?
K. JOHN. Poison'd, ill fare; dead, forsook,
    cast off:
And none of you will bid the winter come
To thrust his icy fingers in my maw;[1]
Nor let my kingdom's rivers take their
    course
Through my burn'd bosom; nor entreat the
    north
To make his bleak winds kiss my parched
    lips
And comfort me with cold.
King John, V, 7:34
[1] maw: stomach.

SECOND MURDERER. I am one, my liege,
Whom the vile blows and buffets of the
    world
Have so incens'd that I am reckless what
I do to spite the world.
FIRST MURDERER. And I another
So weary with disasters, tugg'd with for-
    tune,
That I would set my life on any chance,
To mend it or be rid on 't.
Macbeth, III, 1:108

SALANIO.[1] 'My daughter! O my ducats!
    O my daughter!
Fled with a Christian! O my Christian duc-
    ats!
Justice! the law! my ducats, and my daugh-
    ter!
A sealed bag, two sealed bags of ducats,
Of double ducats, stol'n from me by my
    daughter!'
Merchant of Venice, II, 8:15
[1] Quoting SHYLOCK.

O! that is gone for which I sought to live,
And therefore now I need not fear to die.
Rape of Lucrece: 1051

BOLINGBROKE. Destruction straight shall
    dog them at the heels.
Richard II, V, 3:139

K. RICHARD. I shall despair. There is no
    creature loves me;
And if I die, no soul shall pity me:
Nay, wherefore should they, since that I
    myself
Find in myself no pity to myself?
Richard III, V, 3:200

JULIET. Come weep with me; past hope,
    past cure, past help!
Romeo and Juliet, IV, 1:45

THIRD SERVANT. Leak'd is our bark,
And we, poor mates, stand on the dying
    deck,
Hearing the surges threat.
Timon of Athens, IV, 2:19

HERMIONE [to LEONTES]. Sir, spare your
    threats:
The bug[1] which you would fright me with
    I seek.
To me can life be no commodity:
The crown and comfort of my life, your
    favour,
I do give lost; for I do feel it gone,
But know not how it went.

. . . . .

Now, my liege,
Tell me what blessings I have here alive,
That I should fear to die?
Winter's Tale, III, 2:92, 107
[1] bug: bugbear.

DETERMINATION

LADY M. Glamis thou art, and Cawdor;
    and shalt be
What thou are promis'd.

. . . . .

The raven himself is hoarse
That croaks the fatal entrance of Duncan
Under my battlements.
Macbeth, I, 5:16, 39

JULIET. O! bid me leap, rather than marry
    Paris,
From off the battlements of yonder tower;
Or walk in thievish ways; or bid me lurk
Where serpents are; chain me with roaring
    bears;
Or shut me nightly in a charnel-house,
O'er-cover'd quite with dead men's rattling
    bones,
With reeky shanks, and yellow chapless[1]
    skulls;
Or bid me go into a new-made grave
And hide me with a dead man in his shroud;
Things that, to hear them told, have made
    me tremble;
And I will do it without fear or doubt,
To live an unstain'd wife to my sweet love.
Romeo and Juliet, IV, 1:77
[1] chapless: without jaws.

DEVIL

CLOWN. I am driven on by the flesh; and
he must needs go that the devil drives.
All's Well That Ends Well, I, 3:31

DROMIO SYRACUSE. Marry,[1] he must have
a long spoon that must eat with the devil.
Comedy of Errors, IV, 3:64
[1] Marry: indeed; originally, "by Mary."

GLENDOWER. Why, I can teach you,
    cousin, to command the devil.

HOTSPUR. And I can teach thee, coz, to shame the devil
By telling truth: tell truth and shame the devil.
If thou have power to raise him, bring him hither,
And I'll be sworn I have power to shame him hence,
O! while you live, tell truth and shame the devil.
1 Henry IV, III, 1:56

HOTSPUR. Now I perceive the devil understands Welsh;
And 't is no marvel he is so humorous.[1]
By 'r lady, he 's a good musician.
1 Henry IV, III, 1:233
[1] humorous: capricious.

EDGAR. The prince of darkness is a gentleman.
King Lear, III, 4:148

BANQUO. What! can the devil speak true?
. . . . .
But 't is strange:
And oftentimes, to win us to our harm,
The instruments of darkness tell us truths,
Win us with honest trifles, to betray 's
In deepest consequence.
Macbeth, I, 3:107, 122

ISABELLA. This outward-sainted deputy,
Whose settled visage and deliberate word
Nips youth i' the head, and follies doth emmew,[1]
As falcon doth the fowl, is yet a devil.
Measure for Measure, III, 1:89
[1] emmew: coop-up.

ANTONIO. The devil can cite Scripture for his purpose.
An evil soul, producing holy witness,
Is like a villain with a smiling cheek,
A goodly apple rotten at the heart.
O, what a goodly outside falsehood hath!
Merchant of Venice, I, 3:99

FALSTAFF. I think the devil will not have me damned, lest the oil that is in me should set hell on fire; he would never else cross me thus.
Merry Wives of Windsor, V, 5:37

SIR TOBY. What, man! defy the devil; consider, he's an enemy to mankind.
Twelfth Night, III, 4:108

SIR TOBY. What, man! 't is not for gravity to play at cherry-pit[1] with Satan.
Twelfth Night, III, 4:128
[1] play at cherry-pit: a game of casting cherry-pits into a small hole.

DEVOTION

K. HENRY. I myself will lead a private life,
And in devotion spend my latter days,
To sin's rebuke and my Creator's praise.
III Henry VI, IV, 6:42

MOROCCO. I would outstare the sternest eyes that look,
Outbrave the heart most daring on the earth,
Pluck the young sucking cubs from the she bear,
Yea, mock the lion when he roars for prey,
To win thee, lady.
Merchant of Venice, II, 1:27

HELENA. You[1] in my respect[2] are all the world:
Then how can it be said I am alone,
When all the world is here to look on me?
Midsummer Night's Dream, II, 1:224
[1] DEMETRIUS.   [2] respect: thought.

JULIET. All my fortunes at thy foot I 'll lay,
And follow thee my lord throughout the world.
Romeo and Juliet, II, 2:147

DUKE. You[1] uncivil lady,
To whose ingrate and unauspicious altars
My soul the faithfull'st offerings hath breath'd out
That e'er devotion tender'd!
Twelfth Night, V, 1:115
[1] You: OLIVIA, who has spurned his advances.

FLORIZEL. Were I crown'd the most imperial monarch,
Thereof most worthy, were I the fairest youth
That ever made eye swerve, had force and knowledge
More than was ever man's, I would not prize them
Without her love: for her[1] employ them all;
Commend them and condemn them to her service
Or to their own perdition.
Winter's Tale, IV, 4:382
[1] her: PERDITA.

DIPLOMACY

PHEBE. Faster than his tongue
Did make offence his eye did heal it up.
As You Like It, III, 5:116

MENENIUS. Speak to 'em, I pray you,
In wholesome manner.

CORIOLANUS. Bid them wash their faces,
And keep their teeth clean.
Coriolanus, II, 3:65

CORIOLANUS. Well then, I pray, your
price o' the consulship?
FIRST CITIZEN. The price is, to ask it
kindly.
CORIOLANUS. Kindly! Sir, I pray, let me
ha 't: I have wounds to show you, which
shall be yours in private. Your good voice,
sir; what say you?
Coriolanus, II, 3:79

K. RICHARD. Off goes his[1] bonnet to an
oyster-wench;
A brace of draymen bid God speed him
well,
And had the tribute of his supple knee,
With 'Thanks, my countrymen, my loving
friends';
As were our England in reversion[2] his,
And he our subjects' next degree in hope.
Richard II, I, 4:31
[1] his: BOLINGBROKE'S.   [2] reversion: succession to
the throne.

DISAPPOINTMENT

BEATRICE. A sweet gallant, surely! O! that
I were a man for his sake, or that I had any
friend would be a man for my sake! But
manhood is melted into courtesies, valour
into compliment, and men are only turned
into tongue, and trim ones too: he is now as
valiant as Hercules, that only tells a lie and
swears it. I cannot be a man with wishing,
therefore I will die a woman with griev-
ing.
Much Ado About Nothing, IV, 1:319

The sweets we wish for turn to loathed
sours
Even in the moment that we call them ours.
Rape of Lucrece: 867

GAUNT. Things sweet to taste prove in
digestion sour.
Richard II, I, 3:236

GLOUCESTER.[1] I took him[2] for the plainest
harmless creature
That breath'd upon the earth a Christian;
Made him my book, wherein my soul re-
corded
The history of all her secret thoughts:
So smooth he daub'd his vice with show of
virtue.
Richard III, III, 5:23
[1] Later KING RICHARD III.   [2] him: HASTINGS.

DISCIPLINE

GARDINER.[1] Which reformation must be
sudden, too.
My noble lords; for those that tame wild
horses
Pace 'em not in their hands to make 'em
gentle,
But stop their mouths with stubborn bits,
and spur 'em,
Till they obey the manage.
Henry VIII, V, 3:20
[1] Attacking CRANMER for heresies.

DUKE. Now, as fond[1] fathers,
Having bound up the threat'ning twigs of
birch,
Only to stick it in their children's sight
For terror, not to use, in time the rod
Becomes more mock'd than fear'd; so our
decrees,
Dead[2] to infliction, to themselves are dead,
And liberty plucks justice by the nose;
The baby beats the nurse, and quite athwart
Goes all decorum.
Measure for Measure, I, 3:23
[1] fond: foolish.   [2] Dead to infliction: not en-
forced.

DISCRETION

HAMLET. Let your own discretion be
your tutor.
Hamlet, III, 2:20

FALSTAFF. The better part of valour is
discretion.
I Henry IV, V, 4:122

PISTOL. Look to my chattels and my
moveables:
Let senses rule, the word is 'Pitch[1] and
pay';
Trust none;
For oaths are straws, men's faiths are wafer-
cakes,
And hold-fast is the only dog, my duck:
Therefore, *caveto*[2] be thy counsellor.
Henry V, II, 3:50
[1] Pitch . . . pay: pay ready money; a proverb.
[2] *caveto:* take care, be cautious.

OTHELLO. Let 's teach ourselves that honourable stop,
Not to out-sport[1] discretion.
Othello, II, 3:2
[1] out-sport discretion: go beyond discretion.

DISEASE

SICINIUS. He[1] 's a disease that must be cut
away.

MENENIUS. O! he 's a limb that has but a disease;
Mortal to cut it off; to cure it easy.
                                        Coriolanus, III, 1:295
[1] He: CORIOLANUS.

KING. But, like the owner of a foul disease,
To keep it from divulging, let it feed
Even on the pith of life.
                                        Hamlet, IV, 1:21

KING. Diseases desperate grown
By desperate appliance are reliev'd,
Or not at all.
                                        Hamlet, IV, 3:9

CASSIUS. But soft, I pray you: what! did Caesar swound?
CASCA. He fell down in the market-place, and foamed at mouth, and was speechless.
BRUTUS. 'T is very like: he hath the falling-sickness.
CASSIUS. No, Caesar hath it not: but you, and I, and honest Casca, we have the falling-sickness.
                                        Julius Caesar, I, 2:253

KENT. Kill thy physician, and the fee bestow
Upon the foul disease.
                                        King Lear, I, 1:166

MARINA.[1] For me,
That am a maid, though most ungentle fortune
Hath plac'd me in this sty, where, since I came,
Diseases have been sold dearer than physic,[2]
O! that the gods
Would set me free from this unhallow'd place,
Though they did change me to the meanest bird
That flies i' the purer air.
                                        Pericles, IV, 6:102
[1] MARINA is imprisoned in a house of prostitution. [2] physic: medicine.

DISGRACE

CLEOPATRA. Now, Iras, what think'st thou?
Thou, an Egyptian puppet, shalt be shown
In Rome, as well as I; mechanic slaves
With greasy aprons, rules, and hammers, shall
Uplift us to the view; in their thick breaths,
Rank of gross diet, shall we be enclouded,
And forc'd to drink their vapour.
IRAS. The gods forbid!
CLEOPATRA. Nay, 't is most certain, Iras.
Saucy lictors

Will catch at us, like strumpets, and scald[1] rimers
Ballad us out o' tune; the quick comedians
Extemporally will stage us, and present
Our Alexandrian revels. Antony
Shall be brought drunken forth, and I shall see
Some squeaking Cleopatra boy[2] my greatness
I' the posture of a whore.
                                        Antony and Cleopatra, V, 2:207
[1] scald: scurvy, contemptible. [2] boy: alluding to Elizabethan use of boys for women's parts; notice the use of *boy* as a verb.

FALSTAFF. By the Lord, a buck-basket![1] rammed me in with foul shirts and smocks, socks, foul stockings, greasy napkins; that, Master Brook, there was the rankest compound of villanous smell that ever offended nostril.
                                        Merry Wives of Windsor, III, 5:90
[1] buck-basket: clothes hamper.

DISGUISE

ROSALIND. Were it not better,
Because that I am more than common tall,
That I did suit me all points like a man?
A gallant curtal-axe[1] upon my thigh,
A boar-spear in my hand: and,—in my heart
Lie there what hidden woman's fear there will,—
We 'll have a swashing and a martial outside.
                                        As You Like It, I, 3:116
[1] curtal-axe: a broad, curving sword.

PISANIO. You must forget to be a woman; change
Command into obedience; fear and niceness,[1]
The handmaids of all women, or more truly
Woman it pretty self, into a waggish[2] courage;
Ready in gibes, quick-answer'd, saucy, and
As quarrellous as the weasel;
                                        Cymbeline, III, 4:157
[1] niceness: coyness. [2] waggish: roguish.

IMOGEN.[1] I see a man's life is a tedious one;
I have tir'd[2] myself, and for two nights together
Have made the ground my bed.

·   ·   ·   ·   ·

Best draw my sword; and if mine enemy
But fear the sword like me, he'll scarcely look on 't.
                                        Cymbeline, III, 6, 1:25
[1] In boy's clothes. [2] tir'd: dressed in male costume.

EDGAR. I will preserve myself; and am be-
thought
To take the basest and most poorest shape
That ever penury, in contempt of man,
Brought near to beast

. . . . .

And with this horrible object, from low
farms,
Poor pelting[1] villages, sheep-cotes, and
mills,
Sometime with lunatic bans, sometime with
prayers,
Enforce their charity. Poor Turlygood![2]
poor Tom!
That 's something yet: Edgar I nothing am.
King Lear, II, 3:6, 17
[1] pelting: paltry. [2] Turlygood: a name given
to beggars.

OLIVIA. What is your parentage?
VIOLA.[1] Above my fortunes, yet my state
is well:
I am a gentleman.
Twelfth Night, I, 5:296
[1] Disguised in male attire.

DISHONOUR

ENOBARBUS. Mark Antony . . . will to
his Egyptian dish again; then shall the sighs
of Octavia blow the fire up in Caesar.
Antony and Cleopatra, II, 6:134

ANTONY.[1] Since Cleopatra died,
I have liv'd in such dishonour, that the gods
Detest my baseness. I, that with my sword
Quarter'd the world, and o'er green Nep-
tune's back
With ships made cities, condemn myself to
lack
The courage of a woman.
Antony and Cleopatra, IV, 14:56
[1] ANTONY has been misinformed.

GLOUCESTER.[1] Ah! Humphrey, this dishonour in thine age
Will bring thy head with sorrow to the
ground.
II Henry VI, II, 3:18
[1] HUMPHREY, DUKE OF GLOUCESTER, about the
arrest of his wife, addressing himself.

YORK. I rather would have lost my life
betimes[1]
Than bring a burden of dishonour home,
II Henry VI, III, 1:297
[1] betimes: quickly.

LEONATO. Sweet prince, why speak not
you?
D. PEDRO. What should I speak?

I stand dishonour'd, that have gone about
To link my dear friend to a common stale.[1]
Much Ado About Nothing, IV, 1:64
[1] stale: prostitute.

MOWBRAY [to RICHARD]. My life thou
shalt command, but not my shame:
The one my duty owes; but my fair name,
Despite of death that lives upon my grave,
To dark dishonour's use thou shalt not have.
Richard II, I, 1:166

DISILLUSION

K. RICHARD. O! that I were a mockery
king of snow,
Standing before the sun of Bolingbroke,[1]
To melt myself away in water-drops.
Richard II, IV, 1:260
[1] BOLINGBROKE: HENRY IV, who has dethroned
RICHARD II.

PERDITA. The self-same sun that shines
upon his court
Hides not his[1] visage from our cottage, but
Looks on alike. Will 't please you, sir,[2] be
gone?
I told you what would come of this: be-
seech you,
Of your own state take care: this dream of
mine
Being now awake, I'll queen it no inch fur-
ther,
But milk my ewes and weep.
Winter's Tale, IV, 4:455
[1] his: its.   [2] sir: FLORIZEL.

DISMISSAL

LAFEU. Go thy ways, I begin to be
aweary of thee.
All's Well That Ends Well, IV, 5:59

LADY M. Question enrages him. At once,
good night:
Stand not upon the order[1] of your going.
But go at once.
Macbeth, III, 4:118
[1] order: protocol required them to leave in
order of their rank.

FALSTAFF. Rogues, hence! avaunt! vanish
like hailstones, go:
Trudge, plod away o' the hoof; seek shelter,
pack!
Merry Wives of Windsor, I, 3:90

DEMETRIUS. Hence! get thee gone, and
follow me no more.
Midsummer Night's Dream, II, 1:194

SECOND LORD. Away, unpeaceable dog! or
I'll spurn thee hence.

APEMANTUS. I will fly, like a dog, the heels of the ass.
Timon of Athens, I, 1:281

MARIA. Will you hoist sail, sir? here lies your way.
Twelfth Night, I, 5:216

DISPLEASURE

PAROLLES. I know not how I have deserved to run into my lord's displeasure.
LAFEU. You have made shift to run into 't, boots and spurs and all, like him that leaped into the custard.
All's Well That Ends Well, II, 5:37

CLOWN. Here is a purr of fortune's sir, or of fortune's cat . . . that has fallen into the unclean fishpond of her displeasure.
All's Well That Ends Well, V, 2:20

WILLIAMS. That 's a perilous shot out of an elder-gun[1] that a poor and private displeasure can do against a monarch. You may as well go about to turn the sun to ice with fanning in his face with a peacock's feather.
Henry V, IV, 1:209
[1] elder-gun: a pop-gun.

Q. KATHARINE. Hath my behaviour given to your displeasure,
That thus you should proceed to put me off
And take your good grace from me!
Heaven witness
I have been to you a true and humble wife,
At all times to your will conformable.
Henry VIII, II, 4:20

ULYSSES. You are mov'd, prince; let us depart, I pray you,
Lest your displeasure should enlarge itself
To wrathful terms. This place is dangerous;
The time right deadly: I beseech you, go.
Troilus and Cressida, V, 2:36

DISSEMBLING

CLEOPATRA. I prithee, turn aside and weep for her;
Then bid adieu to me, and say the tears
Belong to Egypt: good now, play one scene
Of excellent dissembling, and let it look
Like perfect honour.
Antony and Cleopatra, I, 3:76
[1] About the news that FULVIA, ANTONY's wife, is dead.

DOGBERRY. Is our whole dissembly appeared?
VERGES. O! a stool and a cushion for the sexton.

SEXTON. Which be the malefactors?
Much Ado About Nothing, IV, 2:1

DUKE. O thou dissembling cub! what wilt thou be
When time hath sow'd a grizzle[1] on thy case?
Or will not else thy craft so quickly grow
That thine own trip shall be thine overthrow?
Twelfth Night, V, 1:167
[1] grizzle: white hair.

DISSENSION

EXETER. This late dissension grown betwixt the peers
Burns under feigned ashes of forg'd love,
And will at last break out into a flame:
As fester'd members rot but by degree,
Till bones and flesh and sinews fall away,
So will this base and envious discord breed.
1 Henry VI, III, 1:190

DISTRESS

ORLANDO. The thorny point
Of bare distress hath ta'en from me the show
Of smooth civility.
As You Like It, II, 7:94

KENT. Who 's there, beside foul weather?
GENTLEMAN. One minded like the weather, most unquietly.
KENT. I know you. Where 's the king?
GENTLEMAN. Contending with the fretful elements;
Bids the wind blow the earth into the sea,
Or swell the curled waters 'bove the main,
That things might change or cease; tears his white hair,
Which the impetuous blasts, with eyeless rage,
Catch in their fury, and make nothing of;
Strives in his little world of man to outscorn
The to-and-fro conflicting wind and rain.
This night, wherein the cub-drawn[1] bear would couch,
The lion and the belly-pinched wolf
Keep their fur dry, unbonneted he runs,
And bids what will take all.
King Lear, III, 1:1
[1] cub-drawn: exhausted by nursing cubs.

TITUS. Therefore I tell my sorrows to the stones,
Who, though they cannot answer my distress,
Yet in some sort they are better than the tribunes,

For that they will not intercept my tale.
When I do weep, they humbly at my feet
Receive my tears, and seem to weep with
    me.
Titus Andronicus, III, 1:37

Third Gentleman. Countenances of
such distraction that they were to be known
by garment, not by favour.[1]
Winter's Tale, V, 2:52
[1] favour: facial appearance.

DIVINITY

King. There 's such divinity doth hedge a
    king,
That treason can but peep to[1] what it
    would,
Acts little of his[2] will.
Hamlet IV, 5:123
[1] to: compared with.   [2] his: its.

Hamlet. There 's a divinity that shapes
    our ends,
Rough-hew them how we will.
Hamlet, V, 2:10

K. Richard. I had forgot myself. Am I
    not king?
Awake, thou sluggard majesty! thou sleep-
    est.
Is not the king's name twenty thousand
    names?
Arm, arm, my name! a puny subject strikes
At thy great glory.
Richard II, III, 2:83

K. Richard. Thoughts of things divine,
    are intermix'd
With scruples, and do set the word itself
Against the word.
Richard II, V, 4:12

Ulysses. The providence that 's in a
    watchful state
Knows almost every grain of Plutus'[1] gold,
Finds bottom in the uncomprehensive deeps,
Keeps place with thought, and almost, like
    the gods,
Does thoughts unveil in their dumb cradles.
There is a mystery, with whom relation
Durst never meddle, in the soul of state,
Which hath an operation more divine
Than breath or pen can give expressure to.
Troilus and Cressida, III, 3:196
[1] Plutus: the god of riches.

DIVORCE

Adriana. Should'st thou but hear I were
    licentious,

And that this body, consecrate to thee,
By ruffian lust should be contaminate!
Would'st thou not spit at me, and spurn at
    me,
And hurl the name of husband in my face,
And tear the stain'd skin off my harlot-
    brow,
And from my false hand cut the wedding-
    ring,
And break it with a deep-divorcing vow?
Comedy of Errors, II, 2:133

Prince. This sleep is sound indeed; this is
    a sleep
That from this golden rigol[1] hath divorc'd
So many English kings.
II Henry IV, IV, 5:35
[1] rigol: circle; the crown.

Norfolk. He[1] counsels a divorce; a loss
    of her,
That like a jewel has hung twenty years
About his neck, yet never lost her lustre;
Of her, that loves him with that excellence
That angels love good men with.
Henry VIII, II, 2:31
[1] He: Wolsey.

Q. Katharine. I have been to you a true
    and humble wife,
At all times to your will conformable;
Ever in fear to kindle your dislike,
Yea, subject to your countenance, glad or
    sorry
As I saw it inclin'd.
Henry VIII, II, 4:23

Q. Katharine. Can you think, lords,
That any Englishman dare give me counsel?
Or be a known friend, 'gainst his highness'
    pleasure?
Henry VIII, III, 1:83.

Q. Katharine [to Wolsey]. Is this your
    Christian counsel? out upon ye!
Heaven is above all yet; there sits a Judge
That no king can corrupt.
Henry VIII, III, 1:99

Norfolk. When returns Cranmer?
Suffolk. He is return'd in his opinions,
    which
Have satisfied the king for his divorce,
Together with all famous colleges
Almost in Christendom. Shortly I believe
His second marriage shall be publish'd, and
Her coronation. Katharine no more
Shall be call'd queen, but princess dowager
And widow to Prince Arthur.[1]
Henry VIII, III, 2:63
[1] Arthur: Henry's elder brother.

Exton. As who should say, 'I would thou
    wert the man

That would divorce this terror from my heart.'

Richard II, V, 3:154

DOG

STEWARD. From courtly friends, with camping foes to live,
Where death and danger dogs the heels of worth.

All's Well That Ends Well, III, 4:14

BRUTUS. They have chose a consul that will from them take
Their liberties; make them of no more voice
Than dogs that are so often beat for barking
As therefore kept to do so.

Coriolanus II, 3:222

DAUPHIN. Turn head, and stop pursuit; for coward dogs
Most spend their mouths when what they seem to threaten
Runs far before them.

Henry V, II, 4:69

ARTHUR. And like a dog that is compell'd to fight,
Snatch at his master that doth tarre[1] him on.

King John, IV, 1:116

[1] tarre: urge.

CORDELIA. Mine enemy's dog,
Though he had bit me, should have stood that night
Against my fire.

King Lear, IV, 7:37

SHYLOCK. Thou call'dst me dog before thou hadst a cause,
But, since I am a dog, beware my fangs:

Merchant of Venice, III, 3:6

BENEDICK. An he had been a dog that should have howled thus, they would have hanged him.

Much Ado About Nothing, II, 3:81

OTHELLO. O! I see that nose of yours, but not that dog I shall throw it to.

Othello, IV, 1:145

LAUNCE. I think Crab my dog be the sourest-natured dog that lives: my mother weeping, my father wailing, my sister crying, our maid howling, our cat wringing her hands, and all our house in a great perplexity, yet did not this cruel-hearted cur shed one tear.

Two Gentlemen of Verona, II, 3:5

DOGGEREL

ROSALIND [*reading* ORLANDO's *verses*].
From the east to western Ind,
No jewel is like Rosalind.
Her worth, being mounted on the wind,
Through all the world bears Rosalind.
All the pictures fairest lin'd
Are but black to Rosalind.
Let no face be kept in mind
But the fair of Rosalind.

TOUCHSTONE. I'll rhyme you so eight years together, dinners and suppers and sleeping hours excepted:

. . . . .

If a hart do lack a hind,
Let him seek out Rosalind.
If the cat will after kind,
So be sure will Rosalind.
Winter garments must be lin'd,
So must slender Rosalind.
They that reap must sheaf and bind,
Then to cart with Rosalind.
Sweetest nut hath sourest rind,
Such a nut is Rosalind.
He that sweetest rose will find
Must find love's prick and Rosalind.

As You like It, III, 2:93, 107

TOUCHSTONE. This is the very false gallop of verses: why do you infect yourself with them?
ROSALIND. Peace! you dull fool: I found them on a tree.
TOUCHSTONE. Truly, the tree yields bad fruit.
ROSALIND. I'll graff it with you, and then I shall graff it with a medlar.[1]

As You like It, III, 2:119

[1] medlar: a kind of apple not eaten until over-ripe.

DOUBT

LUCIO. Our doubts are traitors,
And make us lose the good we oft might win,
By fearing to attempt.

Measure for Measure, I, 4:77

OTHELLO. Make me to see 't; or, at the least, so prove it,
That the probation[1] bear no hinge nor loop
To hang a doubt on; or woe upon thy life!

Othello, III, 3:364

[1] probation: proof.

HECTOR. Modest doubt is call'd
The beacon of the wise, the tent[1] that searches
To the bottom of the worst.

Troilus and Cressida, II, 2:15

[1] tent: probe.

DREAM

IMOGEN. The dream 's here still; even when I wake, it is
Without me, as within me; not imagin'd, felt.
Cymbeline, IV, 2:306

CAESAR. She[1] dream'd to-night she saw my statua,
Which, like a fountain with an hundred spouts,
Did run pure blood; and many lusty Romans
Came smiling, and did bathe their hands in it.
Julius Caesar, II, 2:76
[1] she: CALPURNIA, CAESAR's wife.

CLARENCE. O! I have pass'd a miserable night,
So full of ugly sights, of ghastly dreams,
That, as I am a Christian faithful man,
I would not spend another such a night,
Though 't were to buy a world of happy days.
Richard III, I, 4:2

CLARENCE. Lord, Lord! methought what pain it was to drown:
What dreadful noise of waters in mine ears!
What ugly sights of death within mine eyes!
Methought I saw a thousand fearful wrecks;
A thousand men that fishes gnaw'd upon;
Wedges of gold, great anchors, heaps of pearl,
Inestimable stones, unvalued jewels,
All scatter'd in the bottom of the sea.
Some lay in dead men's skulls; and in those holes
Where eyes did once inhabit, there were crept,
As 't were in scorn of eyes, reflecting gems,
That woo'd the slimy bottom of the deep,
And mock'd the dead bones that lay scatter'd by.
Richard III, I, 4:21

BRAKENBURY. Had you such leisure in the time of death
To gaze upon the secrets of the deep?
CLARENCE. Methought I had; and often did I strive
To yield the ghost; but still the envious flood
Kept in my soul, and would not let it forth
To find the empty, vast, and wandering air;
But smother'd it within my panting bulk.
Richard III, I, 4:34

CLARENCE. I pass'd, methought, the melancholy flood,
With that sour ferryman[1] which poets write of,
Unto the kingdom of perpetual night.
Richard III, I, 4:45
[1] ferryman: Charon, in classical mythology the boatman who ferried souls across the Styx to Hades.

CLARENCE. Then came wandering by
A shadow like an angel, with bright hair
Dabbled in blood; and he shriek'd out aloud,
'Clarence is come; false, fleeting,[1] perjur'd Clarence,
That stabb'd me in the field by Tewksbury;
Seize on him! Furies, take him into torment.'
Richard III, I, 4:52
[1] fleeting: inconstant, unreliable.

K. RICHARD.[1] Give me another horse! bind up my wounds!
Have mercy, Jesu! Soft! I did but dream.
O! coward conscience, how dost thou afflict me.
The lights burn blue. It is now dead midnight.
Cold fearful drops stand on my trembling flesh.
What! do I fear myself? there's none else by.
Richard III, V, 3:177
[1] Awakening from his dream.

MERCUTIO. O! then I see Queen Mab hath been with you.
She is the fairies' midwife, and she comes
In shape no bigger than an agate-stone
On the forefinger of an alderman,
Drawn with a team of little atomies
Athwart men's noses as they lie asleep;
Her waggon-spokes made of long spinners' legs;
The cover, of the wings of grasshoppers;
The traces, of the smallest spider's web;
The collars, of the moonshine's watery beams;
Her whip, of cricket's bone; the lash, of film;
Her waggoner, a small grey-coated gnat,
Not half so big as a round little worm
Prick'd from the lazy finger of a maid;
Her chariot is an empty hazel-nut,
Made by the joiner squirrel or old grub,
Time out o' mind the fairies' coach-makers.
And in this state she gallops night by night
Through lovers' brains, and then they dream of love;
O'er courtiers' knees, that dream on court-'sies straight;
O'er lawyers' fingers, who straight dream on fees;
O'er ladies' lips, who straight on kisses dream;
Which oft the angry Mab with blisters plagues,
Because their breaths with sweetmeats tainted are.

Sometimes she gallops o'er a courtier's nose,
And then dreams he of smelling out a suit;
And sometime comes she with a tithe-pig's[1]
    tail,
Tickling a parson's nose as a'[2] lies asleep,
Then dreams he of another benefice;[3]
Sometime she driveth o'er a soldier's neck,
And then dreams he of cutting foreign
    throats,
Of breaches, ambuscadoes, Spanish blades,
Of healths five fathom deep; and then anon
Drums in his ear, at which he starts and
    wakes;
And, being thus frighted, swears a prayer
    or two,
And sleeps again. This is that very Mab
That plats the manes of horses in the night;
And bakes the elf-locks in foul sluttish hairs,
Which once entangled much misfortune
    bodes;
This is the hag, when maids lie on their
    backs,
That presses them and learns them first to
    bear,
Making them women of good carriage;
This is she—
    ROMEO. Peace, peace! Mercutio, peace!
Thou talk'st of nothing.
    MERCUTIO. True, I talk of dreams,
Which are the children of an idle brain,
Begot of nothing but vain fantasy.
                    Romeo and Juliet, I, 4:53
[1] tithe-pig: a pig given as a church contribu-
tion. [2] a': he. [3] benefice: church position.

    CALIBAN. Then, in dreaming,
The clouds methought would open and
    show riches
Ready to drop upon me, that when I wak'd
I cried to dream again.
                    Tempest, III, 2:149

    SEBASTIAN.[1] Or I am mad, or[2] else this is a
    dream.
Let fancy still my sense in Lethe[3] steep;
If it be thus to dream, still let me sleep!
                    Twelfth Night, IV, 1:65
[1] Mistaken for his sister VIOLA in disguise.
[2] Or . . . or: either . . . or. [3] Lethe: the river
of forgetfulness.

    PERDITA. Of your own state take care: this
    dream of mine
Being now awake, I'll queen it no inch fur-
    ther,
But milk my ewes and weep.
                    Winter's Tale, IV, 4:455

DRINK

Come, thou monarch of the vine,
Plumpy Bacchus[1] with pink eyne![2]

In thy vats our cares be drown'd,
With thy grapes our hairs be crown'd:
Cup us, till the world go round,
Cup us, till the world go round!
                Antony and Cleopatra, II, 7:120
[1] Bacchus, the god of wine. [2] eyne: eyes.

    PETO. Item, A capon . . . . .2s. 2d.
Item, Sauce . . . .   4d.
Item, Sack, two gallons . . . . .5s. 8d.
Item, Anchovies and sack
    after supper . . . . .2s. 6d.
Item, Bread . . . .   ob.
    PRINCE.[1] O monstrous! but one half-
penny-worth of bread to this intolerable
deal of sack!
                    I Henry IV, II, 4:585
[1] About FALSTAFF's diet.

    HAMLET. We'll teach you to drink deep
ere you depart.
                    Hamlet, I, 2:175

    CASSIO. I have very poor and unhappy
brains for drinking: I could well wish courtesy would invent some other custom of
entertainment.
                    Othello, II, 3:34

    IAGO. Now, my sick fool, Roderigo,
Whom love has turn'd almost the wrong
    side out,
To Desdemona hath to-night carous'd
Potations pottle-deep.
                    Othello, II, 3:53

    IAGO. And let me the canakin clink, clink;
And let me the canakin clink:
A soldier 's a man;
A life 's but a span;
Why then let a soldier drink.
                    Othello, II, 3:71

    MONTANO. But is he[1] often thus?
    IAGO. 'T is evermore the prologue to his
    sleep:
He 'll watch the horologe[2] a double set,
If drink rock not his cradle.
                    Othello, II, 3:133
[1] he: CASSIO. [2] horologe . . . set: clock go
round twice.

    JULIET [soliloquy]. My dismal scene I
    needs must act alone.
Come, vial.
What if this mixture do not work at all?
Shall I be married then to-morrow morn-
    ing?
No, no; this shall forbid it: lie thou there.
                    Laying down a dagger.
What if it be a poison, which the friar
Subtly hath minister'd to have me dead,
Lest in this marriage he should be dis-
    honour'd

Because he married me before to Romeo?
I fear it is: and yet, methinks, it should not,
For he hath still been tried a holy man.

. . . . .

O! if I wake, shall I not be distraught,
Environed with all these hideous fears,
And madly play with my forefathers' joints,
And pluck the mangled Tybalt from his
    shroud?
And, in this rage, with some great kinsman's
    bone,
As with a club, dash out my desperate
    brains?
O! look, methinks I see my cousin's ghost
Seeking out Romeo, that did spit his body
Upon a rapier's point. Stay, Tybalt, stay!
Romeo, I come! this do I drink to thee.
        She falls upon her bed within the curtains.
            Romeo and Juliet, IV, 3:20, 49

Sir Toby. I'll drink to her as long as there
is a passage in my throat and drink in Illyria.
            Twelfth Night, I, 3:41

Sir Toby. Does not our life consist of the
four elements?
Sir Andrew. Faith, so they say; but I
think it rather consists of eating and drinking.
Sir Toby. Thou 'rt a scholar; let us therefore eat and drink. Marian, I say! a stoup of
wine.
            Twelfth Night, II, 3:9

DROWNING

Jaques. By my troth, I was seeking for a
fool when I found you.
Orlando. He is drowned in the brook:
look but in, and you shall see him.
            As You Like It, III, 2:305

Falstaff. The rogues slighted[1] me into
the river with as little remorse as they
would have drowned a blind bitch's puppies,
fifteen i' the litter; and you may know by
my size that I have a kind of alacrity in sink-
ing: if the bottom were as deep as hell, I
should down . . . a death that I abhor, for
the water swells a man, and what a thing
should I have been when I had been swelled!
I should have been a mountain of mummy.
            Merry Wives of Windsor, III, 5:9
[1] slighted: threw.

Roderigo. What will I do, think'st thou?
Iago. Why, go to bed, and sleep.
Roderigo. I will incontinently[1] drown my-
self.

. . . . .

Iago. Come, be a man. Drown thyself!
drown cats and blind puppies. I have pro-
fessed me thy friend.
            Othello, I, 3:303, 340
[1] incontinently: immediately.

Gonzalo. I prophesied, if a gallows were
on land,
This fellow could not drown.
            Tempest, V, 1:217

DRUNK

Alexas. We'll know all our fortunes.
Enobarbus. Mine, and most of our fortunes, to-night shall be—drunk to bed.
            Antony and Cleopatra, I, 2:43

Hamlet. It is a custom
More honour'd in the breach than the ob-
    servance.
This heavy-headed revel east and west
Makes us traduc'd and tax'd[1] of other na-
    tions;
They clepe[2] us drunkards, and with swinish
    phrase
Soil our addition.[3]
                    Hamlet, I, 4:12
[1] tax'd: accused, blamed. [2] clepe: call. [3] addi-
tion: title.

Nerissa. How like you the young German, the Duke of Saxony's nephew?
Portia. Very vilely in the morning, when
he is sober, and most vilely in the afternoon,
when he is drunk: when he is best, he is a
little worse than a man, and when he is
worst, he is little better than a beast.
            Merchant of Venice, I, 2:90

Bardolph. Why, sir, for my part, I say
the gentleman had drunk himself out of his
five sentences.[1]
            Merry Wives of Windsor, I, 1:178
[1] sentences: senses.

Slender. I'll ne'er be drunk whilst I live
again, but in honest, civil, godly company.
            Merry Wives of Windsor, I, 1:185

Cassio. Do not think, gentlemen, I am
drunk: this is my ancient;[1] this is my right
hand, and this is my left hand. I am not
drunk now; I can stand well enough, and
speak well enough.
                    Othello, II, 3:116
[1] ancient: an officer next under a lieutenant.

Cassio. Drunk! and speak parrot! and
squabble, swagger, swear, and discourse fustian[1] with one's own shadow! O thou in-

visible spirit of wine! if thou hast no name
to be known by, let us call thee devil.

. . . . .

I remember a mass of things, but nothing
distinctly; a quarrel, but nothing wherefore.
O God! that men should put an enemy in
their mouths to steal away their brains; that
we should, with joy, pleasance, revel, and
applause, transform ourselves into beasts.
Othello, II, 3:282, 288

[1] fustian: nonsense.

CASSIUS. I will ask him for my place
again; he shall tell me I am a drunkard! Had
I as many mouths as Hydra,[1] such an answer would stop them all. To be now a
sensible man, by and by a fool, and presently a beast! O strange! Every inordinate
cup is unblessed and the ingredient is a devil.
Othello, II, 3:306

[1] hydra: many-headed snake.

TRINCULO.[1] A strange fish! Were I in England now, as once I was, and had but this
fish painted, not a holiday fool there but
would give a piece of silver: there would
this monster make a man: any strange beast
there makes a man. When they will not give
a doit to relieve a lame beggar, they will lay
out ten to see a dead Indian. Legged like a
man! and his fins like arms!
Tempest, II, 2:30

[1] Finding the deformed Caliban curled up to
hide.

STEPHANO. The master, the swabber, the
    boatswain and I,
The gunner and his mate
Lov'd Mall, Meg and Marian and Mergery,
But none of us car'd for Kate;
For she had a tongue with a tang,
Would cry to a sailor, 'Go hang!'
She lov'd not the savour of tar nor of pitch,
Yet a sailor might scratch her where-e'er
    she did itch;
Then to sea, boys, and let her go hang.
This is a scurvy tune too; but here 's my
    comfort.
Drinks.
Tempest, II, 2:48

STEPHANO. Prithee, do not turn me about:
    my stomach is not constant.
CALIBAN. These be fine things an if they
    be not sprites.
That's a brave god and bears celestial liquor:
I will kneel to him.
Tempest, II, 2:119

ARIEL. I told you, sir, they were red-hot
    with drinking;
So full of valour that they smote the air

For breathing in their faces; beat the ground
For kissing of their feet.
Tempest, IV, 1:171

OLIVIA. What 's a drunken man like, fool?
CLOWN. Like a drowned man, a fool, and
a madman: one draught above heat makes
him a fool, the second mads him, and the
third drowns him.
Twelfth Night, I, 5:137

MARIA. What a caterwauling do you keep
here!

. . . . .

SIR TOBY. We are politicians . . . 'Three
merry men be we.'

. . . . .

MARIA. For the love of God, peace!
Twelfth Night, II, 3:76, 81, 91

DUTY

POLONIUS. I hold my duty, as I hold my
    soul,
Both to my God and to my gracious king.
Hamlet, II, 2:44

FLUELLEN. A man that I love and honour
with my soul, and my heart, and my duty,
and my life, and my living, and my uttermost power.
Henry V, III, 6:7

K. HENRY. Every subject's duty is the
king's; but every subject's soul is his own.
Henry V, IV, 1:186

KENT. Think'st thou that duty shall have
    dread to speak
When power to flattery bows?
King Lear, I, 1:149

YORK. How long shall I be patient? ah,
    how long
Shall tender duty make me suffer wrong?
Richard II, II, 1:163

BOLINGBROKE [Kneeling]. My noble un-
    cle!
YORK. Show me thy humble heart, and
    not thy knee,
Whose duty is deceivable and false.
Richard II, II, 3:82

SILVIA. And duty never yet did want[1] his[2]
    meed.
Two Gentlemen of Verona, II, 4:112
[1] want . . . meed: lack its reward. [2] his: its.

PROTEUS. But when I call to mind your
    gracious favours

Done to me, undeserving as I am,
My duty pricks me on to utter that
Which else no worldly good should draw
  from me.
Two Gentlemen of Verona, III, 1:6

EAGLE

CYMBELINE. That might'st have had the
  sole son of my queen!
IMOGEN. O bless'd, that I might not! I
  chose an eagle
And did avoid a puttock.[1]
Cymbeline, I, 1:138
[1] puttock: a bird of prey.

Gnats are unnoted wheresoe'er they fly,
But eagles gaz'd upon with every eye.
Rape of Lucrece: 1014

K. RICHARD. We think the eagle-winged
  pride
Of sky-aspiring and ambitious thoughts,
With rival-hating envy, set on you
To wake our peace, which in our country's
  cradle
Draws the sweet infant breath of gentle
  sleep.
Richard II, I, 3:129

EARTH

ENOBARBUS. When it pleaseth their deities[1]
to take the wife of a man from him, it shows
to man the tailors of the earth; comforting
therein, that when old robes are worn out,
there are members to make new.
Antony and Cleopatra, I, 2:170
[1] deities: provide new wife as tailors do new
clothes.

HAMLET. Indeed it goes so heavily[1] with
my disposition that this goodly frame, the
earth, seems to me a sterile promontory;
this most excellent canopy, the air, look you,
this brave o'erhanging firmament, this majestical roof fretted with golden fire, why
it appears no other thing to me than a foul
and pestilent congregation of vapours.
Hamlet, II, 2:309
[1] heavily: sorrowfully.

MACBETH [soliloquy]. Thou sure and
  firm-set earth,
Hear not my steps, which way they walk,
  for fear
The very stones prate of my whereabout.
Macbeth, II, 1:56

MOWBRAY. [May] each day still better
  other's happiness;

Until the heavens, envying earth's good hap,
Add an immortal title to your crown!
Richard II, I, 1:23

GAUNT. This blessed plot, this earth, this
  realm, this England.
Richard II, II, 1:49

The earth can have but earth, which is his[1]
  due;
My spirit is thine, the better part of me.
Sonnet 74
[1] his: its.

TITUS. And sith[1] there 's no justice in
  earth nor hell,
We will solicit heaven and move the gods
To send down Justice for to wreak our
  wrongs.
Titus Andronicus, IV, 3:49
[1] sith: since.

EATING

ABBESS. Thou say'st his meat was sauc'd
  with thy upbraidings:
Unquiet meals make ill digestions;
Thereof the raging fire of fever bred:
And what 's a fever but a fit of madness?
Comedy of Errors, V, 1:73

FALSTAFF. And, I prithee, sweet wag,
when thou art king, as, God save thy grace,
majesty, I should say, for grace thou wilt
have none,—
PRINCE. What! none?
FALSTAFF. No, by my troth; not so much
as will serve to be prologue to an egg and
butter.
I Henry IV, I, 2:17

SILENCE. Do nothing but eat, and make
  good cheer,
And praise heaven for the merry year;
When flesh is cheap and females dear,
And lusty lads roam here and there,
So merrily,
And ever among so merrily.

. . . . .

Be merry, be merry, my wife has all;
For women are shrews, both short and tall:
'T is merry in hall when beards wag all,
And welcome merry Shrovetide.[1]
Be merry, be merry.
II Henry IV, V, 3:18, 35
[1] Shrovetide: a period just before Lent.

CONSTABLE. Give them great meals of beef
and iron and steel, they will eat like wolves
and fight like devils.
Henry V, III, 7:160

BEATRICE. He is a very valiant trencher-man:[1] he hath an excellent stomach.
Much Ado About Nothing, I, 1:51
[1] valiant trencherman: a big eater; by using valiant, she discounts BENEDICK's reputation as a soldier.

ECSTASY

PORTIA. O love! be moderate; allay thy ecstasy;
In measure rain thy joy; scant this excess:
I feel too much thy blessing; make it less,
For fear I surfeit.
Merchant of Venice, III, 2:111

PERICLES. O Helicanus! strike me, honour'd sir;
Give me a gash, put me to present pain,
Lest this great sea of joys rushing upon me
O'erbear the shores of my mortality,[1]
And drown me with their sweetness.
Pericles, V, 1:192
[1] mortality: life.

JULIET [soliloquy]. Gallop apace, you fiery-footed steeds,
Towards Phoebus'[1] lodging; such a waggoner
As Phaethon[2] would whip you to the west,
And bring in cloudy night immediately.
Spread thy close curtain, love-performing night!
That runaway's eyes may wink, and Romeo
Leap to these arms, untalk'd of and unseen!
Lovers can see to do their amorous rites
By their own beauties; or, if love be blind,
It best agrees with night. Come, civil night,
Thou sober-suited matron, all in black,
And learn me how to lose a winning match,
Play'd for a pair of stainless maidenhoods:
Hood my unmann'd blood, bating in my cheeks,
With thy black mantle; till strange love, grown bold,
Think true love acted simple modesty.
Come, night! come, Romeo! come, thou day in night!
For thou wilt lie upon the wings of night
Whiter than new snow on a raven's back,
Come, gentle night; come, loving, black-brow'd night,
Give me my Romeo: and, when he shall die,
Take him and cut him out in little stars,
And he will make the face of heaven so fine
That all the world will be in love with night,
And pay no worship to the garish sun.
O! I have bought the mansion of a love,
But not possess'd it, and though I am sold,
Not yet enjoy'd. So tedious is this day
As is the night before some festival

To an impatient child that hath new robes
And may not wear them.
Romeo and Juliet, III, 2:1
[1] Phoebus: Apollo, Greek god of light, music, song. [2] Phaethon: one who tried to drive the chariot of the sun.

EDUCATION

CADE. Thou hast most traitorously corrupted the youth of the realm in erecting a grammar-school; and whereas, before, our forefathers had no other books but the score and the tally, thou hast caused printing to be used; and, contrary to the king, his crown, and dignity, thou hast built a paper-mill. It will be proved to thy face that thou hast men about thee that usually talk of a noun, and a verb, and such abominable words as no Christian ear can endure to hear.
II Henry VI, IV, 7:36

BIRON. Study is like the heaven's glorious sun,
That will not be deep-search'd with saucy looks;
Small have continual plodders ever won,
Save base authority from others' books.
Love's Labour's Lost, I, 1:84

SIR ANDREW. I would I had bestowed[1] that time in the tongues that I have in fencing, dancing, and bear-baiting. O! had I but followed the arts.
Twelfth Night, I, 3:97
[1] bestowed . . . tongues: spent time learning languages.

EGOTIST

CORIOLANUS. Hear you this Triton[1] of the minnows? mark you
His absolute 'shall'?
Coriolanus, III, 1:89
[1] Triton: sea god.

MENENIUS. He wants nothing of a god but eternity and a heaven to throne in.
Coriolanus, V, 4:25

FALSTAFF. I have a whole school of tongues in this belly of mine, and not a tongue of them all speaks any other word but my name.
II Henry IV, IV, 3:20

ELOPEMENT

LORENZO. She hath directed
How I shall take her from her father's house;

What gold and jewels she is furnish'd with;
What page's suit she hath in readiness.
Merchant of Venice, II, 4:30

LYSANDER. To-morrow night, when
Phoebe[1] doth behold
Her silver visage in the wat'ry glass,
Decking with liquid pearl the bladed grass,
A time that lovers' flights doth still conceal,
Through Athens' gates have we devis'd to
steal.
HERMIA. And in the wood, where often
you[2] and I
Upon faint primrose-beds were wont to lie,
Emptying our bosoms of their counsel
sweet,
There my Lysander and myself shall meet;
And thence from Athens turn away our
eyes,
To seek new friends and stranger com-
panies.
Farewell, sweet playfellow: pray thou for
us;
And good luck grant thee thy Demetrius!
Midsummer Night's Dream, I, 1:209
[1] Phoebe: the moon. [2] you: HELENA.

LUCENTIO. 'T were good, methinks, to
steal our marriage;[1]
Which once perform'd, let all the world say
no,
I'll keep mine own, despite of all the world.
Taming of the Shrew, III, 2:142
[1] marriage: with BIANCA.

ENDURE

JAQUES. What woman in the city do I
name,
When that I say the city-woman bears
The cost of princes on unworthy shoulders!
As You Like It, II, 7:74

MARIA. Folly in fools bears not so strong
a note
As foolery in the wise, when wit doth dote.
Love's Labour's Lost, V, 2:75

PROSPERO. Bear with my weakness; my
old brain is troubled:
Be not disturb'd with my infirmity.
Tempest, IV, 1:159

ENEMY

FLUELLEN. If the enemy is an ass and a
fool and a prating coxcomb, is it meet,
think you, that we should also, look you,
be an ass and a fool and a prating coxcomb?
Henry V, IV, 1:78

K. HENRY [to WOLSEY]. You are not
to be taught[1]
That you have many enemies, that know not
Why they are so, but, like to village curs,
Bark when their fellows do.
Henry VIII, II, 4:157
[1] not . . . taught: do not need to be told.

OCTAVIUS. We are at the stake,
And bay'd about with many enemies;
And some that smile have in their hearts, I
fear,
Millions of mischiefs.
Julius Caesar, IV, 1:48

ANGELO. O cunning enemy! that to catch
a saint,
With saints dost bait thy hook.
Measure for Measure, II, 2:180

BUCKINGHAM. The broken rancour of
your high-swoln hearts,
But lately splinter'd, knit, and join'd together,
Must gently be preserv'd, cherish'd, and
kept.
Richard III, II, 2:116

FLAVIUS. How rarely does it meet with
this time's guise,
When man was wish'd to love his enemies!
Grant I may ever love, and rather woo
Those that would mischief me than those
that do!
Timon of Athens, IV, 3:472

ENGLAND

CLOWN. It was the very day that young
Hamlet was born; he that is mad, and sent
into England.
HAMLET. Ay, marry; why was he sent
into England?
FIRST CLOWN. Why, because he was mad:
he shall recover his wits there; or, if he do
not, 't is no great matter there.
HAMLET. Why?
FIRST CLOWN. 'T will not be seen in him
there; there the men are as mad as he.
Hamlet, V, 1:160

WESTMORELAND. For once the eagle Eng-
land being in prey,
To her unguarded nest the weasel Scot
Comes sneaking and so sucks her princely
eggs;
Playing the mouse in absence of the cat,
To tear and havoc more than she can eat.
Henry V, I, 2:169

CHORUS. O England! model to thy inward
greatness,

Like little body with a mighty heart,
What might'st thou do, that honour would
    thee do,
Were all thy children kind[1] and natural!
            Henry V, II, Introduction: 16
[1] kind and natural: not degenerate and corrupt.

CHARLES. At pleasure we lie near Orleans;
Otherwhiles the famish'd English, like pale
    ghosts,
Faintly besiege us one hour in a month.
    ALENÇON. They want their porridge and
        their fat bull-beeves:
Either they must be dieted like mules
And have their provender tied to their
    mouths,
Or piteous they will look, like drowned
    mice.
            1 Henry VI, I, 2:6

HASTINGS. Why, knows not Montague
    that of itself
England is safe, if true within itself?

            . . . . .

Let us be back'd with God and with the seas
Which he hath given for fence impregna-
    ble.
            III Henry VI, IV, 1:39, 43

AUSTRIA. That white-fac'd shore,
Whose foot spurns back the ocean's roaring
    tides
And coops from other lands her islanders,
Even till that England, hedg'd in with the
    main,
That water-walled bulwark, still secure
And confident from foreign purposes.
            King John, II, 1:23

BASTARD. This England never did, nor
    never shall,
Lie at the proud foot of a conqueror,
But[1] when it first did help to wound itself.
Now these her princes are come home again,
Come the three corners of the world in
    arms,
And we shall shock them. Nought shall
    make us rue,
If England to itself do rest but true.
            King John, V, 7:112
[1] But: except.

GAUNT. This royal throne of kings, this
    sceptred isle,
This earth of majesty, this seat of Mars,
This other Eden, demi-paradise,
This fortress built by Nature for herself
Against infection and the hand of war,
This happy breed of men, this little world,
This precious stone set in the silver sea,
Which serves it in the office of a wall,
Or as a moat defensive to a house,

Against the envy of less happier lands,
This blessed plot, this earth, this realm, this
    England,
This nurse, this teeming womb of royal
    kings,
Fear'd by[1] their breed and famous by their
    birth,
Renowned for their deeds as far from home,
For Christian service and true chivalry,
As is the sepulchre in stubborn Jewry
Of the world's ransom, blessed Mary's son:
This land of such dear souls, this dear, dear
    land,
Dear for her reputation through the world,
Is now leas'd out,[2] I die pronouncing it,
Like to a tenement, or pelting[3] farm:
England, bound in with the triumphant sea,
Whose rocky shore beats back the envious
    siege
Of watery Neptune, is now bound in with
    shame,
With inky blots, and rotten parchment
    bonds:
That England, that was wont to conquer
    others,
Hath made a shameful conquest of itself.
Ah! would the scandal vanish with my life,
How happy then were my ensuing death.
            Richard II, II, 1:40
[1] by: because of. [2] leas'd out: the KING had
pledged government income to France for im-
mediate funds. [3] pelting: paltry.

EQUALITY

IRAS. Royal Egypt! Empress!

            . . . . .

CLEOPATRA. No more, but e'en a woman,
    and commanded
By such poor passion as the maid that milks
And does the meanest chares.[1]
            Antony and Cleopatra, IV, 13:70, 73
[1] chares: chores.

CELIA. Let us sit and mock the good
housewife Fortune from her wheel, that her
gifts may henceforth be bestowed equally.
            As You Like It, I, 2:33

K. HENRY. We few, we happy few, we
    band of brothers;
For he to-day that sheds his blood with me
Shall be my brother; be he ne'er so vile
This day shall gentle his condition.
            Henry V, IV, 3:60

K. RICHARD. I live with bread like you,
    feel want,
Taste grief, need friends: subjected thus,
How can you say to me I am a king?
            Richard II, III, 2:175

ERROR

MESSALA. O hateful error, melancholy's
child!
Why dost thou show to the apt thoughts of
men
The things that are not? O error! soon con-
ceiv'd,
Thou never com'st unto a happy birth,
But kill'st the mother that engender'd thee.
Julius Caesar, V, 3:67

PERICLES. For death remember'd should
be like a mirror,
Who tells us life's but breath, to trust it,
error.
Pericles, I, 1:45

ESCAPE

[KING CLAUDIUS' plot to kill HAMLET by send-
ing him to England is told in the following
sequence.]

Enter SAILORS.
FIRST SAILOR. God bless you, sir.
HORATIO. Let him bless thee too.
SECOND SAILOR. He shall, sir, an 't please
him. There's a letter for you, sir;—it comes
from the ambassador that was bound for
England;—if your name be Horatio, as I
am let to know it is. [*Handing him letter*]
HORATIO. Horatio, when thou shalt have
overlooked this, give these fellows some
means to the king: they have letters for him.
Ere we were two days old at sea, a pirate of
very war-like appointment gave us chase.
Finding ourselves too slow of sail, we put
on a compelled valour, and in the grapple I
boarded them: on the instant they got clear
of our ship, so I alone became their prisoner.
They have dealt with me like thieves of
mercy; but they knew what they did; I am
to do a good turn for them. Let the king
have the letters I have sent: and repair thou
to me with as much haste as thou would'st
fly death. I have words to speak in thine ear
will make thee dumb; yet are they much too
light for the bore of the matter. These good
fellows will bring thee where I am. Rosencrantz and Guildenstern hold their course
for England: of them I have much to tell
thee. Farewell.
Hamlet, IV, 6:6

HAMLET. Sir, in my heart there was a kind
of fighting
That would not let me sleep; methought I
lay
Worse than the mutines in the bilboes.
Rashly,
And prais'd be rashness for it, let us know,

Our indiscretion sometimes serves us well
When our deep plots do fail; and that should
teach us
There 's a divinity that shapes our ends,
Rough-hew them how we will.
HORATIO. That is most certain.
HAMLET. Up from my cabin,
My sea-gown scarf'd about me, in the dark
Grop'd I to find out them, had my desire,
Finger'd their packet, and in fine withdrew
To mine own room again; making so bold,
My fears forgetting manners, to unseal
Their grand commission; where I found,
Horatio,
O royal knavery! an exact command,
Larded with many several sorts of reasons
Importing Denmark's health, and England's
too,
With, ho! such bugs and goblins in my life,
That, on the supervise, no leisure bated,
No, not to stay the grinding of the axe,
My head should be struck off.
Hamlet, V, 2:5

But wilt thou hear me how I did proceed?
HORATIO. I beseech you.
HAMLET. Being thus benetted round with
villanies,—
Ere I could make a prologue to my brains
They had begun the play,—I sat me down,
Devis'd a new commission, wrote it fair;
I once did hold it, as our statists do,
A baseness to write fair, and labour'd much
How to forget that learning; but, sir, now
It did me yeoman's service. Wilt thou know
The effect of what I wrote?
HORATIO. Ay, good my lord.
HAMLET. An earnest conjuration from
the king,
As England was his faithful tributary,
As love between them like the palm should
flourish,
As peace should still her wheaten garland
wear,
And stand a comma 'tween their amities,
And many such-like as's of great charge,
That, on the view and knowing of these
contents,
Without debatement further, more or less,
He should the bearers put to sudden death,
Not shriving-time allow'd.
HORATIO. How was this seal'd!
HAMLET. Why even in that was heaven
ordinant.
I had my father's signet in my purse,
Which was the model of that Danish seal;
Folded the writ up in the form of the other,
Subscrib'd it, gave 't the impression, plac'd
it safely,
The changeling never known. Now, the
next day
Was our sea-fight, and what to this was
sequent

Thou know'st already.

HORATIO. So Guildenstern and Rosen-
crantz go to 't.
HAMLET. Why, man, they did make love
to this employment;
They are not near my conscience; their de-
feat
Does by their own insinuation grow.
'T is dangerous when the baser nature
comes
Between the pass and fell-incensed points
Of mighty opposites.
Hamlet, V, 2:27

HORATIO. It must be shortly known to
him from England
What is the issue of the business there.
HAMLET. It will be short: the interim is
mine;
And a man's life's no more than to say 'One.'
Hamlet, V, 2:71

DROMIO SYRACUSE. As from a bear a man
would run for life,
So fly I from her that would be my wife.
Comedy of Errors, III, 2:158

LAUNCELOT GOBBO. Go to; here 's a simple
line of life: here 's a small trifle of wives:
alas! fifteen wives is nothing: a 'leven widows and nine maids is a simple coming-in
for one man; and then to 'scape drowning
thrice, and to be in peril of my life with the
edge of a feather-bed; here are simple.
'scapes.
Merchant of Venice, II, 2:169

DON PEDRO. Look! here she[1] comes.
BENEDICK. Will your grace command me
any service to the world's end? I will go on
the slightest errand now to the Antipodes
that you can devise to send me on: I will
fetch you a toothpicker now from the furthest inch of Asia; bring you the length of
Prester John's[2] foot; fetch you a hair of the
Great Cham's[3] beard; do you any embassage
to the Pigmies, rather than hold three words'
conference with this harpy.

. . . . .

I cannot endure my Lady Tongue.
Much Ado About Nothing, II, 1:270, 284
[1] she: BEATRICE. [2] Prester John: a fabulous
monarch. [3] Great Cham: Sovereign of Tar-
tary.

CLAUDIO. We had like to have had our
two noses snapped off with two old men
without teeth.
Much Ado About Nothing, V, 1:115

FRANCISCO. Sir, he[1] may live.
I saw him beat the surges under him,

And ride upon their backs: he trod the
water,
Whose enmity he flung aside, and breasted
The surge most swoln that met him: his
bold head
'Bove the contentious waves he kept, and
oar'd
Himself with his good arms in lusty stroke
To the shore, that o'er his[2] wave-worn basis
bow'd,
As stooping to relieve him. I not doubt
He came alive to land.
Tempest, II, 1:114
[1] he: FERDINAND. [2] his: its, the shore's.

EVIL

LUCIANA. Shame hath a bastard fame, well
managed;
Ill deeds are doubled with an evil word.
Comedy of Errors, III, 2:19

QUEEN. Now 't is the spring, and weeds
are shallow-rooted;
Suffer them now and they'll o'ergrow the
garden,
And choke the herbs for want of husbandry.[1]
II Henry VI, III, 1:31
[1] husbandry: cultivation.

K. HENRY. Didst thou never hear
That things ill got had ever bad success?
III Henry VI, II, 2:45

DUKE. Fie, sirrah![1] a bawd, a wicked
bawd![2]
The evil that thou causest to be done,
That is thy means to live. Do thou but think
What 't is to cram a maw[3] or clothe a back
From such a filthy vice: say to thyself,
From their abominable and beastly touches
I drink, I eat, array myself, and live.
Canst thou believe thy living is a life,
So stinkingly depending? Go mend, go
mend.
Measure for Measure, III, 2:20
[1] sirrah: term of address to an inferior. [2] bawd:
procurer for a house of prostitution. [3] maw:
stomach.

CLEON. Thou art like the harpy,
Which, to betray, dost, with thine angel's
face,
Seize with thine eagle's talons.
Pericles, IV, 3:46
[1] harpy: a fabulous evil monster with a woman's head and the body of a bird.

MARINA. Thou hold'st a place,[1] for which
the pained'st fiend
Of hell would not in reputation change;

Thou art the damned door-keeper to every
Coystril[2] that comes inquiring for his Tib;[3]
To the choleric fisting of every rogue
Thy ear is liable; thy food is such
As hath been belch'd on by infected lungs.

BOULT. What would you have me do? go
to the wars, would you? where a man may
serve seven years for the loss of a leg, and
have not money enough in the end to buy
him a wooden one?

MARINA. Do any thing but this thou doest.
Empty
Old receptacles, or common sewers, of filth;
Serve by indenture to the common hang-
man:
Any of these ways are yet better than this;
For what thou professest, a baboon, could
he speak,
Would own a name too dear.
                                    Pericles, IV, 6:173
[1] place: servant to the procurer in a house of
prostitution. [2] Coystril: a low, mean fellow.
[3] Tib: a name for a woman of the lowest class.

'Unruly blasts wait on the tender spring;
Unwholesome weeds take root with pre-
cious flowers;
The adder hisses where the sweet birds sing;
What virtue breeds iniquity devours.'
                                    Rape of Lucrece: 869

ROMEO. O mischief! thou art swift
To enter in the thoughts of desperate men.
                                    Romeo and Juliet, V, 1:35

EXCUSE

PEMBROKE. Oftentimes excusing of a fault
Doth make the fault the worse by the ex-
cuse:
As patches set upon a little breach
Discredit more in hiding of the fault
Than did the fault before it was so patch'd.
                                    King John, IV, 2:30

HOTSPUR. But for these vile guns
He would himself have been a soldier.
                                    I Henry IV, I, 3:63

EDMUND [soliloquy]. This is the excellent foppery of the world, that, when we
are sick in fortune, often the surfeit of our
own behaviour, we make guilty of our disasters the sun, the moon, and the stars; as if
we were villains on necessity, fools by
heavenly compulsion, knaves, thieves and
treachers by spherical[1] predominance,
drunkards, liars and adulterers by an enforced obedience of planetary influence;
and all that we are evil in, by a divine
thrusting on: an admirable evasion of
whoremaster man, to lay his goatish dis-

position to the charge of a star! My father
compounded with my mother under the
dragon's tail,[2] and my nativity was under
ursa major;[3] so that it follows I am rough
and lecherous.[4] Tut! I should have been that
I am had the maidenliest star in the firmament twinkled on my bastardizing.
                                    King Lear, I, 2:127
[1] spherical predominance: power of some
planet. [2] the dragon's tail: a sinister constellation. [3] *ursa major:* the constellation The Great
Bear. [4] lecherous: lustful.

JULIET. The excuse that thou dost make
in this delay
Is longer than the tale thou dost excuse.
                                    Romeo and Juliet, II, 5:33

SIR ANDREW. Methinks sometimes I have
no more wit than a Christian or an ordinary
man has; but I am a great eater of beef, and
I believe that does harm to my wit.
                                    Twelfth Night, I, 3:87

EXPERIENCE

ROSALIND. I had rather have a fool to make
me merry than experience to make me sad;
                                    As You Like It, IV, 1:28

ARMADO. How hast thou purchased this
experience?
MOTH. By my penny of observation.
                                    Love's Labour's Lost, III, 1:27

ANTONIO. Experience is by industry
achiev'd
And perfected by the swift course of time.
                                    Two Gentlemen of Verona, I, 3:22

VALENTINE. His years but young, but his
experience old;
His head unmellow'd, but his judgment ripe.
                                    Two Gentlemen of Verona, II, 4:69

EXTRAVAGANCE

K. HENRY. What piles of wealth hath he
accumulated
To his own portion! and what expense by
the hour
Seems to flow from him! How, i' the name
of thrift,
Does he rake this together?
                                    Henry VIII, III, 2:107

SALISBURY. Therefore, to be possess'd
with double pomp,
To guard a title that was rich before,
To gild refined gold, to paint the lily,
To throw a perfume on the violet,

To smooth the ice, or add another hue
Unto the rainbow, or with taper-light
To seek the beauteous eye of heaven to garnish,
Is wasteful and ridiculous excess.
                                                King John, IV, 2:9

NERISSA. They are as sick that surfeit with too much as they that starve with nothing.
                                                Merchant of Venice, I, 2:6

FLAVIUS. So the gods bless me,
When all our offices have been oppress'd
With riotous feeders, when our vaults have wept
With drunken spilth of wine, when every room
Hath blaz'd with lights and bray'd with minstrelsy,
I have retir'd me to a wakeful couch,
And set mine eyes at flow.
                                                Timon of Athens, II, 2:166

EYE

ABBESS. Hath not else his eye
Stray'd his affection in unlawful love?
A sin prevailing much in youthful men,
Who give their eyes the liberty of gazing.
                                                Comedy of Errors, V, 1:50

IMOGEN. Our very eyes
Are sometimes like our judgments, blind.
                                                Cymbeline, IV, 2:301

BASTARD. Drawn in the flattering table of her eye!
Hang'd in the frowning wrinkle of her brow!
And quarter'd in her heart! he doth espy
Himself love's traitor: this is pity now,
That, hang'd and drawn and quarter'd, there should be
In such a love so vile a lout as he.
                                                King John, II, 1:504

OLD MAN. You cannot see your way.
GLOUCESTER. I have no way, and therefore want no eyes;
I stumbled when I saw.
                                                King Lear, IV, 1:19

PRINCESS. Beauty is bought by judgment of the eye,
Not utter'd by base sale of chapmen's[1] tongues.
                                                Love's Labour's Lost, II, 1:14
[1] chapmen: tradesmen.

KING. So sweet a kiss the golden sun gives not
To those fresh morning drops upon the rose,
As thy eye-beams, when their fresh rays have smote

The night of dew that on my cheeks down flows:
Nor shines the silver moon one half so bright
Through the transparent bosom of the deep,
As doth thy face through tears of mine give light;
Thou shin'st in every tear that I do weep:
                                                Love's Labour's Lost, IV, 3:26

BIRON. For when would you, my lord, or you, or you,
Have found the ground of study's excellence
Without the beauty of a woman's face?
From women's eyes this doctrine I derive:
They are the ground, the books, the academes,
From whence doth spring the true Promethean fire.
                                                . . . . .

For where is any author in the world
Teaches such beauty as a woman's eye?
Learning is but an adjunct to ourself,
And where we are our learning likewise is:
Then when ourselves we see in ladies' eyes,
Do we not likewise see our learning there?
                                                . . . . .

A lover's eyes will gaze an eagle blind;
A lover's ear will hear the lowest sound,
                                                . . . . .

And when love speaks, the voice of all the gods
Make heaven drowsy with the harmony.
Never durst poet touch a pen to write
Until his ink were temper'd with Love's sighs;
O! then his lines would ravish savage ears,
And plant in tyrants mild humility.
From women's eyes this doctrine I derive:
They sparkle still the right Promethean fire;
They are the books, the arts, the academes,
That show, contain, and nourish all the world;
Else none at all in aught proves excellent.
                                                Love's Labour's Lost, IV, 3:299, 312, 334,
                                                                                      344

HELENA [to HERMIA]. Your eyes are lode-stars,[1] and your tongue's sweet air
More tuneable than lark to shepherd's ear,
                                                Midsummer Night's Dream, I, 1:183
[1] lode-stars: to DEMETRIUS.

BEATRICE. I have a good eye, uncle: I can see a church by daylight.
                                                Much Ado About Nothing, II, 1:85

ROMEO. He that is strucken blind cannot forget
The precious treasure of his eyesight lost:
                                                Romeo and Juliet, I, 1:238

ROMEO. Her eyes in heaven
Would through the airy region stream so
   bright
That birds would sing and think it were not
   night.
                    Romeo and Juliet, II, 2:20

If I could write the beauty of your eyes
And in fresh numbers number all your
   graces,
The age to come would say, 'This poet lies;
Such heavenly touches ne'er touch'd earthly
   faces.'
                                  Sonnet 17

Her two blue windows faintly she up-
   heaveth,
Like the fair sun, when in his fresh array
He cheers the morn and all the earth re-
   lieveth:
And as the bright sun glorifies the sky,
So is her face illumin'd with her eye;
                    Venus and Adonis: 482

FACE

MENAS. All men's faces are true, what-
soe'er their hands are.
   ENOBARBUS. But there is never a fair
woman has a true face.
         Antony and Cleopatra, II, 6:102

CLEOPATRA. His[1] face was as the heavens,
   and therein stuck
A sun and moon, which kept their course,
   and lighted
The little O, the earth.
         Antony and Cleopatra, V, 2:79
[1] His: ANTONY's.

FALSTAFF. Do thou amend thy face, and
I'll amend my life: thou art our admiral,
thou bearest the lantern in the poop,[1] but
'tis in the nose of thee: thou art the Knight
of the Burning Lamp.
                    . . . . .

I never see thy face but I think upon hell-
fire and Dives that lived in purple; for there
he is in his robes, burning, burning.
                    1 Henry IV, III, 3:26, 35
[1] poop: stern of a ship.

BOY. Good Bardolph, put thy face between his sheets and do the office of a
warming-pan.
                         Henry V, II, 1:87

QUEEN KATHARINE. Ye have angels' faces,
but heaven knows your hearts.
                      Henry VIII, III, 1:145

FOOL. Thou canst tell why one's nose
stands i' the middle on 's face?
   LEAR. No.
   FOOL. Why, to keep one's eyes of either
side 's nose, that what a man cannot smell
out, he may spy into.
                      King Lear, I, 5:19

BIRON. Vouchsafe to show the sunshine
   of your face,
That we, like savages, may worship it.
         Love's Labour's Lost, V, 2:201

DUNCAN. There 's no art
To find the mind's construction in the face:
He was a gentleman on whom I built
An absolute trust.
                      Macbeth, I, 4:11

LADY MACBETH. Your face, my thane, is as
   a book where men
May read strange matters. To beguile the
   time,
Look like the time; bear welcome in your
   eye,
Your hand, your tongue: look like the innocent flower,
But be the serpent under 't.
                      Macbeth, I, 5:63

MACBETH. Let your remembrance apply
   to Banquo;
Present him eminence, both with eye and
   tongue:
Unsafe the while, that we
Must lave our honours in these flattering
   streams,
And make our faces vizards[1] to our hearts,
Disguising what they are.
                      Macbeth, III, 2:30
[1] vizards: masks.

OTHELLO. Do but encave yourself,
And mark the fleers,[1] the gibes, and notable
   scorns,
That dwell in every region of his face.
                      Othello, IV, 1:82
[1] fleers: mocks.

Then my digression[1] is so vile, so base,
That it will live engraven in my face.
                    . . . . .

Yea, the illiterate, that know not how
To cipher what is writ in learned books,
Will quote my loathsome trespass in my
   looks.
                    . . . . .

It cannot be, I find,
But [2] such a face should bear a wicked mind:
         Rape of Lucrece: 202, 810, 1539
[1] digression: offence.   [2] But: except that.

FAIRIES

DROMIO S. O, for my beads! I cross me
    for a sinner.
This is the fairy land: O! spite of spites,
We talk with goblins, owls, and elvish
    sprites.
If we obey them not, this will ensue,
They'll suck our breath, or pinch us black
    and blue.
             Comedy of Errors, II, 2:190

FAIRY. Over hill, over dale,
Thorough bush, thorough brier,
Over park, over pale,
Thorough flood, thorough fire,
I do wander every where,
Swifter than the moon's sphere;
And I serve the fairy queen.
        Midsummer Night's Dream, II, 1:2

OBERON [to the sleeping TITANIA]. What
    thou seest when thou dost wake,
Do it for thy true-love take;
Love and languish for his sake:
Be it ounce, or cat, or bear,
Pard, or boar with bristled hair,
In thy eye that shall appear
When thou wak'st, it is thy dear.
Wake when some vile thing is near.
                    Exit.
     Midsummer Night's Dream, II, 2:27

PUCK. What hempen home-spuns have we
    swaggering here,
So near the cradle of the fairy queen?
        Midsummer Night's Dream, III, 1:79

Re-enter PUCK, *and* BOTTOM *with an ass's*
                    head.
    BOTTOM. If I were fair, Thisby, I were
    only thine.
    QUINCE. O monstrous! O strange! we are
    haunted.
Pray, masters! fly, masters! help!
                Exeunt CLOWNS.
    PUCK. I'll follow you, I'll lead you about
a round,
Through bog, through bush, through brake,
    through brier:
Sometime a horse I'll be, sometime a hound,
A hog, a headless bear, sometime a fire;
And neigh, and bark, and grunt, and roar,
    and burn,
Like horse, hound, hog, bear, fire, at every
    turn.
                    Exit.
BOTTOM. Why do they run away? this is
a knavery of them to make me afeard.
             Re-enter SNOUT.
SNOUT. O Bottom, thou art changed!
what do I see on thee?

BOTTOM. What do you see? you see an
asshead of your own, do you?
                Exit SNOUT.
  Midsummer Night's Dream, III, 1:107

              Re-enter QUINCE.
QUINCE. Bless thee, Bottom! bless thee!
thou art translated.
                    Exit.
BOTTOM. I see their knavery: this is to
make an ass of me; to fright me, if they
could. But I will not stir from this place, do
what they can: I will walk up and down
here, and I will sing, that they shall hear I
am not afraid.
The ousel-cock,[1] so black of hue,
With orange-tawny bill,
The throstle with his note so true,
The wren with little quill,—
    TITANIA [awaking]. What angel wakes
    me from my flowery bed?

    . . . . .

Mine ear is much enamour'd of thy note;
So is mine eye enthralled to thy shape;
And thy fair virtue's force, perforce, doth
    move me,
On the first view, to say, to swear, I love
    thee.

    . . . . .

Thou art as wise as thou art beautiful.
    BOTTOM. Not so, neither; but if I had wit
enough to get out of this wood, I have
enough to serve mine own turn.
    TITANIA. Out of this wood do not desire
    to go:
Thou shalt remain here, whether thou wilt
    or no.
I am a spirit of no common rate;
The summer still doth tend upon my state;
And I do love thee: therefore, go with me;
I'll give thee fairies to attend on thee,
And they shall fetch thee jewels from the
    deep,
And sing while thou on pressed flowers dost
    sleep:
  Midsummer Night's Dream, III, 1:121, 141,
                              151

[1] ousel-cock: blackbird.

TITANIA. Come, sit thee down upon this
    flowery bed,
While I thy amiable cheeks do coy,
And stick musk-roses in thy sleek smooth
    head,
And kiss thy fair large ears, my gentle joy.
    BOTTOM. Where's Pease-blossom?
    PEASE-BLOSSOM. Ready.
    BOTTOM. Scratch my head, Pease-blossom.
Where's Mounsieur Cobweb?

    . . . . .

TITANIA. What, wilt thou hear some music, my sweet love?

BOTTOM. I have a reasonable good ear in music: let's have the tongs and the bones.

TITANIA. Or say, sweet love, what thou desir'st to eat.

BOTTOM. Truly, a peck of provender: I could munch your good dry oats. Methinks I have a great desire to a bottle of hay: good hay, sweet hay, hath no fellow.[1]

TITANIA. I have a venturous fairy that shall seek
The squirrel's hoard, and fetch thee new nuts.

BOTTOM. I had rather have a handful or two of dried pease. But, I pray you, let none of your people stir me: I have an exposition of sleep come upon me.

TITANIA. Sleep thou, and I will wind thee in my arms. Fairies, be gone, and be all ways away.
Exeunt FAIRIES.
Midsummer Night's Dream, IV, 1:1, 29
[1] fellow: equal.

OBERON. I will undo
This hateful imperfection of her eyes:
And, gentle Puck, take this transformed scalp
From off the head of this Athenian swain,
That, he awaking when the other do,
May all to Athens back again repair,
And think no more of this night's accidents
But as the fierce vexation of a dream.
But first I will release the fairy queen.
Be as thou wast wont to be;
See as thou wast wont to see:
Dian's bud o'er Cupid's flower
Hath such force and blessed power.
Now, my Titania; wake you, my sweet queen.

TITANIA. My Oberon! what visions have I seen!
Methought I was enamour'd of an ass.
Midsummer Night's Dream, IV, 1:65

BOTTOM. The eye of man hath not heard, the ear of man hath not seen, man's hand is not able to taste, his tongue to conceive, nor his heart to report, what my dream was. I will get Peter Quince to write a ballad of this dream.
Midsummer Night's Dream, IV, 1:215

PUCK. Fairy king, attend, and mark;
I do hear the morning lark.

OBERON. Then, my queen, in silence sad,
Trip we after the night's shade;
We the globe can compass soon,
Swifter than the wandering moon.
Midsummer Night's Dream, IV, 1:97

ARIEL. Come unto these yellow sands,
And then take hands:

Court'sied when you have and kiss'd,—
The wild waves whist,—
Foot it featly here and there;
And, sweet sprites, the burthen bear.
Hark! Hark!
Burthen. Bow, wow.
The watch-dogs bark:
Burthen. Bow, wow,
Hark, hark! I hear
The strain of strutting chanticleer
Cry, Cock-a-diddle-dow.
Tempest, I, 2:376

ARIEL. Where the bee sucks, there suck I:
In a cowslip's bell I lie;
There I couch when owls do cry.
On the bat's back I do fly
After summer merrily.
Merrily, merrily shall I live now
Under the blossom that hangs on the bough.

. . . . .

I drink the air before me, and return
Or e'er your pulse twice beat.
Tempest, V, 1:88, 102

FAITH

HELENA. But most it is presumption in us when
The help of heaven we count the act of men.
All's Well That Ends Well, II, 1:154

CORIOLANUS. Now, by the jealous queen of heaven, that kiss
I carried from thee, dear, and my true lip
Hath virgin'd it e'er since.
Coriolanus, V, 3:46

K. HENRY. O! where is faith? O! where is loyalty?
If it be banish'd from the frosty head,
Where shall it find a harbour in the earth?
II Henry VI, V, 1:166

BRUTUS. There are no tricks in plain and simple faith;
But hollow men, like horses hot at hand,
Make gallant show and promise of their mettle;
But when they should endure the bloody spur,
They fall their crests, and, like deceitful jades,
Sink in the trial.
Julius Caesar, IV, 2:22

BEATRICE. He wears his faith but as the fashion of his hat; it ever changes with the next block.[1]
Much Ado About Nothing, I, 1:76
[1] block: model on which hats are shaped.

PERICLES. I'll take thy word for faith, not ask thine oath;
Who shuns not to break one will sure crack both.

Pericles, I, 2:120

FLORIZEL. My desires
Run not before mine honour, nor my lusts
Burn hotter than my faith.

Winter's Tale, IV, 4:35

FALSE

HAMLET. As false as dicers' oaths.

Hamlet, III, 4:45

PERICLES. Falseness cannot come from thee, for thou look'st
Modest as justice, and thou seem'st a palace
For the crown'd truth to dwell in.

Pericles, V, 1:121

CRESSIDA. If I be false, or swerve a hair from truth,
When time is old and hath forgot itself,
When waterdrops have worn the stones of Troy,
And blind oblivion swallow'd cities up,
And mighty states characterless are grated
To dusty nothing, yet let memory,
From false to false, among false maids in love,
Upbraid my falsehood! when they've said 'as false
As air, as water, wind, or sandy earth,
As fox to lamb, as wolf to heifer's calf,
Pard[1] to the hind,[2] or stepdame to her son,'
Yea, let them say, to stick the heart of falsehood,
'As false as Cressid.'

Troilus and Cressida, III, 2:191
[1] Pard: leopard.   [2] hind: female deer.

THERSITES. That same Diomed's a false-hearted rogue, a most unjust knave; I will no more trust him when he leers than I will a serpent when he hisses. He will spend his mouth, and promise, like Brabbler[1] the hound; but when he performs, astronomers foretell it.

Troilus and Cressida, V, 1:95
[1] Brabbler: a hound that barks without seeing the game.

TROILUS. O Cressid! O false Cressid! false, false, false!
Let all untruths stand by thy stained name,
And they'll seem glorious.

Troilus and Cressida, V, 2:177

LEONTES. Women say so,
That will say any thing: but were they false

As o'er-dyed blacks, as wind, as waters, false
As dice are to be wish'd by one that fixes
No bourn[1] 'twixt his and mine.

Winter's Tale, I, 2:130
[1] bourn: boundary, limit.

FAME

BRUTUS. Fame, at the which he aims,
In whom already he's well grac'd, can not
Better be held nor more attain'd than by
A place below the first; for what miscarries
Shall be the general's fault, though he perform
To the utmost of a man.

Coriolanus, I, 1:267

JOAN OF ARC. Glory is like a circle in the water,
Which never ceaseth to enlarge itself
Till by broad spreading it disperse to nought.

I Henry VI, I, 2:133

WOLSEY. And, when I am forgotten, as I shall be,
And sleep in dull cold marble, where no mention
Of me more must be heard of, say, I taught thee,
Say, Wolsey, that once trod the ways of glory,
And sounded all the depths and shoals of honour,
Found thee a way, out of his wreck, to rise in;
A sure and safe one, though thy master miss'd it.
Mark but my fall, and that that ruin'd me.

Henry VIII, III, 2:432

KING. Let fame, that all hunt after in their lives,
Live register'd upon our brazen tombs,
And then grace us in the disgrace of death;
When, spite of cormorant devouring Time,
The endeavour of this present breath may buy
That honour which shall bate his scythe's keen edge,
And make us heirs of all eternity.

Love's Labour's Lost, I, 1:1

BENEDICK. If a man do not erect in this age his own tomb ere he dies, he shall live no longer in monument than the bell rings and the widow weeps.

Much Ado About Nothing, V, 2:79

OTHELLO. But, alas! to make me
A fixed figure for the time of scorn
To point his slow unmoving finger at.

Othello, IV, 2:53

The painful warrior famoused[1] for fight,
After a thousand victories once foil'd,
Is from the book of honour razed quite,
And all the rest forgot for which he toil'd.
                                    Sonnet 25
[1] famoused: renowned.

ALL. He lives in fame that died in virtue's
    cause.
                    Titus Andronicus, I, 1:390

FAREWELL

HELENA. I will be gone;
My being here it is that holds thee hence:[1]
Shall I stay here to do 't? no, no, although
The air of paradise did fan the house,
And angels offic'd all: I will be gone.
            All's Well That Ends Well, III, 2:125
[1] holds . . . hence: keeps BERTRAM away.

IMOGEN. O!
Dissembling courtesy. How fine this tyrant[1]
Can tickle where she wounds! My dearest
    husband,
I something fear my father's wrath; but
    nothing,
Always reserv'd my holy duty, what
His rage can do on me. You must be gone;
And I shall here abide the hourly shot
Of angry eyes, not comforted to live,
But that there is this jewel[2] in the world
That I may see again.
                        Cymbeline, I, 1:84

PISANIO. No madam; for so long
As he could make me with this eye or ear
Distinguish him from others, he did keep
The deck, with glove, or hat, or handker-
    chief,
Still waving, as the fits and stirs of 's mind
Could best express how slow his soul sail'd
    on,
How swift his ship.
                        Cymbeline, I, 3:8

ARVIRAGUS. With fairest flowers
Whilst summer lasts and I live here, Fidele,[1]
I'll sweeten thy sad grave; thou shalt not
    lack
The flower that's like thy face, pale prim-
    rose, nor
The azur'd hare-bell, like thy veins, no, nor
The leaf of eglantine, whom not to slander,
Outsweeten'd not thy breath.
                        Cymbeline, IV, 2:218
[1] Fidele: the name given IMOGEN, disguised in
male attire.

POLONIUS. My honourable lord, I will
most humbly take my leave of you.
HAMLET. You cannot, sir, take from me
anything that I will more willingly part
withal; except my life, except my life, except my life.

POLONIUS. Fare you well, my lord.
HAMLET. These tedious old fools!
                        Hamlet, II, 2:217
[1] withal: with.

MORTIMER. These eyes, like lamps whose
    wasting oil is spent,
Wax dim, as drawing to their exigent.[1]

                · · · · ·

Just death, kind umpire of men's miseries,
With sweet enlargement doth dismiss me
    hence.
                        I Henry VI, II, 5:8, 29
[1] exigent: end.

WOLSEY. Farewell! a long farewell, to all
    my greatness!
This is the state of man: to-day he puts
    forth
The tender leaves of hopes; to-morrow
    blossoms,
And bears his blushing honours thick upon
    him;
The third day comes a frost, a killing frost;
And, when he thinks, good easy man, full
    surely
His greatness is a-ripening, nips his root,
And then he falls, as I do. I have ventur'd,
Like little wanton boys that swim on blad-
    ders,
This many summers in a sea of glory,
But far beyond my depth: my high-blown
    pride
At length broke under me, and now has
    left me,
Weary and old with service, to the mercy
Of a rude stream, that must for ever hide
    me.
Vain pomp and glory of this world, I hate
    ye:
I feel my heart new open'd. O! how
    wretched
Is that poor man that hangs on princes'
    favours,
There is, betwixt that smile we would as-
    pire to,
That sweet aspect of princes, and their ruin,
More pangs and fears than wars or women
    have;
And when he falls, he falls like Lucifer,[1]
Never to hope again.
                        Henry VIII, III, 2:351
[1] Lucifer: a revolting angel hurled from heaven.

GRIFFITH. To whom he[1] gave these words:
'O! father abbot;
An old man, broken with the storms of
    state,
Is come to lay his weary bones among ye;
Give him a little earth for charity.'
                        Henry VIII, IV, 2:20
[1] he: WOLSEY.

BRUTUS. For ever, and for ever, farewell,
  Cassius!
If we do meet again, why, we shall smile;
If not, why then, this parting was well made.
  CASSIUS. For ever, and for ever, farewell,
  Brutus!
If we do meet again, we'll smile indeed;
If not, 't is true this parting was well made.
  BRUTUS. Why then, lead on. O! that a
  man might know
The end of this day's business ere it come;
But it sufficeth that the day will end,
And then the end is known. Come, ho!
                                    Julius Caesar, V, 1:117

LEAR. I prithee, daughter, do not make
  me mad:
I will not trouble thee, my child; farewell.
We'll no more meet, no more see one an-
  other;
But yet thou art my flesh, my blood, my
  daughter;
Or rather a disease that's in my flesh,
Which I must needs call mine: thou art a
  boil,
A plague-sore, an embossed[1] carbuncle . . .
I'll not chide thee;
Let shame come when it will, I do not call
  it:
I do not bid the thunder-bearer shoot,
Nor tell tales of thee to high-judging Jove.
Mend when thou canst; be better at thy
  leisure:
I can be patient; I can stay with Regan,
I and my hundred knights.
                                    King Lear, II, 4:221
[1] embossed: swollen.

CLAUDIO. O Hero! what a Hero hadst
  thou been,
If half thy outward graces had been placed
About thy thoughts and counsels of thy
  heart.
But fare thee well, most foul, most fair!
  farewell,
Thou pure impiety, and impious purity!
For thee I'll lock up all the gates of love,
And on my eyelids shall conjecture hang,
To turn all beauty into thoughts of harm,
And never shall it more be gracious.
                                    Much Ado About Nothing, IV, 1:101

OTHELLO. Farewell the tranquil mind;
  farewell content!
Farewell the plumed troop and the big wars
That make ambition virtue! O, farewell!
Farewell the neighing steed, and the shrill
  trump,
The spirit-stirring drum, the ear-piercing
  fife,
The royal banner, and all quality,
Pride, pomp, and circumstance of glorious
  war!

And, O you mortal engines, whose rude
  throats
The immortal Jove's dread clamours counterfeit,
Farewell! Othello's occupation's gone!
                                    Othello, III, 3:347

FASCINATION

ENOBARBUS. Other women cloy
The appetites they feed, but she makes hun-
  gry
Where most she satisfies; for vilest things
Become themselves in her, that the holy
  priests
Bless her when she is riggish.[1]
                                    Antony and Cleopatra, II, 2:241
[1] she is riggish: CLEOPATRA is unchaste.

DEMETRIUS. O Helen! goddess, nymph,
  perfect, divine!
To what, my love, shall I compare thine
  eyne?[1]
Crystal is muddy. O! how ripe in show
Thy lips, those kissing cherries, tempting
  grow;
That pure congealed white, high Taurus'[2]
  snow,
Fann'd with the eastern wind, turns to a
  crow
When thou hold'st up thy hand. O! let me
  kiss
This princess of pure white, this seal of
  bliss.
                                    Midsummer Night's Dream, III, 2:137
[1] eyne: eyes.   [2] Taurus: mountains in Asia.

My love is as a fever, longing still
For that which longer nurseth the disease;
Feeding on that which doth preserve the ill,
The uncertain sickly appetite to please.
My reason, the physician to my love,
Angry that his prescriptions are not kept,
Hath left me, and I desperate now approve
Desire is death, which physic did except.
Past cure I am, now reason is past care,
And frantic-mad with evermore unrest;
My thoughts and my discourse as madmen's
  are,
At random from the truth, vainly express'd;
For I have sworn thee fair and thought thee
  bright,
Who art as black as hell, as dark as night.
                                    Sonnet 147

LUCENTIO. Tranio, I saw her[1] coral lips to
  move,
And with her breath she did perfume the
  air;
Sacred and sweet was all I saw in her.
                                    Taming of the Shrew, I, 1:179
[1] her: BIANCA's.

FASHION

BIRON. A man in all the world's new fashion planted,
That hath a mint of phrases in his brain.
Love's Labour's Lost, I, 1:165

BORACHIO. Thou knowest that the fashion of a doublet, or a hat, or a cloak, is nothing to a man.
CONRADE. Yes, it is apparel.
BORACHIO. I mean, the fashion.
CONRADE. Yes, the fashion is the fashion.
BORACHIO. Tush! I may as well say the fool's the fool.
Much Ado About Nothing, III, 3:125

BORACHIO. Seest thou not, I say, what a deformed thief this fashion is? how giddily a'[1] turns about all the hot bloods between fourteen and five-and-thirty?

. . . . .

CONRADE. All this I see, and I see the fashion wears out more apparel than the man.
Much Ado About Nothing, III, 3:139, 151
[1] a': he.

MERCUTIO. Strange flies, these fashion-mongers, these *pardonnez-mois*, who stand so much on the new form that they cannot sit at ease on the old bench? O! their *bons*, their *bons*.
Romeo and Juliet, II, 4:34

BIANCO. Old fashions please me best; I am not so nice[1]
To change true rules for odd inventions.
Taming of the Shrew, III, 1:80
[1] nice: fastidious.

FAT

ANTIPHOLUS SYRACUSE. How dost thou mean a fat marriage?
DROMIO SYRACUSE. Marry,[1] sir, she's the kitchenwench, and all grease; and I know not what use to put her to but to make a lamp of her and run from her by her own light. I warrant her rags and the tallow in them will burn a Poland winter: if she lives till doomsday, she'll burn a week longer than the whole world.
Comedy of Errors, III, 2:96
[1] Marry: indeed; originally an oath, "by Mary."

PRINCE. Falstaff sweats to death,
And lards the lean earth as he walks along.
I Henry IV, II, 2:115

PRINCE. How long is't ago, Jack, since thou sawest thine own knee?

FALSTAFF. My own knee! when I was about thy years, Hal, I was not an eagle's talon in the waist; I could have crept into any alderman's thumb-ring.
I Henry IV, II, 4:360

FATE

HAMLET. My fate cries out,
And makes each petty artery in this body
As hardy as the Nemean lion's nerve.
Hamlet, I, 4:81

K. HENRY. O God! that one might read the book of fate,
And see the revolution of the times
Make mountains level, and the continent
Weary of solid firmness, melt itself
Into the sea! and, other times, to see
The beachy girdle of the ocean
Too wide for Neptune's hips; how chances mock,
And changes fill the cup of alteration
With divers liquors! O! if this were seen,
The happiest youth, viewing his progress through,
What perils past, what crosses to ensue,
Would shut the book, and sit him down and die.
II Henry IV, III, 1:45

K. EDWARD. What fates impose, that men must needs abide:
It boots[1] not to resist both wind and tide.
III Henry VI, IV, 3:58
[1] boots: avails.

WARWICK. For who liv'd king but I could dig his grave?
And who durst smile when Warwick bent his brow?
Lo! now my glory smear'd in dust and blood;
My parks, my walks, my manors that I had,
Even now forsake me; and of all my lands
Is nothing left me but my body's length.
Why, what is pomp, rule, reign, but earth and dust?
And, live we how we can, yet die we must.
III Henry VI, V, 2:21

CASSIUS. Men at some time are masters of their fates:
The fault, dear Brutus, is not in our stars,
But in ourselves, that we are underlings.
Julius Caesar I, 2:139

SERGEANT. As whence the sun 'gins his reflection
Shipwrecking storms and direful thunders break,

So from that spring whence comfort seem'd
  to come
Discomfort swells.
                              Macbeth, I, 2:25

DONALBAIN. What should be spoken
Here, where our fate, hid in an auger-hole,
May rush and seize us? Let's away.
                             Macbeth, II, 3:127

MACBETH. Come fate into the list,
And champion[1] me to the utterance!
                              Macbeth, III, 1:71
[1] champion . . . utterance: fight to the finish.

LEONATO. O Fate! take not away thy
  heavy hand:
Death is the fairest cover for her shame
That may be wish'd for.
        Much Ado About Nothing, IV, 1:116

FATHER

ROSALIND. What talk we of fathers, when
there is such a man as Orlando?
                        As You Like It, III, 4:41

IMOGEN. Ere I could
Give him[1] that parting kiss which I had set
Betwixt two charming words, comes in my
  father,
And like the tyrannous breathing of the
  north
Shakes all our buds from growing.
                            Cymbeline, I, 3:33
[1] him: POSTHUMUS, her husband.

KING. 'T is sweet and commendable in
  your nature, Hamlet,
To give these mourning duties to your fa-
  ther:
But, you must know, your father lost a fa-
  ther;
That father lost, lost his . . . but to per-
  sever;
In obstinate condolement is a course
Of impious stubbornness; 't is unmanly
  grief;
It shows a will most incorrect to heaven.
                              Hamlet, I, 2:88

QUEEN. Hamlet, thou hast thy father[1]
  much offended.
HAMLET. Mother, you have my father[2]
  much offended.
QUEEN. Come, come, you answer with an
  idle tongue.
HAMLET. Go, go, you question with a
  wicked tongue.
                             Hamlet, III, 4:9
[1] father: the king. [2] father: HAMLET's dead
father.

KING. Laertes, was your father dear to
  you?
Or are you like the painting of a sorrow,
A face without a heart?
                            Hamlet, IV, 7:108

K. HENRY. Why then, be sad;
But entertain no more of it, good brothers,
Than a joint burden laid upon us all.
For me, by heaven, I bid you be assur'd,
I'll be your father and your brother too;
Let me but bear your love, I'll bear your
  cares:
                          II Henry IV, V, 2:54

RICHARD. As doth a lion in a herd of neat;[1]
Or as a bear, encompass'd round with dogs,
Who having pinch'd a few and made them
  cry,
The rest stand all aloof and bark at him.
So far'd our father with his enemies;
So fled his enemies my war-like father:
Methinks 't is prize enough to be his son.
                           III Henry VI, II, 1:14
[1] neat: cattle.

K. EDWARD.[1] Why, 't is a happy thing
To be the father unto many sons.
Answer no more, for thou shalt be my
  queen.
                        III Henry VI, III, 2:104
[1] To LADY GREY.

FOOL. Fathers that wear rags
Do make their children blind,
But fathers that bear bags
Shall see their children kind.
                           King Lear, II, 4:48

LAUNCELOT GOBBO. O heavens, this is my
true-begotten father.
                     Merchant of Venice, II, 2:36

LAUNCELOT. It is a wise father that knows
his own child.
                     Merchant of Venice, II, 2:80

THESEUS. What say you, Hermia? be ad-
  vis'd, fair maid.
To you your father should be as a god;
One that compos'd your beauties, yea, and
  one
To whom you are but as a form in wax
By him imprinted, and within his power
To leave the figure or disfigure it.
                 Midsummer Night's Dream, I, 1:46

BOLINGBROKE. O loyal father[1] of a treacherous son![2]
Thou sheer, immaculate, and silver fountain,
From whence this stream through muddy
  passages
Hath held his[3] current and defil'd himself!

Thy overflow of good converts to bad,
And thy abundant goodness shall excuse
This deadly blot in thy digressing son.
Richard II, V, 2:60

[1] father: the Black Prince. [2] son: KING RICHARD II. [3] his: its.

ARIEL [singing]. Full fathom five thy father lies;
Of his bones are coral made;
Those are pearls that were his eyes:
Nothing of him that doth fade
But doth suffer a sea-change
Into something rich and strange.
Sea-nymphs hourly ring his knell:
Burthen. Ding-dong.
Hark! now I hear them,—ding-dong, bell.
 FERDINAND. The ditty does remember
 my drown'd father.
This is no mortal[1] business, nor no sound
That the earth owes.[2]
Tempest, I, 2:390

[1] mortal: human. [2] owes: owns.

FAULT

AGRIPPA [about ANTONY]. A rarer spirit never
Did steer humanity; but you, gods, will give us
Some faults to make us men.
Antony and Cleopatra, V, 1:31

FALSTAFF. If sack[1] and sugar be a fault,
God help the wicked!
I Henry IV, II, 4:517

[1] sack: a Spanish wine.

MOTH. If she be made of white and red,
Her faults will ne'er be known,
For blushing cheeks by faults are bred,
And fears by pale white shown:
Then if she fear, or be to blame,
By this you shall not know,
For still her cheeks possess the same
Which native she doth owe.[1]
Love's Labour's Lost, I, 2:104

[1] owe: own.

DUKE. Shame to him whose cruel striking
Kills for faults of his own liking!
Measure for Measure, III, 2:281

MARIANA. They say, best men are moulded out of faults,
And, for the most, become much more the better
For being a little bad.
Measure for Measure, V, 1:444

MISTRESS QUICKLY. His worst fault is, that he is given to prayer; he is something peevish that way, but nobody but has his fault; but let that pass.
Merry Wives of Windsor, I, 4:13

ANNE. O! what a world of vile ill-favour'd[1] faults
Looks handsome in three hundred pounds a year.
Merry Wives of Windsor, III, 4:32

[1] ill-favour'd: ugly looking.

LUCULLUS. Every man has his fault, and honesty is his.
Timon of Athens, III, 1:29

TIMON. Wilt thou whip thine own faults in other men?
Timon of Athens, V, 1:40

OLIVIA. There's something in me that reproves my fault,
But such a headstrong potent fault it is
That it but mocks reproof.
Twelfth Night, III, 4:223

FAVOUR

SECOND LORD. You do not know him, my lord, as we do: certain it is that he will steal himself into a man's favour, and for a week escape a great deal of discoveries.
All's Well That Ends Well, III, 6:99

DUKE SENIOR. I do remember in this shepherd boy
Some lively touches of my daughter's favour.[1]
As You Like It, V, 4:27

[1] favour: countenance.

MARCIUS [later CORIOLANUS]. He that depends
Upon your favours swims with fins of lead,
And hews down oaks with rushes.
Coriolanus, I, 1:184

LADY MACBETH. Only look up clear;
To alter favour[1] ever is to fear.
Leave all the rest to me.
Macbeth, I, 5:72

[1] A change of countenance will show your fear.

PRINCESS. Hold, Rosaline, this favour[1] thou shalt wear,
And then the king will court thee for his dear.
Love's Labour's Lost, V, 2:130

[1] favour: gift or emblem of distinction.

DESDEMONA. My lord is not my lord; nor should I know him,
Were he in favour[1] as in humour alter'd.
Othello, III, 4:125

[1] favour: countenance.

FEAR

GUIDERIUS [singing funeral dirge]. Fear
no more the heat o' the sun,
Nor the furious winter's rages;
Thou thy worldly task hast done,
Home art gone, and ta'en thy wages:
Golden lads and girls all must,
As chimney-sweepers, come to dust.
ARVIRAGUS. Fear no more the frown o' the
great,
Thou art past the tyrant's stroke;
Care no more to clothe and eat;
To thee the reed is as the oak:
The sceptre, learning, physic, must
All follow this, and come to dust.
GUIDERIUS. Fear no more the lightning-
flash,
ARVIRAGUS. Nor the all-dreaded thunder-
stone;
GUIDERIUS. Fear not slander, censure
rash;
ARVIRAGUS. Thou hast finish'd joy and
moan:
BOTH. All lovers young, all lovers must
consign to thee, and come to dust.
GUIDERIUS. No exorciser harm thee!
ARVIRAGUS. Nor no witchcraft charm
thee!
GUIDERIUS. Ghost unlaid forbear thee!
ARVIRAGUS. Nothing ill come near thee!
BOTH. Quiet consummation have;
And renowned be thy grave!
Cymbeline, IV, 2:258

HORATIO. Thrice he[1] walk'd
By their oppress'd and fear-surprised eyes,
Within his truncheon's length; whilst they,
distill'd
Almost to jelly with the act of fear,
Stand dumb and speak not to him.
Hamlet, I, 2:201
[1] he: the ghost of HAMLET's father.

KING. For we will fetters put upon this
fear,
Which now goes too free-footed.
Hamlet, III, 3:25

NORTHUMBERLAND. He that but fears the
thing he would not know
Hath by instinct knowledge from others'
eyes
That what he fear'd is chanced.
II Henry IV, I, 1:85

K. HENRY. The blood weeps from my
heart when I do shape
In forms imaginary the unguided days
And rotten times that you shall look upon
When I am sleeping with my ancestors.
II Henry IV, IV, 4:58

JOAN. Of all base passions, fear is most
accurs'd.
I Henry VI, V, 2:18

YORK. Let pale-fac'd fear keep with the
mean-born man,
And find no harbour in a royal heart.
II Henry VI, III, 1:335

SUFFOLK. True nobility is exempt from
fear:
More can I bear than you dare execute.
II Henry VI, IV, 1:129

BASTARD. But as I travell'd hither through
the land,
I find the people strangely fantasied,
Possess'd with rumours, full of idle dreams,
Not knowing what they fear, but full of
fear.
King John, IV, 2:143

MACBETH. Present fears
Are less than horrible imaginings.
Macbeth, I, 3:137

LADY MACBETH [soliloquy]. Thou 'dst
have, great Glamis,[1]
That which cries 'Thus thou must do, if
thou have it';
And that which rather thou dost fear to do
Than wishest should be undone.
Macbeth, I, 5:23
[1] Glamis is one of MACBETH's titles.

MACBETH [soliloquy]. To be thus is noth-
ing,
But to be safely thus. Our fears in Banquo
Stick deep, and in his royalty of nature
Reigns that which would[1] be fear'd: 't is
much he dares,
And, to that dauntless temper of his mind,
He hath a wisdom that doth guide his valour
To act in safety. There is none but he
Whose being I do fear; and under him
My genius is rebuk'd, as it is said
Mark Antony's was by Caesar. He chid the
sisters
When first they put the name of king upon
me,
And bade them speak to him; then, prophet-
like,
They hail'd him father to a line of kings.
Upon my head they plac'd a fruitless crown,
And put a barren sceptre in my gripe,
Thence to be wrench'd with an unlineal
hand,
No son of mine succeeding. If 't be so,
For Banquo's issue have I fil'd[2] my mind;
For them the gracious Duncan have I mur-
der'd;
Put rancours in the vessel of my peace
Only for them; and mine eternal jewel

Given to the common enemy of man,
To make them kings, the seed of Banquo
    kings!
Rather than so, come fate into the list,
And champion[3] me to the utterance![4]
                        Macbeth, III, 1:48
[1] would: should. [2] fil'd: defiled. [3] champion
me: fight with me. [4] To the utterance: to the
death; a French phrase.

MACBETH. But let the frame of things dis-
    joint, both the worlds suffer,
Ere we will eat our meal in fear, and sleep
In the affliction of these terrible dreams
That shake us nightly.
                        Macbeth, III, 2:16

DUKE. That life is better life, past fearing
    death
Than that which lives to fear.
            Measure for Measure, V, 1:402

LYSANDER. How now, my love! Why is
    your cheek so pale?
How chance the roses there do fade so
    fast?
    Midsummer Night's Dream, I, 1:128

PERICLES. 'T is time to fear when tyrants
seem to kiss.
                        Pericles, I, 2:79

The guilt being great, the fear doth still
    exceed;
And extreme fear can neither fight nor fly,
But coward-like with trembling terror die.
              Rape of Lucrece: 229

CARLISLE. To fear the foe, since fear op-
    presseth strength,
Gives in your weakness strength unto your
    foe,
And so your follies fight against yourself.
              Richard II, III, 2:180

K. RICHARD. Give me a bowl of wine:
I have not that alacrity of spirit,
Nor cheer of mind, that I was wont to have.
              Richard III, V, 3:72

JULIET. I have a faint cold fear thrills
    through my veins,
That almost freezes up the heat of life.
          Romeo and Juliet, IV, 3:15

CRESSIDA. Blind fear, that seeing reason
leads, finds safer footing than blind reason
stumbling without fear: to fear the worst
oft cures the worse.
        Troilus and Cressida, III, 2:76

PETRUCHIO. Tush! tush! fear[1] boys with
bugs.[2]
         Taming of the Shrew, I, 2:211
[1] fear: scare. [2] bugs: bugbears.

FELLOW

LAFEU. A snipt-taffeta[1] fellow[2] there,
whose villanous saffron would have made all
the unbaked and doughy youth of a nation
in his colour.
    All's Well That Ends Well, IV, 5:2
[1] taffeta: a lustrous silk. [2] fellow: often, not
always, used in a sense of disfavor.

K. HENRY. These fellows of infinite
tongue, that can rhyme themselves into ladies' favours, they do always reason themselves out again.
               Henry V, V, 2:163

CAESAR. I am constant as the northern star,
Of whose true-fix'd and resting quality
There is no fellow[1] in the firmament.
           Julius Caesar, III, 1:60
[1] fellow: equal.

ANTONY. A barren-spirited fellow; one
    that feeds
On abjects,[1] orts,[2] and imitations.
           Julius Caesar, IV, 1:36
[1] abjects: things thrown away. [2] orts: leavings.

SALARINO. Nature hath fram'd strange fel-
    lows in her time:
Some that will evermore peep through their
    eyes
And laugh like parrots at a bag-piper;
And other of such vinegar aspect
That they'll not show their teeth in way of
    smile,
Though Nestor swear the jest be laughable.
         Merchant of Venice, I, 1:51

CAMILLO. How now, good fellow! Why
shakest thou so? Fear not, man; here 's no
harm intended to thee.
AUTOLYCUS. I am a poor fellow, sir.
CAMILLO. Why, be so still; here 's nobody
will steal that from thee.
          Winter's Tale, IV, 4:640

CLOWN. Give me thy hand: I will swear
to the prince thou art as honest a true fellow
as any is in Bohemia.
          Winter's Tale, V, 2:177

FIEND

K. HENRY. And whatsoever cunning fiend
    it was
That wrought upon thee so preposterously
Hath got the voice[1] in hell for excellence:
All other devils that suggest by treasons
Do botch and bungle up damnation

120

With patches, colours, and with forms, being fetch'd
From glistering semblances of piety.
                        Henry V, II, 2:111
[1] voice: vote.

ALBANY. See thyself, devil!
Proper deformity[1] seems not in the fiend
So horrid as in woman.

. . . . .

Thou changed and self-cover'd thing, for
shame,
Be-monster not thy feature. Were 't my fitness
To let these hands obey my blood,[2]
They are apt enough to dislocate and tear
Thy flesh and bones; howe'er thou art a
fiend,
A woman's shape doth shield thee.
                        King Lear, IV, 2:59, 62
[1] Proper deformity: that appropriate to the
character. [2] hands . . . blood: hands do as
temper prompts.

MACBETH. And be these juggling fiends[1]
no more believ'd,
That palter with us in a double sense;
That keep the word of promise to our ear,
And break it to our hope.
                        Macbeth, V, 8:19
[1] fiends: the witches.

OLIVIA. Well, . . .
A fiend like thee might bear my soul to hell.
                        Twelfth Night, III, 4:236

FIGHTING

ANTONY. I will be treble-sinew'd, hearted,
breath'd,
And fight maliciously; for when mine hours
Were nice and lucky, men did ransom lives
Of me for jests; but now I'll set my teeth
And send to darkness all that stop me.
                Antony and Cleopatra, III, 11:178

ANTONY. I would they'd fight i' the fire
or i' the air;
We 'd fight there too.
                Antony and Cleopatra, IV, 10:3

HAMLET. Why, I will fight with him[1]
upon this theme
Until my eyelids will no longer wag.
    QUEEN. O my son! what theme?
    HAMLET. I lov'd Ophelia: forty thousand
brothers
Could not, with all their quantity of love,
Make up my sum.
                        Hamlet, V, 1:290
[1] him: LAERTES.

MACBETH. I 'll fight till from my bones my
flesh be hack'd.
                        Macbeth, V, 3:32

OXFORD. Every man's conscience is a
thousand men,
To fight against this guilty homicide.
                        Richard III, V, 2:17

TYBALT. What! drawn, and talk of peace;
I hate the word,
As I hate hell, all Montagues, and thee.
Have at thee, coward!
                        Romeo and Juliet, I, 1:77

MERCUTIO. He fights as you sing prick-
song,[1] keeps time, distance, and proportion;
rests me his minim rest, one, two, and the
third in your bosom; the very butcher of a
silk button, a duellist, a duellist; a gentleman
of the very first house, of the first and second cause. Ah! the immortal passado! the
punto reverso! the hay!
                        Romeo and Juliet, II, 4:22
[1] prick-song: song written by note.

FIRE

CLARENCE. A little fire is quickly trodden
out,
Which, being suffer'd, rivers cannot quench.
                        III Henry VI, IV, 8:7

CASSIUS. Those that with haste will make
a mighty fire
Begin it with weak straws.
                        Julius Caesar, I, 3:107

OTHELLO. Wash me in steep-down gulfs of
liquid fire!
O Desdemona! Desdemona! dead!
Oh! oh! oh!
                        Othello, V, 2:280

ARIEL. The fire and cracks
Of sulphurous roaring the most mighty
Neptune
Seem to besiege and make his bold waves
tremble.
                        Tempest, I, 2:203

JULIA. Didst thou but know the inly[1]
touch of love,
Thou would'st as soon go kindle fire with
snow
As seek to quench the fire of love with
words.
                Two Gentlemen of Verona, II, 7:18
[1] inly: heartfelt.

LEONTES. I 'll ha' thee burn'd.
PAULINA. I care not:

It is an heretic that makes the fire,
Not she which burns in 't.
Winter's Tale, II, 3:115

FISH

HAMLET. A man may fish with the worm that hath eat of a king, and eat of the fish that hath fed of that worm.
Hamlet, IV, 3:29

URSULA. The pleasant'st angling is to see
the fish
Cut with her golden oars the silver stream,
And greedily devour the treacherous bait:
Much Ado About Nothing, III, 1:26

THIRD FISHERMAN. I marvel how the fishes live in the sea.
FIRST FISHERMAN. Why, as men do a-land; the great ones eat up the little ones.
Pericles, II, 1:30

SECOND FISHERMAN. Help, master, help! here 's a fish hangs in the net, like a poor man's right in the law.
Pericles, II, 1:122

TRINCULO. What have we here? a man or a fish? Dead or alive? A fish: he smells like a fish; a very ancient and fish-like smell.
Tempest, II, 2:26

FLATTERY

CELIA. That was laid on with a trowel.
As You Like It, I, 2:112

ROSALIND. 'Tis not her glass, but you, that flatters her.
As You Like It, III, 5:54

MENENIUS. His nature is too noble for the
world:
He[1] would not flatter Neptune for his tri-
dent
Or Jove for 's power to thunder. His heart
's his mouth:
What his breast forges, that his tongue must vent;
And, being angry, does forget that ever
He heard the name of death.
Coriolanus, III, 1:255
[1] He: CORIOLANUS.

HAMLET.[1] Why should the poor be flat-
ter'd?
No; let the candied tongue lick absurd
pomp,
And crook the pregnant[2] hinges of the knee
Where thrift[3] may follow fawning.
Hamlet, III, 2:64

[1] To HORATIO. [2] pregnant: favour-currying.
[3] thrift . . . fawning: profit may follow servile cringing.

ROSENCRANTZ. Take you me for a sponge, my lord?
HAMLET. Ay, sir, that soaks up the king's countenance, his rewards, his authorities. But such officers do the king best service in the end: he keeps them, like an ape, in the corner of his jaw; first mouthed, to be last swallowed.
Hamlet, IV, 2:15

FALSTAFF. Thou dost give me flattering busses.[1]
DOLL TEARSHEET. By my troth, I kiss thee with a most constant heart.
FALSTAFF. I am old, I am old.
DOLL TEARSHEET. I love thee better than I love e'er a scurvy young boy of them all.
FALSTAFF. What stuff wilt thou have a kirtle of? I shall receive money o' Thurs-
day.
II Henry IV, II, 4:291
[1] busses: kisses.

K. HENRY. You were ever good at sud-
den commendations,
Bishop of Winchester; but know, I come not
To hear such flattery now, and in my pres-
ence;
They are too thin and bare to hide offences.
To me you cannot reach; you play the span-
iel,
And think with wagging of your tongue to win me.
Henry VIII, V, 3:122

DECIUS. But when I tell him he hates flat-
terers
He says he does, being then most flattered.
Juluis Caesar, II, 1:207

KENT. Such smiling rogues as these,[1]
. . . smooth every passion
That in the natures of their lords rebel;
Being oil to fire, snow to their colder
moods;
Renege,[2] affirm, and turn their halcyon
beaks
With every gale and vary of their masters,
Knowing nought, like dogs, but following.
King Lear, II, 2:79
[1] these: like OSWALD. [2] Renege: deny.

EDGAR. Yet better thus, and known to be
contemn'd,
Than still[1] comtemn'd and flatter'd. To be
worst,
The lowest and most dejected thing of fortune,
Stands still in esperance,[2] lives not in fear:

The lamentable change is from the best;
The worst returns to laughter.
King Lear, IV, 1:1
[1] still: always. [2] Stands . . . esperance: still
has hope.

HELICANUS. They do abuse[1] the king that
flatter him;
For flattery is the bellows blows up sin.
Pericles, I, 2:38
[1] abuse: deceive, as often in Shakespeare.

GOWER. No visor does become black vil-
lany
So well as soft and tender flattery.
Pericles, IV, 4, Prologue: 44

GAUNT. Though Richard my life's coun-
sel would not hear,
My death's sad tale my yet undeaf his ear.
YORK. No; it is stopp'd with other flatter-
ing sounds,
As praises of his state: then there are found
Lascivious metres, to whose venom sound
The open ear of youth doth always listen.
Richard II, II, 1:15

K. RICHARD. He does me double wrong,
That wounds me with the flatteries of his
tongue.
Richard II, III, 2:215

ANNE. But since you teach me how to
flatter you,
Imagine I have said farewell already.
Richard III, II, 2:224

GLOUCESTER.[1] Because I cannot flatter and
speak fair,
Smile in men's faces, smooth, deceive, and
cog,[2]
Duck with French nods and apish courtesy,
I must be held a rancorous enemy.
Cannot a plain man live and think no harm,
But thus his simple truth must be abus'd
By silken, sly, insinuating Jacks?
Richard III, I, 3:47
[1] Later KING RICHARD III. [2] cog: cheat.

POET. His large fortune,
Upon his good and gracious nature hanging,
Subdues and properties[1] to his love and
tendance
All sorts of hearts; yea, from the glass-fac'd[2]
flatterer
To Apemantus, that few things loves better
Than to abhor himself.
Timon of Athens, I, 1:55
[1] properties, etc.: subdues hearts to his love.
[2] glass-fac'd: one who reflects the looks and
thoughts of his patron.

APEMANTUS. He that loves to be flattered
is worthy o' the flatterer.
Timon of Athens, I, 1:232

CLOWN. Marry,[1] sir, they[2] praise me and
make an ass of me; now my foes tell me
plainly I am an ass: so that by my foes, sir,
I profit in the knowledge of myself.
Twelfth Night, V, 1:19
[1] Marry: indeed. [2] they: his friends.

FLESH

HAMLET. O! that this too too solid flesh
would melt,
Thaw and resolve itself into a dew.
Hamlet, I, 2:129

LAERTES. Lay her i' the earth;
And from her fair and unpolluted flesh
May violets spring!
Hamlet, V, 1:262

SALARINO. Why, I am sure, if he forfeit,
thou will not take his flesh: what 's that
good for?
SHYLOCK. To bait fish withal: if it will
feed nothing else, it will feed my revenge.
Merchant of Venice, II, 1:53

DOGBERRY. I am a wise fellow; and, which
is more, an officer; and, which is more, a
householder; and, which is more, as pretty
a piece of flesh as any in Messina.
Much Ado About Nothing, IV, 2:83

FLIGHT

MORTON. So did our men, heavy[1] in Hot-
spur's loss,
Lend to this weight such lightness with their
fear
That arrows fled not swifter toward their
aim
Than did our soldiers, aiming at their safety,
Fly from the field.
II Henry IV, I, 1:121
[1] heavy: discouraged.

PUCK. I go, I go; look how I go;
Swifter than arrow from the Tartar's bow.
Midsummer Night's Dream, III, 2:100

HASTINGS. To fly the boar[1] before the
boar pursues,
Were[2] to incense the boar to follow us.
Richard III, III, 2:28
[1] boar: GLOUCESTER. [2] Were: would be.

FLIRTATION

LUCIO. I would not, though 't is my familiar sin
With maids to seem the lapwing[1] and to jest,

Tongue far from heart, play with all vir-
gins so.
Measure for Measure, I, 4:31
[1] lapwing: a bird that deceives by pretended
wounds.

BASSANIO. Sometimes from her eyes
I did receive fair speechless messages.
Merchant of Venice, I, 1:163

IAGO. He hath a person and a smooth dispose
To be suspected, fram'd to make women
false.
Othello, I, 3:403

IAGO. Besides, the knave is handsome,
young, and hath all those requisites in him
that folly and green minds look after; a pestilent complete knave! and the woman hath
found him already.
RODERIGO. I cannot believe that in her; she
's full of most blessed condition.
IAGO. Blessed fig's end! the wine she drinks
is made of grapes.
Othello, II, 1:250

FLOWERS

GUIDERIUS. O sweetest, fairest lily!
My brother wears thee not the one half so
well
As when thou grew'st thyself.
Cymbeline, IV, 2:201

OPHELIA. There's rosemary, that's for remembrance; pray you, love, remember: and
there is pansies, that's for thoughts.
Hamlet, IV, 5:174

OBERON. I know a bank whereon the wild
thyme blows,
Where oxlips and the nodding violet grows,
Quite over-canopied with lush woodbine,
With sweet musk-roses, and with eglantine:
There sleeps Titania some time of the night,
Lull'd in these flowers with dances and de-
light.
Midsummer Night's Dream, II, 1:249

MARINA. No, I will rob Tellus[1] of her
weed,
To strew thy green with flowers; the yel-
lows, blues,
The purple violets, and marigolds,
Shall as a carpet hang upon thy grave,
While summer-days do last.
Pericles, IV, 1:13
[1] Tellus: personification of the earth.

But flowers distill'd, though they with winter meet,

Leese[1] but their show; their substance still
lives sweet.
Sonnet 5
[1] Leese: lost; an old form not used elsewhere
by Shakespeare.

The summer's flower is to the summer
sweet,
Though to itself it only live and die.
Sonnet 94

PERDITA. Reverend sirs,[1]
For you there 's rosemary and rue; these
keep
Seeming and savour all the winter long:
Grace and remembrance be to you both,
And welcome to our shearing!

. . . . .

Here 's flowers for you;
Hot lavender, mints, savory, marjoram;
The marigold, that goes to bed wi' the sun,
And with him rises weeping: these are
flowers
Of middle summer, and I think they are
given
To men of middle age.
Winter's Tale, IV, 4:74, 103
[1] Reverend sirs: POLIXENES and CAMILLO.

PERDITA. Daffodils,
That come before the swallow dares, and
take
The winds of March with beauty; violets
dim,
But sweeter than the lids of Juno's[1] eyes
Or Cytherea's[2] breath; pale primroses,
That die unmarried, ere they can behold
Bright Phoebus[3] in his strength, a malady
Most incident to maids; bold oxlips and
The crown-imperial; lilies of all kinds,
The flower-de-luce being one. O! these I
lack
To make you garlands of.
Winter's Tale, IV, 4:118
[1] Juno: wife of Jupiter, goddess of marriage
and childbirth.   [2] Cytherea: Venus.   [3] Phoebus:
god of the sun.

FOOD

BALTHAZAR. Small cheer[1] and great welcome makes a merry feast.
Comedy of Errors, III, 1:26
[1] cheer: food.

SHALLOW. Some pigeons, Davy, a couple
of short-legged hens, a joint of mutton, and
any pretty little tiny kickshaws, tell William
cook.
II Henry IV, V, 1:27

LAUNCELOT GOBBO. I am famished in his[1] service; you may tell[2] every finger I have with my ribs.

Merchant of Venice, II, 2:112

[1] his: SHYLOCK'S. [2] tell: count.

LORENZO. Fair ladies, you drop manna in the way
Of starved people.

Merchant of Venice, V, 1:294

SPEED. Ay, but hearken, sir: though the chameleon Love can feed on the air, I am one that am nourished by my victuals and would fain have meat.

Two Gentlemen of Verona, II, 1:177

FOOL

CELIA. Though Nature hath given us wit to flout at Fortune, hath not Fortune sent in this fool[1] to cut off the argument?

. . . . .

Peradventure this is not Fortune's work neither, but Nature's; who perceiving our natural wits too dull to reason of such goddesses, hath sent this natural[2] for our whetstone: for always the dulness of the fool is the whetstone of the wits. How now, wit! whither wander you?

As You Like It, I, 2:48, 54

[1] fool: jester; like a few of Shakespeare's fools, TOUCHSTONE is far from a fool in our meaning. [2] natural: idiot, a meaning often found in Shakespeare; here CELIA is playing with words.

JAQUES. A fool, a fool! I met a fool i' the forest,
A motley[1] fool; a miserable world!
As I do live by food, I met a fool;
Who laid him down and bask'd him in the sun,
And rail'd on Lady Fortune in good terms,
In good set terms, and yet a motley fool.

. . . . .

And then he drew a dial from his poke,[2]
And looking on it with lack-lustre eye,
Says very wisely, 'It is ten o'clock:
Thus may we see,' quoth he, 'how the world wags:
'Tis but an hour ago since it was nine,
And after one hour more 't will be eleven;
And so from hour to hour we ripe and ripe,
And then from hour to hour we rot and rot,
And thereby hangs a tale.' When I did hear
The motley fool thus moral on the time,
My lungs began to crow like chanticleer,
That fools should be so deep-contemplative,
And I did laugh sans[3] intermission

An hour by his dial. O noble fool!
A worthy fool! Motley 's the only wear.

As You Like It, II, 7:12, 20

[1] motley: costume of jester. [2] poke: pocket.
[3] sans: without.

JAQUES. O worthy fool! One that hath been a courtier,
And says, if ladies be but young and fair,
They have the gift to know it; and in his brain,
Which is as dry as the remainder biscuit
After a voyage, he hath strange places cramm'd
With observation, the which he vents
In mangled forms. O! that I were a fool.
I am ambitious for a motley[1] coat.

As You Like It, II, 7:36

[1] motley coat: the costume of a jester.

TOUCHSTONE. I do now remember a saying, 'the fool doth think he is wise, but the wise man knows himself to be a fool.'

As You Like It, V, 1:33

JAQUES. There is, sure, another flood toward, and these couples are coming to the ark. Here comes a pair[1] of very strange beasts, which in all tongues are called fools.

As You Like It, V, 4:35

[1] pair: TOUCHSTONE and AUDREY.

GUIDERIUS. This Cloten was a fool, an empty purse,
There was no money in 't. Not Hercules
Could have knock'd out his brains, for he had none.

Cymbeline, IV, 2:113

HAMLET. Where 's your father?
OPHELIA. At home, my lord.
HAMLET. Let the doors be shut upon him, that he may play the fool no where but in 's own house.

Hamlet, III, 1:133

NORTHUMBERLAND. Why, what a wasp-stung and impatient fool
Art thou, to break into this woman's mood,
Tying thine ear to no tongue but thine own!

1 Henry IV, I, 3:236

FOOL.[1] Sirrah, you were best take my coxcomb.[2]
KENT. Why, fool?
FOOL. Why? for taking one's part that's out of favour. Nay, an[3] thou canst not smile as the wind sits, thou 'lt catch cold shortly: there, take my coxcomb.

King Lear, I, 4:109

[1] Fool: jester; by no means a fool in present use of the word. [2] coxcomb: the jester's cap, a symbol of his calling. [3] an: if.

FOOL. Dost thou know the difference, my boy, between a bitter fool and a sweet fool?

LEAR. No, lad; teach me.

FOOL. That lord that counsel'd thee
To give away thy land,
Come place him here by me,
Do thou for him stand:
The sweet and bitter fool
Will presently appear;
The one in motley here
The other found out there.

K. LEAR. Dost thou call me fool, boy?

FOOL. All thy other titles thou hast given away; that thou wast born with.

KENT. This is not altogether fool, my lord.

King Lear, I, 4:151

FOOL. Nuncle,[1] give me an egg, and I 'll give thee two crowns.

K. LEAR. What two crowns shall they be?

FOOL. Why, after I have cut the egg i' the middle and eat up the meat, the two crowns of the egg.

King Lear, I, 4:170

[1] Nuncle: the customary address of a licensed fool to his superior.

MARIA. Folly in fools bears not so strong a note
As foolery in the wise, when wit doth dote.[1]

Love's Labour's Lost, V, 2:75

[1] dote: speak irrationally.

PUCK. Lord, what fools these mortals be!

Midsummer Night's Dream, III, 2:115

GREMIO. Sirrah,[1] young gamester, your father were[2] a fool
To give thee all, and in his waning age
Set foot under thy table. Tut! a toy!
An old Italian fox is not so kind, my boy.

Taming of the Shrew, II, 1:402

[1] Sirrah: address to a servant or to one of an inferior class. [2] were: would be.

TRINCULO. They say there 's but five upon this isle: we are three of them; if the other two be brained like us, the state totters.

Tempest, III, 2:6

OLIVIA. Go to, you 're a dry[1] fool; I 'll no more of you: besides, you grow dishonest.

CLOWN. Two faults, madonna, that drink and good counsel will amend: for give the dry fool drink, then is the fool not dry;[2] bid the dishonest man mend himself: if he mend, he is no longer dishonest.

Twelfth Night, I, 5:45

[1] dry: stupid. [2] dry: thirsty.

CLOWN. She[1] will keep no fool,[2] sir, till she be married; and fools are as like hus-bands as pilchards[3] are to herrings, the husband 's the bigger. I am indeed not her fool, but her corrupter of words.

Twelfth Night, III, 1:37

[1] She: OLIVIA. [2] fool: modern sense. [3] pilchards: fish much like herrings.

CLOWN. Foolery,[1] sir, does walk about the orb[2] like the sun; it shines every where.

Twelfth Night, III, 1:43

[1] Foolery: habitual folly. [2] orb: the earth.

FOP

OSRIC. Sir, here is newly come to court Laertes; believe me, an absolute gentleman, full of most excellent differences, of very soft society and great showing; indeed, to speak feelingly of him, he is the card or calendar of gentry, for you shall find in him the continent of what part a gentleman would see.

Hamlet, V, 2:108

HOTSPUR. When I was dry with rage and extreme toil,
Breathless and faint, leaning upon my sword,
Came there a certain lord, neat, and trimly dress'd,
Fresh as a bridegroom; and his chin, new reap'd,
Show'd like a stubble-land at harvest-home:
He was perfumed like a milliner,
And 'twixt his finger and his thumb he held
A pouncet-box,[1] which ever and anon
He gave his nose and took 't away again;

• ` •   •   •

He made me mad
To see him shine so brisk, and smell so sweet,
And talk so like a waiting-gentlewoman.

I Henry IV, I, 3:31, 53

[1] pouncet-box: box for perfumes.

HOTSPUR. As the soldiers bore dead bodies by,
He call'd them untaught knaves, unmannerly,
To bring a slovenly unhandsome corpse
Betwixt the wind and his nobility.

•   •   •   •   •

And but for these vile guns
He would himself have been a soldier.

I Henry IV, I, 3:42, 63

BIRON. This gallant pins the wenches on his sleeve;
Had he been Adam, he had tempted Eve.
A' can carve too, and lisp: why, this is he

That kiss'd away his hand in courtesy;
This is the ape of form, monsieur the nice.[1]
    Love's Labour's Lost, V, 2:321
[1] monsieur the nice: a fastidious fellow.

NERISSA. What say you then to Falconbridge, the young baron of England?

   . . . . .

PORTIA. He is a proper man's picture, but,
alas! who can converse with a dumb-show?
How oddly he is suited! I think he bought
his doublet in Italy, his round hose in
France, his bonnet in Germany, and his behaviour every where.
    Merchant of Venice, I, 2:71, 77

CRESSIDA. O! he smiles valiantly.
    Troilus and Cressida, I, 2:137

FORGETTING

SILVIUS. How many actions most ridiculous
Hast thou been drawn to by thy fantasy?
 CORIN. Into a thousand that I have forgotten.
    As You Like It, II, 4:30

AMIENS. Thy sting is not so sharp
As friend remember'd not.
    As You Like It, II, 7:186

K. HENRY. How might a prince of my
 great hopes forget
So great indignities you laid upon me?
What! rate, rebuke, and roughly send to
 prison
The immediate heir of England! Was this
 easy?
May this be wash'd in Lethe,[1] and forgotten?
 CHIEF JUSTICE. I then did use the person
 of your father;

   . . . . .

And, as you are a king, speak in your state
What I have done that misbecame my place,
My person, or my liege's sovereignty.
 K. HENRY V. You are right, justice; and
 you weigh this well;
Therefore still bear the balance[2] and the
 sword:
And I do wish your honours may increase
Till you do live to see a son of mine
Offend you and obey you, as I did.
    II Henry IV, V, 2:68, 99
[1] Lethe: the river of forgetfulness in the lower
world. [2] balance . . . sword: symbols of judi-
cial justice.

DUMAINE. I would forget her; but a fever
 she

Reigns in my blood, and will remember'd be.
    Love's Labour's Lost, IV, 3:95

K. RICHARD. Or[1] that I could forget what
 I have been,
Or not remember what I must be now.
    Richard II, III, 3:138
[1] Or . . . or: either . . . or.

BUCKINGHAM. Almost shoulder'd[1] in the
 swallowing gulf
Of dark forgetfulness and deep oblivion.
    Richard III, III, 7:128
[1] shoulder'd: shoved.

AGAMEMNON. What's past and what's to
 come is strew'd with husks
And formless ruin of oblivion;
    Troilus and Cressida, IV, 5:166

FORGIVENESS

KING. I have forgiven and forgotten all,
Though my revenges were high bent upon
 him,
    All's Well That Ends Well, V, 3:9

KING. Forgive me my foul murder?
That cannot be; since I am still possess'd
Of those effects for which I did the murder,
My crown, mine own ambition, and my
 queen.
May one be pardon'd and retain the offence?
    Hamlet, III, 3:52

HAMLET.[1] Let my disclaiming from a
 purpos'd evil
Free me so far in your most generous
 thoughts,
That I have shot mine arrow o'er the house,
And hurt my brother.
    Hamlet, V, 2:252
[1] To LAERTES.

BUCKINGHAM.[1] Sir Thomas Lovell, I as
 free forgive you
As I would be forgiven: I forgive all.
There cannot be those numberless offences
'Gainst me that I cannot take peace with:
 no black envy,[2]
Shall mark my grave.
    Henry VIII, II, 1:82
[1] On his way to execution. [2] envy: hate, as
often in Shakespeare.

K. RICHARD. Deep malice makes too deep
 incision:
Forget, forgive; conclude and be agreed.
Our doctors say this is no month to bleed.
    Richard II, I, 1:155

GLOUCESTER.[1] If thy revengeful heart can-
    not forgive,
Lo! here I lend thee this sharp-pointed
    sword;
Which if thou please to hide in this true
    breast,
And let the soul forth that adoreth thee,
I lay it naked to the deadly stroke,
And humbly beg the death upon my knee.
              Richard III, I, 2:174
[1] Later, KING RICHARD III.

No more be griev'd at that which thou hast
    done:
Roses have thorns, and silver fountains mud;
Clouds and eclipses stain both moon and
    sun,
And loathsome canker lives in sweetest bud.
                  Sonnet 35

CLEOMENES. Do as the heavens have done,
    forget your evil;
With them forgive yourself.
            Winter's Tale, V, 1:5

FORTUNE

POMPEY. Well, I know not
What counts harsh fortune casts upon my
    face,
But in my bosom shall she never come
To make my heart her vassal.
        Antony and Cleopatra, II, 6:54

K. HENRY. Will fortune never come with
    both hands full
But write her fair words still[1] in foulest let-
    ters?
She either gives a stomach and no food;
Such are the poor, in health; or else a feast
And takes away the stomach; such are the
    rich,
That have abundance and enjoy it not.
           II Henry IV, IV, 4:103
[1] still: always.

FLUELLEN. Fortune is painted blind, . . .
and she is painted also with a wheel . . .
which is the moral of it, that she is turning
and inconstant . . . and her foot . . . is
fixed on a spherical stone, which rolls, and
rolls, and rolls.
              Henry V, III, 6:32

OLD LADY. And you,[1] O fate!
A very fresh-fish here, fie, fie upon
This compell'd[2] fortune! have your mouth
    fill'd up
Before you open it.
            Henry VIII, II, 3:85
[1] you: ANNE BULLEN. [2] compell'd: enforced,
unsought.

PANDULPH. No, no; when Fortune means
    to men most good,
She looks upon them with a threatening eye.
            King John, III, 4:119

KENT.[1] Fortune, good night; smile once
more; turn thy wheel.
            King Lear, II, 2:180
[1] Said as he is put into the stocks for defending
KING LEAR.

CORDELIA. We are not the first
Who, with best meaning, have incurr'd the
    worst.
For thee, oppressed king, am I cast down;
Myself could else out-frown false fortune's
    frown.
            King Lear, V, 3:3

RODERIGO. What a full fortune does the
    thick-lips[1] owe,[2]
If he can carry[3] 't thus!
            Othello, I, 1:66
[1] thick-lips: OTHELLO. [2] owe: own. [3] carry
. . . thus: hold out against IAGO's deception.

ROMEO. O! I am fortune's fool!
          Romeo and Juliet, III, 1:141

HORTENSIO. And tell me now, sweet
    friend, what happy gale
Blows you to Padua here from old Verona?
    PETRUCHIO. Such wind as scatters young
    men through the world
To seek their fortunes further than at home,
Where small experience grows. But in a few,
Signior Hortensio, thus it stands with me:
Antonio, my father, is deceas'd,
And I have thrust myself into this maze,
Haply[1] to wive and thrive as best I may.

      . . . . .

HORTENSIO. Thou 'dst thank me but a lit-
    tle for my counsel;
And yet I'll promise thee she shall be rich,
And very rich: but thou 'rt too much my
    friend,
And I'll not wish thee to her.
    PETRUCHIO. Signior Hortensio, 'twixt such
    friends as we
Few words suffice; and therefore, if thou
    know
One rich enough to be Petruchio's wife,
As wealth is burthen[2] of my wooing dance,
Be she as foul as was Florentius'[3] love,
As old as Sibyl[4] and as curst[5] and shrewd[6]
As Socrates' Xanthippe, or a worse,
She moves me not, or not removes, at least,
Affection's edge in me, were she as rough
As are the swelling Adriatic seas:
I come to wive it wealthily in Padua;
If wealthily, then happily in Padua.
        Taming of the Shrew, I, 2:48, 61

¹Haply: happily. ²burthen: theme. ³Florentius: a knight who bound himself to marry a deformed hag if she would solve a riddle on which his life depended. ⁴Sibyl: a very old prophetess. ⁵curst: waspish. ⁶shrewd: scolding.

FREEDOM

BELARIUS. This rock and these demesnes¹ have been my world,
Where I have liv'd at honest freedom, paid
More pious debts to heaven than in all
The fore-end of my time.
Cymbeline, III, 3:71
¹demesnes: land possessed.

OTHELLO. 'T is not to make me jealous
To say my wife is fair, feeds well, loves company,
Is free of speech, sings, plays, and dances well;
Where virtue is, these are more virtuous.
Othello, III, 3:183

PROSPERO. As you from crimes would pardon'd be,
Let your indulgence set me free.
Tempest, Epilogue: 19

FRIENDSHIP

CORIOLANUS. O world! thy slippery turns. Friends now fast sworn,
Whose double bosoms seem to wear one heart,
Whose hours, whose bed, whose meal, and exercise,
Are still¹ together, who twin, as 't were, in love
Unseparable, shall within this hour,
On a dissension of a doit,² break out
To bitterest enmity: so, fellest³ foes,
Whose passions and whose plots have broke their sleep
To take the one the other, by some chance,
Some trick not worth an egg, shall grow dear friends
And interjoin their issues.
Coriolanus, IV, 4:12
¹still: always. ²doit: trifle; literally, the smallest piece of money. ³fellest: most savage.

POLONIUS. The friends thou hast, and their adoption tried,
Grapple them to thy soul with hoops of steel.
Hamlet, I, 3:62

PLAYER KING. Who not needs shall never lack a friend;

And who in want a hollow friend doth try
Directly seasons him his enemy.
Hamlet, III, 2:217

FALSTAFF. Call you that backing of your friends? A plague upon such backing! give me them that will face me. Give me a cup of sack.
I Henry IV, II, 4:166

CASSIUS. A friend should bear his friend's infirmities,
But Brutus makes mine greater than they are.
Julius Caesar, IV, 3:86

KING. To wail friends lost
Is not by much so wholesome-profitable
As to rejoice at friends but newly found.
Love's Labour's Lost, V, 2:759

BASSANIO. 'T is not unknown to you, Antonio,
How much I have disabled mine estate,
By something showing a more swelling port¹
Than my faint means would grant continuance.
Merchant of Venice, I, 1:122
¹port: manner of living.

BASSANIO.¹ The dearest friend to me, the kindest man,
The best-condition'd and unwearied spirit
In doing courtesies, and one in whom
The ancient Roman honour more appears
Than any that draws breath in Italy.
Merchant of Venice, III, 2:295
¹About ANTONIO.

HELENA. Is all the counsel that we two have shar'd,
The sisters' vows, the hours that we have spent,
When we have chid the hasty-footed time
For parting us, O! is it all forgot?
All school-days' friendship, childhood innocence?
We, Hermia, like two artificial gods,
Have with our needles created both one flower,
Both on one sampler, sitting on one cushion,
Both warbling of one song, both in one key,
As if our hands, our sides, voices, and minds,
Had been incorporate. So we grew together,
Like to a double cherry, seeming parted,
But yet an union in partition;
Two lovely berries moulded on one stem;
So, with two seeming bodies, but one heart.
. . . . .
And will you rend our ancient love asunder,
To join with men in scorning your poor friend?
Midsummer Night's Dream, III, 2:198, 215

CLAUDIO. Friendship is constant in all other things
Save in the office and affairs of love;
Therefore all hearts in love use their own tongues;
Let every eye negotiate for itself
And trust no agent; for beauty is a witch
Against whose charms faith melteth into blood.
This is an accident of hourly proof.
Which I mistrusted not.
Much Ado About Nothing, II, 1:182

OTHELLO. Thou dost conspire against thy friend, Iago,
If thou but think'st him wrong'd, and mak'st his ear
A stranger to thy thoughts.
Othello, III, 3:142

MARINA. This world to me is like a lasting storm,
Whirring me from my friends.
Pericles, IV, 1:20

STANLEY. The ceremonious vows of love
And ample interchange of sweet discourse,
Which so long sunder'd friends should dwell upon.
Richard III, V, 3:98

Thou art the grave where buried love doth live,
Hung with the trophies of my lovers gone,
Who all their parts of me to thee did give;
That due of many now is thine alone:
Their images I lov'd I view in these.
Sonnet 31

Let me not to the marriage of true minds
Admit impediments. Love is not love
Which alters when it alteration finds,
Or bends with the remover to remove:
O, no! it is an ever-fixed mark,
That looks on tempests and is never shaken;
It is the star to every wandering bark,
Whose worth's unknown, although his height be taken.
Love's not Time's fool, though rosy lips and cheeks
Within his bending sickle's compass come;
Love alters not with his brief hours and weeks,
But bears it out even to the edge of doom.
Sonnet 116

TIMON. I am not of that feather to shake off
My friend when he must need me.
Timon of Athens, I, 1:100

TIMON. May you a better feast never behold,

You knot of mouth-friends! smoke and luke-warm water
Is your perfection. This is Timon's last;
Who, stuck and spangled with your flatteries,
Washes it off, and sprinkles in your faces
Throwing water in their faces.
Your reeking villany. Live loath'd, and long,
Most smiling, smooth, detested parasites,
Courteous destroyers, affable wolves, meek bears,
You fools of fortune, trencher-friends, time's flies,
Cap and knee slaves, vapours,[1] and minute-jacks![2]
Of man and beast the infinite malady
Crust you quite o'er! What! dost thou go?
Soft! take thy physic first,—thou too,—and thou:—
Stay, I will lend thee money, borrow none.
Throws the dishes at them.
What! all in motion? Henceforth be no feast,
Whereat a villain's not a welcome guest.
Timon of Athens, III, 6:98
[1] vapours: those whose friendship vanishes.
[2] minute-jacks: those who change their minds every minute.

FLAVIUS. What viler thing upon the earth than friends
Who can bring noblest minds to basest ends!
How rarely does it meet with this time's guise,
When man was wish'd to love his enemies!
Timon of Athens, IV, 3:470

POLIXENES. We were as twinn'd lambs that did frisk i' the sun,
And bleat the one at the other: what we chang'd
Was innocence for innocence; we knew not
The doctrine of ill-doing, no, nor dream'd
That any did. Had we pursu'd that life,
And our weak spirits ne'er been higher rear'd
With stronger blood, we should have answer'd heaven
Boldly 'not guilty.'
Winter's Tale, I, 2:67

FRIGHT

SIR TOBY. Draw; and, as thou drawest, swear horrible; for it comes to pass oft that a terrible oath, with a swaggering accent sharply twanged off, gives manhood more approbation than ever proof itself would have earned.
Twelfth Night, III, 4:196

SIR TOBY. This will so fright them both that they will kill one another by the look, like cockatrices.[1]

Twelfth Night, III, 4:215

[1] cockatrices: imaginary creatures that killed by their looks.

SIR ANDREW. Plague on 't; an[1] I thought he[2] had been valiant and so cunning in fence I'd have seen him damned ere I'd have challenged him. Let him let the matter slip, and I'll give him my horse, grey Capilet.

Twelfth Night, III, 4:311

[1] an: if.   [2] he: VIOLA.

FRUSTRATION

ORLANDO. I would not have my right Rosalind of this mind, for, I protest, her frown might kill me.

ROSALIND. By this hand, it will not kill a fly.

As You Like It, IV, 1:108

FALSTAFF. Now comes in the sweetest morsel of the night, and we must hence and leave it unpicked.

. . . . .

You see, my good wenches, how men of merit are sought after: the undeserver may sleep when the man of action is called on. Farewell, good wenches. If I be not sent away post,[1] I will see you again ere I go.

DOLL TEARSHEET. I cannot speak; if my heart be not ready to burst,—well, sweet Jack, have a care of thyself.

II Henry IV, II, 4:396, 404

[1] post: in a hurry.

FURY

DUCHESS [to the QUEEN]. Could I come near your beauty with my nails I'd set my ten commandments in your face.

. . . . .

BUCKINGHAM.[1] She's tickled[2] now; her fury needs no spurs, She'll gallop far enough to her destruction.

II Henry VI, I, 3:144, 153

[1] About the DUCHESS.   [2] tickled: vexed, nettled.

DESDEMONA. I understand a fury in your words. But not the words.

Othello, IV, 2:32

FERDINAND. This music crept by me upon the waters, Allaying both their fury and my passion With its sweet air.

Tempest, I, 2:391

FUTILITY

LEPIDUS. What manner o' thing is your crocodile?

ANTONY. It is shaped, sir, like itself, and it is as broad as it hath breadth, it is just so high as it is, and moves with it own organs; it lives by that which nourisheth it; and the elements once out of it, it transmigrates.

LEPIDUS. What colour is it of?

ANTONY. Of it own colour too.

LEPIDUS. 'T is a strange serpent.

ANTONY. 'T is so; and the tears of it are wet.

Antony and Cleopatra, II, 7:46

KING. My arrows, Too slightly timber'd for so loud a wind, Would have reverted to my bow again, And not where I had aim'd them.

Hamlet, IV, 7:21

POINS. Is it not strange that desire should so many years outlive performance?

II Henry IV, II, 4:283

ALBANY. Striving to better, oft we mar what's well.

King Lear, I, 4:369

BIRON. Why, all delights are vain; but that most vain, Which with pain purchas'd doth inherit pain: As, painfully to pore upon a book, To seek the light of truth; while truth the while Doth falsely blind the eyesight of his look.

Love's Labour's Lost, I, 1:72

BIRON. Climb o'er the house to unlock the little gate.

Love's Labour's Lost, I, 1:109

BIRON. This is the ape of form, monsieur the nice,[1] That, when he plays at tables, chides the dice In honourable terms.

Love's Labour's Lost, V, 2:325

[1] nice: fastidious.

GREEN. Alas! poor duke, the task he undertakes Is numbering sands and drinking oceans dry.

Richard II, II, 2:145

FIRST SERVANT. Why should we in the compass of a pale[1] Keep law and form and due proportion, Showing, as in a model, our firm estate, When our sea-walled garden,[2] the whole land,

Is full of weeds, her fairest flowers chok'd
    up,
Her fruit-trees all unprun'd, her hedges
    ruin'd,
Her knots[3] disorder'd, and her wholesome
    herbs
Swarming with caterpillars?
Richard II, III, 4:40
[1] pale: enclosure. [2] sea-walled garden: England. [3] knots: flower beds.

PANDARUS. I have had my labour for my
travail.
Troilus and Cressida, I, 1:70

FUTURE

CLOWN. I am for the house with the narrow gate, which I take to be too little for pomp to enter: some that humble themselves may; but the many will be too chill and tender, and they'll be for the flowery way that leads to the broad gate and the great fire.
All's Well That Ends Well, IV, 5:54

LE BEAU. Hereafter, in a better world
    than this,
I shall desire more love and knowledge of
    you.
As You Like It, I, 2:296

DOLL TEARSHEET. When wilt thou leave fighting o' days, and foining[1] o' nights, and begin to patch up thine old body for heaven?
FALSTAFF. Peace, good Doll! do not speak like a death's-head: do not bid me remember mine end.
II Henry IV, II, 4:256
[1] foining: thrusting with a rapier.

My grief lies onward, and my joy behind.
Sonnet 50

NESTOR. There is seen
The baby figure of the giant mass
Of things to come at large.
Troilus and Cressida, I, 3:344

CAMILLO. A cause more promising
Than a wild dedication of yourselves
To unpath'd waters, undream'd shores.
Winter's Tale, IV, 4:575

GENTLEMAN

PAROLLES. So please your majesty, my master hath been an honourable gentleman: tricks he hath had in him, which gentlemen have.
All's Well That Ends Well, V, 3:238

CHARLES. They say many young gentlemen flock to him every day, and fleet the time carelessly, as they did in the golden world.
As You Like It, I, 1:123

MORTIMER. In faith, he is a worthy gentleman,
Exceedingly well read, and profited
In strange concealments, valiant as a lion
And wondrous affable, and as bountiful
As mines of India.
I Henry IV, III, 1:165

PRINCE [about HOTSPUR]. I do not think
    a braver gentleman,
More active-valiant or more valiant-young,
More daring or more bold, is now alive
To grace this latter age with noble deeds.
I Henry IV, V, 1:89

MOTH. You are a gentleman and a gamester, sir.
ARMADO. I confess both: they are both the varnish of a complete man.
Love's Labour's Lost, I, 2:43

FORD. You are a gentleman of excellent breeding, admirable discourse, of great admittance, authentic in your place and person, generally allowed for your many warlike, court-like, and learned preparations.
Merry Wives of Windsor, II, 2:234

YORK.[1] In war was never lion rag'd more
    fierce,
In peace was never gentle lamb more mild,
Than was that young and princely gentleman.
Richard II, II, 1:173
[1] About K. RICHARD's father, the Black Prince.

GLOUCESTER.[1] A sweeter and a lovelier
    gentleman,
Fram'd in the prodigality of nature,
Young, valiant, wise, and, no doubt, right
    royal,
The spacious world cannot again afford.
Richard III, I, 2:243
[1] Later, KING RICHARD III.

GLOUCESTER.[1] I cannot tell: the world is
    grown so bad
That wrens make prey where eagles dare
    not perch:
Since every Jack became a gentleman
There's many a gentle person made a Jack.[2]
Richard III, I, 3:70
[1] Later, KING RICHARD III. [2] Jack: a term of contempt.

AUTOLYCUS. I know you are now, sir, a gentleman born.

CLOWN. Ay, and have been so any time these four hours.

. . . . .

But I was a gentleman born before my father; for the king's son took me by the hand and called me brother; and then the two kings called my father brother; and then the prince my brother and the princess my sister called my father father; and so we wept: and there was the first gentleman-like tears that ever we shed.

SHEPHERD. We may live, son, to shed many more.

Winter's Tale, V, 2:148, 150

SHEPHERD. We must be gentle, now we are gentlemen.

Winter's Tale, V, 2:164

GHOST

Enter GHOST.

HAMLET. Angels and ministers of grace defend us!
Be thou a spirit of health or goblin damn'd,
Bring with thee airs from heaven or blasts from hell,
Be thy intents wicked or charitable,
Thou com'st in such a questionable shape
That I will speak to thee: I'll call thee Hamlet,
King, father, royal Dane, O! answer me!
Let me not burst in ignorance; but tell
Why thy canoniz'd bones, hearsed in death,
Have burst their cerements.

Hamlet, I, 4:39

HAMLET. My fate cries out,
And makes each petty artery in this body
As hardy as the Nemean lion's nerve.

GHOST *beckons.*
Still am I call'd;—unhand me, gentlemen.

Breaking from them.
By heaven, I'll make a ghost of him that lets[1] me.
I say, away! Go on, I'll follow thee.

Exeunt GHOST *and* HAMLET.

Hamlet, I, 4:81

[1] lets: hinders, stops.

GHOST. I am thy father's spirit;
Doom'd for a certain term to walk the night,
And for the day confin'd to fast in fires,
Till the foul crimes done in my days of nature
Are burnt and purg'd away. But that I am forbid
To tell the secrets of my prison-house,
I could a tale unfold whose lightest word

Would harrow up thy soul, freeze thy young blood,
Make thy two eyes, like stars, start from their spheres,
Thy knotted and combined locks to part,
And each particular hair to stand on end,
Like quills upon the fretful porpentine;[1]
But this eternal blazon must not be
To ears of flesh and blood.

Hamlet, I, 5:9

[1] porpentine: porcupine.

GHOST. 'Tis given out that, sleeping in mine orchard,
A serpent stung me; so the whole ear of Denmark
Is by a forged[1] process of my death
Rankly abus'd:[2] but know, thou noble youth,
The serpent that did sting thy father's life
Now wears his crown.

HAMLET. O my prophetic soul
My uncle!
GHOST. Ay, that incestuous, that adulterate beast,
With witchcraft of his wit, with traitorous gifts,
O wicked wit and gifts, that have the power
So to seduce! won to his shameful lust
The will of my most seeming-virtuous queen.
O Hamlet! what a falling-off was there;
From me, whose love was of that dignity
That it went hand in hand even with the vow
I made to her in marriage; and to decline
Upon a wretch whose natural gifts were poor
To those of mine!
But virtue, as it never will be mov'd,
Though lewdness court it in a shape of heaven,
So lust, though to a radiant angel link'd,
Will sate itself in a celestial bed,
And prey on garbage.
But, soft! methinks I scent the morning air;
Brief let me be. Sleeping within mine orchard,
My custom always in the afternoon,
Upon my secure[3] hour thy uncle stole,
With juice of cursed hebenon[4] in a vial,
And in the porches of mine ears did pour
The leperous distilment; whose effect
Holds such an enmity with blood of man
That swift as quicksilver it courses through
The natural gates and alleys of the body,
And with a sudden vigour it doth posset[5]
And curd, like eager[6] droppings into milk,
The thin and wholesome blood; so did it mine;
And a most instant tetter bark'd about,
Most lazar-like,[7] with vile and loathsome crust,

All my smooth body.
Thus was I, sleeping, by a brother's hand
Of life, of crown, of queen, at once dis-
  patch'd;
Cut off even in the blossoms of my sin,
Unhousel'd,[8] disappointed, unanel'd,[9]
No reckoning made, but sent to my account
With all my imperfections on my head:
O,[10] horrible! O, horrible! most horrible!
If thou hast nature in thee, bear it not;
Let not the royal bed of Denmark be
A couch for luxury and damned incest.
But, howsoever thou pursu'st this act,
Taint not thy mind, nor let thy soul contrive
Against thy mother aught; leave her to
  heaven,
And to those thorns that in her bosom
  lodge,
To prick and sting her. Fare thee well at
  once!
The glow-worm shows the matin to be near,
And 'gins to pale his uneffectual fire;
Adieu, adieu! Hamlet, remember me.
                                                    Exit.
                                    Hamlet, I, 5:35

[1] forged process: a false report. [2] abus'd: a
word often used for deceive. [3] secure: un-
suspicious.   [4] hebenon: probably henbane.
[5] posset: curdle.   [6] eager: sour.   [7] lazar-like
like a leper. [8] Unhousel'd: not having the sac-
rament. [9] Unanel'd: without extreme unction.
[10] O, horrible: in some editions this line is by
HAMLET.

HAMLET. O all you host of heaven! O
  earth! What else?
And shall I couple hell? O fie! Hold, hold,
  my heart;
And you, my sinews, grow not instant old,
But bear me stiffly up! Remember thee!
Ay, thou poor ghost, while memory holds a
  seat
In this distracted globe.[1] Remember thee!
Yea, from the table of my memory
I'll wipe away all trivial fond[2] records,
All saws[3] of books, all forms, all pressures
  past,
That youth and observation copied there;
And thy commandment all alone shall live
Within the book and volume of my brain,
Unmix'd with baser matter: yes, by heaven!
O most pernicious woman!
O villain, villain, smiling, damned villain!
My tables,[4]—meet it is I set it down,
That one may smile, and smile, and be a vil-
  lain;
At least I'm sure it may be so in Denmark:
                                                Writing.
So, uncle, there you are. Now to my word;
It is 'Adieu, adieu! remember me.'
I have sworn 't.
                                    Hamlet, I, 5:92

[1] distracted globe: his head. [2] fond: foolish.
[3] saws: proverbs. [4] tables: notebook, tablets.

BRUTUS. Let me see, let me see; is not the
  leaf turn'd down
Where I left reading? Here it is, I think.
                    Enter the Ghost of CAESAR.
How ill this taper burns! Ha! who comes
  here?
I think it is the weakness of mine eyes
That shapes this monstrous apparition.
It comes upon me. Art thou any thing?
Art thou some god, some angel, or some
  devil,
That mak'st my blood cold and my hair to
  stare?
Speak to me what thou art.
  GHOST. Thy evil spirit, Brutus.
  BRUTUS. Why com'st thou?
  GHOST. To tell thee thou shalt see me at
    Philippi.
  BRUTUS. Well; then I shall see thee again?
  GHOST. Ay, at Philippi.
  BRUTUS. Why, I will see thee at Philippi
    then.
                                    Julius Caesar, IV, 3:273

BRUTUS. O Julius Caesar! thou art mighty
  yet:
Thy spirit walks abroad, and turns our
  swords
In our own proper entrails.
                                    Julius Caesar, V, 3:94

BRUTUS. The ghost of Caesar hath ap-
  pear'd to me
Two several times by night; at Sardis once,
And, this last night, here in Philippi fields.
I know my hour is come.
                                    Julius Caesar, V, 5:17

DUCHESS. Dead life, blind sight, poor
  mortal living ghost,
Woe's scene, world's shame, grave's due by
  life usurp'd,
Brief abstract and record of tedious days,
Rest thy unrest on England's lawful earth.
                                    Richard III, IV, 4:26

                The GHOST *of* HASTINGS *rises.*
GHOST [to KING RICHARD]. Bloody and
  guilty, guiltily awake;
And in a bloody battle end thy days!
Think on Lord Hastings: despair, and die!
[To RICHMOND.] Quiet untroubled soul
  awake, awake!
Arm, fight, and conquer, for fair England's
  sake!
The GHOSTS *of the two young Princes rise.*
GHOSTS [to KING RICHARD]. Dream on
  thy cousins smother'd in the Tower:

Let us be lead within thy bosom, Richard,
And weigh thee down to ruin, shame, and
 death!
Thy nephews' souls bid thee despair, and
 die!
[To RICHMOND.] Sleep, Richmond, sleep in
 peace, and wake in joy;
Good angels guard thee from the boar's[1]
 annoy!
Live, and beget a happy race of kings!
Edward's unhappy sons do bid thee flourish.
    The GHOST *of* LADY ANNE *rises.*
  GHOST [to KING RICHARD]. Richard, thy
   wife, that wretched Anne thy wife,
That never slept a quiet hour with thee,
Now fills thy sleep with perturbations:
To-morrow in the battle think on me,
And fall thy edgeless sword: despair, and
 die!
[To RICHMOND.] Thou, quiet soul, sleep
 thou a quiet sleep;
Dream of success and happy victory!
Thy adversary's wife doth pray for thee.
       Richard III, V, 3:145
[1] boar: a title given RICHARD III.

GIFT

ORLANDO. This nothing that he[1] so plenti-
fully gives me.
       As You Like It, I, 1:19
[1] he: his brother OLIVER.

SIR OLIVER. Is there none here to give the
woman?
TOUCHSTONE. I will not take her on gift of
any man.
       As You Like It, III, 3:68

OPHELIA. Take these again; for to the noble mind
Rich gifts wax poor when givers prove unkind.
       Hamlet, III, 1:100

SHALLOW. Did her grandsire leave her
seven hundred pound?
EVANS. Ay, and her father is make her a
petter penny.
SHALLOW. I know the young gentlewoman; she has good gifts.
EVANS. Seven hundred pounds and possi-
bilities is goot gifts.
   Merry Wives of Windsor, I, 1:60

PERICLES. O you gods!
Why do you make us love your goodly gifts,
And snatch them straight away?
       Pericles, III, 1:23

FLORIZEL. She[1] prizes not such trifles as
these are.

The gifts she looks from me are pack'd and
 lock'd
Up in my heart, which I have given already,
But not deliver'd.
      Winter's Tale, IV, 4:367
[1] She: PERDITA.

GOD

K. HENRY. Now, if these men have defeated the law and outrun native punishment, though they can outstrip men, they
have no wings to fly from God.
       Henry V, IV, 1:175

FLUELLEN. I need not to be ashamed of
your majesty, praised be God, so long as
your majesty is an honest man.
       Henry V, IV, 7:118

K. HENRY. Now, God be prais'd, that to
 believing souls
Gives light in darkness, comfort in despair!
       II Henry VI, II, 1:66

K. HENRY. Poor soul! God's goodness
 hath been great to thee:
Let never day nor night unhallow'd pass,
But still[1] remember what the Lord hath
 done.
       II Henry VI, II, 1:85
[1] still: always.

K. HENRY. God shall be my hope,
My stay, my guide, and lantern to my feet.
       II Henry VI, II, 3:24

K. HENRY. If my suspect be false, forgive
 me, God.
For judgment only doth belong to thee.
       II Henry VI, III, 2:139

SUFFOLK. Rather let my head
Stoop to the block than these knees bow to
 any
Save to the God of heaven, and to my king.
       II Henry VI, IV, 1:124

K. HENRY [soliloquy]. Would I were
 dead! if God's good will were so;
For what is in this world but grief and woe?
O God! methinks it were a happy life,
To be no better than a homely swain.
       III Henry VI, II, 5:19

WOLSEY. Had I but serv'd my God with
 half the zeal
I serv'd my king, he would not in mine age
Have left me naked to mine enemies.
       Henry VIII, III, 2:455

IAGO. 'Zounds! sir; you are one of those
that will not serve God if the devil bid you.
       Othello, I, 1:107

CARLISLE. O! forfend[1] it, God,
That in a Christian climate souls refin'd
Should show so heinous, black, obscene a
    deed.
                              Richard II, IV, 1:129
[1] forfend: forbid.

QUEEN ANNE. O! would to God that the
    inclusive verge
Of golden metal that must round my brow
Were red-hot steel to sear me to the brain.
                              Richard III, IV, 1:59

SIR ANDREW. For the love of God, a surgeon! send one presently[1] to Sir Toby.
                              Twelfth Night, V, 1:175
[1] presently: at once.

GODS

BRUTUS. For let the gods so speed me as
    I love
The name of honour more than I fear death.
                              Julius Caesar, I, 2:88

CASSIUS. Now, most noble Brutus,
The gods to-day stand friendly, that we
    may,
Lovers in peace, lead on our days to age!
                              Julius Caesar, V, 1:94

GLOUCESTER. As flies to wanton boys, are
    we to the gods;
They kill us for their sport.
                              King Lear, IV, 1:37

EDGAR. The gods are just, and of our
    pleasant vices
Make instruments to plague us.
                              King Lear, V, 3:170

GOLD

CLOTEN. 'T is gold
Which buys admittance; oft it doth; yea,
    and makes
Diana's rangers[1] false themselves,[2] yield up
Their deer to the stand o' the stealer; and 't
    is gold
Which makes the true man kill'd and saves
    the thief.
                              Cymbeline, II, 3:72
[1] Diana's rangers: officers protecting game.
[2] false themselves: turn traitors to themselves.

K. HENRY. See, sons, what things you are!
How quickly nature falls into revolt
When gold becomes her object!
For this the foolish over-careful fathers
Have broke their sleep with thoughts,
Their brains with care, their bones with in-
    dustry;

For this they have engrossed and pil'd up
The canker'd heaps of strange-achieved
    gold.
                              II Henry IV, IV, 5:65

YORK. Let them obey that know not how
    to rule;
This hand was made to handle nought but
    gold.
                              II Henry VI, V, 1:6

ROMEO. There is thy gold, worse poison
    to men's souls,
Doing more murders in this loathsome
    world
Than these poor compounds that thou
    may'st not sell.
                              Romeo and Juliet, V, 1:80

The strongest castle, tower, and town,
The golden bullet beats it down.
Sonnets to Sundry Notes of Music, IV: 117

TIMON [soliloquy]. Thus much of this[1]
    will make black white, foul fair,
Wrong right, base noble, old young, coward
    valiant.
Ha! you gods, why this? What this, you
    gods? Why, this
Will lug your priests and servants from your
    sides,
Pluck stout men's pillows from below their
    heads:
This yellow slave
Will knit and break religions; bless the ac-
    curs'd;
Make the hoar leprosy ador'd; place thieves,
And give them title, knee, and approbation
With senators on the bench.
                              Timon of Athens, IV, 3:28
[1] this: gold.

TIMON [looking on the gold]. O thou
    sweet king-killer, and dear divorce
'Twixt natural son and sire! thou bright de-
    filer
Of Hymen's purest bed! thou valiant Mars!
Thou ever young, fresh, lov'd, and delicate
    wooer,
Whose blush doth thaw the consecrated
    snow
That lies on Dian's lap! thou visible god.
                              Timon of Athens, IV, 3:382

TIMON. What a god's gold,
That he is worshipp'd in a baser temple
Than where swine feed!

. . . . .

To thee be worship; and thy saints for aye
Be crown'd with plagues that thee alone
    obey.
                              Timon of Athens, V, 1:50, 55

CLOWN. You're a made old man: if the sins of your youth are forgiven you, you're well to live. Gold! all gold.

SHEPHERD. This is fairy gold, boy, and 't will prove so: up with 't, keep it close.
Winter's Tale, III, 3:124

GOODNESS

ROSALIND. Can one desire too much of a good thing?
As You Like It, IV, 1:123

KING. Goodness, growing to a plurisy, Dies in his[1] own too-much.
Hamlet, IV, 7:118
[1] his: its.

K. HENRY. There is some soul of goodness in things evil,
Would men observingly distil it out;
For our bad neighbors makes us early stirrers,
Which is both healthful and good husbandry.[1]
Besides, they are our outward consciences,
And preachers to us all; admonishing
That we should dress us fairly for our end.
Thus may we gather honey from the weed,
And make a moral of the devil himself.
Henry V, IV, 1:4
[1] husbandry: care for one's business.

LADY MACDUFF. I have done no harm. But I remember now
I am in this earthly world, where to do harm
Is often laudable, to do good sometime
Accounted dangerous folly.
Macbeth, IV, 2:74

FRIAR LAURENCE [soliloquy]. Nought so vile that on the earth doth live
But to the earth some special good doth give,
Nor aught so good but strain'd from that fair use
Revolts from true birth, stumbling on abuse;
Virtue itself turns vice, being misapplied.
Romeo and Juliet, II, 3:17

GOSSIP

NYM. They say he[1] cried out of sack.[2]
HOSTESS. Ay, that a'[3] did.
BARDOLPH. And of women.
HOSTESS. Nay, that a' did not.
BOY. Yes, that a' did; and said they were devils incarnate.
HOSTESS. A' could never abide carnation; 't was a colour he never liked.

BOY. A' said once, the devil would have him about women.
HOSTESS. A' did in some sort, indeed, handle women; but then he was rheumatic, and talked of the whore of Babylon.
BOY. Do you not remember a' saw a flea stick upon Bardolph's nose, and a' said it was a black soul burning in hell-fire?
Henry V, II, 3:29
[1] he: FALSTAFF. [2] sack: wine. [3] a': he.

ROSALINE. Thou art an old love-monger, and speak'st skilfully.
MARIA. He is Cupid's grandfather and learns news of him.
Love's Labour's Lost, II, 1:254

BIRON. Some carry-tale, some please-man, some slight zany,
Some mumble-news, some trencher-knight, some Dick,
That smiles his cheek in years,[1] and knows the trick
To make my lady laugh when she 's dispos'd,
Told our intents before.
Love's Labour's Lost, V, 2:463
[1] smiles . . . years: makes his cheek look old by smiling.

SALANIO. I would she were as lying a gossip in that as ever knapped[1] ginger, or made her neighbours believe she wept for the death of a third husband.
Merchant of Venice, III, 1:10
[1] knapped: bit noisily.

CAPULET. And why, my lady wisdom? hold your tongue,
Good prudence; smatter with your gossips; go.
NURSE. May not one speak?
CAPULET. Peace, you mumbling fool!
Utter your gravity o'er a gossip's bowl,
For here we need it not.
Romeo and Juliet, III, 5:171

PANDARUS. Troilus! why, he esteems her[1] no more than I esteem an addle egg.
CRESSIDA. If you love an addle egg as well as you love an idle head, you would eat chickens i' the shell.
Troilus and Cressida, I, 2:143
[1] her: HELEN.

CAPTAIN. What great ones do the less will prattle of.
Twelfth Night, I, 2:33

Then join they all together,
Like many clouds consulting for foul weather.
Venus and Adonis: 971

GRACE

ADRIANA. His company must do his minions grace,[1]
Whilst I at home starve for a merry look.
Comedy of Errors, II, 1:87
[1] grace: favors.

ANTIPHOLUS SYRACUSE. Her fair sister,
Possess'd with such a gentle sovereign grace,
Of such enchanting presence and discourse,
Hath almost made me traitor to myself.
Comedy of Errors, III, 2:164

MALCOLM. The king-becoming graces,
As justice, verity, temperance, stableness,
Bounty, perseverance, mercy, lowliness,
Devotion, patience, courage, fortitude,
I have no relish of them.
Macbeth, IV, 3:91

LAUNCELOT [to BASSANIO]. The old prov-
erb is very well parted between my master
Shylock and you, sir: you have the grace of
God, sir, and he hath enough.
Merchant of Venice, II, 2:158

YORK.[1] Grace[2] me no grace, nor uncle me
no uncle:
I am no traitor's uncle; and that word
'grace'
In an ungracious mouth is but profane.
Richard II, II, 3:85
[1] Rebuking BOLINGBROKE for returning from
banishment.   [2] Grace: a title of distinction.

HASTINGS.[1] O! momentary grace[2] of mor-
tal men,
Which we more hunt for than the grace of
God.
Who builds his hope in air of your good
looks,
Lives like a drunken sailor on a mast;
Ready with every nod to tumble down
Into the fatal bowels of the deep.
Richard III, III, 4:98
[1] As he is being led to his execution.   [2] grace:
favor.

GRATITUDE

ROSALIND.[1] But, mistress, know yourself:
down on your knees,
And thank heaven, fasting, for a good man's
love:
For I must tell you friendly in your ear,
Sell when you can; you are not for all markets.
As You Like It, III, 5:57
[1] To PHEBE.

PRINCE HENRY. I have a kind soul that
would give you thanks,
And knows not how to do it but with tears.
King John, V, 7:108

DUNCAN [to MACBETH]. More is thy due
than more than all can pay.
Macbeth, I, 4:21

THAISA. Yet my good will is great, though
the gift small.
Pericles, III, 4:18

GRAVE

KING. Our rash faults
Make trivial price of serious things we have,
Not knowing them until we know their
grave:
Oft our displeasures, to ourselves unjust,
Destroy our friends and after weep their
dust.
All's Well That Ends Well, V, 3:60

K. HENRY.[1] What! canst thou not forbear
me half an hour?
Then get thee gone and dig my grave thy-
self,
And bid the merry bells ring to thine ear
That thou art crowned, not that I am dead.
Let all the tears that should bedew my
hearse
Be drops of balm to sanctify thy head.
II Henry IV, IV, 5:110
[1] To PRINCE HENRY, the heir apparent.

TIMON. Timon hath made his everlasting
mansion
Upon the beached verge of the salt flood;
Who once a day with his[1] embossed[2] froth
The turbulent surge shall cover: thither
come,
And let my grave-stone be your oracle.
Timon of Athens, V, 1:218
[1] his: its.   [2] embossed: swollen.

VIOLA. Lady, you are the cruell'st she
alive,
If you will lead these graces to the grave
And leave the world no copy.
Twelfth Night, I, 5:259

PROTEUS. Thus, for my duty's sake, I
rather chose
To cross my friend in his intended drift,
Than, by concealing it, heap on your head
A pack of sorrows which would press you
down,
Being unprevented, to your timeless[1] grave.
Two Gentlemen of Verona, III, 1:17
[1] timeless: untimely.

FIRST CLOWN. This same skull, sir, was
Yorick's skull, the king's jester.

HAMLET. This?

FIRST CLOWN. E'en that.

HAMLET. Let me see. Alas! poor Yorick. I knew him, Horatio; a fellow of infinite jest, of most excellent fancy: he hath borne me on his back a thousand times; and now, how abhorred in my imagination it is! my gorge rises at it. Here hung those lips that I have kissed I know not how oft. Where be your gibes now? your gambols? your songs? your flashes of merriment, that were wont to set the table on a roar? Not one now, to mock your own grinning? quite chapfallen? Now get you to my lady's chamber, and tell her, let her paint an inch thick, to this favour[1] she must come; make her laugh at that. Prithee, Horatio, tell me one thing.

HORATIO. What's that, my lord?

HAMLET. Dost thou think Alexander looked o' this fashion i' the earth?

HORATIO. E'en so.

HAMLET. And smelt so? pah!

Throws down the skull.

HORATIO. E'en so, my lord.

HAMLET. To what base uses we may return, Horatio! Why may not imagination trace the noble dust of Alexander till he find it stopping a bung-hole?

HORATIO. 'Twere to consider too curiously to consider so.

HAMLET. No, faith, not a jot; but to follow him thither with modesty[2] enough, and likelihood to lead it; as thus: Alexander died, Alexander was buried, Alexander returneth into dust; the dust is earth; of earth we make loam; and why of that loam whereto he was converted might they not stop a beer-barrel?

Imperious Caesar, dead and turn'd to clay,
Might stop a hole to keep the wind away:
O, that that earth which kept the world in awe
Should patch a wall to expel the winter's flaw![3]

Hamlet, V, 1:200

[1] favour: countenance. [2] modesty: moderation. [3] flaw: gust of wind.

GREATNESS

HAMLET. Rightly to be great
Is not to stir without great argument,[1]
But greatly to find quarrel in a straw
When honour's at the stake.

Hamlet, IV, 4:53

[1] argument: reason.

EXETER. 'T[1] is no sinister[2] nor no awkward claim,
Pick'd from the worm-holes of long-vanish'd days,

Nor from the dust of old oblivion rak'd,
He sends you this most memorable line.

Henry V, II, 4:85

[1] 'T: it, HENRY's claim to the French crown. [2] sinister: illegitimate; the heraldic bend sinister is popularly understood as a sign of illegitimacy.

DUKE. O place and greatness! millions of false eyes
Are stuck upon thee: volumes of report
Run with these false and most contrarious quests
Upon thy doings: thousand escapes[1] of wit
Make thee the father of their idle dream
And rack[2] thee in their fancies!

Measure for Measure, IV, 1:60

[1] escapes: sallies. [2] rack: misrepresent.

The mightier man, the mightier is the thing
That makes him honour'd, or begets him hate;
For greatest scandal waits on greatest state.

Rape of Lucrece: 1004

ULYSSES. Possess'd he is with greatness,
And speaks not to himself but with a pride
That quarrels at self-breath.

Troilus and Cressida, II, 3:180

ACHILLES. 'T is certain, greatness, once fall'n out with fortune,
Must fall out with men too.

Troilus and Cressida, III, 3:75

MALVOLIO [reading a letter]. If this fall into thy hand, revolve. In my stars I am above thee; but be not afraid of greatness: some are born great, some achieve greatness, and some have greatness thrust upon them.

Twelfth Night, II, 5:155

CLOWN. A great man, I 'll warrant; I know by the picking on 's teeth.

Winter's Tale, IV, 4:778

GRIEF

AEGEON. O! grief hath chang'd me since you saw me last,
And careful hours, with Time's deformed hand,
Have written strange defeatures in my face:
But tell me yet, dost thou not know my voice?

Comedy of Errors, V, 1:297

BELARIUS. Great griefs, I see, medicine[1] the less.

Cymbeline, IV, 2:243

[1] medicine: heal as with medicine.

HAMLET. What is he whose grief
Bears such an emphasis? whose phrase of
    sorrow
Conjures the wandering stars, and makes
    them stand
Like wonder-wounded hearers?
Hamlet, V, 1:277

FALSTAFF. A plague of sighing and grief!
it blows a man up like a bladder.
1 Henry IV, II, 4:365

CONSTANCE. I will instruct my sorrows to
    be proud;
For grief is proud and makes his[1] owner
    stoop.
To me and to the state of my great grief
Let kings assemble; for my grief's so great
That no supporter but the huge firm earth
Can hold it up: here I and sorrows sit;
Here is my throne,[2] bid kings come bow
    to it.
King John, III, 1:68

[1] his: its. [2] Seating herself on the ground.

CONSTANCE. Grief fills the room up of my
    absent child,
Lies in his bed, walks up and down with me,
Puts on his pretty looks, repeats his words,
Remembers me of all his gracious parts,
Stuffs out his vacant garments with his
    form:
Then have I reason to be fond of grief.

    . . . . .

O Lord! my boy, my Arthur, my fair son!
My life, my joy, my food, my all the world!
My widow-comfort, and my sorrow's cure!
King John, III, 4:93, 103

MALCOLM. Give sorrow words; the grief
    that does not speak
Whispers the o'er-fraught heart and bids it
    break.
Macbeth, IV, 3:209

BENEDICK. Well, every one can master a
grief but he that has it.
Much Ado About Nothing, III, 2:28

BRABANTIO. My particular grief
Is of so flood-gate and o'erbearing nature
That it engluts and swallows other sorrows
And it is still[1] itself.
Othello, I, 3:55

[1] still: always.

DUKE. To mourn a mischief that is past
    and gone
Is the next way to draw new mischief on.

    . . . . .

The robb'd that smiles steals something
    from the thief;

He robs himself that spends a bootless grief.
Othello, I, 3:204, 208

CLEON. My Dionyza, shall we rest us here,
And by relating tales of others' griefs,
See if 't will teach us to forget our own?
DIONYZA. That were to blow at fire in
    hope to quench it.
Pericles, I, 4:1

Sad souls are slain in merry company;
Grief best is pleas'd with grief's society:
Rape of Lucrece: 1110

K. RICHARD. 'T is very true, my grief lies
    all within;
And these external manners of laments
Are merely shadows to the unseen grief
That swells with silence in the tortur'd soul;
There lies the substance.
Richard II, IV, 1:294

LADY CAPULET. Some grief shows much
    of love;
But much of grief shows still[1] some want[2] of
    wit.
Romeo and Juliet, III, 5:73

[1] still: always. [2] want: lack.

GUILT

IACHIMO. The heaviness and guilt within
    my bosom
Takes off my manhood.
Cymbeline, V, 2:1

POLONIUS. My lord, I will use them according to their desert.
HAMLET. God's bodikins, man, much
better; use every man after his desert, and
who should 'scape whipping?
Hamlet, II, 2:552

HAMLET. Observe mine uncle; if his oc-
    culted[1] guilt
Do not itself unkennel in one speech,
It is a damned ghost that we have seen,
And my imaginations are as foul
As Vulcan's stithy. Give him heedful note.
Hamlet, III, 2:85

[1] occulted: hidden.

HAMLET. We that have free souls, it
touches us not: let the galled jade wince,
our withers are unwrung.
Hamlet, III, 2:250

KING. My stronger guilt defeats my
    strong intent;
And, like a man to double business bound,
I stand in pause where I shall first begin,
And both neglect.
Hamlet, III, 3:40

QUEEN. To my sick soul, as sin's true nature is,
Each toy seems prologue to some great amiss:
So full of artless jealousy is guilt,
It spills itself in fearing to be spilt.
Hamlet, IV, 5:17

GLOUCESTER.[1] Suspicion always haunts the guilty mind;
The thief doth fear each bush an officer.
III Henry VI, V, 6:11
[1] Later, KING RICHARD III.

IAGO. Guiltiness will speak
Though tongues were out of use.
Othello, V, 1:109

But they whose guilt within their bosoms lie
Imagine every eye beholds their blame.
Rape of Lucrece: 1342

BOLINGBROKE. Since thou hast far to go, bear not along
The clogging burden of a guilty soul.
Richard II, I, 3:199

K. RICHARD. Though some of you with Pilate wash your hands,
Showing an outward pity; yet you Pilates
Have here deliver'd me to my sour cross,
And water cannot wash away your sin.
Richard II, IV, 1:239

GONZALO. All three of them are desperate: their great guilt,
Like poison given to work a great time after,
Now 'gins to bite the spirits.
Tempest, III, 3:104

HABIT

[Shakespeare generally means garb or costume by the word *habit*. Notice the first three quotations below.]

POLONIUS. Costly thy habit as thy purse can buy,
But not express'd in fancy;[1] rich, not gaudy;[2]
For the apparel oft proclaims the man.
Hamlet, I, 3:70
[1] express'd in fancy: singular, unusual. [2] gaudy: showy, "loud."

DUKE. Supply me with the habit, and instruct me
How I may formally in person bear me
Like a true friar.
Measure for Measure, II, 3:46

ANGELO. O place! O form!
How often dost thou with thy case, thy habit,
Wrench awe from fools, and tie the wiser souls
To thy false seeming!
Measure for Measure, II, 4:12

PORTIA. He! why, he hath a horse better than the Neapolitan's, a better bad habit[1] of frowning than the Count Palatine; he is every man in no man.
Merchant of Venice, I, 2:62
[1] habit: here in the usual meaning.

VALENTINE. How use[1] doth breed a habit in a man!
Two Gentlemen of Verona, V, 4:1
[1] use: repeated speech or action.

HAIR

ANTIPHOLUS SYRACUSE. Why is Time such a niggard of hair, being, as it is, so plentiful an excrement?[1]
DROMIO SYRACUSE. Because it is a blessing that he bestows on beasts: and what he hath scanted men in hair he hath given them in wit.
ANTIPHOLUS SYRACUSE. Why, but there 's many a man hath more hair than wit.
DROMIO SYRACUSE. Not a man of those but he hath the wit to lose his hair.
Comedy of Errors, II, 2:78
[1] excrement: often used for hair or beard by Shakespeare.

QUEEN. Your bedded hair, like life in excrements,[1]
Starts up and stands an end.
Hamlet, III, 4:121
[1] excrements: hair or beard.

METELLUS. O! let us have him,[1] for his silver hairs
Will purchase us a good opinion
And buy men's voices to commend our deeds:
It shall be said his judgment rul'd our hands.
Julius Caesar, II, 1:144
[1] him: CICERO.

BASSANIO. So are those crisped snaky golden locks
Which make such wanton gambols with the wind,
Upon supposed fairness, often known
To be the dowry of a second head,
The skull that bred them in the sepulchre.
Merchant of Venice, III, 2:92

BASSANIO. Here in her hairs
The painter plays the spider, and hath woven

A golden mesh to entrap the hearts of men
Faster than gnats in cobwebs.
Merchant of Venice, III, 2:121

HAND

CLEOPATRA. A hand that kings
Have lipp'd, and trembled kissing.
Antony and Cleopatra, II, 5:29

CLEOPATRA. These hands do lack nobility,
that they strike
A meaner[1] than myself.
Antony and Cleopatra, II, 5:82
[1] meaner: of lower class.

PINCH. Give me your hand and let me
feel your pulse.
ANTIPHOLUS OF EPHESUS. There is my
hand, and let it feel your ear.
Strikes him.
Comedy of Errors, IV, 4:55

NORTHUMBERLAND. What valour were it,
when a cur doth grin,[1]
For one to thrust his hand between his teeth,
When he might spurn him with his foot
away?
III Henry VI, I, 4:56
[1] grin: show teeth.

K. HENRY. The fairest hand I ever
touch'd!
O beauty!
Till now I never knew thee.[1]
Henry VIII, I, 4:75
[1] thee: ANNE BULLEN.

MACBETH [soliloquy]. What hands are
here? Ha! they pluck out mine eyes.
Will all great Neptune's ocean wash this
blood
Clean from my hand? No, this my hand will
rather
The multitudinous seas incarnadine,
Making the green one red.
Re-enter LADY MACBETH.
LADY MACBETH. My hands are of your
colour, but I shame
To wear a heart so white.
Macbeth, II, 2:63

LADY MACBETH. Here 's the smell of the
blood still: all the perfumes of Arabia will
not sweeten this little hand. Oh! oh! oh!
Macbeth, V, 1:57

BEATRICE. What! bear[1] her[2] in hand until
they come to take hands,[3] and then with
public accusation, uncovered slander, un-
mitigated rancour,—O God! that I were a
man.
Much Ado About Nothing, IV, 1:306
[1] bear in hand: abuse with false pretenses.
[2] her: HERO.   [3] take hands: be married.

Her lily hand her rosy cheek lies under,
Cozening[1] the pillow of a lawful kiss.
Rape of Lucrece: 386
[1] Cozening: cheating.

YORK. You lose a thousand well-disposed
hearts,
And prick my tender patience to those
thoughts
Which honour and allegiance cannot think.
K. RICHARD. Think what you will: we
seize into our hands
His[1] plate, his goods, his money, and his
lands.
Richard II, II, 1:206
[1] His: JOHN OF GAUNT, father of BOLINGBROKE
who deposed RICHARD.

FLORIZEL. But come; our dance, I pray.
Your hand, my Perdita: so turtles pair
That never mean to part.
Winter's Tale, IV, 4:153

HANGING

FIRST GAOLER. O! the charity of a penny
cord; it sums up thousands in a trice; you
have no true debitor and creditor but it; of
what's past, is, and to come, the discharge.
Cymbeline, V, 4:171

POMPEY. He that drinks all night, and is
hanged betimes in the morning, may sleep
the sounder all the next day.
Measure for Measure, IV, 3:48

NERISSA. The ancient saying is no heresy:
'Hanging and wiving goes by destiny.'
Merchant of Venice, II, 9:82

GONZALO. I have great comfort from this
fellow: methinks he hath no drowning mark
upon him; his complexion is perfect gallows.
Stand fast, good fate, to his hanging! make
the rope of his destiny our cable, for our
own doth little advantage! If he be not born
to be hanged, our case is miserable.
Tempest, I, 1:30

CLOWN. Many a good hanging prevents a
bad marriage.
Twelfth Night, I, 5:20

HAPPINESS

DUKE SENIOR. Thou seest we are not all
alone unhappy:

This wide and universal theatre
Presents more woeful pageants than the
   scene
Wherein we play in.
                               As You Like It, II, 7:136

ORLANDO. O! how bitter a thing it is to
look into happiness through another man's
eyes.
                               As You Like It, V, 2:48

DUKE. Happy thou art not;
For what thou hast not, still thou striv'st to
   get,
And what thou hast, forget'st.
                               Measure for Measure, III, 1:21

NERISSA. It is no mean happiness, therefore, to be seated in the mean: superfluity
comes sooner by white hairs, but competency lives longer.
                               Merchant of Venice, I, 2:8

PORTIA. Happiest of all is that her gentle
   spirit
Commits itself to yours to be directed,
As from her lord, her governor, her king.
                               Merchant of Venice, III, 2:165

LEONATO. Never came trouble to my
house in the likeness of your grace, for trouble being gone, comfort should remain;
but when you depart from me, sorrow
abides and happiness takes his[1] leave.
                               Much Ado About Nothing, I, 1:102
[1] his: its.

O happiness enjoy'd but of a few!
And, if possess'd, as soon decay'd and done
As is the morning's silver-melting dew
Against the golden splendour of the sun;
An expir'd date, cancell'd ere well begun.
                               Rape of Lucrece: 22

BOLINGBROKE. I count myself in nothing
   else so happy
As in a soul remembering my good friends;
And as my fortune ripens with thy love,
It shall be still thy true love's recompense.
                               Richard II, II, 3:48

FRIAR LAURENCE. Happiness courts thee
   in her best array;
But, like a misbehav'd and sullen wench,
Thou pout'st upon thy fortune and thy
   love.
Take heed, take heed, for such die miserable.
                               Romeo and Juliet, III, 3:142

VALENTINE. One feast, one house, one
   mutual happiness.
Two Gentlemen of Verona, V, 4:173

HASTE

HAMLET. What might be toward, that
   this sweaty haste
Doth make the night joint-labourer with
   the day?
                               Hamlet, I, 1:77

BOYET. His tongue, all impatient to speak
   and not see,
Did stumble with haste.
                               Love's Labour's Lost, II, 1:237

K. JOHN. Be Mercury, set feathers to thy
   heels,
And fly like thought from them to me again.
                               King John, IV, 2:174

LENOX. What a haste looks through his
   eyes!
So should he look
That seems to speak things strange.
                               Macbeth, I, 2:46

NORTHUMBERLAND. Here come the
   Lords of Ross and Willoughby,
Bloody with spurring, fiery-red with haste.
                               Richard II, II, 3:57

HATE

CHARMIAN. In time we hate that which
   we often fear.
                               Antony and Cleopatra, I, 3:12

GLENDOWER. Sit, cousin Percy; sit, good
   cousin Hotspur;
For by that name as oft as Lancaster
Doth speak of you, his cheek looks pale and
   with
A rising sigh he wisheth you in heaven.
                               I Henry IV, III, 1:7

EXETER. When envy[1] breeds unkind division:
There comes the ruin, there begins confusion.
                               I Henry VI, IV, 1:193
[1] envy: hatred.

GLOUCESTER.[1] My lord of Winchester, I
   know your mind:
'T is not my speeches that you do mislike,
But 't is my presence that doth trouble ye.
Rancour will out: proud prelate, in thy face
I see thy fury. If I longer stay
We shall begin our ancient bickerings.
                               II Henry VI, I, 1:139
[1] Uncle of KING HENRY VI.

SHYLOCK [aside]. How like a fawning
   publican he looks!

I hate him for he is a Christian;
But more for that in low simplicity
He lends out money gratis, and brings down
The rate of usance[1] here with us in Venice.
If I can catch him once upon the hip,
I will feed fat the ancient grudge I bear him.
He hates our sacred nation, and he rails,
Even there where merchants most do con-
    gregate,
On me, my bargains, and my well-won
    thrift,
Which he calls interest. Cursed be my tribe,
If I forgive him!
                    Merchant of Venice, I, 3:42
[1] usance: interest.

Morocco. Mislike me not for my com-
    plexion,
The shadow'd livery of the burnish'd sun,
To whom I am a neighbour and near bred.
                    Merchant of Venice, II, 1:1

Roderigo. Thou told'st me thou didst
    hold him[1] in thy hate.
Iago. Despise me if I do not. Three great
    ones of the city,
In personal suit to make me his lieutenant,
Off-capp'd to him; and, by the faith of man,
I know my price, I am worth no worse a
    place.
                                Othello, I, 1:7
[1] him: Othello.

K. Richard. Now put it, God, in the
    physician's mind,
To help him[1] to his grave immediately!
The lining of his coffers shall make coats
To deck our soldiers for these Irish wars.
Come, gentlemen, let 's all go visit him:
Pray God we may make haste, and come
    too late!
                            Richard II, I, 4:59
[1] him: Gaunt.

Scroop. Sweet love, I see, changing his[1]
    property,[2]
Turns to the sourest and most deadly hate.
                        Richard II, III, 2:135
[1] his: its, a very frequent use in Shakespeare.
[2] property: quality, character.

K. Richard. The love of wicked friends[1]
    converts to fear;
That fear to hate; and hate turns one or
    both
To worthy danger and deserved death.
                            Richard II, V, 1:66
[1] friends: in First Folio; changed to men in
some texts.

Prince. Capulet! Montague!
See what a scourge is laid upon your hate,

That heaven finds means to kill your joys
    with love!
                    Romeo and Juliet, V, 3:291

Timon. I am *Misanthropos*, and hate
    mankind.
For thy part, I do wish thou[1] wert a dog,
That I might love thee something.
                    Timon of Athens, IV, 3:53
[1] Alcibiades.

Alcibiades.[1] Seek not my name: a plague
    consume you wicked caitiffs left!
Here lie I, Timon; who, alive, all living
    men did hate:
Pass by and curse thy fill; but pass and stay
    not here thy gait.
                    Timon of Athens, V, 4:71
[1] Reading copy of Timon's epitaph.

HEAD

Ghost. Cut off even in the blossoms of
    my sin,
Unhousel'd,[1] disappointed,[2] unanel'd,[3]
No reckoning made, but sent to my account
With all my imperfections on my head.
                                Hamlet, I, 5:76
[1] unhousel'd: without having received the sac-
rament. [2] disappointed: unprepared. [3] unanel'd: without having received extreme unction.

Lucio. Thy head stands so tickle on thy
shoulders that a milkmaid, if she be in love,
may sigh it off.
                    Measure for Measure, I, 2:176

K. Richard.[1] Wert thou not brother to
    great Edward's son,
This tongue that runs so roundly in thy
    head
Should run thy head from thy unreverent
    shoulders.
                        Richard II, II, 1:121
[1] To John of Gaunt.

Cressida. If you love an addle egg as well
as you love an idle head, you would eat
chickens i' the shell.
                    Troilus and Cressida, I, 2:146

HEALTH

Poins. The immortal part needs a physician; but that moves not him: though that
be sick, it dies not.
                        II Henry IV, II, 2:112

K. Henry. Health, alack, with youthful
    wings is flown
From this bare wither'd trunk.
                        II Henry IV, IV, 5:229

SERVANT. If it be so far beyond his health,
Methinks he should the sooner pay his debts,
And make a clear way to the gods.
Timon of Athens, III, 4:75

HEART

ANTONY. Cold-hearted toward me?
CLEOPATRA. Ah! dear, if I be so,
From my cold heart let heaven engender
hail,
And poison it in the source; and the first
stone
Drop in my neck: as it determines, so
Dissolve my life. The next Caesarion smite.
Antony and Cleopatra, III, 13:158

HAMLET. O all you host of heaven! O
earth! What else?
And shall I couple hell? O fie! Hold, hold,
my heart;
And you, my sinews, grow not instant old.
But bear me stiffly up.
Hamlet, I, 5:92

WOLSEY. Love thyself last: cherish those
hearts that hate thee:
Corruption wins not more than honesty.
Henry VIII, III, 2:443

PRINCESS. A heavy heart bears not a nimble tongue.
Love's Labour's Lost, V, 2:747

DON PEDRO. In her bosom I 'll unclasp my
heart,
And take her hearing prisoner with the
force
And strong encounter of my amorous tale.
Much Ado About Nothing, I, 1:325

D. PEDRO. Come, lady, come; you have
lost the heart of Signior Benedick.
BEATRICE. Indeed, my lord, he lent it me
awhile; and I gave him use for it, a double
heart for his single one.
Much Ado About Nothing, II, 1:286

DON PEDRO. He hath a heart as sound as a
bell, and his tongue is the clapper; for what
his heart thinks his tongue speaks.
Much Ado About Nothing, III, 2:11

BENEDICK. I will live in thy heart, die in
thy lap, and be buried in thy eyes; and
moreover I will go with thee to thy uncle's.
Much Ado About Nothing, V, 2:104

BUCKINGHAM. We know each other's
faces; for our hearts,
He knows no more of mine than I of yours;
Nor I of his, my lord, than you of mine.
Richard III, III, 4:10

PROSPERO.[1] Having both the key
Of officer and office, set all hearts i' the
state
To what tune pleas'd his ear; that now he
was
The ivy which had hid my princely trunk,
And suck'd my verdure out on 't.
Tempest, I, 2:83
[1] About his brother ANTONIO who has sup-
planted him.

HEARTBROKEN

COUNTESS. My heart is heavy and mine
age is weak;
Grief would have tears, and sorrow bids
me speak.
All's Well That Ends Well, III, 4:41

ANTONY. The seven-fold shield of Ajax
cannot keep
The battery from my heart. O! cleave, my
sides;
Heart, once be stronger than thy continent.
Crack thy frail case! Apace, Eros, apace.
Antony and Cleopatra, IV, 14:38

K. JOHN. The tackle of my heart is
crack'd and burn'd,
And all the shrouds wherewith my life
should sail
Are turned to one thread, one little hair;
My heart hath one poor string to stay it by,
Which holds but till thy news be uttered;
And then all this thou seest is but a clod
And module of confounded royalty.
King John, V, 7:52

EDGAR. I ask'd his blessing, and from first
to last
Told him[1] my pilgrimage: but his flaw'd
heart,—
Alack, too weak the conflict to support!—
'Twixt two extremes of passion, joy and
grief,
Burst smilingly.
King Lear, V, 3:195
[1] him: EDGAR's father.

PANDARUS. O heart, heavy heart,
Why sigh'st thou without breaking?
Troilus and Cressida, IV, 4:17

HEART—HARD

YORK. O! tiger's heart wrapped in a
woman's hide.
III Henry VI, I, 4:137

RICHARD.[1] Then, Clifford, were thy heart
as hard as steel,

As thou hast shown it flinty by thy deeds,
I come to pierce it, or to give thee mine.
III Henry VI, II, 1:201
[1] Later King Richard III.

OTHELLO. Ay, let her rot, and perish, and
be damned to-night; for she shall not live.
No, my heart is turned to stone; I strike it,
and it hurts my hand.
Othello, IV, 1:191

QUEEN ELIZABETH.[1] No doubt the murderous knife was dull and blunt
Till it was whetted on thy stone-hard heart.
Richard III, IV, 4:227
[1] Widow of KING EDWARD IV.

OLIVIA. I have said too much unto a heart
of stone,
And laid mine honour too unchary[1] out.
Twelfth Night, III, 4:221
[1] unchary: carelessly.

HEART—MERRY

SILENCE. A cup of wine that 's brisk and
fine,
And drink unto the leman[1] mine;
And a merry heart lives long-a.
II Henry IV, V, 3:48
[1] leman: mistress.

DON PEDRO. In faith, lady, you have a
merry heart.
BEATRICE. Yea, my lord; I thank it, poor
fool, it keeps on the windy side of care.
Much Ado About Nothing, II, 1:324

SIR TOBY. But shall we make the welkin
dance indeed? shall we rouse the night-owl
in a catch[1] that will draw three souls out of
one weaver?
Twelfth Night, II, 3:58
[1] catch: a song, now called a *round*.

AUTOLYCUS [singing]. Jog on, jog on,
the foot-path way,
And merrily hent[1] the stile-a:
A merry heart goes all the day,
Your sad tires in a mile-a.
Winter's Tale, IV, 2:132
[1] hent: clear, take.

HEAVEN

COUNTESS. What heaven more will
That thee may furnish, and my prayers
pluck down,
Fall on thy head! Farewell, my lord;
All's Well That Ends Well, I, 1:77

K. HENRY. Five hundred poor I have in
yearly pay,
Who twice a day their wither'd hands
hold up
Toward heaven, to pardon blood;
Henry V, IV, 1:315

GLOUCESTER.[1] I 'll make my heaven in a
lady's lap,
And deck my body in gay ornaments,
And witch sweet ladies with my words and
looks.
O miserable thought!
III Henry VI, III, 2:148
[1] Later RICHARD III.

MARGARET. Though usurpers sway the
rule awhile,
Yet heavens are just, and time suppresseth
wrongs.
III Henry VI, III, 3:76

CONSTANCE. Father cardinal, I have heard
you say
That we shall see and know our friends in
heaven.
If that be true, I shall see my boy again;
For since the birth of Cain, the first male
child,
To him that did but yesterday suspire,
There was not such a gracious creature
born.
King John, III, 4:76

ISABELLA. Could great men thunder
As Jove himself does, Jove would ne'er be
quiet,
For every pelting, petty officer
Would use his heaven for thunder; nothing
but thunder.
Measure for Measure, II, 2:110

MISTRESS PAGE. Heaven guide him to thy
husband's cudgel, and the devil guide his
cudgel afterwards!
Merry Wives of Windsor, IV, 2:87

K. RICHARD. Not shine to-day! Why, what
is that to me
More than to Richmond? for the self-same
heaven
That frowns on me looks sadly upon him.
Richard III, V, 3:285

FRIAR LAURENCE. Peace, ho! for shame!
confusion's cure lives not
In these confusions. Heaven and yourself
Had part in this fair maid; now heaven hath
all,
And all the better is it for the maid:
Your part in her you could not keep from
death,

But heaven keeps his[1] part in eternal life.
Romeo and Juliet, IV, 5:65
[1] his: its.

FRIAR LAURENCE. The heavens do lower
upon you for some ill;
Move them no more by crossing their high
will.
Romeo and Juliet, IV, 5:94

HELL

K. LEAR. There 's hell, there 's darkness,
there 's the sulphurous pit,
Burning, scalding, stench, consumption; fie,
fie, fie! pah, pah! Give me an ounce of
civet,[1] good apothecary, to sweeten my
imagination: there 's money for thee.
King Lear, IV, 6:130
[1] civet: perfume.

PORTER. If a man were porter of hell-
gate he should have old[1] turning the key.

. . . . .

I had thought to have let in some of all pro-
fessions, that go the primrose way to the
everlasting bonfire.
Macbeth, II, 3:1, 18
[1] old: an intensive, as often in Shakespeare.

JESSICA. Our house is hell, and thou, a
merry devil,
Didst rob it of some taste of tediousness.
Merchant of Venice, II, 3:2

GREEN. My comfort is that heaven will
take our souls
And plague injustice with the pains of hell.
Richard II, III, 1:33

ARIEL. [Ferdinand] cried, "Hell is empty.
And all the devils are here."
Tempest, I, 2:214

HERO

K. HENRY. And those that leave their
valiant bones in France,
Dying like men, though buried in your
dunghills,
They shall be fam'd; for there the sun shall
greet them,
And draw their honours reeking up to
heaven.
Henry V, IV, 3:98

MESSENGER. He[1] hath borne himself beyond the promise of his age, doing in the
figure of a lamb the feats of a lion: he hath

indeed better bettered expectation than you
must expect of me to tell you how.
Much Ado About Nothing, I, 1:13
[1] he: CLAUDIO.

HISTORY

WARWICK. There is a history in all men's
lives,
Figuring the nature of the times deceas'd;
The which observ'd a man may prophesy,
With a near aim of the main chance of
things
As yet not come to life, which in their seeds
And weak beginnings lie intreasured.
Such things become the hatch and brood of
time;
II Henry IV, III, 1:80

ARCHBISHOP. And therefore will he wipe
his tables[1] clean,
And keep no tell-tale to his memory
That may repeat and history[2] his loss
To new remembrance.
II Henry IV, IV, 1:201
[1] tables: writing tablet, memoranda. [2] history: used here as a verb.

CANTERBURY. There is no bar
To make against your highness' claim to
France
But this, which they produce from Phara-
mond,[1]
In terram Salicam mulieres ne succedant,
'No woman shall succeed[2] in Salique[3] land.'
Henry V, I, 2:35
[1] Pharamond: a king of the Franks. [2] succeed: inherit the crown. [3] Salique land: France.

K. HENRY. Either our history shall with
full mouth
Speak freely of our acts, or else our grave,
Like Turkish mute, shall have a tongueless
mouth,
Not worshipp'd with a waxen epitaph.
Henry V, I, 2:230

HOBBY

KING. Thus he his special nothing ever
prologues.
All's Well That Ends Well, II, 1:95

Some glory in their birth, some in their skill,
Some in their wealth, some in their body's
force;
Some in their garments, though new-fangled ill;
Some in their hawks and hounds, some in
their horse;
And every humour[1] hath his adjunct pleasure,

Wherein it finds a joy above the rest:
But these particulars are not my measure;
All these I better in one general best.
Thy love is better than high birth to me,
Richer than wealth, prouder than garments'
    cost,
Of more delight than hawks or horses be;
And having thee, of all men's pride I boast.
Sonnet 91

[1] humour: fancy.

Even as the sun with purple-colour'd face
Had ta'en his last leave of the weeping
    morn,
Rose-cheek'd Adonis hied him to the chase;
Hunting he lov'd, but love he laugh'd to
    scorn.
Venus and Adonis: 1

HOLIDAY

K. HENRY. This day, no man think
Has business at his house; for all shall stay:
This little one shall make it holiday.[1]
Henry VIII, V, 5:75

[1] holiday: Elizabeth's birthday.

HONESTY

AUDREY. Would you not have me honest?[1]
TOUCHSTONE. No, truly, unless thou were
hard-favoured;[2] for honesty coupled to
beauty is to have honey a sauce to sugar.
As You Like It, III, 3:28

[1] honest: chaste, a meaning often in Shakespeare. [2] hard-favoured: ill-looking, homely.

TOUCHSTONE. Rich honesty dwells like a
miser, sir, in a poor house, as your pearl in
your foul oyster.
As You Like It, V, 4:62

HAMLET. Ay, sir; to be honest, as this
world goes, is to be one man picked out of
ten thousand.
Hamlet, II, 2:177

DAVY. An honest man, sir, is able to speak
for himself, when a knave is not.
II Henry IV, V, 1:50

CROMWELL.[1] Would you were half so
    honest!
Men's prayers then would seek you, not
    their fears.
Henry VIII, V, 3:82

[1] To GARDINER.

BRUTUS. My heart doth joy that yet in
    all my life
I found no man but he was true to me.
Julius Caesar, V, 5:34

ALBANY. Where I could not be honest,
I never yet was valiant.
King Lear, V, 1:23

DOGBERRY. Verges . . . in faith, honest
as the skin between his brows.
VERGES. Yes, I thank God I am as honest
as any man living that is an old man and no
honester than I.
Much Ado About Nothing, III, 5:13

CASSIO. Dost thou hear, mine honest
friend?
CLOWN. No, I hear not your honest
friend; I hear you.
Othello, III, 1:22

IAGO. O monstrous world! Take note,
    take note, O world!
To be direct and honest is not safe.
Othello, III, 3:377

EMILIA. I durst, my lord, to wager she is
    honest,[1]
Lay down my soul at stake: if you think
    other,
Remove your thought; it doth abuse your
    bosom.
If any wretch hath put this in your head,
Let heaven requite it with the serpent's
    curse!
Othello, IV, 2:12

[1] honest: chaste.

DESDEMONA. I hope my noble lord es-
    teems me honest.
OTHELLO. O! ay; as summer flies are in
    the shambles,
That quicken even with blowing.
Othello, IV, 2:65

AUTOLYCUS [aside]. Though I am not
naturally honest, I am so sometimes by
chance: let me pocket up my pedlar's excrement.
Takes off his false beard.
Winter's Tale, IV, 3:731

AUTOLYCUS. Ha, ha! what a fool Honesty is! and Trust, his sworn brother, a
very simple gentleman! I have sold all my
trumpery: not a counterfeit stone, not a
riband, glass, pomander,[1] brooch, table-
book, ballad, knife, tape, glove, shoe-tie,
bracelet, horn-ring, to keep my pack from
fasting: they throng who should buy first,
as if my trinkets had been hallowed and
brought a benediction to the buyer: by
which means I saw whose purse was best in
picture; and what I saw to my good use I
remembered.
Winter's Tale, IV, 4:605

[1] pomander: a ball of perfume.

Autolycus. If I had a mind to be honest I see Fortune would not suffer me: she drops booties[1] in my mouth. I am courted now with a double occasion, gold and a means to do the prince my master good; which who knows how that may turn back to my advancement?

Winter's Tale, IV, 4:861

[1] booties: favors.

HONOUR

Iachimo. He[1] sits 'mongst men like a descended god;
He hath a kind of honour sets him off,
More than a mortal seeming.

Cymbeline, I, 6:169

[1] He: Posthumus.

Lord. The heavens hold firm
The walls of thy dear honour; keep unshak'd
That temple, thy fair mind; that thou may'st stand,
To enjoy thy banish'd lord and this great land!

Cymbeline, II, 1:67

Hotspur. By heaven methinks it were an easy leap
To pluck bright honour from the pale-fac'd moon,
Or dive into the bottom of the deep,
Where fathom-line could never touch the ground,
And pluck up drowned honour by the locks;
So he that doth redeem her thence might wear
Without corrival all her dignities.

I Henry IV, I, 3:201

Falstaff. Well, 'tis no matter; honour pricks me on. Yea, but how if honour prick me off when I come on? how then? Can honour set to a leg? No. Or an arm? No. Or take away the grief of a wound? No. Honour hath no skill in surgery then? No. What is honour? A word. What is that word honour? Air. A trim reckoning! Who hath it? He that died o' Wednesday. Doth he feel it? No. Doth he hear it? No. Is it insensible then? Yea, to the dead. But will it not live with the living? No. Why? Detraction will not suffer it. Therefore I 'll none of it. Honour is a mere scutcheon;[1] and so ends my catechism.

I Henry IV, V, 1:131

[1] scutcheon: shield with its armorial bearings.

Lady Percy. In the grey vault of heaven; and by his light

Did all the chivalry of England move
To do brave acts: he[1] was indeed the glass
Wherein the noble youth did dress themselves;
He had no legs, that practised not his gait;
And speaking thick, which nature made his blemish,
Became the accents of the valiant;

. . . . .

Never, O! never, do his ghost the wrong
To hold your honour more precise and nice
With others than with him.

II Henry IV, II, 3:21, 39

[1] he: Hotspur.

Fluellen. A man that I love and honour with my soul, and my heart, and my duty, and my life, and my living, and my uttermost powers.

Henry V, III, 6:7

K. Henry. If we are mark'd to die, we are enow
To do our country loss; and if to live,
The fewer men, the greater share of honour.
God's will! I pray thee, wish not one man more.

. . . . .

But if it be a sin to covet honour,
I am the most offending soul alive.

Henry V, IV, 3:20, 28

Cassius. Well, honour is the subject of my story.
I cannot tell what you and other men
Think of this life; but for my single self,
I had as lief not be as live to be
In awe of such a thing as I myself.

Julius Caesar, I, 2:92

Banquo. New honours come upon him,
Like our strange garments, cleave not to their mould
But with the aid of use.

Macbeth, I, 3:145

Banquo. In the great hand of God I stand, and thence
Against the undivulg'd pretence I fight
Of treasonous malice.

Macbeth, II, 3:136

Falstaff. Thinkest thou I'll endanger my soul gratis?

. . . . .

I, I, I myself sometimes, leaving the fear of God on the left hand and hiding mine honour in my necessity, am fain to shuffle, to hedge and to lurch; and yet you, rogue, will ensconce your rags, your cat-a-mountain looks, your red-lattice[1] phrases, and your bold-beating oaths, under the shelter of your honour!

    Merry Wives of Windsor, II, 2:15, 24

[1] red-lattice: lattice window painted red, symbol of an alehouse.

PETRUCHIO. And as the sun breaks through the darkest clouds,
So honour peereth in the meanest habit.[1]

    Taming of the Shrew, IV, 3:174

[1] habit: garb.

TITUS. Give me a staff of honour for mine age,
But not a sceptre to control the world.

    Titus Andronicus, I, 1:198

ACHILLES. Not a man, for being simply man,
Hath any honour, but honour for those honours
That are without him, as place, riches, and favour,
Prizes of accident as oft as merit:
Which when they fall, as being slippery standers,
The love that lean'd on them as slippery too,
Doth one pluck down another, and together
Die in the fall.

    Troilus and Cressida, III, 3:80

HECTOR. Life every man holds dear; but the dear man
Holds honour far more precious-dear than life.

    Troilus and Cressida, V, 3:27

HOPE

HELENA. But will you make it even?
KING. Ay, by my sceptre, and my hopes of heaven.
HELENA. Then shalt thou give me with thy kingly hand
What husband in thy power I will command.

    All's Well That Ends Well, II, 1:194

BARDOLPH. Who lin'd himself with hope,
Eating the air on promise of supply,

    II Henry IV, I, 3:27

BARDOLPH. Indeed the instant action, a cause on foot,
Lives so in hope, as in an early spring
We see the appearing buds; which to prove fruit,
Hope gives not so much warrant as despair
That frosts will bite them.

    II Henry IV, I, 3:37

BANQUO. If there come truth from them,
As upon thee, Macbeth, their speeches shine,
Why, by the verities on thee made good,
May they not be my oracles as well,
And set me up in hope?

    Macbeth, III, 1:6

BUSHY. Despair not, madam.
QUEEN. Who shall hinder me?
I will despair, and be at enmity
With cozening[1] hope: he is a flatterer,
A parasite, a keeper back of death,
Who gently would dissolve the bands of life,
Which false hope lingers in extremity.

    Richard II, II, 2:66

[1] cozening: deceiving.

NORTHUMBERLAND. The present benefit which I possess;
And hope to joy is little less in joy
Than hope enjoy'd.

    Richard II, II, 3:14

RICHMOND. True hope is swift, and flies with swallow's wings;
Kings it makes gods, and meaner creatures kings.

    Richard III, V, 2:23

TROILUS. When I do tell thee, there my hopes lie drown'd,
Reply not in how many fathoms deep
They lie indrench'd. I tell thee I am mad.

    Troilus and Cressida, I, 1:49

PROTEUS. Hope is a lover's staff; walk hence with that
And manage it against despairing thoughts.

    Two Gentlemen of Verona, III, 1:246

HORSE

KING. [The French] can well on horseback; but this gallant
Had witchcraft in 't, he grew unto his seat,
And to such wondrous doing brought his horse,
As he had been incorps'd and demi-natur'd
With the brave beast.

    Hamlet, IV, 7:84

DAUPHIN. When I bestride him, I soar, I am a hawk: he trots the air; the earth sings when he touches it; the basest horn of his hoof is more musical than the pipe of Hermes.[1]

    Henry V, III, 7:16

[1] Hermes: the messenger of the Greek gods.

GRANDPRÉ. The horsemen sit like fixed candlesticks,

With torch-staves in their hand; and their
    poor jades
Lob down their heads, dropping the hides
    and hips,
The gum down-roping from their pale-
    dead eyes,
And in their pale dull mouths the gimmal[1]
    bit
Lies foul with chew'd grass, still and mo-
    tionless.
                                Henry V, IV, 2:45
[1] gimmal: guiding.

FOOL. 'T was her brother that, in pure
kindness to his horse, buttered his hay.
                                King Lear, II, 4:127

GRATIANO. Where is the horse that doth
    untread again
His tedious measures with the unbated fire
That he did pace them first? All things that
    are,
Are with more spirit chased than enjoy'd.
                                Merchant of Venice, II, 6:10

K. RICHARD. Rode he[1] on Barbary? Tell
    me, gentle friend,
How went he under him?
    GROOM. So proudly as if he disdain'd the
    ground.
    K. RICHARD. So proud that Bolingbroke
    was on his back!
That jade hath eat bread from my royal
    hand;
This hand hath made him proud with clap-
    ping him.
Would he not stumble? would he not fall
    down,
Since pride must have a fall, and break the
    neck
Of that proud man that did usurp his back?
Forgiveness, horse! why do I rail on thee,
Since thou, created to be aw'd by man.
Wast born to bear? I was not made a horse;
And yet I bear a burden like an ass,
Spur-gall'd and tir'd by jauncing Boling-
    broke.
                                Richard II, V, 4:81
[1] he: BOLINGBROKE, as King after RICHARD was
dethroned.

K. RICHARD. A horse! a horse! my king-
    dom for a horse!
                                Richard III, V, 4:6

Look, when a painter would surpass the life,
In limning out a well-proportion'd steed,
            . . . . .
Round-hoof'd, short-jointed, fetlocks shag
    and long,
Broad breast, full eye, small head, and nos-
    tril wide,

High crest, short ears, straight legs and
    passing[1] strong,
Thin mane, thick tail, broad buttock, tender
    hide:
Look, what a horse should have he did not
    lack,
Save a proud rider on so proud a back.
                                Venus and Adonis: 289, 295
[1] passing: exceedingly.

HUMILITY

KING. Who were below him
He us'd as creatures of another place,
And bow'd his eminent top to their low
    ranks,
Making them proud of his humility.
                                All's Well That Ends Well, I, 2:41

CLOWN. Though honesty be no puritan,
yet it will do no hurt; it will wear the sur-
plice of humility over the black gown of a
big heart.
                                All's Well That Ends Well, I, 3:97

ANTONY. Hark! the land bids me tread
    no more upon 't;
It is asham'd to bear me.
                                Antony and Cleopatra, III, 9:1

ORLANDO. In the world I fill up a place,
which may be better supplied when I have
made it empty.
                                As You Like It, I, 2:206

CORIOLANUS. Well, I must do 't.[1]
Away, my disposition, and possess me
Some harlot's spirit! my throat of war be
    turn'd,
Which quired with my drum, into a pipe
Small[2] as an eunuch, or the virgin voice
That babies lulls asleep! the smiles of knaves
Tent[3] in my cheeks, and school-boys' tears
    take up
The glasses of my sight! a beggar's tongue
Make motion through my lips, and my
    arm'd knees,
Who bow'd but in my stirrup, bend like his
That hath receiv'd an alms! I will not do 't,
Lest I surcease[4] to honour mine own truth,
And by my body's action teach my mind
A most inherent baseness.
                                Coriolanus, III, 2:110
[1] do 't: flatter the mob. [2] Small: shrill. [3] Tent:
full. [4] surcease: cease.

POLONIUS. Give every man thine ear; but
    few thy voice;
Take each man's censure,[1] but reserve thy
    judgment.
                                Hamlet, I, 3:68
[1] censure: opinion, judgment; not criticism.

[In this soliloquy HAMLET shows that he realizes his great fault, failure to act promptly.]

HAMLET. O! what a rogue and peasant slave am I:
Is it not monstrous that this player here,
But in a fiction, in a dream of passion,
Could force his soul so to his own conceit[1]
That from her working all his visage wann'd,
Tears in his eyes, distraction in 's aspect,
A broken voice, and his whole function suiting
With forms to his conceit?[1] and all for nothing!
For Hecuba!
What 's Hecuba to him or he to Hecuba
That he should weep for her? What would he do
Had he the motive and the cue for passion
That I have? He would drown the stage with tears,
And cleave the general ear with horrid speech,
Make mad the guilty and appal the free,
Confound the ignorant, and amaze indeed
The very faculties of eyes and ears.
Yet I,
A dull and muddy-mettled rascal, peak,[2]
Like John-a-dreams;[3] unpregnant[4] of my cause,
And can say nothing; no, not for a king,
Upon whose property and most dear life
A damn'd defeat was made. Am I a coward?
Who calls me villain? breaks my pate across?
Plucks off my beard and blows it in my face?
Tweaks me by the nose? gives me the lie i' the throat
As deep as to the lungs? Who does me this?
Ha!
'Swounds![5] I should take it, for it cannot be
But I am pigeon-liver'd, and lack[6] gall
To make oppression bitter, or ere this
I should have fatted all the region kites
With this slave's offal. Bloody, bawdy villain!
Remorseless, treacherous, lecherous, kindless[7] villain!
O! vengeance!
Why, what an ass am I! This is most brave,
That I, the son of a dear father murder'd,
Prompted to my revenge by heaven and hell,
Must, like a whore, unpack my heart with words,
And fall a-cursing, like a very drab,
A scullion!
                              Hamlet, II, 2:576
[1] conceit: thought. [2] peak: grow lean. [3] John-a-dreams: a dreamy, idle fellow. [4] unpregnant: not inspired by my cause. [5] 'Swounds: contraction for "God's wounds." [6] lack . . . bitter: lack bitterness of mind to feel the disgrace. [7] kindless: unnatural.

K. HENRY. And then I stole all courtesy from heaven,
And dress'd myself in such humility
That I did pluck allegiance from men's hearts,
Loud shouts and salutations from their mouths,
Even in the presence of the crowned king.
                              1 Henry IV, III, 2:50

K. LEAR. Pray, do not mock me:
I am a very foolish fond old man,
Fourscore and upward, not an hour more nor less;
And, to deal plainly,
I fear I am not in my perfect mind.

. . . . .

Do not laugh at me;
For, as I am a man, I think this lady
To be my child Cordelia.
CORDELIA. And so I am, I am.
K. LEAR. Be your tears wet? Yes, faith. I pray, weep not:
If you have poison for me, I will drink it.
I know you do not love me; for your sisters
Have, as I do remember, done me wrong:
You have some cause, they have not.
CORDELIA. No cause, no cause.
                              King Lear, IV, 7:59, 68

GLOUCESTER.[1] I do not know that Englishman alive
With whom my soul is any jot at odds.
More than the infant that is born to-night:
I thank my God for my humility.
                              Richard III, II, 1:69
[1] Later, KING RICHARD III.

LEONTES.[1] How he glisters
Thorough[2] my rust! and his piety[3]
Does my deeds make the blacker!
                              Winter's Tale, III, 2:171
[1] About CAMILLO. [2] Thorough: often in Shakespeare for through. [3] piety: general virtue.

HUMOUR

LE BEAU. The duke is humorous:[1] what he is indeed,
More suits you to conceive than I to speak of.
                              As You Like It, I, 2:278
[1] humorous: capricious; the word *humour* in Shakespeare seldom has our common meaning.

PRINCE. I am now of all humours[1] that have showed themselves humours since the old days of goodman Adam to the pupil age of this present twelve o'clock at midnight.

I Henry IV, II, 4:105

[1] humours: caprices.

NYM. I will cut thy throat, one time or other, in fair terms; that is the humour[1] of it.

Henry V, II, 1:73

[1] humour: cast of mind, temper.

K. JOHN. It is the curse of kings to be attended
By slaves that take their humours[1] for a warrant
To break within the bloody house of life,
And on the winking of authority
To understand a law, to know the meaning
Of dangerous majesty, when perchance it frowns
More upon humour than advis'd respect.[2]

King John, IV, 2:208

[1] humours: moods. [2] respect: consideration.

PORTIA. Is Brutus sick, and is it physical
To walk unbraced and suck up the humours[1]
Of the dank morning?

Julius Caesar, II, 1:261

[1] humours: dangerous fluids.

SHYLOCK. You 'll ask me, why I rather choose to have
A weight of carrion flesh than to receive
Three thousand ducats: I 'll not answer that:
But, say, it is my humour:[1] is it answer'd?

Merchant of Venice, IV, 1:40

[1] humour: mood.

MALVOLIO. *Seeing the letter.*[1] What employment have we here?
FABIAN. Now is the woodcock near the gin.
SIR TOBY. O, peace! and the spirit of humours[2] intimate reading aloud to him!
MALVOLIO. *Taking up the letter.* By my life, this is my lady's hand!

Twelfth Night, II, 5:91

[1] letter: MARIA's forged letter to make MALVOLIO think OLIVIA loves him. [2] humours: mirth.

HUNT

THESEUS. We will, fair queen, up to the mountain's top,
And mark the musical confusion
Of hounds and echo in conjunction.
HIPPOLYTA. I was with Hercules and Cadmus once,

When in a wood of Crete they bay'd the bear
With hounds of Sparta: never did I hear
Such gallant chiding; for, besides the groves,
The skies, the fountains, every region near
Seem'd all one mutual cry. I never heard
So musical a discord, such sweet thunder.
THESEUS. My hounds are bred out of the Spartan kind,
So flew'd,[1] so sanded; and their heads are hung
With ears that sweep away the morning dew;
Crook-knee'd, and dew-lapp'd like Thessalian bulls;
Slow in pursuit, but match'd in mouth like bells,
Each under each. A cry more tuneable
Was never holla'd to, nor cheer'd with horn.

Midsummer Night's Dream, IV, 1:113.

[1] flew'd . . . sanded: having same hanging chop and sandy color.

TITUS. The hunt is up, the morn is bright and grey,
The fields are fragrant and the woods are green.

Titus Andronicus, II, 2:1

HUSBAND

PAROLLES. Get thee a good husband, and use him as he uses thee: so farewell.

All's Well That Ends Well, I, 1:229

ADRIANA. Thou art an elm, my husband, I a vine,
Whose weakness, married to thy stronger state,
Makes me with thy strength to communicate:
If aught possess thee from me, it is dross,
Usurping ivy, brier, or idle moss.

Comedy of Errors, II, 2:176

ROMAN. The fittest time to corrupt a man's wife is when she's fallen out with her husband.

Coriolanus, IV, 3:33

PLAYER QUEEN. In second husband let me be accurst;
None wed the second but who kill'd the first.
HAMLET [aside]. Wormwood, wormwood.
PLAYER QUEEN. The instances that second marriage move
Are base respects of thrift, but none of love;
A second time I kill my husband dead,
When second husband kisses me in bed.

Hamlet, III, 2:189

MISTRESS QUICKLY. Master Ford, her husband, will be from home. Alas! the sweet woman leads an ill life with him; he 's a very jealousy man; she leads a very frampold[1] life with him, good heart.
Merry Wives of Windsor, II, 2:91
[1] frampold: quarrelsome.

LEONATO. By my troth, niece, thou wilt never get thee a husband, if thou be so shrewd[1] of thy tongue.
. . . . .
BEATRICE. Just, if he send me no husband; for the which blessing I am at him upon my knees every morning and evening.
Much Ado About Nothing, II, 1:19, 29
[1] shrewd: sharp-tongued, waspish.

LEONATO. Well then, go you into hell?
BEATRICE. No; but to the gate; and there will the devil meet me, like an old cuckold, with horns on his head, and say 'Get you to heaven, Beatrice, get you to heaven; here 's no place for you maids': so deliver[1] I up my apes, and away to Saint Peter for the heavens; he shows me where the bachelors sit and there live we as merry as the day is long.
Much Ado About Nothing, II, 1:44
[1] deliver . . . apes: a saying that spinsters were doomed to lead apes in hell.

LEONATO. Well, niece, I hope to see you one day fitted with a husband.
BEATRICE. Not till God make men of some other metal than earth. Would it not grieve a woman to be overmastered with a piece of valiant dust? to make an account of her life to a clod of wayward marl? No, uncle, I 'll none: Adam's sons are my brethren; and, truly, I hold it a sin to match in my kindred.
Much Ado About Nothing, II, 1:59

KATHARINA. Thy husband is thy lord, thy life, thy keeper,
Thy head, thy sovereign; one that cares for thee.
. . . . .
Such duty as the subject owes the prince,
Even such a woman oweth to her husband;
And when she 's froward, peevish, sullen, sour,
And not obedient to his honest will,
What is she but a foul contending rebel,
And graceless traitor to her loving lord?
Taming of the Shrew, V, 2:146, 156

HYPOCRISY

LUCIANA. Be not thy tongue thy own shame's orator;
Look sweet, speak fair, become disloyalty;
Apparel vice like virtue's harbinger;[1]
Bear a fair presence, though your heart be tainted:
Teach sin the carriage of a holy saint.
Comedy of Errors, III, 2:10
[1] harbinger: forerunner.

KING. But now, my cousin[1] Hamlet, and my son,—
HAMLET. A little more than kin,[2] and less than kind.[3]
Hamlet, I, 2:64
[1] cousin: used in Shakespeare for various relationships. [2] kin: family relationship. [3] kind: unworthy our race or kind.

MALCOLM. To show an unfelt sorrow is an office
Which the false man does easy.
Macbeth, II, 3:142

IAGO. Though I do hate him as I do hell-pains,
Yet, for necessity of present life,
I must show out a flag and sign of love.
Othello, I, 1:155

GLOUCESTER.[1] And thus I clothe my naked villany
With old odd ends stol'n forth of holy writ.
And seem a saint when most I play the devil.
Richard III, I, 3:336
[1] Later, KING RICHARD III.

IDOL—IDOLATRY

K. HENRY. What art thou, thou idol ceremony?
What kind of god art thou?
Henry V, IV, 1:257

THERSITES. Why, thou picture of what thou seemest, and idol of idiot-worshippers.
Troilus and Cressida, V, 1:7

IF

TOUCHSTONE. I knew when seven justices could not take up a quarrel; but when the parties were met themselves, one of them thought but of an 'if,' as 'if you said so, then I said so'; and they shook hands and swore brothers. Your 'if' is the only peacemaker; much virtue in 'if.'
As You Like It, V, 4:103

DUKE. Arraign your conscience,
And try your penitence, if[1] it be sound,
Or hollowly put on.
Measure for Measure, II, 3:21
[1] if: whether.

Ford. If money go before, all ways do lie open.

Falstaff. Money is a good soldier, sir, and will on.
Merry Wives of Windsor, II, 2:174

IGNORANCE

Coriolanus. This double worship,
Where one part does disdain with cause, the other
Insult without all reason; where gentry, title, wisdom,
Cannot conclude but by the yea and no
Of general ignorance.
Coriolanus, III, 1:142

Hamlet. Let me not burst in ignorance.
Hamlet, I, 4:46

Lord Say. Ignorance is the curse of God, Knowledge the wing wherewith we fly to heaven.
II Henry VI, IV, 7:78

Holofernes. O! thou monster Ignorance, how deform'd dost thou look.

Nathaniel. Sir, he hath never fed of the dainties that are bred in a book; he hath not eat paper, as it were; he hath not drunk ink: his intellect is not replenished; he is only an animal, only sensible in the duller parts.
Love's Labour's Lost, IV, 2:24

Demetrius. What, man! more water glideth by the mill
Than wots[1] the miller of.
Titus Andronicus, II, 1:85
[1] wots: knows.

Thersites. I had rather be a tick in a sheep than such a valiant ignorance.
Troilus and Cressida, III, 3:316

Clown. I say there is no darkness but ignorance.
Twelfth Night, IV, 2:46

ILLUSION

Edgar. How fearful
And dizzy 't is to cast one's eyes so low!
The crows and choughs that wing the midway air
Show scarce so gross as beetles; half way down
Hangs one that gathers samphire,[1] dreadful trade!
Methinks he seems no bigger than his head.
The fishermen that walk upon the beach
Appear like mice, and yond tall anchoring bark

Diminish'd to her cock,[2] her cock a buoy
Almost too small for sight. The murmuring surge,
That on the unnumber'd idle pebbles chafes,
Cannot be heard so high. I'll look no more,
Lest my brain turn, and the deficient sight
Topple down headlong.
King Lear, IV, 6:11
[1] samphire: an herb that grows among rocks.
[2] Diminish'd . . . cock: reduced to the size of her small boat.

O me! what eyes hath Love put in my head,
Which have no correspondence with true sight;
Or, if they have, where is my judgment fled,
That censures[1] falsely what they see aright?
If that be fair whereon my false eyes dote.

. . . . .

O cunning Love! with tears thou keep'st me blind,
Lest eyes well-seeing thy foul faults should find.
Sonnet 148
[1] censures: judges.

Sly. Am I a lord? and have I such a lady?
Or do I dream? or have I dream'd till now?
I do not sleep; I see, I hear, I speak;
I smell sweet savours, and I feel soft things:
Upon my life, I am a lord indeed,
And not a tinker, nor Christophero Sly.
Well, bring our lady hither to our sight.
Taming of the Shrew, Induction, 2:70

IMAGINATION

Hotspur. Sometime he angers me
With telling me of the moldwarp[1] and the ant,
Of the dreamer Merlin and his prophecies,
And of a dragon, and a finless fish,
A clip-wing'd griffin, and a moulten raven,
A couching lion, and a ramping cat,
And such a deal of skimble-skamble stuff
As puts me from my faith.
I Henry IV, III, 1:148
[1] moldwarp: mole.

Chorus. O! for a Muse of fire, that would ascend
The brightest heaven of invention;
A kingdom for a stage, princes to act
And monarchs to behold the swelling scene.

. . . . .

Can this cockpit hold
The vasty fields of France? or may we cram
Within this wooden O[1] the very casques
That did affright the air at Agincourt?

. . . . .

Think, when we talk of horses, that you see
  them
Printing their proud hoofs i' the receiving
  earth;
For 't is your thoughts that now must deck
  our kings,
Carry them here and there, jumping o'er
  times,
Turning the accomplishment of many years
Into an hour-glass.
Henry V, Introduction: 1, 11, 26
[1] wooden O: Globe Theater.

Think ye see
The very persons of our noble story
As they were living.
Henry VIII, Prologue: 25

THESEUS. Lovers and madmen have such
  seething brains,
Such shaping fantasies, that apprehend
More than cool reason ever comprehends.
The lunatic, the lover, and the poet,
Are of imagination all compact:
One sees more devils than vast hell can hold,
That is the madman; the lover, all as frantic,
Sees Helen's beauty in a brow of Egypt:
The poet's eye, in a fine frenzy rolling,
Doth glance from heaven to earth, from
  earth to heaven;
And, as imagination bodies forth
The forms of things unknown, the poet's
  pen
Turns them to shapes, and gives to airy
  nothing
A local habitation and a name.
Such tricks hath strong imagination,
That, if it would but apprehend some joy,
It comprehends some bringer of that joy,
Or in the night, imagining some fear,
How easy is a bush suppos'd a bear!
Midsummer Night's Dream, V, 1:4

HIPPOLITA. This is the silliest stuff that
e'er I heard.
THESEUS. The best of this kind are but
shadows, and the worst are no worse, if
imagination amend them.
HIPPOLITA. It must be your imagination
then, and not theirs.
THESEUS. If we imagine no worse of them
than they of themselves, they may pass for
excellent men.
Midsummer Night's Dream, V, 1:212

FRIAR. Claudio:
When he shall hear she died upon his words,
The idea of her life shall sweetly creep
Into his study[1] of imagination,
And every lovely organ of her life
Shall come apparell'd in more precious
  habit,
More moving-delicate and full of life,

Into the eye and prospect of his soul,
Than when she liv'd indeed: then shall he
  mourn,
If ever love had interest in his liver,[2]
And wish he had not so accused her.
Much Ado About Nothing, IV, 1:226
[1] study of imagination: imaginative musings.
[2] liver: sometimes believed to be the seat of the
affection.

K. RICHARD. [soliloquy].[1] Thus play I in
  one person many people,
And none contented: sometimes am I king;
Then treasons make me wish myself a beg-
  gar,
And so I am: then crushing penury
Persuades me I was better when a king;
Then am I king'd again; and by and by
Think that I am unking'd by Bolingbroke,
And straight am nothing: but whate'er I be,
Nor I nor any man that but man is
With nothing shall be pleas'd, till he be eas'd
With being nothing.
Richard II, V, 5:31
[1] The king has been deposed and is in prison.

Weary with toil, I haste me to my bed,
The dear repose for limbs with travel tir'd;
But then begins a journey in my head
To work my mind, when body's work 's
  expir'd;
For then my thoughts, from far where I
  abide,
Intend a zealous pilgrimage to thee,
And keep my drooping eyelids open wide,
Looking on darkness which the blind do see:
Save that my soul's imaginary sight
Presents thy shadow to my sightless view,
Which, like a jewel hung in ghastly night,
Makes black night beauteous and her old
  face new.
Sonnet 27

So, either by thy picture or my love,
Thyself away art present still with me;
For thou not farther than my thoughts canst
  move,
And I am still with them and they with thee.
Sonnet 47

TROILUS. I am giddy, expectation whirls
  me round.
The imaginary relish is so sweet
That it enchants my sense.
Troilus and Cressida, III, 2:19

IMMORTALITY

CLEOPATRA. I have
Immortal longings in me; now no more
The juice of Egypt's grape shall moist this
  lip.
. . . . .

I am fire and air; my other elements
I give to baser life.
Antony and Cleopatra, V, 2:283, 292

HAMLET. It will not speak; then I will
  follow it.
HORATIO. Do not, my lord.
HAMLET. Why, what should be the fear?
I do not set my life at a pin's fee;
And for my soul, what can it do to that,
Being a thing immortal as itself?
It waves me forth again; I 'll follow it.
Hamlet, I, 4:63

MACBETH. Mine eternal jewel
Given to the common enemy of man,
To make them kings, the seed of Banquo
  kings!
Macbeth, III, 1:68

BALTHAZAR. Then she is well, and nothing
  can be ill.
Her body sleeps in Capel's monument,
And her immortal part with angels lives.
Romeo and Juliet, V, 1:17

IMPATIENCE

ROSALIND.[1] Alas the day! what shall I do
with my doublet and hose? What did he
when thou sawest him? What said he? How
looked he? Wherein went he? What makes[2]
he here? Did he ask for me? Where remains
he? How parted he with thee, and when
shalt thou see him again? Answer me in one
word.
  CELIA. You must borrow me Gargantua's[3]
mouth first: 'tis a word too great for any
mouth of this age's size. To say ay and no
to these particulars is more than to answer
in a catechism.
As You Like It, III, 2:232
[1] To CELIA who has just seen ORLANDO.
[2] makes: does.   [3] Gargantua: a huge-mouthed,
voracious giant.

PRINCE. I never thought to hear you speak
  again.
K. HENRY. Thy wish was father, Harry,
  to that thought:
I stay too long by thee, I weary thee.
Dost thou so hunger for mine empty chair
That thou wilt needs invest thee with mine
  honours
Before thy hour is ripe? O foolish youth!
Thou seek'st the greatness that will over-
  whelm thee.
II Henry IV, IV, 5:92

JULIET. Where is my mother? why, she is
  within;
Where should she be? How oddly thou re-
  pliest:

'Your love says, like an honest gentleman,
Where is your mother?'
  NURSE. O! God's lady dear.
Are you so hot? Marry, come up, I trow;
Is this the poultice for my aching bones?
Henceforward do your messages yourself.
  JULIET. Here 's such a coil![1] come, what
  says Romeo?
Romeo and Juliet, II, 5:60
[1] coil: confusion.

IMPOSSIBILITY

JOAN OF ARC. Because you want[1] the grace
  that others have,
You judge it straight a thing impossible
To compass wonders but by help of devils.
I Henry VI, V, 4:46
[1] want: lack.

LIGARIUS. Now bid me run,
And I will strive with things impossible;
Yea, get the better of them.
Julius Caesar, II, 1:324

REGAN. How, in one house,
Should many people, under two commands,
Hold amity? 'T is hard; almost impossible.
King Lear, II, 4:243

ISABELLA. Make not impossible that which
  but seems unlike.
Measure for Measure, V, 1:51

INCONSTANCY

MARCIUS.[1] He that trusts to you,
Where he should find you lions, finds you
  hares;
Where foxes, geese: you are no surer, no,
Than is the coal of fire upon the ice,
Or hailstone in the sun. Your virtue is
To make him worthy whose offence subdues
  him,
And curse that justice did it. Who deserves
  greatness
Deserves your hate; and your affections are
A sick man's appetite, who desires most that
Which would increase his evil. He that de-
  pends
Upon your favours swims with fins of lead,
And hews down oaks with rushes.
Coriolanus, I, 1:173
[1] Later CORIOLANUS, to the Roman crowd.

Fair is my love, but not so fair as fickle;
Mild as a dove, but neither true nor trusty;
Brighter than glass, and yet, as glass is, brit-
  tle;
Softer than wax, and yet, as iron, rusty:

A lily pale, with damask dye to grace her,
None fairer, nor none falser to deface her.
    The Passionate Pilgrim, 85

PROTEUS. O heaven! were man
But constant, he were perfect: that one error
Fills him with faults; makes him run through
    all the sins:
Inconstancy falls off ere it begins.
    Two Gentlemen of Verona, V, 4:110

LEONTES. I am a feather for each wind
    that blows.
    Winter's Tale, II, 3:154

INDEPENDENCE

PISANIO. If not at court,
Then not in Britain must you bide.
  IMOGEN. Where then?
Hath Britain all the sun that shines? Day,
    night,
Are they not but in Britain? I' the world's
    volume
Our Britain seems as of it, but not in 't;
In a great pool a swan's nest: prithee, think
There 's livers out of Britain.
    Cymbeline, III, 4:137

BERNADINE. Friar, not I: I have been drinking hard all night, and I will have more time
to prepare me, or they shall beat out my
brains with billets.[1] I will not consent to die
this day, that 's certain.
    Measure for Measure, IV, 3:57
[1] billets: thick sticks.

DON JOHN. I cannot hide what I am: I
must be sad when I have cause, and smile at
no man's jests; eat when I have stomach,
and wait for no man's leisure; sleep when
I am drowsy, and tend[1] on no man's business; laugh when I am merry, and claw[2] no
man in his humour.
    Much Ado About Nothing, I, 3:14
[1] tend: wait. [2] claw: flatter.

VIOLA. I am no fee'd post, lady; keep
your purse.
    Twelfth Night, I, 5:303

INFATUATION

PHILO.[1] Nay, but this dotage of our gen-
    eral's
O'erflows the measure; those his goodly
    eyes,
That o'er the files and musters of the war
Have glow'd like plated Mars, now bend,
    now turn,
The office and devotion of their view
Upon a tawny front; his captain's heart,

Which in the scuffles of great fights hath
    burst
The buckles on his breast, reneges[2] all tem-
    per,
And is become the bellows and the fan
To cool a gipsy's lust . . .
Take but good note, and you shall see in him
The triple pillar[3] of the world transform'd
Into a strumpet's fool.
    Antony and Cleopatra, I, 1:1
[1] About ANTONY. [2] reneges: denies. [3] triple
pillar: one of the three men, Triumvirs, who
ruled Rome.

ANTONY. There 's not a minute of our
    lives should stretch
Without some pleasure now. What sport to-
    night?
    Antony and Cleopatra, I, 1:46

CLEOPATRA. O Charmian!
Where think'st thou he is now? Stand he, or
    sits he?
Or does he walk? or is he on his horse?
O happy horse, to bear the weight of An-
    tony!
Do bravely, horse, for wott'st thou whom
    thou movest?
The demi-Atlas of this earth, the arm
And burgonet[1] of men. He 's speaking now,
Or murmuring 'Where 's my serpent of old
    Nile?'
For so he calls me. Now I feed myself
With most delicious poison. Think on me,
That am with Phoebus'[2] amorous pinches
    black,
And wrinkled deep in time?
    Antony and Cleopatra, I, 5:18
[1] burgonet: a helmet or headpiece. [2] Phoebus:
god of music and sun god.

CHAMBERLAIN.[1] Beauty and honour in her
    are so mingled
That they have caught the king.
    Henry VIII, II, 3:76
[1] About ANNE BULLEN.

ROMEO. One fairer than my love! the all-
    seeing sun
Ne'er saw her[1] match since first the world
    begun.
    Romeo and Juliet, I, 2:97
[1] her: ROSALINE, whom he met before seeing
JULIET.

DUKE. O! when mine eyes did see Olivia
    first,
Methought she purg'd the air of pestilence.
That instant was I turn'd into a hart
And my desires, like fell and cruel hounds,
E'er since pursue me.
    Twelfth Night, I, 1:19

INFIRMITY

MALVOLIO. Infirmity, that decays the wise,
doth ever make the better fool.
CLOWN. God send you, sir, a speedy infirmity, for the better increasing your folly!
Twelfth Night, I, 5:82

INGRATITUDE

AMIENS [singing]. Blow, blow, thou win-
ter wind,
Thou art not so unkind
As man's ingratitude;
Thy tooth is not so keen,
Because thou art not seen,
Although thy breath be rude.
Heigh-ho! sing, heigh-ho! unto the green
holly:
Most friendship is feigning, most loving
mere folly.
Then heigh-ho, the holly!
This life is most jolly.
Freeze, freeze, thou bitter sky,
That dost not bite so nigh
As benefits forgot:
Though thou the waters warp,
Thy sting is not so sharp
As friend remember'd not.
Heigh-ho! sing, heigh-ho! unto the green
holly:
Most friendship is feigning, most loving
mere folly.
Then heigh-ho, the holly!
This life is most jolly.
As You Like It, II, 7:174

K. LEAR. Ingratitude, thou marble-hearted
fiend,
More hideous, when thou show'st thee in a
child,
Than the sea-monster.
King Lear, I, 4:281

ANTONY. This was the most unkindest cut
of all;
For when the noble Caesar saw him stab,
Ingratitude more strong than traitor's arms,
Quite vanquish'd him: then burst his mighty
heart;
Julius Caesar, III, 2:187

K. LEAR. How sharper than a serpent's
tooth it is
To have a thankless child!
King Lear, I, 4:310

K. LEAR. Filial ingratitude!
Is it not as this mouth should tear this hand
For lifting food to 't?
King Lear, III, 4:14

FLAMINIUS.[1] Let molten coin be thy dam-
nation,
Thou disease of a friend, and not himself!
Has friendship such a faint and milky heart
It turns in less than two nights? O you gods!
I feel my master's passion. This slave, unto
his honour,
Has my lord's meat in him:
Why should it thrive and turn to nutriment
When he is turn'd to poison?
Timon of Athens, III, 1:53
[1] Speaking to LUCULLUS, who has refused to
help TIMON.

JULIA. As in revenge of thy ingratitude,
I throw thy name against the bruising stones,
Trampling contemptuously on thy disdain.
Two Gentlemen of Verona, I, 2:110

VIOLA. I hate ingratitude more in a man
Than lying, vainness, babbling, drunken-
ness,
Or any taint of vice whose strong corrup-
tion
Inhabits our frail blood.
Twelfth Night, III, 4:388

INNOCENCE

IMOGEN. False to his bed! What is it to be
false?
To lie in watch there and to think on him?
To weep 'twixt clock and clock? if sleep
charge nature,
To break it with a fearful dream of him,
And cry myself awake? that 's false to 's
bed, is it?
Cymbeline, III, 4:42

HAMLET. Let the galled jade wince, our
withers are unwrung.
Hamlet, III, 2:251

GLOUCESTER. Well, Suffolk's duke, thou
shalt not see me blush,
Nor change my countenance for this arrest:
A heart unspotted is not easily daunted.
II Henry VI, III, 1:98

VIOLA. My remembrance is very free and
clear from any image of offence done to
any man.
Twelfth Night, III, 4:248

HERMIONE. If powers divine
Behold our human actions, as they do,
I dout not then but innocence shall make
False accusation blush, and tyranny
Tremble at patience.
Winter's Tale, III, 2:29

INSULT

MENENIUS. Good den[1] to your worship; more of your conversation would infect my brain.
Coriolanus, II, 1:102

[1] Sometimes God-den, here, good-bye; a salutation usually meaning "God give you good evening."

CORIOLANUS. You[1] common cry[2] of curs! whose breath I hate
As reek o' the rotten fens, whose loves I prize
As the dead carcasses of unburied men
That do corrupt my air, I banish you.
Coriolanus, III, 3:120

[1] you: the common people. [2] cry: pack.

K. HENRY. What treasure, uncle?
EXETER. Tennis-balls, my liege.
K. HENRY. We are glad the Dauphin is so pleasant with us;
His present and your pains we thank you for;
When we have match'd our rackets to these balls,
We will in France, by God's grace, play a set
Shall strike his father's crown into the hazard.[1]
Henry V, I, 2:258

[1] hazard: the risk in a game.

K. LEAR. Do you bandy looks with me, you rascal?
Striking him.
OSWALD. I'll not be struck, my lord.
KENT. Nor tripped neither, you base football player.
Tripping up his heels.
King Lear, I, 4:92

BRABANTIO. Thou art a villain.
IAGO. You are—a senator.
Othello, I, 1:119

THERSITES. Thou mongrel beef-witted lord! I think thy horse will sooner con an oration than thou learn a prayer without book.
Troilus and Cressida, II, 1:14

THERSITES. I would thou didst itch from head to foot, and I had the scratching of thee; I would make thee the loathsomest scab in Greece.
Troilus and Cressida, II, 1:29

INTENTIONS

ROMEO. The time and my intents are savage-wild,

More fierce and more inexorable far
Than empty tigers or the roaring sea.
Romeo and Juliet, V, 3:37

INVITATION

BASSANIO. If it please you to dine with us.
SHYLOCK. Yes, to smell pork; to eat of the habitation which your prophet the Nazarite conjured the devil into. I will buy with you, sell with you, talk with you, walk with you, and so following; but I will not eat with you, drink with you, nor pray with you.
Merchant of Venice, I, 3:33

IAGO. What an eye she has! methinks it sounds a parley to provocation.
Othello, II, 3:22

CAPULET. Such comfort as do lusty young men feel
When well-apparell'd April on the heel
Of limping winter treads, even such delight
Among fresh female buds shall you this night
Inherit at my house; hear all, all see,
And like her most whose merit most shall be.
Romeo and Juliet, I, 2:26

INVOCATION

IRIS.[1] Ceres,[2] most bounteous lady, thy rich leas
Of wheat, rye, barley, vetches,[3] oats, and pease;
Thy turfy mountains, where live nibbling sheep,
And flat meads thatch'd with stover,[4] them to keep;
Thy banks with pioned[5] and twilled brims,
Which spongy April at thy hest betrims,
To make cold nymphs chaste crowns; and thy broom-groves,[6]
Whose shadow the dismissed bachelor loves,
Being lass-lorn; thy pole-clipt vineyard;
And thy sea-marge, sterile, and rocky-hard,
Where thou thyself dost air;—the queen o' the sky,
Whose watery arch and messenger am I,
Bids thee leave these, and with her sovereign grace,
Here on this grass-plot, in this very place,
To come and sport: her peacocks fly amain:
Approach, rich Ceres, her to entertain.
The Tempest, IV, 1:60

[1] IRIS: goddess of the rainbow. [2] CERES: goddess of agriculture. [3] vetches: peas and beans. [4] stover: grass; [5] pioned . . . twilled: probably overgrown with marsh marigolds and reeds. [6] broom-groves: metaphorically, pathless woods.

IRONY

HAMLET. 'Twere good you let him know;
For who, that's but a queen, fair, sober, wise,
Would from a paddock,[1] from a bat, a gib,[2]
Such dear concernings hide?
Hamlet, III, 4:188
[1] paddock: toad.   [2] gib: tomcat.

PAGE. A proper gentlewoman, sir, and a
kinswoman of my master's.
PRINCE. Even such kin as the parish heifers
are to the town bull.
II Henry IV, II, 2:169

FALSTAFF. Well said, good woman's tailor!
well said, courageous Feeble! Thou wilt be
as valiant as the wrathful dove or most
magnanimous mouse. Prick[1] the woman's
tailor: well, Master Shallow.

. . . . .

And this same half-faced fellow, Shadow;
give me this man: he presents no mark to
the enemy; the foeman may with as great
aim level at the edge of a penknife. And for
a retreat; how swiftly will this Feeble the
woman's tailor run off! O! give me the spare
men and spare me the great ones.
II Henry IV, III, 2:170, 282
[1] Prick: list as a soldier under FALSTAFF.

JEALOUSY

CLEOPATRA. Nay, hear them,[1] Antony:
Fulvia[2] perchance is angry; or, who knows
If the scarce-bearded Caesar have not sent
His powerful mandate to you, 'Do this, or
this;
Take in that kingdom, and enfranchise that;
Perform 't, or else we damn thee'?

. . . . .

Thou blushest, Antony, and that blood of
thine
Is Caesar's homager; else so thy cheek pays
shame
When shrill-tongued Fulvia scolds.
Antony and Cleopatra, I, 1:19, 30.
[1] them: messengers from Rome.   [2] FULVIA: AN-
TONY's wife.

CLEOPATRA.[1] Why should I think you can
be mine and true,
Though you in swearing shake the throned
gods,
Who have been false to Fulvia? Riotous
madness,
To be entangled with those mouth-made
vows,
Which break themselves in swearing!

. . . . .

Nay, pray you, seek no colour[2] for your
going,
But bid farewell, and go; when you sued
staying
Then was the time for words; no going
then:
Eternity was in our lips and eyes,
Bliss in our brows' bent; none our parts so
poor
But was a race of heaven; they are so still,
Or thou, the greatest soldier of the world,
Art turn'd the greatest liar.
Antony and Cleopatra, I, 3:27, 32
[1] To ANTONY.   [2] colour: excuse.

LUCIANA. Self-harming jealousy! fie! beat
it hence.
ADRIANA. Unfeeling fools can with such
wrongs dispense.
I know his eye doth homage otherwhere,
Or else what lets[1] it but he would be here?

. . . . .

Since that my beauty cannot please his eye,
I 'll weep what's left away, and weeping die.
LUCIANA. How many fond fools serve
mad jealousy!
Comedy of Errors, II, 1:102, 113
[1] lets: prevents.

ABBESS. And thereof came it that the man
was mad:
The venom clamours of a jealous woman
Poison more deadly than a mad dog's tooth.
Comedy of Errors, V, 1:69

Q. MARGARET. Not all these lords do vex
me half so much
As that proud dame, the lord protector's
wife:

. . . . .

Strangers in court do take her[1] for the
queen:
She bears a duke's revenues on her back,
And in her heart she scorns our poverty.
Shall I not live to be aveng'd on her?
II Henry VI, I, 3:78, 82
[1] her: DUCHESS OF GLOUCESTER.

CASSIUS. This man
Is now become a god, and Cassius is
A wretched creature and must bend his
body
If Caesar carelessly but nod on him.
Julius Caesar, II, 2:115

IAGO. O! beware, my lord, of jealousy;
It is the green-eyed monster which doth
mock
The meat it feeds on; that cuckold lives in
bliss
Who, certain of his fate, loves not his
wronger;

But, O! what damned minutes tells[1] he o'er
Who dotes, yet doubts; suspects, yet
    soundly loves.
                    Othello, III, 3:165
[1] tells: counts.

OTHELLO. No, Iago,
I'll see before I doubt; when I doubt, prove;
And on the proof there is no more but this,
Away at once with love or jealousy!
                    Othello, III, 3:189

DESDEMONA. Alas the day! I never gave
    him cause.
EMILIA. But jealous souls will not be
    answer'd so;
They are not ever jealous for the cause,
But jealous for[1] they are jealous; 't is a
    monster
Begot upon itself, born on itself.

                    Othello, III, 4:158
[1] for: often used for because in Shakespeare.

KATHARINA.[1] Nay, now I see
She[2] is your treasure, she must have a hus-
    band;
I must dance barefoot[3] on her wedding-day,
And, for your love to her, lead apes in hell.[4]
Talk not to me: I will go sit and weep
Till I can find occasion of revenge.
                    Taming of the Shrew, II, 1:32
[1] To BAPTISTA. [2] She: BIANCA, her younger
sister. [3] dance . . . wedding-day: said of an
older sister when a younger one is married
first. [4] lead . . . in hell: supposed consequence
of dying an old maid.

This sour informer, this bate-breeding[1] spy,
This canker that eats up Love's tender
    spring,
This carry-tale, dissentious Jealousy,
That sometime true news, sometime false
    doth bring.
                    Venus and Adonis: 655
[1] bate-breeding: strife breeding.

LEONTES. Still virginalling[1]
Upon his palm!
                    Winter's Tale, I, 2:125
[1] virginalling: playing as on a small instrument
like a piano, so named because used by young
girls.

HERMIONE. Why, lo you now, I have
    spoke to the purpose twice:
The one for ever earn'd a royal husband,
The other for some while a friend.
                    Giving her hand to POLIXENES.
LEONTES [aside]. Too hot, too hot!
To mingle friendship far is mingling bloods.
I have *tremor cordis*[1] on me: my heart
    dances;

But not for joy; not joy. This entertainment
May a free face put on, derive a liberty
From heartiness, from bounty's fertile
    bosom,
And well become the agent: 't may, I grant;
But to be paddling palms, and pinching
    fingers,
As now they are, and making practis'd
    smiles,
As in a looking-glass; and then to sigh, as 't
    were
The mort[2] o' the deer; O! that is entertain-
    ment
My bosom likes not, nor my brows.
                    Winter's Tale, I, 2:106
[1] *tremor cordis:* trembling of the heart. [2] mort:
death.

LEONTES.[1] Arms her with the boldness of a
    wife
To her allowing husband!
                    Winter's Tale, I, 2:184
[1] About POLIXENES and HERMIONE.

LEONTES. Is whispering nothing?
Is leaning cheek to cheek? is meeting noses?
Kissing with inside lip? stopping the career
Of laughter with a sigh? a note infallible
Of breaking honesty; horsing foot on foot?
Skulking in corners? wishing clocks more
    swift?
Hours, minutes? noon, midnight? and all
    eyes
Blind with the pin and web[1] but theirs, theirs
    only,
That would unseen be wicked? is this noth-
    ing?
Why, then the world and all that is in 't is
    nothing;
The covering sky is nothing; Bohemia[2]
    nothing;
My wife is nothing; nor nothing have these
    nothings,
If this be nothing.
                    Winter's Tale, I, 2:284
[1] pin and web: cataract in its early stage.
[2] Bohemia: POLIXENES, King of Bohemia.

JEST—JESTER

BIRON. This jest is dry to me. Fair gentle
    sweet,
Your wit makes wise things foolish.
                    Love's Labour's Lost, V, 2:373

ROSALINE. A jest's prosperity lies in the
    ear
Of him that hears it, never in the tongue
Of him that makes it.
                    Love's Labour's Lost, V, 2:871

IsABELLA. Great men may jest with saints; 't is wit in them,
But in the less foul profanation.
Measure for Measure, II, 2:127

VIOLA. This fellow 's wise enough to play the fool,[1]
And to do that well craves a kind of wit:
He must observe their mood on whom he jests,
The quality of persons, and the time.
Twelfth Night, III, 1:67

[1] fool: jester; as often in Shakespeare.

FABIAN. With some excellent jests, fire-new from the mint, you should have banged the youth into dumbness.
Twelfth Night, III, 2:24

SPEED. O jest unseen, inscrutable, invisible,
As a nose on a man's face, or a weathercock on a steeple!
Two Gentlemen of Verona, II, 1:140

JESUS

K. HENRY. Therefore, friends,
As far as to the sepulchre of Christ,
Whose soldier now, under whose blessed cross
We are impressed and engag'd to fight,

. . . . .

To chase these pagans in those holy fields
Over whose acres walk'd those blessed feet
Which fourteen hundred years ago were nail'd
For our advantage on the bitter cross.
I Henry IV, I, 1:18, 24

GAUNT. Renowned for their[1] deeds as far from home,
For Christian service and true chivalry,
As is the sepulchre in stubborn Jewry
Of the world's ransom, blessed Mary's son.
Richard II, II, 1:53

[1] their: English kings.

JOAN OF ARC—LA PUCELLE

BASTARD. A holy maid hither with me I bring,
Which by a vision sent to her from heaven
Ordained is to raise this tedious siege,
And drive the English forth the bounds of France.
The spirit of deep prophecy she hath,
Exceeding the nine sibyls of old Rome;
What 's past and what 's to come she can descry.
I Henry VI, I, 2:51

PUCELLE. Where is the Dauphin? Come, come from behind;
I know thee well, though never seen before.
Be not amaz'd, there 's nothing hid from me:
I Henry VI, I, 2:66

CHARLES. My heart and hands thou hast at once subdued.
Excellent Pucelle, if thy name be so,
Let me thy servant and not sovereign be:
'T is the French Dauphin sueth to thee thus.
I Henry VI, I, 2:109

PUCELLE. O'ertake me if thou canst; I scorn thy strength.
Go, go, cheer up thy hunger-starved men;
Help Salisbury to make his testament:
This day is ours, as many more shall be.
Exit.
TALBOT. My thoughts are whirled like a potter's wheel;
I know not where I am, nor what I do:

. . . . .

PUCELLE. Advance our waving colours on the walls;
Rescu'd is Orleans from the English.
Thus Joan la Pucelle hath perform'd her word.
I Henry VI, I, 5:15 and I, 6:1

CHARLES. 'T is Joan, not we, by whom the day is won;
For which I will divide my crown with her;
And all the priests and friars in my realm
Shall in procession sing her endless praise.
I Henry VI, I, 6:17

PUCELLE. The regent conquers and the Frenchmen fly.
Now help, ye charming spells and periapts;[1]
And ye choice spirits that admonish me
Appear and aid me in this enterprise!

. . . . .

YORK. Damsel of France, I think I have you fast:
Unchain your spirits now with spelling charms,
And try if they can gain your liberty.
A goodly prize, fit for the devil's grace!
I Henry VI, V, 3:1, 30

[1] periapts: amulets.

YORK. Take her away; for she hath lived too long
To fill the world with vicious qualities.
PUCELLE. First, let me tell you whom you have condemn'd:
Not me begotten of a shepherd swain,
But issu'd from the progeny of kings;
Virtuous and holy; chosen from above,
By inspiration of celestial grace,

To work exceeding miracles on earth.
I never had to do with wicked spirits.
I Henry VI, V, 4:34

PUCELLE. Joan of Arc hath been
A virgin from her tender infancy,
Chaste and immaculate in very thought;
Whose maiden blood, thus rigorously
effus'd,
Will cry for vengeance at the gates of
heaven.
I Henry VI, V, 4:49

JOY

PAROLLES. Make the coming hour o'erflow
with joy,
And pleasure drown the brim.
All's Well That Ends Well, II, 4:47

KING.[1] Therefore our sometime sister,
now our queen,
The imperial jointress of this war-like state
Have we, as 't were with a defeated joy,
With one auspicious and one dropping eye,
With mirth in funeral and with dirge in
marriage,
In equal scale weighing delight and dole,
Taken to wife.
Hamlet, I, 2:8
[1] KING CLAUDIUS announces his marriage to
HAMLET's mother.

GRATIANO. All things that are,
Are with more spirit chased than enjoy'd.
Merchant of Venice, II, 6:12

BASSANIO. And here choose I: joy be the
consequence!
PORTIA [aside]. How all the other passions fleet to air,
As doubtful thoughts, and rash-embrac'd
despair,
And shuddering fear, and green-eyed jealousy!
Merchant of Venice, III, 2:107

THESEUS. Joy, gentle friends! joy and
fresh days of love
Accompany your hearts!
Midsummer Night's Dream, V, 1:29

BOLINGBROKE.[1] Choose out some secret
place, some reverend room
More than thou hast, and with it joy thy
life.
Richard II, V, 6:25
[1] Later, King Henry IV.

ROMEO. Ah! Juliet, if the measure of thy
joy
Be heap'd like mine, and that thy skill be
more

To blazon it, then sweeten with thy breath
This neighbour air, and let rich music's
tongue
Unfold the imagin'd happiness that both
Receive in either by this dear encounter.
Romeo and Juliet, II, 6:24

FRIAR LAURENCE. Beg pardon of the
prince, and call thee back
With twenty hundred thousand times more
joy
Than thou went'st forth in lamentation.
Romeo and Juliet, III, 3:152

PANDARUS. Things won are done; joy's
soul lies in the doing.
Troilus and Cressida, I, 2:313

TROILUS. Swooning destruction, or some
joy too fine,
Too subtle-potent, tun'd too sharp in sweet-
ness
For the capacity of my ruder powers:
I fear it much: and I do fear besides
That I shall lose distinction in my joys.
Troilus and Cressida, III, 2:24

JUDGE—JUDGMENT

HELENA. When judges have been babes;
great floods have flown
From simple sources; and great seas have
dried
When miracles have by the greatest been
denied.
All's Well That Ends Well, II, 1:142

ENOBARBUS. Men's judgments are
A parcel of their fortunes, and things out-
ward
Do draw the inward quality after them,
To suffer all alike.
Antony and Cleopatra, III, 13:31

ANTONY. O misery on 't! the wise gods
seel our eyes;
In our own filth drop our clear judgments;
make us
Adore our errors; laugh at 's, while we strut
To our confusion.
Antony and Cleopatra, III, 13:112

POLONIUS. Give every man thine ear, but
few thy voice;
Take each man's censure,[1] but reserve thy
judgment.
Hamlet, I, 3:68
[1] censure: opinion, as often in Shakespeare.

KING. He[1] 's lov'd of the distracted multitude.

Who like not in their judgment, but their
eyes.
                                       Hamlet, IV, 3:4
[1] He: HAMLET.

WARWICK. Between two hawks, which
flies the higher pitch;
Between two dogs, which hath the deeper
mouth;
Between two blades, which bears the better
temper;
Between two horses, which doth bear him
best;
Between two girls, which hath the merriest
eye;
I have perhaps some shallow spirit of judgment;
But in these nice[1] sharp quillets[2] of the law,
Good faith, I am no wiser than a daw.
                                    I Henry VI, II, 4:11
[1] nice: hair-splitting. [2] quillets: sly tricks in
argument.

K. HENRY. Forbear to judge, for we are
sinners all.
Close up his[1] eyes, and draw the curtain
close;
And let us all to meditation.
                                   II Henry VI, III, 3:31
[1] his: CARDINAL BEAUFORT'S.

K. JOHN. From whom hast thou this great
commission, France,
To draw my answer from thy articles?
K. PHILIP. From that supernal judge, that
stirs good thoughts
In any breast of strong authority.
                                      King John, II, 1:110

K. LEAR [striking his head]. O Lear, Lear,
Lear!
Beat at this gate, that let thy folly in,
And thy dear judgment out!
                                      King Lear, I, 4:292

PROVOST. I have seen,
When, after execution, judgment hath
Repented o'er his[1] doom.
                           Measure for Measure, II, 2:10
[1] his: its.

ANGELO. Condemn the fault and not the
actor of it?
                           Measure for Measure, II, 2:37

ANGELO. Thieves for their robbery have
authority
When judges steal themselves.
                          Measure for Measure, II, 2:176

DUKE. He who the sword of heaven will
bear
Should be as holy as severe.
                         Measure for Measure, III, 2:275

WIDOW. He that is giddy thinks the world
turns round.
                          Taming of the Shrew, V, 2:20

JUSTICE

ANTONY. Things that are past are done
with me.
'T is thus:
Who tells me true, though in his tale lie
death,
I hear him as[1] he flatter'd.
                           Antony and Cleopatra, I, 2:101
[1] as: as if.

CANTERBURY. The sad-ey'd justice, with
his surly hum,
Delivering o'er to executors pale
The lazy yawning drone.
                                    Henry V, I, 2:202

GLOUCESTER.[1] Eleanor,[2] the law, thou
seest, hath judged thee:
I cannot justify whom the law condemns.
                                   II Henry VI, II, 3:15
[1] Uncle of KING HENRY VI. [2] ELEANOR: wife
of GLOUCESTER, is banished.

K. HENRY. What stronger breastplate than
a heart untainted!
Thrice is he arm'd that hath his quarrel just,
And he but naked, though lock'd up in steel,
Whose conscience with injustice is cor-
rupted.
                                   II Henry VI, III, 2:232

K. LEAR. Let the great gods,
That keep this dreadful pother o'er our
heads,
Find out their enemies now. Tremble, thou
wretch,
That hast within thee undivulged crimes,
Unwhipp'd of justice; hide thee, thou
bloody hand,
Thou perjur'd, and thou simular[1] of virtue
That art incestuous; caitiff, to pieces shake,
That under covert and convenient seeming
Hast practis'd on man's life; close pent-up
guilts,[2]
Rive your concealing continents, and cry
These dreadful summoners grace. I am a
man
More sinn'd against than sinning.
                                      King Lear, III, 2:49
[1] simular: counterfeit. [2] guilts . . . grace: de-
stroy your hiding places and beg mercy of the
gods.

MACBETH. This even-handed justice
Commends the ingredients of our poison'd
chalice
To our own lips.
                                    Macbeth, I, 7:10

ANGELO. 'T is one thing to be tempted, Escalus,
Another thing to fall. I not deny,
The jury, passing on the prisoner's life,
May in the sworn twelve have a thief or two
Guiltier than him they try; what's open made to justice,
That justice seizes: what know the laws
That thieves do pass on thieves?

Measure for Measure, II, 1:17

ISABELLA. Justice, O royal duke! Vail[1] your regard
Upon a wrong'd, I would fain have said, a maid!
O worthy prince! dishonour not your eye
By throwing it on any other object,
Till you have heard me in my true complaint,
And given me justice, justice, justice, justice!

Measure for Measure, V, 1:20

[1] Vail: let fall.

PORTIA. Earthly power doth then show likest God's
When mercy seasons justice.

Merchant of Venice, IV, 1:196

PORTIA. As thou urgest justice, be assur'd
Thou shalt have justice, more than thou desirest.

Merchant of Venice, IV, 1:315

KINDNESS

OLIVER. Kindness, nobler ever than revenge.

As You Like It, IV, 3:129

TALBOT. Ne'er trust me then; for when a world of men
Could not prevail with all their oratory,
Yet hath a woman's kindness over-rul'd.

I Henry VI, II, 2:48

MISTRESS QUICKLY. A kind heart he hath: a woman would run through fire and water for such a kind heart.

Merry Wives of Windsor, III, 4:104

MARINA. I never kill'd a mouse, nor hurt a fly;
I trod upon a worm against my will,
But I wept for it. How have I offended?

Pericles, IV, 1:78

KING

HAMLET. So excellent a king; that was, to[1] this,

Hyperion to a satyr; so loving to my mother
That he might not beteem the winds of heaven
Visit her face too roughly. Heaven and earth!
Must I remember? why, she would hang on him,
As if increase of appetite had grown
By what it fed on; and yet, within a month.

Hamlet, I, 2:137

[1] to: compared with.

HAMLET. O God! I could be bounded in a nutshell, and count myself a king of infinite space, were it not that I have bad dreams.

Hamlet, II, 2:261

ROSENCRANTZ. The cease of majesty
Dies not alone; but like a gulf doth draw
What's near it with it: it is a massy wheel,
Fix'd on the summit of the highest mount,
To whose huge spokes ten thousand lesser things
Are mortis'd and adjoin'd; which, when it falls,
Each small annexment, petty consequence,
Attends the boisterous ruin. Never alone
Did the king sigh, but with a general groan.

Hamlet, III, 3:15

HAMLET. A king of shreds and patches.

Hamlet, III, 4:102

HAMLET. A man may fish with the worm that hath eat of a king, and eat of the fish that hath fed of that worm.

Hamlet, IV, 3:29

PISTOL. The king's a bawcock,[1] and a heart of gold,
A lad of life, an imp of fame;
Of parents good, of fist most valiant:
I kiss his dirty shoe and from heart-string
I love the lovely bully.

Henry V, IV, 1:44

[1] bawcock: fine fellow.

K. HENRY. I think the king is but a man, as I am: the violet smells to him as it doth to me; the element shows to him as it doth to me; all his senses have but human conditions: his ceremonies laid by, in his nakedness he appears but a man; and though his affections are higher mounted than ours, yet when they stoop, they stoop with the like wing.

Henry V, IV, 1:105

K. HENRY. Was ever king that joy'd an earthly throne,
And could command no more content than I?
No sooner was I crept out of my cradle
But I was made a king at nine months old:

Was never subject long'd to be a king
As I do long and wish to be a subject.
                              II Henry VI, IV, 9:1

K. HENRY [soliloquy]. O God! me-
   thinks it were a happy life,
To be no better than a homely swain;
To sit upon a hill, as I do now,
To carve out dials quaintly, point by point,
Thereby to see the minutes how they run,
How many make the hour full complete;
How many hours bring about the day;
How many days will finish up the year;
How many years a mortal man may live.
When this is known, then to divide the
   times:
So many hours must I tend my flock;
So many hours must I take my rest;
So many hours must I contemplate;
So many hours must I sport myself;
So many days my ewes have been with
   young;
So many weeks ere the poor fools will ean;[1]
So many years ere I shall shear the fleece:
So minutes, hours, days, months, and years,
Pass'd over to the end they were created,
Would bring white hairs unto a quiet grave.
Ah! what a life were this; how sweet! how
   lovely!
Gives not the hawthorn-bush a sweeter
   shade
To shepherds looking on their silly sheep,
Than doth a rich embroider'd canopy
To kings that fear their subjects' treachery?
O yes! it doth; a thousand-fold it doth.
And to conclude, the shepherd's homely
   curds,
His cold thin drink out of his leather bottle,
His wonted sleep under a fresh tree's shade,
All which secure and sweetly he enjoys,
Is far beyond a prince's delicates,
His viands sparkling in a golden cup,
His body couched in a curious[2] bed,
When care, mistrust, and treason waits on
   him.
                              III Henry VI, II, 5:21
[1] ean: bring forth young. [2] curious: richly
furnished.

WARWICK. Who liv'd king but I could dig
   his grave!
And who durst smile when Warwick bent
   his brow?
                              III Henry VI, V, 2:21

BIRON. O me! with what strict patience
   have I sat,
To see a king transformed to a gnat;
                              Love's Labour's Lost, IV, 3:165

PORTIA. So doth the greater glory dim the
   less:
A substitute shines brightly as a king

Until a king be by, and then his state
Empties itself, as doth an inland brook
Into the main of waters.
                              Merchant of Venice, V, 1:93

K. RICHARD. We were not born to sue, but
   to command;
                              Richard II, I, 1:196

K. RICHARD. I had forgot myself. Am I
   not king?
Awake, thou sluggard majesty! thou sleep-
   est.
Is not the king's name twenty thousand
   names?
Arm, arm, my name! a puny subject strikes
At thy great glory.
                              Richard II, III, 2:83

CARLISLE. What subject can give sentence
   on his king?
And who sits here that is not Richard's sub-
   ject?
Thieves are not judg'd but[1] they are by to
   hear,
Although apparent guilt be seen in them;
And shall the figure of God's majesty,
His captain, steward, deputy elect,
Anointed, crowned, planted many years,
Be judg'd by subject and inferior breath,
And he himself not present? O! forfend[2] it,
   God.
                              Richard II, IV, 1:121
[1] but: unless.   [2] forfend: forbid.

BOATSWAIN. What care these roarers[1] for
   the name of king?
                              Tempest, I, 1:19
[1] roarers: here, waves.

KINGDOM

K. HENRY. O my poor kingdom, sick
   with civil blows!
When that my care could not withhold thy
   riots,
What wilt thou do when riot is thy care?
O! thou wilt be a wilderness again,
Peopled with wolves, thy old inhabitants.
                              II Henry IV, IV, 5:134

K. RICHARD. I weep for joy
To stand upon my kingdom once again.
Dear earth, I do salute thee with my hand,
Though rebels wound thee with their horses
   hoofs.
                              Richard II, III, 2:4

K. RICHARD. Mine ear is open and my
   heart prepar'd:
The worst is worldly loss thou canst unfold.
Say, is my kingdom lost? why, 't was my
   care;
And what loss is it to be rid of care?
                              Richard II, III, 2:93

KISS

ROSALIND. And his kissing is as full of sanctity as the touch of holy bread.
As You Like It, III, 4:14

ROSALIND. What would you say to me now, an[1] I were your very very Rosalind?
ORLANDO. I would kiss before I spoke.
ROSALIND. Nay, you were better speak first, and when you were gravelled for lack of matter, you might take occasion to kiss.
As You Like It, IV, 1:70
[1] an: if.

MORTIMER.[1] I understand thy kisses and thou mine,
And that 's a feeling disputation.
I Henry IV, III, 1:205
[1] To his Welsh wife, whose language he does not understand.

BEATRICE. Speak, cousin; or, if you cannot, stop his mouth with a kiss, and let him not speak neither.
Much Ado About Nothing, II, 1:321

Her lips to mine how often hath she join'd,
Between each kiss her oaths of true love swearing!
How many tales to please me hath she coin'd,
Dreading my love, the loss thereof still fearing!
Yet in the midst of all her pure protestings,
Her faith, her oaths, her tears, and all were jestings.
Passionate Pilgrim: 91

MARCUS. Alas! poor heart; that kiss is comfortless
As frozen water to a starved snake.
Titus Andronicus, III, 1:251

CRESSIDA. The kiss you take is better than you give.
Troilus and Cressida, IV, 5:38

Ten kisses short as one, one long as twenty:
A summer's day will seem an hour but short,
Being wasted in such time-beguiling sport.
. . . . .
Give me one kiss, I'll give it thee again.
Venus and Adonis: 22, 209

A thousand kisses buys my heart from me;
And pay them at thy leisure, one by one.
Venus and Adonis: 517

KNAVE

LAFEU. Whether dost thou profess thyself, a knave or a fool?

CLOWN. A fool, sir, at a woman's service, and a knave at a man's.
All's Well That Ends Well, IV, 5:23
[1] Clown: jester.

LAFEU. Wherein have you played the knave with fortune that she should scratch you, who of herself is a good lady, and would not have knaves thrive long under her?
All's Well That Ends Well, V, 2:32

HAMLET. What should such fellows as I do crawling between earth and heaven? We are arrant knaves all; believe none of us.
Hamlet, III, 1:128

BRUTUS. This is a sleepy tune: O murderous slumber!
Lay'st thou thy leaden mace upon my boy,
That plays thee music? Gentle knave,[1] good night;
I will not do thee so much wrong to wake thee.
If thou dost nod, thou break'st thy instrument;
I'll take it from thee; and, good boy, good night.
Julius Caesar, IV, 3:267
[1] knave: here used in kindly or playful sense.

KENT. Why, madam, if I were your father's dog,
You should not use me so.
REGAN. Sir, being his knave, I will.
King Lear, II, 2:142

FALSTAFF. Hang him, poor cuckoldy[1] knave! I know him not. Yet I wrong him to call him poor: they say the jealous wittolly[2] knave hath masses of money, for the which his wife seems to me well-favoured.[3] I will use her as the key of the cuckoldy rogue's coffer, and there 's my harvest-home.
Merry Wives of Windsor, II, 2:281
[1] cuckoldy: having an unfaithful wife. [2] wittolly: cuckoldy. [3] well-favoured: good-looking.

LABOUR

POINS. How ill it follows, after you have laboured so hard, you should talk so idly!
II Henry IV, II, 2:31

SALISBURY. While these do labour for their own preferment,
Behoves it us to labour for the realm.
II Henry VI, I, 1:181

MACBETH.[1] The rest is labour, which is not us'd for you.
Macbeth, I, 4:44
[1] To KING DUNCAN.

MACBETH. The labour we delight in physics[1] pain.
                                        Macbeth, II, 3:55
[1] physics: acts as a medicine.

Old woes, not infant sorrows, bear them
    mild;
Continuance tames the one; the other wild,
Like an unpractis'd swimmer plunging still,
With too much labour drowns for want of
    skill.
                                        Rape of Lucrece: 1096

LADIES

SONG. Hark! hark! the lark at heaven's
    gate sings,
And Phoebus 'gins arise,
His steeds to water at those springs
On chalic'd flowers that lies;
And winking Mary-buds begin
To ope their golden eyes:
With everything that pretty is,
My lady sweet, arise:
Arise, arise!
                                        Cymbeline, II, 3:21

QUEEN. Forbear sharp speeches to her;
    she 's a lady
So tender of rebukes that words are strokes,
And strokes death to her.
                                        Cymbeline, III, 5:40

BOYET. Fair ladies, mask'd, are roses in
    their bud:
Dismask'd, their damask sweet commixture
    shown,
Are angels vailing clouds, or roses blown.
                                        Love's Labour's Lost, V, 2:295

BOTTOM. God shield us! a lion among ladies is a most dreadful thing.
                                        Midsummer Night's Dream, III, 1:31

LION. You, ladies, you, whose gentle
    hearts do fear
The smallest monstrous mouse that creeps
    on floor.
                                        Midsummer Night's Dream, V, 1:222

FRIAR LAURENCE. Here comes the lady:
    O! so light a foot
Will ne'er wear out the everlasting flint.
                                        Romeo and Juliet, II, 6:16

LANGUAGE

FIRST LORD. When you sally upon him,
speak what terrible language you will:
though you understand it not yourselves.
                                        All's Well That Ends Well, IV, 1:2

MENENIUS. Consider this: he[1] has been
    bred i' the wars
Since he could draw a sword, and is ill
    school'd
In bolted[2] language; meal and bran together
He throws without distinction.
                                        Coriolanus, III, 1:320
[1] he: CORIOLANUS.   [2] bolted: refined.

MOTH. They have been at a great feast of
languages, and stolen the scraps.
                                        Love's Labour's Lost, V, 1:39

ALONSO. You cram these words into mine
    ears against
The stomach of my sense.
                                        Tempest, II, 1:106

GENTLEMAN. There was speech in their
dumbness, language in their very gesture.
                                        Winter's Tale, V, 2:15

LAUGH

FALSTAFF. A man cannot make him laugh;
but that 's no marvel, he drinks no wine.
                                        II Henry IV, IV, 3:95

BIRON. To move wild laughter in the
    throat of death?
It cannot be; it is impossible:
Mirth cannot move a soul in agony.
                                        Love's Labour's Lost, V, 2:865

GRATIANO. With mirth and laughter let
old wrinkles come.
                                        Merchant of Venice, I, 1:80

GONZALO. These gentlemen, who are of
such sensible and nimble lungs that they always use to laugh at nothing.
                                        Tempest, II, 1:173

TRINCULO. I shall laugh myself to death at
this puppy-headed monster.
                                        Tempest, II, 2:157

TIMON. Flinty mankind, whose eyes do
    never give,
But thorough lust and laughter.
                                        Timon of Athens, IV, 3:492

MARIO. Laugh yourselves into stitches.[1]
                                        Twelfth Night, III, 2:73
[1] stitches: sharp pains.

LAW

FALSTAFF. The rusty curb of old Father
Antick the law.
                                        I Henry IV, I, 2:69

SUFFOLK. Faith, I have been a truant in the law,
And never yet could frame my will to it;
And therefore frame the law unto my will.
I Henry VI, II, 4:7

CHAMBERLAIN. Press not a falling man too far; 't is virtue:
His faults lie open to the laws; let them,
Not you, correct him.
Henry VIII, III, 2:333

ANGELO. We must not make a scarecrow of the law,
Setting it up to fear[1] the birds of prey,
And let it keep one shape, till custom make it
Their perch and not their terror.
Measure for Measure, II, 1:1
[1] fear: frighten.

ANGELO. The law hath not been dead, though it hath slept.
Measure for Measure, II, 2:90

PORTIA. The brain may devise laws for the blood,[1] but a hot temper leaps o'er a cold decree.
Merchant of Venice, I, 2:22
[1] blood: here, human frailties.

TRANIO. And do as adversaries do in law,
Strive mightily, but eat and drink as friends.
Taming of the Shrew, I, 2:278

FABIAN. Still you keep o' the windy side of the law: good.
Twelfth Night, III, 4:181

LAW ENFORCEMENT

[The delicious ignorance of the constables, DOGBERRY and VERGES, is one of the finest examples of Shakespeare's satire. With all their faults they prevented HERO's disgrace.]
Enter DOGBERRY *and* VERGES, *with the* WATCH.
DOGBERRY. Are you good men and true?
VERGES. Yea, or else it were pity but they should suffer salvation, body and soul.
DOGBERRY. Nay, that were a punishment too good for them, if they should have any allegiance in them, being chosen for the prince's watch.
VERGES. Well, give them their charge, neighbour Dogberry.
DOGBERRY. First, who think you the most desartless man to be constable?

FIRST WATCH. Hugh Oatcake, sir, or George Seacoal, for they can write and read.
DOGBERRY. Come hither, neighbour Seacoal. God hath blessed you with a good name: to be a well-favoured[1] man is the gift of fortune, but to write and read comes by nature.
Much Ado About Nothing, III, 3:1
[1] well-favoured: good looking.

DOGBERRY. Well, for your favour, sir, why, give God thanks, and make no boast of it; and for your writing and reading, let that appear when there is no need of such vanity. You are thought here to be the most senseless and fit man for the constable of the watch; therefore bear you the lantern. This is your charge: you shall comprehend all vagrom men; you are to bid any man stand, in the prince's name.
WATCH. How if a' will not stand?
DOGBERRY. Why, then take no note of him, but let him go; and presently call the rest of the watch together, and thank God you are rid of a knave.
VERGES. If he will not stand when he is bidden, he is none of the prince's subjects.
DOGBERRY. True, and they are to meddle with none but the prince's subjects. You shall also make no noise in the streets; for the watch to babble and talk is most tolerable and not to be endured.
WATCH. We will rather sleep than talk: we know what belongs to a watch.
DOGBERRY. Why, you speak like an ancient and most quiet watchman, for I cannot see how sleeping should offend; only have a care that your bills[1] be not stolen. Well, you are to call at all the alehouses, and bid those that are drunk get them to bed.
WATCH. How if they will not?
DOGBERRY. Why then, let them alone till they be sober: if they make you not then the better answer, you may say they are not the men you took them for.
WATCH. Well, sir.
DOGBERRY. If you meet a thief, you may suspect him, by virtue of your office, to be no true man; and, for such kind of men, the less you meddle or make with them, why, the more is for your honesty.
WATCH. If we know him to be a thief, shall we not lay hands on him?
DOGBERRY. Truly, by your office you may; but I think they that touch pitch will be defiled. The most peaceable way for you, if you do take a thief, is to let him show himself what he is and steal out of your company.
VERGES. You have been always called a merciful man, partner.

DOGBERRY. Truly, I would not hang a dog by my will, much more a man who hath any honesty in him.

VERGES. If you hear a child cry in the night, you must call to the nurse and bid her still it.

WATCH. How if the nurse be asleep and will not hear us?

DOGBERRY. Why, then depart in peace, and let the child wake her with crying; for the ewe that will not hear her lamb when it baes, will never answer a calf when he bleats.

VERGES. 'T is very true.

Much Ado About Nothing, III, 3:19

[1] bills: weapons.

WATCH. Well, masters, we hear our charge: let us go sit here upon the church-bench till two, and then all to bed.

DOGBERRY. One word more, honest neighbours. I pray you, watch about Signior Leonato's door; for the wedding being there to-morrow, there is a great coil[1] tonight. Adieu; be vigitant, I beseech you.

Exeunt DOGBERRY *and* VERGES.
Much Ado About Nothing, III, 3:94

[1] coil: disturbance.

LAWYER

DICK. The first thing we do, let 's kill all the lawyers.

CADE. Nay, that I mean to do. Is not this a lamentable thing, that of the skin of an innocent lamb should be made parchment? that parchment, being scribbled o'er, should undo a man?

II Henry VI, IV, 2:83

TIMON. Crack the lawyer's voice,
That he may never more false title plead,
Nor sound his quillets[1] shrilly.

Timon of Athens, IV, 3:153

[1] quillets: sly tricks in argument.

LAZINESS

NORTHUMBERLAND. Even such a man, so faint, so spiritless,
So dull, so dead in look, so woe-begone,
Drew Priam's curtain in the dead of night,
And would have told him half his Troy was burn'd;
But Priam found the fire ere he his tongue.

II Henry IV, I, 1:70

FALSTAFF. It hath its original from much grief, from study and perturbation of the brain. I have read the cause of his effects in Galen: it is a kind of deafness.

CHIEF JUSTICE. I think you are fallen into the disease, for you hear not what I say to you.

FALSTAFF. Very well, my lord, very well: rather, an 't please you, it is the disease of not listening, the malady of not marking,[1] that I am troubled withal.[2]

II Henry IV, I, 2:130

[1] marking: paying attention. [2] withal: with.

FALSTAFF. I were better to be eaten to death with rust than to be scoured to nothing with perpetual motion.

II Henry IV, I, 2:245

SHYLOCK. The patch[1] is kind enough, but a huge feeder;
Snail-slow in profit, and he sleeps by day
More than the wild-cat: drones hive not with me.

Merchant of Venice, II, 5:46

[1] patch: referring to LAUNCELOT GOBBO.

LEARNING

VERNON. He[1] made a blushing cital[2] of himself,
And chid his truant youth with such a grace
As if he master'd there a double spirit
Of teaching and of learning instantly.

I Henry IV, V, 2:62

[1] He: PRINCE HAL, later HENRY V. [2] cital: statement about.

FALSTAFF. Learning, a mere hoard of gold kept by a devil till sack[1] commences it and sets it in act and use.

II Henry IV, IV, 3:124

[1] Sack: a strong wine.

REGAN. O! sir, to wilful men,
The injuries that they themselves procure
Must be their schoolmasters.

King Lear, II, 4:305

NURSE. O Lord! I could have stay'd here all the night
To hear good counsel: O! what learning is.

Romeo and Juliet, III, 3:158

Thine[1] eyes, that taught the dumb on high to sing
And heavy ignorance aloft to fly,
Have added feathers to the learned's wing
And given grace a double majesty.

Sonnet 78

[1] Thine: probably the poet.

APEMANTUS. Canst not read?
PAGE. No.
APEMANTUS. There will little learning die then that day thou art hanged.

Timon of Athens, II, 2:84

LETTERS

PRINCESS. We have receiv'd your letters
  full of love;
Your favours, the ambassadors of love;
And, in our maiden council, rated them
At courtship, pleasant jest, and courtesy,
As bombast and as lining to the time.[1]
Love's Labour's Lost, V, 2:787

[1] lining . . . time: from idea of lining filling
out a garment.

PORTIA. You are all amaz'd:
Here is a letter; read it at your leisure;
It comes from Padua, from Bellario:
There you shall find that Portia was the
  doctor,
Nerissa there, her clerk: Lorenzo here
Shall witness I set forth as soon as you
And even but now return'd; I have not yet
Enter'd my house. Antonio, you are wel-
  come;
And I have better news in store for you
Than you expect: unseal this letter soon;
There you shall find three of your argosies
Are richly come to harbour suddenly.
You shall not know by what strange acci-
  dent
I chanced on this letter.
Merchant of Venice, V, 1:266

MISTRESS PAGE. What! have I 'scaped love-
letters in the holiday-time of my beauty,
and am I now a subject for them?
Merry Wives of Windsor, II, 1:1

LAUNCE. Now will he be swinged[1] for
reading my letter. An unmannerly slave,
that will thrust himself into secrets.
Two Gentlemen of Verona, III, 1:392

[1] swinged: whipped.

LIE

HELENA. I love him[1] for his[2] sake;
And yet I know him a notorious liar,
Think him a great way fool, solely a cow-
  ard;
Yet these fix'd evils sit so fit in him,
That they take place, when virtue's steely
  bones
Look bleak i' the cold wind.
All's Well That Ends Well, I, 1:110

[1] him: PAROLLES. [2] his: BERTRAM'S.

PAROLLES. He will lie, sir, with such volubility, that you would think truth were a
fool.
All's Well That Ends Well, IV, 3:284

CLOWN.[1] A very honest woman, but
something given to lie, as a woman should
not do but in the way of honesty.
Antony and Cleopatra, V, 2:252

[1] Clown: a rustic, here giving a sample of his
sly humor.

JAQUES. Can you nominate in order now
the degrees of the lie?
TOUCHSTONE. Upon a lie seven times removed . . . as thus, sir. I did dislike the cut
of a certain courtier's beard: he sent me
word, if I said his beard was not cut well,
he was in the mind it was: this is called the
'retort courteous.' If I sent him word again
it was not well cut, he would send me word
he cut it to please himself: this is called the
'quip modest.' If again, it was not well cut,
he disabled my judgment: this is called the
'reply churlish.' If again, it was not well
cut, he would answer, I spake not true: this
is called the 'reproof valiant.' If again, it
was not well cut, he would say, I lie: this is
called the 'countercheck quarrelsome': and
so to the 'lie circumstantial,' and the 'lie direct.'
JAQUES. And how oft did you say his
beard was not well cut?
TOUCHSTONE. I durst go no further than
the 'lie circumstantial,' nor he durst not give
me the 'lie direct'; and so we measured
swords and parted.
As You Like It, V, 4:71

TOUCHSTONE. O sir, we quarrel in print;
by the book, as you have books for good
manners: I will name you the degrees. The
first, the 'retort courteous'; the second, the
'quip modest'; the third, the 'reply churlish';
the fourth, the 'reproof valiant'; the fifth,
the 'countercheck quarrelsome'; the sixth,
the 'lie with circumstance'; the seventh, the
'lie direct.' All these you may avoid but the
'lie direct'; and you may avoid that too, with
an 'if.'
As You Like It, V, 4:94

IMOGEN [to IACHIMO]. Thou wrong'st a
  gentleman,[1] who is as far
From thy report as thou from honour, and
Solicit'st there a lady that disdains
Thee and the devil alike.
Cymbeline, I, 6:145

[1] gentleman: POSTHUMUS, her banished husband.

IMOGEN. To lapse in fulness[1]
Is sorer than to lie for need, and falsehood
Is worse in kings than beggars.
Cymbeline, III, 6:12

[1] in fulness: having plenty.

FALSTAFF. 'Zounds! I am afraid of this gunpowder Percy though he be dead. How if he should counterfeit too and rise? By my faith I am afraid he would prove the better counterfeit. Therefore I 'll make him sure; yea, and I 'll swear I killed him. Why may not he rise as well as I? Nothing confutes me but eyes, and nobody sees me: therefore, sirrah,

Stabbing him.

with a new wound in your thigh come you along with me.

He takes HOTSPUR *on his back.*
I Henry IV, V, 4:123

Re-enter the PRINCE *and*
JOHN OF LANCASTER.
PRINCE. Why, Percy I killed myself and saw thee dead.
FALSTAFF. Didst thou? Lord, Lord! how this world is given to lying. I grant you I was down and out of breath, and so was he; but we rose both at an instant, and fought a long hour by Shrewsbury clock.
I Henry IV, V, 4:148

FALSTAFF. Lord! how subject we old men are to this vice of lying.
II Henry IV, III, 2:325

FALSTAFF. O! it is much that a lie with a slight oath and a jest with a sad brow will do with a fellow that never had the ache in his shoulders. O!
II Henry IV, V, 1:90

CALPURNIA [to messenger from the Senate]. Say he is sick.
CAESAR. Shall Caesar send a lie?
Have I in conquest stretch'd mine arm so far
To be afeard to tell greybeards the truth?
Decius, go tell them Caesar will not come.
Julius Caesar, II, 2:65

EMILIA. If he say so, may his pernicious soul
Rot half a grain a day! he lies to the heart:

. . . . .

You told a lie, an odious, damned lie;
Upon my soul, a lie, a wicked lie.
Othello, V, 2:155, 180

When my love swears that she is made of truth,
I do believe her, though I know she lies.

. . . . .

I smiling credit her false-speaking tongue,
Outfacing faults in love with love's ill rest.[1]
Passionate Pilgrim, 1:1, 7
[1] This item is missing in some editions.

FITZWATER. I dare eat, or drink, or breathe, or live,
I dare meet Surrey in a wilderness,
And spit upon him, whilst I say he lies,
And lies, and lies.
Richard II, IV, 1:73

THERSITES. The sun borrows of the moon when Diomed keeps his word.
Troilus and Cressida, V, 1:102

LEONTES. I ne'er heard yet
That any of these bolder vices wanted
Less impudence to gainsay what they did
Than to perform it first.
Winter's Tale, III, 2:55

AUTOLYCUS. Let me have no lying; it becomes none but tradesmen.
Winter's Tale, IV, 4:744

LIFE

FIRST LORD. The web of our life is of a mingled yarn, good and ill together: our virtues would be proud if our faults whipped them not; and our crimes would despair if they were not cherished by our virtues.
All's Well That Ends Well, IV, 3:83

BELARIUS. O! this life[1]
Is nobler than attending[2] for a check,
Richer than doing nothing for a bribe,
Prouder than rustling in unpaid-for silk.
Cymbeline, III, 3:21
[1] this life: as hermits, in contrast with the court. [2] attending . . . check: serving only to be rebuked.

HOTSPUR. O gentlemen! the time of life is short;
To spend that shortness basely were too long.
I Henry IV, V, 2:82

MACBETH. Life 's but a walking shadow, a poor player
That struts and frets his hour upon the stage,
And then is heard no more; it is a tale
Told by an idiot, full of sound and fury,
Signifying nothing.
Macbeth, V, 5:24

DUKE.[1] Reason thus with life:
If I do lose thee, I do lose a thing
That none but fools would keep: a breath thou art,
Servile to all the skyey influences,
That do this habitation, where thou keep'st,[2]
Hourly afflict.
Measure for Measure, III, 1:6
[1] Disguised as a monk. [2] keep'st: stay.

DUKE. Thou hast nor youth nor age,
But, as it were, an after-dinner's sleep,
Dreaming on both; for all thy blessed youth
Becomes as aged, and doth beg the alms
Of palsied eld; and when thou art old and
rich,
Thou has neither heat, affection, limb, nor
beauty,
To make thy riches pleasant. What 's yet in
this
That bears the name of life? Yet in this life
Lie hid more thousand deaths; yet death we
fear,
That makes these odds all even.
Measure for Measure, III, 1:32

FALSTAFF. I fear not Goliath with a weaver's beam, because I know also life is a
shuttle.
Merry Wives of Windsor, V, 1:23

NORTHUMBERLAND. Even through the hollow eyes of death
I spy life peering.
Richard II, II, 1:270

ROMEO. My life were better ended by
their hate,
Than death prorogued,[1] wanting[2] of thy
love.
Romeo and Juliet, II, 2:77
[1] prorogued: postponed. [2] wanting: lacking.

But thy eternal summer shall not fade,
Nor lose possession of that fair thou ow'st,[1]
Nor shall death brag thou wander'st in his
shade,
When in eternal lines to time thou grow'st;
So long as men can breathe, or eyes can see,
So long lives this,[2] and this gives life to thee.
Sonnet 18
[1] ow'st: ownest. [2] this: the poem.

Yet do thy worst, old Time: despite thy
wrong,
My love shall in my verse ever live young.
Sonnet 19

Like as the waves make towards the pebbled shore,
So do our minutes hasten to their end.
Sonnet 60

GONZALO. Here is everything advantageous to life.
ANTONIO. True; save means to live.
Tempest, II, 1:49

PROSPERO. We are such stuff
As dreams are made on, and our little life
Is rounded[1] with a sleep.
Tempest, IV, 1:156
[1] rounded . . . sleep: two suggestions for this
passage—one, finished; two, begins and ends
with a sleep.

LIGHTNING

CASSIUS. [I] Have bar'd my bosom to the
thunder-stone,
And when the cross blue lightning seem'd
to open
The breast of heaven, I did present myself
Even in the aim and very flash of it.
Julius Caesar, I, 3:49

LION

HELENA. The hind that would be mated
by the lion
Must die for love.
All's Well That Ends Well, I, 1:102

ENOBARBUS [aside]. 'T is better playing
with a lion's whelp
Than with an old one dying.
Antony and Cleopatra, III, 13:94

ORLEANS. That 's a valiant flea that dare
eat his breakfast on the lip of a lion.
Henry V, III, 7:156

K. HENRY. The man that once did sell
the lion's skin
While the beast liv'd, was kill'd with hunting him.
Henry V, IV, 3:93

QUEEN. Small curs are not regarded when
they grin,
But great men tremble when the lion roars;
II Henry VI, III, 1:18

CLIFFORD. To whom do lions cast their
gentle looks?
Not to the beast that would usurp their den.
Whose hand is that the forest bear doth
lick?
Not his that spoils her young before her
face.
Who scapes the lurking serpent's mortal
sting?
Not he that sets his foot upon her back.
The smallest worm will turn being trodden on,
And doves will peck in safeguard of their
brood
III Henry VI, II, 2:11

WOLSEY. He parted frowning from me, as
if ruin
Leap'd from his eyes: so looks the chafed
lion
Upon the daring huntsman that has gall'd
him;
Then makes him nothing.
Henry VIII, III, 2:205

BASTARD *to* AUSTRIA. Sirrah,[1] were I at
    home,
At your den, sirrah, with your lioness,
I 'd set an ox-head to your lion's hide,
And make a monster of you.
                                        King John, II, 1:289
[1] Sirrah: address to a servant or to an inferior
in rank.

BOYET. Thus dost thou hear the Nemean
    lion roar
'Gainst thee, thou lamb, that standest as his
    prey;
Submissive fall his princely feet before,
And he from forage will incline to play.
                                Love's Labour's Lost, IV, 1:90

LAVINIA. The lion mov'd with pity did en-
    dure
To have his princely paws par'd all away.
                                Titus Andronicus, II, 3:151

LIPS

K. HENRY. You have witchcraft in your
lips, Kate: there is more eloquence in a sugar
touch of them than in the tongues of the
French council.
                                        Henry V, V, 2:300

CASSIUS. His coward lips did from their
    colour fly,
And that same eye whose bend doth awe
    the world
Did lose his[1] lustre; I did hear him groan.
                                        Julius Caesar, I, 2:122
[1] his: its.

BOY [singing]. Take, O take those lips
    away,
That so sweetly were forsworn;
And those eyes, the break of day,
Lights that do mislead the morn:
But my kisses bring again, bring again,
Seals of love, but seal'd in vain, seal'd in
    vain.
                                Measure for Measure, IV, 1:1

BASSANIO. Here are sever'd lips,
Parted with sugar breath; so sweet a bar
Should sunder such sweet friends.
                                Merchant of Venice, III, 2:119

GLOUCESTER.[1] Teach not thy lip such
    scorn, for it was made
For kissing, lady, not for such contempt.
                                        Richard III, I, 2:172
[1] Later, RICHARD III.

LIVER

[The liver is variously referred to as the seat
of courage, love, and the violent passions.]

ROSALIND. This way will I take upon me
to wash your liver as clean as a sound sheep's
heart, that there shall not be one spot of
love in 't.
                                As You Like It, III, 2:443

FALSTAFF. The liver white and pale, which
is the badge of pusillanimity and cowardice.
                                        II Henry IV, IV, 3:113

FERDINAND. The white cold virgin snow
    upon my heart
Abates the ardour of my liver.
                                        Tempest, IV, 1:56

SIR TOBY. For Andrew, if he were opened,
and you find so much blood in his liver as
will clog the foot of a flea, I 'll eat the rest
of the anatomy.
                                Twelfth Night, III, 2:65

LIVERY

ISABELLA. O! 't is the cunning livery of
    hell,
The damned'st body to invest and cover
In princely[1] guards.
                                Measure for Measure, III, 1:95
[1] princely: priestly; readings in various texts
differ.

SIMONIDES. One twelve moons more she
    'll wear Diana's livery;
This by the eye of Cynthia[1] hath she vow'd,
And on her virgin honour will not break it.
                                        Pericles, II, 5:10
[1] Cynthia: the moon goddess.

ROMEO. Arise, fair sun, and kill the en-
    vious moon,
Who is already sick and pale with grief,
That thou her maid art far more fair than
    she:
Be not her maid, since she is envious;
Her vestal livery is but sick and green,
And none but fools do wear it; cast it off.
                                Romeo and Juliet, II, 2:8

LONDON

WARWICK. Why, *Via!* to London will we
    march amain,
And once again bestride our foaming steeds,
And once again cry 'Charge upon our foes!'
But never once again turn back and fly.
                                        III Henry VI, II, 1:182

LORD

ULYSSES. No man is the lord of any thing,
Though in and of him there be much con-
    sisting,

Till he communicate his parts to others:
Nor doth he of himself know them for
    aught
Till he behold them form'd in the applause
Where they 're extended.
                    Troilus and Cressida, III, 3:115

LOSS

FIRST LORD. How mightily sometimes we
make us comforts of our losses!
SECOND LORD. And how mightily some
other times we drown our gain in tears!
            All's Well That Ends Well, IV, 3:77

KING. Praising what is lost
Makes the remembrance dear.
            All's Well That Ends Well, V, 3:19

K. HENRY. And therefore lost that title of
    respect
Which the proud soul ne'er pays but to the
    proud.
                        I Henry IV, I, 3:8

WARWICK. Why stand we like soft-
    hearted women here,
Wailing our losses?
                    III Henry VI, II, 3:25

DUKE. Forgive a moiety[1] of the principal;
Glancing an eye of pity on his losses,
That have of late so huddled on his back,
Enow to press a royal merchant down,
And pluck commiseration of his state
From brassy bosoms and rough hearts of
    flint.
                Merchant of Venice, IV, 1:26
[1] moiety: a half; often used for any portion.

FRIAR. For it so falls out
That what we have we prize not to the
    worth
Whiles we enjoy it, but being lack'd and
    lost,
Why, then we rack[1] the value, then we find
The virtue that possession would not
    show us
Whiles it was ours.
        Much Ado About Nothing, IV, 1:219
[1] rack: increase.

They that lose half with greater patience
    bear it
Than they whose whole is swallow'd in con-
    fusion.
                    Rape of Lucrece: 1158

K. RICHARD. Your cares set up do not
    pluck my cares down.
My care is loss of care, by old care done;
Your care is gain of care, by new care won.
                        Richard II, IV, 1:195

LOVE

ANTONY. There 's beggary[1] in the love
    that can be reckon'd.
CLEOPATRA. I 'll set a bourn[2] how far to be
    belov'd.
ANTONY. Then must thou needs find out
    new heaven, new earth.
                Antony and Cleopatra, I, 1:15
[1] beggary: poverty. [2] bourn: limit.

ROSALIND. I will, coz, . . . devise sports.
Let me see; what think you of falling in
love?
CELIA. Marry, I prithee, do, to make sport
withal:[2] but love no man in good earnest;
nor no further in sport neither, than with
safety of a pure blush thou mayest in honour come off again.
                        As You Like It, I, 2:26
[1] coz: cousin. [2] withal: with it.

CELIA. Why, cousin! why, Rosalind! Cupid have mercy! Not a word?
ROSALIND. Not one to throw at a dog.
CELIA. No, thy words are too precious to
be cast away upon curs; throw some of
them at me; come, lame me with reasons.
ROSALIND. Then there were two cousins
laid up; when the one should be lamed with
reasons and the other mad without any.
CELIA. But is all this for your father?
ROSALIND. No, some of it is for my child's
father: O! how full of briers is this working-day world.
                        As You Like It, I, 3:1

ORLANDO. What were his marks?[1]
ROSALIND. A lean cheek, which you have
not; a blue eye and sunken, which you have
not; an unquestionable spirit, which you
have not; a beard neglected, which you have
not: but I pardon you for that, for simply
your having in beard is a younger[2] brother's
revenue. Then your hose should be ungar-
tered, your bonnet unbanded, your sleeve
unbuttoned, your shoe untied, and every
thing about you demonstrating a careless
desolation.
                    As You Like It, III, 2:391
[1] marks: signs of love. [2] younger . . . revenue: bulk of estate was given to oldest son in
England.

ROSALIND. Love is merely[1] a madness, and
I tell you, deserves as well a dark house and
a whip as madmen do; and the reason why
they are not so punished and cured is, that
the lunacy is so ordinary that the whippers
are in love too. Yet I profess curing it by
counsel.
                    As You Like It, III, 2:420
[1] merely: absolutely.

ORLANDO. Did you ever cure any so?

ROSALIND. Yes, one; and in this manner. He was to imagine me his love, his mistress; and I set him every day to woo me: at which time would I, being but a moonish youth, grieve, be effeminate, changeable, longing and liking, proud, fantastical, apish, shallow, inconstant, full of tears, full of smiles, for every passion something, and for no passion truly any thing, as boys and women are for the most part, cattle of this colour.

As You Like It, III, 2:426

SILVIUS. Then shall you know the wounds invisible
That love's keen arrows make.

As You Like It, III, 5:30

ROSALIND. Well, in her person I say I will not have you.
ORLANDO. Then in mine own person I die.
ROSALIND. No, faith, die by attorney. The poor world is almost six thousand years old, and in all this time there was not any man died in his own person, *videlicet*,[1] in a love-cause.

. . . . .

Men have died from time to time, and worms have eaten them, but not for love.

As You Like It, IV, 1:92, 108

[1] *videlicet:* that is to say.

ROSALIND. O coz,[1] coz, coz, my pretty little coz, that thou didst know how many fathom deep I am in love! But it cannot be sounded: my affection hath an unknown bottom, like the bay of Portugal.

As You Like It, IV, 1:209

[1] coz: cousin.

PHEBE. Good shepherd, tell this youth what 't is to love.
SILVIUS. It is to be all made of sighs and tears

. . . . .

It is to be all made of fantasy,
All made of passion, and all made of wishes;
All adoration, duty, and observance;
All humbleness, all patience, and impatience:
All purity, all trial, all obeisance;

As You Like It, V, 2:89, 100

PLAYER QUEEN. Where love is great, the littlest doubts are fear.

Hamlet, III, 2:181

KING. There lives within the very flame of love
A kind of wick or snuff that will abate it.

Hamlet, IV, 7:115

FRANCE. Love 's not love
When it is mingled with regards that stand
Aloof from the entire point.

King Lear, I, 1:241

O most potential love! vow, bond, nor space,
In thee hath neither sting, knot, nor confine,
For thou art all, and all things else are thine.
When thou impressest, what are precepts worth
Of stale example? When thou wilt inflame,
How coldly those impediments stand forth
Of wealth, of filial fear, law, kindred, fame!
Love's arms are proof, 'gainst rule, 'gainst sense, 'gainst shame,
And sweetens, in the suffering pangs it bears,
The aloes[1] of all forces, shocks, and fears.

A Lover's Complaint: 264

[1] aloes: symbol of bitterness.

ARMADO. I do affect[1] the very ground, which is base, where her shoe, which is baser, guided by her foot, which is basest, doth tread.

. . . . .

Love is a devil: there is no evil angel but Love. Yet was Samson so tempted, and he had an excellent strength; yet was Solomon so seduced, and he had a very good wit.

Love's Labour's Lost, I, 2:172, 178

[1] affect: love.

BIRON. And when Love speaks, the voice of all the gods
Make heaven drowsy with the harmony.

Love's Labour's Lost, IV, 3:344

BOYET. Love doth approach disguis'd,
Armed in arguments; you 'll be surpris'd:
Muster your wits; stand in your own defence;
Or hide your heads like cowards, and fly hence.

Love's Labour's Lost, V, 2:83

BIRON. Love is full of unbefitting strains;
All wanton as a child, skipping and vain;
Form'd by the eye, and therefore, like the eye,
Full of strange shapes, of habits and of forms,
Varying in subjects, as the eye doth roll
To every varied object in his glance.

Love's Labour's Lost, V, 2:770

SALARINO. O! ten times faster Venus' pigeons fly
To seal love's bonds new-made, than they are wont
To keep obliged faith unforfeited.

Merchant of Venice, II, 6:5

JESSICA. But love is blind, and lovers cannot see
The pretty follies that themselves commit.
Merchant of Venice, II, 6:36

PORTIA. Beshrew your eyes,
They have o'erlook'd me and divided me:
One half of me is yours, the other half yours,
Mine own, I would say; but if mine, then yours,
And so all yours.
Merchant of Venice, III, 2:14

SHALLOW. Mistress Anne, my cousin loves you.
SLENDER. Ay, that I do; as well as I love any woman in Glostershire.

. . . . .

ANNE PAGE. What is your will?
SLENDER. My will? od's heartlings! that 's a pretty jest, indeed; I ne'er made my will yet, I thank heaven; I am not such a sickly creature, I give heaven praise.
ANNE PAGE. I mean, Master Slender, what would you with me?
SLENDER. Truly, for mine own part, I would little or nothing with you. Your father and my uncle have made motions: if it be my luck, so; if not, happy man be his dole![1]
Merry Wives of Windsor, III, 4:42, 58
[1] dole: portion.

LYSANDER. Ay me! for aught that ever I could read,
Could ever hear by tale or history,
The course of true love never did run smooth.
Midsummer Night's Dream, I, 1:132

HERMIA. O hell! to choose love by another's eyes.
Midsummer Night's Dream, I, 1:140

HELENA. Things base and vile, holding no quantity,
Love can transpose to form and dignity.
Love looks not with the eyes, but with the mind,
And therefore is wing'd Cupid painted blind.
Midsummer Night's Dream, I, 1:232

LYSANDER. Who will not change a raven for a dove?
Midsummer Night's Dream, II, 2:114

BOTTOM. To say the truth, reason and love keep little company together now-a-days.
Midsummer Night's Dream, III, 1:146

BEATRICE. I had rather hear my dog bark at a crow than a man swear he loves me.
BENEDICK. God keep your ladyship still[1] in that mind; so some gentleman or other shall 'scape a predestinate scratched face.
BEATRICE. Scratching could not make it worse, an[2] 't were such a face as yours were.
Much Ado About Nothing, I, 1:131
[1] still: always. [2] an: if.

BENEDICK. I pray thee now, tell me, for which of my bad parts didst thou first fall in love with me?
BEATRICE. For them all together; which maintained so politic a state of evil that they will not admit any good part to intermingle with them. But for which of my good parts did you first suffer love for me?
BENEDICK. Suffer love! a good epithet. I do suffer love, indeed, for I love thee against my will.
Much Ado About Nothing, V, 2:59

DESDEMONA. I saw Othello's visage in his mind,
And to his honours and his valiant parts
Did I my soul and fortunes consecrate.
So that, dear lords, if I be left behind,
A moth of peace, and he go to the war,
The rights for which I love him are bereft me.
Othello, I, 3:253

OTHELLO. It gives me wonder great as my content
To see you here before me. O my soul's joy!
If after every tempest come such calms,
May the winds blow till they have waken'd death!
And let the labouring bark climb hills of seas
Olympus-high, and duck again as low
As hell 's from heaven! If it were now to die,
'T were now to be most happy, for I fear
My soul hath her content so absolute
That not another comfort like to this
Succeeds[1] in unknown fate.
Othello, II, 1:185
[1] succeeds: follows.

IAGO. They say base men being in love have then a nobility in their natures more than is native to them.
Othello, II, 1:217

OTHELLO. Excellent wretch! Perdition catch my soul
But I do love thee! and when I love thee not,
Chaos is come again.
Othello, III, 3:90

She burn'd with love, as straw with fire
  flameth;
She burn'd out love, as soon as straw out-
  burneth;
She fram'd the love, and yet she foil'd the
  framing;
She bade love last, and yet she fell a-turning,
Was this a lover, or a lecher whether?
Bad in the best, though excellent in neither.
Passionate Pilgrim: 97

Romeo. Love is a smoke made with the
  fume of sighs;
Being purg'd, a fire sparkling in lovers' eyes;
Being vex'd, a sea nourish'd with lovers'
  tears:
What is it else? a madness most discreet,
A choking gall, and a preserving sweet.
Romeo and Juliet, I, 1:196

Romeo. Love goes toward love as school-
  boys from their books;
But love from love toward school with
  heavy looks.
Romeo and Juliet, II, 2:157

Juliet. My true love is grown to such
  excess
I cannot sum up half my sum of wealth.
Romeo and Juliet, II, 6:33

That love is merchandis'd whose rich es-
  teeming
The owner's tongue doth publish every
  where.
Sonnet 102

Two loves I have of comfort and despair,
Which like two spirits do suggest[1] me still:
The better angel is a man, right fair,
The worser spirit a woman, colour'd ill.
To win me soon to hell, my female evil
Tempteth my better angel from my side.
And would corrupt my saint to be a devil,
Wooing his purity with her foul pride.
And whether that my angel be turn'd fiend
Suspect I may, yet not directly tell.
Sonnet 144
[1] suggest . . . still: whisper to me continu-
ously.

Live with me, and be my love,
And we will all the pleasures prove
That hills and valleys, dales and fields,
And all the craggy mountains yields.
Sonnets to Sundry Notes to Music, V: 143

Helen. In love, i' faith, to the very tip
of the nose.
Troilus and Cressida, III, 1:139

Duke. O spirit of love! how quick[1] and
  fresh art thou,

That, notwithstanding thy capacity
Receiveth as the sea, nought enters there,
Of what validity and pitch soe'er,
But falls into abatement and low price,
Even in a minute: so full of shapes is fancy.

. . . . .

O! when mine eyes did see Olivia first,
Methought she purg'd the air of pestilence.
That instant was I turn'd into a hart[2]
And my desires, like fell and cruel hounds,
E'er since pursue me.
Twelfth Night, I, 1:9, 19
[1] quick: sprightly, nimble. [2] hart: a male deer.

Olivia. How does he love me?
Viola. With adorations, with fertile tears,
With groans that thunder love, with sighs of
  fire.

. . . . .

Holla your name to the reverberate hills,
And make the babbling gossip of the air
Cry out 'Olivia!'
Twelfth Night, I, 5:273, 291

Viola [soliloquy; she is disguised in male
  costume]. How will this fadge?[1] My
  master loves her dearly;
And I, poor monster, fond[2] as much on him;
And she,[3] mistaken, seems to dote on me.
What will become of this? As I am man,
My state is desperate for my master's love;
As I am woman, now alas the day!
What thriftless sighs shall poor Olivia
  breathe!
O time! thou must untangle this, not I;
It is too hard a knot for me to untie.
Twelfth Night, II, 2:34
[1] fadge: come out. [2] fond: here a verb, dote.
[3] she: Olivia.

Clown [singing]. O mistress mine! where
  are you roaming?
O! stay and hear; your true love 's coming,
That can sing both high and low.
Trip no further, pretty sweeting;
Journeys end in lovers meeting,
Every wise man's son doth know.
What is love? 't is not hereafter;
Present mirth hath present laughter;
What 's to come is still unsure:
In delay there lies no plenty;
Then come kiss me, sweet-and-twenty,
Youth 's a stuff will not endure.
Twelfth Night, II, 3:40

Duke. There is no woman's sides
Can bide the beating of so strong a passion
As love doth give my heart; no woman's
  heart
So big, to hold so much; they lack retention.

Alas! their love may be call'd appetite,
No motion of the liver;[1] but the palate,
That suffer surfeit, cloyment, and revolt;
But mine is all as hungry as the sea,
And can digest as much. Make no compare
Between that love a woman can bear me
And that I owe Olivia.
Twelfth Night, II, 4:96
[1] liver: supposed seat of affection.

OLIVIA. O! what a deal of scorn looks
    beautiful
In the contempt and anger of his[1] lip.
A murderous guilt shows not itself more
    soon
Than love that would seem hid; love's night
    is noon.
Cesario, by the roses of the spring,
By maidhood, honour, truth, and every
    thing,
I love thee so, that, maugre[2] all thy pride,
Nor[3] wit nor reason can my passion hide.
Do not extort thy reasons from this clause,
For that I woo, thou therefore hast no cause;
But rather reason thus with reason fetter,
Love sought is good, but given unsought is
    better.
Twelfth Night, III, 1:157
[1] CESARIO is VIOLA disguised as a man. [2] mau-
gre: in spite of. [3] Nor . . . nor: neither . . .
nor.

VALENTINE. To be in love, where scorn is
    bought with groans;
Coy looks with heart-sore sighs; one fad-
    ing moment's mirth
With twenty watchful, weary, tedious
    nights:
If haply[1] won, perhaps a hapless[2] gain;
If lost, why then a grievous labour won:
However, but a folly bought with wit,
Or else a wit[3] by folly vanquished.
Two Gentlemen of Verona, I, 1:29
[1] haply: by chance. [2] hapless: unfortunate.
[3] wit: mind.

JULIA. They do not love that do not show
    their love.
LUCETTA. O! they love least that let men
    know their love.
Two Gentlemen of Verona, I, 2:31

JULIA. Fie, fie! how wayward is this fool-
    ish love
That, like a testy babe, will scratch the nurse
And presently[1] all humbled kiss the rod.
Two Gentlemen of Verona, I, 2:57
[1] presently: immediately.

PROTEUS. Sweet love! sweet lines![1] sweet
    life!
Here is her hand, the agent of her heart;

Here is her oath for love, her honour's
    pawn.
Two Gentlemen of Verona, I, 3:45
[1] lines: letter from JULIA.

PROTEUS. O! how this spring of love re-
    sembleth
The uncertain glory of an April day,
Which now shows all the beauty of the sun,
And by and by a cloud takes all away.
Two Gentlemen of Verona, I, 3:84

PROTEUS. Then let her alone.
VALENTINE. Not for the world. Why,
    man, she is mine own,
And I as rich in having such a jewel
As twenty seas, if all their sand were pearl,
The water nectar, and the rocks pure gold.
Two Gentlemen of Verona, II, 4:167

VALENTINE. And why not death rather
    than living torment?
To die is to be banish'd from myself;
And Silvia is myself: banish'd from her
Is self from self; a deadly banishment!
What light is light, if Silvia be not seen?
What joy is joy, if Silvia be not by?
Unless it be to think that she is by
And feed upon the shadow of perfection.
Except I be by Silvia in the night,
There is no music in the nightingale;
Unless I look on Silvia in the day,
There is no day for me to look upon.
Two Gentlemen of Verona, III, 1:170

Who is Silvia? what is she,
That all our swains commend her?
Holy, fair and wise is she;
The heaven such grace did lend her,
That she might admired be.
Is she kind as she is fair?
For beauty lives with kindness:
Love doth to her eyes repair,
To help him of his blindness;
And, being help'd, inhabits there.
Then to Silvia let us sing,
That Silvia is excelling;
She excels each mortal thing
Upon the dull earth dwelling;
To her let us garlands bring.
Two Gentlemen of Verona, IV, 2:39

Love keeps his[1] revels when there are but
    twain.
Venus and Adonis: 123
[1] his: its.

Love is a spirit all compact of fire,
Not gross to sink, but light, and will aspire.
Venus and Adonis: 149

FLORIZEL. The gods themselves,
Humbling their deities to love, have taken

The shapes of beasts upon them: Jupiter
Became a bull, and bellow'd; the green Neptune
A ram, and bleated; and the fire-rob'd god,
Golden Apollo, a poor humble swain,
As I seem now.
Winter's Tale, IV, 4:25

SHEPHERD. He says he loves my daughter:
I think so too; for never gaz'd the moon
Upon the water as he 'll stand and read
As 't were my daughter's eyes; and to be plain,
I think there is not half a kiss to choose
Who loves another best.
Winter's Tale, IV, 4:171

FLORIZEL. Camillo,
Not for Bohemia, nor the pomp that may
Be thereat glean'd, for all the sun sees or
The close earth wombs or the profound sea hides
In unknown fathoms, will I break my oath
To this my fair belov'd.
Winter's Tale, IV, 4:497

LOVE AT FIRST SIGHT

ROSALIND.[1] Wear this for me, one out of suits with fortune,
That could give more, but that her hand lacks means.
          . . . . .

ORLANDO. What passion hangs these weights upon my tongue?
I cannot speak to her, yet she urg'd conference.
O poor Orlando, thou art overthrown!
Or Charles or[2] something weaker masters thee.
As You Like It, I, 2:258, 265
[1] To ORLANDO, as she gives him chain from her neck.   [2] Or . . . or: either . . . or.

PHEBE. Dead shepherd,[1] now I find thy saw[2] of might:
'Who ever lov'd that lov'd not at first sight?'
As You Like It, III, 5:81
[1] shepherd: Christopher Marlowe.   [2] saw: saying.

ROSALIND. Your brother and my sister no sooner met but they looked; no sooner looked but they loved; no sooner loved but they sighed; no sooner sighed but they asked one another the reason; no sooner knew the reason but they sought the remedy: and in these degrees have they made a pair of stairs to marriage which they will climb incontinent,[1] or else be incontinent[2] before marriage. They are in the very wrath of love,

and they will together: clubs cannot part them.
As You Like It, V, 2:36
[1] incontinent: immediately.   [2] incontinent: unchaste.

ROMEO. O! she doth teach the torches to burn bright.
It seems she hangs upon the cheek of night
Like a rich jewel in an Ethiop's ear;
Beauty too rich for use, for earth too dear!
So shows a snowy dove trooping with crows,
As yonder lady o'er her fellows[1] shows.
          . . . . .
Did my heart love till now! forswear it, sight!
For I ne'er saw true beauty till this night.
Romeo and Juliet, I, 5:46, 54
[1] fellows: companions.

LOVE CHARM

OBERON. Flower of this purple dye,
Hit with Cupid's archery,
Sink in apple of his eye.
When his love he doth espy,
Let her shine as gloriously
As the Venus of the sky,
When thou wak'st, if she be by,
Beg of her for remedy.
PUCK. Captain of our fairy band,
Helena is here at hand,
And the youth, mistook by me,
Pleading for a lover's fee.
Shall we their fond pageant see?
Lord, what fools these mortals be!
OBERON. Stand aside: the noise they make
Will cause Demetrius to awake.
PUCK. Then will two at once woo one;
That must needs be sport alone;
And those things do best please me
That befall preposterously.
Midsummer Night's Dream, III, 2:102

PUCK [squeezing juice on LYSANDER's eyes]. On the ground
Sleep sound:
I'll apply
To your eye
Gentle lover, remedy.
When thou wak'st,
Thou tak'st
True delight
In the sight
Of thy former lady's eye:
And the country proverb known,
That every man should take his own,
In your waking shall be shown:
Jack shall have Jill;
Nought shall go ill;

The man shall have his mare again,
And all shall be well.
Midsummer Night's Dream, III, 2:448

OTHELLO. That handkerchief

. . . . .

'T is true; there 's magic in the web of it;
A sibyl, that had number'd in the world
The sun to course two[1] hundred compasses,
In her prophetic fury sew'd the work;
The worms were hallow'd that did breed
the silk,
And it was dy'd in mummy[2] which the skil-
ful
Conserv'd of maidens' hearts.
Othello, III, 4:59, 69
[1] two . . . compasses: 200 years. [2] mummy:
the liquor that oozed from mummies was be-
lieved to have medicinal value.

LOVE—HOPELESS

HELENA. My imagination
Carries no favour[1] in 't but Bertram's.
I am undone: there is no living, none,
If Bertram be away. It were all one
That I should love a bright particular star
And think to wed it, he is so above me:
In his bright radiance and collateral light
Must I be comforted, not in his sphere.[2]
The ambition in my love thus plagues it-
self:
The hind that would be mated by the lion
Must die for love. 'T was pretty, though a
plague,
To see him every hour; to sit and draw
His arched brows, his hawking eye, his
curls,
In our heart's table; heart too capable
Of every line and trick of his sweet favour:
But now he 's gone, and my idolatrous fancy
Must sanctify his relics.[3]
All's Well That Ends Well, I, 1:93
[1] favour: face. [2] sphere: orb in which BER-
TRAM moves. [3] relics: sometimes spelled rel-
iques; things that keep alive his memory.

HELENA. I know I love in vain, strive
against hope;
Yet in this captious and intenible sieve
I still[1] pour in the waters of my love,
And lack not to lose still. Thus, Indian-like,
Religious in mine error, I adore
The sun, that looks upon his worshipper,
But knows of him no more.
All's Well That Ends Well, I, 3:207
[1] still: continuously.

SILVIUS. O! thou didst then ne'er love so
heartily.
If thou remember'st not the slightest folly

That ever love did make thee run into,
Thou has not lov'd.

. . . . .

ROSALIND. Alas, poor shepherd! searching
of thy wound, I have by hard adventure
found mine own.
TOUCHSTONE. And I mine. I remember,
when I was in love I broke my sword upon
a stone, and bid him take that for coming
a-night to Jane Smile; and I remember the
kissing of her batlet[1] and the cow's dugs
that her pretty chopped[2] hands had milked;
and I remember the wooing of a peascod[3]
instead of her, from whom I took two cods,
and giving her them again, said with weeping tears, 'Wear these for my sake.' We that
are true lovers run into strange capers; but
as all is mortal[4] in nature, so is all nature in
love mortal in folly.
As You Like It, II, 4:33, 43
[1] batlet: a small bat used in washing clothes.
[2] chopped: chapped. [3] peascod: husk or pod
of peas. [4] mortal: doomed to death.

SILVIUS. Loose now and then
A scatter'd smile, and that I'll live upon.
As You Like It, III, 5:103

ADRIANA. The time was once when thou
unurg'd would'st vow
That never words were music to thine ear,
That never object pleasing in thine eye,
That never touch well welcome to thy
hand,
That never meat sweet-savour'd in thy
taste,
Unless I spake, or look'd, or touch'd, or
carv'd to thee.
How comes it now, my husband, O! how
comes it,
That thou art thus estranged from thyself?
Comedy of Errors, II, 2:115

BIRON. I will not love; if I do, hang me; i'
faith, I will not. O! but her eye,—by this
light, but for her eye, I would not love her;
yes, for her two eyes. Well, I do nothing in
the world but lie, and lie in my throat. By
heaven, I do love, and it hath taught me to
rhyme, and to be melancholy.
Love's Labour's Lost, IV, 3:10

LYSANDER. She, sweet lady,[1] dotes,
Devoutly dotes, dotes in idolatry,
Upon this spotted[2] and inconstant man.
Midsummer Night's Dream, I, 1:108
[1] lady: HELENA. [2] spotted: guilty.

HERMIA. O! then, what graces in my love
do dwell
That he hath turn'd a heaven unto a hell.
Midsummer Night's Dream, I, 1:206

HELENA. I am your spaniel; and, Deme-
trius,
The more you beat me, I will fawn on you:
Use me but as your spaniel, spurn me,
strike me,
Neglect me, lose me; only give me leave,
Unworthy as I am, to follow you.

. . . . .

Run when you will, the story[1] shall be
chang'd;
Apollo flies, and Daphne holds the chase;
The dove pursues the griffin; the mild hind[2]
Makes speed to catch the tiger: bootless
speed,
When cowardice pursues and valour flies!
Midsummer Night's Dream, II, 1:204, 230
[1] story: Apollo pursued the nymph Daphne
until she was turned into a laurel. [2] hind:
female deer.

FRIAR LAURENCE. Holy Saint Francis!
what a change is here;
Is Rosaline, whom thou didst love so dear,
So soon forsaken? young men's love then
lies
Not truly in their hearts, but in their eyes.
Romeo and Juliet, II, 3:65

VIOLA. If I did love you in my master's
flame,
With such a suffering, such a deadly life,
In your denial I would find no sense;
I would not understand it.
    OLIVIA. Why, what would you?
    VIOLA. Make me a willow cabin at your
    gate,
And call upon my soul within the house;
Write loyal cantons of contemned love,
And sing them loud even in the dead of
night;
                        Twelfth Night, I, 5:283

VIOLA.[1] My father had a daughter lov'd a
man,
As it might be, perhaps, were I a woman,
I should your lordship.
    DUKE. And what's her history?
    VIOLA. A blank, my lord. She[2] never told
    her love,
But let concealment, like a worm i' the bud,
Feed on her damask cheek: she pin'd in
thought,
And with a green and yellow melancholy,
She sat like Patience on a monument,
Smiling at grief. Was not this love indeed?
                        Twelfth Night, II, 4:110
[1] Disguised in male attire. [2] She: VIOLA is in
love with the DUKE.

DUKE. This weak impress of love is as a
figure

Trenched in ice, with which an hour's heat
Dissolves to water and doth lose his[1] form.
A little time will melt her frozen thoughts,
And worthless Valentine shall be forgot.
    Two Gentlemen of Verona, III, 2:6
[1] his: its.

SILVIA. O! 't is the curse in love, and still[1]
approv'd,[2]
When women cannot love where they're belov'd.
    Two Gentlemen of Verona, V, 4:43
[1] still: always. [2] approv'd: experienced.

LOVERS

CELIA. Yes: I think he is not a pick-purse
nor a horse-stealer; but for his verity in love,
I do think him as concave as a covered gob-
let or a worm-eaten nut.
                        As You Like It, III, 4:24

ROSALIND. The sight of lovers feedeth
those in love.
                        As You Like It, III, 4:60

CRESSIDA. They say all lovers swear more
performance than they are able, and yet reserve an ability that they never perform;
vowing more than the perfection of ten and
discharging less than the tenth part of one.
                        Troilus and Cressida, III, 2:91

DUKE. Come hither, boy: if ever thou
shalt love,
In the sweet pangs of it remember me;
For such as I am all true lovers are:
Unstaid and skittish in all motions else
Save in the constant image of the creature
That is belov'd.
                        Twelfth Night, II, 4:15

SPEED. Launce, how sayest thou, that my
master is become a notable lover?
    LAUNCE. I never knew him otherwise.
    Two Gentlemen of Verona, II, 5:43

Foul words and frowns must not repel a
lover;
What though the roses have prickles, yet 't is
pluck'd:
Were beauty under twenty locks kept fast,
Yet love breaks through and picks them all
at last.
                        Venus and Adonis: 573

LOYALTY

ENOBARBUS. He that can endure
To follow with allegiance a fall'n lord,

Does conquer him that did his master con-
quer,
And earns a place i' the story.
Antony and Cleopatra, III, 13:43

ORLANDO. O good old man! how well in
thee appears
The constant service of the antique world,
When service sweat for duty, not for meed![1]
Thou art not for the fashion of these times,
Where none will sweat but for promotion,

. . . . .

ADAM. Master, go on, and I will follow
thee
To the last gasp with truth and loyalty.
As You Like It, II, 3:56, 69
[1] meed: reward.

JOAN OF ARC. O! turn thy edged sword
another way;
Strike those that hurt, and hurt not those
that help.
One drop of blood drawn from thy country's bosom
Should grieve thee more than streams of
foreign gore.
I Henry VI, III, 3:52

K. HENRY. Ah! uncle Humphrey, in thy
face I see
The map of honour, truth, and loyalty.
II Henry VI, III, 1:202

DESDEMONA. My noble father,
I do perceive here a divided duty:
To you I am bound for life and education;
My life and education both do learn me
How to respect you; you are the lord of
duty;
I am hitherto your daughter: but here 's my
husband;
And so much duty as my mother show'd
To you, preferring you before her father,
So much I challenge that I may profess
Due to the Moor my lord.
Othello, I, 3:180

NURSE. Shame come to Romeo!
JULIET. Blister'd be thy tongue
For such a wish! he was not born to shame:
Upon his brow shame is asham'd to sit;
For 't is a throne where honour may be
crown'd
Sole monarch of the universal earth.
O! what a beast was I to chide at him.
NURSE. Will you speak well of him that
kill'd your cousin?
JULIET. Shall I speak ill of him that is my
husband?
Ah! poor my lord, what tongue shall
smooth thy name,

When I, thy three-hours' wife, have mangled it?
But, wherefore, villain, didst thou kill my
cousin?
That villain cousin would have kill'd my
husband.
Romeo and Juliet, III, 2:90

LUCK

DUKE.[1] Then go thou forth,
And fortune play upon thy prosperous helm
As thy auspicious mistress!
All's Well That Ends Well, III, 3:6
[1] To BERTRAM.

CLEOPATRA. I hear him[1] mock
The luck of Caesar, which the gods give
men
To excuse their after wrath.
Antony and Cleopatra, V, 2:286
[1] him: ANTONY.

PISANIO. Fortune brings in some boats that
are not steer'd.
Cymbeline, IV, 3:46

SHYLOCK. No ill luck stirring but what
lights on my shoulders; no sighs but of my
breathing; no tears but of my shedding.
Merchant of Venice, III, 1:99

FALSTAFF. This is the third time; I hope
good luck lies in odd numbers. Away! go.
They say there is divinity in odd numbers,
either in nativity, chance or death.
Merry Wives of Windsor, V, 1:2

STEPHANO. Every man shift for all the rest,
and let no man take care for himself, for all
is but fortune.
Tempest, V, 1:256

LUST

BERTRAM. But I love thee
By love's own sweet constraint, and will for
ever
Do thee all rights of service.
DIANA. Ay, so you serve us
Till we serve you; but when you have our
roses,
You barely leave our thorns to prick our-
selves
And mock us with our bareness.
BERTRAM. How have I sworn!
DIANA. 'T is not the many oaths that make
the truth,
But the plain single vow that is vow'd true.
All's Well That Ends Well, IV, 2:15

GHOST. But virtue, as it never will be mov'd,
Though lewdness court it in a shape of heaven,
So lust, though to a radiant angel link'd,
Will sate itself in a celestial bed,
And prey on garbage.
                                    Hamlet, I, 5:53

HAMLET. O shame! where is thy blush? Rebellious hell,
If thou canst mutine in a matron's bones,
To flaming youth let virtue be as wax,
And melt in her own fire.
                                    Hamlet, III, 4:82

BIRON. And, among three, to love the worst of all;
A wightly[1] wanton[2] with a velvet brow,
With two pitch-balls stuck in her face for eyes;
Ay, and, by heaven, one that will do the deed
Though Argus[3] were her eunuch and her guard.
                                    Love's Labour's Lost, III, 1:197
[1] wightly: sprightly.   [2] wanton: one apt to play; this word has several uses, often lustful, as here.   [3] Argus: in Greek mythology a watchman with a hundred eyes.

FALSTAFF. O! she did so course o'er my exteriors with such a greedy intention, that the appetite of her eye did seem to scorch me up like a burning-glass.
                                    Merry Wives of Windsor, I, 3:72

FALSTAFF. Think on 't, Jove; a foul fault! When gods have hot backs, what shall poor men do?
                                    Merry Wives of Windsor, V, 5:12

[Song]. Fie on sinful fantasy!
Fie on lust and luxury![1]
Lust is but a bloody fire,
Kindled with unchaste desire,
Fed in heart, whose flames aspire
As thoughts do blow them higher and higher.
Pinch him, fairies, mutually;
Pinch him for his villany;
Pinch him, and burn him, and turn him about,
Till candles and star-light and moonshine be out.
                                    Merry Wives of Windsor, V, 5:97
[1] luxury: lust.

IAGO. O! 't is the spite of hell, the fiend's arch-mock,
To lip a wanton in a secure couch,
And to suppose her chaste.
                                    Othello, IV, 1:71

Enjoy'd no sooner but despised straight;
Past reason hunted; and no sooner had,
Past reason hated, as a swallow'd bait
On purpose laid to make the taker mad:
Mad in pursuit, and in possession so;
Had, having, and in quest to have, extreme;
A bliss in proof, and prov'd, a very woe;
Before, a joy propos'd; behind, a dream.
All this the world well knows; yet none knows well
To shun the heaven that leads men to this hell.
                                    Sonnet 129

TAMORA. And curtain'd with a counsel-keeping cave,
We may, each wreathed in the other's arms,
Our pastimes done, possess a golden slumber.
                                    Titus Andronicus, II, 3:24

The sea hath bounds, but deep desire hath none.
                         . . . . .

Call it not love, for Love to heaven is fled,
Since sweating Lust on earth usurp'd his[1] name;
Under whose simple semblance he hath fed
Upon fresh beauty, blotting it with blame;
Which the hot tyrant stains and soon bereaves.
                                    Venus and Adonis: 793
[1] his: its.

Love comforteth like sunshine after rain,
But Lust's effect is tempest after sun;
Love's gentle spring doth always fresh remain,
Lust's winter comes ere summer half be done.
Love surfeits not, Lust like a glutton dies:
Love is all truth, Lust full of forged lies.
                                    Venus and Adonis: 799

MADNESS

[Was HAMLET mad? The following quotations will help the reader to decide whether HAMLET was really mad. After his father's Ghost has told the story of his murder, the Prince pledges his friends to secrecy:]
    HAMLET. But come;
Here, as before, never, so help you mercy,
How strange or odd so e'er I bear myself,
As I perchance hereafter shall think meet
To put an antick[1] disposition on,
That you, at such times seeing me, never shall,
With arms encumber'd thus, or this head-shake,
Or by pronouncing of some doubtful phrase,

As 'Well, well, we know,' or 'We could, an
    if we would,'
Or 'If we list to speak,' or 'There be, an if
    they might,'
Or such ambiguous giving out, to note
That you know aught of me: this not to do,
So grace and mercy at your most need help
    you,
Swear.
                                    Hamlet, I, 5:168
[1] antick: fantastic, grotesque.

[OPHELIA tells her father about HAMLET's
strange behavior:]
    POLONIUS. How now, Ophelia! what 's
        the matter?
    OPHELIA. Alas! my lord, I have been so
        affrighted.
    POLONIUS. With what, i ' the name of God?
    OPHELIA. My lord, as I was sewing in my
        closet[1]
Lord Hamlet, with his doublet all unbrac'd;[2]
No hat upon his head; his stockings foul'd,
Ungarter'd, and down-gyved[3] to his ankle;
Pale as his shirt; his knees knocking each
    other;
And with a look so piteous in purport
As if he had been loosed out of hell
To speak of horrors, he comes before me.
    POLONIUS. Mad for thy love?
    OPHELIA. My lord, I do not know;
But truly I do fear it.
    POLONIUS. What said he?
    OPHELIA. He took me by the wrist and
        held me hard,
Then goes he to the length of all his arm,
And, with his other hand thus o'er his brow,
He falls to such perusal of my face
As he would draw it. Long stay'd he so;
At last, a little shaking of mine arm,
And thrice his head thus waving up and
    down
He rais'd a sigh so piteous and profound
That it did seem to shatter all his bulk
And end his being. That done, he lets me go,
And, with his head over his shoulder turn'd,
He seem'd to find his way without his eyes;
For out o' doors he went without their help,
And to the last bended their light on me.
    POLONIUS. Come, go with me; I will go
        seek the king.
This is the very ecstasy of love,
Whose violent property fordoes itself
And leads the will to desperate undertak-
    ings,
As oft as any passion under heaven,
That does afflict our natures. I am sorry,—
What! have you given him any hard words
    of late?
    OPHELIA. No, my good lord; but, as you
        did command,
I did repel his letters and denied

His access to me.
    POLONIUS. That hath made him mad.
                                    Hamlet, II, 1:74
[1] closet: a private room. [2] unbrac'd: unfast-
ened. [3] down-gyved: hanging loose like fetters.

[In his report to the king and queen POLONIUS
furnishes the all-time high of senile verbosity:]
    POLONIUS. My liege, and madam, to ex-
        postulate
What majesty should be, what duty is,
Why day is day, night night, and time is
    time,
Were nothing but to waste night, day, and
    time.
Therefore, since brevity is the soul of wit,
And tediousness the limbs and outward
    flourishes,
I will be brief. Your noble son is mad:
Mad call I it; for, to define true madness,
What is 't but to be nothing else but mad?
But let that go.
    QUEEN. More matter, with less art.
    POLONIUS. Madam, I swear I use no art
        at all.
That he is mad, 't is true; 't is true 't is pity;
And pity 't is 't is true: a foolish figure;
But farewell it, for I will use no art.
Mad let us grant him, then; and now remains
That we find out the cause of this effect,
Or rather say, the cause of this defect,
For this effect defective comes by cause;
Thus it remains, and the remainder thus.
Perpend:
I have a daughter; have, while she is mine;
Who, in her duty and obedience, mark,
Hath given me this. Now gather, and sur-
    mise.
    *To the celestial, and my soul's idol, the
    most beautified Ophelia,—*
That 's an ill phrase, a vile phrase; 'beauti-
fied' is a vile phrase; but you shall hear.
Thus:
In her excellent white bosom, these, etc.
    QUEEN. Came this from Hamlet to her?
    POLONIUS. Good madam, stay awhile; I
        will be faithful.
Doubt[1] thou the stars are fire;
Doubt that the sun doth move;
Doubt truth to be a liar;
But never doubt I love.
    O dear Ophelia! I am ill at these numbers.[2]
*I have not art to reckon my groans; but
that I love thee best, O most best! believe
it. Adieu.*
    *Thine evermore, most dear lady, whilst
this machine is to him.*
                                    HAMLET
                                    Hamlet, II, 2:86
[1] Doubt: in the first three lines, suspect; in the
fourth line, the usual meaning. [2] numbers:
rhymes.

POLONIUS. And he, repulsed, a short tale
   to make,
Fell into a sadness, then into a fast,
Thence to a watch, thence into a weakness,
Thence to a lightness; and by this declension
Into the madness wherein now he raves,
And all we wail for.
                               Hamlet, II, 2:145

[In a scene with HAMLET, POLONIUS is further
convinced that the Prince is mad:]
   HAMLET. Yourself, sir, should be old as I
am, if, like a crab, you could go backward.
   POLONIUS [aside]. Though this be madness, yet there is method in 't. Will you walk
out of the air, my lord?
   HAMLET. Into my grave?
   POLONIUS. Indeed, that is out o' the air.
[Aside.] How pregnant sometimes his re-
plies are! a happiness that often madness
hits on, which reason and sanity could not
so prosperously be delivered of. I will leave
him, and suddenly contrive the means of
meeting between him and my daughter.
                               Hamlet, II, 2:204

   HAMLET [to ROSENCRANTZ and GUIL-
DENSTERN]. You are welcome; but my uncle-
father and aunt-mother are deceived.
   GUILDENSTERN. In what, my dear lord?
   HAMLET. I am but mad north-north-
west: when the wind is southerly I know a
hawk from a handsaw.[1]
                               Hamlet, II, 2:395
[1] handsaw: probably *hernshaw*, a heron; another interpretation, possibly an old saying for
contrast of dissimilar things.

[From behind the arras (curtains) the KING
and POLONIUS hear HAMLET and OPHELIA.]
   POLONIUS. Ophelia, walk you here. Gracious, so please you,
We will bestow ourselves.   *To* OPHELIA.

Read on this book,
That show of such an exercise may colour
   your loneliness.

                     . . . . .

   HAMLET. We are arrant knaves all; believe none of us. Go thy ways to a nunnery.
Where 's your father?
   OPHELIA. At home, my lord.
   HAMLET. Let the doors be shut upon him,
that he may play the fool no where but in
's own house. Farewell.
   OPHELIA. O! help him, you sweet heavens.
   HAMLET. If thou dost marry, I 'll give
thee this plague for thy dowry: be thou as
chaste as ice, as pure as snow, thou shalt not
escape calumny. Get thee to a nunnery, go;
farewell. Or, if thou wilt needs marry,

marry a fool; for wise men know well
enough what monsters you make of them.
To a nunnery, go; and quickly too. Farewell.
   OPHELIA. O heavenly powers, restore
him!
   HAMLET. I have heard of your paintings
too, well enough; God hath given you one
face, and you make yourselves another; you
jig, you amble, and you lisp, and nickname
God's creatures, and make your wantonness[1] your ignorance. Go to, I 'll no more
on 't; it hath made me mad. I say we will
have no more marriages; those that are married already, all but one shall live; the rest
shall keep as they are. To a nunnery, go.
                                        Exit.
   OPHELIA. O! what a noble mind is here
   o'erthrown:
The courtier's, soldier's, scholar's, eye,
   tongue, sword;
The expectancy and rose of the fair state,
The glass of fashion and the mould of form,
The observ'd of all observers, quite, quite
   down!
And I, of ladies most deject and wretched,
That suck'd the honey of his music vows,
Now see that noble and most sovereign rea-
   son,
Like sweet bells jangled, out of tune and
   harsh;
That unmatch'd form and feature of blown
   youth
Blasted with ecstasy:[2] O! woe is me,
To have seen what I have seen, see what I
   see.
                     Re-enter KING *and* POLONIUS.
   KING. Love! his affections do not that
   way tend;
Nor what he spake, though it lack'd form a
   little,
Was not like madness. There 's something in
   his soul
O'er which his melancholy sits on brood;
And I do doubt[3] the hatch and the disclose
Will be some danger.
                               Hamlet, III, 1:43, 130
[1] wantonness, etc.: excuse wrongdoing by
claiming ignorance. [2] ecstasy: find Greek der-
ivation, here madness. [3] doubt: suspect.

[In the closet scene the GHOST is invisible to
the QUEEN. She thinks HAMLET's excited con-
versation proves his madness.]
   HAMLET. Why, look you there! look how
   it steals away;
My father, in his habit[1] as he liv'd;
Look! where he goes, even now, out at the
   portal.   *Exit* GHOST.
   QUEEN. This is the very coinage of your
   brain:
This bodiless creation ecstasy[2]
Is very cunning in.

HAMLET. Ecstasy!
My pulse, as yours, doth temperately keep time,
And makes as healthful music. It is not madness
That I have utter'd: bring me to the test,
And I the matter will re-word, which madness
Would gambol from. Mother, for love of grace,
Lay not that flattering unction to your soul,
That not your trespass but my madness speaks;
It will but skin and film the ulcerous place,
Whiles rank corruption, mining all within,
Infects unseen.
Hamlet, III, 4:135

[1] habit: garb. [2] ecstasy: madness.

OPHELIA [singing]. They bore him bare-fac'd on the bier;
Hey non nonny, nonny, hey nonny;
And in his grave rain'd many a tear;—

. . . . .

There 's rosemary, that 's for remembrance; pray you, love, remember: and there is pansies, that 's for thoughts.

. . . . .

There 's fennel[1] for you, and columbines; there 's rue[2] for you; and here 's some for me; we may call it herb-grace o' Sundays. O! you[3] must wear your rue with a difference. There 's a daisy; I would give you some violets, but they withered all when my father died. They say he made a good end,— [singing] For bonny sweet Robin is all my joy.

. . . . .

LAERTES. Thought and affliction, passion, hell itself,
She turns to favour and to prettiness.
Hamlet, IV, 5:164, 174, 180

[1] fennel: to the KING, flattery. [2] rue: sorrowful remembrance. [3] you: the QUEEN.

QUEEN. This is mere[1] madness:
And thus awhile the fit will work on him;
Anon, as patient as the female dove,
When that her golden couplets[2] are disclos'd,
His silence will sit drooping.
Hamlet, V, 1:307

[1] mere: absolute. [2] couplets: nestlings.

CONSTANCE. I am not mad: I would to heaven I were!
For then 't is like I should forget myself.
King John, III, 4:48

K. LEAR. O! let me not be mad, not mad, sweet heaven;
Keep me in temper; I would not be mad!
King Lear, I, 5:50

K. LEAR. O! that way madness lies; let me shun that;
No more of that.
King Lear, III, 4:21

EDGAR [feigning madness]. Who gives any thing to poor Tom? whom the foul fiend hath led through fire and through flame, through ford and whirlpool, o'er bog and quagmire; that hath laid knives under his pillow, and halters in his pew; set ratsbane by his porridge; made him proud of heart, to ride on a bay trotting-horse over four-inched bridges, to course his own shadow for a traitor. Bless thy five wits! Tom 's a-cold.
King Lear, III, 4:51

K. LEAR. What has thou been?
EDGAR. A servingman, proud in heart and mind; that curled my hair, wore gloves in my cap, served the lust of my mistress' heart, and did the act of darkness with her; swore as many oaths as I spake words, and broke them in the sweet face of heaven; one that slept in the contriving of lust, and waked to do it. Wine loved I deeply, dice dearly, and in woman out-paramoured the Turk: false of heart, light of ear, bloody of hand; hog in sloth, fox in stealth, wolf in greediness, dog in madness, lion in prey. Let not the creaking of shoes nor the rustling of silks betray thy poor heart to woman: keep thy foot out of brothels, thy hand out of plackets,[1] thy pen from lenders' books, and defy the foul fiend.
King Lear, III, 4:87

[1] plackets: openings in petticoats.

K. LEAR. Unaccommodated[1] man is no more but such a poor, bare, forked animal as thou art. Off, off, you lendings! Come; unbutton here. *Tearing off his clothes.*
FOOL. Prithee, nuncle, be contented; 't is a naughty night to swim in.
King Lear, III, 4:112

[1] Unaccommodated: not clothed.

EDGAR [feigning madness]. Poor Tom; that eats the swimming frog, the toad, the tadpole, the wall-newt.

. . . . .

Who is whipped from tithing to tithing, and stocked, punished, and imprisoned; who hath had three suits to his back, six shirts to his body,

Horse to ride, and weapon to wear,
But mice and rats and such small deer,
Have been Tom's food for seven long year.
King Lear, III, 4:134, 139

KENT. Now, good my lord, lie here and rest awhile.
K. LEAR. Make no noise, make no noise; draw the curtains: so, so, so. We 'll go to supper i' the morning: so, so, so.
FOOL. And I'll go to bed at noon.
King Lear, III, 6:87

CORDELIA. Alack! 't is he: why, he was met even now
As mad as the vex'd sea; singing aloud;
Crown'd with rank fumiter and furrow-weeds,
With burdocks, hemlock, nettles, cuckoo-flowers,
Darnel, and all the idle weeds that grow
In our sustaining corn.
King Lear, IV, 4:1

K. LEAR. No, they cannot touch me for coining; I am the king himself.

. . . . .

Ha! Goneril, with a white beard! They flattered me like a dog, and told me I had white hairs in my beard ere the black ones were there. To say 'ay' and 'no' to every thing I said! 'Ay' and 'no' too was no good divinity. When the rain came to wet me once and the wind to make me chatter, when the thunder would not peace at my bidding, there I found 'em, there I smelt 'em out. Go to, they are not men o' their words: they told me I was every thing; 't is a lie, I am not ague-proof.
King Lear, IV, 6:82, 97

K. LEAR. What! art mad? A man may see how this world goes with no eyes. Look with thine ears: see how yond justice rails upon yond simple thief. Hark, in thine ear: change places; and, handy-dandy, which is the justice, which is the thief? Thou hast seen a farmer's dog bark at a beggar?
GLOUCESTER. Ay, sir.
K. LEAR. And the creature run from the cur? There thou might'st behold the great image of authority; a dog 's obeyed in office.
Thou rascal beadle, hold thy bloody hand!
Why dost thou lash that whore? Strip thine own back;
Thou hotly lusts to use her in that kind
For which thou whipp'st her. The usurer hangs the cozener.
Through tatter'd clothes small vices do appear;
Robes and furr'd gowns hide all. Plate sin with gold,

And the strong lance of justice hurtless breaks;
Arm it in rags, a pigmy's straw does pierce it.
King Lear, IV, 6:153

CORDELIA. How does my royal lord? How fares your majesty?
K. LEAR. You do me wrong to take me out o' the grave;
Thou art a soul in bliss; but I am bound
Upon a wheel of fire, that mine own tears
Do scald like molten lead.
CORDELIA. Sir, do you know me?
K. LEAR. You are a spirit, I know; when did you die?
King Lear, IV, 7:44

CORDELIA. Shall we not see these daughters and these sisters?
K. LEAR. No, no, no, no! Come, let 's away to prison;
We two alone will sing like birds i' the cage:
When thou dost ask me blessing, I 'll kneel down,
And ask of thee forgiveness: so we 'll live,
And pray, and sing, and tell old tales, and laugh
At gilded butterflies, and hear poor rogues
Talk of court news; and we 'll talk with them too,
Who loses and who wins; who 's in, who 's out;
And take upon 's the mystery of things,
As if we were God's spies.
King Lear, V, 3:6

MAGIC

[Solemn and strange music; and PROSPERO above, invisible. Enter several strange Shapes, bringing in a banquet: they dance about it with gentle actions of salutation; and, inviting the King, etc., to eat, they depart.]
ALONZO. What harmony is this? my good friends, hark!
GONZALO. Marvellous sweet music!
ALONZO. Give us kind keepers, heavens! What were these?
SEBASTIAN. A living drollery.
Tempest, III, 3:18

ALONZO. I cannot too much muse
Such shapes, such gesture and such sound, expressing,
Although they want[1] the use of tongue, a kind
Of excellent dumb discourse.
Tempest, III, 3:36

[1] want: lack.

[Thunder and lightning. Enter ARIEL, like a harpy;[1] claps his wings upon the table; and, with a quaint device, the banquet vanishes.]

ARIEL. You are three men of sin, whom Destiny,
That hath to instrument this lower world
And what is in 't, the never-surfeited sea
Hath caus'd to belch up you, and on this island
Where man doth not inhabit; you 'mongst men
Being most unfit to live. I have made you mad;
[Seeing ALONSO, SEBASTIAN, etc., draw their swords.]
You fools! I and my fellows
Are ministers of fate: the elements,
Of whom your swords are temper'd, may as well
Wound the loud winds, or with bemock'd-at stabs
Kill the still-closing waters, as diminish
One dowle[2] that 's in my plume: my fellow-ministers
Are like invulnerable. If you could hurt,
Your swords are now too massy[3] for your strengths,
And will not be uplifted.
Tempest, III, 3:52
[1] harpy: a fabulous monster with a bird's body and wings and a woman's face. [2] dowle: feather. [3] massy: heavy.

IRIS. You nymphs, call'd Naiads, of the wandering brooks,
With your sedg'd crowns, and ever-harmless looks,
Leave your crisp channels and on this green land
Answer your summons: Juno does command.
Come, temperate nymphs, and help to celebrate
A contract[1] of true love; be not too late.
Enter certain Nymphs.
You sunburnt sicklemen, of August weary,
Come hither from the furrow and be merry.
Make holiday; your rye-straw hats put on,
And these fresh nymphs encounter every one
In country footing.
[Enter certain Reapers, properly habited: they join with the Nymphs in a graceful dance; towards the end whereof PROSPERO starts suddenly, and speaks; after which, to a strange, hollow, and confused noise, they heavily vanish.]
Tempest, IV, 1:128
[1] contract: between FERDINAND and MIRANDA.

JUNO and CERES.[1] How does my bounteous sister? Go with me

To bless this twain, that they may prosperous be,
And honour'd in their issue.
Honour, riches, marriage-blessing,
Long continuance, and increasing,
Hourly joys be still upon you!
Juno sings her blessings on you.
CERES. Earth's increase, foison[2] plenty,
Barns and garners never empty;
Vines with clust'ring bunches growing;
Plants with goodly burden bowing;
Spring come to you at the farthest
In the very end of harvest!
Scarcity and want shall shun you;
Ceres' blessing so is on you.
Tempest, IV, 1:103
[1] CERES: goddess of agriculture. [2] foison: harvest.

PROSPERO. Our revels now are ended. These our actors,
As I foretold you, were all spirits and
Are melted into air, into thin air;
And, like the baseless fabric of this vision,
The cloud-capp'd towers, the gorgeous palaces,
The solemn temples, the great globe itself,
Yea, all which it inherit, shall dissolve
And, like this insubstantial pageant faded,
Leave not a rack behind. We are such stuff
As dreams are made on, and our little life
Is rounded with a sleep.
Tempest, IV, 1:148

PROSPERO. I have bedimm'd
The noontide sun, call'd forth the mutinous winds,
And 'twixt the green sea and the azur'd vault
Set roaring war: to the dread rattling thunder
Have I given fire and rifted Jove's stout oak
With his own bolt: the strong bas'd promontory
Have I made shake; and by the spurs pluck'd up
The pine and cedar: graves at my command
Have waked their sleepers, oped, and let them forth
By my so potent art. But this rough magic
I here abjure; and, when I have requir'd
Some heavenly music, which even now I do,
To work mine end upon their senses that
This airy charm is for, I 'll break my staff,
Bury it certain fathoms in the earth,
And, deeper than did ever plummet sound,
I'll drown my book.
Tempest, V, 1:41
[The *Tempest* was Shakespeare's last play. The lines beginning, "But this rough magic" have often been interpreted as his valedictory to his career as an author.]

Prospero. The charm dissolves apace,
And as the morning steals upon the night,
Melting the darkness, so their rising senses
Begin to chase the ignorant fumes that mantle
Their clearer reason.

Tempest, V, 1:64

MAID

Helena. I am a simple maid; and therein wealthiest
That I protest I simply am a maid.

All's Well That Ends Well, II, 3:72

Laertes. The chariest[1] maid is prodigal enough
If she unmask her beauty to the moon;
Virtue itself 'scapes not caluminous strokes.

Hamlet, I, 3:36

[1] chariest: most scrupulous.

Polonius. From this time
Be somewhat scanter of your maiden presence;
Set your entreatments at a higher rate
Than a command to parley.

Hamlet, I, 3:120

France. Not all the dukes of waterish Burgundy
Can buy this unpriz'd precious maid of me.

King Lear, I, 1:261

Angelo. This virtuous maid
Subdues me quite. Ever till now,
When men were fond, I smil'd and wonder'd how.

Measure for Measure, II, 2:185

Portia. But lest you should not understand me well—
And yet a maiden hath no tongue but thought,—
I would detain you here some month or two
Before you venture for me.

Merchant of Venice, III, 2:7

Theseus. For aye to be in shady cloister mew'd,
To live a barren sister all your life,
Chanting faint hymns to the cold fruitless moon.
Thrice blessed they that master so their blood,
To undergo such maiden pilgrimage;

Midsummer Night's Dream, I, 1:71

Oberon. In maiden meditation fancy-free.

Midsummer Night's Dream, II, 1:164

Cassio. Most fortunately: he hath achiev'd a maid[1]
That paragons description and wild fame;
One that excels the quirks of blazoning pens
And in the essential vesture of creation
Does tire[2] the enginer.

Othello, II, 1:61

[1] maid: Desdemona. [2] tire, etc.: various interpretations, e.g., tires the imaginer.

MALAPROPISMS

Quickly. You cannot one bear with another's confirmities.

II Henry IV, II, 4:63

Quickly. I beseek you now, aggravate your choler.

II Henry IV, II, 4:175

Elbow. [I] do bring in here before your good honour two notorious benefactors.

Measure for Measure, II, 1:49

Elbow. My wife, sir, whom I detest before heaven.

Measure for Measure, II, 1:69

Elbow. My wife . . . who if she had been a woman cardinally given.

Measure for Measure, II, 1:81

Slender. All his successors gone before him hath done 't; and all his ancestors that come after him may.

Merry Wives of Windsor, I, 1:14

Quickly. I detest, an honest maid as ever broke bread.

Merry Wives of Windsor, I, 4:160

Bottom. These we may rehearse most obscenely and courageously.

Midsummer Night's Dream, I, 2:110

Quince. He comes to disfigure, or to present, the person of Moonshine.

Midsummer Night's Dream, III, 1:61

Bottom. Flowers of odious savours sweet.

Midsummer Night's Dream, III, 1:84

Quince. A very paramour for a sweet voice.

Midsummer Night's Dream, IV, 2:12

Dogberry. You are thought here to be the most senseless and fit man.

Much Ado About Nothing, III, 3:23

DOGBERRY. You shall comprehend all vagrom men.
Much Ado About Nothing, III, 3:26

DOGBERRY. To babble and talk is most tolerable and not to be endured.
Much Ado About Nothing, III, 3:36

DOGBERRY. Adier; be vigitant, I beseech you.
Much Ado About Nothing, III, 3:101

DOGBERRY. Comparisons are odorous.
Much Ado About Nothing, III, 5:18

DOGBERRY. I hear as good exclamation on your worship.
Much Ado About Nothing, III, 5:27

DOGBERRY. Marry, sir, I would have some confidence with you, that decerns you nearly.
     . . . . .
Only get the learned writer to set down our excommunication and meet me at the gaol.
Much Ado About Nothing, III, 5:3, 69

DOGBERRY. Our watch, sir, have indeed comprehended two aspicious persons
     . . . . .
It shall be suffigance.
Much Ado About Nothing, III, 5:49, 56

DOGBERRY. Is our whole dissembly appeared?
Much Ado About Nothing, IV, 2:1

DOGBERRY. O villain! thou wilt be condemned into everlasting redemption for this.
Much Ado About Nothing, IV, 2:58

DOGBERRY. Dost thou not suspect my place?
Much Ado About Nothing, IV, 2:76

DOGBERRY. No, thou villain, thou art full of piety as shall be proved.
Much Ado About Nothing, IV, 2:81

DOGBERRY. Come, bring away the plaintiffs: by this time our sexton hath reformed Signior Leonato of the matter.
Much Ado About Nothing, V, 1:261

DOGBERRY. God restore you to health! I humbly give you leave to depart, and if a merry meeting may be wished, God prohibit it!
Much Ado About Nothing, V, 1:334

LAUNCE. I have received my proportion like the prodigious son.
Two Gentlemen of Verona, II, 3:3

MAN

JAQUES. All the world 's a stage,
And all the men and women merely players:
They have their exits and their entrances;
And one man in his time plays many parts,
His acts being seven ages. At first the infant,
Mewling and puking in the nurse's arms,
And then the whining school-boy, with his satchel,
And shining morning face, creeping like snail
Unwillingly to school. And then the lover,
Sighing like furnace, with a woeful ballad
Made to his mistress' eyebrow. Then a soldier,
Full of strange oaths, and bearded like the pard,[1]
Jealous in honour, sudden and quick in quarrel,
Seeking the bubble reputation
Even in the cannon's mouth. And then the justice,
In fair round belly with good capon lin'd,
With eyes severe, and beard of formal cut,
Full of wise saws[2] and modern instances;
And so he plays his part. The sixth age shifts
Into the lean and slipper'd pantaloon,[3]
With spectacles on nose and pouch on side,
His youthful hose well sav'd, a world too wide
For his shrunk shank; and his big manly voice,
Turning again toward childish treble, pipes
And whistles in his[4] sound. Last scene of all,
That ends this strange eventful history,
Is second childishness and mere[5] oblivion,
Sans[6] teeth, sans eyes, sans taste, sans every thing.
As You Like It, II, 7:139
[1] pard: leopard.   [2] saws: sayings, proverbs.
[3] pantaloon: an old fool.   [4] his: its.   [5] mere: absolute.   [6] Sans: without.

LUCIANA. Why, headstrong liberty is lash'd with woe.
There 's nothing situate under heaven's eye
But hath his[1] bound[2] in earth, in sea, in sky:
The beasts, the fishes, and the winged fowls,
Are their males' subjects and at their controls.
Men, more divine, the masters of all these,
Lords of the wide world, and wild wat'ry seas,
Indued with intellectual sense and souls,

Of more pre-eminence than fish and fowls,
Are masters to their females, and their
    lords:
Then let your will attend on their accords.[3]
                Comedy of Errors, II, 1:15
[1] his: its.   [2] bound: limitation.   [3] accords: consent.

HAMLET. He was a man, take him for all
    in all,
I shall not look upon his like again.
                            Hamlet, I, 2:187
[1] About his father.

HAMLET. What a piece of work is a man!
how noble in reason! how infinite in faculty! in form and moving how express and
admirable! in action how like an angel! in
apprehension how like a god! the beauty of
the world! the paragon of animals! And
yet, to me, what is this quintessence of dust?
man delights not me; no, nor woman neither, though by your smiling you seem to
say so.
                            Hamlet, II, 2:317

HAMLET. A combination and a form in-
    deed,
Where every god did seem to set his seal,
To give the world assurance of a man.
                            Hamlet, III, 4:60

HAMLET. What is a man,
If his chief good and market of his time
Be but to sleep and feed? a beast, no more.
Sure he that made us with such large dis-
    course,
Looking before and after[1] gave us not
That capability and god-like reason
To fust[2] in us unus'd.
                            Hamlet, IV, 4:33
[1] Looking . . . after: back for causes, forward
for results.   [2] fust: grow mouldy.

ANTONY [about BRUTUS]. His life was
    gentle, and the elements
So mix'd in him that Nature might stand up
And say to all the world, 'This was a man!'
                    Julius Caesar, V, 5:73

FIRST MURDERER. We are men, my liege.
MACBETH. Ay, in the catalogue ye go for
    men;
As hounds and greyhounds, mongrels, span-
    iels, curs,
Shoughs,[1] water-rugs,[2] and demi-wolves, are
    clept[3]
All by the name of dogs: the valu'd file[4]
Distinguishes the swift, the slow, the subtle,
The housekeeper, the hunter, every one

According to the gift which bounteous na-
    ture
Hath in him clos'd.
                            Macbeth, III, 1:91
[1] Shoughs: pronounced shocks, shaggy dogs.
[2] water-rugs: poodles.   [3] clept: called.   [4] valu'd
file: list giving descriptions of each.

PORTIA. God made him, and therefore let
him pass for a man.
                Merchant of Venice, I, 2:60

EMILIA. 'Tis not a year or two shows us a
    man:
They are all but stomachs, and we all but
    food:
They eat us hungerly, and when they are
    full
They belch us.
                    . . . . .

DESDEMONA. Men's natures wrangle with
    inferior things,
Though great ones are their object.
                    Othello, III, 4:103, 144

PERICLES. A man whom both the waters
    and the wind,
In that vast tennis-court, have made the ball
For them to play upon, entreats you pity
    him;
                            Pericles, II, 1:63

APEMANTUS. I wonder men dare trust
    themselves with men:
Methinks they should invite them without
    knives;
Good for their meat, and safer for their
    lives.
                    Timon of Athens, I, 2:43

PANDARUS. Do you know what a man is?
Is not birth, beauty, good shape, discourse,
manhood, learning, gentleness, virtue,
youth, liberality, and so forth, the spice and
salt that season a man?
                    Troilus and Cressida, I, 2:274

ULYSSES. O heavens! what some men do,
While some men leave[1] to do.
How some men creep in skittish fortune's
    hall,
Whiles others play the idiots in her eyes!
                    Troilus and Cressida, III, 3:132
[1] leave to do: do nothing.

MANNERS

CLOWN. Truly, madam, if God have lent
a man any manners, he may easily put it off
at court: he that cannot make a leg, put off
's cap, kiss his hand, and say nothing, has

neither leg, hands, lip, nor cap; and indeed such a fellow, to say precisely, were not for the court.
All's Well That Ends Well, II, 2:9

JAQUES. Of what kind should this cock come of?
As You Like It, II, 7:90

IMOGEN. I am much sorry, sir,
You put me to forget a lady's manners,
By being so verbal.
Cymbeline, II, 3:109

FALSTAFF. Shall I not take mine ease in mine inn but I shall have my pocket picked?
I Henry IV, III, 3:93

BEDFORD. I have heard it said, unbidden guests
Are often welcomest when they are gone.
I Henry VI, II, 2:55

Q. KATHARINE. Nay, we must longer kneel: I am a suitor.
K. HENRY. Arise, and take place by us: half your suit
Never name to us; you have half our power:
The other moiety,[1] ere you ask, is given.
Henry VIII, I, 2:9
[1] moiety: a half; sometimes any part.

GRIFFITH. Men's evil manners live in brass; their virtues
We write in water.
Henry VIII, IV, 2:45

K. HENRY. 'T is well there 's one above 'em yet. I had thought
They had parted so much honesty among 'em.
At least good manners, as not thus to suffer
A man of his place, and so near our favour,
To dance attendance on their lordships' pleasures.
Henry VIII, V, 2:27

KENT. Be Kent unmannerly,
When Lear is mad.
King Lear, I, 1:147

A woeful hostess brooks not merry guests.
Rape of Lucrece: 1125

OLIVIA [to SIR TOBY]. Ungracious wretch!
Fit for the mountains and the barbarous caves,
Where manners ne'er were preach'd. Out of my sight!
Twelfth Night, IV, 1:53

MARRIAGE

BERTRAM. War is no strife
To[1] the dark house[2] and the detested wife.
All's Well That Ends Well, II, 3:308
[1] To: compared with. [2] dark house: house made gloomy by discontent.

PAROLLES. A young man married is a man that's marr'd.
All's Well That Ends Well, II, 3:315

TOUCHSTONE. As the ox hath his bow, sir, the horse his curb, and the falcon her bells, so man hath his desires; and as pigeons bill, so wedlock would be nibbling.
As You Like It, III, 3:80

CELIA. Will you, Orlando, have to wife this Rosalind?
ORLANDO. I will.
ROSALIND. Ay, but when?
ORLANDO. Why now; as fast as she can marry us.
ROSALIND. Then you must say, 'I take thee, Rosalind, for wife.'
ORLANDO. I take thee, Rosalind, for wife.

. . . . .

ROSALIND. Now tell me how long you would have her after you have possessed her.
ORLANDO. For ever and a day.
ROSALIND. Say 'a day,' without the 'ever.' No, no, Orlando; men are April when they woo, December when they wed: maids are May when they are maids, but the sky changes when they are wives.
As You Like It, IV, 1:130, 143

ROSALIND. I will be more jealous of thee than a Barbary cock-pigeon over his hen; more clamorous than a parrot against rain; more new-fangled than an ape; more giddy in my desires than a monkey: I will weep for nothing, like Diana in the fountain, and I will do that when you are disposed to be merry; I will laugh like a hyen, and that when thou art inclined to sleep.
ORLANDO. But will my Rosalind do so?
ROSALIND. By my life, she will do as I do.
As You Like It, IV, 1:150

Song. Wedding is great Juno's crown;
O blessed bond of board and bed!
'T is Hymen peoples every town;
High wedlock then be honoured.
Honour, high honour, and renown,
To Hymen, god of every town!
As You Like It, V, 4:147

JAQUES [to TOUCHSTONE]. And you to wrangling; for thy loving voyage
Is but for two months victuall'd.
As You Like It, V, 4:197

LUCIANA. If you did wed my sister for her wealth,
Then for her wealth's sake use her with more kindness.
Comedy of Errors, III, 2:5

HAMLET. If thou dost marry, I 'll give thee this plague for thy dowry: be thou as chaste as ice, as pure as snow, thou shalt not escape calumny. Get thee to a nunnery, go; farewell. Or, if thou wilt needs marry, marry a fool; for wise men know well enough what monsters you make of them.
Hamlet, III, 1:138

Q. ISABEL. God, the best maker of all marriages,
Combine your hearts in one, your realms in one!
Henry V, V, 2:387

K. HENRY. Marriage, uncle! alas! my years are young,
And fitter is my study and my books
Than wanton dalliance with a paramour.
I Henry VI, V, 1:21

SUFFOLK. Marriage is a matter of more worth
Than to be dealt in by attorneyship.

. . . . .

For what is wedlock forced but a hell,
An age of discord and continual strife?
I Henry VI, V, 5:55, 62

GLOUCESTER.[1] Yet hasty marriage seldom proveth well.
III Henry VI, IV, 1:18
[1] Later, King Richard III.

FIRST CITIZEN. He is the half part of a blessed man,
Left to be finished by such as she;
And she a fair divided excellence,
Whose fulness of perfection lies in him.
O! two such silver currents, when they join,
Do glorify the banks that bound them in;
King John, II, 1:437

SLENDER. I will marry her, sir, at your request; but if there be no great love in the beginning, yet heaven may decrease it upon better acquaintance, when we are married and have more occasion to know one another: I hope, upon familiarity will grow more contempt: but if you say, 'Marry her,' I will marry her; that I am freely dissolved, and dissolutely.
Merry Wives of Windsor, I, 1:253

BEATRICE. For hear me, Hero: wooing, wedding, and repenting, is as a Scotch jig, a measure,[1] and a cinque-pace:[2] the first suit is hot and hasty, like a Scotch jig, and full as fantastical; the wedding, mannerly-modest, as a measure, full of state and ancientry; and then comes repentance, and, with his bad legs, falls into the cinque-pace faster and faster, till he sink into his grave.
Much Ado About Nothing, II, 1:76
[1] measure: a slow dance.   [2] cinque-pace: a lively dance.

DON PEDRO. Will you have me, lady?
BEATRICE. No, my lord, unless I might have another for working-days: your grace is too costly to wear every day.
Much Ado About Nothing, II, 1:339

LEONATO. O Lord! my lord, if they[1] were but a week married, they would talk themselves mad.
Much Ado About Nothing, II, 1:368
[1] they: BEATRICE and BENEDICK.

BENEDICK. I do much wonder that one man, seeing how much another man is a fool when he dedicates his behaviours to love, will, after he hath laughed at such shallow follies in others, become the argument of his own scorn by falling in love.
Much Ado About Nothing, II, 3:7

BRABANTIO. Whether a maid so tender, fair, and happy,
So opposite to marriage that she shunn'd
The wealthy curled darlings of our nation,
Would ever have, to incur a general mock,
Run from her guardage to the sooty bosom
Of such a thing as thou; to fear, not to delight.
Othello, I, 2:166

ANNE.[1] For never yet one hour in his bed
Did I enjoy the golden dew of sleep,
But with his timorous dreams was still[2] awak'd.
Richard III, IV, 1:83
[1] Queen to RICHARD III.   [2] still: always.

ROMEO. Do thou but close our hands with holy words,
Then love-devouring death do what he dare;
It is enough I may but call her mine.
Romeo and Juliet, II, 6:6

GRUMIO. Nothing comes amiss, so money comes withal.[1]

. . . . .

HORTENSIO. She[2] is intolerable curst[3]
And shrewd[4] and froward,[5] so beyond all
  measure,
That, were my state far worser than it is,
I would not wed her for a mine of gold.
  PETRUCHIO. Hortensio, peace!

. . . . .

For I will board her, though she chide as
  loud
As thunder when the clouds in autumn
  crack.
            Taming of the Shrew, I, 2:82, 89, 95
[1] withal: with it. [2] She: KATHARINA. [3] curst:
waspish. [4] shrewd: scolding. [5] froward: disobedient.

BIONDELLO. I knew a wench married in an
afternoon as she went to the garden for
parsley to stuff a rabbit.
            Taming of the Shrew, IV, 4:99

JUNO and CERES.[1] Honour, riches, mar-
  riage-blessing,
Long continuance, and increasing,
Hourly joys be still upon you!
            Tempest, IV, 1:106
[1] Juno: goddess of marriage and childbirth;
CERES: goddess of agriculture.

GONZALO. Look down, you gods,
And on this couple drop a blessed crown!
            Tempest, V, 1:201

DUKE. Let still[1] the woman take
An elder than herself, so wears she to him,
So sways she level in her husband's heart:
For, boy, however we do praise ourselves,
Our fancies are more giddy and unfirm,
More longing, wavering, sooner lost and
  worn,
Than women's are.

. . . . .

Then let thy love be younger than thyself,
Or thy affection cannot hold the bent;[2]
For women are as roses, whose fair flower
Being once display'd, doth fall that very
  hour.
  VIOLA. And so they are: alas! that they
    are so;
To die, even when they to perfection grow.
            Twelfth Night, II, 4:30, 37
[1] still: always. [2] bent: tension, strain.

OLIVIA.[1] Blame not this haste of mine. If
  you mean well,
Now go with me and with this holy man[2]
Into the chantry[3] by; there, before him,
And underneath that consecrated roof,
Plight me the full assurance of your faith;
That my most jealous and too doubtful soul

May live at peace. He shall conceal it
Whiles[4] you are willing it shall come to note,
What time we will our celebration keep
According to my birth. What do you say?
            Twelfth Night, IV, 3:22
[1] To SEBASTIAN, mistaken for VIOLA. [2] holy
man: priest. [3] chantry: chapel. [4] Whiles: until.

MASTER

IMOGEN. There is no more such masters;
  I may wander
From east to occident, cry out for service,
Try many, all good, serve truly, never
Find such another master.
            Cymbeline, IV, 2:371

IAGO. We cannot all be masters, nor all
  masters
Cannot be truly follow'd. You shall mark
Many a duteous and knee-crooking knave,
That, doting on his own obsequious bondage,
Wears out his time, much like his master's
  ass,
For nought but provender, and when he 's
  old, cashier'd.[1]
            Othello, I, 1:43
[1] cashier'd: dismissed.

MEDICINE

LAFEU. I have seen a medicine
That 's able to breathe life into a stone,
Quicken a rock, and make you dance ca-
  nary[1]
With spritely fire and motion.
            All's Well That Ends Well, II, 1:76
[1] canary: a lively dance.

CYMBELINE. By medicine life may be
  prolong'd, yet death
Will seize the doctor too.
            Cymbeline, V, 5:29

MACBETH. Throw physic[1] to the dogs; I
  'll none of it.
            Macbeth, V, 3:47
[1] physic: medicine.

ISABELLA. Besides, he tells me that, if peradventure
He speak against me on the adverse side,
I should not think it strange; for 't is a
  physic.[1]
That 's bitter to sweet end.
            Measure for Measure, IV, 6:5
[1] physic: medicine.

MELANCHOLY

CLOWN. By my troth, I take my young lord to be a very melancholy man.

COUNT. By what observance, I pray you?

CLOWN. Why, he will look upon his boot and sing; mend the ruff and sing; ask questions and sing; pick his teeth and sing. I know a man that had this trick of melancholy sold a goodly manor for a song.

All's Well That Ends Well, III, 2:4

JAQUES. I have neither the scholar's melancholy, which is emulation; nor the musician's, which is fantastical; nor the courtier's, which is proud; nor the soldier's, which is ambitious; nor the lawyer's, which is politic; nor the lady's, which is nice;[1] nor the lover's, which is all these: but it is a melancholy of mine own, compounded of many simples[2] extracted from many objects, and indeed the sundry contemplation of my travels, in which my often rumination wraps me in a most humorous[3] sadness.

As You Like It, IV, 1:10

[1] nice: fastidious. [2] simples: ingredients. [3] humorous: gloomy, capricious.

BELARIUS. O melancholy!
Who ever yet could sound thy bottom? find
The ooze, to show that coast thy sluggish crare[1]
Might earliest harbour in?

Cymbeline, IV, 2:203

[1] crare: small ship.

HAMLET. The devil hath power
To assume a pleasing shape; yea, and perhaps
Out of my weakness and my melancholy,
As he is very potent with such spirits,
Abuses[1] me to damn me.

Hamlet, II, 2:628

[1] Abuses: deceives.

KING. There 's something in his soul
O'er which his melancholy sits on brood.

Hamlet, III, 1:172

FALSTAFF. 'Sblood,[1] I am as melancholy as a gib cat,[2] or a lugged[3] bear.

1 Henry IV, I, 2:83

[1] 'Sblood: an oath, "God's blood." [2] gib cat: tomcat. [3] lugged: dragged.

MEMORY

IACHIMO. Why should I write this down, that 's riveted,
Screw'd to my memory?

Cymbeline, II, 2:43

HAMLET. O heavens! die two months ago, and not forgotten yet? Then there 's hope a great man's memory may outlive his life half a year; but, by 'r lady,[1] he must build churches then, or else shall he suffer not thinking on.

Hamlet, III, 2:139

[1] by 'r lady: oath, "by the Virgin Mary."

BOYET. Why, that contempt will kill the speaker's heart,
And quite divorce his memory from his part.

Love's Labour's Lost, V, 2:149

JULIET. I would forget it fain;
But, O! it presses to my memory,
Like damned guilty deeds to sinners' minds.

Romeo and Juliet, III, 2:109

MERCY

MENENIUS. There is no more mercy in him than there is milk in a male tiger.

Coriolanus, V, 4:30

ISABELLA. Well, believe this,
No ceremony that to great ones 'longs,
Not the king's crown, nor the deputed sword,
The marshal's truncheon,[1] nor the judge's robe,
Become them with one half so good a grace
As mercy does.

Measure for Measure, II, 2:58

[1] truncheon: a symbol of command.

PRINCE. Mercy but murders, pardoning those that kill.

Romeo and Juliet, III, 1:202

TAMORA. Wilt thou draw near the nature of the gods?
Draw near them then in being merciful;
Sweet mercy is nobility's true badge.

Titus Andronicus, I, 1:118

TROILUS. Brother, you have a vice of mercy in you,
Which better fits a lion than a man.

HECTOR. What vice is that, good Troilus? chide me for it.

TROILUS. When many times the captive Grecian falls,
Even in the fan and wind of your fair sword
You bid them rise, and live.

HECTOR. O! 't is fair play.

Troilus and Cressida, V, 3:37

MERIT

Countess. There 's nothing here that is too good for him,[1]
But only she; and she deserves a lord
That twenty such rude boys might tend[2] upon,
And call her hourly mistress.
All's Well That Ends Well, III, 2:82
[1] him: Bertrand. [2] tend: wait.

Hamlet. The spurns
That patient merit of the unworthy takes.
Hamlet, III, 1:73

Arragon. Who shall go about
To cozen[1] fortune and be honourable
Without the stamp of merit?
Merchant of Venice, II, 9:38
[1] cozen: cheat.

MERMAID

Antipholus of Syracuse. O! train me not, sweet mermaid, with thy note,
To drown me in thy sister flood of tears:
Sing, siren, for thyself, and I will dote:
Spread o'er the silver waves thy golden hairs,
And as a bed I 'll take them and there lie;
And in that glorious supposition think
He gains by death that hath such means to die.
Comedy of Errors, III, 2:45

MERRY

Dromio of Syracuse. I am glad to see you in this merry vein:
What means this jest?
Comedy of Errors, II, 2:20

K. Henry. 'T is ever common
That men are merriest when they are from home.
Henry V, I, 2:271

Arthur. So I were out of prison and kept sheep,
I should be as merry as the day is long.
King John, IV, 1:17

Salarino. Why, then you are in love.
Antonio. Fie, fie!
Salarino. Not in love neither? Then let us say you are sad,
Because you are not merry; and 't were as easy

For you to laugh, and leap, and say you are merry,
Because you are not sad.

. . . . .

I would have stay'd till I had made you merry,
If worthier friends had not prevented me.
Merchant of Venice, I, 1:46, 60

MIDNIGHT

Horatio. In the dead vast and middle of the night.
Hamlet, I, 2:198

Hamlet [soliloquy]. 'T is now the very witching time of night,
When churchyards yawn and hell itself breathes out
Contagion to this world: now could I drink hot blood,
And do such bitter business as the day
Would quake to look on.
Hamlet, III, 2:406

Theseus. The iron tongue of midnight hath told[1] twelve;
Lovers, to bed; 't is almost fairy time.
Midsummer Night's Dream, V, 1:370
[1] told: counted.

Puck. Now the hungry lion roars,
And the wolf behowls the moon;
Whilst the heavy ploughman snores,
All with weary task fordone.
Now the wasted brands do glow,
Whilst the screech-owl, screeching loud,
Puts the wretch that lies in woe
In remembrance of a shroud.
Now it is the time of night
That the graves, all gaping wide,
Every one lets forth his sprite,
In the church-way paths to glide:
And we fairies, that do run
By the triple Hecate's team
From the presence of the sun,
Following darkness like a dream,
Now are frolic; not a mouse
Shall disturb this hallow'd house:
I am sent with broom before,
To sweep the dust behind the door.
Midsummer Night's Dream, V, 1:378

Oberon. Through the house give glimmering light
By the dead and drowsy fire;
Every elf and fairy sprite
Hop as light as bird from brier;
And this ditty after me
Sing, and dance it trippingly.
Midsummer Night's Dream, V, 1:398

MIND

K. Henry. All things are ready, if our minds be so.
Westmoreland. Perish the man whose mind is backward now!
Henry V, IV, 3:71

Gloucester. My lord, 't is but a base ignoble mind
That mounts no higher than a bird can soar.
II Henry VI, II, 1:9

Chamberlain.[1] You bear a gentle mind, and heavenly blessings
Follow such creatures.
Henry VIII, II, 3:57

[1] To Anne Bullen.

K. Lear. When the mind 's free
The body 's delicate; the tempest in my mind
Doth from my senses take all feeling else
Save what beats there.
King Lear, III, 4:11

Longaville. The mind shall banquet, though the body pine:
Fat paunches have lean pates, and dainty bits
Make rich the ribs, but bankrupt quite the wits.
Love's Labour's Lost, I, 1:25

Doctor. Unnatural deeds
Do breed unnatural troubles; infected minds
To their deaf pillows will discharge their secrets.
Macbeth, V, 1:79

Morocco. A golden mind stoops not to shows of dross.
Merchant of Venice, II, 7:20

Men have marble, women waxen minds.
Rape of Lucrece: 1240

Achilles. My mind is troubled, like a fountain stirr'd;
And I myself see not the bottom of it.
Troilus and Cressida, III, 3:311

Antonio. In nature there 's no blemish but the mind;
None can be call'd deform'd but the unkind:
Virtue is beauty, but the beauteous evil
Are empty trunks o'erflourished by the devil.
Twelfth Night, III, 4:401

MIRTH

Antonio. I hold the world but as the world, Gratiano;
A stage where every man must play a part,
And mine a sad one.
Gratiano. Let me play the fool:
With mirth and laughter let old wrinkles come.
And let my liver rather heat with wine
Than my heart cool with mortifying groans.
Why should a man, whose blood is warm within,
Sit like his grandsire cut in alabaster?
Sleep when he wakes, and creep into the jaundice
By being peevish? I tell thee what, Antonio,
I love thee, and it is my love that speaks,
There are a sort of men whose visages
Do cream and mantle like a standing pond,
And do a wilful stillness entertain,
With purpose to be dress'd in an opinion
Of wisdom, gravity, profound conceit;
As who should say, 'I am Sir Oracle,
And when I ope my lips let no dog bark!'
Merchant of Venice, I, 1:77

Bassanio. I would entreat you rather to put on
Your boldest suit of mirth, for we have friends
That purpose merriment.
Merchant of Venice, II, 2:210

Theseus. Awake the pert and nimble spirit of mirth;
Turn melancholy forth to funerals.
Midsummer Night's Dream, I, 1:13

Leonato.[1] There 's little of the melancholy element in her, my lord: she is never sad but when she sleeps; and not ever sad then, for I have heard my daughter say, she hath often dreamed of unhappiness and waked herself with laughing.
Much Ado About Nothing, II, 1:355
[1] About Beatrice.

Servant. Therefore they thought it good you hear a play,
And frame your mind to mirth and merriment,
Which bars a thousand harms and lengthens life.
Taming of the Shrew, Induction, II:137

MISCHIEF

Fairy.[1] Either I mistake your shape and making quite,
Or else you are that shrewd and knavish sprite
Call'd Robin Goodfellow: are not you he

That fright the maidens of the villagery;
Skim milk, and sometimes labour in the
  quern,[2]
And bootless make the breathless housewife
  churn;
And sometime make the drink to bear no
  barm;[3]
Mislead night-wanderers, laughing at their
  harm?
  Midsummer Night's Dream, II, 1:32
[1] To Puck.   [2] quern: handmill.   [3] barm: yeast.

PUCK. I am that merry wanderer of the
  night.
I jest to Oberon, and make him smile
When I a fat and bean-fed horse beguile,
Neighing in likeness of a filly foal:
And sometime lurk I in a gossip's bowl,
In very likeness of a roasted crab;
And when she drinks, against her lips I bob
And on her wither'd dewlap[1] pour the ale.
The wisest aunt, telling the saddest tale,
Sometime for three-foot stool mistaketh
  me;
Then slip I from her bum,[2] down topples
  she,
And 'tailor'[3] cries, and falls into a cough;
And then the whole quire[4] hold their hips
  and laugh,
And waxen[5] in their mirth, and neeze,[6] and
  swear
A merrier hour was never wasted there.
  Midsummer Night's Dream, II, 1:43
[1] dewlap: milk.   [2] bum: buttocks.   [3] 'tailor': a
common cry when someone falls.   [4] quire:
company.   [5] waxen: grow.   [6] neeze: sneeze.

MISER

FIRST FISHERMAN. I can compare our rich
misers to nothing so fitly as to a whale; a'[1]
plays and tumbles, driving the poor fry before him, and at last devours them all at a
mouthful.
  Pericles, II, 1:32
[1] a': he.

The aged man that coffers-up his gold
Is plagu'd with cramps and gouts and pain-
  ful fits;
And scarce hath eyes his treasure to behold,
But like still-pining Tantalus[1] he sits,
And useless barns[2] the harvest of his wits;
Having no other pleasure of his gain
But torment that it cannot cure his pain.
  Rape of Lucrece: 855
[1] Tantalus: in Greek mythology, a son of Zeus
who was compelled to hunger and thirst sur-
rounded by water and food.   [2] barns: noun
used as verb.

MISERY

CLAUDIO. The miserable have no other
  medicine
But only hope.
  Measure for Measure, III, 1:2

CALIBAN. They 'll nor pinch,
Fright me with urchin[1]-shows, pitch me i'
  the mire,
Nor lead me, like a firebrand, in the dark
Out of my way, unless he[2] bid 'em; but
For every trifle are they set upon me:
Sometime like apes, that mow and chatter
  at me
And after bite me, then like hedge-hogs
  which
Lie tumbling in my bare-foot way and
  mount
Their pricks at my foot-fall; sometime am I
All wound with adders, who with cloven
  tongues
Do hiss me into madness. Lo, now! lo!
  Tempest, II, 2:4
[1] urchin: hedge-hog.   [2] he: PROSPERO.

TRINCULO. Misery acquaints a man with
strange bedfellows.
  Tempest, II, 2:44

MISFORTUNE

PAROLLES. My lord, I am a man whom
fortune hath cruelly scratched.
  All's Well That Ends Well, V, 2:28

AEGON. By misfortunes was my life pro-
  long'd,
To tell sad stories of my own mishaps.
  Comedy of Errors, I, 1:120

ROMEO. O! give me thy hand
One writ with me in sour misfortune's book.
  Romeo and Juliet, V, 3:82

MODESTY

CORIOLANUS. I had rather have one scratch
  my head i' the sun
When the alarum were struck than idly sit
To hear my nothings monster'd.
  Coriolanus, II, 2:79

MENENIUS. He had rather venture all his
  limbs for honour
Than one on's ears to hear it?
  Coriolanus, II, 2:84

K. EDWARD [Aside]. Her looks do argue
her replete with modesty;

Her words do show her wit incomparable;
All her perfections challenge sovereignty:
One way or other, she is for a king;
And she shall be my love, or else my queen.
III Henry VI, III, 2:84

Duke. My holy sir, none better knows
    than you
How I have ever lov'd the life remov'd,
And held in idle price to haunt assemblies
Where youth, and cost, and witless bravery[1]
    keeps.[2]
                Measure for Measure, I, 3:7
[1] bravery: extravagant finery. [2] keeps: dwells.

Bassanio. Pray thee, take pain
To allay with some cold drops of modesty
Thy skipping spirit, lest through thy wild
    behaviour
I be misconstrued in the place I go to,
And lose my hopes.
                Merchant of Venice, II, 2:194

Demetrius. You do impeach your mod-
    esty too much,
To leave the city, and commit yourself
Into the hands of one that loves you not;
To trust the opportunity of night
And the ill counsel of a desert place
With the rich worth of your virginity.
            Midsummer Night's Dream, II, 1:214

MONEY

Arviragus. All gold and silver rather turn
    to dirt!
As 't is no better reckon'd but of[1] those
Who worship dirty gods.
                    Cymbeline, III, 6:55
[1] but of: except by.

Chief Justice. Your means are very slender, and your waste is great.
Falstaff. I would it were otherwise: I
would my means were greater and my waist
slenderer.
                    II Henry IV, I, 2:160

Falstaff. I can get no remedy against
this consumption of the purse: borrowing
only lingers and lingers it out, but the disease is incurable. Go bear this letter to my
Lord of Lancaster; this to the prince; this to
the Earl of Westmoreland; and this to old
Mistress Ursula, whom I have weekly sworn
to marry since I perceived the first white
hair on my chin.
                    II Henry IV, I, 2:264

Shallow. A friend i' the court is better
than a penny in purse.
                    II Henry IV, V, 1:34

Ford. Love like a shadow flies when substance[1] love pursues;
Pursuing that that flies, and flying what pur-
    sues.
            Merry Wives of Windsor, II, 2:215
[1] substance: material resources.

Iago. Thus do I ever make my fool my
    purse;
For I mine own gain'd knowledge should
    profane,
If I would time expend with such a snipe
But[1] for my sport and profit.
                        Othello, I, 3:389
[1] But: except.

Timon. The learned pate
Ducks to the golden fool.[1]
                Timon of Athens, IV, 3:17
[1] The man of learning bows down to the rich
fool.

MOODS

Don Pedro. Good morrow, Benedick.
    Why, what 's the matter,
That you have such a February face,
So full of frost, of storm and cloudiness?
            Much Ado About Nothing, V, 4:40

Tamora. These two have tic'd me hither
    to this place:
A barren detested vale, you see, it is;
The trees, though summer, yet forlorn and
    lean,
O'ercome with moss and baleful mistletoe:
Here never shines the sun; here nothing
    breeds,
Unless the nightly own or fatal raven:
And when they show'd me this abhorred
    pit,
They told me, here, at dead time of the
    night,
A thousand fiends, a thousand hissing
    snakes,
Ten thousand swelling toads, as many ur-
    chins,
Would make such fearful and confused
    cries,
As any mortal body hearing it
Should straight fall mad, or else die sud-
    denly.
No sooner had they told this hellish tale,
But straight they told me they would bind
    me here
Unto the body of a dismal yew,
And leave me to this miserable death.
                Titus Andronicus, II, 3:92

MOON—MOONLIGHT

MARCIUS [later CORIOLANUS]. They threw
their caps
As they would hang them on the horns o'
the moon,
Shouting their emulation.
Coriolanus, I, 1:216

HAMLET. What may this mean,
That thou, dead corse, again in complete
steel
Revisit'st thus the glimpses of the moon,
Making night hideous.
Hamlet, I, 4:51

BRUTUS. I had rather be a dog, and bay
the moon,
Than such a Roman.
Julius Caesar, IV, 3:27

DULL. What was a month old at Cain's
birth, that 's not five weeks old as yet?
. . . . .

HOLOFERNES. The moon was a month old
when Adam was no more;
And raught[1] not to five weeks when he came
to five-score.
Love's Labour's Lost, IV, 2:36, 40
[1] raught: reached.

ROSALINE. My face is but a moon, and
clouded too.
KING. Blessed are clouds, to do as such
clouds do!
Love's Labour's Lost, V, 2:203

LORENZO. How sweet the moonlight
sleeps upon this bank!
Here we will sit, and let the sounds of music
Creep in our ears: soft stillness and the
night
Become the touches of sweet harmony.
Sit, Jessica: look how the floor of heaven
Is thick inlaid with patines[1] of bright gold:
There 's not the smallest orb which thou
behold'st
But in his[2] motion[3] like an angel sings,
Still quiring to the young-eyed cherubins;
Such harmony is in immortal souls;
But, whilst this muddy vesture of decay
Doth grossly close it in, we cannot hear it.
Merchant of Venice, V, 1:54
[1] patines: plates, sometimes of gold, used in
communion service. [2] his: its. [3] motion: this
refers to a common belief in "music of the
spheres."

OTHELLO. It is the very error of the moon;
She comes more nearer earth than she was
wont,
And makes men mad.
Othello, V, 2:109

The moon being clouded presently is miss'd,
But little stars may hide them when they
list.
Rape of Lucrece: 1007

STEPHANO. How now, moon-calf? how
does thine ague?
CALIBAN. Hast thou not dropped from
heaven?
STEPHANO. Out o' the moon, I do assure
thee: I was the man in the moon, when
time was.
Tempest, II, 2:139

MORNING

HORATIO. But look, the morn, in russet
mantle clad,
Walks o'er the dew of yon high eastern hill.
Hamlet, I, 1:166

GHOST. The glow-worm shows the matin[1]
to be near,
And 'gins to pale his uneffectual fire.
Hamlet, I, 5:89
[1] matin: morning.

RICHARD.[1] See how the morning opes her
golden gates,
And takes her farewell of the glorious sun;
How well resembles it the prime of youth,
Trimm'd like a younker prancing to his
love.
III Henry VI, II, 1:21
[1] Later, GLOUCESTER.

PUCK. My fairy lord, this must be done
with haste,
For night's swift dragons cut the clouds
full fast,
And yonder shines Aurora's harbinger.[1]
Midsummer Night's Dream, III, 2:378
[1] harbinger: forerunner.

DON PEDRO. Look, the gentle day,
Before the wheels of Phoebus,[1] round about
Dapples the drowsy east with spots of grey.
Much Ado About Nothing, V, 3:25
[1] Phoebus: the sun god.

RATCLIFF. The early village cock
Hath twice done salutation to the morn.
Richard III, V, 3:209

BENVOLIO. An hour before the worshipp'd
sun
Peer'd forth the golden window of the east.
Romeo and Juliet, I, 1:125

FRIAR LAURENCE. The grey-eyed morn
smiles on the frowning night,
Chequering the eastern clouds with streaks
of light,

And flecked darkness like a drunkard reels
From forth day's path and Titan's fiery
wheels.
Romeo and Juliet, II, 3:1

Full many a glorious morning have I seen
Flatter the mountain tops with sovereign
eye,
Kissing with golden face the meadows
green,
Gilding pale streams with heavenly alchemy.[1]
Sonnet 33
[1] alchemy: transmutation of base metals into
gold.

Lo! here the gentle lark, weary of rest,
From his moist cabinet mounts up on high,
And wakes the morning, from whose silver
breast
The sun ariseth in his majesty.
Venus and Adonis: 853

MOTHER

AEGEON. The pleasing punishment that
women bear.
Comedy of Errors, I, 1:47

CORIOLANUS [as his mother kneels]. What
is this?
Your knees to me! to your corrected son!
Then let the pebbles on the hungry beach
Fillip the stars; then let the mutinous winds
Strike the proud cedars 'gainst the fiery sun.
Coriolanus, V, 3:57

VOLUMNIA. There 's no man in the world
More bound to 's mother; yet here he lets
me prate
Like one i' the stocks. Thou hast never in
thy life
Show'd thy dear mother any courtesy;
When she, poor hen! fond of no second
brood,
Has cluck'd thee to the wars, and safely
home,
Loaden with honour.
Coriolanus, V, 3:158

GHOST. Taint not thy mind, nor let thy
soul contrive
Against thy mother aught; leave her to
heaven,
And to those thorns that in her bosom
lodge,
To prick and sting her.
Hamlet, I, 5:85

K. RICHARD. Though rebels wound thee
with their horses' hoofs:
As a long-parted mother with her child

Plays fondly with her tears and smiles in
meeting,
So, weeping, smiling, greet I thee, my earth.
Richard II, III, 2:7

MOURNING

LAFEU. Moderate lamentation is the right
of the dead, excessive grief the enemy to
the living.
All's Well That Ends Well, I, 1:63

GUIDERIUS. I cannot sing; I 'll weep, and
word it with thee;
For notes of sorrow out of tune are worse
Than priests and fanes[1] that lie.
Cymbeline, IV, 2:240
[1] fanes: temples.

QUEEN. Do not for ever with thy vailed
lids
Seek for thy noble father in the dust;
Thou know'st 't is common; all that lives
must die,
Passing through nature to eternity.
HAMLET. Ay, madam, it is common.
QUEEN. If it be,
Why seems it so particular with thee?
HAMLET. Seems, madam! nay, it is; I
know not 'seems.'
'T is not alone my inky cloak, good mother,
Nor customary suits of solemn black,
Nor windy suspiration of forc'd breath,
No, nor the fruitful river in the eye,
Nor the dejected haviour of the visage,
Together with all forms, modes, shows of
grief,
That can denote me truly; these indeed
seem,
For they are actions that a man might play;
But I have that within which passeth show;
These but the trappings and the suits of
woe.
. . . . .
KING. Fie! 't is a fault to heaven,
A fault against the dead, a fault to nature,
To reason most absurd, whose common
theme
Is death of fathers, and who still[1] hath cried,
From the first corse till he that died to-day,
'This must be so.' We pray you, throw to
earth
This unprevailing woe, and think of us
As of a father; for let the world take note,
You are the most immediate to our throne.
Hamlet, I, 2:70, 101
[1] still: continuously.

BEDFORD. Hung be the heavens with black,
yield day to night!

Comets, importing change of times and
   states,
Brandish your crystal tresses in the sky,
And with them scourge the bad revolting
   stars
That have consented unto Henry's death!
King Henry the Fifth, too famous to live
   long!
England ne'er lost a king of so much worth.
                           1 Henry VI, I, 1:1

Paris. Sweet flower, with flowers thy
   bridal bed I strew,
O woe! thy canopy is dust and stones;
Which with sweet water nightly I will dew,
Or, wanting that, with tears distill'd by
   moans:
The obsequies that I for thee will keep
Nightly shall be to strew thy grave and
   weep.
                     Romeo and Juliet, V, 3:12

No longer mourn for me when I am dead
Than you shall hear the surly sullen bell
Give warning to the world that I am fled
From this vile world, with vilest worms to
   dwell.
                                   Sonnet 71

Paulina. I, an old turtle,[1]
Will wing me to some wither'd bough, and
   there
My mate, that's never to be found again,
Lament till I am lost.
                     Winter's Tale, V, 3:132
[1] turtle: turtle dove.

MURDER

King. No place, indeed, should murder
   sanctuarize;
Revenge should have no bounds. But, good
   Laertes,
Will you do this, keep close within your
   chamber.
Hamlet return'd shall know you are come
   home;
We 'll put on those shall praise your ex-
   cellence,
And set a double varnish on the fame
The Frenchman gave you, bring you, in
   fine, together
And wager on your heads: he, being remiss,
Most generous and free from all contriving,
Will not peruse the foils; so that with ease
Or with a little shuffling, you may choose
A sword unbated, and in a pass of practice
Requite him for your father.
Laertes. I will do 't;
And, for that purpose, I 'll anoint my
   sword.
I bought an unction of a mountebank,

So mortal that, but dip a knife in it,
Where it draws blood no cataplasm so rare,
Collected from all simples that have virtue
Under the moon, can save the thing from
   death
That is but scratch'd withal;[1] I 'll touch my
   point
With this contagion, that, if I gall him
   slightly,
It may be death.
   King. Let 's further think of this;
Weigh what convenience both of time and
   means
May fit us to our shape. If this should fail,
And that our drift look through our bad
   performance
'T were better not assay'd;[2] therefore this
   project
Should have a back or second, that might
   hold,
If this should blast in proof. Soft! let me see;
We 'll make a solemn wager on your cun-
   nings:
I ha 't:
When in your motion you are hot and dry,
As make your bouts more violent to that
   end,
And that he calls for drink, I 'll have pre-
   par'd him
A chalice for the nonce, whereon but sip-
   ping,
If he by chance escape your venom'd stuck,
Our purpose may hold there.
                              Hamlet, IV, 7:128
[1] withal: with it. [2] assay'd: attempted.

Hamlet. Another hit; what say you?
Laertes. A touch, a touch, I do confess.
King. Our son shall win.
Queen. He 's fat, and scant of breath.
   Here, Hamlet, take my napkin, rub thy
   brows;
The queen carouses to thy fortune, Hamlet.
Hamlet. Good madam!
King. Gertrude, do not drink.
Queen. I will, my lord; I pray you,
   pardon me.
King [aside]. It is the poison'd cup! it is
   too late.
Hamlet. I dare not drink yet, madam;
   by and by.
Queen. Come, let me wipe thy face.
Laertes. My lord, I 'll hit him now.
King. I do not think 't.
Laertes [aside]. And yet 't is almost
   'gainst my conscience.
Hamlet. Come, for the third, Laertes.
   you but dally;
I pray you, pass with your best violence.
I am afeard you make a wanton of me.
Laertes. Say you so? come on.
Osric. Nothing, neither way.
Laertes. Have at you now.

KING. Part them! they are incens'd.
HAMLET. Nay, come again.
                                 The QUEEN *falls.*
OSRIC. Look to the queen there, ho!
HORATIO. They bleed on both sides. How
  is it, my lord?

          . . . . .

Treachery! seek it out.
                                 LAERTES *falls.*
LAERTES. It is here, Hamlet. Hamlet, thou
  art slain;
No medicine in the world can do thee good;
In thee there is not half an hour of life;
The treacherous instrument is in thy hand,
Unbated and envenom'd. The foul practice
Hath turn'd itself on me; lo! here I lie,
Never to rise again. Thy mother's poison'd.
I can no more. The king, the king 's to
  blame.
HAMLET. The point envenom'd too!
Then, venom, to thy work. *Stabs the* KING.

          . . . . .

Follow my mother.   KING *dies.*
  LAERTES. He is justly serv'd;
It is a poison temper'd by himself.
Exchange forgiveness with me, noble Ham-
  let:
Mine and my father's death come not upon
  thee,
Nor thine on me!   *Dies.*
  HAMLET. Heaven make thee free of it! I
  follow thee.
I am dead, Horatio. Wretched queen, adieu!
Had I but time, as this fell sergeant, Death,
Is strict in his arrest, O! I could tell you,—
But let it be. Horatio, I am dead;
Thou liv'st; report me and my cause aright
To the unsatisfied.
  HORATIO. Never believe it;
I am more an antique Roman than a Dane:
Here 's yet some liquor left.
  HAMLET. As thou 'rt a man,
Give me the cup: let go; by heaven, I 'll
  have 't.
O God! Horatio, what a wounded name,
Things standing thus unknown, shall live
  behind me.
If thou didst ever hold me in thy heart,
Absent thee from felicity awhile,
And in this harsh world draw thy breath
  in pain,
To tell my story.

          . . . . .

—the rest is silence.
                                       Dies.
  HORATIO. Now cracks a noble heart.
  Good night, sweet prince,
And flights of angels sing thee to thy rest!
          Hamlet V, 2:296, 323, 338, 347, 369

SUFFOLK. And do not stand on quillets[1]
  how to slay him:[2]
Be it by gins, by snares, by subtilty,
Sleeping or waking, 't is no matter how,
So he be dead; for that is good deceit
Which mates him first that first intends de-
  ceit.
          II Henry VI, III, 1:261
[1] quillets: legal tricks.   [2] him: GLOUCESTER.

K. JOHN. Good Hubert! Hubert, Hubert,
  throw thine eye
On yon young boy:[1] I 'll tell thee what, my
  friend,
He is a very serpent in my way;
And wheresoe'er this foot of mine doth
  tread,
He lies before me: dost thou understand
  me?
Thou art his keeper.
  HUBERT. And I 'll keep him so
That he shall not offend your majesty.
  K. JOHN. Death.
  HUBERT. My lord?
  K. JOHN. A grave.
  HUBERT. He shall not live.
  K. JOHN. Enough.
I could be merry now. Hubert, I love thee.
          King John, III, 3:59
[1] boy: PRINCE ARTHUR.

SALISBURY. This[1] is the very top,
The height, the crest, or crest unto the crest,
Of murder's arms: this is the bloodiest
  shame,
The wildest savagery, the vilest stroke,
That ever wall-eyed[2] wrath or staring rage
Presented to the tears of soft remorse.[3]
  PEMBROKE. All murders past do stand ex-
  cus'd in this:
And this, so sole and so unmatchable,
Shall give a holiness, a purity,
To the yet unbegotten sin of times;
And prove a deadly bloodshed but a jest.
          King John, IV, 3:45
[1] This: the supposed murder of PRINCE AR-
THUR.   [2] wall-eyed: fierce looking.   [3] remorse:
pity.

BRUTUS. Since Cassius first did whet me
  against Caesar,
I have not slept.
Between the acting of a dreadful thing
And the first motion, all the interim is
Like a phantasma,[1] or a hideous dream;
The genius and the mortal instruments
Are then in council; and the state of man,
Like to a little kingdom, suffers then
The nature of an insurrection.
          Julius Caesar, II, 1:61
[1] phantasma: vision.

BRUTUS. Give me your hands all over, one by one.

CASSIUS. And let us swear our resolution.

BRUTUS. No, not an oath: if not the face of men,
The sufferance of our souls, the time's abuse,
If these be motives weak, break off betimes,
And every man hence to his idle bed;
So let high-sighted tyranny range on,
Till each man drop by lottery.[1]

Julius Caesar, II, 1:112

[1] by lottery: in turn at order of a dictator.

DECIUS. Shall no man else be touch'd but only Caesar?

CASSIUS. Decius, well urg'd. I think it is not meet,
Mark Antony, so well belov'd of Caesar,
Should outlive Caesar: we shall find of him
A shrewd contriver; and, you know, his means,
If he improve them, may well stretch so far
As to annoy us all.

BRUTUS. Our course will seem too bloody, Caius Cassius.
To cut the head off and then hack the limbs,
Like wrath in death and envy afterwards;
For Antony is but a limb of Caesar.
Let us be sacrificers, but not butchers, Caius.
We all stand up against the spirit of Caesar;
And in the spirit of men there is no blood:
O! that we then could come by Caesar's spirit,
And not dismember Caesar. But, alas!
Caesar must bleed for it.

Julius Caesar, II, 1:154

BRUTUS. Let 's kill him boldly, but not wrathfully;
Let 's carve him as a dish fit for the gods,
Not hew him as a carcass fit for hounds:
And let our hearts, as subtle masters do,
Stir up their servants to an act of rage,
And after seem to chide 'em.

Julius Caesar, II, 1:172

DECIUS. The senate have concluded
To give this day a crown to mighty Caesar.
If you shall send them word you will not come,
Their minds may change. Besides, it were a mock
Apt to be render'd, for some one to say
'Break up the senate till another time,
When Caesar's wife shall meet with better dreams.'

. . . . .

CAESAR. How foolish do your fears seem now, Calpurnia!

I am ashamed I did yield to them.
Give me my robe, for I will go.

Julius Caesar, II, 2:93, 105

CAESAR.[1] The ides of March are come.

SOOTHSAYER. Ay, Caesar; but not gone.

Julius Caesar, III, 1:1

[1] To SOOTHSAYER.

CALPURNIA. When beggars die there are no comets seen;
The heavens themselves blaze forth the death of princes.

CAESAR. Cowards die many times before their deaths;
The valiant never taste of death but once.
Of all the wonders that I yet have heard,
It seems to me most strange that men should fear;
Seeing that death, a necessary end,
Will come when it will come.

Julius Caesar, II, 2:30

DECIUS. Where is Metellus Cimber? Let him go,
And presently prefer his suit to Caesar.

BRUTUS. He is address'd; press near and second him.

CINNA. Casca, you are the first that rears your hand.

CAESAR. Are we all ready? What is now amiss
That Caesar and his senate must redress?

METELLUS. Most high, most mighty, and most puissant Caesar,
Metellus Cimber throws before thy seat
An humble heart,—   *Kneeling.*

CAESAR. I must prevent thee, Cimber.
These couchings and these lowly courtesies,
Might fire the blood of ordinary men,
And turn pre-ordinance and first decree
Into the law of children. Be not fond,[1]
To think that Caesar bears such rebel blood
That will be thaw'd from the true quality.

. . . . .

If I could pray to move, prayers would move me;
But I am constant as the northern star,
Of whose true-fix'd and resting quality
There is no fellow[2] in the firmament.

. . . . .

That I was constant Cimber should be banish'd,
And constant do remain to keep him so.

CINNA. O Caesar,—

CAESAR. Hence! Wilt thou lift up Olympus?

DECIUS. Great Caesar,—

CAESAR. Doth not Brutus bootless kneel?

CASCA. Speak, hands, for me!

They stab CAESAR.

Caesar. *Et tu, Brute!*[3] Then fall, Caesar!
                                        Dies.
Cinna. Liberty! Freedom! Tyranny is
   dead!
                    Julius Caesar, III, 1:27, 59, 72
[1] fond: foolish.   [2] fellow: equal.   [3] *Et tu, Brute:*
And you, Brutus.

Brutus. Fates,[1] we will know your pleas-
   ures.
That we shall die, we know; 't is but the
   time
And drawing days out, that men stand upon.
   Cassius. Why, he that cuts off twenty
   years of life
Cuts off so many years of fearing death.
   Brutus. Grant that, and then is death a
   benefit:
So are we Caesar's friends, that have
   abridg'd
His time of fearing death. Stoop, Romans,
   stoop,
And let us bathe our hands in Caesar's
   blood
Up to the elbows, and besmear our swords:
Then walk we forth, even to the market-
   place;
And, waving our red weapons o'er our
   heads,
Let 's all cry 'Peace, freedom, and liberty!'
   Cassius. Stoop then, and wash. How
   many ages hence
Shall this our lofty scene be acted over,
In states unborn and accents yet unknown!
                          Julius Caesar, III, 1:98
[1] Fates: Clotho, Lachesis and Atropos, the three
fates in Greek mythology, spun and cut off the
threads of human lives.

Macbeth [soliloquy]. Is this a dagger
   which I see before me,
The handle toward my hand? Come, let me
   clutch thee:
I have thee not, and yet I see thee still.
Art thou not, fatal vision, sensible
To feeling as to sight? or art thou but
A dagger of the mind, a false creation,
Proceeding from the heat-oppressed brain?
I see thee yet, in form as palpable
As this which now I draw.
Thou marshall'st me the way that I was
   going;
And such an instrument I was to use.
Mine eyes are made the fools o' the other
   senses,
Or else worth all the rest: I see thee still;
And on thy blade and dudgeon[1] gouts[2] of
   blood,
Which was not so before. There 's no such
   thing:
It is the bloody business which informs
Thus to mine eyes. Now o'er the one half-
world

Nature seems dead, and wicked dreams
   abuse[3]
The curtain'd sleep; witchcraft celebrates
Pale Hecate's[4] offerings; and wither'd mur-
   der,
Alarum'd by his sentinel, the wolf,
Whose howl's his watch, thus with his
   stealthy pace,
With Tarquin's ravishing strides, towards
   his design
Moves like a ghost. Thou sure and firm-set
   earth,
Hear not my steps, which way they walk,
   for fear
Thy very stones prate of my whereabout,
And take the present horror from the time,
Which now suits with it. Whiles I threat he
   lives:
Words to the heat of deeds too cold breath
   gives.
                                   A bell rings.
I go, and it is done; the bell invites me.
Hear it not, Duncan; for it is a knell
That summons thee to heaven or to hell.
                                        Exit.
                             Macbeth, II, 1:33
[1] dudgeon: hilt.   [2] gouts: drops.   [3] abuse: de-
ceive.   [4] Hecate: goddess of witchcraft.

                        Enter Lady Macbeth.
Lady Macbeth. That which hath made
   them drunk hath made me bold,
What hath quench'd them hath given me
   fire. Hark! Peace!
It was the owl that shriek'd, the fatal bell-
   man,
Which gives the stern'st good-night. He is
   about it:
The doors are open, and the surfeited
   grooms
Do mock their charge with snores: I have
   drugg'd their possets,
That death and nature do contend about
   them,
Whether they live or die.
   Macbeth. *Within.* Who 's there? what,
   ho!
   Lady Macbeth. Alack! I am afraid they
   have awak'd,
And 't is not done; the attempt and not the
   deed
Confounds us. Hark! I laid their daggers
   ready;
He could not miss 'em. Had he not resem-
   bled
My father as he slept I had done 't.
                             Enter Macbeth.
My husband!
   Macbeth. I have done the deed.

                     .   .   .   .   .

   Macbeth. Methought I heard a voice cry
   'Sleep no more!'

Macbeth does murder sleep,' the innocent sleep,
Sleep that knits up the ravell'd sleave of care
The death of each day's life, sore labour's bath,
Balm of hurt minds, great nature's second course,
Chief nourisher in life's feast,—
    LADY MACBETH. What do you mean?
    MACBETH. Still it cried 'Sleep no more!' to all the house:
'Glamis hath murder'd sleep, and therefore Cawdor
Shall sleep no more, Macbeth shall sleep no more!'
    LADY MACBETH. Who was it that thus cried?
Why worthy thane,
You do unbend your noble strength to think
So brainsickly of things. Go get some water,
And wash this filthy witness from your hand.
Why did you bring these daggers from the place?
They must lie there: go carry them, and smear
The sleepy grooms with blood.
    MACBETH. I 'll go no more:
I am afraid to think what I have done;
Look on 't again I dare not.
    LADY MACBETH. Infirm of purpose!
Give me the daggers. The sleeping and the dead
Are but as pictures; 't is the eye of child-hood
That fears a painted devil. If he do bleed,
I 'll gild the faces of the grooms withal;
For it must seem their guilt.
                    Exit. Knocking within.
    MACBETH. Whence is that knocking?
How is 't with me, when every noise appals me?
What hands are here? Ha! they pluck out mine eyes.
Will all great Neptune's ocean wash this blood
Clean from my hand? No, this my hand will rather
The multitudinous seas incarnadine,
Making the green one red.
                    Re-enter LADY MACBETH.
    LADY MACBETH. My hands are of your colour, but I shame
To wear a heart so white.
                    Knocking within.
I hear a knocking
At the south entry; retire we to our cham-ber;
A little water clears us of this deed;
How easy is it then! Your constancy
Hath left you unattended.
                    Knocking within.

Hark! more knocking.
Get on your night-gown, lest occasion call us,
And show us to be watchers. Be not lost
So poorly in your thoughts.
    MACBETH. To know my deed 't were best not know myself.
                    Knocking within.
Wake Duncan with thy knocking! I would thou could'st!
                    Exeunt.
                Macbeth, II, 2:1, 35

    Ross. Let not your ears despise my tongue for ever,
Which shall possess them with the heaviest sound
That ever yet they heard.
    MACDUFF. Hum! I guess at it.
    Ross. Your castle is supris'd; your wife and babes
Savagely slaughter'd.
                    . . . . .

    MACDUFF. My children too?
    Ross. Wife, children, servants, all
That could be found.
    MACDUFF. And I must be from thence!
My wife kill'd too?
                    . . . . .

    MACDUFF. He has no children. All my pretty ones?
Did you say all? O hell-kite! All?
What! all my pretty chickens and their dam
At one fell swoop?
                Macbeth, IV, 3:201, 211, 217

    HERMIA. It cannot be but thou hast mur-der'd him;
So should a murderer look, so dead, so grim.
            Midsummer Night's Dream, III, 1:56

    EXTON.[1] For now the devil, that told me I did well,
Says that this deed is chronicled in hell.
                Richard II, V, 5:116
[1] Who has just killed KING RICHARD II.

    GLOUCESTER.[1] Go, tread the path that thou shalt ne'er return,
Simple, plain Clarence! I do love thee so
That I will shortly send thy soul to heaven,
If heaven will take the present at our hands.
                Richard III, I, 1:117
[1] Later, KING RICHARD III.

    CLARENCE. I charge you, as you hope to have redemption
By Christ's dear blood shed for our griev-ous sins,
That you depart and lay no hands on me.
                    . . . . .

SECOND MURDERER. And he that hath commanded is the king.
CLARENCE. Erroneous vassals! the great king of kings
Hath in the table of his law commanded
That thou shall do no murder: will you then
Spurn at his edict and fulfil a man's?
Take heed; for he holds vengeance in his hand,
To hurl upon their heads that break his law.

.   .   .   .   .

Relent and save your souls.
FIRST MURDERER. Relent! 't is cowardly and womanish.
CLARENCE. Not to relent, is beastly, savage, devilish.
                        Richard III, I, 4:194, 199, 262

TYRREL. When Dighton[1] thus told on: 'We smothered
The most replenished sweet work of nature,
That from the prime creation e'er she fram'd.'

.   .   .   .   .

K. RICHARD. The sons of Edward sleep in Abraham's bosom,
And Anne my wife hath bid this world good night.
                        Richard III, IV, 3:17, 38
[1] Dighton: the murderer of the two princes.

MUSIC

CLEOPATRA. Give me some music; music, moody food
Of us that trade in love.
                        Antony and Cleopatra, II, 5:1

DUKE SENIOR. If he,[1] compact of jars, grow musical,
We shall have shortly discord in the spheres.[2]
                        As You Like It, II, 7:5
[1] he: Jaques.   [2] discord . . . spheres: reference to belief that heavenly bodies make music.

Orpheus[1] with his lute made trees,
And the mountain tops that freeze,
Bow themselves when he did sing:
To his music plants and flowers
Ever sprung; as sun and showers
There had made a lasting spring.
Every thing that heard him play,
Even the billows of the sea,
Hung their heads, and then lay by.
In sweet music is such art,
Killing care and grief of heart
Fall asleep, or hearing, die.
                        Henry VIII, III, 1:5
[1] Orpheus: a fabulous Greek musician.

GLENDOWER. And those musicians that shall play to you
Hang in the air a thousand leagues from hence,
And straight they shall be here: sit, and attend.
                        I Henry IV, III, 1:226

DUKE. Music oft hath such a charm
To make bad good, and good provoke to harm.
                        Measure for Measure, IV, 1:14

SHYLOCK. And the vile squeaking of the wry-neck'd fife.
                        Merchant of Venice, II, 5:30

LORENZO. Come, ho! and wake Diana[1] with a hymn:
With sweetest touches pierce your mistress'[2] ear,
And draw her home with music.
                        Merchant of Venice, V, 1:66
[1] Diana: goddess of the moon and of chastity.
[2] mistress: Portia.

JESSICA. I am never merry when I hear sweet music.
LORENZO. The reason is, your spirits are attentive:
For do but note a wild and wanton herd,
Or race of youthful and unhandled colts,
Fetching mad bounds, bellowing and neighing loud,
Which is the hot condition of their blood;
If they but hear perchance a trumpet sound,
Or any air of music touch their ears,
You shall perceive them make a mutual stand,
Their savage eyes turn'd to a modest gaze
By the sweet power of music: therefore the poet
Did feign that Orpheus[1] drew trees, stones, and floods;
Since nought so stockish, hard, and full of rage,
But music for the time doth change his nature.
The man that hath no music in himself,
Nor is not mov'd with concord of sweet sounds,
Is fit for treasons, stratagems, and spoils;
The motions of his spirit are dull as night,
And his affections dark as Erebus:[2]
Let no such man be trusted.
                        Merchant of Venice, V, 1:69
[1] Orpheus: son of Apollo, Greek god of music.
[2] Erebus: sometimes used for the lower world in mythology—a place of utter darkness.

OBERON. My gentle Puck, come hither: thou remember'st
Since once I sat upon a promontory,

And heard a mermaid on a dolphin's back
Uttering such dulcet and harmonious breath,
That the rude sea grew civil at her song,
And certain stars shot madly from their spheres,
To hear the sea-maid's music.
Midsummer Night's Dream, II, 1:148

TITANIA. Music, ho! music! such as charmeth sleep.
· · · · ·

OBERON. Sound, music! Come, my queen, take hands with me,
And rock the ground whereon these sleepers be.
Midsummer Night's Dream, IV, 1:87, 89

CLOWN. But, masters, here 's money for you; and the general so likes your music, that he desires you, for love's sake, to make no more noise with it.
· · · · ·

If you have any music that may not be heard, to 't again; but, as they say, to hear music the general does not greatly care.
Othello, III, 1:11, 15

If music and sweet poetry agree,
As they must needs, the sister and the brother,
Then must the love be great 'twixt thee and me,
Because thou lov'st the one, and I the other.
· · · · ·

One god is god of both, as poets feign;
One knight loves both, and both in thee remain.
Passionate Pilgrim: 103, 115

PERICLES. Rarest sounds! Do ye not hear?
LYSIMACHUS. My lord, I hear.
PERICLES. Most heavenly music:
It nips me unto list'ning, and thick slumber
Hangs upon mine eyes; let me rest.
Pericles, V, 1:233

K. RICHARD. Music do I hear?
Ha, ha! keep time. How sour sweet music is
When time is broke and no proportion kept!
So is it in the music of men's lives.
And here have I the daintiness of ear
To check time broke in a disorder'd string;
But for the concord of my state and time
Had not an ear to hear my true time broke.
· · · · ·

This music mads me: let it sound no more;
For though it hath holp[1] madmen to their wits,

In me it seems it will make wise men mad.
Richard II, V, 4:41, 61
[1] holp: helped.

PETER. When griping grief the heart doth wound,
And doleful dumps the mind oppress,
Then music with her silver sound—
· · · · ·
With speedy help doth lend redress.
Romeo and Juliet, IV, 5:128, 144

Music to hear, why hear'st thou music sadly?
Sweets with sweets war not, joy delights in joy:
Why lov'st thou that which thou receiv'st not gladly,
Or else receiv'st with pleasure thine annoy?
· · · · ·
Mark how one string, sweet husband to another,
Strikes each in each by mutual ordering;
Resembling sire and child and happy mother,
Who, all in one, one pleasing note do sing.
Sonnet 8

LORD. Wilt thou have music? hark! Apollo plays,
And twenty caged nightingales do sing.
Taming of the Shrew, Induction 2:37

CALIBAN. Be not afeard; the isle is full of noises,
Sounds and sweet airs, that give delight and hurt not.
Sometimes a thousand twangling instruments
Will hum about mine ears; and sometime voices
That, if I then had wak'd after long sleep,
Will make me sleep again.
Tempest, III, 2:144

ARIEL. Then I beat my tabor,[1]
At which, like unback'd colts, they prick'd their ears,
Advanc'd their eyelids, lifted up their noses
As they smelt music: so I charm'd their ears.
Tempest, IV, 1:175
[1] tabor: a small drum.

DUKE. If music be the food of love, play on;
Give me excess of it, that, surfeiting,
The appetite may sicken, and so die.
That strain again! it had a dying fall:
O! it came o'er my ear like the sweet sound
That breathes upon a bank of violets,
Stealing and giving odour.
Twelfth Night, I, 1:1

JULIA. The current that with gentle mur-
    mur glides,
Thou know'st, being stopp'd, impatiently
    doth rage;
But when his fair course is not hindered,
He makes sweet music with the enamell'd
    stones,
Giving a gentle kiss to every sedge
He overtaketh in his pilgrimage.
            Two Gentlemen of Verona, II, 7:24

NAGGING

ADRIANA. In bed, he slept not for my
    urging it;
At board, he fed not for my urging it;
Alone, it was the subject of my theme;
In company I often glanced it:
Still[1] did I tell him it was vile and bad.
    ABBESS. And thereof came it that the man
        was mad:
The venom clamours of a jealous woman
Poison more deadly than a mad dog's tooth.
It seems, his sleeps were hinder'd by thy
    railing,
And thereof comes it that his head is light.
Thou say'st his meat was sauc'd with thy
    upbraidings:
Unquiet meals make ill digestions;
Thereof the raging fire of fever bred:
And what 's a fever but a fit of madness?
Thou say'st his sports were hinder'd by thy
    brawls:
Sweet recreation barr'd, what doth ensue
But moody and dull melancholy,
Kinsman to grim and comfortless despair,
And at their heels a huge infectious troop
Of pale distemperatures and foes to life?
In food, in sport, and life-preserving rest
To be disturb'd, would mad or man or
    beast:
The consequence is then thy jealous fits
Have scar'd thy husband from the use of
    wits.
            Comedy of Errors, V, 1:63
[1] still: always, repeated action.

DESDEMONA. Good love, call him back.
OTHELLO. Not now, sweet Desdemona;
    some other time.
DESDEMONA. But shall 't be shortly?
OTHELLO. The sooner, sweet, for you.
DESDEMONA. Shall 't be to-night at sup-
    per?
OTHELLO. No, not to-night.
DESDEMONA. To-morrow dinner then?
OTHELLO. I shall not dine at home
I meet the captains at the citadel.
DESDEMONA. Why, then, to-morrow
    night; or Tuesday morn;
On Tuesday noon, or night; on Wednesday
    morn:

I prithee name the time, but let it not
Exceed three days.
            Othello, III, 3:54

NAME

FALSTAFF. I would to God thou and I
knew where a commodity of good names
were to be bought.
            I Henry IV, I, 2:92

BASTARD. And if his name be George, I 'll
    call him Peter;
For new-made honour doth forget men's
    names.
            King John, I, 1:186

MISTRESS PAGE. I cannot tell what the
dickens his name is.
            Merry Wives of Windsor, III, 2:19

IAGO. Good name in man and woman, dear
    my lord,
Is the immediate jewel of their souls:
Who steals my purse steals trash; 't is some-
    thing, nothing;
'T was mine, 't is his, and has been slave to
    thousands:
But he that filches from me my good name
Robs me of that which not enriches him,
And makes me poor indeed.
            Othello, III, 3:155

NATURE

DUKE SENIOR. And this our life, exempt
    from public haunt,
Finds tongues in trees, books in the run-
    ning brooks,
Sermons in stones, and good in every thing.
            As You Like It, II, 1:15

SICINIUS. Nature teaches beasts to know
their friends.
            Coriolanus, II, 1:5

BELARIUS. How hard it is to hide the
    sparks of nature!
            Cymbeline, III, 3:79

BELARIUS. Thou divine Nature, how thy-
    self thou blazon'st
In these two princely boys.[1] They are as
    gentle
As zephyrs, blowing below the violet,
Not wagging his sweet head; and yet as
    rough,
Their royal blood enchaf'd, as the rud'st
    wind,
That by the top doth take the mountain
    pine,

And make him stoop to the vale. 'T is won-
der
That an invisible instinct should frame them
To royalty unlearn'd, honour untaught,
Civility, not seen from other, valour
That wildly grows in them, but yields a
crop
As if it had been sow'd!
Cymbeline, IV, 2:170
[1] boys: sons of the king, stolen as babes and
brought up in the woods.

LAERTES. For nature crescent[1] does not
grow alone
In thews[2] and bulk; but, as this temple
waxes,
The inward service of the mind and soul
Grows wide withal.
Hamlet, I, 3:11
[1] crescent: developing. [2] thews: bodily
strength.

LAERTES. Nature is fine in love, and where
't is fine
It sends some precious instance of itself
After the thing it loves.
Hamlet, IV, 5:161

HOTSPUR. Diseased nature oftentimes
breaks forth
In strange eruptions; oft the teeming earth
Is with a kind of colic pinch'd and vex'd
By the imprisoning of unruly wind
Within her womb; which, for enlargement
striving,
Shakes the old beldam earth, and topples
down
Steeples and moss-grown towers.
I Henry IV, III, 1:27

K. LEAR. Allow not nature more than
nature needs,
Man's life is cheap as beast's. Thou art a lady;
If only to go warm were gorgeous,
Why nature needs not what thou gorgeous
wear'st,
Which scarcely keeps thee warm.
King Lear, II, 4:269

MACBETH. Our fears in Banquo
Stick deep, and in his royalty of nature
Reigns that which would be fear'd: 't is
much he dares,
And, to that dauntless temper of his mind,
He hath a wisdom that doth guide his
valour
To act in safety. There is none but he.
Macbeth, III, 1:49

CLAUDIO. Our natures do pursue,
Like rats that ravin[1] down their proper
bane,[2]

A thirsty evil, and when we drink we die.
Measure for Measure, I, 2:132
[1] ravin: eat ravenously. [2] bane: poison.

DOGBERRY. To be a well-favoured[1] man
is the gift of fortune, but to write and read
comes by nature.
Much Ado About Nothing, III, 3:14
[1] well-favoured: good looking.

APEMANTUS. What! think'st
That the bleak air, thy boisterous chamber-
lain,
Will put thy shirt on warm? will these
moss'd trees,
That have outliv'd the eagle, page thy heels
And skip when thou point'st out! will the
cold brook,
Candied with ice, caudle[1] thy morning taste
To cure thy o'er-night's surfeit?
Timon of Athens, IV, 3:221
[1] caudle: provide a soothing drink.

TIMON. Why should you want? Behold,
the earth hath roots:
Within this mile break forth a hundred
springs;
The oaks bear mast,[1] the briers scarlet hips;[2]
The bounteous housewife, nature, on each
bush
Lays her full mess before you. Want! why
want?
Timon of Athens, IV, 3:420
[1] mast: acorns. [2] hips: a berry-like fruit.

ULYSSES. One touch of nature makes the
whole world kin,
That all with one consent praise new-born
gawds.[1]
Troilus and Cressida, III, 3:175
[1] gawds: trinkets.

NECESSITY

K. LEAR. My wits begin to turn.
Come on, my boy. How dost, my boy? Art
cold?
I am cold myself. Where is this straw, my
fellow?
The art of our necessities is strange,
That can make vile things precious. Come,
your hovel.
Poor fool and knave, I have one part in
my heart
That 's sorry yet for thee.
King Lear, III, 2:67

BIRON. Necessity will make us all forsworn
Three thousand times within this three
years' space;
For every man with his affects[1] is born,

Not by might master'd, but by special
grace.
If I break faith, this word shall speak for
me,
I am forsworn on 'mere[2] necessity.'
Love's Labour's Lost, I, 1:150
[1] affects: inclinations. [2] mere: absolute.

GAUNT. Teach thy necessity to reason
thus;
There is no virtue like necessity.
Richard II, I, 3:277

SECOND OUTLAW.[1] Are you content to be
our general?
To make a virtue of necessity
And live, as we do, in this wilderness?
Two Gentlemen of Verona, IV, 1:61
[1] To VALENTINE.

NEWS

MESSENGER. The nature of bad news infects the teller.
Antony and Cleopatra, I, 2:99

CLEOPATRA. O! from Italy;
Ram thou thy fruitful tidings in mine ears,
That long time have been barren.
Antony and Cleopatra, II, 5:23

MESSENGER. Madam, he's married to Octavia.

. . . . .

CLEOPATRA. Though it be honest, it is
never good
To bring bad news; give to a gracious mes-
sage
An host of tongues, but let ill tidings tell
Themselves when they be felt.
Antony and Cleopatra, II, 5:60, 85

CELIA. Here comes Monsieur Le Beau.
ROSALIND. With his mouth full of news.
CELIA. Which he will put on us, as pigeons
feed their young.
ROSALIND. Then shall we be news-
crammed.
CELIA. All the better; we shall be the more
marketable.
As You Like It, I, 2:98

IMOGEN. Why tender'st thou that paper
to me with
A look untender? If 't be summer news,
Smile to 't before; if winterly, thou need'st
But keep that countenance still.
Cymbeline, III, 4:11

NORTHUMBERLAND. The first bringer of
unwelcome news

Hath but a losing office, and his tongue
Sounds ever after as a sullen bell,
Remember'd knolling a departing friend.
II Henry IV, I, 1:100

OLD LADY. Sir, your queen
Desires your visitation, and to be
Acquainted with this stranger: 't is as like
you
As cherry is to cherry.

. . . . .

K. HENRY. Give her an hundred marks.
I 'll to the queen.
OLD LADY. An hundred marks! By this
light, I 'll ha' more.
An ordinary groom is for such payment:
I will have more, or scold it out of him.
Said I for this the girl was like to him?
Henry VIII, V, 1:166, 170
[1] stranger: new-born daughter, later Queen
Elizabeth.

K. RICHARD. Say, Scroop, where lies our
uncle with his power?
Speak sweetly, man, although thy looks be
sour.
SCROOP. Men judge by the complexion of
the sky
The state and inclination of the day;
So may you by my dull and heavy eye,
My tongue hath but a heavier tale to say.
Richard II, III, 2:192

JULIET. Though news be sad, yet tell
them merrily;
If good, thou sham'st the music of sweet
news
By playing it to me with so sour a face.
Romeo and Juliet, II, 5:22

NIGHT

HORATIO. In the dead vast and middle of
the night.
Hamlet, I, 2:198

BOLINGBROKE. Deep night, dark night, the
silent of the night,
The time of night when Troy was set on
fire;
The time when screech-owls cry, and ban-
dogs howl,
And spirits walk, and ghosts break up their
graves.
II Henry VI, I, 4:18

BANQUO. I must become a borrower of
the night
For a dark hour or twain.
MACBETH. Fail not our feast.
BANQUO. My lord, I will not.
Macbeth, III, 1:27

ANGELO. This will last out a night in Russia,
When nights are longest there.
Measure for Measure, II, 1:139

LORENZO. The moon shines bright: in such a night as this,
When the sweet wind did gently kiss the trees
And they did make no noise, in such a night
Troilus methinks mounted the Trojan walls,
And sigh'd his soul toward the Grecian tents,
Where Cressid lay that night.
JESSICA. In such a night
Did Thisbe fearfully o'ertrip the dew,
And saw the lion's shadow ere himself,
And ran dismay'd away.
LORENZO. In such a night
Stood Dido with a willow in her hand
Upon the wild sea-banks, and wav'd her love
To come again to Carthage.
JESSICA. In such a night
Medea gather'd the enchanted herbs
That did renew old Æson.
LORENZO. In such a night
Did Jessica steal from the wealthy Jew,
And with an unthrift love did run from Venice,
As far as Belmont.
JESSICA. In such a night
Did young Lorenzo swear he lov'd her well,
Stealing her soul with many vows of faith,
And ne'er a true one.
LORENZO. In such a night
Did pretty Jessica, like a little shrew,
Slander her love, and he forgave it her.
JESSICA. I would out-night you, did no body come;
But hark! I hear the footing of a man.
Merchant of Venice, V, 1:1

PORTIA. This night methinks is but the daylight sick;
It looks a little paler: 't is a day,
Such as the day is when the sun is hid.
Merchant of Venice, V, 1:124

HELENA. It is not night when I do see your face,
Therefore I think I am not in the night;
Nor doth this wood lack worlds of company.
Midsummer Night's Dream, II, 1:221

HERMIA. Dark night, that from the eye his[1] function takes,
The ear more quick of apprehension makes;
Wherein it doth impair the seeing sense,
It pays the hearing double recompense.
Midsummer Night's Dream, III, 2:177
[1] his: its.

PUCK. Night's swift dragons cut the clouds full fast,
And yonder shines Aurora's harbinger;[1]
At whose approach, ghosts, wandering here and there,
Troop home to churchyards: damned spirits all,
That in crossways and floods have burial,
Already to their wormy beds are gone;
For fear lest day should look their shames upon.
Midsummer Night's Dream, III, 2:379
[1] Aurora's harbinger: forerunner of Aurora, goddess of the dawn.

HELENA. O weary night, O long and tedious night,
Abate thy hours! shine comforts from the east!
Midsummer Night's Dream, III, 2:431

PYRAMUS. O grim-look'd night! O night with hue so black!
O night, which ever art when day is not!
O night! O night! alack, alack, alack!
Midsummer Night's Dream, V, 1:171

Sable Night, mother of Dread and Fear,
Upon the world dim darkness doth display,
And in her vaulty prison stows the Day.

. . . . .

'O comfort-killing Night, image of hell!
Dim register and notary of shame!
Black stage for tragedies and murders fell!
Vast sin-concealing chaos! nurse of blame!
Blind muffled bawd! dark harbour for defame!
Grim cave of death! whispering conspirator
With close-tongu'd treason and the ravisher!

. . . . .

'O Night! thou furnace of foul-reeking smoke,
Let not the jealous Day behold that face
Which underneath thy black all-hiding cloak
Immodestly lies martyr'd with disgrace:
Keep still possession of thy gloomy place,
That all the faults which in thy reign are made
May likewise be sepulchred in thy shade.'
Rape of Lucrece: 117, 764, 799

K. RICHARD. When the searching eye of heaven is hid
Behind the globe, and lights the lower world,
Then thieves and robbers range abroad unseen,
In murders and in outrage bloody here;
But when from under this terrestrial ball
He fires the proud tops of the eastern pines

And darts his light through every guilty
    hole,
Then murders, treasons, and detested sins,
The cloak of night being pluck'd from off
    their backs,
Stand bare and naked, trembling at them-
    selves?
                        Richard II, III, 2:37

CRESSIDA. Night hath been too brief.
TROILUS. Beshrew the witch! with ven-
    omous wights she stays
As tediously as hell, but flies the grasps of
    love
With wings more momentary-swift than
    thought.
                Troilus and Cressida, IV, 2:11

ACHILLES. The dragon wing of night
    o'erspreads the earth.
                Troilus and Cressida, V, 8:17

NOTHING

CLOWN. To say nothing, to do nothing,
to know nothing, and to have nothing, is to
be a great part of your title; which is within
a very little of nothing.
        All's Well That Ends Well, II, 4:25

IMOGEN. 'T was but a bolt of nothing,
    shot at nothing,
Which the brain makes of fumes.
                    Cymbeline, IV, 2:301

FALSTAFF. Nay, and a'[1] do nothing but
speak nothing, a' shall be nothing here.
                    II Henry IV, II, 4:206
[1] an a': if he.

ANNE. I do not know
What kind of my obedience[1] I should ten-
    der;
More than my all is nothing, nor my pray-
    ers
Are not words duly hallow'd, nor my
    wishes
More worth than empty vanities; yet pray-
    ers and wishes
Are all I can return.
                    Henry VIII, II, 3:65
[1] obedience: to QUEEN KATHARINE.

FOOL. Can you make no use of nothing,
nuncle?[1]
    K. LEAR. Why no, boy; nothing can be
    made out of nothing.
                    King Lear, I, 4:144
[1] nuncle: the customary address of a jester to a
superior.

FOOL. Thou wast a pretty fellow when
thou hadst no need to care for her frowning; now thou art an O without a figure. I
am better than thou art; I am a fool, thou
art nothing.
                    King Lear, I, 4:210

GRATIANO. O! my Antonio, I do know of
    these,
That therefore only are reputed wise
For saying nothing.
            Merchant of Venice, I, 1:95

K. RICHARD. Make me, that nothing have,
    with nothing griev'd.
                    Richard II, IV, 1:216

NOVELTY

DUKE. Novelty is only in request; and it
is as dangerous to be aged in any kind of
course, as it is virtuous to be constant in
any undertaking.
            Measure for Measure, III, 2:237

ULYSSES. All with one consent praise
    new-born gawds,[1]
Though they are made and moulded of
    things past,
And give to dust that is a little gilt
More laud[2] than gilt o'er-dusted.
                Troilus and Cressida, III, 3:176
[1] gawds: worthless things.   [2] laud: praise.

OAK

OLIVER. Under an oak, whose boughs
    were moss'd with age,
And high top bald with dry antiquity.
                    As You Like It, IV, 3:105

PROSPERO.[1] If thou more murmur'st, I will
    rend an oak
And peg thee in his knotty entrails till
Thou hast howl'd away twelve winters.
                    Tempest, I, 2:294
[1] To ARIEL.

OATH

DIANA. 'T is not the many oaths that
    make the truth,
But the plain single vow that is vow'd true.
        All's Well That Ends Well, IV, 2:21

PAROLLES. He professes not keeping of
oaths; in breaking 'em he is stronger than
Hercules; he will lie, sir, with such volubility, that you would think truth were a
fool.
        All's Well That Ends Well, IV, 3:281

AUFIDIUS. Breaking his oath and resolution like
A twist of rotten silk.

Coriolanus, V, 6:95

HOTSPUR. Swear me, Kate,[1] like a lady as thou art,
A good mouth-filling oath; and leave 'in sooth,'
And such protest of pepper-gingerbread,
To velvet-guards and Sunday-citizens.

I Henry IV, III, 1:258

[1] KATE: HOTSPUR's wife.

K. HENRY. It may be his enemy is a gentleman of great sort, quite from the answer[1] of his degree.
FLUELLEN. Though he be as good a gentleman as the devil is, as Lucifer and Belzebub himself, it is necessary, look your grace, that he keep his vow and his oath.

Henry V, IV, 7:141

[1] answer . . . degree: a gentleman of high rank could not fight one of lower rank.

SALISBURY. It is great sin to swear unto a sin,
But greater sin to keep a sinful oath.
Who can be bound by any solemn vow
To do a murderous deed, to rob a man,
To force a spotless virgin's chastity,
To reave the orphan of his patrimony,
To wring the widow from her custom'd right,
And have no other reason for this wrong
But that he was bound by a solemn oath?

II Henry VI, V, 1:182

AUSTRIA. Upon thy cheek lay I this zealous kiss,
As seal to this indenture of my love,
That to my home I will no more return
Till Angiers, and the right thou hast in France,
Together with that pale, that white-fac'd shore,
Whose foot spurns back the ocean's roaring tides
And coops from other lands her islanders,
Even till that England, hedg'd in with the main,
That water-walled bulwark, still secure
And confident from foreign purposes,
Even till that utmost corner of the west
Salute thee for her king: till then, fair boy,
Will I not think of home, but follow arms.

King John, II, 1:19

BRUTUS. Swear priests and cowards and men cautelous,[1]
Old feeble carrions and such suffering souls
That welcome wrongs; unto bad causes swear
Such creatures as men doubt; but do not stain
The even virtue of our enterprise,
Nor the insuppressive mettle of our spirits,
To think that or our cause or our performance
Did need an oath; when every drop of blood
That every Roman bears, and nobly bears,
Is guilty of a several bastardy,
If he do break the smallest particle
Of any promise that hath pass'd from him.

Julius Caesar, II, 1:129

[1] cautelous: tricky, deceitful.

BIRON. I'll lay my head to any good man's hat,
These oaths and laws will prove an idle scorn.

Love's Labour's Lost, I, 1:310

BIRON. What fool is not so wise
To lose an oath to win a paradise?

Love's Labour's Lost, IV, 3:72

SHYLOCK. An oath, an oath, I have an oath in heaven:
Shall I lay perjury upon my soul?
No, not for Venice.

Merchant of Venice, IV, 1:228

PORTIA. Mark you but that!
In both my eyes he doubly sees himself;
In each eye, one: swear by your double self,
And there's an oath of credit.

Merchant of Venice, V, 1:243

JULIET. At lovers' perjuries,
They say, Jove laughs.

Romeo and Juliet, II, 2:92

AARON. An idiot holds his bauble for a god,
And keeps the oath which by that god he swears.

Titus Andronicus, V, 1:79

OBEDIENCE

ANGUS. Those he[1] commands move only in command,
Nothing in love.

Macbeth, V, 2:19

[1] he: MACBETH.

LADY CAPULET. The County Paris, at Saint Peter's church,
Shall happily make thee there a joyful bride.

JULIET. Now, by Saint Peter's church, and Peter too,
He shall not make me there a joyful bride.

. . . . .

CAPULET. Thank me no thankings, nor proud me no prouds,
But fettle[1] your fine joints 'gainst Thursday next,
To go with Paris to Saint Peter's church,
Or I will drag thee on a hurdle[2] thither.

. . . . .

JULIET. Good father, I beseech you on my knees,
Hear me with patience but to speak a word,
CAPULET. Hang thee, young baggage! disobedient wretch!
   Romeo and Juliet, III, 5:115, 153, 159
[1] fettle: prepare. [2] hurdle: vehicle on which criminals were drawn to execution.

ARIEL. Pardon, master:
I will be correspondent to command,
And do my spriting gently.
   Tempest, I, 2:296

OFFENCE

KING. O! my offence is rank, it smells to heaven.
   Hamlet, III, 3:36

KING. May one be pardon'd and retain the offence?
   Hamlet, III, 3:56

WESTMORELAND. That argues but the shame of your offence:
A rotten case abides no handling.
   II Henry IV, IV, 1:160

GONERIL. All's not offence that indiscretion finds
And dotage terms so.
   King Lear, II, 4:199

All my offences that abroad you see
Are errors of the blood,[1] none of the mind.
   Lover's Complaint: 183
[1] blood: emotion.

OVERDONE. But what 's his[1] offence?
POMPEY. Groping for trouts in a peculiar river.
   Measure for Measure, I, 2:90
[1] his: CLAUDIO's.

CLAUDIO. Thus stands it with me: upon a true contract
I got possession of Julietta's bed:
You know the lady; she is fast my wife,
Save that we do the annunciation lack
Of outward order.
   Measure for Measure, I, 2:150

OLD AGE

KING. He[1] lasted long;
But on us both did haggish age steal on,
And wore us out of act.
   All's Well That Ends Well, I, 2:28
[1] He: HELENA's father.

ADAM. But do not so. I have five hundred crowns,
The thrifty hire I sav'd under your father,
Which I did store to be my foster-nurse
When service should in my old limbs lie lame,
And unregarded age in corners thrown.
Take that; and He that doth the ravens feed,
Yea, providently caters for the sparrow,
Be comfort to my age! Here is the gold.

. . . . .

For in my youth I never did apply
Hot and rebellious liquors in my blood.

. . . . .

Therefore my age is as a lusty winter,
Frosty, but kindly. Let me go with you.
   As You Like It, II, 3:38, 48, 52

JAQUES. Last scene of all,
That ends this strange eventful history,
Is second childishness and mere[1] oblivion,
Sans[2] teeth, sans eyes, sans taste, sans every thing.
   As You Like It, II, 7:163
[1] mere: absolute. [2] Sans: without.

ADRIANA. He is deformed, crooked, old, and sere,
Ill'-fac'd, worse bodied, shapeless everywhere;
Vicious, ungentle, foolish, blunt, unkind.
   Comedy of Errors, IV, 2:19

AEGEON. Though now this grained face of mine be hid
In sap-consuming winter's drizzled snow,
And all the conduits of my blood froze up,
Yet hath my night of life some memory,
My wasting lamps some fading glimmer left,
My dull deaf ears a little use to hear.
   Comedy of Errors, V, 1:311

POLONIUS. By heaven, it is as proper[1] to our age
To cast beyond ourselves[2] in our opinions
As it is common for the younger sort
To lack discretion.
   Hamlet, II, 1:114
[1] proper: appropriate. [2] cast . . . ourselves: be mistaken when too certain.

PRINCE.[1] That villanous abominable mis-leader of youth, Falstaff, that old white-bearded Satan.

I Henry IV, II, 4:507

[1] Pretending to speak for his father, KING HENRY IV.

FALSTAFF. Your lordship,[1] though not clean past your youth, hath yet some smack of age in you, some relish of the saltness of time; and I most humbly beseech your lord-ship to have a reverent care of your health.

II Henry IV, I, 2:109

[1] lordship: CHIEF JUSTICE.

FALSTAFF. You that are old consider not the capacities of us that are young; you do measure the heat of our livers[1] with the bit-terness of your galls.[2]

. . . . .

CHIEF JUSTICE. Have you not a moist eye, a dry hand, a yellow cheek, a white beard, a decreasing leg, an increasing belly? Is not your voice broken, your wind short, your chin double, your wit single[3] and every part about you blasted with antiquity, and will you yet call yourself young? Fie, fie, fie, Sir John!

II Henry IV, I, 2:195, 203

[1] livers: seat of passion. [2] galls: bitterness of mind. [3] single: silly.

FALSTAFF. A man can no more separate age and covetousness than a'[1] can part young limbs and lechery.[2]

II Henry IV, I, 2:256

[1] a': he. [2] lechery: indulgence of lust.

CLARENCE. The old folk, time's doting chronicles.

II Henry IV, IV, 4:126

FOOL.[1] Thou should'st not have been old till thou hadst been wise.

King Lear, I, 5:48

[1] Fool: jester.

MACBETH. I have liv'd long enough: my way of life
Is fall'n into the sear, the yellow leaf;
And that which should accompany old age,
As honour, love, obedience, troops of friends,
I must not look to have; but, in their stead,
Curses, not loud but deep, mouth-honour, breath,
Which the poor heart would fain deny, and dare not.

Macbeth, V, 3:22

DOGBERRY. A good old man, sir; he will be talking: as they say, 'When the age is in, the wit is out.'

Much Ado About Nothing, III, 5:35

LEONATO. I speak not like a dotard nor a fool,
As, under privilege of age, to brag
What I have done being young, or what would do,
Were I not old.

Much Ado About Nothing, V, 1:59

The aim of all is but to nurse the life
With honor, wealth, and ease, in waning age.

Rape of Lucrece: 141

Thus is his cheek the map of days outworn,
When beauty liv'd and died as flowers do now.

Sonnet 68

That time of year thou may'st in me behold
When yellow leaves, or none, or few, do hang
Upon those boughs which shake against the cold,
Bare ruin'd choirs, where late the sweet birds sang.

Sonnet 73

To me, fair friend, you never can be old,
For as you were when first your eye I eyed,
Such seems your beauty still.

Sonnet 104

And wherefore say not I that I am old?
O! love's best habit is in seeming trust,
And age in love loves not to have years told.

Sonnet 138

THERSITES. There 's Ulysses and old Nes-tor, whose wit[1] was mouldy ere your grand-sires had nails on their toes.

Troilus and Cressida, II, 1:114

[1] wit: intelligence.

HECTOR.[1] Let me embrace thee, good old chronicle,
Thou hast so long walk'd hand in hand with time.

Troilus and Cressida, IV, 5:202

[1] To NESTOR.

'Were I hard-favour'd,[1] foul, or wrinkled-old,
Ill-nurtur'd, crooked, churlish, harsh in voice,
O'erworn, despised, rheumatic, and cold,
Thick-sighted, barren, lean, and lacking juice,

Then might'st thou pause, for then I were
    not for thee;
But having no defects, why dost abhor me?'
               Venus and Adonis: 133
[1] hard-favour'd: ill-looking.

OLD MEN

POLONIUS. What do you read, my lord?
HAMLET. Words, words, words.

    . . . . .

POLONIUS. I mean the matter that you
read, my lord.
HAMLET. Slanders, sir: for the satirical
rogue says here that old men have grey
beards, that their faces are wrinkled, their
eyes purging thick amber and plum-tree
gum, and that they have a plentiful lack of
wit, together with most weak hams: all
which, sir, though I most powerfully and
potently believe, yet I hold it not honesty to
have it thus set down; for yourself, sir,
should be old as I am, if like a crab you
could go backward.
               Hamlet, II, 2:193, 197

GONERIL. Idle old man,
That still would manage those authorities
That he hath given away! Now, by my life,
Old fools are babes again, and must be us'd
With checks[1] as flatteries, when they are
    seen abus'd.
               King Lear, I, 3:16
[1] checks . . . abus'd: forcible checks where
flatteries are abused.

REGAN. O, sir! you are old;
Nature in you stands on the very verge
Of her confine: you should be rul'd and led
By some discretion that discerns your state
Better than you yourself.
               King Lear, II, 4:148

K. LEAR. O heavens,
If you do love old men, if your sweet sway
Allow obedience, if yourselves are old,
Make it your cause; send down and take my
    part!
               King Lear, II, 4:193

OPINION

MARCIUS.[1] What 's the matter, you dis-
    sentious rogues,
That, rubbing the poor itch of your opinion,
Make yourselves scabs?
               Coriolanus, I, 1:168
[1] Later CORIOLANUS.

SIMONIDES. Opinion 's but a fool, that
    makes us scan

The outward habit[1] by the inward man.
               Pericles, II, 2:56
[1] habit: costume; this phrase means judge the
man by his dress—"a reversal."

THERSITES. A plague of opinion! a man
may wear it on both sides, like a leather
jerkin.[1]
            Troilus and Cressida, III, 3:268
[1] jerkin: a short coat.

FABIAN. You are now sailed into the north
of my lady's opinion; where you will hang
like an icicle on a Dutchman's beard, unless
you do redeem it by some laudable attempt,
either of valour or policy.
               Twelfth Night, III, 2:27

PAULINA. The root of his opinion, which
    is rotten
As ever oak or stone was sound.
               Winter's Tale, II, 3:89

OPPORTUNITY

MENAS. These three world-sharers,[1] these
    competitors,[2]
Are in thy vessel: let me cut the cable;
And, when we are put off, fall to their
    throats:
All there is thine.
POMPEY. Ah! this thou should'st have
    done,
And not have spoke on 't. In me 't is villany;
In thee 't had been good service.

    . . . . .

MENAS. Who seeks, and will not take
    when once 't is offer'd.
Shall never find it more.
         Antony and Cleopatra, II, 7:76, 89
[1] world-sharers: CAESAR, ANTONY, and LEPIDUS.
[2] competitors: associates.

BRUTUS. There is a tide in the affairs of
    men,
Which, taken at the flood, leads on to for-
    tune;
Omitted, all the voyage of their life
Is bound in shallows and in miseries.
               Julius Caesar, IV, 3:218

K. JOHN. How oft the sight of means to
    do ill deeds
Makes deeds ill done!
               King John, IV, 2:219

OWNERSHIP

HELENA. I am not worthy of the wealth I
    owe,[1]

Nor dare I say 't is mine, and yet it is;
But, like a timorous thief, most fain would
    steal
What law does vouch mine own.
        All's Well That Ends Well, II, 5:84
[1] owe: own.

DUKE. What 's mine is yours and what is
    yours is mine.
        Measure for Measure, V, 1:543

LEONATO. But mine, and mine I lov'd, and
    mine I prais'd,
And mine that I was proud on, mine so
    much
That I myself was to myself not mine.
        Much Ado About Nothing, IV, 1:138

GREMIO. I have a hundred milch-kine to
    the pail,
Six score fat oxen standing in my stalls,
And all things answerable to this portion.
Myself am struck in years, I must confess;
And if I die to-morrow, this is hers,
If whilst I live she will be only mine.
        Taming of the Shrew, II, 1:359

PETRUCHIO. But for my bonny Kate, she
    must with me.
Nay, look not big, nor stamp, nor stare, nor
    fret;
I will be master of what is mine own.
She is my goods, my chattels; she is my
    house,
My household stuff, my field, my barn,
My horse, my ox, my ass, my anything;
And here she stands, touch her whoever
    dare.
        Taming of the Shrew, III, 2:229

PAGEANTRY

VERNON. All furnish'd, all in arms,
All plum'd like estridges[1] that wing the
    wind,
Baited[2] like eagles having lately bath'd,
Glittering in golden coats, like images,
As full of spirit as the month of May,
And gorgeous as the sun at midsummer;
Wanton[3] as youthful goats, wild as young
    bulls.
I saw young Harry, with his beaver[4] on,
His cuisses on his thighs, gallantly arm'd,
Rise from the ground like feather'd Mer-
    cury,
And vaulted with such ease into his seat,
As if an angel dropp'd down from the
    clouds,
To turn and wind a fiery Pegasus

And witch the world with noble horseman-
    ship.
        I Henry IV, IV, 1:97
[1] estridges: ostriches. [2] baited: fluttered; falconry. [3] Wanton: frolicsome. [4] beaver: helmet; literally the visor of the helmet.

NORFOLK. To-day the French
All clinquant,[1] all in gold, like heathen gods,
Shone down the English; and to-morrow
    they
Made Britain India: every man that stood
Show'd like a mine. Their dwarfish pages
    were
As cherubins, all gilt: the madams too,
Not us'd to toil, did almost sweat to bear
The pride upon them.
        Henry VIII, I, 1:18
[1] clinquant: glittering.

PANDER

PANDARUS. I 'll be the witness. Here I hold
your hand, here my cousin's. If ever you
prove false one to another, since I have
taken such pains to bring you together, let
all pitiful goers-between be called to the
world's end after my name; call them all
Pandars; let all constant men be Troiluses,
all false women Cressids, and all brokers-
between Pandars!
        Troilus and Cressida, III, 2:205

PARDON

SILVIUS. The common executioner,
Whose heart the accustom'd sight of death
    makes hard,
Falls not the axe upon the humbled neck
But first begs pardon.
        As You Like It, III, 5:3

KING. May one be pardon'd and retain the
    offence?
        Hamlet, III, 3:56

FORD. Pardon me, wife. Henceforth do
    what thou wilt;
I rather will suspect the sun with cold
Than thee with wantonness:[1] now doth thy
    honour stand,
In him that was of late an heretic,
As firm as faith.
        Merry Wives of Windsor, IV, 4:6
[1] wantonness: unchastity.

DUCHESS. Nay, do not say 'stand up';
But 'pardon' first, and afterwards 'stand up.'
And if I were thy nurse, thy tongue to
    teach,

'Pardon' should be the first word of thy
    speech.
I never long'd to hear a word till now;
Say 'pardon,' king; let pity teach thee how:
The word is short, but not so short as sweet.
                                    Richard II, V, 3:112

PARROT

HAMLET. Do you see yonder cloud that 's
almost in shape of a camel?
    POLONIUS. By the mass, and 't is like a
camel, indeed.
    HAMLET. Methinks it is like a weasel.
    POLONIUS. It is backed like a weasel.
    HAMLET. Or like a whale?
    POLONIUS. Very like a whale.
    HAMLET. Then will I come to my mother
by and by.[1] They fool me to the top of my
bent. I will come by and by.
                                    Hamlet, III, 2:393
[1] by and by: at once.

PRINCE. It would be every man's thought;
and thou art a blessed fellow to think as every man thinks; never a man's thought in the
world keeps the roadway better than thine.
                                    II Henry IV, II, 2:60

PARTING

SUFFOLK.[1] If I depart from thee I cannot
    live;
And in thy sight to die, what were it else
But like a pleasant slumber in thy lap?

            . . . . .

QUEEN MARGARET.[2] Let me hear from
    thee;
For wheresoe'er thou art in this world's
    globe,
I 'll have an Iris[3] that shall find thee out.
                                    II Henry VI, III, 2:388, 405
[1] To QUEEN MARGARET. [2] To SUFFOLK. [3] Iris:
the messenger of Juno.

QUEEN MARGARET. So part we sadly in
    this troublous world,
To meet with joy in sweet Jerusalem.
                                    III Henry VI, V, 5:7

K. RICHARD.[1] Twice for one step I 'll
    groan, the way being short,
And piece the way out with a heavy heart.
Come, come, in wooing sorrow let's be
    brief,
Since, wedding it, there is such length in
    grief.

One kiss shall stop our mouths, and dumbly
    part:
Thus give I mine, and thus take I thy heart.
                                    Richard II, V, 1:91
[1] To his wife, banished to France.

JULIET. Wilt thou be gone? it is not yet
    near day:
It was the nightingale, and not the lark,
That pierc'd the fearful hollow of thine ear;
Nightly she sings on yon pomegranate tree:
Believe me, love, it was the nightingale.
    ROMEO. It was the lark, the herald of the
    morn,
No nightingale: look, love, what envious
    streaks
Do lace the severing clouds in yonder east:
Night's candles are burnt out, and jocund
    day
Stands tiptoe on the misty mountain tops:
I must be gone and live, or stay and die.

            . . . . .

JULIET. It is, it is; hie hence, be gone,
    away!
It is the lark that sings so out of tune,
Straining harsh discords and unpleasing
    sharps.

            . . . . .

O! think'st thou we shall ever meet again?
    ROMEO. I doubt it not; and all these woes
    shall serve
For sweet discourses in our time to come.
    JULIET. O God! I have an ill-divining
    soul:
Methinks I see thee, now thou art so low,
As one dead in the bottom of a tomb:
Either my eyesight fails, or thou look'st
    pale.
    ROMEO. And trust me, love, in my eye
    so do you:
Dry sorrow drinks our blood. Adieu! adieu!
                                    Romeo and Juliet, III, 5:1, 26, 51

PASSION

ENOBARBUS. Alack! sir, no; her[1] passions
are made of nothing but the finest part of
pure love. We cannot call her winds and waters sighs and tears; they are greater storms
and tempests than almanacs can report; this
cannot be cunning in her; if it be, she makes
a shower of rain as well as Jove.
                                    Antony and Cleopatra, I, 2:151
[1] her: CLEOPATRA'S.

HAMLET. O! it offends me to the soul to
hear a robustious periwig-pated[1] fellow tear
a passion to tatters, to very rags, to split the
ears of the groundlings,[2] who for the most
part are capable of nothing but inexplicable
dumb-shows and noise: I would have such a

fellow whipped for o'erdoing Termagant;[3]
it out-herods Herod:[4] pray you, avoid it.
Hamlet, III, 2:10
[1] periwig-pated: wearing a wig. [2] groundlings:
people in the pit, the cheapest part of the
theatre. [3] Termagant: an imaginary violent
god of the Mohammedans. [4] Herod: a blustering tyrant of the mystery plays.

HAMLET. Give me that man
That is not passion's slave, and I will wear
him
In my heart's core, ay, in my heart of heart,
As I do thee.[1]
Hamlet, III, 2:76
[1] thee: HORATIO.

THESEUS. This passion, and the death of a
dear friend, would go near to make a man
look sad.
Midsummer Night's Dream, V, 1:293

OTHELLO. My blood[1] begins my safer
guides to rule,
And passion, having my best judgment collied,[2]
Assays[3] to lead the way.
Othello, II, 3:205
[1] blood: temper. [2] collied: clouded. [3] Assays:
tries.

DESDEMONA. Alas! why gnaw you so your
nether lip?
Some bloody passion shakes your very
frame;
These are portents,[1] but yet I hope, I hope
They do not point on me.
Othello, V, 2:43
[1] portents: omens of ill.

PERICLES. Then it is thus: the passions of
the mind,
That have their first conception by mis-
dread,
Have after-nourishment and life by care;
And what was first but fear what might be
done,
Grows elder now and cares it be not done.
Pericles, I, 2:11

PATIENCE

SERVANT. My master preaches patience to
him, and the while
His man with scissors nicks him like a fool.
Comedy of Errors, V, 1:174

QUEEN. O gentle son!
Upon the heat and flame of thy distemper
Sprinkle cool patience.
Hamlet, III, 4:122

NYM. Though patience be a tired mare,
yet she will plow.
Henry V, II, 1:26

K. LEWIS. Renowned queen, with patience
calm the storm,
While we bethink a means to break it off.
III Henry VI, III, 3:38

ANTONIO. I do oppose
My patience to his fury, and am arm'd
To suffer with a quietness of spirit
The very tyranny and rage of his.
Merchant of Venice, IV, 1:10

MISTRESS QUICKLY. Here will be an old
abusing of God's patience and the king's
English.
Merry Wives of Windsor, I, 4:5

LEONATO. I pray thee, peace! I will be flesh
and blood;
For there was never yet philosopher
That could endure the tooth-ache patiently.
Much Ado About Nothing, V, 1:34

GLOUCESTER.[1] Since you will buckle for-
tune on my back,
To bear her burden, whether I will or no,
I must have patience to endure the load:
But if black scandal or foul-fac'd reproach
Attend the sequel of your imposition,
Your mere[2] enforcement shall acquit-
tance me
From all the impure blots and stains
thereof;
For God doth know, and you may partly
see,
How far I am from the desire of this.
Richard III, III, 7:228
[1] Later, KING RICHARD III, to BUCKINGHAM, with
whom he has conspired to be offered the
crown. [2] mere: absolute.

VIOLA. She sat like Patience on a monu-
ment,
Smiling at grief.
Twelfth Night, II, 4:117

HERMIONE. There's some ill planet reigns:
I must be patient till the heavens look
With an aspect more favourable.
Winter's Tale, II, 1:105

PATRIOTISM

VOLUMNIA. Had I a dozen sons, each in
my love alike, and none less dear than thine
and my good Marcius,[1] I had rather had

eleven die nobly for their country than one voluptuously surfeit out of action.
Coriolanus, I, 3:24
[1] Marcius: CORIOLANUS.

COMINIUS. I do love
My country's good with a respect more tender,
More holy and profound, than mine own life.
Coriolanus, III, 3:111

CLOTEN. Britain is
A world by itself, and we will nothing pay
For wearing our own noses.
. . . . .

QUEEN. Remember, sir, my liege,
The kings your ancestors, together with
The natural bravery of your isle, which stands
As Neptune's park, ribbed and paled in
With rocks unscaleable and roaring waters,
With sands that will not bear your enemies' boats,
But suck them up to the topmast.
. . . . .

CLOTEN. Why should we pay tribute? If Caesar can hide the sun from us with a blanket, or put the moon in his pocket, we will pay him tribute for light; else, sir, no more tribute, pray you now.
Cymbeline, III, 1:12, 16, 43

K. PHILIP. This blessed day
Ever in France shall be kept festival:
To solemnize this day the glorious sun
Stays in his course and plays the alchemist,
Turning with splendour of his precious eye
The meagre cloddy earth to glittering gold:
The yearly course that brings this day about
Shall never see it but a holiday.
King John, III, 1:77

PAYMENT

CHIEF JUSTICE.[1] Prithee, peace. Pay her the debt you owe her, and unpay the villany you have done with her: the one you may do with sterling money, and the other with current repentance.
II Henry IV, II, 1:129
[1] To FALSTAFF.

DANCER. Bate[1] me some and I will pay you some; and as most debtors do, promise you infinitely.
II Henry IV, V, Epilogue: 17
[1] Bate: deduct.

DUKE. Haste still[1] pays haste, and leisure answers leisure,

Like doth quit[2] like, and Measure still[1] for Measure.
Measure for Measure, V, 1:415
[1] still: always. [2] quit: repay.

PORTIA. He is well paid that is well satisfied.
Merchant of Venice, IV, 1:415

PEACE

OCTAVIUS CAESAR. The time of universal peace is near:
Prove this a prosperous day, the three-nook'd world
Shall bear the olive freely.
Antony and Cleopatra, IV, 6:5

ARCHBISHOP. And therefore be assur'd, my good lord marshal,
If we do not now make our atonement well,
Our peace will, like a broken limb united,
Grow stronger for the breaking.
II Henry IV, IV, 1:220

ARCHBISHOP OF YORK. A peace is of the nature of a conquest;
For then both parties nobly are subdued,
And neither party loser.
II Henry IV, IV, 2:89

BURGUNDY. I demand before this royal view,
What rub or what impediment there is,
Why that the naked, poor, and mangled Peace,
Dear nurse of arts, plenties, and joyful births,
Should not in this best garden of the world,
Our fertile France, put up her lovely visage?
Alas! she hath from France too long been chas'd,
And all her husbandry[1] doth lie on heaps,
Corrupting in its own fertility.
Henry V, V, 2:32
[1] husbandry: cultivation.

GLOUCESTER [soliloquy]. Now is the winter of our discontent
Made glorious summer by this sun of York;
And all the clouds that lour'd upon our house
In the deep bosom of the ocean buried.
Now are our brows bound with victorious wreaths;
Our bruised arms hung up for monuments;
Our stern alarums chang'd to merry meetings;
Our dreadful marches to delightful measures.[2]
Grim-visag'd war hath smooth'd his wrinkled front;

And now, instead of mounting barbed steeds
To fright the souls of fearful adversaries,
He capers nimbly in a lady's chamber
To the lascivious pleasing of a lute.
Richard III, I, 1:1
[1] Later, KING RICHARD III; EDWARD IV is king.
[2] measures: dancing.

PETRUCHIO. Marry, peace it bodes, and
    love, and quiet life,
And awful[1] rule and right supremacy;
And, to be short, what not that 's sweet and
    happy?
Taming of the Shrew, V, 2:108
[1] awful: respectful.

PEDANT

KING. A man in all the world's new fash-
    ion planted,
That hath a mint of phrases in his brain;
One whom the music of his own vain tongue
Doth ravish like enchanting harmony.

. . . . .

How you delight, my lords, I know not, I;
But, I protest, I love to hear him lie.

. . . . .

BIRON. Armado is a most illustrious wight,
A man of fire-new words, fashion's own
    knight.
Love's Labour's Lost, I, 1:165, 175, 178

HOLOFERNES. The deer was, as you know,
sanguis, in blood; ripe as the pomewater,[1]
who now hangeth like a jewel in the ear of
caelo, the sky, the welkin, the heaven; and
anon falleth like a crab on the face of *terra*,
the soil, the land, the earth.

. . . . .

This is a gift that I have, simple, simple; a
foolish extravagant spirit, full of forms, figures, shapes, objects, ideas, apprehensions,
motions, revolutions: these are begot in the
ventricle of memory, nourished in the womb
of *pia mater*,[2] and delivered upon the mel-
lowing of occasion. But the gift is good in
those in whom it is acute, and I am thankful
for it.
Love's Labour's Lost, IV, 2:3, 67
[1] pomewater: a kind of apple. [2] *pia mater*: a
membrane of the brain.

NATHANIEL. Your reasons at dinner have
been sharp and sententious; pleasant without scurrility, witty without affection,[1] au-
dacious without impudency, learned without opinion, and strange without heresy.
Love's Labour's Lost, V, 1:2
[1] affection: affectation.

HOLOFERNES. His humour is lofty, his discourse peremptory, his tongue filed,[1] his eye
ambitious, his gait majestical, and his general behaviour vain, ridiculous, and thrasonical.[2] He is too picked, too spruce, too affected, too odd, as it were, too peregrinate,[3]
as I may call it.
Love's Labour's Lost, V, 1:11
[1] filed: polished. [2] thrasonical: boastful. [3] peregrinate: having air of foreign travel.

PERFECTION

CLOTON. I love and hate her; for she 's fair
    and royal,
And that she hath all courtly parts more ex-
    quisite
Than lady, ladies, woman; from every one
The best she hath, and she, of all com-
    pounded,
Outsells them all.
Cymbeline, III, 5:70

SUFFOLK. The chief perfections of that
    lovely dame,
Had I sufficient skill to utter them,
Would make a volume of enticing lines,
Able to ravish any dull conceit.[1]
I Henry VI, V, 5:12
[1] conceit: imagination.

But no perfection is so absolute,
That some impurity doth not pollute.
Rape of Lucrece: 853

ANNE.[1] His better doth not breathe upon
    the earth.
Richard III, I, 2:140
[1] About EDWARD, her former husband.

PERSUASION

HOTSPUR. Arm, arm with speed! and, fel-
    lows, soldiers, friends,
Better consider what you have to do,
Than I, that have not well the gift of
    tongue,
Can lift your blood up with persuasion.
I Henry IV, V, 2:76

LUCIO. Go to Lord Angelo,
And let him learn to know, when maidens
    sue,
Men give like gods; but when they weep
    and kneel,
All their petitions are as freely theirs
As they themselves would owe[1] them.
Measure for Measure, I, 4:79
[1] owe: own.

LUCIO.[1] Give 't not o'er so: to him again,
    entreat him;

Kneel down before him, hang upon his
    gown;
You are too cold; if you should need a pin,
You could not with more tame a tongue de-
    sire it.
                            Measure for Measure, II, 2:43
[1] To ISABELLA.

BAWD. She[1] would make a puritan of the
devil.
                                        Pericles, IV, 6:9
[1] She: MARINA.

PHILOSOPHY

LAFEU. They say miracles are past; and
we have our philosophical persons, to make
modern[1] and familiar, things supernatural
and causeless. Hence is it that we make trifles of terrors, ensconcing ourselves into
seeming knowledge, when we should sub-
mit ourselves to an unknown fear.
                    All's Well That Ends Well, II, 3:1
[1] modern: commonplace.

FIRST LORD. The web of our life is of a
mingled yarn, good and ill together: our
virtues would be proud if our faults
whipped them not; and our crimes would
despair if they were not cherished by our
virtues.
                All's Well That Ends Well, IV, 3:83

FIRST LORD. To-day my Lord of Amiens
    and myself
Did steal behind him as he lay along
Under an oak whose antique root peeps out
Upon the brook that brawls along this
    wood;
To the which place a poor sequester'd stag,
That from the hunter's aim had ta'en a hurt,
Did come to languish.

                    . . . . .

DUKE SENIOR. But what said Jaques?
Did he not moralize this spectacle?

                    . . . . .

FIRST LORD. 'Poor deer,' quoth he, 'thou
    mak'st a testament
As worldings do, giving thy sum of more
To that which had too much': then, being
    there alone,
Left and abandon'd of his velvet friends;
' 'T is right,' quoth he; 'thus misery doth
    part
The flux of company': anon, a careless herd
Full of the pasture, jumps along by him
And never stays to greet him; 'Ay,' quoth
    Jaques.
'Sweep on, you fat and greasy citizens;
'T is just the fashion; wherefore do you
    look

:Upon that poor and broken bankrupt
    there?'
Thus most invectively he pierceth through
The body of the country, city, court,
Yea, and of this our life; swearing that we
Are mere[1] usurpers, tyrants, and what 's
    worse,
To fright the animals and to kill them up
In their assign'd and native dwelling-place.
                        As You Like It, II, 1:29, 43, 47
[1] mere: absolute.

CORIN. And how like you this shepherd's
life, Master Touchstone?
TOUCHSTONE. Truly, shepherd, in respect
of itself, it is a good life; but in respect that
it is a shepherd's life, it is naught. In respect
that it is solitary, I like it very well; but in
respect that it is private, it is a very vile life.
Now, in respect it is in the fields, it pleaseth
me well; but in respect it is not in the court,
it is tedious. As it is a spare[1] life, look you,
it fits my humour well; but as there is no
more plenty in it, it goes much against my
stomach. Hast any philosophy in thee, shepherd?
CORIN. No more but that I know the more
one sickens the worse at ease he is; and that
he that wants[2] money, means, and content, is
without three good friends; that the property of rain is to wet, and fire to burn; that
good pasture makes fat sheep, and that a
great cause of the night is lack of the sun;
that he that hath learned no wit by nature
nor art may complain of good breeding, or
comes of a very dull kindred.
                                As You Like It, III, 2:11
[1] spare: parsimonious, frugal. [2] wants: lacks.

CORIN. Sir, I am a true labourer: I earn
that I eat, get that I wear, owe no man hate,
envy no man's happiness, glad of other
men's good, content with my harm; and
the greatest of my pride is to see my ewes
graze and my lambs suck.
TOUCHSTONE. That is another simple sin
in you, to bring the ewes and the rams together, and to offer to get your living by
the copulation of cattle; to be bawd to a
bell-wether, and to betray a she-lamb of a
twelvemonth to a crooked-pated, old, cuck-
oldly ram, out of all reasonable match. If
thou be'st not damned for this, the devil
himself will have no shepherds: I cannot see
else how thou shouldst 'scape.
                                As You Like It, III, 2:77

IACHIMO. What! are men mad? Hath na-
ture given them eyes
To see this vaulted arch, and the rich crop
Of sea and land, which can distinguish
    'twixt
The fiery orbs above and the twinn'd stones

Upon the number'd beach, and can we not
Partition make with spectacles so precious
'Twixt fair and foul?
Cymbeline, I, 6:32

HAMLET. There are more things in heaven
and earth, Horatio,
Than are dreamt of in your philosophy.
Hamlet, I, 5:166

HAMLET. There is something in this more
than natural, if philosophy could find it out.
Hamlet, II, 2:385

DUMAINE. The grosser manner of these
world's delights
He throws upon the gross world's baser
slaves:
To love, to wealth, to pomp, I pine and die;
With all these living in philosophy.
Love's Labour's Lost, I, 1:29

DUKE. Heaven doth with us as we with
torches do,
Not light them for themselves; for if our
virtues
Did not go forth of us, 't were all alike
As if we had them not. Spirits are not finely
touch'd
But to fine issues, nor Nature never lends
The smallest scruple of her excellence,
But, like a thrifty goddess, she determines
Herself the glory of a creditor.
Measure for Measure, I, 1:33

PORTIA. How far that little candle throws
his[1] beams!
So shines a good deed in a naughty world.
Merchant of Venice, V, 1:90
[1] his: its, as often in Shakespeare.

FRIAR. I 'll give thee armour to keep off
that word;[1]
Adversity's sweet milk, philosophy.

. . . . .

ROMEO. Hang up philosophy!
Unless philosophy can make a Juliet.
Romeo and Juliet, III, 3:54, 57
[1] word: banishment.

And yet love knows it is a greater grief
To bear love's wrong than hate's known in-
jury.
Sonnet 40

PHRASES

CELIA. Well said: that was laid on with a
trowel.
As You Like It, I, 2:112

ADAM. Unregarded age in corners
thrown.
As You Like It, II, 3:42

ROSALIND. Falser than vows made in wine.
As You Like It, III, 5:73

OLIVER. Chewing the food of sweet and
bitter fancy.[1]
As You Like It, IV, 3:102
[1] fancy: imagination.

SECOND PAGE. Both in a tune, like two gip-
sies on a horse.
As You Like It, V, 3:16

DROMIO SYRACUSE. A back-friend, a
shoulder-clapper.
Comedy of Errors, IV, 2:37

SICINIUS. What is the city but the people?
Coriolanus, III, 1:199

THIRD SERVANT. The wars for my money.
Coriolanus, IV, 5:249

IMOGEN. Society is no comfort
To one not sociable.
Cymbeline, IV, 2:12

HAMLET. I must be cruel only to be kind.
Hamlet, III, 4:178

K. HENRY. My scepter and my soul to
boot.
I Henry IV, III, 2:97

QUICKLY. He hath eaten me out of house
and home.
II Henry IV, II, 1:80

CHAMBERLAIN. This bold bad man.[1]
Henry VIII, II, 2:44
[1] man: WOLSEY.

CASCA. For mine own part, it was Greek
to me.
Julius Caesar, I, 2:287

EDGAR. The worst is not
So long as we can say 'This is the worst.'
King Lear, IV, 1:29

ARMADO. The naked truth.
Love's Labour's Lost, V, 2:716

PORTER. The primrose way to the everlasting bonfire.
Macbeth, II, 3:18

SHYLOCK. A harmless necessary cat.
Merchant of Venice, IV, 1:55

QUICKLY. Thereby hangs a tale.
Merry Wives of Windsor, I, 4:159

MISTRESS PAGE. Dispense with trifles.
Merry Wives of Windsor, II, 1:48

NYM. There's the humour of it.
Merry Wives of Windsor, II, 1:141

QUICKLY. This is the short and the long of it.
Merry Wives of Windsor, II, 2:60

FALSTAFF. As good luck would have it.
Merry Wives of Windsor, III, 5:84

THESEUS. Grows, lives, and dies, in single blessedness.
Midsummer Night's Dream, I, 1:78

LYSANDER. True love never did run smooth.
Midsummer Night's Dream, I, 1:134

BOTTOM. A part to tear a cat in.
Midsummer Night's Dream, I, 2:31

OBERON. In maiden meditation fancy free.
Midsummer Night's Dream, II, 1:164

QUINCE. He comes to disfigure or to present, the person of Moonshine.
Midsummer Night's Dream, III, 1:62

QUINCE. He goes but to see a noise he has heard.
Midsummer Night's Dream, III, 1:93

PUCK. Lord, what fools these mortals be.
Midsummer Night's Dream, III, 2:115

YORK. Everything is left at six and seven.
Richard II, II, 2:122

K. RICHARD. The worst is death, and death will have his day.
Richard II, III, 2:103

GARDENER. Superfluous branches
We lop away that bearing boughs may live.
Richard II, III, 4:63

BUCKINGHAM. I dance attendance here.
Richard III, III, 7:56

MERCUTIO. A plague o' both your houses.
Romeo and Juliet, III, 1:103

GONZALO. To excel the golden age.
Tempest, II, 1:168

ALONZO. A kind of excellent dumb discourse.
Tempest, III, 3:38

MIRANDA. O brave new world.
Tempest, V, 1:183

MARIA. My purpose is, indeed, a horse of that colour.
Twelfth Night, II, 3:181

ANTONIO. Out of the jaws of death.
Twelfth Night, III, 4:394

PROTEUS. The uncertain glory of an April day.
Two Gentlemen of Verona, I, 3:85

PICTURE

PORTIA. He is a proper man's picture.
Merchant of Venice, I, 2:78

SECOND SERVANT. Dost thou love pictures? we will fetch thee straight
Adonis painted by a running brook,
And Cytherea[1] all in sedges hid,
Which seem to move and wanton with her breath,
Even as the waving sedges play with wind.
Taming of the Shrew, Induction, 2:51
[1] Cytherea: Venus.

OLIVIA. Here; wear this jewel for me, 'tis my picture:
Refuse it not; it hath no tongue to vex you;
Twelfth Night, III, 4:228

PROTEUS. Vouchsafe me yet your picture for my love,
The picture that is hanging in your chamber:
To that I'll speak, to that I'll sigh and weep;
For since the substance of your perfect self
Is else devoted, I am but a shadow,
And to your shadow will I make true love.
Two Gentlemen of Verona, IV, 2:121

PITY

DUKE SENIOR. Come, shall we go and kill us venison?
And yet it irks me, the poor dappled fools,
Being native burghers of this desert city,
Should, in their own confines, with forked heads[1]
Have their round haunches gor'd.
As You Like It, II, 1:21
[1] forked heads: arrows.

ORLANDO. Speak you so gently? Pardon me, I pray you:
I thought that all things had been savage here,

And therefore put I on the countenance
Of stern commandment. But whate'er you
    are
That in this desert inaccessible,
Under the shade of melancholy boughs,
Lose and neglect the creeping hours of time;
If ever you have look'd on better days,
If ever been where bells have knoll'd[1] to
    church,
If ever sat at any good man's feast,
If ever from your eyelids wip'd a tear,
And know what 't is to pity, and be pitied,
Let gentleness my strong enforcement be:
In the which hope I blush, and hide my
    sword.
    DUKE SENIOR. True is it that we have seen
    better days,
And have with holy bell been knoll'd to
    church,
And sat at good men's feasts, and wip'd our
    eyes
Of drops that sacred pity hath engender'd;
And therefore sit you down in gentleness
And take upon command what help we have
That to your wanting may be minister'd.
               As You Like It, II, 7:106
[1] knoll'd: rung, tolled.

K. HENRY. My pity hath been balm to
    heal their wounds,
My mildness hath allay'd their swelling
    griefs,
My mercy dry'd their water-flowing tears;
               III Henry VI, IV, 8:41

GLOUCESTER. The sea, with such a storm
    as his bare head
In hell-black night endur'd, would have
    buoy'd up,
And quench'd the stelled[1] fires;
Yet, poor old heart, he holp[2] the heavens to
    rain.
If wolves had at thy gate howl'd that stern
    time,
Thou should'st have said 'Good porter, turn
    the key.'
               King Lear, III, 7:59
[1] stelled: referring to the stars.   [2] holp: helped.

CORDELIA. Was this a face
To be oppos'd against the warring winds?
To stand against the deep dread-bolted
    thunder?
In the most terrible and nimble stroke
Of quick cross lightning? to watch, poor
    perdu!
With this thin helm? Mine enemy's dog,
Though he had bit me, should have stood
    that night
Against my fire. And wast thou fain, poor
    father,
To hovel thee with swine and rogues for-
    lorn,

In short and musty straw? Alack, alack!
'T is wonder that thy life and wits at once
Had not concluded all.
               King Lear, IV, 7:32

ISABELLA. Yet show some pity.
ANGELO. I show it most of all when I show
    justice;
For then I pity those I do not know,
Which a dismiss'd offence would after gall,
And do him right, that, answering one foul
    wrong,
Lives not to act another.
          Measure for Measure, II, 2:99

OTHELLO. O! Iago, the pity of it, Iago.
               Othello, IV, 1:207

ANNE. No beast so fierce but knows some
    touch of pity.
               Richard III, I, 2:71

JULIET. Is there no pity sitting in the
    clouds,
That sees into the bottom of my grief?
          Romeo and Juliet, III, 5:198

ARIEL. Your charm so strongly works
    them,
That if you now beheld them, your affec-
    tions
Would become tender.
    PROSPERO. Dost thou think so, spirit?
    ARIEL. Mine would, sir, were I human.
    PROSPERO. And mine shall.
Hast thou, which art but air, a touch, a feel-
    ing
Of their afflictions, and shall not myself,
One of their kind, that relish[1] all as sharply,
Passion as they, be kindlier mov'd than thou
    art?
               Tempest, V, 1:17
[1] relish: feel.

PLAINNESS

DROMIO SYRACUSE. Marry, sir, by a rule
as plain as the plain bald pate of Father
Time himself.
               Comedy of Errors, II, 2:70

KENT. Sir, 't is my occupation to be plain:
I have seen better faces in my time
Than stands on any shoulder that I see
Before me at this instant.
    CORNWALL. This is some fellow,
Who, having been prais'd for bluntness,
    doth affect
A saucy roughness, and constrains the garb
Quite from his nature: he cannot flatter, he,
An honest mind and plain, he must speak
    truth:

An they will take it, so; if not, he 's plain.
These kind of knaves I know, which in this
    plainness
Harbour more craft and more corrupter
    ends
Than twenty silly-ducking observants,
That stretch their duties nicely.
                            King Lear, II, 2:98

LAUNCELOT. I was always plain with you,
and so now I speak my agitation of the matter: therefore, be of good cheer; for truly
I think you are damned.
                    Merchant of Venice, III, 5:4

PLAY

HAMLET. The play, I remember, pleased
not the million; 't was caviare[1] to the general.
                            Hamlet, II, 2:454
[1] caviare: a Russian delicacy not appreciated by
the common people.

HAMLET. Will you play upon this pipe?
GUILDENSTERN. My lord, I cannot.
HAMLET. I pray you.
GUILDENSTERN. Believe me, I cannot.

. . . . .

HAMLET. Why, look you now, how unworthy a thing you make of me. You would
play upon me; you would seem to know my
stops; you would pluck out the heart of
my mystery; you would sound me from my
lowest note to the top of my compass; and
there is much music, excellent voice, in this
little organ, yet cannot you make it speak.
'Sblood! do you think I am easier to be
played on than a pipe? Call me what instrument you will, though you can fret me, you
cannot play upon me.
                        Hamlet, III, 2:365, 381

PRINCE. If all the year were playing holi-
    days,
To sport would be as tedious as to work;
                        I Henry IV, I, 2:227

PRINCESS. Since you can cog,[1] I 'll play no
    more with you.
                    Love's Labour's Lost, V, 2:235
[1] cog: cheat.

LORENZO. When you shall please to play
    the thieves for wives,
I 'll watch as long for you then.
                    Merchant of Venice, II, 6:23

CAPULET. You are welcome, gentlemen!
    Come, musicians, play.
A hall! a hall! give room, and foot it, girls.
                    Romeo and Juliet, I, 5:27

LEONTES. Go play, boy, play; thy mother
    plays, and I
Play too, but so disgrac'd a part, whose is-
sue
Will hiss me to my grave.
                    Winter's Tale, I, 2:187

PLAYBOY

OCTAVIUS CAESAR [about ANTONY]. It is
    not Caesar's natural vice to hate
Our great competitor.[1] From Alexandria
This is the news: he fishes, drinks, and
    wastes
The lamps of night in revel; is not more
    man-like
Than Cleopatra, nor the queen of Ptolemy
More womanly than he; hardly gave au-
    dience, or
Vouchsaf'd to think he had partners: you
    shall find there
A man who is the abstract[2] of all faults
That all men follow.
                    Antony and Cleopatra, I, 4:2
[1] competitor: colleague or partner.   [2] abstract:
summary.

POINS. Where has been, Hal?
PRINCE. With three or four loggerheads[1]
amongst three or four score hogsheads.

. . . . .

To conclude, I am so good a proficient in
one quarter of an hour, that I can drink with
any tinker in his own language during my
life.
                        I Henry IV, II, 4:3, 20
[1] loggerheads: blockheads.

PRINCE. Well, thus we play the fools with
the time, and the spirits of the wise sit in
the clouds and mock us.
                    II Henry IV, II, 2:154

GRATIANO. Let me play the fool.
                    Merchant of Venice, I, 1:79

PORTIA. God made him, and therefore let
him pass for a man.

. . . . .

If a throstle sing, he falls straight a-capering;
he will fence with his own shadow.
                    Merchant of Venice, I, 2:60, 65

PLEADING

ARTHUR. O! spare mine eyes,
Though to no use but still to look on you.
Lo! by my troth, the instrument is cold
And would not harm me.

HUBERT. I can heat it, boy.
ARTHUR. No, in good sooth; the fire is
  dead with grief,
Being create for comfort, to be us'd
In undeserv'd extremes: see else yourself;
There is no malice in this burning coal;
The breath of heaven hath blown his[1] spirit
  out
And strew'd repentant ashes on his head.
HUBERT. But with my breath I can revive
  it, boy.
ARTHUR. An if you do you will but make
  it blush
And glow with shame of your proceedings,
  Hubert:
Nay, it perchance will sparkle in your eyes;
And like a dog that is compell'd to fight,
Snatch at his master that doth tarre[2] him on.
All things that you should use to do me
  wrong
Deny their office; only you do lack
That mercy which fierce fire and iron ex-
  tends.
King John, IV, 1:102
[1] his: its. [2] tarre: urge, incite.

O! if no harder than a stone thou art,
Melt at my tears and be compassionate.
Rape of Lucrece: 593

PLEASURE

ANTONY. The present pleasure,
By revolution lowering, does become
The opposite of itself:
Antony and Cleopatra, I, 2:128

JAQUES. So, to your pleasures:
I am for other than for dancing measures.
As You Like It, V, 4:198

GLOUCESTER. Do as I bid thee, or rather
  do thy pleasure;
Above the rest, be gone.
King Lear, IV, 1:49

DUKE. What pleasure was he given to?
ESCALUS. Rather rejoicing to see another
merry, than merry at any thing which pro-
fessed to make him rejoice:
Measure for Measure, III, 2:248

IAGO. Pleasure and action make the hours
seem short.
Othello, II, 3:385

Why should the private pleasure of some
  one
Become the public plague of many moe?[1]
Rape of Lucrece: 1478
[1] moe: more.

LUCENTIO. No profit grows where is no
  pleasure ta'en:
In brief, sir, study what you most affect.[1]
Taming of the Shrew, I, 1:39
[1] affect: enjoy.

PLOT

HELENA. Let us assay[1] our plot; which, if
  it speed,[2]
Is wicked meaning in a lawful deed,
And lawful meaning in a lawful act,
Where both not sin, and yet a sinful fact.
All's Well That Ends Well, III, 7:44
[1] assay: try. [2] speed: succeed.

POLONIUS. Your bait of falsehood takes
  this carp of truth;
And thus do we of wisdom[1] and of reach,
With windlasses[2] and with assays of bias,[3]
By indirections find directions out.
Hamlet, II, 1:63
[1] wisdom . . . reach: wise and shrewd. [2] windlasses: roundabout ways. [3] assays of bias: indirect ways.

HAMLET [soliloquy]. I have heard
That guilty creatures sitting at a play
Have by the very cunning of the scene
Been struck so to the soul that presently[1]
They have proclaim'd their malefactions;
For murder, though it have no tongue, will
  speak
With most miraculous organ. I 'll have these
  players
Play something like the murder of my fa-
  ther
Before mine uncle; I 'll observe his looks;
I 'll tent him to the quick:[2] if he but blench
I know my course. The spirit that I have
  seen
May be the devil; and the devil hath power
To assume a pleasing shape; yea, and per-
  haps
Out of my weakness and my melancholy,
As he is very potent with such spirits,
Abuses[3] me to damn me. I 'll have grounds
More relative than this: the play 's the thing
Wherein I 'll catch the conscience of the
  king.
Hamlet, II, 2:617
[1] presently: immediately. [2] tent . . . quick:
probe to the flesh. [3] Abuse: deceive, as often
in Shakespeare.

HAMLET. Madam, how like you this play?
QUEEN. The lady protests too much, me-
thinks.
HAMLET. O! but she 'll keep her word.
KING. Have you heard the argument? Is
there no offence in 't?
HAMLET. No, no, they do but jest, poison
in jest; no offence i' the world. . . . We that

have free souls, it touches us not: let the galled jade wince, our withers are unwrung.

. . . . .

He poisons him 'i the garden for 's estate.
His name 's Gonzago; the story is extant, and writ in choice Italian. You shall see anon how the murderer gets the love of Gonzago's wife.

OPHELIA. The king rises.
HAMLET. What! frighted with false fire?
QUEEN. How fares my lord?
POLONIUS. Give o'er the play.
KING. Give me some light: away!
ALL. Lights, lights, lights!
          Exeunt all but HAMLET *and* HORATIO.

HAMLET. Why, let the stricken deer go weep,
The hart ungalled play;
For some must watch, while some must sleep:
So runs the world away.
                                    Hamlet, III, 2:239, 271

HAMLET. O good Horatio! I 'll take the ghost's word for a thousand pound. Didst perceive?
HORATIO. Very well, my lord.
HAMLET. Upon the talk of the poisoning?
HORATIO. I did very well note him.
HAMLET. Ah, ha! Come, some music! come, the recorders!
For if the king like not the comedy,
Why then, belike, he likes it not, perdy.
                                    Hamlet, III, 2:297

KING. Now, Hamlet, where 's Polonius?
HAMLET. At supper.
KING. At supper! Where?
HAMLET. Not where he eats, but where he is eaten: a certain convocation of politic worms are e'en at him. Your worm is your only emperor for diet: we fat all creatures else to fat us, and we fat ourselves for maggots: your fat king and your lean beggar is but variable service; two dishes, but to one table: that 's the end.
KING. Alas, alas!
HAMLET. A man may fish with the worm that hath eat of a king, and eat of the fish that hath fed of that worm.
KING. What dost thou mean by this?
HAMLET. Nothing, but to show you how a king may go a progress[1] through the guts of a beggar.
KING. Where is Polonius?
HAMLET. In heaven; send thither to see: if your messenger find him not there, seek him i' the other place yourself. But, indeed, if you find him not within this month, you shall nose him as you go up the stairs into the lobby.

KING [to some ATTENDANTS]. Go seek him there.
HAMLET. He will stay till you come.
                                    Exeunt Attendants.
KING. Hamlet, this deed, for thine especial safety,
Which we do tender, as we dearly grieve
For that which thou hast done, must send thee hence
With fiery quickness: therefore prepare thyself;
The bark is ready, and the wind at help,
The associates tend, and every thing is bent
For England.
HAMLET. For England!
KING. Ay, Hamlet.
HAMLET. Good.
KING. So is it, if thou knew'st our purposes.
HAMLET. I see a cherub that sees them. But come; for England! Farewell, dear mother.
KING. Thy loving father, Hamlet.
HAMLET. My mother: father and mother is man and wife, man and wife is one flesh, and so, my mother. Come, for England!   •
                                    Exit.
                                    Hamlet, IV, 3:17
[1] go a progress: an official visit by royalty.

KING. And, England, if my love thou hold'st at aught,
As my great power thereof may give thee sense,
Since yet thy cicatrice[1] looks raw and red
After the Danish sword, and thy free awe
Pays homage to us, thou may'st not coldly set
Our sovereign process, which imports at full,
By letters conjuring to that effect,
The present death of Hamlet. Do it, England;
For like the hectic in my blood he rages,
And thou must cure me.
                                    Hamlet, IV, 3:60
[1] cicatrice: scar after a wound.

HOTSPUR. Our plot is as good a plot as ever was laid; our friends true and constant: a good plot, good friends, and full of expectation; an excellent plot, very good friends.
                                    I Henry IV, II, 3:20

SUFFOLK. Madam, myself have lim'd[1] a bush for her,
And plac'd a quire of such enticing birds
That she will light to listen to the lays,
And never mount to trouble you again.
                                    II Henry VI, I, 3:91
[1] lim'd: referring to plan of catching birds by smearing branches with pitch.

York. My brain, more busy than the labouring spider,
Waves tedious snares to trap mine enemies.
II Henry VI, III, 1:339

Ford. Good plots! They are laid; and our revolted wives share damnation together.
Merry Wives of Windsor, III, 2:38

Puck. When I did him[1] at this advantage take;
An ass's nowl[2] I fixed on his head:
Anon his Thisbe must be answered,
And forth my mimic comes. When they him spy,
As wild geese that the creeping fowler eye,
Or russet-pated choughs, many in sort,
Rising and cawing at the gun's report,
Sever themselves, and madly sweep the sky;
So, at his sight, away his fellows fly.
Midsummer Night's Dream, III, 2:16
[1] him: Bottom. [2] nowl: head.

Buckingham. Now, my lord, what shall we do if we perceive Lord Hastings will not yield to our complots?
Gloucester.[1] Chop off his head; something we will determine:
And, look, when I am king, claim thou of me
The earldom of Hereford, and the moveables
Whereof the king my brother stood possess'd.
Richard III, III, 1:191
[1] Later, King Richard III.

Buckingham. Ah, ah! my lord, this prince[1] is not an Edward,
He is not lolling on a lewd day-bed,
But on his knees at meditation;
Not dallying with a brace of courtezans,
But meditating with two deep divines;
Not sleeping, to engross his idle body,
But praying, to enrich his watchful soul.
Happy were England, would this virtuous prince
Take on his grace the sovereignty thereof:
But, sure, I fear, we shall not win him to it.
Richard III, III, 7:71
[1] prince: Gloucester, later Richard III.

Prospero. In few, they hurried us aboard a bark,
Bore us some leagues to sea; where they prepar'd
A rotten carcase of a boat, not rigg'd,
Nor tackle, sail, nor mast; the very rats
Instinctively had quit it; there they hoist us,
To cry to the sea that roar'd to us; to sigh
To the winds whose pity, sighing back again,
Did us but loving wrong.

Miranda. Alack! what trouble
Was I then to you.
Tempest, I, 2:144

Ariel. Safely in harbour
Is the king's ship; in the deep nook, where once
Thou call'dst me up at midnight to fetch dew
From the still-vex'd Bermoothes; there she's hid.
Tempest, I, 2:224

Leontas. Break up the seals and read.[1]
Officer. Hermione is chaste; Polixenes blameless; Camillo a true subject; Leontes a jealous tyrant; his innocent babe truly begotten; and the king shall live without an heir if that which is lost be not found!
Winter's Tale, III, 2:132
[1] Apollo's Oracle, the key to the plot.

POETRY

Orlando. Hang there, my verse, in witness of my love;
And thou, thrice-crowned queen of night, survey
With thy chaste eye, from thy pale sphere above,
Thy huntress'[1] name, that my full life doth sway.
O Rosalind! these trees shall be my books,
And in their barks my thoughts I'll character.[2]
As You Like It, III, 2:1
[1] huntress: goddess of the hunt, Diana. [2] character: write.

Touchstone. I'll rhyme you so eight years together, dinners and suppers and sleeping hours excepted.
As You Like It, III, 2:101

Touchstone. Truly, I would the gods had made thee poetical.
Audrey. I do not know what 'poetical' is. Is it honest in deed and word? Is it a true thing?
Touchstone. No, truly, for the truest poetry is the most feigning; and lovers are given to poetry, and what they swear in poetry may be said as lovers they do feign.
As You Like It, III, 3:16

Armado. Assist me, some extemporal god of rhyme, for I am sure I shall turn sonneter. Devise, wit; write, pen.
Love's Labour's Lost, I, 2:189

Longaville. Did not the heavenly rhetoric of thine eye,

'Gainst whom the world cannot hold argument,
Persuade my heart to this false perjury?
Love's Labour's Lost, IV, 3:60

BIRON. Fie, painted rhetoric! O! she needs it not:
To things of sale a seller's praise belongs;
She passes praise; then praise too short doth blot.
Love's Labour's Lost, IV, 3:239

BIRON. O! then his lines would ravish savage ears,
And plant in tyrants mild humility.
Love's Labour's Lost, IV, 3:348

BENEDICK. I can find out no rhyme to 'lady' but 'baby,' an innocent rhyme; for 'scorn,' 'horn,' a hard rhyme; for 'school,' 'fool,' a babbling rhyme; very ominous endings. No, I was not born under a rhyming planet.
Much Ado About Nothing, V, 2:36

Not marble, nor the gilded monuments
Of princes, shall outlive this powerful rhyme;
But you shall shine more bright in these contents
Than unswept stone, besmear'd with sluttish time.
When wasteful war shall statues overturn,
And broils root out the work of masonry,
Nor Mars his sword nor war's quick fire shall burn
The living record of your memory.
'Gainst death and all-oblivious enmity
Shall you pace forth; your praise shall still find room
Even in the eyes of all posterity
That wear this world out to the ending doom.
Sonnet 55

DUKE. Much is the force of heaven-bred poesy

. . . . .

PROTEUS. For Orpheus'[1] lute was strung with poets' sinews,
Whose golden touch could soften steel and stones,
Make tigers tame and huge leviathans[2]
Forsake unsounded deeps to dance on sands.
Two Gentlemen of Verona, III, 2:72, 78
[1] Orpheus: the Greek god of music. [2] leviathans: whales.

POISON

CORNELIUS. I do not like her.[1] She doth think she has

Strange lingering poisons; I do know her spirit,
And will not trust one of her malice with
A drug of such damn'd nature. Those she has
Will stupefy and dull the sense awhile;
Which first, perchance, she 'll prove[2] on cats and dogs,
Then afterward up higher; but there is
No danger in what show of death it makes,
More than the locking-up the spirits a time,
To be more fresh, reviving.
Cymbeline, I, 5:33
[1] her: the QUEEN. [2] prove: test.

IMOGEN. O! get thee from my sight;
Thou gav'st me poison: dangerous fellow, hence!
Breathe not where princes are.
Cymbeline, V, 5:237

HOTSPUR. And that same sword-and-buckler Prince of Wales,
But that I think his father loves him not,
And would be glad he met with some mischance,
I would have him poison'd with a pot of ale.
I Henry IV, I, 3:230

K. HENRY. Hide not thy poison with such sugar'd words.
II Henry VI, III, 2:45

YORK. She-wolf of France, but worse than wolves of France,
Whose tongue more poisons than the adder's tooth!
How ill-beseeming is it in thy sex.
III Henry VI, I, 4:111

OTHELLO. Get me some poison, Iago; this night: I 'll not expostulate with her, lest her body and beauty unprovide my mind again. This night, Iago.
IAGO. Do it not with poison, strangle her in her bed, even the bed she hath contaminated.
Othello, IV, 1:215

GLOUCESTER.[1] Why dost thou spit at me?
ANNE.[2] Would it were mortal[3] poison, for thy sake!
GLOUCESTER. Never came poison from so sweet a place.
ANNE. Never hung poison on a fouler toad. Out of my sight! thou dost infect mine eyes.
GLOUCESTER. Thine eyes, sweet lady, have infected mine.
Richard III, I, 2:145
[1] GLOUCESTER: later RICHARD III. [2] ANNE: later RICHARD'S wife. [3] mortal: deadly.

ROMEO. Hold, there is forty ducats; let
    me have
A dram of poison, such soon-speeding gear
As will disperse itself through all the veins
That the life-weary talker may fall dead.
                          Romeo and Juliet, V, 1:59

LEONTES. Bespice a cup,
To give mine enemy a lasting wink;
Which draught to me were cordial.[1]
                          Winter's Tale, I, 2:316
[1] cordial: a pleasing drink.

POLITICS

KING. And oft 't is seen the wicked prize
    itself
Buys out the law.
                          Hamlet, III, 3:59

HAMLET. This might be the pate of a politician, . . . that would circumvent God.
                          Hamlet, V, 1:85

BISHOP OF ELY. But how, my lord, shall
    we resist it[1] now?
ARCHBISHOP OF CANTERBURY. It must be
    thought on. If it pass against us,
We lose the better half of our possession;
For all the temporal lands which men de-
    vout
By testament have given to the church
Would they strip from us.
                    . . . . .

And to the coffers of the king beside,
A thousand pounds by the year. Thus runs
    the bill.
ELY. This would drink deep.
CANTERBURY. 'T would drink the cup
    and all.
                          Henry V, I, 1:6, 18
[1] it: a bill giving certain church possessions
to the crown. War would take attention from
the bill.

BASTARD. Search out thy wit for secret
    policies,
And we will make thee famous through the
    world.
                          I Henry VI, III, 3:12

POPULARITY

FIRST SERVANT. To be called into a huge
sphere, and not to be seen to move in 't, are
the holes where eyes should be, which piti-
fully disaster the cheeks.
                          Antony and Cleopatra, II, 7:16

BRUTUS [about CORIOLANUS]. All tongues
    speak of him, and the bleared sights

Are spectacled to see him: your prattling
    nurse
Into a rapture lets her baby cry
While she chats him: the kitchen malkin[1]
    pins
Her richest lockram[2] 'bout her reechy neck,
Clambering the walls to eye him: stalls,
    bulks, windows,
Are smother'd up, leads[3] fill'd, and ridges
    hors'd[4]
With variable complexions, all agreeing
In earnestness to see him.
                          Coriolanus, II, 1:221
[1] malkin: untidy female servant. [2] lockram: a
linen fabric. [3] leads: roofs covered with lead.
[4] hors'd: people astride them.

MESSENGER.[1] You are sent for to the Capi-
    tol. 'T is thought
That Marcius[2] shall be consul.
I have seen the dumb men throng to see him,
    and
The blind to hear him speak: matrons flung
    gloves,
Ladies and maids their scarfs and handker-
    chers,
Upon him as he pass'd; the nobles bended,
As to Jove's statue, and the commons made
A shower and thunder with their caps and
    shouts:
I never saw the like.
                          Coriolanus, II, 1:276
[1] To BRUTUS and SICINIUS, Tribunes. [2] MAR-
CIUS: later CORIOLANUS.

K. HENRY [to PRINCE HAL]. Had I so
    lavish of my presence been,
So common-hackney'd in the eyes of men,
So stale and cheap to vulgar company,
Opinion, that did help me to the crown,
Had[1] still kept loyal to possession
And left me in reputeless banishment,
A fellow of no mark nor likelihood.
By being seldom seen, I could not stir
But like a comet I was wonder'd at;
That men would tell their children 'This
    is he';
Others would say 'Where? which is Boling-
    broke?'
And then I stole all courtesy from heaven,
And dress'd myself in such humility
That I did pluck allegiance from men's
    hearts,
Loud shouts and salutations from their
    mouths,
Even in the presence of the crowned king.
                    . . . . .

The skipping king,[2] he ambled up and down
With shallow jesters and rash bavin[3] wits,
Soon kindled and soon burnt; carded[4] his
    state,

Mingled his royalty with capering fools,
Had his great name profaned with their
    scorns,
And gave his countenance, against his name,
To laugh at gibing boys and stand the push
Of every beardless vain comparative;[5]
Grew a companion to the common streets,
Enfeoff'd[6] himself to popularity;
That, being daily swallow'd by men's eyes,
They surfeited with honey and began
To loathe the taste of sweetness, whereof a
    little
More than a little is by much too much.
                          I Henry IV, III, 2:39, 60
[1] Had: would have.   [2] king: RICHARD II.
[3] bavin: soon burned out.   [4] carded: debased
by mixing.   [5] comparative: one fond of making
comparisons.   [6] Enfeoff'd: enslaved himself to
popularity.

DUKE. I 'll privily away: I love the peo-
    ple,
But do not like to stage me to their eyes.
Though it do well, I do not relish well
Their loud applause and Aves vehement,
Nor do I think the man of safe discretion
That does affect[1] it.
                          Measure for Measure, I, 1:68
[1] affect: love.

MOROCCO. The Hyrcanian deserts[1] and the
    vasty wilds
Of wide Arabia are as throughfares now,
For princes to come view fair Portia:
The watery kingdom, whose ambitious
    head
Spits in the face of heaven, is no bar
To stop the foreign spirits, but they come,
As o'er a brook, to see fair Portia.
                          Merchant of Venice, II, 7:41
[1] Hyrcanian deserts: southeast of Caspian Sea.

POSTERITY

When forty winters shall besiege thy brow
And dig deep trenches in thy beauty's field,
Thy youth's proud livery, so gaz'd on now,
Will be a tatter'd weed, of small worth held:
Then being ask'd where all thy beauty lies,
Where all the treasure of thy lusty days,
To say, within thine own deep-sunken eyes,
Were an all-eating shame and thriftless
    praise.
Now much more praise deserv'd thy
    beauty's use,
If thou could'st answer 'This fair child of
    mine
Shall sum my count and make my old ex-
    cuse,'
Proving his beauty by succession thine!
                          Sonnet 2

'By law of nature thou art bound to breed,
That thine may live when thou thyself art
    dead;
And so in spite of death thou dost survive,
In that thy likeness still is left alive.'
                          Venus and Adonis: 171

POLIXENES. You see, sweet maid, we
    marry
A gentler scion to the wildest stock,
And make conceive a bark of baser kind
By bud of nobler race: this is an art
Which does mend nature, change it rather,
    but
The art itself is nature.
                          Winter's Tale, IV, 4:92

POVERTY

FALSTAFF. I am as poor as Job, my lord,
but not so patient.
                          II Henry IV, I, 2:144

GLOUCESTER.[1] Suffolk, the new-made
    duke that rules the roast,
Hath given the duchy of Anjou and Maine
Unto the poor King Reignier,[2] whose large
    style
Agrees not with the leanness of his purse.
                          II Henry VI, I, 1:109
[1] Uncle of KING HENRY VI.   [2] King Reignier:
father of QUEEN MARGARET.

K. LEAR. Poor naked wretches, whereso-
    e'er you are,
That bide the pelting of this pitiless storm.
How shall your houseless heads and unfed
    sides,
Your loop'd and window'd raggedness, de-
    fend you
From seasons such as these? O! I have ta'en
Too little care of this. Take physic,[1] pomp;
Expose thyself to feel what wretches feel,
That thou may'st shake the superflux[2] to
    them,
And show the heavens more just.
                          King Lear, III, 4:28
[1] physic: medicine.   [2] superflux: superfluity.

EDGAR. A most poor man, made tame to
    fortune's blows;
Who, by the art of known and feeling sor-
    rows,
Am pregnant to good pity.
                          King Lear, IV, 6:225

ROMEO. Famine is in thy cheeks,
Need and oppression starveth in thine eyes,
Contempt and beggary hang upon thy back;
The world is not thy friend nor the world's
    law:
The world affords no law to make thee rich;

Then be not poor, but break it, and take this.
APOTHECARY. My poverty, but not my will, consents.
ROMEO. I pay thy poverty and not thy will.
Romeo and Juliet, V, 1:69

OLIVIA. O world! how apt the poor are to be proud.
Twelfth Night, III, 1:138

VALENTINE. Then know that I have little wealth to lose.
A man I am cross'd with adversity;
My riches are these poor habiliments,[1]
Of which if you should here disfurnish me,
You take the sum and substance that I have.
Two Gentlemen of Verona, IV, 1:11
[1] habiliments: clothing.

POWER

SICINIUS. We charge you, that you have contriv'd to take
From Rome all season'd[1] office, and to wind
Yourself into a power tyrannical;
For which you are a traitor to the people.
Coriolanus, III, 3:63
[1] season'd: well-established.

ANTONY. When Caesar says 'Do this,' it is perform'd.
Julius Caesar, I, 2:10

MALCOLM. Macbeth
Is ripe for shaking, and the powers above
Put on their instruments. Receive what cheer you may;
The night is long that never finds the day.
Macbeth, IV, 3:237

CARLISLE. Fear not, my lord: that power that made you king
Hath power to keep you king in spite of all.
The means that heaven yields must be embrac'd,
And not neglected; else, if heaven would,
And we will not, heaven's offer we refuse,
The proffer'd means of succour and redress.
Richard II, III, 2:27

K. RICHARD. They well deserve to have
That know the strong'st and surest way to get.
Richard II, III, 3:200

TAMORA. The eagle suffers little birds to sing,
And is not careful what they mean thereby,
Knowing that with the shadow of his wings
He can at pleasure stint[1] their melody.
Titus Andronicus, IV, 4:83
[1] stint: stop.

ADAM. Your prai[...]
home before you[...]
Know you not, maste[...]
Their graces serve the[...]
No more do yours:[...]
master,
Are sanctified and holy[...]
O, what a world is [...]
comely
Envenoms him that bears[...]
As You Like It, II, 3:9

BELARIUS to CYMBELINE. Here are your sons again; and I must lose
Two of the sweet'st companions in the world.
The benediction of these covering heavens
Fall on their heads like dew! for they are worthy
To inlay heaven with stars.
Cymbeline, V, 5:348

CANTERBURY. And make her[1] chronicles as rich with praise
As is the ooze and bottom of the sea
With sunken wreck and sumless treasuries.
Henry V, I, 2:163
[1] her: England's.

ANTONY. Friends, Romans, countrymen, lend me your ears;
I come to bury Caesar, not to praise him.
The evil that men do lives after them,
The good is oft interred with their bones;
So let it be with Caesar. The noble Brutus
Hath told you Caesar was ambitious;
If it were so, it was a grievous fault,
And grievously hath Caesar answer'd it.
Here, under leave of Brutus and the rest,
For Brutus is an honourable man;
So are they all, all honourable men;
Come I to speak in Caesar's funeral.
He was my friend, faithful and just to me:
But Brutus says he was ambitious;
And Brutus is an honourable man.
He hath brought many captives home to Rome,
Whose ransoms did the general coffers fill:
Did this in Caesar seem ambitious?
When that the poor have cried, Caesar hath wept;
Ambition should be made of sterner stuff:
Yet Brutus says he was ambitious;
And Brutus is an honourable man.
You all did see that on the Lupercal
I thrice presented him a kingly crown,
Which he did thrice refuse: was this ambition?
Yet Brutus says he was ambitious;
And, sure, he is an honourable man.
I speak not to disprove what Brutus spoke,

am to speak what I do know.
ll did love him once, not without
cause:
What cause withholds you then to mourn
for him?
O judgment! thou art fled to brutish beasts,
And men have lost their reason. Bear
with me;
My heart is in the coffin there with Caesar,
And I must pause till it come back to me.
Julius Caesar, III, 2:78

PORTIA. No more, I pray thee: I am half
afeard
Thou wilt say anon he is some kin to thee,
Thou spend'st such high-day[1] wit in praising
him.
Merchant of Venice, II, 9:96
[1] high-day: holiday.

PORTIA. This comes too near the praising
of myself;
Therefore no more of it.
Merchant of Venice, III, 4:22

BEATRICE. There 's not one wise man
among twenty that will praise himself.
Much Ado About Nothing, V, 2:75

Who is it that says most? which can say
more
Than this rich praise, that you alone are
you?
Sonnet 84

TIMON. A mere[1] satiety of commendations.
Timon of Athens, I, 1:166
[1] mere: absolute.

FLAVIUS. Ah! when the means are gone
that buy this praise,
The breath is gone whereof this praise is
made:
Feast-won, fast-lost; one cloud of winter
showers.
Timon of Athens, II, 2:178

ALCIBIADES. He is a man, setting his fate
aside,
Of comely virtues.
Timon of Athens, III, 5:14

AENEAS. The worthiness of praise distains[1] his worth,
If that the prais'd himself bring the praise
forth;
But what the repining enemy commends,
That breath fame blows; that praise, sole
pure, transcends.
Troilus and Cressida, I, 3:241
[1] distains: dishonours.

HERMIONE. One good deed dying tongue-
less
Slaughters a thousand waiting upon that.
Our praises are our wages: you may ride 's[1]
With one soft kiss a thousand furlongs ere
With spur we heat an acre.
Winter's Tale, I, 2:92
[1] 's: us, women.

PRAYER

HELENA. O you leaden messengers,
That ride upon the violent speed of fire,
Fly with false aim; move the still-piecing[1]
air,
That sings with piercing; do not touch my
lord!
Whoever shoots at him, I set him there;
Whoever charges on his forward breast,
I am the caitiff that do hold him to it;
And, though I kill him not, I am the cause
His death was so effected: better 't were
I met the ravin lion when he roar'd
With sharp constraint of hunger.
All's Well that Ends Well, III, 2:111
[1] still-piecing: motionless.

MENECRATES. We, ignorant of ourselves,
Beg often our own harms, which the wise
powers
Deny us for our good; so find we profit
By losing of our prayers.
Antony and Cleopatra, II, 1:5

HAMLET. Soft you now!
The fair Ophelia! Nymph, in thy orisons
Be all my sins remember'd.
Hamlet, III, 1:88

KING [soliloquy]. O! my offence is rank,
it smells to heaven;
It hath the primal eldest curse upon 't;
A brother's murder! Pray can I not,
Though inclination be as sharp as will:
My stronger guilt defeats my strong intent;
And, like a man to double business bound,
I stand in pause where I shall first begin,
And both neglect. What if this cursed hand
Were thicker than itself with brother's
blood,
Is there not rain enough in the sweet heavens
To wash it white as snow? Whereto serves
mercy
But to confront the visage of offence?
And what 's in prayer but this two-fold
force,
To be forestalled ere we come to fall,
Or pardon'd being down? Then I'll look up;
My fault is past. But, O! what form of
prayer

Can serve my turn? 'Forgive me my foul
    murder?'
That cannot be; since I am still possess'd
Of those effects for which I did the murder,
My crown, mine own ambition, and my
    queen.
May one be pardon'd and retain the of-
    fence?
In the corrupted currents of this world
Offence's gilded hand may shove by justice,
And oft 't is seen the wicked prize itself
Buys out the law; but 't is not so above;
There is no shuffling, there the action lies
In his[1] true nature, and we ourselves com-
    pell'd
Even to the teeth and forehead of our faults
To give in evidence. What then? what rests?
Try what repentance can: what can it not?
Yet what can it, when one can not repent?
O wretched state! O bosom black as death!
O limed soul[2] that struggling to be free
Art more engaged! Help, angels! make as-
    say[3]
Bow, stubborn knees; and, heart with strings
    of steel,
Be soft as sinews of the new-born babe.
All may be well.   *Retires and kneels.*
    Enter HAMLET, *unseen and unheard*
    by the KING.

HAMLET [soliloquy]. Now might I do it
    pat, now he is praying;
And now I 'll do 't: and so he goes to
    heaven;
And so am I reveng'd. That would be
    scann'd:[4]
A villain kills my father; and for that,
I, his sole son, do this same villain send
To heaven.
Why, this is hire and salary, not revenge.
He took my father grossly, full of bread,
With all his crimes broad blown, as flush as
    May;
And how his audit stands who knows save
    heaven?
But in our circumstance and course of
    thought
'T is heavy with him. And am I then re-
    veng'd,
To take him in the purging of his soul,
When he is fit and season'd for his passage?
No.
Up, sword, and know thou a more horrid
    hent;[5]
When he is drunk asleep, or in his rage,
Or in the incestuous pleasure of his bed,
At gaming, swearing, or about some act
That has no relish of salvation in 't:
Then trip him, that his heels may kick at
    heaven,
And that his soul may be as damn'd and
    black
As hell, whereto it goes.

KING. My words fly up, my thoughts re-
    main below:
Words without thoughts never to heaven
    go.
                  Hamlet, III, 3:36
[1] his: its. [2] limed soul: metaphor of birds that
were caught by sticky bird-lime smeared on
branches; the more they struggled the more
they were entangled. [3] assay: effort, trial.
[4] scann'd: interpreted. [5] hent: occasion.

CANTERBURY. God and his angels guard
    your sacred throne,
And make you long become it!
                  Henry V, I, 2:7

K. HENRY. O God of battles! steel my
    soldiers' hearts;
Possess them not with fear; take from them
    now
The sense of reckoning, if the opposed num-
    bers
Pluck their hearts from them.
               Henry V, IV, 1:306

QUEEN KATHARINE. God mend all!
              Henry VIII, I, 2:201

KING. Sir, I will pronounce your sentence:
you shall fast a week with bran and water.
    COSTARD. I had rather pray a month with
mutton and porridge.
        Love's Labour's Lost, I, 1:302

ANGELO. How, bribe me?
        . . . . .

ISABELLA. Not with fond[1] shekels of the
    tested gold,
Or stones whose rates are either rich or poor
As fancy values them; but with true prayers
That shall be up at heaven and enter there
Ere sunrise: prayers from preserved souls,
From fasting maids whose minds are dedi-
    cate
To nothing temporal.
      Measure for Measure, II, 2:146, 149
[1] fond: foolish.

ANGELO. When I would pray and think, I
    think and pray
To several subjects: heaven hath my empty
    words,
Whilst my invention, hearing not my
    tongue,
Anchors on Isabel: heaven in my mouth,
As if I did but only chew his[1] name.
        Measure for Measure, II, 4:1
[1] his: its.

LEONINE. If you require a little space for
    prayer,

I grant it. Pray; but be not tedious,
For the gods are quick of ear.
Pericles, IV, 1:68

RICHMOND. O! thou, whose captain I account myself,
Look on my forces with a gracious eye;
Put in their hands thy bruising irons of wrath,
That they may crush down with a heavy fall
The usurping helmets of our adversaries.
Make us thy ministers of chastisement,
That we may praise thee in thy victory!
To thee I do commend my watchful soul,
Ere I let fall the windows of mine eyes;
Sleeping and waking, O! defend me still.
Richard III, V, 3:108

PROSPERO. Now my charms are all o'er-thrown,
And what strength I have 's mine own;

. . . . .

And my ending is despair,
Unless I be reliev'd by prayer.
Tempest, V, 1, Epilogue: 319, 333

HERMIONE. You gods, look down,
And from your sacred vials pour your graces
Upon my daughter's head!
Winter's Tale, V, 3:121

PREACHER

ROSALIND. O most gentle pulpiter! what tedious homily of love have you wearied your parishioners withal,[1] and never cried, 'Have patience, good people!'
As You Like It, III, 2:164
[1] withal: with it.

LANCASTER. Who hath not heard it spoken
How deep you[1] were within the books of God?
To us the speaker in his parliament;
To us the imagin'd voice of God himself;
The very opener and intelligencer
Between the grace, the sanctities of heaven,
And our dull workings: O! who shall believe
But you misuse the reverence of your place,
Employ the countenance and grace of heaven,
As a false favourite doth his prince's name,
In deeds dishonourable?
II Henry IV, IV, 2:16
[1] ARCHBISHOP OF YORK.

PREMONITION

NORTHUMBERLAND. Yea, this man's brow, like to a title-leaf,
Foretells the nature of a tragic volume.
II Henry IV, I, 1:60

K. EDWARD. But, in the midst of this bright-shining day,
I spy a black, suspicious, threat'ning cloud
That will encounter with our glorious sun,
Ere he attain his easeful western bed.
III Henry VI, V, 3:3

ROSS. Thou seest, the heavens, as troubled with man's act,
Threaten his bloody stage: by the clock 't is day,
And yet dark night strangles the travelling lamp.
Is 't night's predominance, or the day's shame,
That darkness does the face of earth entomb,
When living light should kiss it?
Macbeth, II, 4:5

ANTONIO. In sooth, I know not why I am so sad:
It wearies me; you say it wearies you;
But how I caught it, found it, or came by it,
What stuff 't is made of, whereof it is born,
I am to learn;
And such a want-wit sadness makes of me,
That I have much ado to know myself.
Merchant of Venice, I, 1:1

SHYLOCK. I am right loath to go:
There is some ill a-brewing towards my rest,
For I did dream of money-bags to-night.
Merchant of Venice, II, 5:16

OTHELLO. O! it comes o'er my memory,
As doth the raven o'er the infected house,
Boding to all.
Othello, IV, 1:20

QUEEN. Yet again, methinks,
Some unborn sorrow, ripe in fortune's womb,
Is coming towards me, and my inward soul
With nothing trembles; at some thing it grieves
More than with parting from my lord the king.
BUSHY. Each substance of a grief hath twenty shadows,
Which show like grief itself, but are not so.
Richard II, II, 2:9

SALISBURY. Ah! Richard, with the eyes of heavy mind

I see thy glory like a shooting star
Fall to the base earth from the firmament.
Thy sun sets weeping in the lowly west,
Witnessing storms to come, woe, and unrest.
Thy friends are fled to wait upon thy foes,
And crossly to thy good all fortune goes.
Richard II, II, 4:18

BENVOLIO. Supper is done, and we shall
come too late.
ROMEO. I fear, too early; for my mind mis-
gives
Some consequence yet hanging in the stars
Shall bitterly begin his[1] fearful date
With this night's revels, and expire the term
Of a despised life clos'd in my breast
By some vile forfeit of untimely death.
But he, that hath the steerage of my course,
Direct my sail! On, lusty gentlemen.
. . . . .

Is she a Capulet?
O dear account! my life is my foe's debt.
Romeo and Juliet, I, 4:105 and 5:119
[1] his: its.

JULIET. My only love sprung from my
only hate!
Too early seen unknown, and known too
late!
Prodigious birth of love it is to me,
That I must love a loathed enemy.
Romeo and Juliet, I, 5:140

ROMEO. If I may trust the flattering truth
of sleep,
My dreams presage some joyful news at
hand:
My bosoms's lord sits lightly in his throne;
And all this day an unaccustom'd spirit
Lifts me above the ground with cheerful
thoughts.
I dreamt my lady came and found me dead;
Strange dream, that gives a dead man leave
to think!
And breath'd such life with kisses in my
lips,
That I reviv'd, and was an emperor.
Romeo and Juliet, V, 1:1

PREPARATION

BARDOLPH. When we mean to build,
We first survey the plot, then draw the
model;
And when we see the figure of the house,
Then must we rate the cost of the erection;
Which if we find outweighs ability,
What do we then but draw anew the model
In fewer offices, or at last desist
To build at all?
II Henry IV, I, 3:41

DAUPHIN. It is most meet we arm us
'gainst the foe;
For peace itself should not so dull a king-
dom,
Though war nor no known quarrel were in
question,
But that defences, musters, preparations,
Should be maintain'd, assembled, and col-
lected,
As were a war in expectation.
Henry V, II, 4:15

WINCHESTER. Com'st thou with deep premeditated lines,
With written pamphlets studiously devis'd?
1 Henry VI, III, 1:1

LORENZO. Go in, sirrah:[1] bid them prepare
for dinner.
LAUNCELOT. That is done, sir; they have
all stomachs.
Merchant of Venice, III, 5:52
[1] sirrah: form of address to a servant or to one
of inferior rank.

PRETENSE

K. LEAR. Get thee glass eyes;
And, like a scurvy politician, seem
To see the things thou dost not.
King Lear, IV, 6:174

EGEUS. Thou hast by moonlight at her
window sung,
With feigning voice, verses of feigning love.
Midsummer Night's Dream, I, 1:30

SATURNIUS. But if I live, his feigned ec-
stasies
Shall be no shelter to these outrages.
Titus Andronicus, IV, 4:21

PRIDE

ANTONY. Now, gods and devils!
Authority melts from me: of late, when I
cried 'Ho!'
Like boys unto a muss,[1] kings would start
forth,
And cry 'Your will?' Have you no ears?
I am
Antony yet.
Antony and Cleopatra, III, 13:90
[1] muss: scramble.

ROSALIND. My pride fell with my fortunes.
As You Like It, I, 2:264

JAQUES. Why, who cries out on pride,
That can therein tax[1] any private party?
Doth it not flow as hugely as the sea.
As You Like It, II, 7:70

[1] tax: blame, accuse.

MENENIUS. You talk of pride: O! that
you could turn your eyes toward the napes
of your necks,[1] and make but an interior
survey of your good selves. O! that you
could.
Coriolanus, II, 1:41

[1] napes . . . necks: fable that every man has a
bag hanging before him for faults of others,
and one behind for his own.

PISTOL. Discuss unto me; art thou officer?
Or art thou base, common and popular?
K. HENRY. I am a gentleman of a company.
PISTOL. Trail'st thou the puissant pike?
Henry V, IV, 1:37

ABERGAVENNY.[1] I can see his pride
Peep through each part of him: whence has
he that?
If not from hell, the devil is a niggard.
Henry VIII, I, 1:68

[1] About WOLSEY.

BEATRICE. Stand I condemn'd for pride
and scorn so much?
Contempt, farewell! and maiden pride,
adieu!
No glory lives behind the back of such.
And, Benedick, love on; I will requite thee,
Taming my wild heart to thy loving hand.
Much Ado About Nothing, III, 1:108

SLY. The Slys are no rogues; look in the
chronicles; we came in with Richard Conqueror.
Taming of the Shrew, Induction, 1:3

AGAMEMNON. He that is proud eats up
himself; pride is his own glass, his own
trumpet, his own chronicle.
Troilus and Cressida, II, 3:164

ULYSSES. Possess'd he is with greatness,
And speaks not to himself but with a pride
That quarrels at self-breath: imagin'd worth
Holds in his blood such swoln and hot discourse,
That 'twixt his mental and his active parts
Kingdom'd Achilles in commotion rages
And batters 'gainst itself.
Troilus and Cressida, II, 3:180

PRINCE—PRINCESS

WOLSEY. The hearts of princes kiss obedience,

So much they love it; but to stubborn spirits
They swell, and grow as terrible as storms.
Henry VIII, III, 1:162

TYRREL.[1] Their lips were four red roses
on a stalk,
And in their summer beauty kiss'd each
other.
Richard III, IV, 3:12

[1] Tyrrel: murderer of the two princes.

SIMONIDES. Princes in this should live like
gods above,
Who freely give to every one that comes
To honour them;
And princes not doing so are like to gnats,
Which make a sound, but kill'd are wonder'd at.
Pericles, II, 3:59

LEONTES. His princess, say you, with him?
GENTLEMAN. Ay, the most peerless piece
of earth, I think,
That e'er the sun shone bright on.
Winter's Tale, V, 1:93

PRODIGAL

ORLANDO. Shall I keep your hogs, and eat
husks with them? What prodigal portion
have I spent, that I should come to such
penury?
As You Like It, I, 1:40

DROMIO SYRACUSE. He that goes in the
calf's skin that was killed for the Prodigal.
Comedy of Errors, IV, 3:16

PROMISE

ROSALIND. Break an hour's promise in
love! He that will divide a minute into a
thousand parts, and break but a part of the
thousandth part of a minute in the affairs of
love, it may be said of him that Cupid hath
clapped him o' the shoulder, but I 'll warrant him heart-whole.
As You Like It, IV, 1:44

KING. How fares our cousin[1] Hamlet?
HAMLET. Excellent, i' faith; of the chameleon's[2] dish: I eat the air, promise-crammed;
you cannot feed capons so.
Hamlet, III, 2:98

[1] cousin: used for various relatives. [2] chameleon: idea that this bird fed on air.

CHARLES. How shall I honour thee[1] for
this success?
Thy promises are like Adonis' gardens,

That one day bloom'd and fruitful were the
next.
1 Henry VI, I, 6:5

[1] thee: JOAN.

LUCIO. He was ever precise in promise-
keeping.
Measure for Measure, I, 2:77

RODERIGO.[1] Faith, I have heard too much,
for your words and performances are no
kin together.
Othello, IV, 2:184

[1] To IAGO.

FLAVIUS [aside]. His[1] promises fly so be-
yond his state[2]
That what he speaks is all in debt; he owes
For every word.
Timon of Athens, I, 2:203

[1] his: TIMON'S.   [2] state: resources.

PROOF

IACHIMO. She[1] stripp'd it from her arm; I
see her yet;
Her pretty action did outsell her gift,
And yet enrich'd it too.
Cymbeline, II, 4:101

[1] She: IMOGEN.

DOGBERRY. Masters, it is proved already
that you are little better than false knaves.
Much Ado About Nothing, IV, 2:23

DUKE. To vouch this, is no proof,
Without more wider and more overt test
Than these thin habits and poor likelihoods
Of modern seeming[1] do prefer against him.
Othello, I, 3:106

[1] modern seeming: trivial import.

IAGO. Trifles light as air
Are to the jealous confirmations strong
As proofs of holy writ.
Othello, III, 3:322

PAULINA. Behold, my lords,
Although the print[1] be little, the whole mat-
ter
And copy of the father; eye, nose, lip,
The trick of 's frown, his[2] forehead, nay,
the valley,
The pretty dimples of his chin and cheek,
his smiles,
The very mould and frame of hand, nail,
finger:
And thou, good goddess Nature, which hast
made it
So like to him that got it.
Winter's Tale, II, 3:97

[1] print: HERMIONE'S baby.   [2] his: its.

PROPHECY

HELENA. Ere twice the horses of the sun
shall bring
Their fiery torcher his diurnal ring,
Ere twice in murk and occidental damp
Moist Hesperus[1] hath quench'd his sleepy
lamp,
Or four-and-twenty times the pilot's glass
Hath told the thievish minutes how they
pass,
What is infirm from your sound parts shall
fly,
Health shall live free, and sickness freely
die.
All's Well That Ends Well, II, 1:164

[1] Hesperus: the evening star.

SOOTHSAYER. In nature's infinite book of
secrecy
A little I can read.
Antony and Cleopatra, I, 2:9

SOOTHSAYER.[1] You shall be yet far fairer
than you are.

. . . . .

You shall be more beloving than belov'd.

. . . . .

You shall outlive the lady whom you serve.
CHARMIAN. O excellent! I love long life
better than figs.
Antony and Cleopatra, I, 2:16, 22, 31

[1] To CHARMIAN.

ANTONY. Say to me,
Whose fortunes shall rise higher, Caesar's or
mine?

. . . . .

SOOTHSAYER. If thou dost play with him[1]
at any game
Thou art sure to lose, and of that natural
luck,
He beats thee 'gainst the odds; thy lustre
thickens
When he shines by. I say again, thy spirit
Is all afraid to govern thee near him,
But he away, 't is noble.
Antony and Cleopatra, II, 3:16, 25

[1] OCTAVIUS CAESAR.

K. HENRY.[1] Come hither, England's hope.
If secret powers
Suggest but truth to my divining thoughts,
This pretty lad[2] will prove our country's
bliss.
His looks are full of peaceful majesty,
His head by nature fram'd to wear a crown,

His hand to wield a sceptre, and himself
Likely in time to bless a regal throne.
                                    III Henry VI, IV, 6:69

[1] To EARL OF RICHMOND, laying his hand upon his head. [2] lad: later King Henry VII, after overthrowing Richard III.

CRANMER. This royal infant, heaven still
    move about her!
Though in her cradle, yet now promises
Upon this land a thousand thousand bless-
    ings,
Which time shall bring to ripeness: she
    shall be,
But few now living can behold that good-
    ness,
A pattern to all princes living with her,
And all that shall succeed: Saba[1] was never
More covetous of wisdom and fair virtue
Than this pure soul shall be: all princely
    graces,
That mould up such a mighty piece as this
    is,
With all the virtues that attend the good,
Shall still[2] be doubled on her; truth shall
    nurse her;
Holy and heavenly thoughts still[2] counsel
    her;
She shall be lov'd and fear'd; her own shall
    bless her;
Her foes shake like a field of beaten corn,
And hang their heads with sorrow; good
    grows with her.
In her days every man shall eat in safety
Under his own vine what he plants; and sing
The merry songs of peace to all his neigh-
    bours.
God shall be truly known; and those about
    her
From her shall read the perfect ways of
    honour,
And by those claim their greatness, not by
    blood.
                                    Henry VIII, V, 5:18

[1] Saba: the queen of Sheba.   [2] still: always.

CRANMER [prophecy about ELIZABETH's
    successor]. Wherever the bright sun of
    heaven shall shine,
His honour and the greatness of his name
Shall be, and make new nations.
                                    Henry VIII, V, 5:51

GAUNT. Methinks I am a prophet new in-
    spir'd,
And thus expiring do foretell of him:[1]
His rash fierce blaze of riot cannot last,
For violent fires soon burn out themselves;
Small showers last long, but sudden storms
    are short;

He tires betimes[2] that spurts too fast be-
    times.[3]
                                    Richard II, II, 1:31
[1] him: KING RICHARD.   [2] betimes: soon.   [3] betimes: at an early hour.

CARLISLE. The blood of English shall ma-
    nure the ground
And future ages groan for this foul act;[1]
Peace shall go sleep with Turks and infidels,
And in this seat of peace tumultuous wars
Shall kin with kin and kind with kind con-
    found;
Disorder, horror, fear, and mutiny
Shall here inhabit, and this land be call'd
The field of Golgotha[2] and dead men's
    skulls.
                                    Richard II, IV, 1:137
[1] foul act: deposition of RICHARD.   [2] Golgotha:
a place of execution.

HASTINGS. O bloody Richard! miserable
    England!
I prophesy the fearfull'st time to thee
That ever wretched age hath look'd upon.
Come, lead me to the block; bear him my
    head:
They smile at me who shortly shall be dead.
                                    Richard III, III, 4:105

PROSPERO. What seest thou else
In the dark backward and abysm of time?
                                    Tempest, I, 2:49

GONZALO. I prophesied, if a gallows were
    on land,
This fellow could not drown.
                                    Tempest, V, 1:217

PROVERBS

ROSALIND. O! how full of briers is this
working-day world.
                                    As You Like It, I, 3:12

JAQUES. The 'why' is plain as way to par-
    ish church.
                                    As You Like It, II, 7:52

ROSALIND [reads]. Why, your godhead
    laid apart,
Warr'st thou with a woman's heart?
                                    As You Like It, IV, 3:43

DROMIO SYRACUSE. Every why hath a
wherefore.
                                    Comedy of Errors, II, 2:45

DROMIO SYRACUSE. Neither rhyme nor
reason.
                                    Comedy of Errors, II, 2:49

ANTIPHOLUS SYRACUSE. There's a time for all things.
Comedy of Errors, II, 2:66

ANTIPHOLUS EPHESUS. There's something in the wind.
Comedy of Errors, III, 1:69

DROMIO EPHESUS. We'll pluck a crow together.
Comedy of Errors, III, 1:83

HAMLET. By and by is easily said.
Hamlet, III, 2:404

HAMLET. A knavish speech sleeps in a foolish ear.
Hamlet, IV, 2:25

HAMLET. There's a special providence in the fall of a sparrow.
Hamlet, V, 2:230

WESTMORELAND. A rotten case abides no handling.
II Henry IV, IV, 1:161

LORD CHAMBERLAIN. Two women plac'd together makes cold weather.
Henry VIII, I, 4:22

ALBANY. Striving to better, oft we mar what's well.
King Lear, I, 4:369

ALBANY. Wisdom and goodness to the vile seem vile;
Filths savour[1] but themselves.
King Lear, IV, 2:38
[1] savour: smell.

NERISSA. They are as sick that surfeit with too much as they that starve with nothing.
Merchant of Venice, I, 2:6

LAUNCELOT GOBBO. It is a wise father that knows his own child.
Merchant of Venice, II, 2:80

GRATIANO. All things that are,
Are with more spirit chased than enjoy'd.
Merchant of Venice, II, 6:13

PORTIA. A light wife doth make a heavy[1] husband.
Merchant of Venice, V, 1:130
[1] heavy: sad.

MISTRESS FORD. We burn daylight.
Merry Wives of Windsor, II, 1:54

FORD. Better three hours too soon than a minute too late.
Merry Wives of Windsor, II, 2:327

DOGBERRY. They that touch pitch will be defiled.
Much Ado About Nothing, III, 3:61

QUEEN ELIZABETH. Pitchers have ears.
Richard III, II, 4:37

SECOND SERVANT. Marry, sir, 't is an ill cook that cannot lick his own fingers.
Romeo and Juliet, IV, 2:6

GREMIO. Our cake's dough on both sides.
Taming of the Shrew, I, 1:110

HORTENSIO. There's small choice in rotten apples.
Taming of the Shrew, I, 1:139

STEPHANO. He that dies pays all debts.
Tempest, III, 2:140

PANDARUS. He that will have a cake out of the wheat must needs tarry the grinding.
Troilus and Cressida, I, 1:14

SECOND OUTLAW. Make a virtue of necessity.
Two Gentlemen of Verona, IV, 1:62

PUNISHMENT

AEGEON. The pleasing punishment that women bear.
Comedy of Errors, I, 1:47

FIRST SERVANT. He was too hard for him directly, to say the truth on 't: before Corioli he scotched[1] him and notched him like a carbonado.[2]
SECOND SERVANT. An[3] he had been cannibally given, he might have broiled and eaten him too.
Coriolanus, IV, 5:195
[1] scotched: cut, slashed.   [2] carbonado: meat scored across.   [3] An: if.

ALBANY. This[1] shows you are above,
You justicers, that these our nether crimes
So speedily can venge!
King Lear, IV, 2:78
[1] This: death of CORNWALL.

CLAUDIO. Thus can the demi-god Authority
Make us pay down for our offence by weight.
. . . . .

LUCIO. Why, how now, Claudio! whence comes this restraint?

CLAUDIO. From too much liberty, my
Lucio, liberty:
As surfeit is the father of much fast,
So every scope by the immoderate use
Turns to restraint.
Measure for Measure, I, 2:124, 128

FALSTAFF. Since I plucked geese,[1] played
truant, and whipped top, I knew not what
't was to be beaten till lately.
Merry Wives of Windsor, V, 1:20
[1] plucked geese: pulling feathers from geese
was boyish mischief.

DOGBERRY. This plaintiff here, the offender, did call me ass: I beseech you, let it
be remembered in his punishment.
Much Ado About Nothing, V, 1:315

PURSE

HORATIO. His purse is empty already; all
's[1] golden words are spent.
Hamlet, V, 2:136
[1] 's: his.

FALSTAFF. We that take purses go by the
moon and the seven stars, and not by
Phoebus.[1]
1 Henry IV, I, 2:15
[1] Phoebus: the sun god.

ANTONIO. My purse, my person, my ex-
tremest means,
Lie all unlock'd to your occasions.
Merchant of Venice, I, 1:138

PAGE. There is either liquor in his pate or
money in his purse when he looks so merrily.
Merry Wives of Windsor, II, 1:198

BAGOT. Their love lies in their purses, and
whoso empties them
By so much fills their hearts with deadly
hate.
Richard II, II, 2:129

PETRUCHIO. Our purses shall be proud,
our garments poor:
For 't is the mind that makes the body rich.
Taming of the Shrew, IV, 3:173

PROTEUS. You have a quick wit.
SPEED. And yet it cannot overtake your
slow purse.
Two Gentlemen of Verona, I, 1:132

PYTHAGORAS

GRATIANO [to SHYLOCK]. O! be thou
damn'd, inexecrable dog,

And for thy life let justice be accus'd.
Thou almost mak'st me waver in my faith
To hold opinion with Pythagoras,
That souls of animals infuse themselves
Into the trunks of men: thy currish spirit
Govern'd a wolf, who, hang'd for human
slaughter,
Even from the gallows did his fell soul fleet,
And whilst thou lay'st in thy unhallow'd
dam,
Infus'd itself in thee; for thy desires
Are wolfish, bloody, starv'd, and ravenous.
Merchant of Venice, IV, 1:128

CLOWN. What is the opinion of Pythagoras concerning wild fowl?
MALVOLIO. That the soul of our grandam
might haply[1] inhabit a bird.
Twelfth Night, IV, 2:54
[1] haply: perchance.

QUARREL

POLONIUS. Beware
Of entrance to a quarrel, but being in,
Bear 't that the opposed may beware of
thee.
Hamlet, I, 3:66

FLUELLEN. I pray you to serve God, and
keep you out of prawls, and prabbles, and
quarrels, and dissensions, and I warrant you,
it is the better for you.
Henry V, IV, 8:68

CASSIUS. That you have wrong'd me doth
appear in this:
You have condemn'd and noted Lucius
Pella
For taking bribes here of the Sardians;
. . . . .

BRUTUS. Let me tell you, Cassius, you
yourself
Are much condemned to have an itching
palm;
To sell and mart your offices for gold
To undeservers.
CASSIUS. I an itching palm!
You know that you are Brutus that speak
this,
Or, by the gods, this speech were else your
last.
. . . . .

BRUTUS. Remember March, the ides of
March remember:
Did not great Julius bleed for justice' sake?
What villain touch'd his body, that did stab,
And not for justice? What! shall one of us,
That struck the foremost man of all this
world
But for supporting robbers, shall we now

Contaminate our fingers with base bribes,
And sell the mighty space of our large hon-
ours
For so much trash as may be grasped thus?
I had rather be a dog, and bay the moon,
Than such a Roman.
Julius Caesar, IV, 3:1, 9, 48

Cassius. Urge me no more, I shall forget
myself;
Have mind upon your health; tempt me no
further.

. . . . .

Brutus. Go show your slaves how chol-
eric you are,
And make your bondmen tremble. Must I
budge?
Must I observe you? Must I stand and
crouch
Under your testy humour? By the gods,
You shall digest the venom of your spleen,
Though it do split you; for from this day
forth
I 'll use you for my mirth, yea, for my
laughter,
When you are waspish.

. . . . .

There is no terror, Cassius, in your threats,
For I am arm'd so strong in honesty
That they pass by me as the idle wind,
Which I respect not. I did send to you
For certain sums of gold, which you denied
me;
For I can raise no money by vile means:
By heaven, I had rather coin my heart,
And drop my blood for drachmas, than to
wring
From the hard hands of peasants their vile
trash
By any indirection. I did send
To you for gold to pay my legions,
Which you denied me: was that done like
Cassius?
Should I have answer'd Caius Cassius so?
When Marcus Brutus grows so covetous,
To lock such rascal counters from his
friends,
Be ready, gods, with all your thunderbolts;
Dash him to pieces!

. . . . .

Cassius. A friend should bear his friend's
infirmities,
But Brutus makes mine greater than they
are.
Julius Caesar, IV, 3:35, 43, 66, 85

Cassius. Come, Antony, and young Oc-
tavius, come,
Revenge yourselves alone on Cassius,
For Cassius is aweary of the world;

Hated by one he loves; brav'd by his
brother;
Check'd like a bondman; all his faults observ'd,
Set in a note-book, learn'd, and conn'd by
rote,
To cast into my teeth.

. . . . .

Brutus. Sheathe your dagger:
Be angry when you will, it shall have scope;
Do what you will, dishonour shall be hu-
mour,
O Cassius! you are yoked with a lamb
That carries anger as the flint bears fire,
Who, much enforced, shows a hasty spark,
And straight is cold again.
Julius Caesar, IV, 3:93, 108

Brutus. O Cassius! I am sick of many
griefs.
Cassius. Of your philosophy you make
no use
If you give place to accidental evils.
Brutus. No man bears sorrow better:
Portia is dead.
Cassius. Ha! Portia!
Brutus. She is dead.
Cassius. How 'scap'd I killing when I
cross'd you so?
O insupportable and touching loss!

. . . . .

Brutus. Why, farewell, Portia. We must
die, Messala:
With meditating that she must die once,
I have the patience to endure it now.
Messala. Even so great men great losses
should endure.
Julius Caesar, IV, 3:145, 190

Brutus. The deep of night is crept upon
our talk,
And nature must obey necessity,
Which we will niggard with a little rest.
There is no more to say?

. . . . .

Cassius. O my dear brother!
This was an ill beginning of the night:
Never come such division 'tween our souls!
Let it not, Brutus.
Brutus. Every thing is well.
Cassius. Good night, my lord.
Brutus. Good night, good brother.
Julius Caesar, IV, 3:226, 234

Titania [to Oberon]. These are the
forgeries of jealousy:
And never, since the middle summer's
spring,
Met we on hill, in dale, forest, or mead,
By paved fountain, or by rushy brook,
Or in the beached margent of the sea,

To dance our ringlets[1] to the whistling wind,
But with thy brawls thou hast disturb'd our sport.

. . . . .

The spring, the summer,
The chiding autumn, angry winter, change
Their wonted liveries, and the mazed[2] world,
By their increase, now knows not which is which.
And this same progeny of evils comes
From our debate, from our dissension:
We are their parents and original.[3]
Midsummer Night's Dream, II, 1:81, 111
[1] ringlets: rings formed in dance of fairies.
[2] mazed: perplexed. [3] original: origin.

DON PEDRO. In the managing of quarrels you may say he[1] is wise; for either he avoids them with great discretion, or undertakes them with a most Christian-like fear.
Much Ado About Nothing, II, 3:197
[1] he: BENEDICK.

BENEDICK. In a false quarrel there is no true valour.
Much Ado About Nothing, V, 1:120

MERCUTIO. Thy head is as full of quarrels as an egg is full of meat, and yet thy head hath been beaten as addle[1] as an egg for quarrelling. Thou hast quarrelled with a man for coughing in the street, because he hath wakened thy dog that hath lain asleep in the sun. Didst thou not fall out with a tailor for wearing his new doublet before Easter? with another, for tying his new shoes with old riband? and yet thou wilt tutor me from quarrelling!
Romeo and Juliet, III, 1:24
[1] addle: in a morbid state.

FIRST SENATOR. Your words have took such pains as if they labour'd
To bring manslaughter into form, and set quarrelling
Upon the head of valour; which indeed
Is valour misbegot, and came into the world
When sects and factions were newly born.
Timon of Athens, III, 5:26

QUEEN

ANTONY. Fie, wrangling queen!
Whom every thing becomes, to chide, to laugh,
To weep; whose every passion fully strives
To make itself, in thee, fair and admir'd.
Antony and Cleopatra, I, 1:48

Q. MARGARET. To be a queen in bondage is more vile
Than is a slave in base servility;
For princes should be free.
1 Henry VI, V, 3:112

LADY GREY. And that is more than I will yield unto.
I know I am too mean to be your queen,
And yet too good to be your concubine.
III Henry VI, III, 2:96

OLD LADY. You would not be a queen?
ANNE. No, not for all the riches under heaven.
OLD LADY. 'T is strange: a three-pence bow'd[1] would hire me,
Old as I am, to queen it.
Henry VIII, II, 3:34
[1] bow'd: bent.

K. HENRY. That man i' the world who shall report he has
A better wife, let him in nought be trusted,
For speaking false in that: thou art, alone,
If thy rare qualities, sweet gentleness,
Thy meekness saint-like, wife-like government,
Obeying in commanding, and thy parts
Sovereign and pious else, could speak thee out,
The queen of earthly queens.
Henry VIII, II, 4:134

Q. ELIZABETH.[1] I had rather be a country servant maid
Than a great queen, with this condition,
To be so baited,[2] scorn'd and stormed at.
Richard III, I, 3:107
[1] Queen of EDWARD IV. [2] baited: taunted.

Q. MARGARET. Poor painted queen, vain flourish of my fortune!
Why strew'st thou sugar on that bottled spider,
Whose deadly web ensnareth thee about?
Richard III, I, 3:241

TROILUS. He[1] brought a Grecian queen,[2] whose youth and freshness
Wrinkles Apollo's, and makes stale the morning.
Why keep we her? the Grecians keep our aunt.[3]
Is she worth keeping? why, she is a pearl,
Whose price hath launch'd above a thousand ships,
And turn'd crown'd kings to merchants.
Troilus and Cressida, II, 2:78
[1] He: PARIS. [2] queen: HELEN. [3] aunt: KING PRIAM's sister.

PANDARUS. Fair be to you, my lord, and to all this fair company! fair desires, in all fair measure, fairly guide them! especially to you, fair queen! fair thoughts be your fair pillow!

Troilus and Cressida, III, 1:45

RABBLE

FIRST CITIZEN. He[1] himself stuck not to call us the many-headed multitude.

THIRD CITIZEN. We have been called so of many; not that our heads are some brown, some black, some auburn, some bald, but that our wits are so diversely coloured: and truly I think if all our wits were to issue out of one skull, they would fly east, west, north, south; and their consent of one direct way should be at once to all the points o' the compass.

Coriolanus, II, 3:17

[1] He: CORIOLANUS.

VOLUMNIA. 'T was you incens'd the rabble:
Cats, that can judge as fitly of his worth
As I can of those mysteries which heaven
Will not have earth to know.

Coriolanus, IV, 2:33

DUCHESS. Ah! Gloucester, teach me to forget myself;
For whilst I think I am thy married wife,
And thou a prince, protector of this land,
Methinks I should not thus be led along,
Mail'd up in shame, with papers on my back,
And follow'd with a rabble that rejoice
To see my tears and hear my deep-fet[1] groans.
The ruthless flint doth cut my tender feet,
And when I start, the envious people laugh
And bid me be advised how I tread.

II Henry VI, II, 4:27

[1] deep-fet: deep-fetched.

GONERIL. Your disorder'd rabble
Make servants of their betters.

King Lear, I, 4:278

RASCAL

BERTRAM [about PAROLLES]. What of him?
He's quoted[1] for a most perfidious slave,
With all the spots o' the world tax'd[2] and debosh'd;[3]
Whose nature sickens but to speak a truth.
Am I or that or[4] this for what he 'll utter,
That will speak any thing?

All's Well That Ends Well, V, 3:204

[1] quoted: written down. [2] tax'd: accused. [3] debosh'd: debased. [4] Or . . . or: either . . . or.

HAMLET. Yet I,
A dull and muddy-mettled rascal, peak,[1]
Like John-a-dreams,[2] unpregnant[3] of my cause.

Hamlet, II, 2:593

[1] peak: mope. [2] John-a-dreams: a dreamy, idle fellow. [3] unpregnant: not quickened in desire for revenge.

BOY. For Pistol, he hath a killing tongue and a quiet sword; by the means whereof a' breaks words, and keeps whole weapons. For Nym, he hath heard that men of few words are the best men; and therefore he scorns to say his prayers, lest a' should be thought a coward: but his few bad words are matched with as few good deeds; for a'[1] never broke any man's head but his own, and that was against a post when he was drunk. They will steal anything and call it purchase.

Henry V, III, 2:38

[1] a': he.

EMILIA. O heaven! that such companions thou 'dst unfold,
And put in every honest hand a whip
To lash the rascals naked through the world.

Othello, IV, 2:141

HECTOR. Art thou of blood and honour?
THERSITES. No, no; I am a rascal; a scurvy railing knave; a very filthy rogue.

Troilus and Cressida, V, 4:29

READING—WRITING

POSTHUMUS. Thither write, my queen,
And with mine eyes I 'll drink the words you send,
Though ink be made of gall.

Cymbeline, I, 1:99

CYMBELINE. O most delicate fiend!
Who is 't can read a woman? Is there more?
CORNELIUS. More, sir, and worse. She did confess she had
For you a mortal[1] mineral.

Cymbeline, V, 5:47

[1] mortal: deadly.

HAMLET. I once did hold it, as our statists do,
A baseness to write fair, and labour'd much
How to forget that learning.

Hamlet, V, 2:33

CAESAR. If my name were liable to fear,
I do not know the man I should avoid
So soon as that spare Cassius. He reads much;

He is a great observer, and he looks
Quite through the deeds of men.
                            Julius Caesar, I, 2:199

LADY MACBETH. Your face, my thane, is as
    a book where men
May read strange matters.
                            Macbeth, I, 5:64

DOGBERRY. To be a well-favoured[1] man
is the gift of fortune, but to write and read
comes by nature.

                    . . . . .

Well, for your favour, sir, why, give God
thanks, and make no boast of it; and for
your writing and reading, let that appear
when there is no need of such vanity.
        Much Ado About Nothing, III, 3:14, 20
[1] well-favoured: good looking.

REALITY

My mistress' eyes are nothing like the sun;
Coral is far more red than her lips' red:
If snow be white, why then her breasts are
    dun;
If hairs be wires, black[1] wires grow on her
    head.
I have seen roses damask'd,[2] red and white,
But no such roses see I in her cheeks;
And in some perfumes is there more delight
Than in the breath that from my mistress
    reeks.[3]
I love to hear her speak, yet well I know
That music hath a far more pleasing sound:
I grant I never saw a goddess go,
My mistress, when she walks, treads on the
    ground:
And yet, by heaven, I think my love as rare
As any she[4] belied with false compare.
                            Sonnet 130
[1] black: to Elizabethans, only blondes were
beautiful. [2] damask'd: mingled red and white.
[3] reeks: word used for rhyme. [4] she: woman.
This sonnet is a burlesque on exaggeration
about beauties.

REASON

HAMLET. Sure he that made us with such
    large discourse,
Looking before and after, gave us not
That capability and god-like reason
To fust[1] in us unus'd.
                            Hamlet, IV, 4:36
[1] fust: grow musty.

FALSTAFF. Give you a reason on compulsion! if reasons were as plenty as blackber-

ries I would give no man a reason upon
compulsion, I.
                            I Henry IV, II, 4:264

WARWICK. Who finds the heifer dead, and
    bleeding fresh,
And sees fast by a butcher with an axe,
But will suspect 't was he that made the
    slaughter?
Who finds the partridge in the puttock's[1]
    nest,
But may imagine how the bird was dead,
Although the kite soar with unbloodied
    beak?
Even so suspicious is this tragedy.
                            II Henry VI, III, 2:188
[1] puttock: bird of prey.

NORFOLK. I say again, there is no English
    soul
More stronger to direct you than yourself,
If with the sap of reason you would quench,
Or but allay, the fire of passion.
                            Henry VIII, I, 1:146

BANQUO. Were such things here as we do
    speak about?
Or have we eaten on the insane root
That takes the reason prisoner?
                            Macbeth, I, 3:83

BOTTOM. To say the truth, reason and
love keep little company together now-a-
days. The more the pity.
        Midsummer Night's Dream, III, 1:146

IAGO. If the balance of our lives had not
one scale of reason to poise another of sen-
suality, the blood and baseness of our natures would conduct us to most preposter-
ous conclusions; but we have reason to cool
our raging motions, our carnal stings, our
unbitted lusts.
                            Othello, I, 3:331

LUCETTA. I have no other but a woman's
    reason:
I think him so because I think him so.
        Two Gentlemen of Verona, I, 2:22

REBELLION

COUNTESS. And I beseech your majesty
    to make it
Natural rebellion, done i' the blaze of youth;
When oil and fire, too strong for reason's
    force,
O'erbears it and burns on.
        All's Well That Ends Well, V, 3:6

MENENIUS. There was a time when all
    the body's members

Rebell'd against the belly; thus accus'd it:
That only like a gulf it did remain
I' the midst o' the body, idle and unactive,
Still cupboarding the viand, never bearing
Like labour with the rest, where the other
    instruments
Did see and hear, devise, instruct, walk, feel,
And, mutually participate, did minister
Unto the appetite and affection common
Of the whole body.
Coriolanus, I, 1:99

CORIOLANUS. In soothing them we nour-
    ish 'gainst our senate
The cockle of rebellion, insolence, sedition,
Which we ourselves have plough'd for,
    sow'd and scatter'd.
Coriolanus, III, 1:69

K. HENRY. Never yet did insurrection
    want[1]
Such water-colours to impaint his cause;
Nor moody beggars, starving for a time
Of pell-mell havoc and confusion.
I Henry IV, V, 1:79
[1] want: lack.

SALISBURY. The king hath dispossess'd
    himself of us:
We will not line his thin bestained cloak
With our pure honours, nor attend the foot
That leaves the print of blood where'er it
    walks.
King John, IV, 3:23

MELUN. Fly, noble English; you are
    bought and sold;
Unthread the rude eye of rebellion.
And welcome home again discarded faith.
King John, V, 4:10

NORTHUMBERLAND. If then we shall shake
    off our slavish yoke,
Imp out[1] our drooping country's broken
    wing,
Redeem from broking pawn the blemish'd
    crown,
Wipe off the dust that hides our sceptre's
    gilt,
And make high majesty look like itself,
Away with me in post to Ravenspurgh.
Richard II, II, 1:291
[1] Imp out: supply with new feathers; a term of
falconry.

CALIBAN [singing]. No more dams I'll
    make for fish;
Nor fetch in firing
At requiring;
Nor scrape trencher, nor wash dish;
'Ban, 'Ban, Ca Caliban
Has a new master; get a new man.

Freedom, hey-day! hey-day, freedom!
Freedom! hey-day, freedom!
Tempest, II, 2:199

RECONCILIATION

PAGE. I hope we shall drink down all unkindness.
Merry Wives of Windsor, I, 1:203

O benefit of ill! now I find true
That better is by evil still made better;
And ruin'd love, when it is built anew,
Grows fairer than at first, more strong, far
    greater.
Sonnet 119

LUCENTIO. At last, though long, our jar-
    ring notes agree:
And time it is, when raging war is done,
To smile at scapes and perils overblown.
Taming of the Shrew, V, 2:1

RECOVERY

Ross. Things at the worst will cease, or
    else climb upward
To what they were before.
Macbeth, IV, 2:24

PROSPERO. A turn or two I'll walk
To still my beating mind.
Tempest, IV, 1:162

RELIEF

SILVIUS. Wherever sorrow is, relief would
    be:
If you do sorrow at my grief in love,
By giving love your sorrow and my grief
Were both extermin'd.
As You Like It, III, 5:86

RELIGION

HAMLET. He took my father grossly, full
    of bread,
With all his crimes broad blown, as flush as
    May;
And how his audit stands who knows save
    heaven?
But in our circumstance and course of
    thought
'T is heavy with him.
Hamlet, III, 3:80

HAMLET. O! such a deed
As from the body of contraction[1] plucks

The very soul, and sweet religion makes
A rhapsody of words.
                                    Hamlet, III, 4:45
[1] contraction: marriage contract.

K. HENRY. We are in God's hand,
  brother, not in theirs.
                                    Henry V, III, 6:178

K. HENRY. Every subject's soul is his
own. Therefore should every soldier in the
wars do as every sick man in his bed, wash
every mote out of his conscience; and dying so, death is to him advantage.
                                    Henry V, IV, 1:186

QUEEN. But all his[1] mind is bent to holi-
    ness,
To number Ave-Maries on his beads;
His champions are the prophets and apos-
    tles,
His weapons holy saws[2] of sacred writ,
His study is his tilt-yard, and his loves
Are brazen images of canoniz'd saints.
                                    II Henry VI, I, 3:58
[1] his: KING HENRY's.   [2] saws: sayings, proverbs.

WARWICK. As surely as my soul intends to
    live
With that dread King that took our state
    upon him
To free us from his father's wrathful curse.
                                    II Henry VI, III, 2:153

CRANMER. Love and meekness, lord,
Become a churchman better than ambition:
Win straying souls with modesty again,
Cast none away.
                                    Henry VIII, V, 3:62

PANDULPH. It is religion that doth make
    vows kept;
But thou hast sworn against religion.
                                    King John, III, 1:279

BASSANIO. In religion,
What damned error, but some sober brow
Will bless it and approve it with a text.
                                    Merchant of Venice, III, 2:77

CARLISLE. Many a time hath banish'd Nor-
    folk fought
For Jesu Christ in glorious Christian field,
Streaming the ensign of the Christian cross
Against black pagans, Turks, and Saracens;
And toil'd with works of war, retir'd him-
    self
To Italy; and there at Venice gave
His body to that pleasant country's earth,
And his pure soul unto his captain Christ,
Under whose colours he had fought so long.
                                    Richard II, IV, 1:92

K. EDWARD IV. I every day expect an
    embassage
From my Redeemer to redeem me hence;
And now in peace my soul shall part to
    heaven,
Since I have set my friends at peace on
    earth.
Rivers and Hastings, take each other's hand;
Dissemble not your hatred, swear your love.

                  . . . . .

Take heed you dally not before your king;
Lest he that is the supreme King of kings
Confound your hidden falsehood, and
    award
Either of you to be the other's end.
                                    Richard III, II, 1:3, 12

HECTOR. 'T is mad idolatry
To make the service greater than the god.
                                    Troilus and Cressida, II, 2:56

POLIXENES. O! then my blest blood turn
To an infected jelly, and my name
Be yok'd with his[1] that did betray the Best;
Turn then my freshest reputation to
A savour that may strike the dullest nostril
Where I arrive; and my approach be
    shunn'd.
Nay, hated too, worse than the great'st in-
    fection
That e'er was heard or read!
                                    Winter's Tale, I, 2:417
[1] his . . . Best: Judas Iscariot.

REMEMBRANCE

PRINCE. Thy ignomy sleep with thee in
    the grave,
But not remember'd in thy epitaph!
                                    I Henry IV, V, 4:100

DEMETRIUS. As the remembrance of an
    idle gaud[1]
Which in my childhood I did dote upon.
                                    Midsummer Night's Dream, IV, 1:171
[1] gaud: trinket.

K. RICHARD [to his QUEEN]. Join not
    with grief, fair woman, do not so,
To make my end too sudden: learn, good
    soul,
To think our former state a happy dream;
From which awak'd, the truth of what we
    are
Show us but this. I am sworn brother, sweet,
To grim Necessity; and he and I
Will keep a league till death.
                                    Richard II, V, 1:16

CAPULET. I have seen the day
That I have worn a visor, and could tell

A whispering tale in a fair lady's ear
Such as would please; 't is gone, 't is gone,
   't is gone.
     . . . . .

Nay, sit, nay, sit, good cousin Capulet,[1]
For you and I are past our dancing days.
     Romeo and Juliet, I, 5:23, 32
[1] Cousin Capulet, a relative, guest of the speaker.

When in the sessions of sweet silent thought
I summon up remembrance of things past,
I sigh the lack of many a thing I sought,
And with old woes new wail my dear time's
   waste:
Then can I drown an eye, unus'd to flow,
For precious friends hid in death's dateless
   night,
And weep afresh love's long since cancell'd
   woe,
And moan the expense of many a vanish'd
   sight:
Then can I grieve at grievances foregone,
And heavily from woe to woe tell o'er
The sad account of fore-bemoaned moan,
Which I new pay as if not paid before.
But if the while I think on thee, dear friend,
All losses are restor'd and sorrows end.
     Sonnet 30

Thou art the grave where buried love doth
   live,
Hung with the trophies of my lovers gone.
     Sonnet 31

Your monument shall be my gentle verse,
Which eyes not yet created shall o'er-read;
And tongues to be your being shall rehearse,
When all the breathers of this world are
   dead;
You still shall live, such virtue hath my pen,
Where breath most breathes, even in the
   mouths of men.
     Sonnet 81

REMORSE

COUNTESS. Ah! what sharp stings are in
   her mildest words.
   All's Well That Ends Well, III, 4:18

BERTRAM [about HELEN]. Thence it came
That she, whom all men prais'd, and whom
   myself,
Since I have lost, have lov'd, was in mine
   eye
The dust that did offend it.
   KING. Well excus'd:
That thou didst love her, strikes some
   scores away
From the great compt. But love, that comes
   too late,

Like a remorseful pardon slowly carried,
To the great sender turns a sour offence.
Crying, 'That's good that's gone.'
   All's Well That Ends Well, V, 3:52

KING. Oft our displeasures, to ourselves
   unjust,
Destroy our friends and after weep their
   dust:
Our own love waking cries to see what's
   done.
   All's Well That Ends Well, V, 3:63

ANTONY. My very hairs do mutiny, for
   the white
Reprove the brown for rashness, and they
   them
For fear and doting.
   Antony and Cleopatra, III, 11:13

K. HENRY. So shaken as we are, so wan
   with care,
Find we a time for frighted peace to pant,
And breathe short-winded accents of new
   broils
To be commenc'd in strands afar remote.[1]
     1 Henry IV, I, 1:1
[1] KING HENRY IV, the BOLINGBROKE of *King
Richard II*, frequently shows remorse for this
overthrow of RICHARD and his questionable
right to the throne.

CARDINAL.[1] O! torture me no more, I will
   confess.
Alive again? then show me where he is:
I'll give a thousand pound to look upon
   him.
He hath no eyes, the dust hath blinded
   them.
Comb down his hair; look! look! it stands
   upright,
Like lime-twigs[2] set to catch my winged
   soul.
     II Henry VI, III, 3:11
[1] Dying after the murder of GLOUCESTER.
[2] lime-twigs: branches smeared with cement
to catch birds.

LADY MACBETH. Stop up the access and
   passage to remorse,
That no compunctious visitings of nature
Shake my fell[1] purpose, nor keep peace between
The effect[2] and it!
     Macbeth, I, 5:45
[1] fell: cruel. [2] effect: the murder of DUNCAN.

MACBETH. To know my deed 't were best
   not know myself.
     Knocking within.
Wake Duncan with thy knocking! I would
   thou could'st!
     Macbeth, II, 2:73

K. Edward. My brother kill'd no man,
  his fault was thought,
And yet his punishment was bitter death.
Who sued to me for him? who, in my wrath,
Kneel'd at my feet, and bade me be advis'd?
Who spoke of brotherhood? who spoke of
  love?
Who told me how the poor soul did forsake
The mighty Warwick, and did fight for me?
Who told me, in the field at Tewksbury,
When Oxford had me down, he rescu'd me
And said, 'Dear brother, live, and be a king'?
Who told me, when we both lay in the field
Frozen almost to death, how he did lap me
Even in his garments; and did give himself,
All thin and naked, to the numb cold night?
All this from my remembrance brutish
  wrath
Sinfully pluck'd, and not a man of you
Had so much grace to put it in my mind.

. . . . .

O God! I fear thy justice will take hold
On me and you and mine and yours for this.
               Richard III, II, 1:104, 131
[1] About Clarence's death, which Edward had
ordered but revoked too late.

K. Richard. Look, what is done cannot
  be now amended:
Men shall deal unadvisedly sometimes,
Which after-hours give leisure to repent.
               Richard III, IV, 4:291

Alonso. O! it is monstrous; monstrous!
Methought the billows spoke and told me
  of it;
The winds did sing it to me; and the thun-
  der,
That deep and dreadful organ-pipe, pro-
  nounc'd
The name of Prosper: it did bass my tres-
  pass.
Therefore my son i' the ooze is bedded; and
I 'll seek him deeper than e'er plummet
  sounded,
And with him there lie mudded.
               Tempest, III, 3:96

Paulina. What's gone and what's past
  help
Should be past grief.
               Winter's Tale, III, 2:223

REPENTANCE

King. Try what repentance can: what
  can it not?
Yet what can it, when one can not repent?
               Hamlet, III, 3:65

Hamlet. Confess yourself to heaven;
Repent what 's past; avoid what is to come.
               Hamlet, III, 4:149

Falstaff. Well, I 'll repent, and that suddenly, while I am in some liking; I shall be
out of heart shortly, and then I shall have
no strength to repent.
               I Henry IV, III, 3:5

Portia. I never did repent for doing
  good,
Nor shall not now.
               Merchant of Venice, III, 4:10

Valentine. Who by repentance is not satisfied
Is nor[1] of heaven nor earth; for these are
  pleas'd.
By penitence the Eternal's wrath 's appeas'd.
            Two Gentlemen of Verona, V, 4:79
[1] nor . . . nor: neither . . . nor.

REPUTATION

Widow. Though my estate be fall'n, I was
  well born,
Nothing acquainted with these businesses;
And would not put my reputation now
In any staining act.
        All's Well That Ends Well, III, 7:4

Antony. My Octavia,
Read not my blemishes in the world's report,
I have not kept my square,[1] but that to
  come
Shall all be done by the rule.
          Antony and Cleopatra, II, 3:4
[1] kept . . . square: a clear record.

Lieutenant.[1] I do not know what witch-
  craft 's in him, but
Your soldiers use him as the grace fore
  meat,
Their talk at table, and their thanks at end;
And you are darken'd in this action, sir,
Even by your own.
               Coriolanus, IV, 7:2
[1] To Aufidius about Coriolanus.

Othello. The gravity and stillness of
  your youth
The world hath noted, and your name is
  great
In mouths of wisest censure:[1] what 's the
  matter,
That you unlace your reputation thus
And spend your rich opinion for the name
Of night-brawler?
               Othello, II, 3:191
[1] censure: judgment, not necessarily criticism.

Cassio. Reputation, reputation, reputation! O! I have lost my reputation. I have lost the immortal part of myself, and what remains is bestial. My reputation, Iago, my reputation!

Othello, II, 3:262

Iago. Reputation is an idle and most false imposition; oft got without merit, and lost without deserving: you have lost no reputation at all, unless you repute yourself such a loser.

Othello, II, 3:269

Mowbray. The purest treasure mortal times afford
Is spotless reputation; that away,
Men are but gilded loam or painted clay.

Richard II, I, 1:177

Achilles. My fame is shrewdly gor'd.
Patroclus. O! then beware;
Those wounds heal ill that men do give themselves.

Troilus and Cressida, III, 3:229

RESIGNATION

K. Lear. Give me the map there. Know that we have divided
In three our kingdom; and 't is our fast intent
To shake all cares and business from our age,
Conferring them on younger strengths, while we
Unburden'd crawl toward death.

King Lear, I, 1:38

Bolingbroke. Are you contented to resign the crown?
K. Richard. Ay, no; no, ay; for I must nothing be;
Therefore no no, for I resign to thee.

Richard II, IV, 1:200

Juliet. O! break, my heart; poor bankrupt, break at once!
To prison, eyes; ne'er look on liberty!
Vile earth, to earth resign; end motion here;
And thou and Romeo press one heavy bier!

Romeo and Juliet, III, 2:57

RESOLUTION

Antony. These strong Egyptian fetters I must break,
Or lose myself in dotage.

. . . . .

Would I had never seen her!
Enobarbus. O, sir! you had then left unseen a wonderful piece of work, which not to have been blessed withal would have discredited your travel.

Antony and Cleopatra, I, 2:120, 158

Coriolanus. Let them pull all about mine ears; present me
Death on the wheel, or at wild horses' heels;
Or pile ten hills on the Tarpeian rock,
That the precipitation might down stretch
Below the beam of sight; yet will I still
Be thus to them.

Coriolanus, III, 2:1

RESOURCES

K. Lear. What services canst thou do?
Kent. I can keep honest counsel, ride, run, mar a curious tale in telling it, and deliver a plain message bluntly; that which ordinary men are fit for, I am qualified in, and the best of me is diligence.
K. Lear. How old art thou?
Kent. Not so young, sir, to love a woman for singing, nor so old to dote on her for any thing.

King Lear, I, 4:33

Bianca. My books and instruments shall be my company,
On them to look and practise by myself.

Taming of the Shrew, I, 1:82

Titus. Come, and take choice of all my library,
And so beguile thy sorrow.

Titus Andronicus, IV, 1:34

RESPONSIBILITY

Bates. We know we are the king's subjects. If his cause be wrong, our obedience to the king wipes the crime of it out of us.
Williams. But if the cause be not good, the king himself hath a heavy reckoning to make; when all those legs and arms and heads, chopped off in a battle, shall join together at the latter day, and cry all 'We died at such a place.'

. . . . .

Now, if these men do not die well, it will be a black matter for the king that led them to it.

Henry V, IV, 1:136, 150

K. Henry [soliloquy]. Upon the king! let us our lives, our souls,
Our debts, our careful wives,

Our children, and our sins lay on the king!
We must bear all. O hard condition!
Twin-born with greatness, subject to the breath
Of every fool, whose sense no more can feel
But his own wringing. What infinite heart's ease
Must kings neglect that private men enjoy!
And what have kings that privates have not too,
Save ceremony, save general ceremony?
Henry V, IV, 1:247

REST

IACHIMO. The crickets sing, and man's o'er-labour'd sense
Repairs itself by rest.
Cymbeline, II, 2:12

HAMLET [to the GHOST]. Rest, rest, perturbed spirit.
Hamlet, I, 5:182

WORCESTER. For mine own part, I could be well content
To entertain the lag-end of my life
With quiet hours.
1 Henry IV, V, 1:23

WOLSEY. Nature does require
Her times of preservation, which perforce
I, her frail son, amongst my brethren mortal,
Must give my tendance to.
Henry VIII, III, 2:145

Q. KATHARINE. So may he[1] rest; his faults lie gently on him!
Henry VIII, IV, 2:31
[1] he: WOLSEY.

KENT. Oppress'd nature sleeps:
This rest might yet have balm'd thy broken sinews.
King Lear, III, 6:105

PORTIA. I will make haste; but till I come again,
No bed shall e'er be guilty of my stay,
Nor rest be interposer 'twixt us twain.
Merchant of Venice, III, 2:328

RESTRAINT

BERTRAM. I am commanded here, and kept[1] a coil with,—
'Too young,' and 'the next year,' and ''tis too early.'

. . . . .

I shall stay here the forehorse[2] to a smock,
Creaking my shoes on the plain masonry,
Till honour be bought up and no sword worn
But one to dance with. By heaven! I 'll steal away.
All's Well That Ends Well, II, 1:27, 30
[1] kept a coil: kept confused. [2] forehorse . . . smock: usher or attendant on ladies.

SHALLOW. Keep a gamester from the dice, and a good student from his book, and it is wonderful.
Merry Wives of Windsor, III, 1:38

Ross. My heart is great; but it must break with silence
Ere 't be disburden'd with a liberal tongue.
Richard II, II, 1:228

RETRIBUTION

MACBETH. This even-handed justice
Commends the ingredients of our poison'd chalice
To our own lips.
Macbeth, I, 7:10

LADY MACBETH [soliloquy]. Nought 's had, all 's spent,
Where our desire is got without content:
'T is safer to be that which we destroy
Than by destruction dwell in doubtful joy.
Enter MACBETH.
How now, my lord! why do you keep alone,
Of sorriest fancies your companions making,
Using those thoughts which should indeed have died
With them they think on? Things without all remedy
Should be without regard: what 's done is done.
MACBETH. We have scotch'd the snake, not kill'd it:
She 'll close and be herself, whilst our poor malice
Remains in danger of her former tooth.
But let the frame of things disjoint, both the worlds suffer,
Ere we will eat our meal in fear, and sleep
In the affliction of these terrible dreams
That shake us nightly. Better be with the dead,
Whom we, to gain our peace, have sent to peace,
Than on the torture of the mind to lie
In restless ecstasy. Duncan is in his grave;
After life's fitful fever he sleeps well;
Treason has done his worst: nor steel, nor poison,

Malice domestic, foreign levy, nothing
Can touch him further!
Macbeth, III, 2:5

BUCKINGHAM [on the way to his execu-
tion]. That high All-Seer which I dal-
lied with
Hath turn'd my feigned prayer on my head,
And given in earnest what I begg'd in jest.
Thus doth he force the swords of wicked
men
To turn their own points on their masters'
bosoms: . . .
Come, lead me, officers, to the block of
shame;
Wrong hath but wrong, and blame the due
of blame.
Richard III, V, 1:20

RICHMOND. The day is ours, the bloody
dog is dead.
STANLEY. Courageous Richmond, well
hast thou acquit thee.
Lo! here, this long-usurped royalty
From the dead temples of this bloody
wretch
Have I pluck'd off, to grace thy brows
withal.[1]
Richard III, V, 5:2

[1] withal: with it.

REVELS

ANTONY. Let 's have one other gaudy
night: call to me
All my sad captains; fill our bowls once
more;
Let 's mock the midnight bell.
Antony and Cleopatra, III, 13:183

HAMLET. The king doth wake to-night
and takes his rouse,
Keeps wassail,[1] and the swaggering up-
spring[2] reels;
And as he drains his draughts of Rhenish
down,
The kettle-drum and trumpet thus bray out
The triumph of his pledge.
Hamlet, I, 4:8

[1] wassail: drinking bout. [2] up-spring: a dance.

PLAYER KING. Where joy most revels grief
doth most lament,
Grief joys, joy grieves, on slender accident.
Hamlet, III, 2:208

REVENGE

HAMLET [to his father's GHOST]. Haste
me to know 't, that I with wings as
swift

As meditation or the thoughts of love,
May sweep to my revenge.
Hamlet, I, 5:29

HAMLET. They[1] bear the mandate;[2] they
must sweep my way,
And marshall me to knavery. Let it work;
For 't is the sport to have the enginer
Hoist with his own petar:[3] an 't shall go hard
But I will delve one yard below their mines,
And blow them at the moon.
Hamlet, III, 4:203

[1] They: ROSENCRANTZ and GUILDENSTERN, the
KING's spies on HAMLET. [2] mandate: the
KING's order that HAMLET shall be killed;
HAMLET has substituted an order that the two
spies shall be executed. [3] petar: bomb.

ANTONY [soliloquy]. And Caesar's spirit,
ranging for revenge,
With Ate[1] by his side come hot from hell,
Shall in these confines with a monarch's
voice
Cry 'Havoc!' and let slip the dogs of war.
Julius Caesar, III, 1:270

[1] Ate: goddess of mischief.

GLOUCESTER. All ports I 'll bar; the vil-
lain[1] shall not 'scape;
The duke must grant me that: besides, his
picture
I will send far and near, that all the kingdom
May have due note of him.
King Lear, II, 1:82

[1] villain: his loyal son, EDGAR, whom his bastard
son, EDMUND, has falsely accused of plotting
against their father.

LEAR. You see me here, you gods, a poor
old man,
As full of grief as age; wretched in both!
If it be you that stirs these daughters' hearts
Against their father, fool me not so much
To bear it tamely; touch me with noble
anger,
And let not women's weapons, water-drops,
Stain my man's cheeks! No, you unnatural
hags,
I will have such revenges on you both
That all the world shall—I will do such
things,
What they are yet I know not, but they
shall be
The terrors of the earth. You think I 'll
weep;
No, I 'll not weep:
I have full cause of weeping, but this heart
Shall break into a hundred thousand flaws[1]
Or ere I 'll weep. O fool! I shall go mad.
King Lear, II, 4:275

[1] flaws: fragments.

MACDUFF. O! I could play the woman
with mine eyes,

And braggart with my tongue. But, gentle
   heavens
Cut short all intermission; front to front
Bring thou this fiend of Scotland and my-
   self;
Within my sword's length set him; if he
   'scape,
Heaven forgive him too!
                                    Macbeth, IV, 3:230

SALANIO. Never did I know
A creature, that did bear the shape of man,
So keen and greedy to confound[1] a man.
                       Merchant of Venice, III, 2:277
[1] confound: ruin, destroy.

MISTRESS PAGE [about FALSTAFF]. Why,
I 'll exhibit a bill in the parliament for the
putting down of men. How shall I be revenged on him? for revenged I will be, as
sure as his guts are made of puddings.
                            . . . . .

MISTRESS FORD. I would have sworn his
disposition would have gone to the truth
of his words; but they do no more adhere
and keep place together than the Hundredth
Psalm to the tune of 'Green Sleeves.'[1] What
tempest, I trow, threw this whale, with so
many tuns of oil in his belly, ashore at Windsor? How shall I be revenged on him?
           Merry Wives of Windsor, II, 1:29, 60
[1] 'Green Sleeves': a popular song sometimes still
heard.

OTHELLO. O! that the slave had forty
   thousand lives;
One is too poor, too weak for my revenge.
                                       Othello, III, 3:442

TAMORA. I am Revenge, sent from the infernal kingdom.
To ease the gnawing vulture of thy mind,
By working wreakful vengeance on thy
   foes.
                          Titus Andronicus, V, 2:30

HECTOR. The reasons you allege do more
   conduce
To the hot passion of distemper'd blood
Than to make up a free determination
'Twixt right and wrong; for pleasure and
   revenge
Have ears more deaf than adders to the
   voice
Of any true decision.
                    Troilus and Cressida, II, 2:168

REVERENCE

BELARIUS. Though mean and mighty, rot-
   ting
Together, have one dust, yet reverence,

That angel of the world, doth make distinction
Of place 'tween high and low. Our foe was
   princely,
And though you took his life, as being our
   foe,
Yet bury him as a prince.
                                 Cymbeline, IV, 2:246

ANTONY. But yesterday the word of Caesar might
Have stood against the world; now lies he
   there,
And none so poor to do him reverence.
                               Julius Caesar, III, 2:123

LUCIO [to ISABELLA]. I hold you as a
   thing ensky'd and sainted;
By your renouncement an immortal spirit,
And to be talked with in sincerity,
As with a saint.
                      Measure for Measure, I, 4:34

REWARD

FALSTAFF. I 'll follow, as they say, for reward. He that rewards me, God reward
him! If I do grow great, I 'll grow less; for
I 'll purge, and leave sack, and live cleanly,
as a nobleman should do.
                                  I Henry IV, V, 4:167

HELICANUS. A fire from heaven came and
   shrivell'd up
Their bodies, even to loathing.
                            . . . . .
And yet but just; for though
This king were great, his greatness was no
   guard
To bar heaven's shaft, but sin had his[1] reward.
                                    Pericles, II, 4:9, 14
[1] his: its.

FIRST MURDERER. Where 's thy conscience
now?
SECOND MURDERER. In the Duke of Gloucester's purse.
FIRST MURDERER. So when he opens his
purse to give us our reward, thy conscience
flies out.
                                 Richard III, I, 4:130

RHETORIC

TOUCHSTONE. Then learn this of me: to
have, is to have; for it is a figure in rhetoric,
that drink, being poured out of a cup into a
glass, by filling the one doth empty the
other.
                            As You Like It, V, 1:44

K. Henry. This man so complete,
Who was enroll'd 'mongst wonders, and
    when we,
Almost with ravish'd listening, could not
    find
His hour of speech a minute.
                                    Henry VIII, I, 2:118

RICHES

Hamlet. Spacious in the possession of
dirt.
                                    Hamlet, V, 2:89

Bastard. Well, whiles I am a beggar, I will
    rail
And say there is no sin but to be rich;
And being rich, my virtue then shall be
To say there is no vice but beggary.
                                    King John, II, 1:593

France. Fairest Cordelia, that art most
    rich, being poor;
Most choice, forsaken; and most lov'd, de-
    spis'd!
                                    King Lear, I, 1:253

Duke. If thou art rich, thou'rt poor;
For, like an ass whose back with ingots
    bows,
Thou bear'st thy heavy riches but a journey,
And death unloads thee.
                                    Measure for Measure, III, 1:25

Iago. Poor and content is rich and rich
    enough,
But riches fineless[1] is as poor as winter
To him that ever fears he shall be poor.
                                    Othello, III, 3:172

[1] fineless: endless.

But, poorly rich, so wanteth in his store,
That, cloy'd with much, he pineth still for
    more.
                                    Rape of Lucrece: 97

Juliet. Conceit,[1] more rich in matter than
    in words,
Brags of his substance, not of ornament:
They are but beggars that can count their
    worth;
But my true love is grown to such excess
I cannot sum up half my sum of wealth.
                                    Romeo and Juliet, II, 6:30

[1] Conceit: thought.

Flavius. My dearest lord, bless'd, to be
    most accurs'd,
Rich, only to be wretched, thy great for-
    tunes
Are made thy chief afflictions.
                                    Timon of Athens, IV, 2:42

RIDICULE

Mercutio. Romeo! humours! madman!
    passion! lover!
Appear thou in the likeness of a sigh;
Speak but one rhyme and I am satisfied;
Cry but 'Ay me!' pronounce but 'love' and
    'dove';
Speak to my gossip Venus one fair word,
One nickname for her purblind[1] son and
    heir,
Young Adam Cupid, he that shot so trim
When King Cophetua lov'd the beggar-
    maid.
He heareth not, he stirreth not, he moveth
    not;
The ape is dead, and I must conjure him.
                                    Romeo and Juliet, II, 1:7
[1] purblind: partly or wholly blind.

Anne. Corrupt, corrupt, and tainted in
    desire!
About him, fairies, sing a scornful rhyme
And, as you trip, still[1] pinch him to your
    time.
                                    Merry Wives of Windsor, V, 5:94
[1] still . . . time: keep pinching him in time
with your song.

RING

Portia. This house, these servants, and
    this same myself
Are yours, my lord. I give them with this
    ring;
Which when you part from, lose, or give
    away,
Let it presage the ruin of your love,
And be my vantage to exclaim on you.

                    . . . . .

Bassanio. But when this ring
Parts from this finger, then parts life from
    hence:
O! then be bold to say Bassanio's dead.
                                    Merchant of Venice, III, 2:172, 185

Bassanio. Sweet Portia,
If you did know to whom I gave the ring,
If you did know for whom I gave the ring,
And would conceive for what I gave the
    ring,
And how unwillingly I left the ring,
When nought would be accepted but the
    ring,
You would abate the strength of your dis-
    pleasure.
Portia. If you had known the virtue of
    the ring,
Or half her worthiness that gave the ring,
Or your own honour to contain the ring,

You would not then have parted with the ring.

. . . . .

BASSANIO. Pardon me, good lady,
For, by these blessed candles of the night,
Had you been there, I think you would have begg'd
The ring of me to give the worthy doctor.
PORTIA. Let not that doctor e'er come near my house.
Since he hath got the jewel that I lov'd,
And that which you did swear to keep for me,
I will become as liberal as you;
I 'll not deny him any thing I have;
No, not my body, nor my husband's bed.
                    Merchant of Venice, V, 1:192, 219

ANTONIO. I once did lend my body for his wealth,
Which, but for him that had your husband's ring,
Had quite miscarried: I dare be bound again,
My soul upon the forfeit, that your lord
Will never more break faith advisedly.
PORTIA. Then you shall be his surety. Give him this,
And bid him keep it better than the other.
ANTONIO. Here, Lord Bassanio; swear to keep this ring.
BASSANIO. By heaven! it is the same I gave the doctor.
                    Merchant of Venice, V, 1:249

RISK

HOTSPUR. Were it good
To set the exact wealth of all our states
All at one cast? to set so rich a main
On the nice[1] hazard of one doubtful hour?
It were not good; for therein should we read
The very bottom and the soul of hope,
The very list, the very utmost bound
Of all our fortunes.
                    1 Henry IV, IV, 1:45
[1] nice: precarious.

CASSIUS. Why now, blow wind, swell billow, and swim bark!
The storm is up, and all is on the hazard.
                    Julius Caesar, V, 1:67

RIVAL

CLEOPATRA [as she hears that ANTONY has married OCTAVIA in Rome]. Lead me from hence;
I faint: O Iras! Charmian! 'T is no matter.

Go to the fellow, good Alexas; bid him
Report the feature of Octavia, her years,
Her inclinations, let him not leave out
The colour of her hair: bring me word quickly.
                    Exit ALEXAS.
Let him for ever go:—let him not—Charmian!
Though he be painted one way like a Gorgon,[1]
The other way 's a Mars.
                    To MARDIAN.
Bid you Alexas
Bring me word how tall she is. Pity me, Charmian,
But do not speak to me. Lead me to my chamber.
                    Antony and Cleopatra, II, 5:109
[1] Gorgons: three sisters whose appearance was so terrible that gazers were turned to stone.

[A messenger reports about OCTAVIA.]
CLEOPATRA. Is she as tall as me?
MESSENGER. She is not, madam.
CLEOPATRA. Didst hear her speak? is she shrill-tongued or low?
MESSENGER. Madam, I heard her speak; she is low-voiced.
CLEOPATRA. That 's not so good. He cannot like her long.
CHARMIAN. Like her! O Isis! 't is impossible.
CLEOPATRA. I think so, Charmian: dull of tongue, and dwarfish!
What majesty is in her gait? Remember,
If e'er thou look'dst on majesty.
MESSENGER. She creeps;
Her motion and her station are as one;
She shows a body rather than a life,
A statue than a breather.
CLEOPATRA. Is this certain?
MESSENGER. Or I have no observance.
CHARMIAN. Three in Egypt
Cannot make better note.
CLEOPATRA. He 's very knowing,
I do perceive 't. There 's nothing in her yet.
The fellow has good judgment.
CHARMIAN. Excellent.
CLEOPATRA. Guess at her years, I prithee,
MESSENGER. Madam,
She was a widow,—
CLEOPATRA. Widow! Charmian, hark.
MESSENGER. And I do think she 's thirty.
CLEOPATRA. Bear'st thou her face in mind? is 't long or round?
MESSENGER. Round even to faultiness.
CLEOPATRA. For the most part, too, they are foolish that are so.
Her hair, what colour?
MESSENGER. Brown, madam; and her forehead
As low as she would wish it.
CLEOPATRA. There 's gold for thee:

Thou must not take my former sharpness
   ill.
I will employ thee back again; I find thee
Most fit for business. Go make thee ready;
Our letters are prepar'd.
        Antony and Cleopatra, III, 3:14

  HOTSPUR. My name is Harry Percy.
  PRINCE. Why, then I see
A very valiant rebel of that name.
I am the Prince of Wales; and think not,
   Percy,
To share with me in glory any more;
Two stars keep not their motion in one
   sphere;
Nor can one England brook a double reign,
Of Harry Percy and the Prince of Wales.
        1 Henry IV, V, 4:61

Tell me thou lov'st elsewhere; but in my
   sight,
Dear heart, forbear to glance thine eye
   aside;
What need'st thou wound with cunning,
   when thy might
Is more than my o'er-press'd defence can
   bide?
        Sonnet 139

RIVER

  EVANS. To shallow rivers, to whose falls
Melodious birds sing madrigals.
        Merry Wives of Windsor, III, 1:17

  TITANIA. The winds, piping to us in vain,
As in revenge, have suck'd up from the sea
Contagious fogs; which falling in the land
Have every pelting river made so proud,
That they have overborne their continents.
        Midsummer Night's Dream, II, 1:88

ROGUE

  BERTRAM. Damnable both-sides rogue.
        All's Well That Ends Well, IV, 3:251

  HAMLET. O! what a rogue and peasant
   slave am I.
        Hamlet, II, 2:576

  FALSTAFF. An[1] 't were not as good a deed
as drink to turn true man and to leave these
rogues, I am the veriest varlet that ever
chewed with a tooth.
        1 Henry IV, II, 2:25
[1] An: if.

  MISTRESS QUICKLY. Ah! thou honey-
suckle villain! wilt thou kill God's officers
and the king's? Ah! thou honey-seed[1] rogue!

thou art a honey-seed, a man-queller;[2] and a
woman-queller.
        II Henry IV, II, 1:56
[1] honey-seed: MISTRESS QUICKLY's blunder for
homicide.   [2] queller: killer.

  KENT. Draw, you rogue; for though it be
night, yet the moon shines; I 'll make a sop
o' the moonshine of you.
        King Lear, II, 2:33

ROMAN

  CYMBELINE. Till the injurious Romans
   did extort
This tribute from us, we were free; Caesar's
   ambition
Which swell'd so much that it did almost
   stretch
The sides o' the world, against all colour
   here
Did put the yoke upon 's; which to shake off
Becomes a war-like people.
        Cymbeline, III, 1:48

  CASSIUS. Romans now
Have thews[1] and limbs like to their ancestors;
But, woe the while! our fathers' minds are
   dead,
And we are govern'd with our mothers'
   spirits;
        Julius Caesar, I, 3:80
[1] thews: physical strength.

  BRUTUS. Now, as you are a Roman, tell
   me true.
  MESSALA. Then like a Roman bear the
   truth I tell:
        Julius Caesar, IV, 3:187

  BRUTUS.[1] The last of all the Romans, fare
   thee well!
It is impossible that ever Rome
Should breed thy fellow.[2] Friends, I owe
   more tears
To this dead man than you shall see me pay.
I shall find time, Cassius, I shall find time.
        Julius Caesar, V, 3:99
[1] Speaking as he finds the body of CASSIUS.
[2] fellow: equal.

ROME

  CLEOPATRA. Sink Rome, and their tongues
   rot
That speak against us! A charge we bear i'
   the war,
And, as the president of my kingdom, will
Appear there for a man. Speak not against it.
        Antony and Cleopatra, III, 7:16

CORIOLANUS. Keep Rome in safety, and the chairs of justice
Supplied with worthy men! plant love among us!
Throng our large temples with the shows of peace,
And not our streets with war!
Coriolanus, III, 3:34

SECOND CAPTAIN. Lay hands on him; a dog!
A leg of Rome shall not return to tell
What crows have peck'd them here.
Cymbeline, V, 3:91

TITANIUS. The sun of Rome is set. Our day is gone;
Clouds, dews, and dangers come; our deeds are done.
Julius Caesar, V, 3:63

SATURNIUS. Rome, be as just and gracious unto me
As I am confident and kind to thee.
Titus Andronicus, I, 1:60

ROSE

DON JOHN. I had rather be a canker in a hedge than a rose in his grace.
Much Ado About Nothing, I, 3:28

OTHELLO. When I have pluck'd the rose,
I cannot give it vital growth again,
It needs must wither.
Othello, V, 2:13

JULIET. That which we call a rose
By any other name would smell as sweet.
Romeo and Juliet, II, 2:43

RUIN

KING. For you have seen him open 't. Read o'er this;[1]
Giving him papers.
And after, this; and then to breakfast with
What appetite you have.
Henry VIII, III, 2:201
[1] this: a paper showing WOLSEY's duplicity.

WOLSEY. I have touch'd the highest point of all my greatness;
And from that full meridan of my glory
I haste now to my setting: I shall fall
Like a bright exhalation in the evening,
And no man see me more.
Henry VIII, III, 2:223

SHYLOCK. Thou but offend'st thy lungs to speak so loud:

Repair thy wit, good youth, or it will fall
To cureless ruin.
Merchant of Venice, IV, 1:140

K. RICHARD. They break their faith to God as well as us:
Cry woe, destruction, ruin, loss, decay;
The worst is death, and death will have his day.
Richard II, III, 2:101

K. RICHARD. All the ruins of distressful times
Repair'd with double riches of content.
What! we have many goodly days to see;
The liquid drops of tears that you have shed
Shall come again, transform'd to orient pearl.
Richard III, IV, 4:318

RUMOUR

Enter RUMOUR, *painted full of tongues.*
Open your ears; for which of you will stop
The vent of hearing when loud Rumour speaks?
I, from the orient to the drooping west,
Making the wind my post-horse, still unfold
The acts commenced on this ball of earth:
Upon my tongues continual slanders ride,
The which in every language I pronounce,
Stuffing the ears of men with false reports.
I speak of peace, while covert enmity
Under the smile of safety wounds the world:
. . . . .
Rumour is a pipe
Blown by surmises, jealousies, conjectures,
And of so easy and so plain a stop
That the blunt monster with uncounted heads,
The still-discordant wavering multitude.
II Henry IV, Induction: 1, 15

WARWICK. Rumour doth double, like the voice and echo.
The numbers of the fear'd.
II Henry IV, III, 1:97

MESSENGER. This from rumour's tongue
I idly heard; if true or false I know not.
King John, IV, 2:123

HUBERT. My lord, they say five moons were seen to-night;
Four fixed, and the fifth did whirl about
The other four in wondrous motion.
K. JOHN. Five moons!
HUBERT. Old men and beldams[1] in the streets

Do prophesy upon it dangerously:
Young Arthur's death is common in their
  mouths;
And when they talk of him, they shake their
  heads
And whisper one another in the ear;
And he that speaks doth gripe the hearer's
  wrist,
Whilst he that hears makes fearful action,
With wrinkled brows, with nods, with roll-
  ing eyes.
I saw a smith stand with his hammer, thus,
The whilst his iron did on the anvil cool,
With open mouth swallowing a tailor's
  news;
Who, with his shears and measure in his
  hand,
Standing on slippers, which his nimble haste
Had falsely thrust upon contrary feet,
Told of a many thousand war-like French,
That were embattailed and rank'd in Kent.
Another lean unwash'd artificer
Cuts off his tale and talks of Arthur's death.
King John, IV, 2:182
¹ beldams: a term of contempt for old women.

Ross. I dare not speak much further;
But cruel are the times, when we are traitors
And do not know ourselves, when we hold
  rumour
From what we fear, yet know not what we
  fear.
Macbeth, IV, 2:18

RUTHLESSNESS

MACBETH [aside]. Time, thou anticipat'st
  my dread exploits;
The flighty purpose never is o'ertook
Unless the deed go with it; from this mo-
  ment
The very firstlings of my heart shall be
The firstlings of my hand. And even now,
To crown my thoughts with acts, be it
  thought and done:
The castle of Macduff I will surprise;
Seize upon Fife; give to the edge o' the
  sword
His wife, his babes, and all unfortunate souls
That trace him in his line. No boasting like
  a fool;
This deed I 'll do before this purpose cool.
Macbeth, IV, 1:144

GLOUCESTER.¹ Talk'st thou to me of 'ifs'?
  Thou² art a traitor:
Off with his head! now, by Saint Paul I
  swear,
I will not dine until I see the same.
Richard III, III, 4:77
¹ Later, RICHARD III.   ² Thou: HASTINGS.

SACK

FALSTAFF. A good sherris-sack hath a two-
fold operation in it. It ascends me into the
brain; dries me there all the foolish and dull
and crudy vapours which environ it; makes
it apprehensive, quick, forgetive, full of
nimble, fiery and delectable shapes; which,
delivered o'er to the voice, the tongue,
which is the birth, becomes excellent wit.

. . . . .

If I had a thousand sons, the first human
principle I would teach them should be, to
forswear thin potations and to addict themselves to sack.
II Henry IV, IV, 3:104, 132

TRINCULO. Why, thou deboshed fish thou,
was there ever man a coward that hath
drunk so much sack as I to-day?
Tempest, III, 2:28

SADNESS

ORLANDO. If I be foiled, there is but one
shamed that was never gracious; if killed,
but one dead that is willing to be so. I shall
do my friends no wrong, for I have none to
lament me; the world no injury, for in it I
have nothing; only in the world I fill up a
place, which may be better supplied when I
have made it empty.
As You Like It, I, 2:199

ABBESS. Hath he not lost much wealth by
  wreck of sea?
Buried some dear friend? Hath not else his
  eye
Stray'd his affection in unlawful love?
A sin prevailing much in youthful men,
Who give their eyes the liberty of gazing.
Comedy of Errors, V, 1:49

BENVOLIO. What sadness lengthens Romeo's hours?
ROMEO. Not having that, which, having,
  makes them short.
Romeo and Juliet, I, 1:169

PROSPERO. Let us not burden our remem-
  brance with
A heaviness that 's gone.
Tempest, V, 1:198

SAFETY

HOTSPUR [reading a letter]. *The purpose
you undertake is dangerous;—*
why, that 's certain: 't is dangerous to take a
cold, to sleep, to drink; but I tell you, my

lord fool, out of this nettle, danger, we
pluck this flower, safety.
I Henry IV, II, 3:8

BOY. Would I were in an alehouse in London! I would give all my fame for a pot of
ale, and safety.
Henry V, III, 2:12

Q. MARGARET. The duke is made protec-
tor of the realm;
And yet shalt thou be safe? such safety finds
The trembling lamb environed with
wolves.
III Henry VI, I, 1:240

GONZALO. Now would I give a thousand
furlongs of sea for an acre of barren ground;
long heath, brown furze, any thing. The
wills above be done! but I would fain die a
dry death.
Tempest, I, 1:68

SAIL

CHORUS. Behold the threaden sails,
Borne with the invisible and creeping wind,
Draw the huge bottoms through the fur-
row'd sea,
Breasting the lofty surge.
Henry V, III, Prologue: 10

FIRST WITCH. But in a sieve I 'll thither
sail,
And, like[1] a rat without a tail,
I 'll do, I 'll do, and I 'll do.
Macbeth, I, 3:8
[1] like . . . tail: in the guise of.

TITANIA. When we have laugh'd to see the
sails conceive
And grow big-bellied with the wanton
wind;
Midsummer Night's Dream, II, 1:128

ROMEO. As is a winged messenger of
heaven
Unto the white-upturned wond'ring eyes
Of mortals, that fall back to gaze on him
When he bestrides the lazy-pacing clouds,
And sails upon the bosom of the air.
Romeo and Juliet, II, 2:28

NESTOR. In the reproof[1] of chance
Lies the true proof of men: the sea being
smooth,
How many shallow bauble boats dare sail
Upon her patient breast, making their way
With those of nobler bulk!
Troilus and Cressida, I, 3:33
[1] reproof: refutation.

SAINT

CHAMBERLAIN. I know thou worshippest
Saint Nicholas[1] as truly as a man of falsehood may.
I Henry IV, II, 1:71
[1] Saint Nicholas: the patron saint of scholars;
highwaymen were sometimes called "St. Nicholas' clerks."

BASTARD. Saint George, that swing'd the
dragon and e'er since
Sits on his horse back at mine hostess' door.
King John, II, 1:288

Q. MARGARET. Earth gapes, hell burns,
fiends roar, saints pray,
To have him suddenly convey'd from hence.
Richard III, IV, 4:75

RICHMOND. The prayers of holy saints
and wronged souls,
Like high-rear'd bulwarks, stand before our
faces;
Richard III, V, 3:241

SARCASM

CELIA. How prove you that, in the great
heap of your knowledge?
ROSALIND. Ay, marry: now unmuzzle
your wisdom.
As You Like It, I, 2:72

TOUCHSTONE. It is the first time that ever
I heard breaking of ribs was sport for ladies.
As You Like It, I, 2:145

FALSTAFF. Well said, good woman's tailor!
well said, courageous Feeble! Thou wilt be
as valiant as the wrathful dove or most magnanimous mouse.
II Henry IV, III, 2:169

Q. ELINOR [to PRINCE ARTHUR, heir to
the crown]. Come to thy grandam,
child.
CONSTANCE. Do, child, go to it[1] grandam,
child;
Give grandam kingdom, and it grandam
will
Give it a plum, a cherry, and a fig:
There 's a good grandam.
King John, II, 1:154
[1] it: its; the possessive pronoun *its* is seldom
found in Shakespeare. Note that *his* often takes
its place.

DUKE. Hast thou or[1] word, or wit, or impudence,
That yet can do thee office?
Measure for Measure, V, 1:368
[1] or . . . or: either . . . or.

BEATRICE. I pray you, how many hath he killed and eaten in these wars? But how many hath he killed? for indeed I promised to eat all of his killing.
Much Ado About Nothing, I, 1:43

DON PEDRO. Lady, will you walk about with your friend?
HERO. So you walk softly[1] and look sweetly and say nothing, I am yours for the walk; and especially when I walk away.
Much Ado About Nothing, II, 1:90
[1] softly: leisurely.

OTHELLO [to officers coming to arrest him]. Keep up your bright swords, for the dew will rust them.
Good signior, you shall more command with years
Than with your weapons.
Othello, I, 2:59

SATIETY

IACHIMO. The cloyed will,
That satiate yet unsatisfied desire, that tub
Both fill'd and running, ravening[1] first the lamb,
Longs after for the garbage.
Cymbeline, I, 6:47
[1] ravening: devouring.

KING. Goodness, growing to a plurisy,
Dies in his[1] own too-much.
Hamlet, IV, 7:118
[1] his: its.

K. HENRY. They surfeited with honey and began
To loathe the taste of sweetness, whereof a little
More than a little is by much too much.
I Henry IV, III, 2:71

NERISSA. They are as sick that surfeit with too much as they that starve with nothing.
Merchant of Venice, I, 2:6

FRIAR LAURENCE. These violent delights have violent ends.
And in their triumph die, like fire and powder,
Which as they kiss consume: the sweetest honey
Is loathsome in his own deliciousness
And in the taste confounds the appetite:
Romeo and Juliet, II, 6:9

SCANDAL

CASSIUS. If you know
That I do fawn on men and hug them hard,

And after scandal them; . . . then hold me dangerous.
Julius Caesar, I, 2:73

DUKE. Shall we thus permit
A blasting and a scandalous breath to fall
On him so near us?
Measure for Measure, V, 1:121

The mightier man, the mightier is the thing
That makes him honour'd, or begets him hate;
For greatest scandal waits on greatest state.
Rape of Lucrece: 1004

GAUNT. Ah! would the scandal[1] vanish with my life,
How happy then were my ensuing death.
Richard II, II, 1:67
[1] scandal: disgraceful loan from France made to RICHARD.

Your love and pity doth the impression fill
Which vulgar scandal stamp'd upon my brow;
For what care I who calls me well or ill,
So you o'er-green my bad, my good allow?
Sonnet 112

SCHOLAR

GRIFFITH. He[1] was a scholar, and a ripe and good one;
Exceeding wise, fair-spoken, and persuading;
Lofty and sour to them that lov'd him not;
But to those men that sought him sweet as summer.
Henry VIII, IV, 2:51
[1] He: WOLSEY.

KING. My fellow-scholars, and to keep those statutes
That are recorded in this schedule here:
Your oaths are pass'd; and now subscribe your names,
That his own hand may strike his honour down.
Love's Labour's Lost, I, 1:17

NATHANIEL. The epithets are sweetly varied, like a scholar at the least.
Love's Labour's Lost, IV, 2:9

SCOLD

ABBESS. Thou say'st his meat was sauc'd with thy upbraidings:
Unquiet meals make ill digestions;
Thereof the raging fire of fever bred:
And what's a fever but a fit of madness?
Comedy of Errors, V, 1:74

Lewis. We grant thou can'st outscold us:
  fare thee well;
We hold our time too precious to be spent
With such a brabbler.
                                    King John, V, 2:160

Mistress Page. Better a little chiding than
a great deal of heart-break.
                  Merry Wives of Windsor, V, 3:10

Helena [about Hermia]. O! when she 's
  angry, she is keen and shrewd![1]
She was a vixen when she went to school:
And though she be but little, she is fierce.
                  Midsummer Night's Dream, III, 2:323
[1] shrewd: sharp of tongue.

Benedick [about Beatrice]. She speaks
poniards, and every word stabs. . . . Come,
talk not of her; you shall find her the infernal Ate[1] in good apparel. I would to God
some scholar would conjure her, for certainly, while she is here, a man may live as
quiet in hell as in a sanctuary.
Much Ado About Nothing, II, 1:255, 263
[1] Ate: goddess of mischief and vengeance.

Katharina. Doubt not her care should be
To comb your noddle with a three-legg'd
  stool.
              Taming of the Shrew, I, 1:63

Gremio. O! sir, such a life, with such a
  wife, were strange;
But if you have a stomach, to 't i' God's
  name:
You shall have me assisting you in all.
But will you woo this wild-cat?
    Petruchio. Will I live?
  Gremio. Will he woo her? ay, or I 'll hang
  her.
  Petruchio. Why came I hither but to that
  intent?
Think you a little din can daunt mine ears?
Have I not in my time heard lions roar?
Have I not heard the sea, puff'd up with
  winds,
Rage like an angry boar chafed with sweat?
Have I not heard great ordnance in the field,
And heaven's artillery thunder in the skies?
Have I not in a pitched battle heard
Loud 'larums, neighing steeds, and trumpets'
  clang?
And do you tell me of a woman's tongue,
That gives not half so great a blow to hear
As will a chestnut in a farmer's fire?
              Taming of the Shrew, I, 2:194

Leontes [about Paulina]. A callat[1]
Of boundless tongue, who late hath beat her
  husband
And now baits me!
                          Winter's Tale, II, 3:90
[1] callat: scold.

SCORN

Third Citizen. He[1] said he had wounds,
  which he could show in private;
And with his hat, thus waving it in scorn,
'I would be consul,' says he: 'aged custom,
But[2] by your voices, will not so permit me;
Your voices therefore.' When we granted
  that,
Here was, 'I thank you for your voices,
  thank you;
Your most sweet voices: now you have left
  your voices
I have no further with you.' Was not this
  mockery?
                          Coriolanus, II, 3:174
[1] He: Coriolanus. [2] But: only by your votes.

Ulysses. But he already is too insolent;
And we were better parch in Afric sun
Than in the pride and salt scorn of his eyes,
              Troilus and Cressida, I, 3:369

Olivia. O! what a deal of scorn looks
  beautiful
In the contempt and anger of his lip.
                          Twelfth Night, III, 1:157

SEA

Aegeon. The always-wind-obeying deep.
                  Comedy of Errors, I, 1:64

Coriolanus. You were us'd ʌo say
That when the sea was calm all boats alike
Show'd mastership in floating.
                          Coriolanus, IV, 1:3

K. Henry. Now sways it this way, like a
  mighty sea
Forc'd by the tide to combat with the wind;
Now sways it[1] that way, like the self-same
  sea
Forc'd to retire by fury of the wind:
                          III Henry VI, II, 5:5
[1] it: the battle.

Second Gentlemen. Do but stand upon
  the foaming shore,
The chidden billow seems to pelt the
  clouds;
The wind-shak'd surge, with high and monstrous mane,
Seems to cast water on the burning Bear[1]
And quench the guards of the ever-fixed
  pole:
                          Othello, II, 1:11
[1] Bear: the constellation *Ursa Major*.

Cassio. Tempests themselves, high seas,
  and howling winds,

The gutter'd rocks, and congregated sands,
Traitors ensteep'd to clog the guiltless keel,
As having sense of beauty, do omit
Their mortal natures, letting go safely by
The divine Desdemona.
Othello, II, 1:68

Titus. When heaven doth weep, doth not
the earth o'erflow?
If the winds rage, doth not the sea wax mad,
Threat'ning the welkin with his big-swoln
face?
And wilt thou have a reason for this coil?[1]
Titus Andronicus, III, 1:222
[1] coil: fuss, turmoil.

SECRECY

Lady Percy. Some heavy business hath
my lord in hand,
And I must know it, else he loves me not.
I Henry IV, II, 3:66

Lady Percy. In faith, I 'll break thy little
finger, Harry,
An if thou wilt not tell me all things true.

. . . . .

Hotspur. I know you wise; but yet no
further wise
Than Harry Percy's wife: constant you are,
But yet a woman: and for secrecy,
No lady closer; for I well believe
Thou wilt not utter what thou dost not
know;
And so far will I trust thee, gentle Kate.
I Henry IV, II, 3:90, 110

Benedick. Old signior, walk aside with
me: I have studied eight or nine wise words
to speak to you, which these hobby-horses
must not hear.
Much Ado About Nothing, III, 2:73

Montague. But he, his own affections'
counsellor,
Is to himself, I will not say how true,
But to himself so secret and so close,
So far from sounding and discovery,
As is the bud bit with an envious worm,
Ere he can spread his sweet leaves to the air,
Or dedicate his beauty to the sun.
Romeo and Juliet, I, 1:154

Nurse. Two may keep counsel, putting
one away?
Romeo and Juliet, II, 4:208

Captain. When my tongue blabs, then let
mine eyes not see.
Twelfth Night, I, 2:63

Viola. She never told her love,
But let concealment, like a worm i' the bud,
Feed on her damask cheek.
Twelfth Night, II, 4:113

SECURITY

Falstaff. A rascally yea-forsooth knave!
to bear[1] a gentleman in hand, and then stand
upon security . . .

. . . . .

I had as lief they would put ratsbane in my
mouth as offer to stop it with security. I
looked a'[2] should have sent me two-and-
twenty yards of satin, as I am a true knight,
and he[3] sends me security.
II Henry IV, I, 2:41, 45
[1] bear . . . hand: deceive with false pretences.
[2] a': he.   [3] he . . . security: silences me by
the word security.

K. Edward. Thus have we swept suspi-
cion from our seat,
And made our footstool of security.
III Henry VI, V, 7:13

Hecate. And you all know security
Is mortals' chiefest enemy.
Macbeth, III, 5:32

Lucullus [to Timon's servant]. Thou
knowest well enough, although thou comest to me, that this is no time to lend money,
especially upon bare friendship, without security. Here 's three solidares for thee; good
boy, wink at me, and say thou sawest me
not. Fare thee well.
Timon of Athens, III, 1:43

SEEMING

Imogen. Men's vows are women's traitors.
All good seeming,
By thy revolt, O husband! shall be thought
Put on for villany; not born where 't grows,
But worn a bait for ladies.
Cymbeline, III, 4:56

Hamlet. Seems, madam! nay, it is; I
know not 'seems.'
Hamlet, I, 2:76

Kent. I do profess to be no less than I
seem; to serve him truly that will put me in
trust; to love him that is honest; to converse
with him that is wise, and says little; to fear
judgment; to fight when I cannot choose;
and to eat no fish.
King Lear, I, 4:13

ISABELLA. Let your reason serve
To make the truth appear where it seems
   hid,
And hide the false seems true.
Measure for Measure, V, 1:65

DEMETRIUS. But, my good lord, I wot not
   by what power,
But by some power it is, my love to Hermia,
Melted as doth the snow, seems to me now
As the remembrance of an idle gaud
Which in my childhood I did dote upon;
Midsummer Night's Dream, IV, 1:168

IAGO. Men should be what they seem;
Or those that be not, would they might
   seem none!
Othello, III, 3:126

SELF

PAROLLES. Our remedies oft in ourselves
   do lie
Which we ascribe to heaven.
All's Well That Ends Well, I, 1:231

KING. Break not your sleeps for that; you
   must not think
That we are made of stuff so flat and dull
That we can let our beard be shook with
   danger
And think it pastime.
Hamlet, IV, 7:30

DESDEMONA. I am not merry, but I do be-
   guile
The thing I am by seeming otherwise.
Othello, II, 1:123

GLOUCESTER[1] [soliloquy]. I, that am not
   shap'd for sportive tricks,
Nor made to court an amorous looking-
   glass;
I, that am rudely stamp'd, and want love's
   majesty
To strut before a wanton ambling nymph;
I, that am curtail'd of this fair proportion,
Cheated of feature by dissembling nature,
Deform'd, unfinish'd, sent before my time
Into this breathing world, scarce half
   made up,
And that so lamely and unfashionable
That dogs bark at me as I halt by them;
Why, I, in this weak piping time of peace,
Have no delight to pass away the time,
Unless to see my shadow in the sun
And descant on mine own deformity:
And therefore, since I cannot prove a lover,
To entertain these fair well-spoken days,
I am determined to prove a villain.
Richard III, I, 1:14

[1] Later KING RICHARD III.

FLAVIUS. It is in vain that you would
   speak with Timon;
For he is set so only to himself,
That nothing but himself, which looks like
   man,
Is friendly with him.
Timon of Athens, V, 1:119

PROTEUS. I to myself am dearer than a
   friend.
Two Gentlemen of Verona, II, 6:23

SELF-CONTROL

ANTONY. I . . . condemn myself to lack
The courage of a woman; less noble mind
Than she which by her death our Caesar
   tells
'I am conqueror of myself.'
Antony and Cleopatra, IV, 12:59

FIRST LORD. Your lordship is the most patient man in loss, the most coldest that ever
turned up ace.
Cymbeline, II, 3:1

HAMLET. Refrain to-night;
And that shall lend a kind of easiness
To the next abstinence.
Hamlet, III, 4:165

PRINCE. Presume not that I am the thing
   I was;
For God doth know, so shall the world per-
   ceive,
That I have turn'd away my former self;
So will I those that kept me company.
II Henry IV, V, 5:60

DUKE. He doth with holy abstinence sub-
   due
That in himself which he spurs on his
   power
To qualify in others: were he meal'd[1] with
   that
Which he corrects, then were he tyrannous;
But this being so, he 's just.
Measure for Measure, IV, 2:84

[1] meal'd: defiled.

SELF-LOVE

DAUPHIN. Good my sovereign,
Take up the English short, and let them
   know
Of what a monarchy you are the head:
Self-love, my liege, is not so vile a sin
As self-neglecting.
Henry V, II, 4:71

Sin of self-love possesseth all mine eye
And all my soul and all my every part;

And for this sin there is no remedy,
It is so grounded inward in my heart.
Methinks no face so gracious is as mine,
No shape so true, no truth of such account;
And for myself mine own worth do define,
As I all other in all worths surmount.
But when my glass shows me myself indeed,
Bated and chopp'd with tann'd antiquity
Mine own self-love quite contrary I read;
Self so self-loving were iniquity.
Sonnet 62

APEMANTUS. Immortal gods, I crave no
    pelf;
I pray for no man but myself:
Grant I may never prove so fond,[1]
To trust man on his oath or bond;
Or a harlot for her weeping;
Or a dog that seems a-sleeping;
Or a keeper with my freedom;
Or my friends, if I should need 'em.
Timon of Athens, I, 2:63
[1] fond: foolish.

OLIVIA. O! you are sick of self-love, Malvolio, and taste with a distempered appetite.
To be generous, guiltless, and of free disposition, is to take those things for bird-
bolts[1] that you deem cannon bullets.
Twelfth Night, I, 5:97
[1] bird-bolts: short arrows without sharp points
used to kill birds.

SELF-PITY

K. RICHARD. Feed not thy sovereign's foe,
    my gentle earth,
Nor with thy sweets comfort his ravenous
    sense;
But let thy spiders, that suck up thy venom,
And heavy-gaited toads lie in their way,
Doing annoyance to the treacherous feet
Which with usurping steps do trample thee.
Yield stinging nettles to mine enemies;
And when they from thy bosom pluck a
    flower,
Guard it, I pray thee, with a lurking adder
Whose double tongue may with a mortal
    touch
Throw death upon thy sovereign's enemies.
Mock not my senseless conjuration, lords:
This earth shall have a feeling and these
    stones
Prove armed soldiers, ere her native king
Shall falter under foul rebellion's arms.
Richard II, III, 2:12

K. RICHARD. Not all the water in the
    rough rude sea
Can wash the balm from an anointed king;
The breath of wordly men cannot depose
The deputy elected by the Lord.
Richard II, III, 2:54

K. RICHARD. Of comfort no man speak:
Let 's talk of graves, of worms, and epi-
    taphs;
Make dust our paper, and with rainy eyes
Write sorrow on the bosom of the earth;
Let 's choose executors and talk of wills:
And yet not so, for what can we bequeath
Save our deposed bodies to the ground?
Our lands, our lives, and all are Boling-
    broke's,
And nothing can we call our own but death,
And that small model of the barren earth
Which serves as paste and cover to our
    bones.
For God's sake, let us sit upon the ground
And tell sad stories of the death of kings;
How some have been depos'd, some slain in
    war,
Some haunted by the ghosts they have de-
    pos'd,
Some poison'd by their wives, some sleeping
    kill'd;
All murder'd: for within the hollow crown
That rounds the mortal temples of a king
Keeps Death his court, and there the antick
    sits,
Scoffing his state and grinning at his pomp;
Allowing him a breath, a little scene,
To monarchize, be fear'd, and kill with
    looks,
Infusing him with self and vain conceit,
As if this flesh which walls about our life
Were brass impregnable; and humour'd thus
Comes at the last and with a little pin
Bores through his castle wall, and farewell
    king!
Cover your heads, and mock not flesh and
    blood
With solemn reverence: throw away re-
    spect,
Tradition, form, and ceremonious duty,
For you have but mistook me all this while:
I live with bread like you, feel want,
Taste grief, need friends: subjected thus,
How can you say to me I am a king?
Richard II, III, 2:144

K. RICHARD. The king shall be contented:
    must he lose
The name of king? O' God's name, let it go:
I 'll give my jewels for a set of beads;
My gorgeous palace for a hermitage,
My gay apparel for an almsman's gown,
My figur'd goblets for a dish of wood,
My sceptre for a palmer's walking-staff,
My subjects for a pair of carved saints,
And my large kingdom for a little grave,
A little little grave, an obscure grave;
Or I 'll be buried in the king's highway,
Some way of common trade, where sub-
    jects' feet
May hourly trample on their sovereign's
    head;

For on my heart they tread now whilst I
    live;
And buried once, why not upon my head?
                                Richard II, III, 3:145

K. RICHARD. What says King Bolingbroke?
    will his majesty
Give Richard leave to live till Richard die?
You make[1] a leg, and Bolingbroke says ay.
    NORTH. My lord, in the base court he doth
        attend
To speak with you; may't please you to
    come down?
    K. RICHARD. Down, down I come; like
        glistering Phaethon;[2]
Wanting the manage of unruly jades.
In the base court? Base court, where kings
    grow base,
To come at traitors' calls and do them
    grace.
In the base court? Come down? Down,
    court! down, king!
For night-owls shriek where mounting larks
    should sing.
                                Richard II, III, 3:172
[1] make a leg: an obeisance made by drawing
back one leg and bending the other. [2] Phae-
thon: who was killed driving the horses of the
sun.

K. RICHARD. You may my glories and my
    state depose,
But not my griefs; still am I king of those.
                                Richard II, IV, 1:192

K. RICHARD. Give me the glass, and
    therein will I read.
No deeper wrinkles yet? hath sorrow
    struck
So many blows upon this face of mine
And made no deeper wounds? O flattering
    glass!
Like to my followers in prosperity,
Thou dost beguile me. Was this face the face
That every day under his household roof
Did keep ten thousand men? was this the
    face
That like the sun did make beholders wink?
Was this the face that fac'd so many follies,
And was at last out-fac'd by Bolingbroke?
A brittle glory shineth in this face:
As brittle as the glory is the face;
                                Richard II, IV, 1:276

K. RICHARD. In winter's tedious nights sit
    by the fire
With good old folks, and let them tell thee
    tales
Of woeful ages, long ago betid;
And ere thou bid good night, to quit their
    grief,
Tell thou the lamentable tale of me,
And send the hearers weeping to their beds.
                                Richard II, V, 1:40

K. RICHARD. I give this heavy weight from
    off my head,
And this unwieldy sceptre from my hand,
The pride of kingly sway from out my
    heart;
With mine own tears I wash away my balm,
With mine own hands I give away my
    crown,
With mine own tongue deny my sacred
    state,
With mine own breath release all duty's
    rites:
All pomp and majesty I do forswear;
My manors, rents, revenues I forego;
My acts, decrees, and statutes I deny:
God pardon all oaths that are broke to me!
                                Richard II, IV, 1:204

TIMON. But myself,
Who had the world as my confectionary,
The mouths, the tongues, the eyes and
    hearts of men
At duty, more than I could frame employ-
    ment,
That numberless upon me stuck as leaves
Do on the oak, have with one winter's brush
Fell from their boughs and left me open,
    bare
For every storm that blows; I, to bear this,
That never knew but better, is some burden.
                                Timon of Athens, IV, 3:259

SELF-REPROACH

HAMLET [soliloquy]. Now, whether it be
Bestial oblivion, or some craven scruple
Of thinking too precisely on the event,
A thought, which, quarter'd, hath but one
    part wisdom
And ever three parts coward, I do not know
Why yet I live to say 'This thing[1] 's to do';
Sith[2] I have cause and will and strength and
    means
To do 't. Examples gross as earth exhort
    me:
Witness this army of such mass and charge
Led by a delicate and tender prince,
Whose spirit with divine ambition puff'd
Makes mouths at the invisible event,
Exposing what is mortal and unsure
To all that fortune, death and danger dare,
Even for an egg-shell. Rightly to be great
Is not to stir without great argument,
But greatly to find quarrel in a straw
When honour's at the stake. How stand I
    then,
That have a father kill'd, a mother stain'd,
Excitements of my reason and my blood,
And let all sleep, while, to my shame, I see
The imminent death of twenty thousand
    men,
That, for a fantasy and trick of fame,
Go to their graves like beds, fight for a plot

Whereon the numbers cannot try the cause,
Which is not tomb enough and continent
To hide the slain? O! from this time forth,
My thoughts be bloody, or be nothing
worth.
Hamlet, IV, 4:39
[1] This thing: murder of the king.   [2] Sith: since.

SELLING

Enter AUTOLYCUS, *singing.*
Lawn as white as driven snow;
Cyprus[1] black as e'er was crow;
Gloves as sweet as damask roses;
Masks for faces and for noses;
Bugle-bracelet, necklace-amber,
Perfume for a lady's chamber;
Golden quoifs[2] and stomachers,
For my lads to give their dears;
Pins and poking-sticks[3] of steel;
What maids lack from head to heel:
Come buy of me, come; come buy, come
buy;
Buy, lads, or else your lasses cry: Come buy.
Winter's Tale, IV, 4:220
[1] Cyprus: a crape-like fabric.   [2] quoifs: close-fitting caps.   [3] poking-sticks: rods used to
stiffen the pleats in ruffles.

AUTOLYCUS. Will you buy any tape,
Or lace for your cape,
My dainty duck, my dear-a?
Any silk, any thread,
Any toys for your head,
Of the new'st and fin'st, fin'st wear-a?
Come to the pedlar;
Money 's a meddler,
That doth utter all men's ware-a.
Winter's Tale, IV, 4:322

SEPARATION

K. LEAR. He that parts us shall bring a
brand from heaven,
And fire[1] us hence like foxes.
King Lear, V, 3:22
[1] fire . . . foxes: referring to practice of smoking foxes out of their holes.

All days are nights to see till I see thee,
And nights bright days when dreams do
show thee me.
Sonnet 43

Summer and his[1] pleasures wait on thee,
And, thou away, the very birds are mute:
Or, if they sing, 't is with so dull a cheer
That leaves look pale, dreading the winter's
near.
Sonnet 97
[1] his: its.

TROILUS. O Cressida! but that the busy
day,
Wak'd by the lark, hath rous'd the ribald
crows,
And dreaming night will hide our joys no
longer,
I would not from thee.
Troilus and Cressida, IV, 2:8

SERPENT

GHOST. The serpent that did sting thy fa-
ther's life
Now wears his crown.
HAMLET. O my prophetic soul! My
uncle!
Hamlet, I, 5:39

SALISBURY. Were there a serpent seen,
with forked tongue,
That slily glided towards your majesty,
It were but necessary you were wak'd,
Lest, being suffer'd in that harmful slumber,
The mortal worm might make the sleep
eternal.
II Henry VI, III, 2:259

BRUTUS. And therefore think him as a ser-
pent's egg
Which, hatch'd, would, as his kind, grow
mischievous,
And kill him in the shell.
Julius Caesar, II, 1:32

HERMIA [awaking]. Help me, Lysander,
help me! do thy best
To pluck this crawling serpent from my
breast,
Ay me, for pity! what a dream was here!
Lysander, look how I do quake with fear:
Methought a serpent eat my heart away,
And you sat smiling at his cruel prey.
Midsummer Night's Dream, II, 2:145

SERVANT

POSTHUMUS. Every good servant does not
all commands;
No bond but to do just ones.
Cymbeline, V, 1:6

K. HENRY. If a servant, under his master's
command transporting a sum of money, be
assailed by robbers and die in many irrecon-
ciled iniquities, you may call the business
of the master the author of the servant's
damnation. But this is not so: the king is not
bound to answer the particular endings of
his soldiers, the father of his son, nor the
master of his servant.
Henry V, IV, 1:158

Lady Macbeth [to Duncan]. Your serv-
    ants ever
Have theirs, themselves, and what is theirs,
    in compt,[1]
To make their audit at your highness'
    pleasure.
                                    Macbeth, I, 6:23
[1] in compt: subject to a reckoning.

Ariel. Remember I have done thee
    worthy service;
Told thee no lies, made thee no mistakings,
    serv'd
Without or[1] grudge or grumblings.
                                    Tempest, I, 2:247
[1] or . . . or: either or.

SHAME

Antony. Would'st thou be window'd in
    great Rome, and see
Thy master thus with pleach'd[1] arms, bend-
    ing down
His corrigible neck, his face subdued
To penetrative shame, whilst the wheel'd
    seat
Of fortunate Caesar, drawn before him,
    branded[2]
His baseness that ensued?
                        Antony and Cleopatra, IV, 12:72
[1] pleach'd: folded. [2] branded: etc.: the one
who followed.

Prince [to Falstaff]. What a slave art
thou, to hack thy sword as thou hast done,
and then say it was in fight! What trick,
what device, what starting-hole canst thou
now find out to hide thee from this open
and apparent shame?
                                    I Henry IV, II, 4:289

Dauphin. Reproach and everlasting
    shame
Sit mocking in our plumes.
                                    Henry V, IV, 5:5

Lewis. Bitter shame hath spoil'd the
    sweet world's taste,
That it yields nought but shame and bitter-
    ness.
                                    King John, III, 4:110

K. Lear. Let shame come when it will, I
    do not call it:
I do not bid the thunder-bearer shoot,
Nor tell tales of thee to high-judging Jove.
Mend when thou canst; be better at thy
    leisure:
I can be patient; I can stay with Regan,
I and my hundred knights.
                                    King Lear, II, 4:229

Friar. I have mark'd
A thousand blushing apparitions
To start into her face; a thousand innocent
    shames
In angel whiteness beat away those blushes.
                        Much Ado About Nothing, IV, 1:160

Shame folded up in blind concealing night,
When most unseen, then most doth tyran-
    nize.
                                    Rape of Lucrece: 675

SHEPHERD

Rosalind. You foolish shepherd, where-
    fore do you follow her,
Like foggy south puffing with wind and
    rain?
You are a thousand times a properer man
Than she a woman.
                                    As You Like It, III, 5:49

Rosalind. Art thou god to shepherd
    turn'd,
That a maiden's heart hath burn'd?
                                    As You Like It, IV, 3:40

Edgar. Sleepest or wakest thou, jolly
    shepherd?
Thy sheep be in the corn;
And for one blast of thy minikin[1] mouth,
Thy sheep shall take no harm.
                                    King Lear, III, 6:42
[1] minikin: small and pretty.

SHIP

Shylock. Ships are but boards, sailors but
men: there be land-rats and water-rats, wa-
ter-thieves and land-thieves, I mean pirates:
and then there is the peril of waters, winds,
and rocks.
                                    Merchant of Venice, I, 3:22

Autolycus. The king is not at the palace; he is gone aboard a new ship to purge
melancholy and air himself.
                                    Winter's Tale, IV, 4:788

SHIRT

Antony. The shirt of Nessus[1] is upon me;
teach me, Alcides,[2] thou mine ancestor, thy
rage;
                        Antony and Cleopatra, IV, 10:56
[1] shirt of Nessus: a poisoned garment that
brought certain evil fates. [2] Alcides: Hercules,
whom Antony claimed to be his ancestor.

Prince. What a disgrace is it to me to remember thy name, or to know thy face to-

morrow! or . . . to bear the inventory of thy shirts; as, one for superfluity, and one other for use!

II Henry IV, II, 2:16

SHORE

K. HENRY. The tide of pomp
That beats upon the high shore of this world,

Henry V, IV, 1:281

BASSANIO. Thus ornament is but the guiled[1] shore
To a most dangerous sea; the beauteous scarf
Veiling an Indian beauty.

Merchant of Venice, III, 2:97

[1] guiled: treacherous.

SILENCE

JAQUES. Why, 't is good to be sad and say nothing.
ROSALIND. Why then, 't is good to be a post.

As You Like It, IV, 1:8

HAMLET. But break, my heart, for I must hold my tongue!

Hamlet, I, 2:159

HAMLET [dying]. The rest is silence.

Hamlet, V, 2:368

GLOUCESTER.[1] I hear, yet say not much, but think the more.

III Henry VI, IV, 1:83

[1] Later, KING RICHARD III.

DUKE. Silence that fellow: I would he had some cause
To prattle for himself.

Measure for Measure, V, 1:181

CLAUDIO. Silence is the perfectest herald of joy: I were but little happy, if I could say much how. Lady, as you are mine, I am yours: I give away myself for you and dote upon the exchange.

Much Ado About Nothing, II, 1:316

CALIBAN. Pray you, tread softly, that the blind mole may not
Hear a foot fall.

Tempest, IV, 1:194

EMILIA. The silence often of pure innocence
Persuades when speaking fails.

Winter's Tale, II, 2:41

SIN

K. HENRY. Have you a ruffian that will swear, drink, dance,
Revel the night, rob, murder, and commit
The oldest sins the newest kind of ways?

II Henry IV, IV, 5:125

K. JOHN. Then God forgive the sin of all those souls
That to their everlasting residence,
Before the dew of evening fall, shall fleet,
In dreadful trial of our kingdom's king!

King John, II, 1:283

K. LEAR. I am a man
More sinn'd against than sinning.

King Lear, III, 2:59

ESCALUS. Well, heaven forgive him, and forgive us all!
Some rise by sin, and some by virtue fall:
Some run from brakes[1] of vice, and answer none,
And some condemned for a fault alone.

Measure for Measure, II, 1:37

[1] brakes: thickets; a much discussed passage.

CLAUDIO. Sweet sister, let me live.
What sin you do to save a brother's life,
Nature dispenses with the deed so far
That it becomes a virtue.
ISABELLA. O you beast!
O faithless coward! O dishonest wretch!
Wilt thou be made a man out of my vice?

. . . . .

Thy sin 's not accidental, but a trade.
Mercy to thee would prove itself a bawd:
'T is best that thou diest quickly.

Measure for Measure, III, 1:133, 149

PERICLES. Great king,
Few love to hear the sins they love to act;
'T would braid[1] yourself too near for me to tell it.
Who has a book of all that monarchs do,
He 's more secure to keep it shut than shown;

. . . . .

Kings are earth's gods; in vice their law 's their will;

Pericles, I, 1:91, 103

[1] braid: upbraid, criticize.

PERICLES. One sin, I know, another doth provoke;
Murder 's as near to lust as flame to smoke.
Poison and treason are the hands of sin,
Ay, and the targets, to put off the shame:

Pericles, I, 1:137

Who buys a minute's mirth to wail a week?
Or sells eternity to get a toy?

. . . . .

Bearing away the wound that nothing heal-
  eth,
The scar that will despite of cure remain.
                    Rape of Lucrece: 213, 731

Think but how vile a spectacle it were,
To view thy present trespass in another.
Men's faults do seldom to themselves ap-
  pear;
Their own transgressions partially they
  smother:
This guilt would seem death-worthy in thy
  brother.
                           Rape of Lucrece: 631

ROMEO [to PARIS]. I beseech thee, youth,
Put not another sin upon my head
By urging me to fury: O! be gone:
By heaven, I love thee better than myself,
For I come hither arm'd against myself:
Stay not, be gone; live, and hereafter say
A madman's mercy bade thee run away.
                    Romeo and Juliet, V, 3:61

SINGER

PORTIA. The crow doth sing as sweetly as
  the lark
When neither is attended, and I think
The nightingale, if she should sing by day,
When every goose is cackling, would be
  thought
No better a musician than the wren.
                  Merchant of Venice, V, 1:102

DON PEDRO. Come, Balthazar, we 'll hear
  that song again.
BALTHAZAR. O! good my lord, tax not so
  bad a voice
To slander music any more than once.
              Much Ado About Nothing, II, 3:45

GOWER. She sings like one immortal, and
  she dances
As goddess-like to her admired lays.
                         Pericles, V, Prologue: 3

FLORIZEL. When you sing,
I 'd have you buy and sell so; so give alms;
Pray so; and, for the ordering your affairs,
To sing them too.
                       Winter's Tale, IV, 4:137

SERVANT. He[1] sings several tunes faster
than you 'll tell[2] money: he utters them as
he had eaten ballads and all men's ears grew
to his tunes.
                       Winter's Tale, IV, 4:184
[1] He: AUTOLYCUS.   [2] tell: count.

SISTER

CELIA [about ORLANDO]. A nun of winter's sisterhood kisses not more religiously;
the very ice of chastity is in them.
                    As You Like It, III, 4:18

LAERTES. And so have I a noble father lost;
A sister driven into desperate terms,
Whose worth, if praises may go back again,
Stood challenger on mount of all the age
For her perfections. But my revenge will
  come.
                            Hamlet, IV, 7:25

PISTOL. Then death rock me asleep,
  abridge my doleful days!
Why then, let grievous, ghastly, gaping
  wounds
Untwine the Sisters Three![1] Come, Atropos,
  I say!
                         II Henry IV, II, 4:211
[1] The Fates, Clotho, Lachesis, and Atropos, in
Greek mythology spun and cut off the threads
of life.

PANDARUS. Go thy way, Troilus, go thy
way! Had I a sister were a grace, or a daughter a goddess, he should take his choice. O
admirable man!
                Troilus and Cressida, I, 2:256

SKY

BOLINGBROKE. The more fair and crystal is
  the sky,
The uglier seem the clouds that in it fly.
                          Richard II, I, 1:41

MARINER. The skies look grimly
And threaten present blusters. In my con-
  science,
The heavens with that we have in hand are
  angry,
And frown upon 's.
                       Winter's Tale, III, 3:3

SLANDER

BALTHAZAR. Slander lives upon succession,[1]
For ever housed where it gets possession.
                    Comedy of Errors, III, 1:105
[1] succession: repetition.

PISANIO. What shall I need to draw my
  sword? the paper
Hath cut her throat already. No, 't is slander,
Whose edge is sharper than the sword, whose
  tongue
Outvenoms all the worms of Nile, whose
  breath

Rides on the posting winds and doth belie
All corners of the world; kings, queens, and
 states,
Maids, matrons, nay, the secrets of the grave
This viperous slander enters.
Cymbeline, III, 4:34

King. Slander,
Whose whisper o'er the world's diameter,
As level as the cannon to his[1] blank,[2]
Transports his poison'd shot.
Hamlet, IV, 1:40
[1] his: its. [2] blank: target.

Duke. No might nor greatness in mortality[1]
Can censure 'scape: back-wounding calumny
The whitest virtue strikes. What king so
 strong
Can tie the gall up in the slanderous tongue?
Measure for Measure, III, 2:196
[1] mortality: human life.

Claudio [reads from a scroll].
Done to death by slanderous tongues
Was the Hero that here lies:
Death, in guerdon[1] of her wrongs,
Gives her fame which never dies,
So the life that died with shame
Lives in death with glorious fame.
Much Ado About Nothing, V, 3:3
[1] guerdon: recompense.

Othello. If thou dost slander her and
 torture me,
Never pray more; abandon all remorse,[1]
On horror's head horrors accumulate;
Do deeds to make heaven weep, all earth
 amaz'd;
For nothing canst thou to damnation add
Greater than that.
Othello, III, 3:368
[1] remorse: pity.

Mowbray. Pierc'd to the soul with slander's venom'd spear.
Richard II, I, 1:171

That thou art blam'd shall not be thy defect,
For slander's mark was ever yet the fair;
The ornament of beauty is suspect,
A crow that flies in heaven's sweetest air.
Sonnet 70

Nestor. A slave whose gall coins slanders
 like a mint,
To match us in comparisons with dirt;
Troilus and Cressida, I, 3:193

SLAVE

Being your slave, what should I do but tend
Upon the hours and times of your desire?

I have no precious time at all to spend,
Nor services to do, till you require.
Sonnet 57

Lucius. Say, wall-eyed[1] slave, whither
 would'st thou convey
This growing image of thy fiend-like face?
Titus Andronicus, V, 1:44
[1] wall-eyed: fierce-looking.

SLEEP

Cleopatra. Give me to drink mandra-
gora.[1]
Charmian. Why madam?
Cleopatra. That I might sleep out this
great gap of time
My Antony is away.
Antony and Cleopatra, I, 5:4
[1] mandragora: a sleep-producing drug.

Peto. Falstaff! Fast asleep behind the
arras, and snorting like a horse.
1 Henry IV, II, 4:577

K. Henry [soliloquy]. How many thou-
 sand of my poorest subjects
Are at this hour asleep! O Sleep! O gentle
 Sleep!
Nature's soft nurse, how have I frighted
 thee,
That thou no more wilt weigh my eyelids
 down
And steep my senses in forgetfulness?
Why rather, Sleep, liest thou in smoky cribs,
Upon uneasy pallets stretching thee,
And hush'd with buzzing night-flies to thy
 slumber,
Than in the perfum'd chambers of the
 great,
Under the canopies of costly state,
And lull'd with sound of sweetest melody?
O thou dull god! why liest thou with the
 vile
In loathsome beds, and leav'st the kingly
 couch
A watch-case[1] or a common larum bell?
Wilt thou upon the high and giddy mast
Seal up the ship-boy's eyes, and rock his
 brains
In cradle of the rude imperious surge,
And in the visitation of the winds,
Who take the ruffian billows by the top,
Curling their monstrous heads, and hanging
 them
With deaf'ning clamour in the slippery
 clouds,
That with the hurly death itself awakes?
Canst thou, O partial Sleep! give thy repose
To the wet sea-boy in an hour so rude,
And in the calmest and most stillest night,
With all appliances and means to boot,

Deny it to a king? Then happy low, lie
   down!
Uneasy lies the head that wears a crown.
                          II Henry IV, III, 1:4
[1] watch-case: sentry-box.

BRUTUS. I would it were my fault to sleep
   so soundly.
                          Julius Caesar, II, 1:4

BRUTUS. Boy! Lucius! Fast asleep? It is
   no matter;
Enjoy the honey-heavy dew of slumber:
Thou hast no figures nor no fantasies
Which busy care draws in the brains of men;
Therefore thou sleep'st so sound.
                       Julius Caesar, II, 1:229

FIRST WITCH. Sleep shall neither night nor
   day
Hang upon his pent-house lid;
                             Macbeth, I, 3:19

BANQUO. A heavy summons[1] lies like lead
   upon me,
And yet I would not sleep: merciful powers!
Restrain in me the cursed thoughts[2] that nature
Gives way to in repose.
                             Macbeth, II, 1:6
[1] heavy   summons: sleepiness.   [2] cursed
thoughts: possibly suspicion of MACBETH, possibly ambition.

MACBETH. Now o'er the one-half world
Nature seems dead, and wicked dreams
   abuse[1]
The curtain'd sleep:
                            Macbeth, II, 1:49
[1] abuse: deceive, as often in Shakespeare.

MACBETH. Methought I heard a voice cry
   'Sleep no more!'
Macbeth does murder sleep,' the innocent
   sleep,
Sleep that knits up the ravell'd sleave of
   care,
The death of each day's life, sore labour's
   bath,
Balm of hurt minds, great nature's second[1]
   course,
Chief nourisher in life's feast.
   LADY M. What do you mean?
   MACBETH. Still[2] it cried 'Sleep no more!'
   to all the house:
Glamis hath murder'd sleep, and therefore
   Cawdor
Shall sleep no more, Macbeth shall sleep no
   more!'
                            Macbeth, II, 2:35
[1] second course: the chief course at a meal.
[2] Still: showing continuous action.

MACDUFF. Shake off this downy sleep,
   death's counterfeit,
And look on death itself!
                            Macbeth, II, 3:81

MACBETH. Duncan is in his grave;
After life's fitful fever he sleeps well.
                           Macbeth, III, 2:22

LADY M. You lack the season of all natures, sleep.
                          Macbeth, III, 4:141

DOCTOR. I have two nights watched with
you but can perceive no truth in your report. When was it she last walked?
   GENTLEWOMAN. Since his majesty went
into the field, I have seen her rise from her
bed, throw her nightgown upon her, unlock
her closet, take forth paper, fold it, write
upon 't, read it, afterwards seal it, and again
return to bed; yet all this while in a most
fast sleep.
   DOCTOR. A great perturbation in nature,
to receive at once the benefit of sleep and
do the effects of watching! In this slumbery
agitation, besides her walking and other ac-
tual performances, what, at any time, have
you heard her say?
   GENTLEWOMAN. That, sir, which I will
not report after her.
   DOCTOR. You may to me, and 't is most
meet you should.
   GENTLEWOMAN. Neither to you nor any
one, having no witness to confirm my
speech.
          Enter, LADY MACBETH, *with a taper*.
Lo you! here she comes. This is her very
guise; and, upon my life, fast asleep. Observe her; stand close.
   DOCTOR. How came she by that light?
   GENTLEWOMAN. Why, it stood by her:
she has light by her continually; 't is her
command.
   DOCTOR. You see, her eyes are open.
   GENTLEWOMAN. Ay, but their sense is
shut.
   DOCTOR. What is it she does now? Look,
how she rubs her hands.
   GENTLEWOMAN. It is an accustomed action with her, to seem thus washing her
hands. I have known her continue in this a
quarter of an hour.
   LADY MACBETH. Yet here 's a spot.
   DOCTOR. Hark! she speaks. I will set down
what comes from her, to satisfy my remembrance the more strongly.
   LADY M. Out, damned spot! out, I say!
One; two: why, then 't is time to do 't. Hell
is murky! Fie, my lord, fie! a soldier, and
afeard? What need we fear who knows it,
when none can call our power to account?

Yet who would have thought the old man to have had so much blood in him?

DOCTOR. Do you mark that?

LADY M. The Thane of Fife had a wife: where is she now? What! will these hands ne'er be clean? No more o' that, my lord, no more o' that: you mar all with this starting.

DOCTOR. Go to, go to; you have known what you should not.

GENTLEWOMAN. She has spoke what she should not, I am sure of that: heaven knows what she has known.

LADY M. Here 's the smell of the blood still: all the perfumes of Arabia will not sweeten this little hand. Oh! oh! oh!

DOCTOR. What a sigh is there! The heart is sorely charged.

GENTLEWOMAN. I would not have such a heart in my bosom for the dignity of the whole body.

DOCTOR. Well, well, well.

GENTLEWOMAN. Pray God it be, sir.

DOCTOR. This disease is beyond my practice: yet I have known those which have walked in their sleep who have died holily in their beds.

LADY M. Wash your hands, put on your nightgown; look not so pale. I tell you yet again, Banquo 's buried; he cannot come out on 's grave.

DOCTOR. Even so?

LADY M. To bed, to bed: there 's knocking at the gate. Come, come, come, come, give me your hand. What 's done cannot be undone. To bed, to bed, to bed.

Exit.

DOCTOR. Will she go now to bed?

GENTLEWOMAN. Directly.

DOCTOR. Foul whisperings are abroad. Unnatural deeds

Do breed unnatural troubles; infected minds

To their deaf pillows will discharge their secrets;

More needs she the divine than the physician.

God, God forgive us all! Look after her;

Remove from her the means of all annoyance,

And still keep eyes upon her. So, good night:

My mind she has mated,[1] and amaz'd my sight.

Macbeth, V, 1:10

[1] mated: stupefied.

OBERON. O'er their brows death-counterfeiting sleep

With leaden legs and batty[1] wings doth creep.

Midsummer Night's Dream, III, 2:364

[1] batty: bat-like.

HELENA. And sleep, that sometimes shuts up sorrow's eye,

Steal me awhile from mine own company.

Midsummer Night's Dream, III, 2:435

ROMEO. Sleep dwell upon thine eyes, peace in thy breast!

Would I were sleep and peace, so sweet to rest!

Romeo and Juliet, II, 2:187

ALONSO. What! all so soon asleep? I wish mine eyes

Would, with themselves, shut up my thoughts.

Tempest, II, 1:191

ANTONIO. This is a strange repose, to be asleep

With eyes wide open; standing, speaking, moving,

And yet so fast asleep.

Tempest, II, 1:213

TROILUS. To bed, to bed: sleep kill those pretty eyes,

And give as soft attachment to thy senses

As infants' empty of all thought!

Troilus and Cressida, IV, 2:4

SMELL

BIRON. Your nose smells 'no,' in this, most tender-smelling knight.

Love's Labour's Lost, V, 2:568

HOST. What say you to young Master Fenton? he capers, he dances, he has eyes of youth, he writes verses, he speaks holiday, he smells April and May.

Merry Wives of Windsor, III, 2:66

DON PEDRO. A'[1] rubs him with civet;[2] can you smell him out by that?

Much Ado About Nothing, III, 2:50

[1] A': he.   [2] civet: perfume.

The rose looks fair, but fairer we it deem

For that sweet odour which doth in it live.

Sonnet 54

SMILE

HAMLET. O villain, villain, smiling, damned villain!

My tables,[1]—meet it is I set it down,

That one may smile, and smile, and be a villain;

Hamlet, I, 5:106

[1] tables: memorandum tablet.

Julius Caesar. Seldom he[1] smiles, and
smiles in such a sort
As if he mock'd himself, and scorn'd his
spirit
That could be mov'd to smile at any thing.
Julius Caesar, I, 2:205
[1] he: Cassius.

Gentleman. You have seen
Sunshine and rain at once; her smiles and
tears
Were like a better way; those happy smilets
That play'd on her ripe lip seem'd not to
know
What guests were in her eyes; which parted
thence,
As pearls from diamonds dropp'd.
King Lear, IV, 3:19

Hermia. I frown upon him, yet he loves
me still.
Helena. O! that your frowns would
teach my smiles such skill.
Midsummer Night's Dream, I, 1:194

Paris. Venus smiles not in a house of
tears.
Romeo and Juliet, IV, 1:8

Second Senator. Thou rather shalt en-
force it with thy smile
Than hew to 't with thy sword.
Timon of Athens, V, 4:45

Maria. He does smile his face into more
lines than are in the new map with the aug-
mentation of the Indies.
Twelfth Night, III, 2:84

A smile recures the wounding of a frown.
Venus and Adonis: 465

SOLDIER

Falstaff [about his recruits]. Such a
commodity of warm slaves, as had as lief
hear the devil as a drum;

. . . . .

indeed I had the most of them out of prison.
There 's but a shirt and a half in all my company; and the half shirt is two napkins[1]
tacked together.
I Henry IV, IV, 2:19, 44
[1] napkins: handkerchiefs.

Falstaff. You would think that I have a
hundred and fifty tattered prodigals, lately
come from swine-keeping, from eating
draff[1] and husks.
I Henry IV, IV, 2:37
[1] draff: refuse.

Prince. I did never see such pitiful rascals.
Falstaff. Tut, tut; good enough to toss;
food for powder, food for powder; they 'll
fill a pit as well as better: tush, man, mortal
men, mortal men.
I Henry IV, IV, 2:70

Falstaff [soliloquy]. I am as hot as molten lead, and as heavy too: God keep lead
out of me! I need no more weight than mine
own bowels. I have led my ragamuffins
where they are peppered: there 's not three
of my hundred and fifty left alive, and
they are for the town's end, to beg during
life.
I Henry IV, V, 3:34

Ross. Your son, my lord, has paid a sol-
dier's debt:
He only liv'd but till he was a man;
The which no sooner had his prowess con-
firm'd
In the unshrinking station where he fought,
But like a man he died.

. . . . .

Siward. Had he his hurts before?
Ross. Ay, on the front.
Siward. Why then, God's soldier be he!
Had I as many sons as I have hairs,
I would not wish them to a fairer death:
And so, his knell is knoll'd.
Macbeth, V, 7:68, 75

Messenger. And a good soldier too, lady.
Beatrice. And a good soldier to a lady;
but what is he to a lord?
Messenger. A lord to a lord, a man to a
man; stuffed with all honourable virtues.
Much Ado About Nothing, I, 1:53

Othello. Come, Desdemona; 't is the soldiers' life
To have their balmy slumbers wak'd with
strife.
Othello, II, 3:257

SON

King. But now, my cousin[1] Hamlet, and
my son,
Hamlet [Aside]. A little more than kin,
and less than kind.[2]
Hamlet, I, 2:64
[1] cousin: term used for nephew, cousin, or
sometimes for other relatives; the King is
Hamlet's uncle and his step-father.   [2] kind:
not emotional; cf. "our kind of people."

Hamlet [soliloquy]. Why, what an ass
am I! This is most brave,

That I, the son of a dear father murder'd,
Prompted to my revenge by heaven and
  hell,
Must, like a whore, unpack my heart with
  words,
And fall a-cursing, like a very drab,
A scullion!
Hamlet, II, 2:611

K. HENRY.[1] Yea, there thou mak'st me
  sad, and mak'st me sin
In envy that my Lord Northumberland
Should be the father to so blest a son;
A son who is the theme of honour's tongue;
Amongst a grove the very straightest plant;
Who is sweet Fortune's minion and her
  pride;
Whilst I, by looking on the praise of him,
See riot and dishonour stain the brow
Of my young Harry. O! that it could be
  prov'd
That some night-tripping fairy had ex-
  chang'd
In cradle-clothes our children where they
  lay,
And call'd mine Percy, his Plantagenet.
Then would I have his Harry, and he mine.
I Henry IV, I, 1:78
[1] The king laments the wildness of PRINCE
HENRY, his son, and contrasts him with HOT-
SPUR.

JOHN TALBOT [to his father]. Surely, by
  all the glory you have won,
An if I fly, I am not Talbot's son:
Then talk no more of flight.
I Henry VI, IV, 6:50

K. HENRY. And happy always was it for
  that son
Whose father for his hoarding went to hell?
I'll leave my son my virtuous deeds behind;
And would my father had left me no more!
For all the rest is held at such a rate
As brings a thousand-fold more care to
  keep
Than in possession any jot of pleasure.
III Henry VI, II, 2:47

Q. MARGARET [to mother of KING]. From
  forth the kennel of thy womb hath
  crept
A hell-hound that doth hunt us all to death:
That dog, that had his teeth before his eyes,
To worry lambs and lap their gentle blood,
That foul defacer of God's handiwork,
That excellent grand-tyrant of the earth,
That reigns in galled eyes of weeping souls,
Thy womb let loose, to chase us to our
  graves.
Richard III, IV, 4:47

LEONTES. Looking on the lines
Of my boy's face, methought I did recoil

Twenty-three years, and saw myself un-
  breech'd,[1]
In my green velvet coat, my dagger muz-
  zled,
Lest it should bite its master, and so prove,
As ornaments oft do, too dangerous:
How like, methought, I then was to this
  kernel,[2]
This squash,[3] this gentleman.

. . . . .

He makes a July's day short as December,
And with his varying childness cures in me
Thoughts that would thick my blood.
Winter's Tale, I, 2:153, 169
[1] unbreech'd: without grown-up clothes. [2] kernel: seed from which man grows. [3] squash:
unripe pea-pod.

SONG

FIRST LORD. Have you no song, forester,
for this purpose?
FORESTER. Yes, sir.
JAQUES. Sing it: 't is no matter how it be
in tune so it make noise enough.
As You Like It, IV, 2:6

CRANMER. In her[1] days every man shall
  eat in safety
Under his own vine what he plants; and sing
The merry songs of peace to all his neighbours.
Henry VIII, V, 5:34
[1] her: QUEEN ELIZABETH'S.

PRINCE HENRY.[1] I am the cygnet to this
  pale faint swan,
Who chants a doleful hymn[2] to his[3] own
  death,
And from the organ-pipe of frailty sings
His[3] soul and body to their lasting rest.
King John, V, 7:20
[1] PRINCE HENRY: son of K. JOHN, who is dying.
[2] hymn . . . death: tradition that the swan sang
its own death song. [3] his: its.

BOTTOM [singing]. The finch, the spar-
  row, and the lark,
The plain-song[1] cuckoo gray,
Whose note full many a man doth mark,
And dares not answer nay;
Midsummer Night's Dream, III, 1:134
[1] plain-song: a simple melody.

DESDEMONA. She had a song of 'willow';
An old thing 't was, but it express'd her fortune.

. . . . .

The poor soul sat sighing by a sycamore
  tree,

Sing all a green willow;
Her hand on her bosom, her head on her
    knee,
Sing willow, willow, willow:
The fresh streams ran by her, and mur-
    mur'd her moans;
Sing willow, willow, willow;
Her salt tears fell from her, and soften'd
    the stones;—
. . . Sing willow, willow, willow.
                    Othello, IV, 3:28, 41

Gower [as chorus]. Sing a song that old
    was sung,
Assuming man's infirmities,
To glad your ear, and please your eyes.
It hath been sung at festivals,
On ember-eves[1] and holy-ales;
And lords and ladies in their lives
Have read it for restoratives:
The purchase is to make men glorious.
                    Pericles, I, Prelude: 1
[1] ember-eves, etc.: religious observances.

Duke. Now, good Cesario but that piece
    of song,
That old and antique song we heard last
    night;
Methought it did relieve my passion much,
More than light airs and recollected terms
Of these most brisk and giddy-paced times.
                    Twelfth Night, II, 4:2

SORROW

King. When sorrows come, they come not
    single spies,
But in battalions.
                    Hamlet, IV, 5:78

Malcolm. Let us seek out some desolate
    shade, and there
Weep our sad bosoms empty.
                    . . . . .

Macduff. Each new morn
New widows howl, new orphans cry, new
    sorrows
Strike heaven on the face, that it resounds
As if it felt with Scotland and yell'd out
Like syllable of dolour.[1]
                    Macbeth, IV, 3:1, 4
[1] dolour: sorrow.

Cleon. One sorrow never comes but
    brings an heir
That may succeed as his[1] inheritor.
                    Pericles, I, 4:65
[1] his: its.

Though woe be heavy, yet it seldom sleeps;
And they that watch see time how slow it
    creeps.
                    . . . . .

It easeth some, though none it ever cur'd,
To think their dolour[1] others have endur'd.
                    Rape of Lucrece: 1574, 1581
[1] dolour: sorrow.

Brakenbury. Sorrow breaks seasons and
    reposing hours,
Makes the night morning, and the noontide
    night.
                    Richard III, I, 4:76

Duchess of York.[1] Eighty odd years of
    sorrow have I seen,
And each hour's joy wreck'd with a week
    of teen.[2]
                    Richard III, IV, 1:96
[1] Gloucester's mother.   [2] teen: grief.

Marcus. Sorrow concealed, like an oven
    stopp'd,
Doth burn the heart to cinders where it is.
                    Titus Andronicus, II, 4:36

Marcus. To weep with them that weep
    doth ease some deal,
But sorrow flouted at is double death.
                    Titus Andronicus, III, 1:245

Proteus. Cease to lament for that thou
    canst not help,
And study help for that which thou la-
    ment'st.
Time is the nurse and breeder of all good.
                    Two Gentlemen of Verona, III, 1:241

For lovers say, the heart hath treble wrong
When it is barr'd the aidance of the tongue.
An oven that is stopp'd, or river stay'd[1]
Burneth more hotly, swelleth with more
    rage:
So of concealed sorrow may be said;
Free vent of words love's fire doth assuage.
                    Venus and Adonis: 329
[1] river stay'd: river that is held back.

SOUL

Antony. Where souls do couch on flow-
    ers, we'll hand in hand,
And with our sprightly port make the
    ghosts gaze.
                    Antony and Cleopatra, IV, 14:51

Hamlet. I do not set my life at a pin's
    fee;
And for my soul, what can it[1] do to that,
Being a thing immortal as itself.
                    Hamlet, I, 4:65
[1] it: the Ghost.

King. O limed[1] soul, that struggling to be
    free

Art more engaged! Help, angels! make assay;²
Bow, stubborn knees; and heart with strings
   of steel,
Be soft as sinews of the new-born babe.
                     Hamlet, III, 3:68
¹ limed: metaphor of bird caught in bird-lime
smeared on branches. ² assay: effort.

GHOST. But, look! amazement¹ on thy
   mother sits;
O! step between her and her fighting soul;
Conceit² in weakest bodies strongest works:
Speak to her, Hamlet.
                   Hamlet, III, 4:112
¹ amazement: terror. ² Conceit: imagination.

YORK. Open thy gate of mercy, gracious
   God!
My soul flies through these wounds to seek
   out thee.
                III Henry VI, I, 4:177

K. JOHN. We owe thee much: within this
   wall of flesh
There is a soul counts thee her creditor,
And with advantage means to pay thy love.
               King John, III, 3:20

K. LEAR [to CORDELIA]. You do me
   wrong to take me out o' the grave;
Thou art a soul in bliss; but I am bound
Upon a wheel of fire, that mine own tears
Do scald like molten lead.
               King Lear, IV, 7:46

ISABELLA. Why, all the souls that were
   were forfeit once;
And He that might the vantage best have
   took,
Found out the remedy. How would you be,
If He, which is the top of judgment, should
But judge you as you are?
        Measure for Measure, II, 2:73

LORENZO. Such harmony¹ is in immortal
   souls;
But, whilst this muddy vesture of decay
Doth grossly close it in, we cannot hear it.
         Merchant of Venice, V, 1:63
¹ harmony: music of the heavenly bodies.

IAGO. There are a kind of men so loose of
   soul
That in their sleeps will mutter their affairs.
               Othello, III, 3:416

My body or my soul, which was the dearer,
When the one pure, the other made divine?
Whose love of either to myself was nearer,
When both were kept for heaven and Col-
   latine?¹
Ay me! the bark peel'd from the lofty pine,

His² leaves will wither and his sap decay;
So must my soul, her bark being peel'd
   away.
              Rape of Lucrece: 1163
¹ COLLATINE: her husband. ² His: its.

K. RICHARD. Mount, mount, my soul! thy
   seat is up on high,
Whilst my gross flesh sinks downward, here
   to die.
               Richard II, V, 5:112

ROMEO. Now, Tybalt, take the villain
   back again
That late thou gav'st me; for Mercutio's
   soul
Is but a little way above our heads,
Staying¹ for thine to keep him company:
Either thou, or I, or both, must go with him.
       Romeo and Juliet, III, 1:130
¹ Staying: waiting.

FLAMINIUS. You only speak from your
   distracted soul.
        Timon of Athens, III, 4:114

TROILUS. No, Pandarus: I stalk about her
   door,
Like a strange soul upon the Stygian¹ banks
Staying² for waftage. O! be thou my Charon,³
And give me swift transportation to those
   fields
Where I may wallow in the lily-beds
Propos'd for the deserver. O gentle Pandarus!
From Cupid's shoulder pluck his painted
   wings,
And fly with me to Cressid.
       Troilus and Cressida, III, 2:8
¹ Stygian bank: shore of the river between
this world and the next. ² Staying: waiting.
³ Charon: the boatman who takes souls to the
next world.

SPEECH

LEPIDUS. Your speech is passion;
But, pray you, stir no embers up.
       Antony and Cleopatra, II, 2:12

ORLANDO. Your accent is something finer
than you could purchase in so removed a
dwelling.
           As You Like It, III, 2:359

HAMLET. We must speak by the card, or
equivocation will undo us.
               Hamlet, V, 1:149

FALSTAFF. Peace, good pint-pot! peace,
good tickle-brain!
             I Henry IV, II, 4:438

CANTERBURY. When he[1] speaks,
The air, a charter'd libertine, is still,
And the mute wonder lurketh in men's ears
To steal his sweet and honey'd sentences.
                              Henry V, I, 1:47

[1] he: KING HENRY V.

K. HENRY. Under this conjuration speak,
   my lord,
And we will hear, note, and believe in heart
That what you speak is in your conscience
   wash'd
As pure as sin with baptism.
                              Henry V, I, 2:29

K. HENRY. The gentleman[1] is learned,
and a most rare speaker.
                              Henry VIII, I, 2:111

[1] BUCKINGHAM.

Q. KATHARINE. Pray, speak in English:
   here are some will thank you,
If you speak truth.
                              Henry VIII, III, 1:46

K. JOHN. Give me thy hand. I had a thing
   to say,
But I will fit it with some better time.
                              King John, III, 3:25

FOOL. I marvel what kin thou and thy
daughters are: they 'll have me whipped
for speaking true, thou 'lt have me whipped
for lying; and sometimes I am whipped for
holding my peace.
                              King Lear, I, 4:200

ISABELLA. Who 's that which calls?
FRANCISCA. It is a man's voice. Gentle Isa-
   bella,
Turn you the key, and know his business of
   him:
You may, I may not; you are yet unsworn.
When you have vow'd, you must not speak
   with men
But in the presence of the prioress:
Then, if you speak, you must not show your
   face,
Or, if you show your face, you must not
   speak.
                         Measure for Measure, I, 4:6

ISABELLA. It oft falls out,
To have what we would have, we speak not
   what we mean.
                      Measure for Measure, II, 4:118

DON PEDRO. Runs not this speech like iron
   through your blood?
CLAUDIO. I have drunk poison whiles he
   utter'd it.
                  Much Ado About Nothing, V, 1:252

EMILIA. Let heaven and men and devils,
   let them all,
All, all, cry shame against me, yet I 'll speak.
                              Othello, V, 2:222

ULYSSES. When he speaks,
'T is like a chime a-mending.
                  Troilus and Cressida, I, 3:158

STEPHANO. A most delicate monster! His
forward voice now is to speak well of his
friend; his backward voice is to utter foul
speeches and to detract.
                              Tempest, II, 2:93

SPEED

CLEOPATRA. Celerity is never more admir'd
Than by the negligent.
                  Antony and Cleopatra, III, 7:25

IMOGEN. O! for a horse with wings.
   Hear'st thou, Pisanio?
He is at Milford-Haven; read, and tell me
How far 't is thither. If one of mean affairs
May plod it in a week, why may not I
Glide thither in a day?

                    . . . . .

Why, one that rode to 's execution, man,
Could never go so slow.
                     Cymbeline, III, 2:50, 71

FALSTAFF. That sprightly Scot of Scots,
Douglas, that runs o' horseback up a hill
perpendicular.
                         I Henry IV, II, 4:377

MESSENGER. The copy of your speed is
   learn'd by them;
For when you should be told they do prepare,
The tidings comes that they are all arriv'd.
                          King John, IV, 2:113

PORTIA. I would have had thee there, and
   here again,
Ere I can tell thee what thou should'st do
   there.
                          Julius Caesar, II, 4:4

PUCK. I'll put a girdle round about the
   earth
In forty minutes.
              Midsummer Night's Dream, II, 1:175

FRIAR LAURENCE. Wisely and slow; they
   stumble that run fast.

                    . . . . .

Too swift arrives as tardy as too slow.
              Romeo and Juliet, II, 3:94 and 6:15

PROSPERO. I must use you
In such another trick. Go bring the rabble,
O'er whom I give thee power, here to this
place:
Incite them to quick motion.

. . . . .

ARIEL. Presently?[1]
PROSPERO. Ay, with a twink.
ARIEL. Before you can say 'come' and 'go,'
And breathe twice and cry 'so so,'
Each one, tripping on his toe,
Will be here with mop and mow.[2]
Do you love me, master? no?
Tempest, IV, 1:36, 42
[1] Presently: at once. [2] mop and mow: grimaces.

ARIEL. I drink the air before me, and return
Or e'er your pulse twice beat.
Tempest, V, 1:102

SPIRIT

KING. Methinks in thee some blessed spirit
doth speak
His powerful sound within an organ weak.
All's Well That Ends Well, II, 1:178

COMINIUS. When by and by the din of
war 'gan pierce
His ready sense; then straight his doubled
spirit
Re-quicken'd what in flesh was fatigate,
And to the battle came he.
Coriolanus, II, 2:119

LADY PERCY. Thy spirit within thee hath
been so at war,
And thus hath so bestirr'd thee in thy sleep,
That beads of sweat have stood upon thy
brow,
Like bubbles in a late-disturbed stream.
I Henry IV, II, 3:59

CASSIUS. Nor[1] stony tower, nor walls of
beaten brass,
Nor airless dungeon, nor strong links of
iron,
Can be retentive to the strength of spirit.
Julius Caesar, I, 3:93
[1] Nor . . . nor: neither nor.

BENVOLIO. That gallant spirit hath aspir'd
the clouds,
Which too untimely here did scorn the
earth.
Romeo and Juliet, III, 1:122

BAPTISTA. For shame, thou hilding[1] of a
devilish spirit,

Why dost thou wrong her that did ne'er
wrong thee?
Taming of the Shrew, II, 1:26
[1] hilding: a term of contempt.

ARIEL. All hail, great master! grave sir,
hail! I come
To answer thy best pleasure; be 't to fly,
To swim, to dive into the fire, to ride
On the curl'd clouds: to thy strong bidding
task
Ariel and all his quality.[1]
Tempest, I, 2:189
[1] quality: powers as a spirit.

ARIEL. I boarded the king's ship; now on
the beak,
Now in the waist, the deck, in every cabin,
I flam'd amazement: sometimes I'd divide
And burn in many places; on the topmast,
The yards and bowsprit, would I flame distinctly,
Then meet and join. Jove's lightnings, the
precursors
O' the dreadful thunder-claps, more momentary
And sight-outrunning were not: the fire
and cracks
Of sulphurous roaring the most mighty
Neptune[1]
Seem to besiege and make his bold waves
tremble;
Yes, his dread trident shake.
Tempest, I, 2:196
[1] Neptune: god of the sea.

SPIRITS

BELARIUS. When on my three-foot stool I
sit and tell
The war-like feats I have done, his spirits
fly out
Into my story: say 'Thus mine enemy fell,
And thus I set my foot on 's neck;' even then
The princely blood flows in his cheek, he
sweats,
Strains his young nerves, and puts himself
in posture
That acts my words.
Cymbeline, III, 3:90

LADY M. [soliloquy]. Come, you spirits
That tend on mortal[1] thoughts! unsex me
here,
And fill me from the crown to the toe top
full
Of direst cruelty; make thick my blood,
Stop up the access[2] and passage to remorse,[3]
That no compunctious visitings of nature
Shake my fell[4] purpose, nor keep peace between

The effect and it! Come to my woman's
  breasts,
And take my milk for gall, you murdering
  ministers,
Wherever in your sightless[5] substances
You wait on nature's mischief! Come, thick
  night,
And pall thee in the dunnest smoke of hell,
That my keen knife see not the wound it
  makes,
Nor heaven peep through the blanket of the
  dark,
To cry 'Hold,[6] hold!'
                                    Macbeth, I, 5:41
[1] mortal: deadly. [2] access: entrance. [3] remorse: pity. [4] fell: cruel. [5] sightless: invisible. [6] Hold: military law made it a capital
offence for a duelist to strike an opponent after
a third person had cried, "Hold, hold!"

AUMERLE. I have a thousand spirits in one
  breast,
To answer twenty thousand such as you.
                                    Richard II, IV, 1:58

FERDINAND. May I be bold
To think these spirits?
  PROSPERO. Spirits, which by mine art
I have from their confines call'd to enact
My present fancies.
                                    Tempest, IV, 1:119

SPRING

AMIENS. Under the greenwood tree
Who loves to lie with me,
And turn his merry note
Unto the sweet bird's throat,
Come hither, come hither, come hither:
Here shall he see
No enemy
But winter and rough weather.
                                    As You Like It, II, 5:1

TWO PAGES. It was a lover and his lass,
With a hey, and a ho, and a hey nonino,
That o'er the green corn-field did pass,
In the spring time, the only pretty ring time,
When birds do sing, hey ding a ding, ding;
Sweet lovers love the spring.
Between the acres of the rye,
With a hey, and a ho, and a hey nonino,
These pretty country folks would lie,
In the spring time, the only pretty ring time,
When birds do sing, hey ding a ding, ding;
Sweet lovers love the spring.
This carol they began that hour
With a hey, and a ho, and a hey nonino,
How that a life was but a flower
In the spring time, the only pretty ring time,
When birds do sing, hey ding a ding, ding;
Sweet lovers love the spring.

And therefore take the present time,
With a hey, and a ho, and a hey nonino,
For love is crowned with the prime
In the spring time, the only pretty ring time,
                                    As You Like It, V, 3:17

KING. Biron is like an envious sneaping[1]
  frost
That bites the first-born infants[2] of the
  spring.
                                    Love's Labour's Lost, I, 1:100
[1] sneaping: nipping. [2] infants . . . spring:
buds.

                          Enter AUTOLYCUS, *singing.*
When daffodils begin to peer,
With heigh! the doxy[1] over the dale,
Why, then comes in the sweet o' the year;
For the red blood reigns in the winter's pale.
The white sheet bleaching on the hedge,
With heigh! the sweet birds, O! how they
  sing,
Doth set my pugging[2] tooth on edge;
For a quart of ale is a dish for a king.
The lark, that tirra-lirra chants,
With heigh! with heigh! the thrush and the
  jay,
Are summer songs for me and my aunts,[3]
While we lie tumbling in the hay.
                                    Winter's Tale, IV, 3:1
[1] doxy: mistress. [2] pugging: thieving. [3] aunts:
prostitutes.

STAGE

NORTHUMBERLAND. Now let not Nature's
  hand
Keep the wild flood confin'd! let order die!
And let this world no longer be a stage
To feed contention in a lingering act.
                                    II Henry IV, I, 1:153

O! for a Muse of fire, that would ascend
The brightest heaven of invention;
A kingdom for a stage, princes to act
And monarchs to behold the swelling scene.
                                    Henry V, I, Prologue: 1

JAQUES. All the world's a stage,
And all the men and women merely players:
                                    As You Like It, II, 7:139

STARS

ANTONY. My good stars, that were my
  former guides,
Have empty left their orbs, and shot their
  fires
Into the abysm of hell.
                                    Antony and Cleopatra, III, 13:145

HORATIO. The moist star
Upon whose influence Neptune's[1] empire stands
Was sick almost to doomsday with eclipse.
Hamlet, I, 1:118
[1] Neptune: god of the sea.

CASSIUS. The fault, dear Brutus, is not in our stars,
But in ourselves, that we are underlings.
Julius Caesar, I, 2:140

KENT. It is the stars,
The stars above us, govern our conditions;
Else one self[1] mate and mate could not beget
Such different issues.
King Lear, IV, 3:34
[1] self . . . mate: the same husband and wife.

JULIET. Give me my Romeo: and, when he shall die,
Take him and cut him out in little stars,
And he will make the face of heaven so fine
That all the world will be in love with night.
And pay no worship to the garish sun.
Romeo and Juliet, III, 2:21

PROSPERO. I find my zenith doth depend upon
A most auspicious star, whose influence
If now I court not but omit, my fortunes
Will ever after droop.
Tempest, I, 2:181

STOCKS

CORNWALL. Fetch forth the stocks!
You stubborn ancient knave, you reverend braggart,
We 'll teach you.
KENT. Sir, I am too old to learn.
Call not your stocks for me; I serve the king,
On whose employment I was sent to you.

. . . . .

CORNWALL. Fetch forth the stocks!
As I have life and honour, there shall he sit till noon.
REGAN. Till noon! till night, my lord; and all night too.
KENT. Why, madam, if I were your father's dog,
You should not use me so.
King Lear, II, 2:132, 140

KENT.[1] Some time I shall sleep out, the rest I 'll whistle.
A good man's fortune may grow out at heels.
King Lear, II, 2:162
[1] In the stocks.

STORM

YORK. I will stir up in England some black storm
Shall blow ten thousand souls to heaven or hell;
And this fell[1] tempest shall not cease to rage
Until the golden circuit on my head,
Like to the glorious sun's transparent beams,
Do calm the fury of this mad-bred flaw.[2]
II Henry VI, III, 1:348
[1] fell: cruel. [2] flaw: blast of wind.

K. LEAR. Blow, winds, and crack your cheeks! rage! blow!
You cataracts and hurricanoes, spout
Till you have drench'd our steeples, drown'd the cocks!
You sulphurous and thought-executing fires,
Vaunt-couriers of oak-cleaving thunder-bolts,
Singe my white head! And thou, all-shaking thunder,
Strike flat the thick rotundity o' the world!
Crack nature's moulds, all germens spill at once
That make ingrateful man!
FOOL.[1] O nuncle,[2] court holy-water in a dry house is better than this rain-water out o' door. Good nuncle, in, and ask thy daughters' blessing; here 's a night pities neither wise men nor fools.
K. LEAR. Rumble thy bellyful! Spit, fire! spout, rain!
Nor rain, wind, thunder, fire, are my daughters:
I tax[3] not you, you elements, with unkindness;
I never gave you kingdom, call'd you children,
You owe me no subscription: then let fall
Your horrible pleasure; here I stand, your slave,
A poor, infirm, weak, and despis'd old man.
But yet I call you servile ministers,
That have with two pernicious daughters join'd
Your high-engender'd battles 'gainst a head
So old and white as this. O! O! 't is foul.
King Lear, III, 2:1
[1] Fool: jester. [2] nuncle: the customary address of a licensed fool to his superior. [3] tax: accuse.

K. LEAR. This tempest will not give me leave to ponder
On things would hurt me more.
King Lear, III, 4:25

SECOND GENTLEMAN. For do but stand upon the foaming shore,
The chidden billow seems to pelt the clouds;

The wind-shak'd surge, with high and
    monstrous mane,
Seems to cast water on the burning Bear[1]
And quench the guards of the ever-fixed
    pole:
I never did like[2] molestation view
On the enchafed flood.
                            Othello, II, 1:11
[1] Bear: a constellation.   [2] like: similar.

Cassio. Tempests themselves, high seas,
    and howling winds,
The gutter'd rocks, and congregated sands,
Traitors ensteep'd[1] to clog the guiltless keel,
As having sense of beauty, do omit
Their mortal[2] natures, letting go safely by
The divine Desdemona.
                            Othello, II, 1:68
[1] ensteep'd: lying under water.   [2] mortal:
deadly.

Pericles. Thou god of this great vast, re-
    buke these surges,
Which wash both heaven and hell; and thou,
    that hast
Upon the winds command, bind them in
    brass,
Having call'd them from the deep. O! still
Thy deafening, dreadful thunders; gently
    quench
Thy nimble, sulphurous flashes.
                            Pericles, III, 1:1

STRENGTH

Isabella. O! it is excellent
To have a giant's strength, but it is tyran-
    nous
To use it like a giant.
                    Measure for Measure, II, 2:107

Juliet. Love give me strength! and
    strength shall help afford.
                    Romeo and Juliet, IV, 1:125

Ariel. If you could hurt,
Your swords are now too massy[1] for your
    strengths,
And will not be uplifted.
                            Tempest, III, 3:67
[1] massy: heavy.

STUDY

Biron. O! these are barren tasks, too hard
    to keep,
Not to see ladies, study, fast, not sleep.
                    Love's Labour's Lost, I, 1:47

Biron. What is the end of study? let me
    know.

King. Why, that to know which else we
    should not know.
Biron. Things hid and barr'd, you mean,
    from common sense?
King. Ay, that is study's god-like recom-
    pense.
Biron. Come on then; I will swear to
    study so
To know the thing I am forbid to know;
As thus: to study where I well may dine,
When I to feast expressly am forbid;
Or study where to meet some mistress fine,
When mistresses from common sense are
    hid;
Or, having sworn too hard-a-keeping oath,
Study to break it, and not break my troth.
                    Love's Labour's Lost, I, 1:55

Biron. Study me how to please the eye in-
    deed,
By fixing it upon a fairer eye.
                    Love's Labour's Lost, I, 1:80

Biron. Small have continual plodders
    ever won,
Save base authority from others' books.
These earthly godfathers of heaven's lights
That give a name to every fixed star,
Have no more profit of their shining nights
Than those that walk and wot[1] not what
    they are.
                    Love's Labour's Lost, I, 1:86
[1] wot: know.

Pistol. He hath studied her well, and
translated her well, out of honesty into
English.
                    Merry Wives of Windsor, I, 3:54

Tranio. No profit grows where is no
    pleasure ta'en:
In brief, sir, study what you most affect.[1]
                    Taming of the Shrew, I, 1:39
[1] affect: love.

Prospero. I, thus neglecting worldly ends,
    all dedicated
To closeness and the bettering of my mind,
. . . in my false brother
Awak'd an evil nature.
                            Tempest, I, 2:89

SUCCESS

Dolabella [to Cleopatra]. Hear me,
    good madam.
Your loss is as yourself, great; and you bear
    it
As answering to the weight: would I might
    never
O'ertake pursu'd success, but I do feel,

By the rebound of yours, a grief that smites
My very heart at root.
Antony and Cleopatra, V, 2:100

K. HENRY. Now, lords, if God doth give
  successful end
To this debate that bleedeth at our doors
We will our youth lead on to higher fields
And draw no swords but what are sancti-
  fied.
II Henry IV, IV, 4:1

FRIAR. Let this be so, and doubt not but
  success
Will fashion the event in better shape
Than I can lay it down in likelihood.
Much Ado About Nothing, IV, 1:236

SUFFERING

SICILIUS. Why did you suffer[1] Iachimo,
Slight thing of Italy,
To taint his nobler heart and brain
With needless jealousy.
Cymbeline, V, 4:63

[1] suffer: permit.

HAMLET. Since my dear soul was mistress
  of her choice
And could of men distinguish, her election
Hath seal'd thee for herself; for thou hast
  been
As one, in suffering all, that suffers nothing,
A man that fortune's buffets and rewards
Has ta'en with equal thanks.
Hamlet, III, 2:68

EDGAR. Who alone suffers suffers most i'
  the mind,
Leaving free things and happy shows behind;
But then the mind much sufferance doth
  o'erskip,
When grief hath mates, and bearing fellowship.
King Lear, III, 6:111

SUICIDE

CLEOPATRA. Patience is sottish, and im-
  patience does
Become a dog that 's mad; then is it sin
To rush into the secret house of death,
Ere death dare come to us?
Antony and Cleopatra, IV, 15:79

CLEOPATRA. We 'll bury him; and then,
  what 's brave, what 's noble,
Let 's do it after the high Roman fashion,
And make death proud to take us.
Antony and Cleopatra, IV, 15:86

IMOGEN. Against self-slaughter
There is a prohibition so divine
That cravens[1] my weak hand.
Cymbeline, III, 4:78

[1] cravens: frightens.

POSTHUMUS. Yet am I better
That one that 's sick o' the gout, since he
  had rather
Groan so in perpetuity than be cur'd
By the sure physician, death.
Cymbeline, V, 4:4

HAMLET. O! that this too too solid flesh
  would melt,
Thaw and resolve itself into a dew;
Or that the Everlasting had not fix'd
His canon 'gainst self-slaughter!
Hamlet, I, 2:129

HAMLET [soliloquy]. To be, or not to be:
  that is the question:
Whether 't is nobler in the mind to suffer
The slings and arrows of outrageous for-
  tune,
Or to take arms against a sea of troubles,
And by opposing end them? To die: to
  sleep;
No more; and by a sleep to say we end
The heart-ache and the thousand natural
  shocks
That flesh is heir to, 't is a consummation
Devoutly to be wish'd. To die, to sleep;
To sleep; perchance to dream: ay, there 's
  the rub;
For in that sleep of death what dreams may
  come
When we have shuffled off this mortal coil,
Must give us pause. There 's the respect
That makes calamity of so long life;
For who would bear the whips and scorns
  of time,
The oppressor's wrong, the proud man's
  contumely,
The pangs of dispriz'd love, the law's delay,
The insolence of office, and the spurns
That patient merit of the unworthy takes,
When he himself might his quietus[1] make
With a bare bodkin?[2] who would fardels[3]
  bear,
To grunt and sweat under a weary life,
But that the dread of something after death,
The undiscover'd country from whose
  bourn
No traveller returns, puzzles the will,
And makes us rather bear those ills we have
Than fly to others that we know not of?
Thus conscience does make cowards of us
  all;
And thus the native hue of resolution
Is sicklied[4] o'er with the pale cast of
  thought,
And enterprises of great pith and moment

With this regard their currents turn awry,
And lose the name of action.

Hamlet, III, 1:56

[1] quietus: end. [2] bodkin: a tool for making holes by piercing; here, a dagger. [3] fardels: burdens. [4] sicklied o'er: tainted and over-spread.

QUEEN. Your sister's drown'd, Laertes.
LAERTES. Drown'd! O! where?
QUEEN. There is a willow grows aslant a brook,
That shows his hoar leaves in the glassy stream;
There with fantastic garlands did she come,
Clambering to hang, an envious sliver broke,
When down her weedy trophies and herself
Fell in the weeping brook. Her clothes spread wide,
And mermaid-like, awhile they bore her up;
Which time she chanted snatches of old tunes,

. . . . .

Till that her garments, heavy with their drink,
Pull'd the poor wretch from her melodious lay
To muddy death.
LAERTES. Alas! then, she is drown'd?

Hamlet, IV, 7:165

SECOND CLOWN. Will you ha' the truth on 't? If this had not been a gentlewoman she should have been buried out o' Christian burial.
FIRST CLOWN. Why, there thou sayest; and the more pity that great folk shall have countenance in this world to drown or hang themselves more than their even Christian.

Hamlet, V, 1:26

LAERTES. What ceremony else?
PRIEST. Her obsequies have been as far enlarg'd
As we have warrantise; her death was doubtful,
And, but that great command o'ersways the order,
She should in ground unsanctified have lodg'd
Till the last trumpets.

. . . . .

No more be done:
We should profane the service of the dead,
To sing a requiem and such rest to her
As to peace-parted souls.
LAERTES. Lay her i' the earth;
And from her fair and unpolluted flesh
May violets spring! I tell thee, churlish priest,

A ministering angel shall my sister be,
When thou liest howling.

Hamlet, V, 1:245, 258

CASCA. So every bondman in his own hand bears
The power to cancel his captivity.

Julius Caesar, I, 3:101

CASSIUS. Guide thou the sword. Caesar, thou art reveng'd,
Even with the sword that kill'd thee.

Julius Caesar, V, 3:44

BRUTUS. Hold then my sword, and turn away thy face,

. . . . .

Farewell, good Strato. Caesar, now be still:
I kill'd not thee with half so good a will.

Julius Caesar, V, 5:47, 50

GLOUCESTER. You ever-gentle gods, take my breath from me:
Let not my worser spirit tempt me again
To die before you please!

King Lear, IV, 6:221

SUITORS

IMOGEN. A foolish suitor to a wedded lady,
That hath her husband banish'd.

Cymbeline, I, 6:2

NERISSA. First, there is the Neapolitan prince.
PORTIA. Ay, that 's a colt indeed, for he doth nothing but talk of his horse; and he makes it a great appropriation to his own good parts that he can shoe him himself . . .
NERISSA. Then is there the County Palatine.
PORTIA. He doth nothing but frown, as who should say, 'If you will not have me, choose.' He hears merry tales, and smiles not: I fear he will prove the weeping philosopher when he grows old, being so full of unmannerly sadness in his youth. I had rather be married to a death's-head with a bone in his mouth than to either of these. God defend me from these two!
NERISSA. How say you by the French lord, Monsieur Le Bon?
PORTIA. God made him, and therefore let him pass for a man. In truth, I know it is a sin to be a mocker; but he! why he hath a horse better than the Neapolitan's, a better bad habit of frowning than the Count Palatine; he is every man in no man; if a throstle sing, he falls straight a-capering; he will fence with his own shadow: if I should marry him, I should marry twenty hus-

bands. If he would despise me, I would forgive him, for if he love me to madness, I shall never requite him.

NERISSA. What say you then to Falconbridge, the young baron of England?

PORTIA. You know I say nothing to him, for he understands not me, nor I him: he hath neither Latin, French, nor Italian, and you will come into the court and swear that I have a poor pennyworth in the English. He is a proper man's picture, but, alas! who can converse with a dumb-show? How oddly he is suited![1] I think he bought his doublet in Italy, his round hose in France, his bonnet in Germany, and his behaviour every where.

. . . . .

NERISSA. How like you the young German, the Duke of Saxony's nephew?

PORTIA. Very vilely in the morning, when he is sober, and most vilely in the afternoon, when he is drunk: when he is best, he is a little worse than a man, and when he is worst, he is little better than a beast. An[2] the worst fall that ever fell, I hope I shall make shift to go without him.

NERISSA. If he should offer to choose, and choose the right casket, you should refuse to perform your father's will, if you should refuse to accept him.

PORTIA. Therefore, for fear of the worst, I pray thee, set a deep glass of Rhenish wine on the contrary casket, for if the devil be within and that temptation without, I know he will choose it. I will do anything, Nerissa, ere I'll be married to a sponge.

NERISSA. You need not fear, lady, the having any of these lords: they have acquainted me with their determinations; which is, indeed, to return to their home and to trouble you with no more suit, unless you may be won by some other sort than your father's imposition depending on the caskets.

PORTIA. If I live to be as old as Sibylla,[3] I will die as chaste as Diana,[4] unless I be obtained by the manner of my father's will. I am glad this parcel of wooers are so reasonable, for there is not one among them but I dote on his very absence, and I pray God grant them a fair departure.

Merchant of Venice, I, 2:42, 91

[1] suited: dressed. [2] An: if. [3] Sibylla: a priestess of Apollo gifted for prophecy. [4] Diana: goddess of the hunt, noted for her chastity.

TRANIO. Thus it stands:
Her elder sister is so curst and shrewd,
That till the father rid his hands of her,
Master, your love must live a maid at home;

And therefore has he closely mew'd[1] her up,
Because she will not be annoy'd with suitors.
Taming of the Shrew, I, 1:185
[1] mew'd: cooped.

SIR TOBY. He[1] 's as tall[2] a man as any 's in Illyria.

MARIA. What 's that to the purpose?

SIR TOBY. Why, he has three thousand ducats a year.

MARIA. Ay, but he 'll have but a year in all these ducats: he 's a very fool and a prodigal.

SIR TOBY. Fie, that you 'll say so! he plays o' the viol-de-gamboys,[3] and speaks three or four languages word for word without book.
Twelfth Night, I, 3:20
[1] He: SIR ANDREW. [2] tall: stout, sturdy. [3] viol-de-gamboys. Toby's mistake for *vol di gamba*.

SUMMER

K. JOHN. There is so hot a summer in my bosom
That all my bowels crumble up to dust:
I am a scribbled form, drawn with a pen
Upon a parchment, and against his fire
Do I shrink up.
King John, V, 7:30

Shall I compare thee to a summer's day?
Thou art more lovely and more temperate:
Rough winds do shake the darling buds of May,
And summer's lease hath all too short a date:
Sometimes too hot the eye of heaven shines,
And often is his gold complexion dimm'd;
And every fair from fair sometime declines,
By chance of nature's changing course untrimm'd;
But thy eternal summer shall not fade;
Nor lose possession of that fair thou ow'st.[1]
Sonnet 18
[1] ow'st: ownest.

SUN

FALSTAFF. Shall the blessed sun of heaven prove a micher[1] and eat blackberries? a question not to be asked. Shall the son of England prove a thief and take purses? a question to be asked.
I Henry IV, II, 4:449
[1] micher: truant.

LEWIS. The sun of heaven methought was loath to set,
But stay'd and made the western welkin blush.
King John, V, 5:1

GAUNT. More are men's ends mark'd than their lives before:
The setting sun, and music at the close,
As the last taste of sweets, is sweetest last,
Writ in remembrance more than things long past.
Richard II, II, 1:11

MONTAGNE. But all so soon as the all-cheering sun
Should in the furthest east begin to draw
The shady curtains from Aurora's[1] bed,
Away from light steals home my heavy son.
Romeo and Juliet, I, 1:140
[1] Aurora: goddess of the dawn.

AARON. As when the golden sun salutes the morn,
And, having gilt the ocean with his beams,
Gallops the zodiac in his glistering coach,
And overlooks the highest-peering hills;
Titus Andronicus, II, 1:5

TITUS. Heaven shall hear our prayers,
Or with our sighs we 'll breathe the welkin dim,
And stain the sun with fog, as sometime clouds
When they do hug him in their melting bosoms.
Titus Andronicus, III, 1:211

TROILUS. I have, as when the sun doth light a storm,
Buried this sigh in wrinkle of a smile.
Troilus and Cressida, I, 1:37

SUPERSTITION

HORATIO. In the most high and palmy state of Rome,
A little ere the mighty Julius fell,
The graves stood tenantless and the sheeted dead
Did squeak and gibber in the Roman streets;
As stars with trains of fire and dews of blood,
Disasters in the sun; and the moist star[1]
Upon whose influence Neptune's[2] empire stands
Was sick almost to doomsday with eclipse.
Hamlet, I, 1:113
[1] moist star: the moon. [2] Neptune: god of the sea.

HORATIO. I have heard,
The cock, that is the trumpet to the morn,
Doth, with his lofty and shrill-sounding throat
Awake the god of day; and, at his warning,
Whether in sea or fire, in earth or air,
The extravagant[1] and erring[2] spirit hies

To his confine; and of the truth herein
This present object made probation.
MARCELLUS. It faded on the crowing of the cock.
Some say that ever 'gainst that season comes
Wherein our Saviour's birth is celebrated,
The bird of dawning singeth all night long;
And then, they say, no spirit can walk abroad;
The nights are wholesome; then no planets strike,
No fairy takes, nor witch hath power to charm,
So hallow'd and so gracious is the time.
Hamlet, I, 1:149
[1] extravagant: wandering beyond its place of confinement. [2] erring: wandering.

GADSHILL. We steal as in a castle, cock-sure; we have the receipt of fern-seed, we walk invisible.
I Henry IV, II, 1:95

CASCA. Are not you mov'd, when all the sway of earth
Shakes like a thing unfirm? O Cicero!
I have seen tempests, when the scolding winds
Have riv'd the knotty oaks; and I have seen
The ambitious ocean swell and rage and foam,
To be exalted with the threat'ning clouds:
But never till to-night, never till now.
Did I go through a tempest dropping fire.
Either there is a civil strife in heaven,
Or else the world, too saucy with the gods,
Incenses them to send destruction.

. . . . .

CASSIUS. But if you would consider the true cause
Why all these fires, why all these gliding ghosts,
Why birds and beasts, from quality and kind;
Why old men fool, and children calculate;
Why all these things change from their or-dinance,
Their natures, and preformed faculties,
To monstrous quality, why, you shall find
That heaven hath infus'd them with these spirits
To make them instruments of fear and warning
Unto some monstrous state.
Julius Caesar, I, 3:3, 62

GLOUCESTER. These late eclipses in the sun and moon portend[1] no good to us; though the wisdom of nature can reason it thus and thus, yet nature finds itself scourged by the sequent[2] effects. Love cools, friendship falls off, brothers divide: in cities, mutinies; in countries, discord; in palaces, treason; and the bond cracked 'twixt son and father.

King Lear, I, 2:112

[1] portend: foretell. [2] sequent: following.

CAPTAIN. The bay-trees in our country are all wither'd
And meteors fright the fixed stars of heaven,
The pale-fac'd moon looks bloody on the earth
And lean-look'd prophets whisper fearful change,
These signs forerun the death or fall of kings.

Richard II, II, 4:8

GONZALO. Who would believe that there were mountaineers
Dew-lapp'd like bulls, whose throats had hanging at them
Wallets of flesh? or that there were such men,
Whose heads stood in their breasts? which now we find
Each putter-out[1] of five for one will bring us
Good warrant of.

Tempest, III, 3:44

[1] putter-out . . . one: gambler giving odds of five for one.

SUSPENSE

ROSALIND. Nay, I prithee now with most petitionary vehemence, tell me who it is.
CELIA. O! wonderful, wonderful, and most wonderful wonderful! and yet again wonderful! and after that, out of all whooping!
ROSALIND. Good my complexion! dost thou think, though I am caparisoned like a man, I have a doublet and hose in my disposition? One inch of delay more is a South-sea of discovery;[1] I prithee, tell me who is it.

As You Like It, III, 2:200

[1] South-sea . . . discovery: delay as bad as a voyage of discovery.

CHORUS. From camp to camp, through the foul womb of night,
The hum of either army stilly sounds,
That the fix'd sentinels almost receive
The secret whispers of each other's watch:
Fire answers fire, and through their paly flames
Each battle[1] sees the other's umber'd[2] face;
Steed threatens steed, in high and boastful neighs

Piercing the night's dull ear; and from the tents
The armourers, accomplishing the knights,
With busy hammers closing rivets up,
Give dreadful note of preparation.

. . . . .

The royal captain[3] of this ruin'd band
Walking from watch to watch, from tent to tent,
Let him cry 'Praise and glory on his head!'
For forth he goes and visits all his host,
Bids them good morrow with a modest smile,
And calls them brothers, friends and countrymen.

Henry V, IV, Prologue: 4, 29

[1] battle: army. [2] umber'd: darkened. [3] captain: KING HENRY.

SUSPICION

GLOUCESTER. Suspicion always haunts the guilty mind;
The thief doth fear each bush an officer.

III Henry VI, V, 6:11

BANQUO [soliloquy]. Thou hast it now: king, Cawdor, Glamis, all,
As the weird women promis'd; and, I fear,
Thou play'dst most foully for 't; yet it was said
It should not stand in thy posterity,
But that myself should be the root and father
Of many kings. If there come truth from them,
As upon thee, Macbeth, their speeches shine,
Why, by the verities[1] on thee made good,
May they not be my oracles[2] as well,
And set me up in hope?

Macbeth, III, 1:1

[1] verities: truths. [2] oracles: those who tell the decisions of the gods.

LENNOX. Things have been strangely borne.[1] The gracious Duncan
Was pitied of Macbeth: marry, he was dead:
And the right-valiant Banquo walk'd too late;
Whom, you may say, if 't please you, Fleance kill'd,
For Fleance fled: men must not walk too late.

Macbeth, III, 6:3

[1] borne: managed.

IAGO. Not poppy, nor mandragora,
Nor all the drowsy syrups of the world,
Shall ever medicine thee to that sweet sleep
Which thou ow'dst[1] yesterday.
OTHELLO. Ha! ha! false to me?

IAGO. Why, how now, general! no more of that.

OTHELLO. Avaunt! be gone! thou hast set me on the rack;
I swear 't is better to be much abus'd
Than but to know 't a little.
Othello, III, 3:330

[1] ow'dst: owned.

LEONTES. Cease! no more.
You smell this business with a sense as cold
As is a dead man's nose; but I do see 't and feel 't,
As you feel doing thus, and see withal[1]
The instruments that feel.
Winter's Tale, II, 1:150

[1] withal: with it.

SWEAR

CLOTEN. I had a hundred pound on 't; and then a whoreson jackanapes must take me up for swearing, as if I borrowed mine oaths of him and might not spend them at pleasure.
Cymbeline, II, 1:3

FALSTAFF. If thou wert any way given to virtue, I would swear by thy face; my oath should be, 'By this fire.'
1 Henry IV, III, 3:38

CONSTANCE. What a fool art thou,
A ramping fool, to brag and stamp and swear.
King John, III, 1:120

Q. ELIZABETH [to K. RICHARD]. If something thou would'st swear to be believ'd,
Swear then by something that thou hast not wrong'd.
Richard III, IV, 4:372

GONZALO. He 'll be hang'd yet,
Though every drop of water swear against it.
Tempest, I, 1:62

SWORD

PRINCE. Faith, tell me now in earnest, how came Falstaff's sword so hacked?
PETO. Why, he hacked it with his dagger, and said he would swear truth out of England but he would make you believe it was done in fight, and persuaded us to do the like.
1 Henry IV, II, 4:334

EDMUND. To be tender-minded
Does not become a sword.
King Lear, V, 3:31

[Prologue.] Whereat with blade, with bloody blameful blade,
He bravely broach'd his boiling bloody breast;
Midsummer Night's Dream, V, 1:147

AUMERLE. No, good my lord; let 's fight with gentle words
Till time lend friends and friends their helpful swords.
Richard II, III, 3:131

MERCUTIO. Thou art like one of those fellows that when he enters the confines of a tavern claps me his sword upon the table and says, 'God send me no need of thee!' and by the operation of the second cup draws it on the drawer, when indeed there is no need.
Romeo and Juliet, III, 1:5

HECTOR. Now is my day's work done; I 'll take good breath:
Rest, sword; thou hast thy fill of blood and death.
Troilus and Cressida, V, 8:3

TACT

MENENIUS. He was not taken well; he had not din'd:
The veins unfill'd, our blood is cold, and then
We pout upon the morning, are unapt
To give or to forgive; but when we have stuff'd
These pipes and these conveyances of our blood
With wine and feeding, we have suppler souls
Than in our priest-like fasts: therefore, I 'll watch him
Till he be dieted to my request,
And then I 'll set upon him.
BRUTUS. You know the very road into his kindness,
And cannot lose your way.
Coriolanus, V, 1:50

HAMLET. Suit the action to the word, the word to the action; with this special observance, that you o'erstep not the modesty[1] of nature.
Hamlet, III, 2:20

[1] modesty: moderation.

DESDEMONA. Those that do teach young babes
Do it with gentle means and easy tasks;
He might have chid me so; for, in good faith,
I am a child to chiding.
Othello, IV, 2:111

VALENTINE. Win her with gifts, if she respect not words.
Dumb jewels often in their silent kind
More than quick words do move a woman's mind.
Two Gentlemen of Verona, III, 1:89

TALE

FLUELLEN. It is not well done, mark you now, to take the tales out of my mouth, ere it is made and finished.
Henry V, IV, 7:44

EDGAR. List a brief tale;
And when 't is told, O! that my heart would burst!
King Lear, V, 3:181

CLOWN. O, thereby hangs a tale.
Othello, III, 1:8

Q. ELIZABETH. An honest tale speeds best being plainly told.
Richard III, IV, 4:358

TALKER

PAROLLES. Why, I say nothing.
CLOWN. Marry, you are the wiser man; for many a man's tongue shakes out his[1] master's undoing.
All's Well That Ends Well, II, 4:22
[1] his: its.

ROSALIND. Pray you, no more of this: 't is like the howling of Irish wolves against the moon.
As You Like It, V, 2:116

MENENIUS. [He] talks like a knell, and his hum is a battery.
Coriolanus, V, 4:22

K. JOHN. They shoot but calm words folded up in smoke,
To make a faithless error in your ears.
King John, II, 1:229

KING. A man in all the world's new fashion planted,
That hath a mint of phrases in his brain.
Love's Labour's Lost, I, 1:165

LORENZO. I must be one of these same dumb wise men,
For Gratiano never lets me speak.
GRATIANO. Well, keep me company but two years more,
Thou shalt not know the sound of thine own tongue.
. . . . .

BASSANIO. Gratiano speaks an infinite deal of nothing, more than any man in all Venice. His reasons are as two grains of wheat hid in two bushels of chaff: you shall seek all day ere you find them, and when you have them, they are not worth the search.
Merchant of Venice, I, 1:106, 114

LORENZO. How every fool can play upon the word! I think the best grace of wit will shortly turn into silence, and discourse grow commendable in none only but parrots.
Merchant of Venice, III, 5:48

LORENZO. The fool hath planted in his memory
An army of good words.
Merchant of Venice, III, 5:71

BEATRICE. I wonder that you will still be talking, Signior Benedick: nobody marks you.
BENEDICK. What! my dear Lady Disdain, are you yet living?
BEATRICE. Is it possible disdain should die while she hath such meet food to feed it as Signior Benedick?
Much Ado About Nothing, I, 1:117

BENEDICK. He was wont to speak plain and to the purpose, like an honest man and a soldier; and now is he turned orthography:[1] his words are a very fantastical banquet, just so many strange dishes.
Much Ado About Nothing, II, 3:19
[1] orthography: meticulous correctness.

BENEDICK. I 'll tell thee what, prince; a college of wit-crackers cannot flout me out of my humour.
Much Ado About Nothing, V, 4:101

NORTHUMBERLAND. These high wild hills and rough uneven ways
Draw out our miles and make them wearisome;
And yet your fair discourse hath been as sugar,
Making the hard way sweet and delectable.
Richard II, II, 3:4

FIRST MURDERER. Talkers are no good doers: be assur'd
We go[1] to use our hands and not our tongues.
Richard III, I, 3:352
[1] go: sent by RICHARD to murder his brother CLARENCE.

ROMEO. A gentleman, nurse, that loves to hear himself talk, and will speak more in a minute than he will stand to in a month.
Romeo and Juliet, II, 4:155

ANTONIO. Fie, what a spendthrift is he of
  his tongue!
                              Tempest, II, 1:23

SILVIA. A fine volley of words, gentlemen,
and quickly shot off.
    Two Gentlemen of Verona, II, 4:32

TAMING

BAPTISTA. What will be said? what mock-
  ery will it be
To want[1] the bridegroom when the priest
  attends
To speak the ceremonial rites of marriage!
What says Lucentio to this shame of ours?
    KATHARINA. No shame but mine: I must,
      forsooth, be forc'd
To give my hand oppos'd against my heart
Unto a mad-brain rudesby, full of spleen;
Who woo'd in haste and means to wed at
  leisure
I told you, I, he was a frantic fool.

                · · · · ·

Now must the world point at poor Katha-
  rine
And say, 'Lo! there is mad Petruchio's wife,
If it would please him come and marry her.'

                · · · · ·

BIONDELLO. Why, Petruchio is coming, in
a new hat and an old jerkin; a pair of old
breeches thrice turned; a pair of boots that
have been candle-cases, one buckled, another laced; an old rusty sword ta'en out
of the town-armoury, with a broken hilt,
and chapeless;[2] with two broken points:[3]
his horse hipped[4] with an old mothy saddle
and stirrups of no kindred.
    Taming of the Shrew, III, 2:4, 18, 43
[1] want: lack. [2] chapeless: without the metal
tip of the scabbard. [3] points: substitutes for
buttons. [4] hipped: lame in the hip.

GREMIO. Tell thou the tale: but hadst
thou not crossed me thou shouldst have
heard how her horse fell, and she under her
horse; thou shouldst have heard in how
miry a place, how she was bemoiled;[1] how
he left her with the horse upon her; how he
beat me because her horse stumbled; how
she waded through the dirt to pluck him
off me; how he swore; how she prayed, that
never prayed before.
            Taming of the Shrew, IV, 1:74
[1] bemoiled: befouled with mire.

PETRUCHIO. There, take it to you, trench-
  ers, cups, and all.
        Throws the meat, etc. at them.
You heedless joltheads and unmanner'd
  slaves!

What! do you grumble? I'll be with you
  straight.
    KATHARINA. I pray you, husband, be not
      so disquiet:
The meat was well if you were so con-
  tented.
PETRUCHIO. I tell thee, Kate, 't was burnt
  and dried away,
And I expressly am forbid to touch it,
For it engenders choler, planteth anger;
And better 't were that both of us did fast,
Since, of ourselves,[1] ourselves are choleric,[1]
Than feed it with such over-roasted flesh.
            Taming of the Shrew, IV, 1:167
[1] ourselves . . . choleric: we become choleric
(angry) with ourselves.

PETRUCHIO. She eat no meat to-day, nor
  none shall eat;
Last night she slept not, nor to-night she
  shall not:
As with the meat, some undeserved fault
I 'll find about the making of the bed;
And here I 'll fling the pillow, there the
  bolster,
This way the coverlet, another way the
  sheets:
Ay, and amid this hurly I intend
That all is done in reverend care of her;
And in conclusion she shall watch all night:
And if she chance to nod I'll rail and
  brawl,
And with the clamour keep her still awake.
This is a way to kill a wife with kindness;
And thus I 'll curb her mad and headstrong
  humour.[1]
            Taming of the Shrew, IV, 1:200
[1] humour: temper.

PETRUCHIO. Here, love; thou seest how
  diligent I am
To dress thy meat myself and bring it thee:
I am sure, sweet Kate, this kindness merits
  thanks.
What! not a word? Nay, then thou lov'st it
  not,
And all my pains is sorted[1] to no proof.
Here, take away this dish.
    KATHARINA. I pray you, let it stand.
    PETRUCHIO. The poorest service is repaid
      with thanks,
And so shall mine, before you touch the
  meat.
    KATHARINA. I thank you, sir.
            Taming of the Shrew, IV, 3:39
[1] sorted . . . proof: proved to be to no pur-
pose.

TAX

Q. KATHARINE. Language unmannerly;
  yea, such which breaks

The sides of loyalty, and almost appears
In loud rebellion.
    NORFOLK. Not almost appears,
It doth appear; for upon these taxations,
The clothiers all, not able to maintain
The many to them longing;[1] have put off
The spinsters, carders, fullers, weavers,
    who,
Unfit for other life, compell'd by hunger
And lack of other means, in desperate man-
    ner
Daring the event to the teeth, are all in up-
    roar,
And danger serves among them.
    K. HENRY. Taxation!
Wherein? and what taxation? My lord car-
    dinal,
You that are blam'd for it alike with us,
Know you of this taxation?
               Henry VIII, I, 2:27
[1] longing: belonging.

    Q. KATHARINE. The subjects' grief
Comes through commissions, which compel
    from each
The sixth part of his substance, to be levied
Without delay; and the pretence for this
Is nam'd your wars in France. This makes
    bold mouths:[1]
Tongues spit their duties out, and cold
    hearts freeze
Allegiance in them; their curses now
Live where their prayers did.
               Henry VIII, I, 2:55
[1] bold mouths: bold criticisms.

TEARS

    EXETER. And all my mother came into
    mine eyes
And gave me up to tears.
               Henry V, IV, 6:31

    RICHARD.[1] To weep is to make less the
    depth of grief:
Tears then for babes; blows and revenge
    for me!
            III Henry VI, II, 1:85
[1] Sometimes called GLOUCESTER; later still, K.
RICHARD III.

    HUBERT. I honour'd him, I lov'd him;[1]
and will weep
My date of life out for his sweet life's loss.
    SALISBURY. Trust not those cunning wa-
    ters of his eyes,
For villany is not without such rheum;
And he, long traded in it, makes it seem
Like rivers of remorse and innocency.
             King John, IV, 3:105
[1] him: PRINCE ARTHUR whom JOHN wanted
HUBERT to kill.

O! father! what a hell of witchcraft lies
In the small orb of one particular tear.
            Lover's Complaint, 288

    OTHELLO. O devil, devil!
If that the earth could teem[1] with woman's
    tears,
Each drop she falls would prove a crocodile.
Out of my sight!
              Othello, IV, 1:255
[1] teem: conceive.

    K. RICHARD. Aumerle, thou weep'st, my
    tender-hearted cousin!
We 'll make foul weather with despised
    tears;
Our sighs and they shall lodge the summer
    corn,
And make a dearth in this revolting land.
Or shall we play the wantons with our woes,
And make some pretty match with shedding
    tears?
As thus; to drop them still upon one place,
Till they have fretted us a pair of graves.
            Richard II, III, 3:160

    CAPULET. Thou counterfeit'st a bark, a
    sea, a wind;
For still thy eyes, which I may call the sea,
Do ebb and flow with tears; the bark thy
    body is,
Sailing in this salt flood; the winds, thy sighs;
Who, raging with thy tears, and they with
    them,
Without a sudden calm, will overset
Thy tempest-tossed body.
       Romeo and Juliet, III, 5:132

    LORD. And if the boy[1] have not a wom-
    an's gift[2]
To rain a shower of commanded tears,
An onion will do well for such a shift,
Which in a napkin being close convey'd,
Shall in despite enforce a watery eye.
    Taming of the Shrew, Induction, 1:124
[1] boy: the actor playing part of SLY's wife.
[2] woman's gift: ability to weep.

TEDIOUSNESS

    POLONIUS. My liege, and madam, to ex-
    postulate
What majesty should be, what duty is,
Why day is day, night night, and time is
    time,
Were nothing but to waste night, day, and
    time.
Therefore, since brevity is the soul of wit,
And tediousness the limbs and outward
    flourishes,
I will be brief. Your noble son is mad:
Mad call I it; for, to define true madness,

What is 't but to be nothing else but mad?
But let that go.
   QUEEN. More matter, with less art.
   POLONIUS. Madam, I swear I use no art at
all.
That he is mad, 't is true; 't is true 't is pity;
And pity 't is 't is true: a foolish figure;
But farewell it, for I will use no art.
Mad let us grant him, then; and now remains
That we find out the cause of this effect,
Or rather say, the cause of this defect,
For this effect defective comes by cause;
Thus it remains, and the remainder thus.
Perpend:
I have a daughter; have, while she is mine;
Who, in her duty and obedience, mark,
Hath given me this. Now gather, and sur-
   mise.
                   Hamlet, II, 2:86

HOTSPUR. O! he 's as tedious
As a tired horse, a railing wife;
Worse than a smoky house. I had rather live
With cheese and garlic in a windmill, far,
Then feed on cates[1] and have him talk to
   me.
              I Henry IV, III, 1:159
[1] cates: dainties.

BURGUNDY. Speak on; but be not over-
tedious.
               I Henry VI, III, 3:43

LEWIS. Life is as tedious as a twice-told
   tale
Vexing the dull ear of a drowsy man.
            King John, III, 4:108

BENEDICK. I would my horse had the
speed of your tongue, and so good a continuer.[1]
    Much Ado About Nothing, I, 1:142
[1] continuer: one having ability to keep going.

LEONATO. Neighbours, you are tedious.
   DOGBERRY. It pleases your worship to say
so, but we are the poor duke's officers; but,
truly, for mine own part, if I were as tedious as a king, I could find in my heart to
bestow it all of your worship.
   Much Ado About Nothing, III, 5:20

TEMPER

ALEXAS [to CLEOPATRA]. Good majesty,
Herod of Jewry dare not look upon you
But when you are well pleas'd.
       Antony and Cleopatra, III, 3:3

BRUTUS.[1] Being once chaf'd, he[2] cannot
Be rein'd again to temperance; then he
   speaks

What 's in his heart; and that is there which
   looks
With us to break his neck.
         Coriolanus, III, 3:27
[1] Tribune of the People. [2] he: CORIOLANUS.

PORTIA. The brain may devise laws for
the blood,[1] but a hot temper leaps o'er a
cold decree.
      Merchant of Venice, I, 2:19
[1] blood: often used for emotion, impulse,
temper.

K. RICHARD. High-stomach'd[1] are they
   both,[2] and full of ire,
In rage deaf as the sea, hasty as fire.
          Richard II, I, 1:19
[1] High-stomach'd: fiercely angry; the stomach
is sometimes referred to as seat of passions.
[2] both: BOLINGBROKE and MOWBRAY.

GREMIO. I say, a devil. Thinkest thou,
Hortensio, though her[1] father be very rich,
any man is so very a fool to be married to
hell?
      Taming of the Shrew, I, 1:127
[1] her: KATHARINA, the shrew.

TEMPTATION

ROMAN. I have heard it said, the fittest
time to corrupt a man's wife is when she 's
fallen out with her husband.
        Coriolanus, IV, 3:33

MACBETH [soliloquy]. Two truths are
   told,
As happy prologues to the swelling act
Of the imperial theme . . .
This supernatural soliciting
Cannot be ill, cannot be good; if ill,
Why hath it given me earnest[1] of success,
Commencing in a truth? I am Thane of
   Cawdor:
If good, why do I yield to that suggestion[2]
Whose horrid image doth unfix my hair
And make my seated heart knock at my
   ribs,
Against the use of nature? Present fears
Are less than horrible imaginings;
My thought, whose murder yet is but fan-
   tastical,[3]
Shakes so my single state of man that func-
   tion
Is smother'd in surmise,[4] and nothing is
But what is not.
         . . . . .

DUNCAN. We will establish our estate
   upon
Our eldest, Malcolm, whom we name hereafter
The Prince of Cumberland.
         . . . . .

MACBETH. The Prince of Cumberland!
   That is a step
On which I must fall down, or else o'erleap,
For in my way it lies. Stars, hide your fires!
Let not light see my black and deep desires;
The eye wink at the hand; yet let that be
Which the eye fears, when it is done, to see.
                    Macbeth, I, 3:127 and 4:37, 47
[1] earnest: a part paid as pledge. [2] suggestion:
murder of the king. [3] fantastical: imaginary.
[4] function . . . surmise: ability to act, over-
come by wonder.

ANGELO [soliloquy]. What 's this? what 's
   this? Is this her fault or mine?
The tempter or the tempted, who sins most
Ha!
Not she, nor doth she tempt; but it is I,
That, lying by the violet in the sun,
Do as the carrion does, not as the flower,
Corrupt with virtuous season. Can it be
That modesty may more betray our sense
Than woman's lightness? Having waste
   ground enough,
Shall we desire to raze the sanctuary,
And pitch our evils there? O! fie, fie, fie.
What dost thou, or what art thou, Angelo?
Dost thou desire her foully for those things
That make her good? O! let her brother
   live,
Thieves for their robbery have authority
When judges steal themselves. What! do I
   love her,
That I desire to hear her speak again,
And feast upon her eyes? What is 't I dream
   on?
O cunning enemy! that, to catch a saint,
With saints dost bait thy hook. Most dan-
   gerous
Is that temptation that doth goad us on
To sin in loving virtue; never could the
   strumpet,
With all her double vigour, art and nature,
Once stir my temper; but this virtuous maid
Subdues me quite. Ever till now,
When men were fond,[1] I smil'd and won-
   der'd how.
                    Measure for Measure, II, 2:163
[1] fond: foolish.

CLAUDIO. Bait the hook well, this fish will
   bite.
         Much Ado About Nothing, II, 3:113

To win me soon to hell, my female evil
Tempteth my better angel from my side,
And would corrupt a saint to be a devil.
                    Passionate Pilgrim: 19

Q. ELIZABETH. Shall I be tempted of the
   devil thus?
K. RICHARD. Ay, if the devil tempt thee
   to do good.
                    Richard III, IV, 4:418

ANTONIO. Here lies your brother,
No better than the earth he lies upon,
If he were that which now he 's like, that
   's dead;
Whom I, with this obedient steel, three
   inches of it,
Can lay to bed for ever; whiles you, doing
   thus,
To the perpetual wink for aye might put
This ancient morsel, this Sir Prudence.
                    Tempest, II, 1:280

THANKS

KING. Proffers[1] not took reap thanks for
   their reward.
         All's Well That Ends Well, II, 3:150
[1] Proffers: offers.

K. HENRY. O God! thy arm was here;
And not to us, but to thy arm alone,
Ascribe we all. When, without stratagem,
But in plain shock and even play of battle,
Was ever known so great and little loss
On one part and on the other? Take it, God,
For it is none but thine!
                    Henry V, IV, 8:111

K. HENRY. O Lord! that lends me life,
Lend me a heart replete with thankful-
   ness;
For thou hast given me in this beauteous
   face[1]
A world of earthly blessings to my soul,
If sympathy of love unite our thoughts.
                    . . . . .

Her sight did ravish, but her grace in
   speech,
Her words yclad with wisdom's majesty,
Makes me from wondering fall to weeping
   joys;
Such is the fullness of my heart's content.
                    II Henry VI, I, 1:19, 32
[1] face: QUEEN MARGARET'S.

K. HENRY. Now, God be prais'd, that to
   believing souls
Gives light in darkness, comfort in despair!
                    II Henry VI, II, 1:66

PERICLES. This, this: no more, you gods!
   your present kindness
Makes my past miseries sports.
                    Pericles, V, 3:40

BOLINGBROKE. Evermore thanks, the exchequer of the poor.
                    Richard II, II, 3:65

SEBASTIAN. My kind Antonio,
I can no other answer make but thanks,

And thanks, and ever thanks; and oft good
   turns
Are shuffled off with such uncurrent pay.
                  Twelfth Night, III, 3:13

THEME OF PLAY

KING. What do you call the play?
HAMLET. The Mouse-trap. Marry, how?
Tropically.[1] This play is the image of a murder done in Vienna: Gonzago is the duke's
name; his wife, Baptista. You shall see anon;
't is a knavish piece of work: but what o'
that? your majesty and we that have free
souls, it touches us not: let the galled jade
wince, our withers are unwrung.
                    Hamlet, III, 2:246
[1] Tropically: figuratively.

QUINCE. Marry, our play is, The most
lamentable comedy, and most cruel death
of Pyramus and Thisby.
        Midsummer Night's Dream, I, 2:11

CHORUS. From forth the fatal loins of
   these two foes
A pair of star-cross'd lovers take their life;
Whose misadventur'd piteous overthrows
Do with their death bury their parents'
   strife.
          Romeo and Juliet, Prologue: 5

THIEF

FALSTAFF. Marry, then, sweet wag, when
thou art king, let not us that are squires[1] of
the night's body be called thieves of the
day's beauty: let us be Diana's[2] foresters,
gentlemen of the shade, minions of the
moon; and let men say we be men of good
government, being governed as the sea is,
by our noble and chaste mistress the moon,
under whose countenance we steal.
               1 Henry IV, I, 2:25
[1] squires . . . body: a squire of the body was
an attendant on a knight. [2] Diana: goddess of
the moon.

PRINCE. I see a good amendment of life
in thee; from praying to purse-taking.
FALSTAFF. Why, Hal, 't is my vocation,[1]
Hal; 't is no sin for a man to labour in his
vocation.
               1 Henry IV, I, 2:116
[1] vocation: purse-taking.

POINS. But, my lads, my lads, to-morrow
morning, by four o'clock, early at Gadshill!
There are pilgrims going to Canterbury
with rich offerings, and traders riding to
London with fat purses: I have vizards for
you all; you have horses for yourselves.
               1 Henry IV, I, 2:137

PRINCE. Who, I rob? I a thief? not I, by
my faith.
FALSTAFF. There 's neither honesty, manhood, nor good fellowship in thee, nor thou
camest not of the blood royal, if thou darest
not stand for ten shillings.
PRINCE. Well then, once in my days I 'll
be a madcap.
               1 Henry IV, I, 2:154

POINS [to PRINCE HAL]. Now, my good
sweet honey lord, ride with us to-morrow:
I have a jest to execute that I cannot manage
alone. Falstaff, Bardolph, Peto, and Gadshill
shall rob those men that we have already
waylaid; yourself and I will not be there;
and when they have the booty, if you and I
do not rob them, cut this head off from my
shoulders.
               1 Henry IV, I, 2:179

POINS. The virtue of this jest will be, the
incomprehensible lies that this same fat
rogue will tell us when we meet at supper:
how thirty, at least, he fought with; what
wards, what blows, what extremities he
endured; and in the reproof[1] of this lies the
jest.
               1 Henry IV, I, 2:207
[1] reproof: proving its falsehood.

PRINCE. Peace, ye fat-guts! lie down; lay
thine ear close to the ground and list if thou
canst hear the tread of travellers.
FALSTAFF. Have you any levers to lift me
up again, being down? 'Sblood! I 'll not
bear mine own flesh so far afoot again for
all the coin in thy father's exchequer.
               1 Henry IV, II, 2:33

PRINCE. The thieves have bound the true
men. Now could thou and I rob the thieves
and go merrily to London, it would be argument for a week, laughter for a month,
and a good jest for ever.
               1 Henry IV, II, 2:98

[FALSTAFF and companions have robbed some
travellers.]
FALSTAFF. Come, my masters; let us share,
and then to horse before day. An[1] the
Prince and Poins be not two arrant cowards,
there 's no equity stirring: there 's no more
valour in that Poins than in a wild duck.
PRINCE. Your money!
POINS. Villains!
[As they are sharing, the PRINCE and POINS set
upon them. They all run away, and FALSTAFF,

after a blow or two, runs away too, leaving the booty behind them.]

PRINCE. Got with much ease. Now merrily to horse:
The thieves are scatter'd and possess'd with fear
So strongly that they dare not meet each other;
Each takes his fellow[2] for an officer.

1 Henry IV, II, 2:104

[1] An: if.   [2] fellow: companion.

FALSTAFF. Are you not a coward? answer me to that; and Poins there?
POINS. 'Zounds! ye fat paunch, an ye call me coward, I 'll stab thee.
FALSTAFF. I call thee coward! I 'll see thee damned ere I call thee coward; but I would give a thousand pound I could run as fast as thou canst. You are straight enough in the shoulders; you care not who sees your back: call you that backing of your friends? A plague upon such backing! give me them that will face me. Give me a cup of sack: I am a rogue if I drunk to-day.
PRINCE. O villain! thy lips are scarce wiped since thou drunkest last.
FALSTAFF. All 's one for that.

He drinks.

A plague of all cowards, still say I.

1 Henry IV, II, 4:157

FALSTAFF. I am a rogue, if I were not at half-sword[1] with a dozen of them two hours together. I have 'scaped by miracle. I am eight times thrust through the doublet, four through the hose; my buckler cut through and through; my sword hacked like a handsaw: *ecce signum!*[2] I never dealt better since I was a man: all would not do. A plague of all cowards!

1 Henry IV, II, 4:182

[1] half-sword: close quarters.   [2] *ecce signum:* see the proof.

GADSHILL. As we were sharing, some six or seven fresh men set upon us,—
FALSTAFF. And unbound the rest, and then come in the other.
PRINCE. What! fought you with them all?
FALSTAFF. All! I know not what you call all; but if I fought not with fifty of them, I am a bunch of radish: if there were not two or three and fifty upon poor old Jack, then am I no two-legged creature.
PRINCE. Pray God you have not murdered some of them.
FALSTAFF. Nay, that 's past praying for: I have peppered two of them: two I am sure I have paid, two rogues in buckram suits. I tell thee what, Hal, if I tell thee a lie, spit in my face, call me horse.

1 Henry IV, II, 4:199

PRINCE. We two saw you four set on four and bound them, and were masters of their wealth. Mark now, how a plain tale shall put you down. Then did we two set on you four, and, with a word, out-faced you from your prize, and have it; yea, and can show it you here in the house. And, Falstaff, you carried your guts away as nimbly, with as quick dexterity, and roared for mercy, and still ran and roared, as ever I heard bull-calf. What a slave art thou, to hack thy sword as thou hast done, and then say it was in fight! What trick, what device, what starting-hole canst thou now find out to hide thee from this open and apparent shame?
POINS. Come, let 's hear, Jack; what trick hast thou now?
FALSTAFF. By the Lord, I knew ye as well as he that made ye. Why, hear you, my masters: was it for me to kill the heir apparent? should I turn upon the true prince? why, thou knowest I am as valiant as Hercules; but beware instinct: the lion will not touch the true prince. Instinct is a great matter, I was a coward on instinct.

1 Henry IV, II, 4:279

PRINCE. These lies are like their father that begets them; gross as a mountain, open, palpable. Why, thou clay-brained guts, thou knotty-pated fool, thou whoreson, obscene, greasy tallow-ketch.[1]

1 Henry IV, II, 4:249

[1] tallow-ketch: a vessel filled with tallow.

PISTOL. Fortune is Bardolph's foe, and frowns on him;
For he hath stol'n a pax,[1] and hanged must a'[2] be.
A damned death!
Let gallows gape for dog, let man go free
And let not hemp his wind-pipe suffocate.
But Exeter hath given the doom of death
For pax of little price.

Henry V, III, 6:41

[1] pax: the cover of the chalice at Mass.   [2] a': he.

PISTOL. To England will I steal, and there I 'll steal:
And patches will I get unto these cudgell'd scars,
And swear I got them in the Gallia[1] wars.

Henry V, V, 1:92

[1] Gallia: French.

CLIFFORD. What makes robbers bold but too much lenity?

III Henry VI, II, 6:24

ABHORSON. Every true man's apparel fits your thief.

Measure for Measure, IV, 2:46

TIMON. I 'll example you with thievery:
The sun 's a thief, and with his great attraction
Robs the vast sea; the moon 's an arrant thief,
And her pale fire she snatches from the sun;
The sea 's a thief, whose liquid surge resolves
The moon into salt tears; the earth 's a thief,
That feeds and breeds by a composture[1] stolen
From general excrement; each thing 's a thief;
The laws, your curb and whip, in their rough power
Have uncheck'd theft.
                                        Timon of Athens, IV, 3:438
[1] composture: fertilizer.

AUTOLYCUS. A snapper-up of unconsidered trifles.
                                        Winter's Tale, IV, 3:27

THOUGHT

HAMLET. There is nothing either good or bad, but thinking makes it so.
                                        Hamlet, II, 2:256

HOTSPUR. But thought 's the slave of life, and life time's fool;
And time, that takes survey of all the world,
Must have a stop. O! I could prophesy;
But that the earthy and cold hand of death
Lies on my tongue. No, Percy, thou art dust,
And food for—
                                        Dies.
PRINCE. For worms, brave Percy. Fare thee well, great heart!
                                        I Henry IV, V, 4:81

FALSTAFF. Do you think me a swallow, an arrow, or a bullet? have I, in my poor and old motion, the expedition of thought?
                                        II Henry IV, IV, 3:37

YORK. Faster than spring-time showers comes thought on thought;
                                        II Henry VI, III, 1:337

ROMEO. She[1] hath forsworn to love, and in that vow
Do I live dead, that live to tell it now.
BENVOLIO. Be rul'd by me; forget to think of her.
ROMEO. O! teach me how I should forget to think.
BENVOLIO. By giving liberty unto thine eyes:
Examine other beauties.
                                        Romeo and Juliet, I, 1:229
[1] She: Rosaline, the one ROMEO thought he loved before he met JULIET.

For nimble thought can jump both sea and land,
As soon as think the place where he would be.
                                        Sonnet 44

POLONIUS. Give thy thoughts no tongue
Nor any unproportion'd[1] thought his[2] act.
                                        Hamlet, I, 3:59
[1] unproportion'd: disorderly.   [2] his: its.

THOUGHTS

PLAYER KING. Our thoughts are ours, their ends none of our own.
                                        Hamlet, III, 2:223

TALBOT. My thoughts are whirled like a potter's wheel;
I know not where I am, nor what I do:
                                        I Henry VI, I, 5:19

K. RICHARD [soliloquy]. Thoughts tending to ambition, they do plot
Unlikely wonders; how these vain weak nails
May tear a passage through the flinty ribs
Of this hard world, my ragged prison walls;
And, for[1] they cannot, die in their own pride.
Thoughts tending to content flatter themselves
That they are not the first of fortune's slaves,
Nor shall not be the last; like silly beggars
Who sitting in the stocks refuge[2] their shame,
That many have and others must sit there:
And in this thought they find a kind of ease,
Bearing their own misfortune on the back
Of such as have before endur'd the like.
                                        Richard II, V, 5:18
[1] for: because.   [2] refuge: find excuse for.

JULIET. O! she is lame: love's heralds should be thoughts,
Which ten times faster glide than the sun's beams
Driving back shadows over lowering hills.
                                        Romeo and Juliet, II, 5:4

VALENTINE. I have done penance for contemning love;
Whose high imperious thoughts have punish'd me
With bitter fasts, with penitential groans,
With nightly tears and daily heart-sore sighs;
For in revenge of my contempt of love,
Love hath chas'd sleep from my enthralled eyes,

And made them watchers of mine own heart's sorrow.
Two Gentlemen of Verona, II, 4:129

PARIS. He eats nothing but doves, love; and that breeds hot blood, and hot blood begets hot thoughts, and hot thoughts beget hot deeds, and hot deeds is love.
Troilus and Cressida, III, 1:140

CRESSIDA. My thoughts were like unbridled children, grown
Too headstrong for their mother.
Troilus and Cressida, III, 2:130

[VALENTINE's letter.] My thoughts do harbour with my Silvia nightly;
And slaves they are to me that send them flying;
O! could their master come and go as lightly.
Two Gentlemen of Verona, III, 1:140

THREAT

CLEOPATRA. What say you?[1] Hence, Horrible villain! or I 'll spurn thine eyes
Like balls before me; I 'll unhair thy head:
Thou shalt be whipp'd with wire, and stew'd in brine,
Smarting in lingering pickle.
Antony and Cleopatra, II, 5:62
[1] you: messenger telling that ANTONY has married OCTAVIA.

TOUCHSTONE. Therefore, you clown, abandon—which is in the vulgar, leave—the society,—which in the boorish is, company,—of this female,—which in the common is, woman; which together is, abandon the society of this female, or, clown, thou perishest; or, to thy better understanding, diest; or, to wit, I kill thee, make thee away, translate thy life unto death, thy liberty into bondage. I will deal in poison with thee, or in bastinado, or in steel.
As You Like It, V, 1:52

K. LEAR. Five days we do allot thee[1] for provision
To shield thee from diseases of the world;
And on the sixth to turn thy hated back
Upon our kingdom: if on the tenth day following
Thy banish'd trunk be found in our dominions,
The moment is thy death.
King Lear, I, 1:176
[1] thee: the faithful KENT.

PROSPERO [to CALIBAN]. Shrug'st thou, malice?

If thou neglect'st, or dost unwillingly
What I command, I 'll rack thee with old[1] cramps,
Fill all thy bones with aches, make thee roar,
That beasts shall tremble at thy din.
Tempest, I, 2:367
[1] old: used simply as an epithet, or intensive.

DIOMEDES. Our bloods are now in calm, and, so long, health!
But when contention and occasion meet,
By Jove, I 'll play the hunter for thy life
With all my force, pursuit, and policy.
Troilus and Cressida, IV, 1:15

THRIFT

HAMLET. Thrift, thrift, Horatio! the funeral bak'd meats
Did coldly furnish forth the marriage tables.
Would I had met my dearest[1] foe in heaven
Or ever I had seen that day, Horatio!
Hamlet, I, 2:180
[1] dearest: most ardent.

BASSANIO. I have a mind presages me such thrift,
That I should questionless be fortunate.
Merchant of Venice, I, 1:175

SHYLOCK. Thrift is blessing, if men steal it not.
Merchant of Venice, I, 3:91

TROILUS. The remainder viands
We do not throw in unrespective[1] sieve,
Because we now are full.
Troilus and Cressida, II, 2:70
[1] unrespective: undiscriminating.

TIME

KING. For we are old, and on our quick'st decrees
The inaudible and noiseless foot of time
Steals ere we can effect them.
All's Well That Ends Well, V, 3:40

ENOBARBUS. Every time
Serves for the matter that is then born in 't.
Antony and Cleopatra, II, 2:9

ORLANDO. Under the shade of melancholy boughs,
Lose and neglect the creeping hours of time.
As You Like It, II, 7:111

ROSALIND. I pray you, what is 't o'clock?
ORLANDO. You should ask me what time o' day; there 's no clock in the forest.
ROSALIND. Then there is no true lover in

the forest; else sighing every minute and groaning every hour would detect the lazy foot of Time as well as a clock.

ORLANDO. And why not the swift foot of Time? had not that been as proper?

ROSALIND. By no means, sir. Time travels in divers[1] paces with divers persons. I 'll tell you who Time ambles withal,[2] who Time trots withal, who Time gallops withal, and who he stands still withal.

ORLANDO. I prithee, who doth he trot withal?

ROSALIND. Marry, he trots hard with a young maid between the contract of her marriage and the day it is solemnized; if the interim be but a se'nnight,[3] Time's pace is so hard that it seems the length of seven year.

ORLANDO. Who ambles time withal?

ROSALIND. With a priest that lacks Latin, and a rich man that hath not the gout: for the one sleeps easily because he cannot study, and the other lives merrily because he feels no pain; the one lacking the burden of lean and wasteful learning, the other knowing no burden of heavy tedious penury. These Time ambles withal.

ORLANDO. Who doth he gallop withal?

ROSALIND. With a thief to the gallows; for though he go as softly as foot can fall, he thinks himself too soon there.

ORLANDO. Who stays it still withal?

ROSALIND. With lawyers in the vacation; for they sleep between term and term, and then they perceive not how Time moves.
                              As You Like It, III, 2:319
[1] divers: different. [2] withal: with. [3] se'nnight: seven nights, a week.

ROSALIND. Well, Time is the old justice that examines all such offenders, and let Time try.
                              As You Like It, IV, 1:203

LUCIANA. A man is master of his liberty: Time is their master, and, when they see time,
They 'll go or come.
                              Comedy of Errors, II, 1:7

HAMLET. The time is out of joint; O cursed spite,
That ever I was born to set it right!
                              Hamlet, I, 5:189

HORATIO. It must be shortly known to him from England
What is the issue of the business there.
   HAMLET. It will be short: the interim is mine;
And a man's life's no more than to say 'One.'
                              Hamlet, V, 2:71

FALSTAFF. Now, Hal, what time of day is it, lad?

PRINCE. Thou art so fat-witted, with drinking of old sack, and unbuttoning thee after supper, and sleeping upon benches after noon, that thou hast forgotten to demand that truly which thou would'st truly know. What a devil hast thou to do with the time of the day? Unless hours were cups of sack, and minutes capons, and clocks the tongues of bawds, and dials the signs of leaping-houses, and the blessed sun himself a fair hot wench in flame-coloured taffeta, I see no reason why thou should'st be so superfluous to demand the time of the day.
                              I Henry IV, I, 2:1

ARCHBISHOP OF YORK. Past and to come seems best; things present worst.
                              II Henry IV, I, 3:108

BASTARD. Old Time the clock-setter, that bald sexton Time,
Is it as he will? well then, France[1] shall rue.
                              King John, III, 1:324
[1] France: PHILIP, KING OF FRANCE.

EDMUND. Pat he comes, like the catastrophe of the old comedy.
                              King Lear, I, 2:146

MACBETH [Aside]. Come what come may,
Time and the hour runs through the roughest day.
                              Macbeth, I, 3:146

HIPPOLYTA. Four days will quickly steep themselves in night;
Four nights will quickly dream away the time;
And then the moon, like to a silver bow
New-bent in heaven, shall behold the night
Of our solemnities.
                              Midsummer Night's Dream, I, 1:7

PERICLES. Time 's the king of men;
He 's both their parent, and he is their grave,
And gives them what he will, not what they crave.
                              Pericles, II, 3:45

Time's office is to fine[1] the hate of foes;
To eat up errors by opinion bred,
Not spend the dowry of a lawful bed.
Time's glory is to calm contending kings,
To unmask falsehood and bring truth to light,
To stamp the seal of time in aged things,
To wake the morn and sentinel the night,
To wrong the wronger till he render right,
                              Rape of Lucrece: 936
[1] fine: a verb, end.

SALISBURY. O! call back yesterday, bid time return.

To-day, to-day, unhappy day, too late,
O'erthrows thy joys, friends, fortune, and
    thy state.
                        Richard II, III, 2:69

Ruin hath taught me thus to ruminate,
That Time will come and take my love
    away.
This thought is as a death, which cannot
    choose
But weep to have that which it fears to lose.
                        Sonnet 64

Since brass, nor stone, nor earth, nor bound-
    less sea,
But sad mortality[1] o'ersways their power,
How with this rage shall beauty hold a plea,
Whose action is no stronger than a flower?
O! how shall summer's honey breath hold
    out
Against the wreckful siege of battering
    days,
When rocks impregnable are not so stout,
Nor gates of steel so strong, but Time de-
    cays?
                        Sonnet 65
[1] mortality: death.

ULYSSES. Time hath, my lord, a wallet at
    his back,
Wherein he puts alms for oblivion,
A great-siz'd monster for ingratitudes:
Those scraps are good deeds past; which are
    devour'd
As fast as they are made, forgot as soon
As done.
                Troilus and Cressida, III, 3:145

ULYSSES. For time is like a fashionable
    host,
That slightly shakes his parting guest by the
    hand,
And with his arms outstretch'd, as he would
    fly,
Grasps in the comer: welcome ever smiles,
And farewell goes out sighing.
                Troilus and Cressida, III, 3:165

TROILUS. Injurious time now with a rob-
    ber's haste
Crams his rich thievery up, he knows not
    how:
As many farewells as be stars in heaven,
With distinct breath and consign'd kisses to
    them,
He fumbles up into a loose adieu,
And scants us with a single famish'd kiss,
Distasting with the salt of broken tears.
                Troilus and Cressida, IV, 4:44

HECTOR. The end crowns all,
And that old common arbitrator, Time,
Will one day end it.
                Troilus and Cressida, IV, 5:224

OLIVIA. The clock upbraids me with the
    waste of time.
                Twelfth Night, III, 1:141

CLOWN. And thus the whirligig of time
brings in his[1] revenges.
                Twelfth Night, V, 1:385
[1] his: its.

TIME.[1] I, that please some, try all, both
    joy and terror
Of good and bad, that makes and unfolds
    error,
Now take upon me, in the name of Time,
To use my wings. Impute it not a crime
To me or my swift passage, that I slide
O'er sixteen years, and leave the growth un-
    tried
Of that wide gap; since it is in my power
To o'erthrow law, and in one self-born hour
To plant and o'erwhelm custom.
                Winter's Tale, IV, Chorus: 1
[1] As Chorus.

TONGUE

PAROLLES. I must put you into a butter-
woman's mouth, and buy myself another of
Bajazet's mule, if you prattle me into these
perils.
                All's Well That Ends Well, IV, 1:45

CELIA. Cry 'holla!' to thy tongue, I
prithee, it curvets[1] unseasonably.
                As You Like It, III, 2:257
[1] curvets: leaps, bounds.

K. HENRY. You play the spaniel,
And think with wagging of your tongue to
win me.
                Henry VIII, V, 3:126

CONSTANCE. O! that my tongue were in
    the thunder's mouth;
Then with a passion would I shake the
    world.
                King John, III, 4:38

REGAN. Return you to my sister.
LEAR. Never, Regan.
She hath abated me of half my train;
Look'd black upon me; struck me with her
    tongue,
Most serpent-like, upon the very heart.
All the stor'd vengeances of heaven fall
On her ingrateful top! Strike her young
    bones,
You taking[1] airs, with lameness!
                King Lear, II, 4:159
[1] taking: infectious.

'So on the tip of his subduing tongue
All kind of arguments and question deep,
All replication[1] prompt and reason strong,

For his advantage still did wake and sleep:
To make the weeper laugh, the laugher
    weep,
He had the dialect and different skill,
Catching all passions in his craft of will.'
                    Lover's Complaint: 120
[1] replication: reply.

KING. One whom the music of his own
    vain tongue
Doth ravish like enchanting harmony.
            Love's Labour's Lost, I, 1:167

BOYET. The tongues of mocking wenches
    are as keen
As is the razor's edge invisible,
Cutting a smaller hair than may be seen,
Above the sense of sense; so sensible
Seemeth their conference; their conceits[1]
    have wings
Fleeter than arrows, bullets, wind, thought,
    swifter things.
            Love's Labour's Lost, V, 2:256
[1] conceits: thoughts.

ROSALINE. The world's large tongue
Proclaims you for a man replete with
    mocks;
Full of comparisons and wounding flouts,
Which you on all estates will execute
That lie within the mercy of your wit.
            Love's Labour's Lost, V, 2:852

BENEDICK. I cannot endure my Lady[1]
Tongue.
            Much Ado About Nothing, II, 1:284
[1] Lady: BEATRICE.

GAUNT O! but they say the tongues of
    dying men
Enforce attention like deep harmony:
Where words are scarce, they are seldom
    spent in vain,
For they breathe truth that breathe their
    words in pain.
He that no more must say is listen'd more
Than they whom youth and ease have
    taught to gloze.
                    Richard II, II, 1:5

GLOUCESTER.[1] I never sued to friend nor
    enemy;
My tongue could never learn sweet smooth-
    ing words;
But now thy beauty is propos'd my fee,
My proud heart sues, and prompts my
    tongue to speak.
                    Richard III, I, 2:168
[1] Later K. RICHARD III.

VALENTINE. That man that hath a tongue,
    I say, is no man,
If with his tongue he cannot win a woman.
    Two Gentlemen of Verona, III, 1:104

TORTURE

JULIET. What says he of our marriage?
    what of that?
NURSE. Lord! how my head aches; what
    a head have I!
It beats as it would fall in twenty pieces.
My back o' t' other side; O! my back, my
    back.
                    . . . . .

JULIET. Sweet, sweet, sweet nurse, tell me,
    what says my love?
NURSE. Your love says, like an honest
gentleman, and a courteous, and a kind, and
a handsome, and, I warrant, a virtuous,—
Where is your mother?
            Romeo and Juliet, II, 5:48, 55

PROSPERO [to ARIEL]. Refusing her[1] grand
    hests, she did confine thee,
By help of her more potent ministers
And in her most unmitigable rage,
Into a cloven pine; within which rift
Imprison'd thou didst painfully remain
A dozen years; within which space she died
And left thee there, where thou didst vent
    thy groans
As fast as mill-wheels strike.
                    . . . . .

Thou best know'st
What torment I did find thee in; thy groans
Did make wolves howl and penetrate the
    breasts
Of ever-angry bears.
                    Tempest, I, 2:274, 286
[1] her: "this damned witch, Sycorax."

STEPHANO. O! touch me not: I am not
Stephano, but a cramp.
                    Tempest, V, 1:286

TRAITOR—TREASON

ENOBARBUS. O sovereign mistress[1] of true
    melancholy,
The poisonous damp of night disponge
    upon me,
That life, a very rebel to my will,
May hang no longer on me; throw my heart
Against the flint and hardness of my fault,
Which, being dried with grief, will break to
    powder,
And finish all foul thoughts. O Antony!
Nobler than my revolt is infamous,
Forgive me in thine own particular;[2]
But let the world rank me in register
A master-leaver and a fugitive.
O Antony! O Antony!
            Antony and Cleopatra, IV, 9:12
[1] mistress: the moon. [2] particular: personal
relation.

AUFIDIUS. At a few drops of women's
  rheum,[1] which are
As cheap as lies, he[2] sold the blood and
  labour
Of our great action: therefore shall he die.
                                Coriolanus, V, 6:46
[1] rheum: tears.   [2] he: CORIOLANUS.

IMOGEN. Thus may poor fools
Believe false teachers; though those that are
  betray'd
Do feel the treason sharply, yet the traitor
Stands in worse case of woe.
                                Cymbeline, III, 4:86

WORCESTER. Suspicion all our lives shall be
  stuck full of eyes;
For treason is but trusted like the fox,
Who, ne'er so tame, so cherish'd, and
  lock'd up,
Will have a wild trick of his ancestors.
                                I Henry IV, V, 2:8

CAMBRIDGE. Never was monarch better
  fear'd and lov'd
Than is your majesty.
                . . . . .

GREY. True: those that were your father's
  enemies
Have steep'd their galls in honey, and do
  serve you
With hearts create of duty and of zeal.
                . . . . .

SCROOP. So service shall with steeled
  sinews toil,
And labour shall refresh itself with hope,
To do your grace incessant services.
  K. HENRY. We judge no less. Uncle of
    Exeter,
Enlarge[1] the man committed yesterday
That rail'd against our person: we consider
It was excess of wine that set him on;
And on his more advice we pardon him.
  SCROOP. That's mercy, but too much se-
    curity.
                . . . . .

  K. HENRY. See you, my princes and my
    noble peers,
These English monsters! My Lord of Cam-
  bridge here,
You know how apt our love was to accord
To furnish him with all appertinents
Belonging to his honour; and this man
Hath, for a few light crowns, lightly con-
  spir'd,
And sworn unto the practices of France,
To kill us here in Hampton.
                . . . . .

God quit you in his mercy!
Hear your sentence.

You have conspir'd against our royal person,
Join'd with an enemy proclaim'd, and from
  his coffers
Receiv'd the golden earnest[2] of our death;
Wherein you would have sold your king to
  slaughter.
                . . . . .

Get you therefore, hence,
Poor miserable wretches, to your death.
        Henry V, II, 2:25, 29, 36, 84, 166, 177
[1] Enlarge: set free.   [2] earnest: money paid to
bind a bargain.

  K. HENRY. Treason and murder ever kept
    together,
As two yoke-devils sworn to either's purpose.
                                Henry V, II, 2:105

  CADE. He can speak French; and therefore
he is a traitor.
                . . . . .

Away with him! away with him! he speaks
  Latin.
                II Henry VI, IV, 2:176 and 7:63

EDGAR.[1] I protest,
Maugre[2] thy strength, youth, place, and emi-
  nence,
Despite thy victor sword and fire-new for-
  tune,
Thy valour and thy heart, thou art a traitor,
False to thy gods, thy brother, and thy fa-
  ther,
Conspirant 'gainst this high illustrious
  prince,
And, from the extremest upward of thy
  head
To the descent and dust below thy foot,
A most toad-spotted traitor.
                                King Lear, V, 3:130
[1] Edgar: to his bastard brother, EDMUND.
[2] Maugre: in spite of.

BIRON. To fast, to study, and to see no
  woman;
Flat treason 'gainst the kingly state of
  youth.
                Love's Labour's Lost, IV, 3:292

MOWBRAY. If ever I were traitor,
My name be blotted from the book of life,
And I from heaven banish'd as from hence!
                                Richard II, I, 3:201

  K. RICHARD. Give sorrow leave awhile to
    tutor me
To this submission. Yet I well remember
The favours[1] of these men: were they not
  mine?
Did they not sometime cry 'All hail!' to me?

So Judas did to Christ: but he, in twelve,
Found truth in all but one; I, in twelve thou-
    sand, none.
                    Richard II, IV, 1:166
[1] favours: faces.

APEMANTUS. I should fear those that
    dance before me now
Would one day stamp upon me: 't has been
    done;
Men shut their doors against a setting sun.
               Timon of Athens, I, 2:148

TRANSFORMATION

PRINCE. So, when this loose behaviour I
    throw off,
And pay the debt I never promised,
By how much better than my word I am
By so much shall I falsify men's hopes;
And like bright metal on a sullen ground,
My reformation, glittering o'er my fault,
Shall show more goodly and attract more
    eyes
Than that which hath no foil to set it off.
               I Henry IV, I, 2:231

K. HENRY.[1] I know thee not, old man:
    fall to thy prayers;
How ill white hairs become a fool and
    jester!
I have long dream'd of such a kind of man,
So surfeit-swell'd, so old, and so profane;
But being awak'd, I do despise my dream.
             II Henry IV, V, 5:51
[1] As King, PRINCE HAL dismisses FALSTAFF.

ARCHBISHOP OF CANTERBURY. The breath
    no sooner left his father's body
But that his wildness, mortified in him,
Seem'd to die too; yea, at that very moment,
Consideration like an angel came,
And whipp'd the offending Adam out of
    him,
Leaving his body as a paradise,
To envelop and contain celestial spirits.

      . . . . .

BISHOP OF ELY [about HENRY V]. We are
    blessed in the change.
CANTERBURY. Hear him but reason in di-
    vinity,
And, all-admiring, with an inward wish
You would desire the king were made a prel-
    ate:
Hear him debate of commonwealth affairs,
You would say it hath been all in all his
    study:
List his discourse of war, and you shall hear
A fearful battle render'd you in music:
Turn him to any cause of policy,
The Gordian knot of it he will unloose,

Familiar as his garter; that, when he speaks,
The air, a charter'd libertine, is still,
And the mute wonder lurketh in men's ears
To steal his sweet and honey'd sentences;
So that the art and practic part of life
Must be the mistress to this theoric:
Which is a wonder how his grace should
    glean it,
Since his addiction was to courses vain;
His companies unletter'd, rude, and shallow;
His hours filled up with riots, banquets,
    sports;
And never noted in him any study,
Any retirement, any sequestration
From open haunts and popularity.
             Henry V, I, 1:25, 37

TRAVEL

TOUCHSTONE. Ay, now am I in Arden;
the more fool I: when I was at home, I was
in a better place: but travellers must be content.
             As You Like It, II, 4:16

ROSALIND. A traveller! By my faith, you
have great reason to be sad. I fear you have
sold your own lands to see other men's; then,
to have seen much and to have nothing, is to
have rich eyes and poor hands.

      . . . . .

Farewell, Monsieur Traveller: look you lisp
and wear strange suits, disable[1] all the benefits of your own country, be out of love
with your nativity, and almost chide God
for making you that countenance you are;
or I will scarce think you have swam in a
gondola.
          As You Like It, IV, 1:21, 31
[1] disable: disparage.

BASTARD. For he is but a bastard to the
    time,
That doth not smack of observation.[1]
             King John, I, 1:207
[1] smack of observation: show knowledge gained
by observation.

FIRST MURDERER. The west yet glimmers
    with some streaks of day:
Now spurs the lated traveller apace
To gain the timely inn.
             Macbeth, III, 3:5

VALENTINE. I rather would entreat thy
    company
To see the wonders of the world abroad,
Than, living dully sluggardiz'd at home,
Wear out thy youth with shapeless idleness.

      . . . . .

PROTEUS. Go, go, be gone, to save your
    ship from wreck,

Which cannot perish, having thee aboard,
Being destin'd to a drier death on shore.[1]
Two Gentlemen of Verona, I, 1:5, 156
[1] Allusion to adage, "who's born to be hanged will never be drowned."

TREACHERY

Worcester. And we shall feed like oxen at a stall,
The better cherish'd, still the nearer death.
I Henry IV, V, 2:14

Exeter. Nay, but the man that was his bed-fellow,
Whom he hath dull'd and cloy'd with gracious favours,
That he should, for a foreign purse, so sell
His sovereign's life to death and treachery!
Henry V, II, 2:8

K. Henry. Smooth runs the water where the brook is deep,
And in his[1] simple show he harbours treason.
The fox barks not when he would steal the lamb:
II Henry VI, III, 1:53
[1] his: Gloucester's, later Richard III.

TROUBLE

Q. Katharine. Take thy lute, wench: my soul grows sad with troubles;
Sing, and disperse 'em, if thou canst.
Henry VIII, III, 1:1

Pistol. Thou art the Mars of malecontents:
I second thee; troop on.
Merry Wives of Windsor, I, 3:113

Queen. Uncle, for God's sake, speak comfortable words.
York. Should I do so, I should belie my thoughts:
Comfort 's in heaven; and we are on the earth,
Where nothing lives but crosses,[1] cares, and grief.
Richard II, II, 2:76
[1] crosses: burdens.

Stephano. Trinculo, if you trouble him any more in his tale, by this hand, I will supplant some of your teeth.
Tempest, III, 2:55

TRUST

Hamlet. My two schoolfellows,
Whom I will trust as I will adders fang'd.
Hamlet, III, 4:201

Q. Elizabeth.[1] Trust not him that hath once broken faith.
III Henry VI, IV, 4:30
[1] Formerly Lady Grey, wife of Edward IV.

Macbeth. He 's here in double trust:
First, as I am his kinsman and his subject,
Strong both against the deed; then, as his host,
Who should against his murderer shut the door,
Not bear the knife myself.
Macbeth, I, 7:12

Thersites. I will no more trust him when he leers than I will a serpent when he hisses.
Troilus and Cressida, V, 1:96

Valentine. Who should be trusted now, when one's right hand
Is perjur'd to the bosom? Proteus,
I am sorry I must never trust thee more,
But count the world a stranger for thy sake.
The private wound is deepest. O time most accurst!
'Mongst all foes that a friend should be the worst!
Two Gentlemen of Verona, V, 4:67

TRUTH

Polonius. This above all: to thine own self be true,
And it must follow, as the night the day,
Thou canst not then be false to any man.
Hamlet, I, 3:78

Hotspur. Tell truth and shame the devil.
I Henry IV, III, 1:59

Plantagenet. The truth appears so naked on my side
That any purblind[1] eye may find it out.
I Henry VI, II, 4:20
[1] purblind: half-blind; sometimes, wholly blind.

Cordelia. I want[1] that glib and oily art
To speak and purpose not.
. . . . .
But even for want of that for which I am richer,
A still-soliciting eye, and such a tongue
That I am glad I have not.
King Lear, I, 1:227, 233
[1] want: lack.

Fool. Truth 's a dog must to kennel; he must be whipped out when Lady the brach[1] may stand by the fire and stink.
King Lear, I, 4:124
[1] brach: a female hound.

Isabella. Nay, it is ten times true; for truth is truth
To the end of reckoning.
Measure for Measure, V, 1:43

Launcelot Gobbo. Truth will come to light; murder cannot be hid long; a man's son may, but in the end truth will out.
Merchant of Venice, II, 2:84

Marina. If I should tell my history, it would seem
Like lies, disdain'd in the reporting.
Pericles. Prithee, speak;
Falseness cannot come from thee, for thou look'st
Modest as justice, and thou seem'st a palace
For the crown'd truth to dwell in. I 'll believe thee.
Pericles, V, 1:119

Mowbray. As gentle and as jocund as to jest,
Go I to fight: truth hath a quiet breast.
Richard II, I, 3:95

Prospero. My trust,
Like a good parent, did beget of him
A falsehood in it's contrary as great
As my trust was;

. . . . .

But what my power might else exact, like one
Who having, unto truth, by telling of it,
Made such a sinner of his memory,
To credit his own lie.
Tempest, I, 2:93, 99

Troilus. Whiles others fish with craft for great opinion,
I with great truth catch mere[1] simplicity;
Whilst some with cunning gild their copper crowns,
With truth and plainness I do wear mine bare.
Fear not my truth; the moral of my wit
Is 'plain and true'; there 's all the reach of it.
Troilus and Cressida, IV, 4:106
[1] mere: absolute.

Viola. By innocence I swear, and by my youth,
I have one heart, one bosom, and one truth,
And that no woman has; nor never none
Shall mistress be of it, save I alone.
Twelfth Night, III, 1:169

TYRANT—TYRANNY

Warwick. Tyranny, which never quaff'd but blood,

Would, by beholding him, have wash'd his knife
With gentle eye-drops.
II Henry IV, IV, 5:86

King. We are no tyrant, but a Christian king.
Henry V, I, 2:246

Q. Margaret. How can tyrants safely govern home,
Unless abroad they purchase great alliance.
III Henry VI, III, 3:69

K. John to the Bastard. Cousin,[1] away for England! haste before;
And, ere our coming, see thou shake the bags
Of hoarding abbots; imprisoned angels[2]
Set thou at liberty: the fat ribs of peace
Must by the hungry now be fed upon:
Use our commission in his[3] utmost force,
Bastard. Bell, book, and candle[4] shall not drive me back
When gold and silver becks me to come on.
King John, III, 3:6
[1] Cousin: a term used for any relationship.
[2] angels: gold coins. [3] his: its. [4] Bell . . . candle: symbols of ex-communication.

Macduff. Bleed, bleed, poor country!
Great tyranny, lay thou thy basis sure,
For goodness dare not check[1] thee? wear thou thy wrongs;
The title is affeer'd![2]
Macbeth, IV, 3:31
[1] check: stop. [2] affeer'd: two interpretations possible, 1) a legal term, confirmed, established; 2) the lawful owner of the title is afraid.

Bottom. My chief humour is for a tyrant:
I could play Ercles rarely, or a part to tear a cat in.[1]
Midsummer Night's Dream, I, 2:30
[1] tear a cat: a saying to describe ranting.

Pericles. I knew him tyrannous; and tyrants' fears
Decrease not, but grow faster than the years.
Pericles, I, 2:84

UNCERTAINTY

Imogen. Since doubting[1] things go ill often hurts more
Than to be sure they do; for certainties
Either are past remedies, or, timely knowing,
The remedy then born,—discover to me
What both you spur and stop.
Cymbeline, I, 6:95
[1] doubting: suspecting or fearing.

NORTHUMBERLAND. 'T is with my mind
As with the tide swell'd up unto his[1] height,
That makes a still-stand, running neither
way.
II Henry IV, II, 3:62
[1] his: its.

CLAUDIO. O! what men dare do! what men
may do! what men daily do, not knowing
what they do!
Much Ado About Nothing, IV, 1:19

JULIA. Since maids, in modesty, say 'No'
to that
Which they would have the profferer construe 'Ay.'
Two Gentlemen of Verona, I, 2:55

LEONTES. I am a feather for each wind
that blows.
Winter's Tale, II, 3:154

USE

HAMLET. How weary, stale, flat, and unprofitable
Seem to me all the uses[1] of this world.
Hamlet, I, 2:133
[1] uses: customs, practices.

HAMLET. To what base uses we may return, Horatio! Why may not imagination
trace the noble dust of Alexander, till he
find it stopping a bung-hole?
Hamlet, V, 1:223

Torches are made to light, jewels to wear,
Dainties to taste, fresh beauty for the use,
Herbs for their smell, and sappy plants to
bear;
Things growing to themselves are growth's
abuse.
Venus and Adonis: 163

VALOUR

ENOBARBUS. When valour preys on reason
It eats the sword it fights with.
Antony and Cleopatra, III, 11:199

POSTHUMUS. Myself I 'll dedicate. Let me
make men know
More valour in me than my habits show.
Cymbeline, V, 1:29

ELY. Awake remembrance of these val-
iant dead,
And with your puissant arm renew their
feats:
You are their heir, you sit upon their throne.
Henry V, I, 2:115

ARMADO. Adieu, valour! rust, rapier! be
still, drum! for your manager is in love; yea,
he loveth.
Love's Labour's Lost, I, 2:189

LYSANDER. This lion is a very fox for his
valour.
THESEUS. True; and a goose for his discretion.
Midsummer Night's Dream, V, 1:233

ARIEL. They were red-hot with drinking;
So full of valour that they smote the air
For breathing in their faces; beat the ground
For kissing of their feet;
Tempest, IV, 1:171

FABIAN. She did show favour to the youth
in your sight only to exasperate you, to
awake your dormouse[1] valour, to put fire in
your heart, and brimstone in your liver.
Twelfth Night, III, 2:20
[1] dormouse: a small hibernating rodent whose
sleepiness is proverbial.

FABIAN. Assure thyself, there is no love-
broker in the world can more prevail in
man's commendation with woman than report of valour.
Twelfth Night, III, 2:39

VALUE

JEWELLER. Things of like value, differing
in the owners,
Are prized by their masters. Believe 't, dear
lord,
You mend the jewel by the wearing it.
Timon of Athens, I, 1:170

VANITY

BRUTUS. Our veil'd dames
Commit the war of white and damask in
Their nicely-gawded cheeks, to the wanton
spoil
Of Phoebus'[1] burning kisses.
Coriolanus, II, 1:231
[1] Phoebus: the sungod.

HOTSPUR. I can no longer brook thy vanities.
I Henry IV, V, 4:74

CONSTABLE. And you shall find his vanities
forespent
Were but the outside of the Roman Brutus,
Covering discretion with a coat of folly;
As gardeners do with ordure hide those
roots
That shall first spring and be most delicate.
Henry V, II, 4:36

GAUNT. Light vanity, insatiate cormorant,
Consuming means, soon preys upon itself.
Richard II, II, 1:38

FRIAR LAURENCE. A lover may bestride
the gossamer
That idles in the wanton summer air,
And yet not fall; so light is vanity.[1]
Romeo and Juliet, II, 6:18
[1] vanity: illusion.

VENTURE

IACHIMO. Diseas'd ventures
That play with all infirmities for gold
Which rottenness can lend nature! such
boil'd stuff
As well might poison poison!
Cymbeline, I, 6:123

WOLSEY. I have ventur'd,
Like little wanton boys that swim on blad-
ders,
This many summers in a sea of glory.
Henry VIII, III, 2:358

BASSANIO. In Belmont is a lady richly left,
And she is fair, and, fairer than that word,
Of wondrous virtues: sometimes from her
eyes
I did receive fair speechless messages:
Her name is Portia; nothing undervalued
To Cato's daughter, Brutus' Portia:
Nor is the wide world ignorant of her
worth,
For the four winds blow in from every
coast
Renowned suitors; and her sunny locks
Hang on her temples like a golden fleece,
Which makes her seat of Belmont Colchos'[1]
strand,
And many Jasons come in quest of her.
O my Antonio! had I but the means
To hold a rival place with one of them,
I have a mind presages me such thrift,
That I should questionless be fortunate.
Merchant of Venice, I, 1:161
[1] Colchos' strand: where Jayson sought the
golden fleece.

Things out of hope are compass'd oft with
venturing,
Chiefly in love, whose leave exceeds commission:
Affection faints not like a pale-fac'd coward.
Venus and Adonis: 567

VERSE

CELIA. Didst thou hear these verses?
ROSALIND. O! yes, I heard them all, and

more too; for some of them had in them
more feet than the verses would bear.
As You Like It, III, 2:172

JAQUES. I pray you, mar no more trees
with writing lovesongs in their barks.
ORLANDO. I pray you, mar no more of my
verses with reading them ill-favouredly.
As You Like It, III, 2:278

CINNA. I am Cinna the poet, I am Cinna
the poet.
FOURTH CITIZEN. Tear him for his bad
verses, tear him for his bad verses.
Julius Caesar, III, 3:32

Who will believe my verse in time to come,
If it were fill'd with your most high deserts?
Though yet, heaven knows, it is but as a
tomb
Which hides your life and shows not half
your parts.
Sonnet 17

Lord of my love, to whom in vassalage
Thy merit hath my duty strongly knit,
To thee I send this written ambassage,
To witness duty, not to show my wit.
Sonnet 26

If my slight Muse do please these curious
days,
The pain be mine, but thine shall be the
praise.
Sonnet 38

Was it the proud full sail of his great verse,
Bound for the prize of all too precious you,
That did my ripe thoughts in my brain in-
hearse.
Sonnet 86

VICE

LUCIANA. Apparel vice like virtue's harbinger;[1]
Bear a fair presence, though your heart be
tainted.
Comedy of Errors, III, 2:12
[1] harbinger: forerunner.

BASSANIO. There is no vice so simple but
assumes
Some mark of virtue on his[1] outward parts.
Merchant of Venice, III, 2:81
[1] his: its.

GLOUCESTER.[1] So smooth he daub'd his
vice with show of virtue.
Richard III, III, 5:29
[1] Later, KING RICHARD III.

O! what a mansion have those vices got
Which for their habitation chose out thee,

Where beauty's veil doth cover every blot,
And all things turn to fair that eyes can see.
Sonnet 95

VICTORY

CLEOPATRA. Upon your sword
Sit laurel victory, and smooth success
Be strew'd before your feet!
Antony and Cleopatra, I, 3:99

ARCHBISHOP OF CANTERBURY.[1] O noble
English! that could entertain
With half their forces the full pride of
France,
And let another half stand laughing by,
All out of work, and cold for action.
Henry V, I, 2:111
[1] About the Black Knight at Battle of Poitiers
in 1356.

CHORUS. Behold the English beach
Pales in the flood with men, with wives, and
boys,
Whose shouts and claps out-voice the deep-
mouth'd sea,
Which, like a mighty whiffler,[1] fore the king
Seems to prepare his way: so let him land,
And solemnly see him set on to London.

· · · · ·

As in good time he may, from Ireland coming,
Bringing rebellion broached on his sword.
Henry V, V, Prologue: 9, 31
[1] whiffler: tin officer who makes way for a
procession.

VILLAIN

COUNTESS. A very tainted fellow,[1] and full
of wickedness.
All's Well That Ends Well, III, 2:89
[1] fellow: PAROLLES.

FIRST LORD. He[1] hath out-villained villany
so far that the rarity redeems him.
All's Well That Ends Well, IV, 3:305
[1] He: PAROLLES.

ANTIPHOLUS OF SYRACUSE. They say this
town is full of cozenage;[1]
As, nimble jugglers that deceive the eye,
Dark-working sorcerers that change the
mind,
Soul-killing witches that deform the body,
Disguised cheaters, prating mountebanks,
And many such like liberties[2] of sin.
Comedy of Errors, I, 2:97
[1] cozenage: cheating. [2] liberties: improper free-
dom.

FIRST GENTLEMAN. He[1] that hath miss'd
the princess is a thing
Too bad for bad report.
Cymbeline, I, 1:16
[1] He: CLOTEN.

HAMLET. My tables,[1]—meet[2] it is I set it
down,
That one may smile, and smile, and be a villain.
Hamlet, I, 5:107
[1] tables: writing tablet. [2] meet: proper, fitting.

HAMLET. There's ne'er a villain dwelling
in all Denmark
But he's an arrant knave.
HORATIO. There needs no ghost, my lord,
come from the grave,
To tell us this.
Hamlet, I, 5:123

HAMLET. Bloody, bawdy villain!
Remorseless, treacherous, lecherous, kindless[1] villain!
Hamlet, II, 2:608
[1] kindless: unnatural; no thought of common
meaning of *kind*.

FALSTAFF. O! if men were to be saved by
merit, what hole in hell were hot enough
for him? This is the most omnipotent villain that ever cried 'Stand!'[1] to a true man.
1 Henry IV, I, 2:116
[1] Stand: the order of a robber—like "Hands
up!" today.

CHAMBERLAIN. Heaven will one day open
The king's eyes, that so long have slept upon
This bold bad man.[1]
SUFFOLK. And free us from his slavery.
Henry VIII, II, 2:42
[1] man: WOLSEY.

Q. KATHARINE. He[1] was a man
Of an unbounded stomach,[2] ever ranking
Himself with princes; one, that by sugges-
tion
Tied all the kingdom; simony[3] was fair-
play;
His own opinion was his law; i' the pres-
ence[4]
He would say untruths, and be ever double
Both in his words and meaning. He was
never,
But where he meant to ruin, pitiful;
His promises were, as he then was, mighty;
But his performance, as he is now, nothing.
Henry VIII, IV, 2:33
[1] He: WOLSEY. [2] stomach: pride. [3] simony:
traffic in sacred things. [4] i'. . . presence:
among persons of rank.

EDMUND. A credulous father, and a
brother noble,

Whose nature is so far from doing harms
That he suspects none; on whose foolish
    honesty
My practices[1] ride easy!
                                      King Lear, I, 2:195
[1] practices: insidious devices.

EDGAR. I know thee[1] well: a serviceable
    villain;
As duteous to the vices of thy mistress
As badness would desire.
                                      King Lear, IV, 6:257
[1] thee: OSWALD.

EDMUND. To both these sisters have I
    sworn my love;
Each jealous of the other, as the stung
Are of the adder. Which of them shall I
    take?
Both? one? or neither? Neither can be en-
    joy'd
If both remain alive.
                                      King Lear, V, 1:55

ARMADO. Villain, thou shalt fast for thy
offences ere thou be pardoned.
COSTARD. Well, sir, I hope, when I do it, I
shall do it on a full stomach.
                                 Love's Labour's Lost, I, 2:151

BASSANIO. I like not fair terms and a villain's mind.
                                 Merchant of Venice, I, 3:181

BORACHIO. When rich villains have need of
poor ones, poor ones may make what price
they will.
                           Much Ado About Nothing, III, 3:121

LEONATO. Which is the villain? Let me see
    his eyes,
That when I note another man like him,
I may avoid him: which of these is he?
                           Much Ado About Nothing, V, 1:269

IAGO. And what 's he then that says I play
    the villain?
When this advice is free I give and honest.
                                      Othello, II, 3:342

IAGO. Divinity of hell!
When devils will their blackest sins put on,
They do suggest at first with heavenly
    shows,
As I do now.

                    .   .   .   .   .

She shall undo her credit with the Moor.
So will I turn her virtue into pitch,
And out of her own goodness make the net
That shall enmesh them all.
                                      Othello, II, 3:356, 365

BOLINGBROKE. The caterpillars of the com-
    monwealth,
Which I have sworn to weed and pluck
    away.
                                      Richard II, II, 3:166

K. RICHARD. O villains, vipers, damn'd
    without redemption!
Dogs, easily won to fawn on any man!
Snakes, in my heart-blood warm'd, that
    sting my heart!
Three Judases, each one thrice worse than
    Judas!
                                      Richard II, III, 2:129

AARON. Tut! I have done a thousand
    dreadful things
As willingly as one would kill a fly,
And nothing grieves me heartily indeed
But that I cannot do ten thousand more.

                    .   .   .   .   .

If there be devils, would I were a devil,
To live and burn in everlasting fire,
So I might have your company in hell,
But to torment you with my bitter tongue!
                           Titus Andronicus, V, 1:141, 147

AUTOLYCUS. I understand the business; I
hear it. To have an open ear, a quick eye,
and a nimble hand, is necessary for a cut-
purse;[1] a good nose is requisite also, to smell
out work for the other senses. I see this is the
time that the unjust man doth thrive.
                                      Winter's Tale, IV, 4:683
[1] cut-purse: pick-pocket.

VIRGIN

HERMIA. So will I grow, so live, so die,
    my lord,
Ere I will yield my virgin patent up
Unto his lordship, whose unwished yoke
My soul consents not to give sovereignty.
                           Midsummer Night's Dream, I, 1:79

MARINA. If fires be hot, knives sharp, or
    waters deep,
Untied I still my virgin knot will keep.
                                      Pericles, IV, 2:159

PROSPERO. Take my daughter: but
If thou dost break her virgin-knot before
All sanctimonious ceremonies may
With full and holy rite be minister'd,
No sweet aspersion shall the heavens let fall
To make this contract grow; but barren
    hate,
Sour-eyed disdain and discord shall bestrew
The union of your bed with weeds so
    loathly

That you shall hate it both: therefore take
  heed,
As Hymen's lamps shall light you.
  FERDINAND. As I hope
For quiet days, fair issue and long life,
With such love as 't is now,—the murkiest
  den,
The most opportune place, the strong'st
  suggestion
Our worser genius can, shall never melt
Mine honour into lust, to take away
The edge of that day's celebration
When I shall think, or[1] Phoebus'[2] steeds are
  founder'd,
Or Night kept chain'd below.
                              Tempest, IV, 1:13
[1] or . . . Or: either, or. [2] Phoebus: the sun-
god.

VIRGINITY

HELENA. Man is enemy to virginity; how
may we barricado it against him?
  PAROLLES. Keep him out.
  HELENA. But he assails; and our virginity,
though valiant in the defence, yet is weak.
Unfold to us some war-like resistance.
                    All's Well That Ends Well, I, 1:124

THESEUS. Therefore, fair Hermia, ques-
tion your desires;
Know of your youth, examine well your
  blood,
Whether, if you yield not to your father's
  choice,
You can endure the livery of a nun.
For aye to be in shady cloister mew'd,
To live a barren sister all your life,
Chanting faint hymns to the cold fruitless
  moon.
Thrice blessed they that master so their
  blood,
To undergo such maiden pilgrimage;
But earthlier happy is the rose distill'd,
Than that which withering on the virgin
  thorn
Grows, lives, and dies, in single blessedness.
  HERMIA. So will I grow, so live, so die,
  my lord,
Ere I will yield my virgin patent up
              Midsummer Night's Dream, I, 1:67

VIRTUE

HAMLET. Forgive me this my virtue;
For in the fatness of these pursy[1] times
Virtue itself of vice must pardon beg,
Yea, curb[2] and woo for leave to do him
  good.
                          Hamlet, III, 4:152
[1] pursy: short of breath. [2] curb: bow down.

HAMLET. Assume a virtue, if you have it
  not.
                          Hamlet, III, 4:160

FALSTAFF. Virtue is of so little regard in
these costermonger[1] times that true valour is
turned bear-herd:[2] pregnancy is made a
tapster, and hath his quick wit wasted in giving reckonings: all the other gifts apperti-
nent to man, as the malice of this age shapes
them, are not worth a gooseberry.
                          II Henry IV, I, 2:191
[1] costermonger: a seller of things of little value;
used contemptuously. [2] bear-herd: one who
leads a tame bear at a show.

YORK. 'T is beauty that doth oft make
  women proud;
But God he knows, thy share thereof is
  small:
'T is virtue that doth make them most admir'd;
The contrary doth make thee wonder'd at:
                          III Henry VI, I, 4:128

DUKE. Virtue is bold, and goodness never
fearful.
                  Measure for Measure, III, 1:215

CERIMON. I held it ever,
Virtue and cunning[1] were endowments
  greater
Than nobleness and riches; careless heirs
May the two latter darken and expend,
But immortality attends the former,
Making a man a god.
                          Pericles, III, 2:25
[1] cunning: knowledge.

FRIAR LAURENCE. Virtue itself turns vice,
being misapplied.
                  Romeo and Juliet, II, 3:21

CLOWN. Virtue that transgresses is but
patched with sin; and sin that amends is but
patched with virtue.
                  Twelfth Night, I, 5:53

SIR TOBY. Dost thou think, because thou
art virtuous, there shall be no more cakes
and ale?
                  Twelfth Night, II, 3:123

ANTONIO. Virtue is beauty, but the beauteous evil
Are empty trunks o'erflourished by the
  devil.
                  Twelfth Night, III, 4:403

VOICE

JAQUES. More! I prithee, more. I can suck
melancholy out of a song as a weasel sucks
eggs. More! I prithee, more.

AMIENS. My voice is ragged; I know I cannot please you.

JAQUES. I do not desire you to please me; I do desire you to sing.
As You Like It, II, 5:12

FALSTAFF. For my voice, I have lost it with the hallooing and singing of anthems.
II Henry IV, I, 2:212

BOY. I did never know so full a voice issue from so empty a heart: but the saying is true, 'The empty vessel makes the greatest sound.'
Henry V, IV, 4:71

K. LEAR [about CORDELIA]. Her voice was ever soft,
Gentle and low, an excellent thing in woman.
King Lear, V, 3:272

PORTIA. He knows me as the blind man knows the cuckoo,
By the bad voice.
Merchant of Venice, V, 1:112

ROMEO. How silver-sweet sound lovers' tongues by night,
Like softest music to attending ears!
Romeo and Juliet, II, 2:166

VOWS

ROSALIND. I pray you, do not fall in love with me,
For I am falser than vows made in wine.
As You Like It, III, 5:72

POSTHUMUS. Where there 's another man; the vows of women
Of no more bondage be to where they are made
Than they are to their virtues, which is nothing.
Cymbeline, II, 4:110

LONGAVILLE. A woman I forswore; but I will prove,
Thou being a goddess, I forswore not thee;
My vow was earthly, thou a heavenly love;
Love's Labour's Lost, IV, 3:64

PRINCESS. This field shall hold me, and so hold your vow:
Nor God, nor I, delights in perjur'd men.
KING. Rebuke me not for that which you provoke:
The virtue of your eye must break my oath.
Love's Labour's Lost, V, 2:345

HERMIA. My good Lysander!
I swear to thee by Cupid's strongest bow,

By his best arrow with the golden head,
By the simplicity of Venus' doves,
By that which knitteth souls and prospers loves,
And by that fire which burn'd the Carthage queen,
When the false Troyan under sail was seen,
By all the vows that ever men have broke,
In number more than ever women spoke,
In that same place thou hast appointed me,
To-morrow truly will I meet with thee.
Midsummer Night's Dream, I, 1:169

SERVANT. So his familiars to his buried fortunes
Slink all away, leave their false vows with him,
Like empty purses pick'd.
Timon of Athens, IV, 2:10

TROILUS. We vow to weep seas, live in fire, eat rocks, tame tigers; thinking it harder for our mistress to devise imposition enough than for us to undergo any difficulty imposed. This is the monstruosity in love, lady, that the will is infinite, and the execution confined; that the desire is boundless.
Troilus and Cressida, III, 2:84

PROTEUS. Unheedful vows may heedfully be broken;
And he wants[1] wit that wants resolved will
To learn his wit to exchange the bad for better.
Two Gentlemen of Verona, II, 6:11
[1] wants: lacks.

WANT

OCTAVIUS CAESAR. Women are not
In their best fortunes strong, but want will perjure
The ne'er-touch'd vestal.
Antony and Cleopatra, III, 12:29

CORIN. He that wants[1] money, means, and content, is without three good friends.
As You Like It, III, 2:26
[1] wants: lacks, as often in Shakespeare.

WAR

OCTAVIA. Wars' twixt you twain[1] would be
As if the world should cleave, and that slain men
Should solder up the rift.
Antony and Cleopatra, III, 4:30
[1] you twain: her brother OCTAVIUS and ANTONY.

MARCIUS.[1] What would you have, you curs,

That like nor[2] peace nor war? the one affrights you,
The other makes you proud.
                        Coriolanus, I, 1:172
[1] MARCIUS: later CORIOLANUS.   [2] nor . . . nor:
neither—nor.

FIRST SERVANT. Let me have war, say I: it
exceeds peace as far as day does night; it 's
spritely, waking, audible, and full of vent.
Peace is a very apoplexy, lethargy; mulled,[1]
deaf, sleepy, insensible; a getter of more
bastard children than war 's a destroyer of
men.
   SECOND SERVANT. 'T is so: and as war, in
some sort, may be said to be a ravisher, so it
cannot be denied but peace is a great maker
of cuckolds.[2]
   THIRD SERVANT. The wars for my money.
                        Coriolanus, IV, 5:235
[1] mulled: dispirited.   [2] cuckold: husbands of
unfaithful wives.

BELARIUS. The toil o' the war,
A pain that only seems to seek out danger
I' the name of fame and honour; which dies
   i' the search,
And hath as oft a slanderous epitaph
As record of fair act.
                        Cymbeline, III, 3:49

CAPTAIN. We go to gain a little patch of
   ground
That hath in it no profit but the name.
To pay five ducats, five, I would not farm it;
Nor will it yield to Norway or the Pole
A ranker rate, should it be sold in fee.
   HAMLET. Why, then the Polack never will
      defend it.
   CAPTAIN. Yes, 't is already garrison'd.
   HAMLET. Two thousand souls and twenty
      thousand ducats
Will not debate the question of this straw:
This is the imposthume[1] of much wealth and
   peace,
That inward breaks, and shows no cause
   without
Why the man dies.
                        Hamlet, IV, 4:18
[1] imposthume: an inward sore or abscess.

HOTSPUR. Let them come;
They come like sacrifices in their trim,
And to the fire-eyed maid of smoky war
All hot and bleeding will we offer them:
The mailed Mars shall on his altar sit
Up to the ears in blood.
                        I Henry IV, IV, 1:112

WESTMORELAND.[1] Wherefore do you so ill
   translate yourself
Out of the speech of peace that bears such
   grace,

Into the harsh and boisterous tongue of war;
Turning your books to graves, your ink to
   blood,
Your pens to lances, and your tongue divine
To a loud trumpet and a point of war?
                        II Henry IV, IV, 1:47
[1] To ARCHBISHOP OF YORK.

PRINCE JOHN OF LANCASTER.[1] My Lord of
   York, it better show'd with you,
When that your flock, assembled by the bell,
Encircled you to hear with reverence
Your exposition on the holy text
Than now to see you here an iron man,
Cheering a rout of rebels with your drum,
Turning the word to sword and life to
   death.
                        II Henry IV, IV, 2:4
[1] Son of KING HENRY IV.

ARCHBISHOP OF CANTERBURY. As many ar-
   rows, loosed several ways,
Come to one mark; as many ways meet in
   one town;
As many fresh streams meet in one salt sea;
As many lines close in the dial's centre;
So many a thousand actions, once afoot,
End in one purpose, and be all well borne
Without defeat. Therefore to France, my
   liege.
Divide your happy England into four;
Whereof take you one quarter into France,
And you withal[1] shall make all Gallia[2] shake.
                        Henry V, I, 2:207
[1] withal: with it.   [2] Gallia: France.

CHORUS. Now all the youth of England
   are on fire
And silken dalliance in the wardrobe lies;
Now thrive the armourers, and honour's
   thought
Reigns solely in the breast of every man.
                        Henry V, II, Prologue: 1

K. HENRY. What is it then to me, if im-
   pious war,
Array'd in flames like to the prince of
   fiends,
Do, with his smirch'd complexion, all fell[1]
   feats
Enlink'd to waste and desolation?
What is 't to me, when you yourselves are
   cause,
If your pure maidens fall into the hand
Of hot and forcing violation?
                        Henry V, III, 3:15
[1] fell: savage.

K. HENRY. Ay, marry,[1] uncle; for I always
   thought
It was both impious and unnatural

That such immanity[2] and bloody strife
Should reign among professors of one faith.
I Henry VI, V, 1:11
[1] marry: indeed; originally an oath or invocation to the Virgin Mary. [2] immanity: ferocity.

YOUNG CLIFFORD. O war! thou son of hell,
Whom angry heavens do make their minister,
Throw in the frozen bosoms of our part
Hot coals of vengeance! Let no soldier fly:
He that is truly dedicate to war
Hath no self-love; nor he that loves himself
Hath not essentially, but by circumstance,
The name of valour.
II Henry VI, V, 2:33

YOUNG CLIFFORD. Wast thou ordain'd, dear father,
To lose thy youth in peace, and to achieve
The silver livery of advised age,
And, in thy reverence and thy chair-days, thus
To die in ruffian battle? Even at this sight
My heart is turn'd to stone: and while 't is mine
It shall be stony.
II Henry VI, V, 2:45

SON. Ill blows the wind that profits nobody.
This man, whom hand to hand I slew in fight,
May be possessed with some store of crowns;
. . . . .
Who's this? O God! it is my father's face,
Whom in this conflict I unwares have kill'd.
O heavy times! begetting such events.
III Henry VI, II, 5:55, 61

FATHER. Thou that so stoutly hast resisted me,
Give me thy gold, if thou hast any gold,
For I have bought it with an hundred blows.
But let me see: is this our foeman's face?
Ah! no, no, no; it is mine only son.
Ah! boy, if any life be left in thee,
Throw up thine eye: see, see! what showers arise,
Blown with the windy tempest of my heart,
Upon thy wounds, that kill mine eye and heart.
III Henry VI, II, 5:79

FRENCH HERALD. Many a widow's husband grovelling lies,
Coldly embracing the discolour'd earth;
And victory, with little loss, doth play
Upon the dancing banners of the French.
. . . . .

FIRST CITIZEN. Blood hath bought blood, and blows have answer'd blows;
Strength march'd with strength, and power confronted power.
King John, II, 1:305, 329

BASTARD.[1] Ha, majesty! how high thy glory towers
When the rich blood of kings is set on fire!
O! now doth death line his dead chaps[2] with steel;
The swords of soldiers are his teeth, his fangs;
And now he feasts, mousing the flesh of men,
In undetermin'd differences of kings.
Why stand these royal fronts amazed thus?
Cry, 'havoc'! kings; back to the stained field,
You equal-potents, fiery-kindled spirits!
Then let confusion of one part confirm
The other's peace; till then, blows, blood, and death!
King John, II, 1:350
[1] To KING PHILIP. [2] chaps: jaws.

BASTARD. Now for the bare-pick'd bone of majesty
Doth dogged war bristle his angry crest,
And snarleth in the gentle eyes of peace:
King John, IV, 3:148

RICHMOND. In God's name, cheerly on, courageous friends,
To reap the harvest of perpetual peace
By this one bloody trial of sharp war.
Richard III, V, 2:14

LUCENTIO. At last, though long, our jarring notes agree:
And time it is, when raging war is done,
To smile at scapes and perils overblown.
Taming of the Shrew, V, 2:1

WARNING

KING OF FRANCE. Those girls of Italy, take heed of them:
They say our French lack language to deny
If they demand: beware of being captives.
All's Well That Ends Well, II, 1:19

LAERTES [to OPHELIA]. For Hamlet, and the trifling of his favour,
Hold it a fashion and a toy in blood,
A violet in the youth of primy nature,
Forward, not permanent, sweet, not lasting,
The perfume and suppliance of a minute;
No more.
. . . . .

The chariest maid is prodigal enough
If she unmask her beauty to the moon;
Virtue itself 'scapes not caluminous strokes;

The canker galls the infants of the spring
Too oft before their buttons be disclos'd.
And in the morn and liquid dew of youth
Contagious blastments are most imminent.
    Ophelia. I shall the effect of this good les-
      son keep,
As watchman to my heart. But, good my
    brother,
Do not, as some ungracious pastors do,
Show me the steep and thorny way to
    heaven,
Whiles, like a puff'd and reckless libertine,
Himself the primrose path of dalliance
    treads,
And recks[1] not his own rede.
                        Hamlet, I, 3:5, 36
[1] recks . . . rede: regards not his own lesson.

    Ophelia. And hath given countenance to
      his[1] speech, my lord,
With almost all the holy vows of heaven.
    Polonius. Ay, springes to catch wood-
      cocks. I do know,
When the blood burns, how prodigal the
    soul
Lends the tongue vows; these blazes, daugh-
    ter,
Giving more light than heat, extinct in both,
Even in their promise, as it is a-making,
You must not take for fire.
         . . . . .

Do not believe his vows, for they are bro-
    kers
Not of that dye which their investments
    show,
But mere implorators of unholy suits,
Breathing like sanctified and pious bawds,
The better to beguile.
                Hamlet, I, 3:113, 127
[1] his: Hamlet's.

    K. Henry. Therefore take heed how you
      impawn[1] our person,
How you awake our sleeping sword of war:
We charge you, in the name of God, take
    heed.
                   Henry V, I, 2:21
[1] impawn: pledge, make responsible.

    Plantagenet. I'll note you in my book
      of memory,
To scourge you for this apprehension.
               I Henry VI, II, 4:101

    Gloucester.[1] Ah! gracious lord, these
      days are dangerous.
Virtue is chok'd with foul ambition,
And charity chas'd hence by rancour's hand;
Foul subornation is predominant,
And equity exil'd your highness' land.
I know their complot is to have my life;
             II Henry VI, III, 1:142
[1] Uncle of King Henry VII, to King Henry.

    Gloucester. Many men that stumble at
      the threshold
Are well foretold that danger lurks within.
             III Henry VI, IV, 7:11
[1] Later, King Richard III.

    Soothsayer [to Caesar]. Beware the ides[1]
of March.
    Caesar. He is a dreamer; let us leave him:
pass.
               Julius Caesar, I, 2:23
[1] ides: the fifteenth.

    Pandulph. France,[1] thou may'st hold a
      serpent by the tongue,
A chafed lion by the mortal[2] paw,
A fasting tiger safer by the tooth,
Than keep in peace that hand which thou
    dost hold.
               King John, III, 1:258
[1] France: i.e., King of France. [2] mortal:
deadly.

    Demetrius. There is no following her in
this fierce vein.
      Midsummer Night's Dream, III, 2:82

    Roderigo. If 't be your pleasure and most
      wise consent,
As partly I find it is, that your fair daugh-
    ter,
At this odd-even and dull watch o' the
    night,
Transported with no worse nor better
    guard
But with a knave of common hire, a gondo-
    lier,
To the gross clasps of a lascivious Moor,—
If this be known to you and your allowance,
We then have done you bold and saucy
    wrongs.
                 Othello, I, 1:122

    Brabantio. Look to her, Moor, if thou
      hast eyes to see:
She has deceiv'd her father, and may thee.
                 Othello, I, 3:293

    Katharine. If I be waspish, best beware
    my sting.
        Taming of the Shrew, II, 1:211

WEAKNESS

    K. Lear. We are not ourselves
When nature, being oppress'd, commands
    the mind
To suffer with the body.
               King Lear, II, 4:108

    Queen. The lion dying thrusteth forth
    his paw

And wounds the earth, if nothing else, with
    rage
To be o'erpower'd; and wilt thou, pupil-
    like,
Take thy correction mildly, kiss the rod,
And fawn on rage with base humility?
                  Richard II, V, 1:29

K. RICHARD [about RICHMOND]. A milk-
    sop, one that never in his life
Felt so much cold as over shoes in snow?
                Richard III, V, 3:325

TROILUS. But I am weaker than a woman's
    tear,
Tamer than sleep, fonder[1] than ignorance,
Less valiant than the virgin in the night,
And skilless as unpractis'd infancy.
           Troilus and Cressida, I, 1:9
[1] fonder: more foolish.

CRESSIDA. Ah! poor our sex; this fault in
    us I find,
The error of our eye directs our mind.
What error leads must err. O! then conclude
Minds sway'd by eyes are full of turpitude.
        Troilus and Cressida, V, 2:109

WEARINESS

ROSALIND. O Jupiter! how weary are my
    spirits.
TOUCHSTONE. I care not for my spirits if
my legs were not weary.
               As You Like It, II, 4:1

BELARIUS. Weariness
Can snore upon the flint when resty sloth
Finds the down pillow hard.
             Cymbeline, III, 6:33

PRINCE. Before God, I am exceeding
weary.
POINS. Is it come to that? I had thought
weariness durst not have attached one of so
high blood.
                II Henry IV, II, 2:1

BIONDELLO. I am dog weary.
         Taming of the Shrew, IV, 2:60

WEEDS

ANTONY. O! then we bring forth weeds
When our quick minds lie still; and our ills
    told us
Is as our earing.[1]
         Antony and Cleopatra, I, 2:113
[1] as . . . earing; according to our cultivation,
or mental growth.

AUFIDIUS. Each word thou hast spoke
    hath weeded from my heart
A root of ancient envy.[1]
            Coriolanus, IV, 5:108
[1] envy: hatred.

GHOST [to HAMLET]. I find thee apt:
And duller should'st thou be than the fat
    weed
That roots itself in ease on Lethe[1] wharf,
Would'st thou not stir in this.
               Hamlet, I, 5:31
[1] Lethe: the river of forgetfulness in the under
world.

LONGAVILLE. He weeds[1] the corn, and still
    lets grow the weeding.
          Love's Labour's Lost, I, 1:96
[1] weeds: cuts out the corn.

DUKE. Twice treble shame on Angelo,
To weed[1] my vice and let his grow!
O! what may man within him hide,
Though angel on the outward side.
         Measure for Measure, III, 2:283
[1] weed: uproot.

GARDENER. I will go root away
The noisome weeds, that without profit
    suck
The soil's fertility from wholesome flowers.
            Richard II, III, 4:37

YORK. 'Ay,' quoth my uncle Gloucester,
'Small herbs have grace, great weeds do
    grow apace':
And since, methinks, I would not grow so
    fast,
Because sweet flowers are slow and weeds
    make haste.
              Richard III, II, 4:12

WEEPING

ENOBARBUS. Look, they weep;
And I, an ass, am onion-eyed:[1] for shame,
Transform us not to women.
         Antony and Cleopatra, IV, 2:34
[1] onion-eyed: weeping.

RICHARD.[1] I cannot weep, for all my
    body's moisture
Scarce serves to quench my furnace-burn-
    ing heart:
Nor can my tongue unload my heart's great
    burden;
For self-same wind that I should speak
    withal
Is kindling coals that fire all my breast,
And burn me up with flames that tears
    would quench.
To weep is to make less the depth of grief:

Tears then for babes; blows and revenge for
me!
III Henry VI, II, 1:79
[1] Later KING RICHARD III.

K. LEAR. No, I 'll not weep:
I have full cause of weeping, but this heart
Shall break into a hundred thousand flaws[1]
Or ere I 'll weep. O fool! I shall go mad.
King Lear, II, 4:286
[1] flaws: gusts of passion.

LEONATO. How much better is it to weep
at joy than to joy at weeping!
Much Ado About Nothing, I, 1:28

GLOUCESTER.[1] All the standers-by had
wet their cheeks,
Like trees bedash'd with rain.
Richard III, I, 2:163
[1] Later, RICHARD III.

WELCOME

MARCIUS. O! let me clip[1] ye
In arms as sound as when I woo'd, in heart
As merry as when our nuptial day was
done,
And tapers burn'd to bedward.
Coriolanus, I, 6:29
[1] clip: embrace.

GUILDFORD. Ladies, a general welcome
from his grace
Salutes ye all: this night he dedicates
To fair content and you. None here, he
hopes,
In all this noble bevy, has brought with her
One care abroad; he would have all as
merry
As, first, good company, good wine, good
welcome
Can make good people.
Henry VIII, I, 4:1

LORD. Go, sirrah,[1] take them to the but-
tery,
And give them friendly welcome every
one:
Let them want[2] nothing that my house affords.
Taming of the Shrew, Induction, 1:102
[1] sirrah: term used for a servant. [2] want: lack.

CAMILLO. You pay a great deal too dear
for what 's given freely.
Winter's Tale, I, 1:19

LEONTES. Welcome hither, as is the spring
to the earth.
Winter's Tale, V, 1:151

WHORE

CLEOPATRA. O! is 't come to this?
ANTONY. I found you as a morsel cold
upon
Dead Caesar's[1] trencher, nay; you were a
fragment
Of Cneius Pompey's; besides what hotter
hours,
Unregister'd in vulgar frame, you have
Luxuriously[2] pick'd out; for I am sure,
Though you can guess what temperance
should be,
You know not what it is.
Antony and Cleopatra, III, 13:116
[1] Caesar: JULIUS. [2] Luxuriously: lustfully.

LEONATO. O! she is fallen
Into a pit of ink, that the wide sea
Hath drops too few to wash her clean again,
And salt too little which may season give
To her foul-tainted flesh.
Much Ado About Nothing, IV, 1:141

IAGO. 'Tis the strumpets' plague
To beguile many and be beguil'd by one.
Othello, IV, 1:97

EMILIA. He call'd her whore; a beggar in
his drink
Could not have laid such terms upon his
callat.[1]

. . . . .

Hath she forsook so many noble matches,
Her father and her country and her friends,
To be call'd whore? would it not make one
weep?
Othello, IV, 2:120, 125
[1] callat: prostitute.

DESDEMONA. His unkindness may defeat
my life,
But never taint my love. I cannot say
'whore':
It does abhor me now I speak the word;
To do the act that might the addition[1] earn
Not the world's mass of vanity could make
me.
Othello, IV, 2:160
[1] addition: title.

TIMON. This fell[1] whore of thine
Hath in her more destruction than thy
sword,
For all her cherubim look.
Timon of Athens, IV, 3:61
[1] fell: cruel.

TIMANDRA. Be a whore still; they love
thee not that use thee;
Give them diseases, leaving with thee their
lust.

Make use of thy salt hours; season the slaves
For tubs and baths; bring down rose-
    cheeked youth
To the tub-fast[1] and the diet.
                        Timon of Athens, IV, 3:82
[1] tub-fast: strict abstinence during treatment
for venereal disease.

WIDOW

GLOUCESTER. The jealous o'erworn
    widow and herself,
Since that our brother dubb'd them gentle-
women,
Are mighty gossips in our monarchy.
                        Richard III, I, 1:81

BUCKINGHAM. A beauty-waning and dis-
    tressed widow,[1]
Even in the afternoon of her best days,
Made prize and purchase of his[2] wanton eye.
                        Richard III, III, 7:185
[1] widow: ELIZABETH WOODVILLE.   [2] his: ED-
WARD IV.

TRANIO. I' faith, he 'll have a lusty widow
    now,
That shall be woo'd and wedded in a day.
                        Taming of the Shrew, IV, 2:50

WIFE

DIANA. Alas! poor lady;
'T is a hard bondage to become the wife
Of a detesting lord.
                        All's Well That Ends Well, III, 5:66

LAFEU. He[1] lost a wife
Whose beauty did astonish the survey
Of richest eyes, whose words all ears took
    captive.
                        All's Well That Ends Well, V, 3:15
[1] He: BERTRAM.

KING. I wonder, sir, sith[1] wives are mon-
    sters to you,
And that you fly them as you swear them
    lordship,
Yet you desire to marry.
                        All's Well That Ends Well, V, 3:155
[1] sith: since.

ANTIPHOLUS EPHESUS. My wife is shrewish[1] when I keep not hours.
                        Comedy of Errors, III, 1:2
[1] shrewish: cross.

CORIOLANUS. Resume that spirit, when
    you were wont to say,
If you had been the wife of Hercules,

Six of his labours you'd have done, and
    sav'd
Your husband so much sweat.
                        Coriolanus, IV, 1:16

IMOGEN. Why did you throw your
    wedded lady from you?
Think that you are upon a rock; and now
Throw me again.
                        Embracing him.
POST. Hang there like fruit, my soul,
Till the tree die!
                        Cymbeline, V, 5:261

WINCHESTER.[1] Thy wife is proud; she
    holdeth thee in awe,
More than God or religious churchmen
    may.
                        I Henry VI, I, 1:39
[1] To GLOUCESTER, uncle of KING HENRY.

PORTIA. Within the bonds of marriage, tell
    me, Brutus,
Is it excepted I should know no secrets
That appertain to you? Am I yourself
But, as it were, in sort or limitation,
To keep with you at meals, comfort your
    bed,
And talk to you sometimes? Dwell I but in
    the suburbs
Of your good pleasure? If it be no more,
Portia is Brutus' harlot, not his wife.
    BRUTUS. You are my true and honour-
    able wife,
As dear to me as are the ruddy drops
That visit my sad heart.
                        Julius Caesar, II, 1:280

BIRON. What, I! I love! I sue! I seek a wife!
A woman, that is like a German clock,
Still a-repairing, ever out of frame,
And never going aright, being a watch,
But being watch'd that it may still go right!
                        Love's Labour's Lost, III, 1:191

BIRON. And I to sigh for her! to watch for
    her!
To pray for her! Go to; it is a plague
That Cupid will impose for my neglect
Of his almighty dreadful little might.
Well, I will love, write, sigh, pray, sue, and
    groan:
Some men must love my lady, and some
    Joan.
                        Love's Labour's Lost, III, 1:202

BASSANIO. Antonio, I am married to a wife
Which is as dear to me as life itself;
But life itself, my wife, and all the world,
Are not with me esteem'd above thy life;
I would lose all, ay, sacrifice them all,
Here to this devil, to deliver you.

PORTIA. Your wife would give you little thanks for that,
If she were by to hear you make the offer.
Merchant of Venice, IV, 1:282

MISTRESS PAGE. Wives may be merry, and yet honest[1] too.
Merry Wives of Windsor, IV, 2:105
[1] honest: chaste.

BENEDICK. One woman is fair, yet I am well; another is wise, yet I am well; another virtuous, yet I am well; but till all graces be in one woman, one woman shall not come in my grace. Rich she shall be, that 's certain; wise, or I 'll none; virtuous, or I 'll never cheapen her; fair, or I 'll never look on her; mild, or come not near me; noble, or not I for an angel; of good discourse, an excellent musician, and her hair shall be of what colour it please God.
Much Ado About Nothing, II, 3:28

IAGO. Sir, would she[1] give you so much of her lips
As of her tongue she oft bestows on me,
You'd have enough.
Othello, II, 1:101
[1] she: EMILIA, his wife.

IAGO. Look to your wife; observe her well with Cassio;
Wear your eye thus, not jealous nor secure:
I would not have your free and noble nature
Out of self-bounty be abus'd; look to 't.
I know our country disposition well;
In Venice they do let heaven see the pranks
They dare not show their husbands; their best conscience
Is not to leave 't undone, but keep 't unknown.
Othello, III, 3:197

EMILIA. Let husbands know
Their wives have sense like them; they see and smell,
And have their palates both for sweet and sour,
As husbands have. What is it that they do
When they change us for others? Is it sport?
I think it is; and doth affection breed it?
I think it doth; is 't frailty that thus errs?
It is so too; and have not we affections,
Desires for sport, and frailty, as men have?
Then let them use us well; else let them know,
The ills we do, their ills instruct us so.
Othello, IV, 3:94

PERICLES. My dearest wife was like this maid, and such a one

My daughter might have been: my queen's square brows;
Her stature to an inch: as wand-like straight;
As silver-voic'd; her eyes as jewel-like,
And cas'd as richly; in pace another Juno;
Who starves the ears she feeds, and makes them hungry,
The more she gives them speech.
Pericles, V, 1:108

KATHARINA [to the other wives after she has been tamed].
Fie, fie! unknit that threatening unkind brow,
And dart not scornful glances from those eyes,
To wound thy lord, thy king, thy governor:
It blots thy beauty as frosts do bite the meads,
Confounds thy fame as whirlwinds shake fair buds,
And in no sense is meet or amiable.
A woman mov'd is like a fountain troubled,
Muddy, ill'seeming, thick, bereft of beauty;
And while it is so, none so dry or thirsty
Will deign to sip or touch one drop of it.
Thy husband is thy lord, thy life, thy keeper,
Thy head, thy sovereign; one that cares for thee,
And for thy maintenance commits his body
To painful labour both by sea and land,
To watch the night in storms, the day in cold,
Whilst thou liest warm at home, secure and safe;
And craves no other tribute at thy hands
But love, fair looks, and true obedience;
Too little payment for so great a debt,
Such duty as the subject owes the prince,
Even such a woman oweth to her husband;
And when she 's froward,[1] peevish, sullen, sour,
And not obedient to his honest will,
What is she but a foul contending rebel,
And graceless traitor to her loving lord?
I am asham'd that women are so simple
To offer war where they should kneel for peace,
Or seek for rule, supremacy, and sway,
When they are bound to serve, love, and obey.
Why are our bodies soft, and weak, and smooth,
Unapt to toil and trouble in the world,
But that our soft conditions and our hearts
Should well agree with our external parts?
Come, come, you froward and unable worms!
My mind hath been as big as one of yours,
My heart as great, my reason haply more,

To bandy word for word and frown for
  frown;
But now I see our lances are but straws,
Our strength as weak, our weakness past
  compare,
That seeming to be most which we indeed
  least are.
Then vail[2] your stomachs, for it is no boot,[3]
And place your hands below your husband's
  foot:
In token of which duty, if he please,
My hand is ready; may it do him ease.
  PETRUCHIO. Why, there 's a wench! Come
  on, and kiss me, Kate.
                    Taming of the Shrew, V, 2:136
[1] froward: disobedient.   [2] vail . . . stomachs:
curb your pride.   [3] boot: advantage.

  TROILUS. I take to-day a wife, and my
  election[1]
Is led on in the conduct of my will;
My will enkindled by mine eyes and ears,
Two traded pilots 'twixt the dangerous
  shores
Of will and judgment.
                    Troilus and Cressida, II, 2:61
[1] election: choice.

WILL

  PERICLES. I 'll make my will then; and as
  sick men do,
Who know the world, see heaven, but feel-
  ing woe,
Gripe not at earthly joys as erst they did:
So I bequeath a happy peace to you
And all good men, as every prince should
  do;
My riches to the earth from whence they
  came.
                                    Pericles, I, 1:41

WINE

  ANTONY. Come, let us all take hands,
Till that the conquering wine hath steep'd
  our sense
In soft and delicate Lethe.[1]
                    Antony and Cleopatra, II, 7:112
[1] Lethe: forgetfulness.

  MENENIUS. I am known to be a humorous[1] patrician, and one that loves a cup of
hot wine with not a drop of allaying Tiber
in 't.
                                Coriolanus, II, 1:51
[1] humorous: capricious.

  MACBETH. All is but toys; renown and
  grace is dead,

The wine of life is drawn, and the mere
  lees[1]
Is left this vault to brag of.
                                Macbeth, II, 3:99
[1] lees: dress, dregs.

  TIMON. Go, suck the subtle blood o' the
  grape,
Till the high fever seethe your blood to
  froth,
And so 'scape hanging.
                    Timon of Athens, IV, 3:432

WINTER

  DUKE SR. Here feel we but the penalty
  of Adam,
The seasons' difference; as the icy fang
And churlish chiding of the winter's wind.
                                As You Like It, II, 1:5

  PHILARIO. What means do you make to
  him?
  POSTHUMUS. Not any, but abide the
  change of time,
Quake in the present winter's state and wish
That warmer days would come.
                                Cymbeline, II, 4:3

  BIRON. A wither'd hermit, five-score winters worn,
Might shake off fifty, looking in her eye:
                    Love's Labour's Lost, IV, 3:242

Song. When icicles hang by the wall,
And Dick the shepherd blows his nail,
And Tom bears logs into the hall,
And milk comes frozen home in pail,
When blood is nipp'd, and ways be foul,
Then nightly sings the staring owl,
Tu-whit;
To-who, a merry note,
While greasy Joan doth keel[1] the pot.
When all aloud the wind doth blow,
And coughing drowns the parson's saw,
And birds sit brooding in the snow,
And Marian's nose looks red and raw,
When roasted crabs hiss in the bowl,
Then nightly sings the staring owl,
Tu-whit;
Tu-who, a merry note,
While greasy Joan doth keel[1] the pot.
                    Love's Labour's Lost, V, 2:922
[1] keel: stir.

For never-resting time leads summer on
To hideous winter, and confounds him
  there;
Sap check'd with frost, and lusty leaves
  quite gone,
Beauty o'ersnow'd and bareness everywhere:
                                    Sonnet 5

When they see
Return of lo, more bless'd may be the view;
Else call it winter, which, being full of care
Makes summer's welcome thrice more
wish'd, more rare.
Sonnet 56

WISDOM

HELENA. Full oft we see
Cold wisdom waiting on superfluous folly.
All's Well That Ends Well, I, 1:115

PAROLLES. Well, I shall be wiser.
LAFEU. E'en as soon as thou canst, for
thou hast to pull[1] at a smack o' the contrary.
All's Well That Ends Well, II, 3:235
[1] pull . . . contrary: work against a taste of
the opposite of wisdom.

GUIDERIUS. Those that I reverence, those
I fear, the wise;
At fools I laugh, not fear them.
Cymbeline, IV, 2:95

ALBANY. Wisdom and goodness to the vile
seem vile;
Filths savour[1] but themselves.
King Lear, IV, 2:38
[1] savour: have relish for.

GRATIANO. There are a sort of men whose
visages
Do cream and mantle like a standing pond,
And do a wilful stillness entertain,
With purpose to be dress'd in an opinion
Of wisdom, gravity, profound conceit;[1]
As who should say, 'I am Sir Oracle,
And when I ope my lips let no dog bark!'
Merchant of Venice, I, 1:88
[1] conceit: knowledge.

ULYSSES. The amity that wisdom knits
not, folly may easily untie.
Troilus and Cressida, II, 3:110

WISH

ALEXAS. You think none but your sheets
are privy to your wishes.
Antony and Cleopatra, I, 2:41

PISTOL. If wishes would prevail with me,
My purpose should not fail with me,
But thither would I hie.
Henry V, III, 2:15

PRINCESS. Sweet health and fair desires
consort your grace!
Love's Labour's Lost, II, 1:178

WIT

TOUCHSTONE. The more pity, that fools[1]
may not speak wisely what wise men do
foolishly.
CELIA. By my troth, thou sayest true; for
since the little wit that fools have was si-
lenced, the little foolery that wise men have
makes a great show.
As You Like It, I, 2:92
[1] fools: jesters.

ROSALIND. Thou speakest wiser than thou
art ware of.
TOUCHSTONE. Nay, I shall ne'er be ware
of mine own wit till I break my shins against
it.
As You Like It, II, 4:58

DUKE SENIOR. He[1] uses his folly like a
stalking-horse,[2] and under the presentation
of that he shoots his wit.
As You Like It, V, 4:111
[1] He: TOUCHSTONE. [2] stalking-horse: a real or
artificial horse behind which a hunter hides.

THIRD CITIZEN. Nay, your wit will not so
soon out as another man's will; 't is strongly
wedged up in a blockhead.
Coriolanus, II, 3:29

FALSTAFF. I am not only witty in myself,
but the cause that wit is in other men.
II Henry IV, I, 2:11

FOOL. I had rather be any kind o' thing
than a fool; and yet I would not be thee,
nuncle;[1] thou hast pared thy wit o' both
sides, and left nothing i' the middle: here
comes one o' the parings.
King Lear, I, 4:203
[1] nuncle: term used by a jester to his master.

FOOL. He that has and a little tiny wit,—
With hey, ho, the wind and the rain,—
Must make content with his fortunes fit,
For the rain it raineth every day.
King Lear, III, 2:74

BIRON. Your wit 's too hot, it speeds too
fast, 't will tire.
Love's Labour's Lost, II, 1:120

BIRON. This fellow pecks up wit, as pi-
geons pease,
And utters it again when God doth please.
He is wit's pedlar, and retails his wares
At wakes, and wassails, meetings, markets,
fairs.
Love's Labour's Lost, V, 2:315

LEONATO. They[1] never meet but there 's a
skirmish of wit between them.
Much Ado About Nothing, I, 1:63
[1] They: BEATRICE and BENEDICK.

BEATRICE [about BENEDICK]. In our last conflict four of his five wits went halting off, and now is the whole man governed with one.

Much Ado About Nothing, I, 1:65

BEATRICE. If he have wit enough to keep himself warm, let him bear it for a difference between himself and his horse.

Much Ado About Nothing, I, 1:68

DON PEDRO. What a pretty thing man is when he goes in his doublet and hose and leaves off his wit!

Much Ado About Nothing, V, 1:202

BENEDICK. Thy wit is as quick as the grey-hound's mouth; it catches.
MARGARET. And yours as blunt as the fencer's foils, which hit, but hurt not.
BENEDICK. A most manly wit, Margaret; it will not hurt a woman.

Much Ado About Nothing, V, 2:11

BENEDICK. Come, I will have thee; but, by this light, I take thee for pity.
BEATRICE. I would not deny you; but, by this good day, I yield upon great persuasion, and partly to save your life, for I was told you were in a consumption.
BENEDICK. Peace! I will stop your mouth.
Kisses her.

Much Ado About Nothing, V, 4:92

FRIAR LAURENCE. Thy wit, that ornament to shape and love,
Misshapen in the conduct of them both,
Like powder in a skilless soldier's flask,
Is set a-fire by thine own ignorance.

Romeo and Juliet, III, 3:130

SEBASTIAN. Look; he 's winding up the watch of his wit: by and by it will strike.

Tempest, II, 1:12

AJAX. An[1] all men were o' my mind,—
ULYSSES [aside]. Wit would be out of fashion.

Troilus and Cressida, II, 3:224

[1] An: if.

CLOWN. Wit, an 't[1] be thy will, put me into good fooling! Those wits that think they have thee, do very oft prove fools; and I, that am sure I lack thee, may pass for a wise man: for what says Quinapalus?[2] 'Better a witty fool than a foolish wit.'

Twelfth Night, I, 5:35

[1] an 't: if it. [2] Quinapalus: an imaginary philosopher.

VALENTINE. Home-keeping youth have ever homely[1] wits.[2]

Two Gentlemen of Verona, I, 1:2

[1] homely: plain, not refined. [2] wits: understanding, knowledge.

WITCHES

FIRST WITCH. When shall we three meet again
In thunder, lightning, or in rain?
SECOND WITCH. When the hurlyburly 's done,
When the battle 's lost and won.
THIRD WITCH. That will be ere the set of sun.

Macbeth, I, 1:1

FIRST WITCH. Her husband 's to Aleppo gone, master o' the Tiger:
But in a sieve I 'll thither sail,
And, like a rat[1] without a tail,
I 'll do, I 'll do, and I 'll do.

. . . . .

I will drain him dry as hay:
Sleep shall neither night nor day
Hang upon his pent-house lid;
He shall live a man forbid.
Weary se'nnights[2] nine times nine
Shall he dwindle, peak and pine:

. . . . .

Drum within.
THIRD WITCH. A drum! a drum!
Macbeth doth come.
ALL. The weird sisters, hand in hand,
Posters of the sea and land,
Thus do go about, about:
Thrice to thine, and thrice to mine,
And thrice again, to make up nine.
Peace! the charm 's wound up.

Macbeth, I, 3:7, 18, 30

[1] like a rat: in guise of a rat. [2] se'nnights: seven nights.

MACBETH. So foul and fair a day I have not seen.
BANQUO. How far is 't call'd to Forres? What are these,
So wither'd and so wild in their attire,
That look not like th' inhabitants o' the earth,
And yet are on 't? Live you? or are you aught
That man may question? You seem to understand me,
By each at once her choppy finger laying
Upon her skinny lips: you should be women,
And yet your beards forbid me to interpret
That you are so.

Macbeth, I, 3:38

MACBETH. Speak, if you can: what are you?
FIRST WITCH. All hail, Macbeth! hail to thee, Thane of Glamis!

SECOND WITCH. All hail, Macbeth! hail to thee, Thane of Cawdor!
THIRD WITCH. All hail, Macbeth! that shalt be king hereafter.

Macbeth, I, 3:47

BANQUO. If you can look into the seeds of time,
And say which grain will grow and which will not,
Speak then to me, who neither beg nor fear
Your favours nor your hate.

. . . . .

FIRST WITCH. Lesser than Macbeth, and greater.
SECOND WITCH. Not so happy, yet much happier.
THIRD WITCH. Thou shalt get kings, though thou be none.

Macbeth, I, 3:58, 65

BANQUO. The earth hath bubbles, as the water has,
And these are of them. Whither are they vanish'd?
MACBETH. Into the air, and what seem'd corporal melted
As breath into the wind. Would they had stay'd!

. . . . .

Do you not hope your children shall be kings,
When those that gave the Thane of Cawdor to me
Promis'd no less to them?
BANQUO. That, trusted home,
Might yet enkindle you unto the crown,
Besides the Thane of Cawdor. But 't is strange:
And oftentimes, to win us to our harm,
The instruments of darkness tell us truths,
Win us with honest trifles, to betray 's
In deepest consequence.

Macbeth, I, 3:79, 118

FIRST WITCH. Round about the cauldron go;
In the poison'd entrails throw.
Toad, that under cold stone
Days and nights has thirty-one
Swelter'd venom sleeping got,
Boil thou first i' the charmed pot.
ALL. Double, double toil and trouble;
Fire burn and cauldron bubble.

. . . . .

SECOND WITCH. By the pricking of my thumbs,
Something wicked this way comes.

Macbeth, IV, 1:5, 45

Thunder. First Apparition, an armed Head.
MACBETH. Tell me, thou unknown power,—
FIRST WITCH. He knows thy thought:
Hear his speech, but say thou nought
FIRST APP. Macbeth! Macbeth! Macbeth! beware Macduff:
Beware the Thane of Fife. Dismiss me. Enough.

Descends.

. . . . .

SECOND APP. Be bloody, bold, and resolute; laugh to scorn
The power of man, for none of woman born
Shall harm Macbeth.

Descends.

MACBETH. Then live, Macduff: what need I fear of thee?
But yet I 'll make assurance double sure,
And take a bond of fate: thou shalt not live;
That I may tell pale-hearted fear it lies,
And sleep in spite of thunder.

. . . . .

THIRD APP. Be lion-mettled, proud, and take no care
Who chafes, who frets, or where conspirers are:
Macbeth shall never vanquish'd be until
Great Birnam wood to high Dunsinane hill
Shall come against him.

Descends.

. . . . .

Yet my heart
Throbs to know one thing: tell me, if your art
Can tell so much, shall Banquo's issue ever
Reign in this kingdom?
ALL. Seek to know no more.

. . . . .

MACBETH. Thou art too like the spirit of Banquo; down!

Macbeth, IV, 1:68, 79, 90, 100, 112

MACBETH. Thy crown does sear mine eye-balls: and thy hair,
Thou other gold-bound brow, is like the first:
A third is like the former. Filthy hags!
Why do you show me this? A fourth! Start, eyes!
What! will the line stretch out to the crack of doom?
Another yet! A seventh! I 'll see no more:
And yet the eighth appears, who bears a glass
Which shows me many more; and some I see
That two-fold balls and treble sceptres carry.

Horrible sight! Now, I see, 't is true;
For the blood-bolter'd Banquo smiles upon
me,
And points at them for his.
Macbeth, IV, 1:113

WOE

HAMLET. I have that within which passeth show;
These but the trappings and the suits of
woe.
Hamlet, I, 2:85

QUEEN. One woe doth tread upon an-
other's heel,
So fast they follow.
Hamlet, IV, 7:165

ANGELO. Alack! when once our grace[1] we
have forgot,
Nothing goes right: we would, and we
would not.
Measure for Measure, IV, 4:36
[1] grace: virtue.

GAUNT. Woe doth the heavier sit,
Where it perceives it is but faintly borne.

. . . . .

For gnarling[1] sorrow hath less power to bite
The man that mocks at it and sets it light.
Richard II, I, 3:280, 292
[1] gnarling: snarling.

YORK. God for his mercy! what a tide of
woes
Comes rushing on this woeful land at once!
Richard II, II, 2:98

CARLISLE. Wise men ne'er sit and wail
their woes,
But presently[1] prevent the ways to wail.
Richard II, III, 2:178
[1] presently: at once.

ABBOT. A woeful pageant have we here
beheld.
CARLISLE. The woe 's to come; the chil-
dren yet unborn
Shall feel this day as sharp to them as thorn.
Richard II, IV, 1:321

ROMEO. All these woes shall serve
For sweet discourses in our time to come.
Romeo and Juliet, III, 5:52

WOLF

ARVIRAGUS. We are beastly, subtle as the
fox for prey,
Like war-like as the wolf for what we eat.
Cymbeline, III, 3:40

CHIEF JUSTICE. Since all is well, keep it
so: wake not a sleeping wolf.
FALSTAFF. To wake a wolf is as bad as to
smell a fox.
II Henry IV, I, 2:173

Q. MARGARET. Is he[1] a lamb? his skin is
surely lent him,
For he 's inclin'd as is the ravenous wolf.
Who cannot steal a shape that means deceit?
II Henry VI, III, 1:77
[1] he: GLOUCESTER, later RICHARD III.

BUCKINGHAM. This holy fox,[1]
Or wolf, or both, for he is equal ravenous
As he is subtle, and as prone to mischief
As able to perform.
Henry VIII, I, 1:158
[1] fox: CARDINAL WOLSEY.

CASSIUS. Poor man![1] I know he would not
be a wolf
But that he sees the Romans are but sheep;
He were no lion were not Romans hinds.[2]
Julius Caesar, I, 3:104
[1] man: CAESAR. [2] hinds: female deer.

ANTONIO. You may as well use question
with the wolf,
Why he hath made the ewe bleat for the
lamb;
You may as well forbid the mountain pines
To wag their high tops, and to make no
noise
When they are fretted with the gusts of
heaven.
Merchant of Venice, IV, 1:73

How many lambs might the stern wolf be-
tray,
If like a lamb he could his looks translate!
Sonnet 96

WOMAN

KING. Come, come, to the purpose: did
he love this woman?
PAROLLES. Faith, sir, he did love her; but
how?
KING. How, I pray you?
PAROLLES. He did love her, sir, as a gen-
tleman loves a woman.
KING. How is that?
PAROLLES. He loved her, sir, and loved
her not.   . . . . .

He loved her, for indeed he was mad for
her, and talked of Satan, and of limbo, and
of Furies, and I know not what.
All's Well That Ends Well, V, 3:241, 258

CLEOPATRA. My resolution 's placed, and
I have nothing

Of woman in me; now from head to foot
I am marble-constant, now the fleeting moon
No planet is of mine.
Antony and Cleopatra, V, 2:238

CLOWN. A very honest woman, but something given to lie, as a woman should not do but in the way of honesty.
Antony and Cleopatra, V, 2:252
[This speech is an example of some clowns' sly humor.]

CLOWN.[1] You must not think I am so simple but I know the devil himself will not eat a woman; I know that a woman is a dish for the gods, if the devil dress her not. But, truly, these same whoreson[2] devils do the gods great harm in their women, for in every ten that they make, the devils mar five.
Antony and Cleopatra, V, 2:273
[1] CLOWN: a rustic, not a comedian. [2] whoreson: a term of reproach, sometimes used playfully.

ROSALIND. The bountiful blind woman[1] doth most mistake in her gifts to woman.
CELIA. 'T is true; for those that she makes fair she scarce makes honest, and those that she makes honest she makes very ill-favouredly.[2]
As You Like It, I, 2:31
[1] blind woman: Fortune. [2] ill-favouredly: homely.

ROSALIND. Do you not know I am a woman? when I think, I must speak.
As You Like It, III, 2:263

ORLANDO. Can you remember any of the principal evils that he laid to the charge of women?
ROSALIND. There were none principal; they were all like one another as half-pence are; every one fault seeming monstrous till his[1] fellow fault came to match it.
As You Like It, III, 2:369
[1] his: its.

ROSALIND. Make[1] the doors upon a woman's wit, and it will out at the casement; shut that, and 't will out at the keyhole; stop that, 't will fly with the smoke out at the chimney.
ORLANDO. A man that had a wife with such a wit, he might say, 'Wit, whither wilt?'
ROSALIND. Nay, you might keep that check for it till you met your wife's wit going to your neighbour's bed.
ORLANDO. And what wit could wit have to excuse that?
ROSALIND. Marry, to say she came to seek

you there. You shall never take her without her answer, unless you take her without her tongue. O! that woman that cannot make her fault her husband's occasion,[2] let her never nurse her child herself, for she will breed it like a fool.
As You Like It, IV, 1:163
[1] Make: close. [2] occasion: fault.

HAMLET. Frailty, thy name is woman!
Hamlet, I, 2:146

K. HENRY. She 's a woman to be pitied much:
Her sighs will make a battery in his breast;
Her tears will pierce into a marble heart;
The tiger will be mild whiles she doth mourn.
III Henry VI, III, 1:36

PRINCE. Methinks a woman of this valiant spirit
Should, if a coward heard her speak these words,
Infuse his breast with magnanimity,
And make him, naked, foil a man at arms.
III Henry VI, V, 4:39

Q. KATHARINE. Bring me a constant woman to her husband,
One that ne'er dream'd a joy beyond his pleasure,
And to that woman, when she has done most,
Yet will I add an honour, a great patience.
Henry VIII, III, 1:134

PORTIA. I grant I am a woman, but withal[1]
A woman that Lord Brutus took to wife;
I grant I am a woman, but withal
A woman well-reputed, Cato's daughter.
Think you I am no stronger than my sex,
Being so father'd and so husbanded?
Tell me your counsels, I will not disclose 'em.
Julius Caesar, II, 1:292
[1] withal: with it.

PORTIA. How hard it is for women to keep counsel!
Julius Caesar, II, 4:9

FOOL.[1] For there was never yet fair woman but she made mouths in a glass.
King Lear, III, 2:35
[1] Fool: jester.

KING. A child of our grandmother Eve, a female; or, for thy more sweet understanding, a woman.
Love's Labour's Lost, I, 1:266

BIRON. From women's eyes this doctrine I derive;

They sparkle still the right Promethean fire;
They are the books, the arts, the academes,
That show, contain, and nourish all the
    world;
                        Love's Labour's Lost, IV, 3:350

IAGO. You are pictures out of doors,
Bells in your parlours, wild cats in your
    kitchens,
Saints in your injuries, devils being of-
    fended,
Players in your housewifery, and house-
    wives in your beds.
                        Othello, II, 1:110

IAGO. She never yet was foolish that was
    fair,
For even her folly help'd her to an heir.
DESDEMONA. These are old fond[1] para-
doxes to make fools laugh i' the alehouse.
                        Othello, II, 1:137
[1] fond: foolish.

DESDEMONA. But what praise could'st
thou bestow on a deserving woman indeed?
                . . . . .

IAGO. She that was ever fair and never
    proud,
Had a tongue at will and yet was never
    loud,
Never lack'd gold and yet went never gay,
Fled from her wish and yet said 'Now I
    may,'
She that being anger'd, her revenge being
    nigh,
Bade her wrong stay and her displeasure fly,
She that in wisdom never was so frail
To change[1] the cod's head for the salmon's
    tail,
She that could think and ne'er disclose her
    mind,
See suitors following and not look behind,
She was a wight, if ever such wight were,
DESDEMONA. To do what?
IAGO. To suckle fools and chronicle[2] small
    beer.
                        Othello, II, 1:145, 149
[1] To change, etc.: to change a choice bit for a
poorer one. [2] chronicle: keep household ac-
counts.

OTHELLO. O! the world hath not a sweeter
creature; she might lie by an emperor's side
and command him tasks.
                        Othello, IV, 1:194

FRIAR LAURENCE. Women may fall, when
there's no strength in men.
                        Romeo and Juliet, II, 3:80

HORTENSIO. Kindness in women, not their
    beauteous looks,
Shall win my love: and so I take my leave.
                        Taming of the Shrew, IV, 2:41

KATHARINA. A woman mov'd is like a
    fountain troubled,
Muddy, ill-seeming, thick, bereft of beauty;
And while it is so, none so dry or thirsty
Will deign to sip or touch one drop of it.
                        Taming of the Shrew, V, 2:142

DEMETRIUS. She is a woman, therefore
    may be woo'd;
She is a woman, therefore may be won;
She is Lavinia, therefore must be lov'd.
                        Titus Andronicus, II, 1:82

CRESSIDA. To be wise and love
Exceeds man's might; that dwells with gods
    above.
TROILUS. O! that I thought it could be in
    a woman,
As if it can I will presume in you,
To feed for aye her lamp and flames of
    love;
To keep her constancy in plight and youth,
Outliving beauty's outward, with a mind
That doth renew swifter than blood decays.
                        Troilus and Cressida, III, 2:163

PATROCLUS. A woman impudent and
    mannish grown
Is not more loath'd than an effeminate man.
                        Troilus and Cressida, III, 3:217

VIOLA. How easy is it for the proper-
    false[1]
In women's waxen hearts to set their forms!
Alas! our frailty is the cause, not we,
For such as we are made of, such we be.
                        Twelfth Night, II, 2:30
[1] proper-false: good-looking and deceitful.

SECOND LADY. Who taught you this?
MAXIMILLIUS. I learn'd it out of women's
    faces.
                        Winter's Tale, II, 1:12

PAULINA. If one by one you wedded all
    the world,
Or from the all that are took something
    good,
To make a perfect woman, she[1] you kill'd
Would be unparallel'd.
                . . . . .

GENTLEMAN. Women will love her,[2] that
    she is a woman
More worth than any man; men, that she is
The rarest of all women.
                        Winter's Tale, V, 1:13, 110
[1] she: HERMIONE.   [2] her: PERDITA.

WONDER

ROSALIND. I was seven of the nine days
out of the wonder before you came; for

look here what I found on a palm-tree: I was never so be-rhymed since Pythagoras'[1] time, that I was an Irish rat, which I can hardly remember.

As You Like It, III, 2:185

[1] Pythagoras: a philosopher who taught the transmigration of souls.

DUCHESS. I, his forlorn duchess,
Was made a wonder and a pointing-stock
To every idle rascal follower.

II Henry VI, II, 4:45

MACBETH. Can such things be,
And overcome us like a summer's cloud,
Without our special wonder?

Macbeth, III, 4:110

ANNE. O! wonderful, when devils tell the truth.
GLOUCESTER. More wonderful when angels are so angry.

Richard III, I, 2:73

WOOING

ROSALIND. Come, woo me, woo me; for now I am in a holiday humour, and like enough to consent. What would you say to me now, an[1] I were your very very Rosalind?

As You Like It, IV, 1:68

[1] an: if.

K. HENRY. Fair Katharine, and most fair, Will you vouchsafe to teach a soldier terms Such as will enter at a lady's ear And plead his love-suit to her gentle heart?
PRINCESS KATHARINE. Your majesty sall mock at me; I cannot speak your England.
K. HENRY. O fair Katharine! if you will love me soundly with your French heart, I will be glad to hear you confess it brokenly with your English tongue. Do you like me, Kate?
KATHARINE. *Pardonnez-moy*, I cannot tell vat is 'like me.'
K. HENRY. An angel is like you, Kate, and you are like an angel.

Henry V, V, 2:98

K. HENRY.[1] If thou canst love a fellow of this temper, Kate, whose face is not worth sun-burning, that never looks in his glass for love of any thing he sees there, let thine eye be thy cook. I speak to thee plain soldier: if thou canst love me for this, take me; if not, to say to thee that I shall die, is true; but for thy love, by the Lord, no; yet I love thee too.

Henry V, V, 2:153

[1] To PRINCESS KATHARINE OF FRANCE.

PRINCESS KATHARINE. Is it possible dat I sould love de enemy of France?
K. HENRY. No; it is not possible you should love the enemy of France, Kate; but, in loving me, you should love the friend of France, for I love France so well that I will not part with a village of it; I will have it all mine: and Kate, when France is mine and I am yours, then yours is France and you are mine.

Henry V, V, 2:178

K. HENRY. No, Kate? I will tell thee in French, which I am sure will hang upon my tongue like a new-married wife about her husband's neck, hardly to be shook off.

Henry V, V, 2:187

K. HENRY. Now beshrew my father's ambition! he was thinking of civil wars when he got me: therefore was I created with a stubborn outside, with an aspect of iron, that when I come to woo ladies I fright them. But, in faith, Kate, the elder I wax the better I shall appear.

Henry V, V, 2:242

K. HENRY. My comfort is, that old age, that ill layer-up of beauty, can do no more spoil upon my face: thou hast me, if thou hast me, at the worst; and thou shalt wear me, if thou wear me, better and better.

Henry V, V, 2:249

SUFFOLK. She 's beautiful and therefore to be woo'd;
She is a woman, therefore to be won.

I Henry VI, V, 3:78

FALSTAFF. Have I caught my heavenly jewel?

Merry Wives of Windsor, III, 3:45

FALSTAFF. What made me love thee? let that persuade thee there 's something extraordinary in thee. Come, I cannot cog[1] and say thou art this and that, like a many of these lisping hawthorn-buds, that come like women in men's apparel, and smell like Bucklersbury[2] in simple[3] time: I cannot; but I love thee, none but thee, and thou deservest it.

Merry Wives of Windsor, III, 3:73

[1] cog: deceive. [2] Bucklersbury: a street of many druggists. [3] simple: herbs used as medicines.

FENTON. Albeit I will confess thy father's wealth
Was the first motive that I woo'd thee, Anne:
Yet, wooing thee, I found thee of more value

Than stamps in gold or sums in sealed bags;
And 't is the very riches of thyself
That now I aim at.
Merry Wives of Windsor, III, 4:13

EGEUS. This man hath bewitch'd the
bosom of my child:
Thou, thou, Lysander, thou hast given her
rhymes,
And interchang'd love-tokens with my
child;
Thou hast by moonlight at her window
sung,
With feigning[1] voice, verses of feigning[2]
love;
And stol'n the impression of her fantasy
With bracelets of thy hair, rings, gawds,[3]
conceits,
Knacks, trifles, nosegays, sweetmeats, messengers
Of strong prevailment in unharden'd youth.
Midsummer Night's Dream, I, 1:27
[1] feigning: soft, perhaps crooning. [2] feigning:
pretending. [3] gawds: trinkets.

HELENA. We cannot fight for love, as men
may do;
We should be woo'd and were not made to
woo.
Midsummer Night's Dream, II, 1:241

BENEDICK [to BEATRICE]. Thou and I are
too wise to woo peaceably.
Much Ado About Nothing, V, 2:73

GLOUCESTER.[1] Fairer than tongue can
name thee, let me have
Some patient leisure to excuse myself.
ANNE.[2] Fouler than heart can think thee,
thou canst make
No excuse current, but to hang thyself.

· · · · ·

GLOUCESTER. Is not the causer of the
timeless deaths
Of these Plantagenets, Henry and Edward,
As blameful as the executioner?
ANNE. Thou art the cause, and most ac-
curs'd effect.
GLOUCESTER. Your beauty was the cause
of that effect;
Your beauty, that did haunt me in my sleep
To undertake the death of all the world,
So I might live one hour in your sweet
bosom.
Richard III, I, 2:81, 117
[1] GLOUCESTER: later, KING RICHARD III.
[2] ANNE: widow of EDWARD, PRINCE OF WALES,
whom GLOUCESTER murdered.

GLOUCESTER.[1] Look! how this ring en-
compasseth thy finger,

Even so thy breast encloseth my poor
heart;
Wear both of them, for both of them are
thine.
Richard III, I, 2:204
[1] Later, KING RICHARD III to ANNE, widow of
EDWARD, son of HENRY VI.

GLOUCESTER.[1] Was ever woman in this
humour woo'd?
Was ever woman in this humour won?
I'll have her; but I will not keep her long.
What! I, that kill'd her husband and his
father,
To take her in her heart's extremest hate;
With curses in her mouth, tears in her eyes,
The bleeding witness of her hatred by.

· · · · ·

And yet to win her, all the world to nothing!
Richard III, I, 2:228, 238
[1] Later KING RICHARD III.

Gentle thou art, and therefore to be won,
Beauteous thou art, therefore to be assail'd;
And when a woman woos, what woman's
son
Will sourly leave her till she[1] have prevail'd?
Sonnet 41
[1] she: some critics think *he* is the right word;
first Folio says *he*.

BAPTISTA. Gentlemen, importune me no
further,
For how I firmly am resolv'd you know;
That is, not to bestow my youngest daugh-
ter
Before I have a husband for the elder.
If either of you both love Katharina,
Because I know you well and love you well,
Leave shall you have to court her at your
pleasure.

· · · · ·

KATHARINA. I pray you, sir, is it your will
To make a stale[1] of me amongst these
mates?[2]
Taming of the Shrew, I, 1:48, 56
[1] stale: laughing stock. [2] mates: fellows, a
term of contempt.

PETRUCHIO. Now, by the world, it is a
lusty wench!
I love her ten times more than e'er I did:
O! how I long to have some chat with her.

· · · · ·

Say that she rail; why then I 'll tell her plain
She sings as sweetly as a nightingale:
Say that she frown; I 'll say she looks as
clear
As morning roses newly wash'd with dew:

Say she be mute and will not speak a word;
Then I 'll commend her volubility,
And say she uttereth piercing eloquence:
If she do bid me pack; I 'll give her thanks,
As though she bid me stay by her a week:
If she deny to wed; I 'll crave the day
When I shall ask the banns, and when be
   married.
      Taming of the Shrew, II, 1:161, 171
[1] About KATHARINA.

KATHARINA. They call me Katharine that
   do talk of me.
PETRUCHIO. You lie, in faith; for you are
   call'd plain Kate,
And bonny Kate, and sometimes Kate the
   curst;[1]
But Kate, the prettiest Kate in Christendom;
Kate of Kate-Hall, my super-dainty Kate
For dainties are all Kates:[2] and therefore,
   Kate,
Take this of me, Kate of my consolation;
Hearing thy mildness prais'd in every town,
Thy virtues spoke of, and thy beauty
   sounded,
Yet not so deeply as to thee belongs,
Myself am mov'd to woo thee for my wife.
        Taming of the Shrew, II, 1:185
[1] curst: waspish.   [2] Kates: a pun on *cates*,
dainty food.

PETRUCHIO. 'T was told me you were
   rough and coy and sullen,
And now I find report a very liar;
For thou art pleasant, gamesome, passing
   courteous,
But slow in speech, yet sweet as spring-time
   flowers.
Thou canst not frown, thou canst not look
   askance,
Nor bite the lip, as angry wenches will;
Nor hast thou pleasure to be cross in talk;
But thou with mildness entertain'st thy
   wooers,
With gentle conference, soft and affable.
Why does the world report that Kate doth
   limp?
O slanderous world!
Thus in plain terms: your father hath con-
   sented
That you shall be my wife; your dowry
   'greed on;
And, will you, nill you, I will marry you.
Now, Kate, I am a husband for your turn;
For, by this light, whereby I see thy beauty,
Thy beauty that doth make me like thee
   well,
Thou must be married to no man but me.
       Taming of the Shrew, II, 1:244, 271

KATHARINA. Call you me daughter? now,
   I promise you

You have show'd a tender fatherly regard,
To wish me wed to one half lunatic;
A mad-cap ruffian and a swearing Jack,
That thinks with oaths to face the matter
   out.
        Taming of the Shrew, II, 1:287

PETRUCHIO. And to conclude, we have
   'greed so well together,
That upon Sunday is the wedding-day.
   KATHARINA. I 'll see thee hang'd on Sunday first.

      . . . . .

PETRUCHIO. Be patient, gentlemen; I
   choose her for myself:
If she and I be pleas'd, what 's that to you?
'T is bargain'd 'twixt us twain, being alone,
That she shall still be curst[1] in company.
I tell you, 't is incredible to believe
How much she loves me: O! the kindest
   Kate,
She hung about my neck, and kiss on kiss
She vied so fast, protesting oath on oath,
That in a twink she won me to her love.

      . . . . .

We will have rings, and things, and fine array;
And kiss me, Kate, we will be married o'
   Sunday.
    Taming of the Shrew, II, 1:299, 304, 325
[1] curst: waspish.

CRESSIDA. But, though I lov'd you well, I
   woo'd you not;
And yet, good faith, I wish'd myself a man,
Or that we women had men's privilege
Of speaking first.
       Troilus and Cressida, III, 2:134

VALENTINE. A woman sometimes scorns
   what best contents her.
Send her another; never give her o'er,
For scorn at first makes after-love the more.
If she do frown, 't is not in hate of you,
But rather to beget more love in you;
If she do chide, 't is not to have you gone;
For why, the fools are mad if left alone.
Take no repulse, whatever she doth say;
For 'get you gone,' she doth not mean
   'away!'
Flatter and praise, commend, extol their
   graces;
Though ne'er so black, say they have an-
   gels' faces.
     Two Gentlemen of Verona, III, 1:93

PROTEUS. You must lay lime[1] to tangle her
   desires
By wailful sonnets, whose composed
   rhymes

Should be full-fraught with serviceable
vows.
Two Gentlemen of Verona, III, 2:68
[1] lime: metaphor of catching birds by smearing bird-lime on branches.

WORDS

KING. Methinks I hear him now: his plau-
sive words
He scatter'd not in ears, but grafted them,
To grow there and to bear.
All's Well That Ends Well, I, 2:54

DUKE. If their purgation did consist in
words,
They are as innocent as grace itself.
As You Like It, I, 3:55

HORATIO. These are but wild and whirl-
ing words.
Hamlet, I, 5:133

POLONIUS. What do you read, my lord?
HAMLET. Words, words, words.
Hamlet, II, 2:193

OPHELIA. Words of so sweet breath com-
pos'd
As made the things more rich.
Hamlet, III, 1:98

KING. My words fly up, my thoughts remain below:
Words without thoughts never to heaven
go.
Hamlet, III, 3:97

PRINCE. That ever this fellow should have
fewer words than a parrot, and yet the son
of a woman!
1 Henry IV, II, 4:110

K. HENRY. Ah! kill me with thy weapon,
not with words,
My breast can better brook thy dagger's
point
Than can my ears that tragic history.
III Henry VI, V, 6:26

K. HENRY. 'T is well said again;
And 't is kind of good deed to say well:
And yet words are no deeds.
Henry VIII, III, 2:152

BASTARD. 'Zounds! I was never so be-
thump'd with words
Since I first call'd my brother's father dad.
King John, II, 1:466

BRUTUS. Words before blows: is it so,
countrymen?

OCTAVIUS. Not that we love words bet-
ter, as you do.
BRUTUS. Good words are better than bad
strokes, Octavius.
ANTONY. In your bad strokes, Brutus, you
give good words:
Witness the hole you made in Caesar's heart,
Crying 'Long live! hail, Caesar!'
CASSIUS. Antony,
The posture of your blows are yet un-
known;
But for your words, they rob the Hybla
bees,
And leave them honeyless.
ANTONY. Not stingless too.
Julius Caesar, V, 1:27

COSTARD. O! they have lived long on the
alms-basket of words. I marvel thy master
hath not eaten thee for a word.
Love's Labour's Lost, V, 1:41

Ross. I have words
That would be howl'd out in the desert air,
Where hearing should not latch them.
Macbeth, IV, 3:193

BENEDICK. His words are a very fantastical banquet, just so many strange dishes.
Much Ado About Nothing, II, 3:20

HERO. One doth not know
How much an ill word may empoison lik-
ing.
Much Ado About Nothing, III, 1:85

BEATRICE. Foul words is but foul wind,
and foul wind is but foul breath, and foul
breath is noisome; therefore, I will depart
unkissed.
Much Ado About Nothing, V, 2:52

PANDARUS. Words pay no debts.
Troilus and Cressida, III, 2:58

WORK

PRINCE. Hotspur of the North; he that
kills me some six or seven dozen of Scots at
a breakfast, washes his hands, and says to
his wife 'Fie upon this quiet life! I want
work.'
1 Henry IV, II, 4:115

OFFICER. I cannot draw a cart nor eat
dried oats;
If it be man's work I'll do it.
King Lear, V, 3:38

MARIA. Nay, but say true; does it work
upon him?

Sir Toby. Like aqua-vitae[1] with a mid-wife.

Twelfth Night, II, 5:214

[1] aqua-vitae: liquor.

Autolycus. Every lane's end, every shop, church, session, hanging, yields a careful man work.

Winter's Tale, IV, 4:702

WORLD

Rosalind. O! how full of briers is this working-day world.

Celia. They are but burrs, cousin, thrown upon thee in holiday foolery: if we walk not in the trodden paths, our very petti-coats will catch them.

Rosalind. I could shake them off my coat: these burrs are in my heart.

Celia. Hem them away.

Rosalind. I would try, if I could cry 'hem' and have him.

As You Like It, I, 3:12

Antipholus Syracuse. I to the world am like a drop of water
That in the ocean seeks another drop.

Comedy of Errors, I, 2:35

Hamlet. Why, let the stricken deer go weep,
The hart ungalled play;
For some must watch, while some must sleep:
So runs the world away.

Hamlet, III, 2:282

K. Henry. Upon thy eye-balls murder-ous tyranny
Sits in grim majesty to fright the world.

II Henry VI, III, 2:49

Bastard. Come the three corners of the world in arms,
And we shall shock them.

King John, V, 7:116

Edgar. My father, poorly led? World, world, O world!
But that thy strange mutations make us hate thee
Life[1] would not yield to age.

King Lear, IV, 1:10

[1] Life . . . age: hate life, welcome age and death.

Pistol. Why, then the world's mine oys-ter,
Which I with sword will open.

Merry Wives of Windsor, II, 2:2

Timon. What would'st thou do with the world, Apemantus, if it lay in thy power?

Apemantus. Give it the beasts, to be rid of the men.

Timon of Athens, IV, 3:321

Miranda. How beauteous mankind is! O brave new world,
That has such people in 't!

Tempest, V, 1:183

WORRY

Clarence. The incessant care and labour of his mind
Hath wrought the mure[1] that should con-fine it in
So thin that life looks through and will break out.

II Henry IV, IV, 4:118

[1] mure: wall.

Salanio. Believe me, sir, had I such ven-ture forth,
The better part of my affections would
Be with my hopes abroad. I should be still[1]
Plucking the grass to know where sits the wind,
Peering in maps for ports, and piers, and roads;[2]
And every object that might make me fear
Misfortune to my ventures, out of doubt
Would make me sad.

Salarino. My wind, cooling my broth,
Would blow me to an ague, when I thought
What harm a wind too great might do at sea.
I should not see the sandy hour-glass run
But I should think of shallows and of flats,
And see my wealthy Andrew, dock'd in sand,
Vailing her high-top lower than her ribs
To kiss her burial.

. . . . .

Antonio. Believe me, no: I thank my for-tune for it,
My ventures are not in one bottom trusted,
Nor to one place; nor is my whole estate
Upon the fortune of this present year:
Therefore my merchandise makes me not sad.

Merchant of Venice, I, 1:15, 41

[1] still: always. [2] roads: havens.

Sir Toby. I am sure care's an enemy to life.

Twelfth Night, I, 3:2

WOUND

Scarus. Room for six scotches[1] more.

Antony and Cleopatra, IV, 7:9

[1] scotches: gashes.

ROSALIND. Alas, poor shepherd! searching of thy wound, I have by hard adventure found mine own.
As You Like It, II, 4:44

CORIOLANUS. I had rather have my wounds to heal again
Than hear say how I got them.
Coriolanus, II, 2:73

FALSTAFF. I gave him this wound in the thigh: if the man were alive and would deny it, 'zounds! I would make him eat a piece of my sword.
I Henry IV, V, 4:154

MESSENGER. Stop the rage betime,[1]
Before the wound do grow incurable.
II Henry VI, III, 1:286
[1] betime: soon, or in time.

IAGO. What wound did ever heal but by degrees?
Othello, II, 3:377

JULIA. Poor wounded name! my bosom as a bed
Shall lodge thee till thy wound be throughly[1] heal'd;
And thus I search it with a sovereign kiss.
Two Gentlemen of Verona, I, 2:114
[1] throughly: thoroughly.

WRONG

MARCELLUS. We do it[1] wrong, being so majestical,
To offer it the show of violence;
For it is, as the air, invulnerable,
And our vain blows malicious mockery.
Hamlet, I, 1:143
[1] it: the ghost of HAMLET's father.

HOTSPUR [about HENRY IV]. Broke oath on oath, committed wrong on wrong;
And in conclusion drove us to seek out
This head of safety; and withal[1] to pry
Into his title, the which we find
Too indirect for long continuance.
I Henry IV, IV, 3:101
[1] withal: with it.

YORK. I have in equal balance justly weigh'd
What wrongs our arms may do, what wrongs we suffer,
And find our griefs heavier than our offences.
II Henry IV, IV, 1:67

Celestial as thou art, O! do not love that wrong,

To sing heaven's praise with such an earthly tongue.
Passionate Pilgrim: 69

K. RICHARD. So in the Lethe[1] of thy angry soul
Thou drown the sad remembrance of those wrongs
Which thou supposest I have done to thee.
Richard III, IV, 4:251
[1] Lethe: the river of forgetfulness in the lower world.

Then need I not fear the worst of wrongs,
When in the least of them my life hath end.
Sonnet 92

HECTOR. Thus to persist
In doing wrong extenuates not wrong,
But makes it much more heavy.
Troilus and Cressida, II, 2:186

YEARNING

When, in disgrace with fortune and men's eyes,
I all alone beweep my outcast state,
And trouble deaf heaven with my bootless cries,
And look upon myself, and curse my fate,
Wishing me like to one more rich in hope,
Featur'd like him, like him with friends possess'd,
Desiring this man's art, and that man's scope,
With what I most enjoy contented least;
Yet in these thoughts myself almost despising,
Haply[1] I think on thee, and then my state,
Like to the lark at break of day arising
From sullen earth, sings hymns at heaven's gate:
For thy sweet love remember'd such wealth brings
That then I scorn to change my state with kings.
Sonnet 29
[1] Haply: fortunately.

YOUTH

KING. 'Let me not live,' quoth he,
'After my flame lacks oil, to be the snuff
Of younger spirits, whose apprehensive senses
All but new things disdain; whose judgments[1] are
Mere fathers of their garments; whose constancies
Expire before their fashions.'
All's Well That Ends Well, I, 2:58
[1] judgments . . . garments: discernment confined to garments.

COUNTESS. Even so it was with me when
I was young:
If ever we are nature's, these are ours; this
thorn[1]
Doth to our rose of youth rightly belong;
Our blood to us, this to our blood is born:
It is the show and seal of nature's truth,
Where love's strong passion is impress'd in
youth:
By our remembrances of days foregone,
Such were our faults; or then we thought
them none.
All's Well That Ends Well, I, 3:134
[1] thorn: loving the wrong person.

All's brave that youth mounts and folly
guides.
As You Like It, III, 4:48

LAERTES. The canker galls the infants of
the spring
Too oft before their buttons[1] be disclos'd.
And in the morn and liquid dew of youth
Contagious blastments are most imminent.
Hamlet, I, 3:39
[1] buttons: buds.

KING. Youth no less becomes
The light and careless livery that it wears
Than settled age his sables and his weeds,
Importing health and graveness.
Hamlet, IV, 7:79

SILENCE. You were called 'lusty Shallow'
then, cousin.
SHALLOW. By the mass, I was called any
thing; and I would have any thing indeed
too, and roundly too.
II Henry IV, III, 2:17

ELY. You are their heir, you sit upon their
throne,
The blood and courage that renowned them
Runs in your veins; and my thrice-puissant
liege
Is in the very May-morn of his youth,
Ripe for exploits and mighty enterprises.
Henry V, I, 2:117

PORTER. These are the youths that thunder
at a playhouse, and fight for bitten apples;
that no audience but the Tribulation of
Tower-hill,[1] or the Limbs of Limehouse,
their dear brothers, are able to endure.
Henry VIII, V, 4:63
[1] Tower-hill . . . Limehouse: references have
not been discovered; probably a local gibe.

BIRON. Young blood doth not obey an old
decree.
Love's Labour's Lost, IV, 3:217

PORTIA. The brain may devise laws for the
blood,[1] but a hot temper leaps o'er a cold
decree: such a hare is madness, the youth,
to skip o'er the meshes of good counsel, the
cripple.
Merchant of Venice, I, 2:20
[1] blood: passions, desires.

SHALLOW. Though we are justices and
doctors and churchmen, Master Page, we
have some salt of our youth in us; we are
the sons of women.
Merry Wives of Windsor, II, 3:47

Crabbed age and youth cannot live to-
gether:
Youth is full of pleasance, age is full of care:
Youth like summer morn, age like winter
weather;
Youth like summer brave, age like winter
bare.
Youth is full of sport, age's breath is short;
Youth is nimble, age is lame;
Youth is hot and bold, age is weak and cold
Youth is wild, and age is tame.
Age, I do abhor thee; youth, I do adore thee.
Passionate Pilgrim: 157

Misshapen[1] Time, copesmate[2] of ugly Night,
Swift subtle post, carrier of grisly care,
Eater of youth, false slave to false delight,
Base watch of woes, sin's pack-horse, vir-
tue's snare;
Rape of Lucrece: 925
[1] Misshapen: badly used. [2] copesmate: com-
panion.

Then the conceit[1] of this inconstant stay
Sets you most rich in youth before my sight,
Where wasteful Time debateth with Decay,
To change your day of youth to sullied
night.
Sonnet 15
[1] conceit: thought.

SHEPHERD. I would there were no age between sixteen and three-and-twenty, or that
youth would sleep out the rest; for there is
nothing in the between but getting wenches
with child, wronging the ancientry,[1] stealing, fighting. Hark you now! Would any
but these boiled brains of nineteen and two-
and-twenty hunt this weather?
Winter's Tale, III, 3:58
[1] ancientry: old people.

INDEX